Sport Inside Out

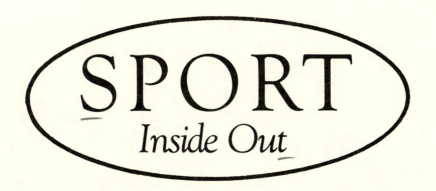

SPORT
Inside Out

Readings in Literature and Philosophy

Edited by
David L. Vanderwerken
and
Spencer K. Wertz

Texas Christian University

TEXAS CHRISTIAN UNIVERSITY PRESS • FORT WORTH

Library of Congress Cataloging in Publication Data
Main entry under title:

Sport inside out.

   Bibliography: p.
   1. Sports—Philosophy—Addresses, essays, lectures.
2. Sports in literature—Addresses, essays, lectures.
I. Vanderwerken, David L.   II. Wertz, Spencer K.
GV706.S746 1985   796'.01   84-23951
ISBN 0-87565-003-1
ISBN 0-87565-006-6 (pbk.)

Designed by Whitehead & Whitehead • Austin
Illustrations by Walle Conoly

For Linda, Karen, Brian, Eric, Shari
and *Pippin, Daño, Cali*

Contents

Preface

In John Updike's *Rabbit, Run*, Harry "Rabbit" Angstrom's former basketball coach argues that a "boy who has had his heart enlarged by an inspiring coach can never become, in the deepest sense, a failure in the greater game of life." The coach's remark expresses several commonly held assumptions about the relationship between sport and life. One is that sport is life in miniature, life reduced to essentials, a microcosm of the "greater game." Closely related to the microcosm idea is the belief in the efficacy of sport to shape character traits and to teach values assumed necessary for proper and successful living. And finally, there is the faith that sport is a humanizing endeavor, that the athlete undergoes unique and intense experiences closed to others—experiences that make him more human somehow. The athlete savors certain possibilities of existence that make him different from, and probably better than, his fellows. He who has played *knows* something unshareable. Surely a kind of mysticism attributed to the sport experience underlies the compelling appeal of sport for the human imagination.

This analogy between sport and life, so easily and often drawn, is part of America's conventional wisdom. But we believe that it demands examination. Hence, this anthology of sports-centered fiction and poetry, speculative and informal essays, and philosophical meditations. The purpose of this disparate compilation is to raise, but hardly to resolve, focal and ongoing questions about the relationship between sport and life. Where does the analogy hold, where does it mislead, where does it deceive? If correspondences do indeed exist between elements of sport and that which is not sport, precisely where do they reside? Or is sport an autonomous world tangential at best, unrelated at worst, to anything outside itself? The readings we have selected reflect such concerns.

We have divided the book into four parts, moving from subjective to objective, from the experience of sport to ideas about sport. Part I, Sport and the Individual, explores the impact of sport upon the player, the individual fan, and the collective—the hometown crowd. Part II, Sport and Society, focuses attention on the social mythology surrounding sport. The readings in Part III, The Meanings of Sport, examine what sport has to do with religion, myth, and philosophy—problematic matters all. Finally, Part IV touches upon other Dimensions of Sport, including Language, Fantasy, Humor, Space and Time, and Death. This list of topics could be extended indefinitely.

Each part leads off with some brief keynoting remarks. Selections of fiction and poetry precede expository material that speaks to issues raised by the creative works. We feel that the dual perspectives, the imaginative and the analytical, illuminate more than either form of discourse alone. In one instance, the section on Sport and Social Myths, we have reversed ourselves by opening with former President Ford's essay and letting the fiction comment on it.

Inevitably, our groupings and categories are arbitrary. Many selections could be interchanged, and the instructor will likely wish to add and delete or skip around. The guides for further study at the end of each section include some of our suggestions on this matter. We have tried to include enough variety to encourage modifications appropriate to specific needs. These readings should be workable in English and philosophy classes, as well as for more eclectic humanities classes and interdisciplinary sequences. The great majority of pieces are quite recent, reflecting the burgeoning interest in sports in the last ten years or so. Thus, our bias is toward contemporary writing simply because of its availability, bulk, and quality. We have largely restricted the creative works to those concerned with major American team sports—baseball, football, basketball—because of their broad cultural impact and because of the abundance of excellent material. A good anthology is flexible, and above all, useful, and we hope to have approached these ideals.

Most of the material included in this anthology has been used in our classes in Sport in Modern American Literature and Thinking About Sport. Although the collection is aimed at a collegiate audience, it is our hope that the sports-minded public who seek an understanding of their own involvement in sport or a society's preoccupation with sport will find this book a faithful guide and companion.

The American academic world has discovered that it had best take sport seriously. The Seventies witnessed the appearance of courses on sport in several disciplines, philosophical inquiries into the nature and aesthetics of sport, anthologies of sports-centered creative literature, and collections of sociological and psychological studies of sport. (For openers, see the selected bibliography.) The *Journal of the Philosophy of Sport*, *Journal of Sport History*, and *Arete: The Journal of Sport Literature* now exist. Even James A. Michener, after chronicling Hawaii, Spain, and North America from the year zero onward, has turned his attention upon *Sports in America*. In short, studying sport has become not only legitimate but even respectable.

Of course, many outside the academy regard these developments with a sense of alarm, hostility, and woe. The intrusive academic, notecards in hand, with his penchant for interrogation, speculation, and analysis is now investigating nearly virgin territory. The sentiment seems to run "Can't they leave sports alone? Must the damn professors make a field out of *the field?*" We offer this collection in rebuttal to such an anti-intellectual stance. We believe that understanding enhances, rather than spoils, enjoyment, whether of Wallace Stevens's poetry, Kant's thought, Alfred Hitchcock's films, or the National Football League.

In the movie *The Sands of Iwo Jima*, a dying William Bendix claims that he fought the Axis powers not only for mom and apple pie but for the Brooklyn Dodgers. It behooves us to understand the genesis of such a statement. "Know thyself" goes for nations as well as for individuals.

. . .

The editors of this anthology owe much to many. Without the contributors and their representatives, of course, there would be no book. Special thanks go to Dr. Lyle Olsen, San Diego State University and Dr. Robert J. Trevas, Ohio University who read and commented shrewdly on the manuscript.

Finally, while we can never repay the generosity of Karen and Linda, who put up with us daily, we sure do enjoy trying.

DAVID L. VANDERWERKEN
SPENCER K. WERTZ
Fort Worth
January, 1985

Part I:

Sport and the Individual

Introduction

The sport experience is both private and shared, intensely personal for the player and the spectator yet unifying and communicable within the larger group, the team and the crowd. Beyond the spectacle in the stadium lies the community, whether town, state, or nation, and its involvement forms the third side of the triangle out of which the full complexity of the sport experience emerges. These three viewpoints—the participant, the spectator, the community—are explored in the readings in Part I: Sport and the Individual.

All five literature pieces in Section I: The Participant concern athletes a bit past their prime who are caught between their memories and achievements and the harsh realities of time and circumstance. Whether amateur or professional, each athlete fears hanging them up and strives to extend the transition period.

A common tension in these writings is the contrast between the extraordinary experiences available to the athlete and the boring ordinariness of the nonsports world. Sport offers the athlete occasional entry into an extra dimension of human experience. The magic moment—mystical, incommunicable—is best articulated by Irwin Shaw's description of Christian Darling's eighty-yard run with a screen pass, by Glendon Swarthout's aging catcher, Al, when he stages a private home run derby for his wife in the empty Arizona ball park, and by David Hilton's joyous jump shot even as his left leg disintegrates. Yet the fleeting transcendent moment, our writers maintain, is of sport alone and cannot be approximated in everyday life. The message is clear: sport is better than life. Perhaps this is so because the spirit of play is triumphant in such scenes.

Despite these isolated and rare moments of joyous transcendence, the prevailing mood of these works consists of anxiety, disillusionment, and alienation. The main characters sense that their sport has become work, that their games play them. Consider the fear and desperation of Swarthout's Al, trying to make the roster with a good spring performance, or Hemingway's exhausted welterweight champion, Jack Brennan, preparing for a fight he can't win, or the terrifying futuristic gladiator, Jonathan E, in William Harrison's "Roller Ball Murder," who feels that he has a "deep rupture" in his soul. In identifying the participant's experience of sport, these negatives must be accounted for as well as the epiphanies.

Justifiers of sport have long insisted that the sport experience builds character, teaches values, prepares one for the "game of life," and so on. However, several of the readings question such assumptions, asking whether in the lives of these maturing athletes sport has in fact promoted or retarded personal growth and an increase in wisdom. The issue is often dramatized in the players' relationships with women. The most complete analysis may be found in Shaw's "The Eighty-Yard Run." Over fifteen years, we see Christian Darling's wife, Louise, become increasingly mature while Christian stands pat, refusing to grow beyond his college football experiences, retreating to mental instant replays of his magical run. At the end of the story, when he attempts to re-enact his run at age 35, he becomes a sympathetic yet pathetic victim of his sport experience, which hardly prepared him for life. As he admits to himself: "He hadn't practiced for 1929 and New York City and a girl who would turn into a woman." In Swarthout's story, Al and Babe try to hold their marriage together. She like her husband is hanging on, bitter, frustrated, playing putt-putt with other baseball wives, and drinking too much to avoid thinking of what the future holds beyond baseball. Harrison's Jonathan E stages a reunion with his ex-wife, Ella, and discovers that she is a part of the corporate nightmare—dehumanized, impersonal, brutal—that roller ball itself so accurately mirrors: "She plays like a biker, I decide; she rides up there high above the turmoil, decides when to swoop down, and makes a clean kill." Finally, Hemingway's Jack Brennan claims to miss "the wife" in his spartan training camp although the reader can only surmise about the quality of their union. These stories demand that the easy analogy between the sport experience and life be rigorously scrutinized. Yet the question remains concerning precisely what the participant gains, learns, or knows through the sport experience.

The three philosophical essays by Adam Smith, Margaret Steel, and R. Scott Kretchmar suggest some other ways of looking at the problem of knowing in the sport experience. In other realms of human endeavor, knowing is equated with thinking. But in sport, thinking about the movements to be performed inhibits, even paralyzes action rather than releasing it. One might ask, How is the action released? By feeling. In sport, knowing is feeling. Smith foresees no verbal counterpart to feeling, whereas Steel and Kretchmar attempt to analyze this affective region.

Smith describes the athletic yogi, pursuing a carefully planned course of physical and mental exercises in order to concentrate the mind. As an ancient Hindu proverb reports: breath is the lord of the mind. To play in a trance, as Nicklaus does on the golf course, is to suit up in Smith's "mental scuba gear." Smith pushes this thesis to the point where we begin asking if playing is really "playing without your head." There are times when participants are supposed to think. A participant must think about the whole game, about the dynamics of the game, the strategies employed by himself and his opponent. There are times to be mindful. But executing an action is obviously different from thinking about an action.

Smith's mysticism is replaced by analysis in Steel's and Kretchmar's studies. Steel claims that learning a sport, such as tennis, is like learning a science: "In learning science we *do* science by working through the exemplars, the problems and classical experiments. Once the science is learned we can go on to new discoveries." Steel continues by showing that this is also how we learn games. Kretchmar goes even further, showing how the bodily *gestalt* of "distancing" works in sport—that thinking does take place in the form of detaching oneself from one's own immediacy. "Don't dwell on the mechanics—concentrate on the whole game, the game before you," yells the coach. Steel and Kretchmar help explain how such remarks are meaningful.

The bodily *gestalt* also serves as an explanation of the problems of the aging athlete: as the body wanes, so do one's skills. That knowing is feeling in sport could be the reason why such a gulf lies between participant and spectator. This gulf is further explored by the next section: The Spectator.

One of the shrewdest insights into the spectator's side of the sport experience appears in Don DeLillo's definition of the "exemplary spectator," from his novel *End Zone*, as the "person who understands that sport is a benign illusion, the illusion that order is possible." At the same time, as we know, some spectators aren't so exemplary, whose vicarious identification with sports figures shades into obsession, neurosis, and violence. The readings in Section II: The Spectator cover the range of possible spectator responses, from the aesthetic appreciation of a Roger Angell through the disordered Frank Gifford fetish of a Frederick Exley to those who make death threats against Reggie Jackson.

Of the pieces below, those by Dickey, Humphries, Epstein, and Angell illustrate DeLillo's notion of exemplary spectatorship. Dickey's "For the Death of Vince Lombardi" stresses the galvanizing cultural power of Lombardi and his Green Bay Packers over "those who played for you / And those who entered the bodies / Of Bart Starr, Donny Anderson, Ray Nitschke, Jerry Kramer / Through the snowing tube on Sunday afternoons." Yet Dickey asks hard questions about the Lombardi ethic ("Does your death set us free?"),

finally deciding that "We've got to believe there's such a thing / As winning."
On the other hand, Rolfe Humphries's "Night Game" comments less ambiguously on fan identification. The tone is joyous as the crowd crosses the outfield after the game, "So wonderful underfoot, so right, so perfect / That each of us was a player for a moment." More analytically, Joseph Epstein, the editor of *The American Scholar*, in his essay "Obsessed with Sport" discovers the features that he finds most satisfying as a spectator—craftsmanship of a high order, an absence of fraudulence, clarity in both situation and character, and levels of physical intelligence. Perhaps the most exemplary spectator of all is Roger Angell in "The Interior Stadium." For Angell, baseball is art—rich, inexhaustible, timeless, memorable. After describing the geometry of a routine grounder to short, Angell writes: "Scientists speak of the profoundly moving aesthetic beauty of mathematics, and perhaps the baseball field is one of the few places where the rest of us can glimpse this mystery." Angell bears out DeLillo's claim that the exemplary spectator finds in sport "not just order but civilization." Baseball's philosophical lessons are made explicit by James Memmott's sensitive critical study and Harold VanderZwaag's reply. They guide the reader through Angell's images and suggest questions for us to contemplate.

Would that all fans were as civilized as these, but, of course, they're not. The darker side of the spectator psyche emerges in the pieces by Exley, Vecsey, and Gilbert and Twyman. Harmless vicarious identification with George Brett is one thing, but Frederick Exley's twisted involvement with Frank Gifford is quite another. As a whole, *A Fan's Notes* is a penetrating study of all the cultural icons involved in America's success mythology and how failure to measure up to that mythology can lead to psychosis. More particularly, Frank Gifford becomes the incarnation of our success mythology for Exley, the measure for everything Exley isn't, an ideal alter ego who can never be realized. In the excerpt below, Exley tells of his one chance encounter with Gifford at USC at a campus hangout in which Exley discovers that Gifford is a fellow mortal. At least Exley never projects his love-hate fixation into overt violence on Gifford. George Vecsey in "Fans" and Bil Gilbert and Lisa Twyman in "Violence: Out of Hand in the Stands" exlore the problem of spectator hooliganism. The conventional notion that sport provides a release of spectator aggression, a catharsis, that keeps society docile is discredited by these two essays. Some plausible causes offered for spectator rowdyism are the availability of liquor, the frustrations of contemporary living, the absence of internal restraint, and media-induced exhibitionism. Gilbert and Twyman suggest that the sportsworld itself must "reeducate fans" to see that "these are games, not genuine confrontations of world-shaking significance."

When the University of Arkansas Razorbacks are playing, the state of Arkansas essentially closes for three hours. The public effects and implications of sport are the subjects addressed in Section III: The Community.

In Gary Gay's story "Ishmael in Arlis," we grasp the powerful bond between any small town and its high school football team. As reported by the narrator, the players are conscious of the enormous, intimidating pressure of the community on them. All the hopes, fears, frustrations, and anxieties of Arlis, Texas ride the players' backs every Friday night. Town vindication and redemption depend on the team's performance, an awesome burden for forty teenagers. When the narrator decides to quit football, he knows ostracism will result. Sitting atop the town water tower, he wonders "what it'd be like not being a football player anymore," a radical heretic in the community's eyes.

Roger Kahn's preface to *The Boys of Summer* reflects upon the Brooklyn Dodgers of the Jackie Robinson era and their relationship with the borough of Brooklyn. The ethnic and racial mix of the Dodgers perfectly mirrored the melting pot that was Brooklyn itself. Dodger rooters illustrate what Michael Novak suggests is the meaning of rooting, of being "rooted" in a specific place. Kahn argues that when the Dodgers "uprooted" and moved to Los Angeles, when Ebbets Field was leveled, Brooklyn itself changed irrevocably. Change and loss and bittersweet sadness prevail: "I covered a team that no longer exists in a demolished ball park for a newspaper that is dead." Community identity, so inextricably welded to the Dodgers, vanished as well. And Kahn believes that the nation lost something too, for the Dodgers (along with the hated Yankees) were one of America's teams long before the Dallas Cowboys (or the Atlanta Braves) arrogated that title.

In a provocative social analysis, Michael Novak's "Regional Religions" from his *The Joy of Sports* suggests that a region's character is revealed in the style of football played. To support this thesis, Novak examines Pennsylvania, the South and Southwest, the Midwestern style of the Big Ten, California, and the Ivy League. Each region's ethos, cultural values, world view, and fundamental attitudes find expression in its football teams. The shrewd observer, Novak believes, can discern the community's deepest convictions in its teams.

Edwin Cady generally agrees with Novak's perceptions of state and regional teams but dissents from Novak's viewing sport as a form of secular religion. The whole of Cady's *The Big Game: College Sports and American Life* is "about the games we play in the seats, in the stands or at home." In the following excerpt, "Pop Art and the American Dream," Cady sees sport as fulfilling a community need, not for a sacred ritual, but for festival, for public participatory art: "The great team games are, then, instant and collective art forms. Hence they are, though Walt Whitman never saw one, ideally Whitmanian—democratic, organic." In a Puritan country that has few holidays (look at a Mexican calendar sometime), Cady believes that college football and basketball provide feast days, celebrations, where restraint and decorum can be thrown aside and homo ludens can emerge: "The best party in American life, the Big Game enacts itself as the most vitally folkloristic event in our culture." Something like Texas-Oklahoma weekend, then, dramatizes for Cady a basic community need—the need for renewal of the play spirit. And, Cady continues, no more appropriate context exists than the University—that institution devoted to studying the full range of humankind—to display this legitimate, basic, and profound side of human nature.

The last article of Part I, by Peter S. Wenz, deals with issues of social justice, in particular, human equality in sport. Given that the monetary and funding patterns of men's and women's sports are presently neither obvious nor agreed upon, Wenz's philosophical strategy is to develop an ideal case which employs a distinction between value in use and value in exchange: "The exchange value of a sport to an individual is the fame and fortune he or she derives from participating in that sport. The use value of a sport to an individual, by contrast, is the value to that individual which is intrinsic to his or her participation in that sport." The relationship between these two values comes down to this: "playing increases watching, [but] watching tends to depress rather than increase the level of participation. I call this the inverse relationship thesis (IRT)." Wenz analyzes several sports and concludes that there are several strong reasons for adopting the idea of a society in which sport is deprofessionalized. Greater use of sports is to be gained for both men and women by increased deprofessionalization. Exchange values must be replaced by use values if a more general *human* equality in sports is to be attainable.

Section I: The Participant

IRWIN SHAW

The Eighty-Yard Run

The pass was high and wide and he jumped for it, feeling it slap flatly against his hands, as he shook his hips to throw off the halfback who was diving at him. The center floated by, his hands desperately brushing Darling's knee as Darling picked his feet up high and delicately ran over a blocker and an opposing linesman in a jumble on the ground near the scrimmage line. He had ten yards in the clear and picked up speed, breathing easily, feeling his thigh pads rising and falling against his legs, listening to the sound of cleats behind him, pulling away from them, watching the other backs heading him off toward the sideline, the whole picture, the men closing in on him, the blockers fighting for position, the ground he had to cross, all suddenly clear in his head, for the first time in his life not a meaningless confusion of men, sounds, speed. He smiled a little to himself as he ran, holding the ball lightly in front of him with his two hands, his knees pumping high, his hips twisting in the almost girlish run of a back in a broken field. The first halfback came at him and he fed him his leg, then swung at the last moment, took the shock of the man's shoulders without breaking stride, ran right through him, his cleats biting securely into the turf. There was only the safety man now, coming warily at him, his arms crooked, hands spread. Darling tucked the ball in, spurted at him, driving hard, hurling himself along, all two hundred pounds bunched into controlled attack. He was sure he was going to get past the safety man. Without thought, his arms and legs working beautifully together, he headed right for the safety man, stiff-armed him, feeling blood spurt instantaneously from the man's nose onto his hand, seeing his face go awry, head turned, mouth pulled to one side. He pivoted away, keeping the arm locked, dropping the safety man as he ran easily toward the goal line, with the drumming of cleats diminishing behind him.

How long ago? It was autumn then, and the ground was getting hard be- cause the nights were cold and leaves from the maples around the stadium

Originally appeared in *Esquire* (1941).

blew across the practice fields in gusts of wind, and the girls were beginning to put polo coats over their sweaters when they came to watch practice in the afternoon. . . . Fifteen years. Darling walked slowly over the same ground in the spring twilight, in his neat shoes, a man of thirty-five dressed in a double-breasted suit, ten pounds heavier in the fifteen years, but not fat, with the years between 1925 and 1940 showing in his face.

The coach was smiling quietly to himself and the assistant coaches were looking at each other with pleasure the way they always did when one of the second stringers suddenly did something fine, bringing credit to them, making their $2,000 a year a tiny bit more secure.

Darling trotted back, smiling, breathing deeply but easily, feeling wonderful, not tired, though this was the tail end of practice and he'd run eighty yards. The sweat poured off his face and soaked his jersey and he liked the feeling, the warm moistness lubricating his skin like oil. Off in a corner of the field some players were punting and the smack of leather against the ball came pleasantly through the afternoon air. The freshmen were running signals on the next field and the quarterback's sharp voice, the pound of the eleven pairs of cleats, the "Dig, now *dig!*" of the coaches, the laughter of the players all somehow made him feel happy as he trotted back to midfield, listening to the applause and shouts of the students along the sidelines, knowing that after that run the coach would have to start him Saturday against Illinois.

Fifteen years, Darling thought, remembering the shower after the workout, the hot water steaming off his skin and the deep soapsuds and all the young voices singing with the water streaming down and towels going and managers running in and out and the sharp sweet smell of oil of wintergreen and everybody clapping him on the back as he dressed and Packard, the captain, who took being captain very seriously, coming over to him and shaking his hand and saying, "Darling, you're going to go places in the next two years."

The assistant manager fussed over him, wiping a cut on his leg with alcohol and iodine, the little sting making him realize suddenly how fresh and whole and solid his body felt. The manager slapped a piece of adhesive tape over the cut, and Darling noticed the sharp clean white of the tape against the ruddiness of the skin, fresh from the shower.

He dressed slowly, the softness of his shirt and the soft warmth of his wool socks and his flannel trousers a reward against his skin after the harsh pressure of the shoulder harness and thigh and hip pads. He drank three glasses of cold water, the liquid reaching down coldly inside of him, soothing the harsh dry places in his throat and belly left by the sweat and running and shouting of practice.

Fifteen years.

The sun had gone down and the sky was green behind the stadium and he laughed quietly to himself as he looked at the stadium, rearing above the trees, and knew that on Saturday when the 70,000 voices roared as the team came running out onto the field, part of that enormous salute would be for him. He walked slowly, listening to the gravel crunch satisfactorily under his shoes in the still twilight, feeling his clothes swing lightly against his skin, breathing the thin evening air, feeling the wind move softly in his damp hair, wonderfully cool behind his ears and at the nape of his neck.

Louise was waiting for him at the road, in her car. The top was down and he noticed all over again, as he always did when he saw her, how pretty she was, the rough blonde hair and the large, inquiring eyes and the bright mouth, smiling now.

She threw the door open. "Were you good today?" she asked.

"Pretty good," he said. He climbed in, sank luxuriously into the soft leather, stretched his legs far out. He smiled, thinking of the eighty yards. "Pretty damn good."

She looked at him seriously for a moment, then scrambled around, like a little girl, kneeling on the seat next to him, grabbed him, her hands along his ears, and kissed him as he sprawled, head back, on the seat cushion. She let go of him, but kept her head close to his, over his. Darling reached up slowly and rubbed the back of his hand against her cheek, lit softly by a street lamp a hundred feet away. They looked at each other, smiling.

Louise drove down to the lake and they sat there silently, watching the moon rise behind the hills on the other side. Finally he reached over, pulled her gently to him, kissed her. Her lips grew soft, her body sank into his, tears formed slowly in her eyes. He knew, for the first time, that he could do whatever he wanted with her.

"Tonight," he said. "I'll call for you at seven-thirty. Can you get out?"

She looked at him. She was smiling, but the tears were still full in her eyes. "All right," she said. "I'll get out. How about you? Won't the coach raise hell?"

Darling grinned. "I got the coach in the palm of my hand," he said. "Can you wait till seven-thirty?"

She grinned back at him. "No," she said.

They kissed and she started the car and they went back to town for dinner. He sang on the way home.

Christian Darling, thirty-five years old, sat on the frail spring grass, greener now than it ever would be again on the practice field, looked thoughtfully up at the stadium, a deserted ruin in the twilight. He had started on the first

team that Saturday and every Saturday after that for the next two years, but it
had never been as satisfactory as it should have been. He never had broken
away, the longest run he'd ever made was thirty-five yards, and that in a game
that was already won, and then that kid had come up from the third team,
Diederich, a blank-faced German kid from Wisconsin, who ran like a bull,
ripping lines to pieces Saturday after Saturday, plowing through, never getting hurt, never changing his expression, scoring more points, gaining more
ground than all the rest of the team put together, making everybody's All-
American, carrying the ball three times out of four, keeping everybody else
out of the headlines. Darling was a good blocker and he spent his Saturday
afternoons working on the big Swedes and Polacks who played tackle and end
for Michigan, Illinois, Purdue, hurling into huge pile-ups, bobbing his head
wildly to elude the great raw hands swinging like meat-cleavers at him as he
went charging in to open up holes for Diederich coming through like a locomotive behind him. Still, it wasn't so bad. Everybody liked him and he did
his job and he was pointed out on the campus and boys always felt important
when they introduced their girls to him at their proms, and Louise loved him
and watched him faithfully in the games, even in the mud, when your own
mother wouldn't know you, and drove him around in her car keeping the top
down because she was proud of him and wanted to show everybody that she
was Christian Darling's girl. She bought him crazy presents because her father
was rich, watches, pipes, humidors, an icebox for beer for his room, curtains,
wallets, a fifty-dollar dictionary.

"You'll spend every cent your old man owns," Darling protested once when
she showed up at his rooms with seven different packages in her arms and
tossed them onto the couch.

"Kiss me," Louise said, "and shut up."

"Do you want to break your poor old man?"

"I don't mind. I want to buy you presents."

"Why?"

"It makes me feel good. Kiss me. I don't know why. Did you know that
you're an important figure?"

"Yes," Darling said gravely.

"When I was waiting for you at the library yesterday two girls saw you coming and one of them said to the other, 'That's Christian Darling. He's an important figure.'"

"You're a liar."

"I'm in love with an important figure."

"Still, why the hell did you have to give me a forty-pound dictionary?"

"I wanted to make sure," Louise said, "that you had a token of my esteem. I
wanted to smother you in tokens of my esteem."

Fifteen years ago.

They'd married when they got out of college. There'd been other women for him, but all casual and secret, more for curiosity's sake, and vanity, women who'd thrown themselves at him and flattered him, a pretty mother at a summer camp for boys, an old girl from his home town who'd suddenly blossomed into a coquette, a friend of Louise's who had dogged him grimly for six months and had taken advantage of the two weeks that Louise went home when her mother died. Perhaps Louise had known, but she'd kept quiet, loving him completely, filling his rooms with presents, religiously watching him battling with the big Swedes and Polacks on the line of scrimmage on Saturday afternoons, making plans for marrying him and living with him in New York and going with him there to the night clubs, the theaters, the good restaurants, being proud of him in advance, tall, white-teethed, smiling, large, yet moving lightly, with an athlete's grace, dressed in evening clothes, approvingly eyed by magnificently dressed and famous women in theater lobbies, with Louise adoringly at his side.

Her father, who manufactured inks, set up a New York office for Darling to manage and presented him with three hundred accounts, and they lived on Beekman Place with a view of the river with fifteen thousand dollars a year between them, because everybody was buying everything in those days, including ink. They saw all the shows and went to all the speakeasies and spent their fifteen thousand dollars a year and in the afternoons Louise went to the art galleries and the matinees of the more serious plays that Darling didn't like to sit through and Darling slept with a girl who danced in the chorus of *Rosalie* and with the wife of a man who owned three copper mines. Darling played squash three times a week and remained as solid as a stone barn and Louise never took her eyes off him when they were in the same room together, watching him with a secret, miser's smile, with a trick of coming over to him in the middle of a crowded room and saying gravely, in a low voice, "You're the handsomest man I've ever seen in my whole life. Want a drink?"

Nineteen twenty-nine came to Darling and to his wife and father-in-law, the maker of inks, just as it came to everyone else. The father-in-law waited until 1933 and then blew his brains out and when Darling went to Chicago to see what the books of the firm looked like he found out all that was left were debts and three or four gallons of unbought ink.

"Please, Christian," Louise said, sitting in their neat Beekman Place apartment, with a view of the river and prints of paintings by Dufy and Braque and Picasso on the wall, "please, why do you want to start drinking at two o'clock in the afternoon?"

"I have nothing else to do," Darling said, putting down his glass, emptied of its fourth drink. "Please pass the whisky."

Louise filled his glass. "Come take a walk with me," she said. "We'll walk along the river."

"I don't want to walk along the river," Darling said, squinting intensely at the prints of paintings by Dufy, Braque and Picasso.

"We'll walk along Fifth Avenue."

"I don't want to walk along Fifth Avenue."

"Maybe," Louise said gently, "you'd like to come with me to some art galleries. There's an exhibition by a man named Klee. . . ."

"I don't want to go to any art galleries. I want to sit here and drink Scotch whisky," Darling said. "Who the hell hung these goddam pictures up on the wall?"

"I did," Louise said.

"I hate them."

"I'll take them down," Louise said.

"Leave them there. It gives me something to do in the afternoon. I can hate them." Darling took a long swallow. "Is that the way people paint these days?"

"Yes, Christian. Please don't drink any more."

"Do you like painting like that?"

"Yes, dear."

"Really?"

"Really."

Darling looked carefully at the prints once more. "Little Louise Tucker. The middle-western beauty. I like pictures with horses in them. Why should you like pictures like that?"

"I just happen to have gone to a lot of galleries in the last few years . . ."

"Is that what you do in the afternoon?"

"That's what I do in the afternoon," Louise said.

"I drink in the afternoon."

Louise kissed him lightly on the top of his head as he sat there squinting at the pictures on the wall, the glass of whisky held firmly in his hand. She put on her coat and went out without saying another word. When she came back in the early evening, she had a job on a woman's fashion magazine.

They moved downtown and Louise went out to work every morning and Darling sat home and drank and Louise paid the bills as they came up. She made believe she was going to quit work as soon as Darling found a job, even though she was taking over more responsibility day by day at the magazine, interviewing authors, picking painters for the illustrations and covers, getting actresses to pose for pictures, going out for drinks with the right people, making a thousand new friends whom she loyally introduced to Darling.

"I don't like your hat," Darling said, once, when she came in in the evening and kissed him, her breath rich with Martinis.

"What's the matter with my hat, Baby?" she asked, running her fingers through his hair. "Everybody says it's very smart."

"It's too damned smart," he said. "It's not for you. It's for a rich, sophisticated woman of thirty-five with admirers."

Louise laughed. "I'm practicing to be a rich, sophisticated woman of thirty-five with admirers," she said. He stared soberly at her. "Now, don't look so grim, Baby. It's still the same simple little wife under the hat." She took the hat off, threw it into a corner, sat on his lap. "See? Homebody Number One."

"Your breath could run a train," Darling said, not wanting to be mean, but talking out of boredom, and sudden shock at seeing his wife curiously a stranger in a new hat, with a new expression in her eyes under the little brim, secret, confident, knowing.

Louise tucked her head under his chin so he couldn't smell her breath. "I had to take an author out for cocktails," she said. "He's a boy from the Ozark Mountains and he drinks like a fish. He's a Communist."

"What the hell is a Communist from the Ozarks doing writing for a woman's fashion magazine?"

Louise chuckled. "The magazine business is getting all mixed up these days. The publishers want to have a foot in every camp. And anyway, you can't find an author under seventy these days who isn't a Communist."

"I don't think I like you to associate with all those people, Louise," Darling said. "Drinking with them."

"He's a very nice, gentle boy," Louise said. "He reads Ernest Dowson."

"Who's Ernest Dowson?"

Louise patted his arm, stood up, fixed her hair. "He's an English poet."

Darling felt that somehow he had disappointed her. "Am I supposed to know who Ernest Dowson is?"

"No, dear. I'd better go in and take a bath."

After she had gone, Darling went over to the corner where the hat was lying and picked it up. It was nothing, a scrap of straw, a red flower, a veil, meaningless on his big hand, but on his wife's head a signal of something . . . big city, smart and knowing women drinking and dining with men other than their husbands, conversation about things a normal man wouldn't know much about, Frenchmen who painted as though they used their elbows instead of brushes, composers who wrote whole symphonies without a single melody in them, writers who knew all about politics and women who knew all about writers, the movement of the proletariat, Marx, somehow mixed up with five-dollar dinners and the best looking women in America and fairies who made them laugh and half-sentences immediately understood and secretly hilarious and wives who called their husbands "Baby." He put the hat down, a scrap of straw and a red flower, and a little veil. He drank some whisky straight and went into the bathroom where his wife was lying deep in her bath, singing to herself and smiling from time to time like a little girl, paddling the water gently with her hands, sending up a slight spicy fragrance from the bath salts she used.

He stood over her, looking down at her. She smiled up at him, her eyes half closed, her body pink and shimmering in the warm, scented water. All over again, with all the old suddenness, he was hit deep inside him with the knowledge of how beautiful she was, how much he needed her.

"I came in here," he said, "to tell you I wish you wouldn't call me 'Baby.'"

She looked up at him from the bath, her eyes quickly full of sorrow, half-understanding what he meant. He knelt and put his arms around her, his sleeves plunged heedlessly in the water, his shirt and jacket soaking wet as he clutched her wordlessly, holding her crazily tight, crushing her breath from her, kissing her desperately, searchingly, regretfully.

He got jobs after that, selling real estate and automobiles, but somehow, although he had a desk with his name on a wooden wedge on it, and he went to the office religiously at nine each morning, he never managed to sell anything and he never made any money.

Louise was made assistant editor, and the house was always full of strange men and women who talked fast and got angry on abstract subjects like mural painting, novelists, labor unions. Negro short-story writers drank Louise's liquor, and a lot of Jews, and big solemn men with scarred faces and knotted hands who talked slowly but clearly about picket lines and battles with guns and leadpipe at mine-shaft-heads and in front of factory gates. And Louise moved among them all, confidently, knowing what they were talking about, with opinions that they listened to and argued about just as though she were a man. She knew everybody, condescended to no one, devoured books that Darling had never heard of, walked along the streets of the city, excited, at home, soaking in all the million tides of New York without fear, with constant wonder.

Her friends liked Darling and sometimes he found a man who wanted to get off in the corner and talk about the new boy who played fullback for Princeton, and the decline of the double wing-back, or even the state of the stock market, but for the most part he sat on the edge of things, solid and quiet in the high storm of words. "The dialectics of the situation . . . The theater has been given over to expert jugglers . . . Picasso? What man has a right to paint old bones and collect ten thousand dollars for them? . . . I stand firmly behind Trotsky . . . Poe was the last American critic. When he died they put lilies on the grave of American criticism. I don't say this because they panned my last book, but . . ."

Once in a while he caught Louise looking soberly and consideringly at him through the cigarette smoke and the noise and he avoided her eyes and found an excuse to get up and go into the kitchen for more ice or to open another bottle.

"Come on," Cathal Flaherty was saying, standing at the door with a girl, "you've got to come down and see this. It's down on Fourteenth Street, in the old Civic Repertory, and you can only see it on Sunday nights and I guarantee you'll come out of the theater singing." Flaherty was a big young Irishman with a broken nose who was the lawyer for a longshoreman's union, and he had been hanging around the house for six months on and off, roaring and shutting everybody else up when he got in an argument. "It's a new play, *Waiting for Lefty*; it's about taxi-drivers."

"Odets," the girl with Flaherty said. "It's by a guy named Odets."

"I never heard of him," Darling said.

"He's a new one," the girl said.

"It's like watching a bombardment," Flaherty said. "I saw it last Sunday night. You've got to see it."

"Come on, Baby," Louise said to Darling, excitement in her eyes already. "We've been sitting in the Sunday *Times* all day, this'll be a great change."

"I see enough taxi-drivers every day," Darling said, not because he meant that, but because he didn't like to be around Flaherty, who said things that made Louise laugh a lot and whose judgment she accepted on almost every subject. "Let's go to the movies."

"You've never seen anything like this before," Flaherty said. "He wrote this play with a baseball bat."

"Come on," Louise coaxed, "I bet it's wonderful."

"He has long hair," the girl with Flaherty said. "Odets. I met him at a party. He's an actor. He didn't say a goddam thing all night."

"I don't feel like going down to Fourteenth Street," Darling said, wishing Flaherty and his girl would get out. "It's gloomy."

"Oh, hell!" Louise said loudly. She looked coolly at Darling, as though she'd just been introduced to him and was making up her mind about him, and not very favorably. He saw her looking at him, knowing there was something new and dangerous in her face and he wanted to say something, but Flaherty was there and his damned girl, and anyway, he didn't know what to say.

"I'm going," Louise said, getting her coat. "I don't think Fourteenth Street is gloomy."

"I'm telling you," Flaherty was saying, helping her on with her coat, "it's the Battle of Gettysburg, in Brooklynese."

"Nobody could get a word out of him," Flaherty's girl was saying as they went through the door. "He just sat there all night."

The door closed. Louise hadn't said good night to him. Darling walked around the room four times, then sprawled out on the sofa, on top of the Sunday *Times*. He lay there for five minutes looking at the ceiling, thinking of Flaherty walking down the street talking in that booming voice, between the girls, holding their arms.

Louise had looked wonderful. She'd washed her hair in the afternoon and it had been very soft and light and clung close to her head as she stood there angrily putting her coat on. Louise was getting prettier every year, partly because she knew by now how pretty she was, and made the most of it.

"Nuts," Darling said, standing up. "Oh, nuts."

He put on his coat and went down to the nearest bar and had five drinks off by himself in a corner before his money ran out.

The years since then had been foggy and downhill. Louise had been nice to him, and in a way, loving and kind, and they'd fought only once, when he said he was going to vote for Landon. ("Oh, Christ," she'd said, "doesn't *anything* happen inside your head? Don't you read the papers? The penniless Republican!") She'd been sorry later and apologized for hurting him, but apologized as she might to a child. He'd tried hard, had gone grimly to the art galleries, the concert halls, the bookshops, trying to gain on the trail of his wife, but it was no use. He was bored, and none of what he saw or heard or dutifully read made much sense to him and finally he gave it up. He had thought, many nights as he ate dinner alone, knowing that Louise would come home late and drop silently into bed without explanation, of getting a divorce, but he knew the loneliness, the hopelessness, of not seeing her again would be too much to take. So he was good, completely devoted, ready at all times to go any place with her, do anything she wanted. He even got a small job, in a broker's office and paid his own way, bought his own liquor.

Then he'd been offered a job of going from college to college as a tailor's representative. "We want a man," Mr. Rosenberg had said, "who as soon as you look at him, you say, 'There's a university man.'" Rosenberg had looked approvingly at Darling's broad shoulders and well-kept waist, at his carefully brushed hair and his honest, wrinkleless face. "Frankly, Mr. Darling, I am willing to make you a proposition. I have inquired about you, you are favorably known on your old campus. I understand you were in the backfield with Alfred Diederich."

Darling nodded. "Whatever happened to him?"

"He is walking around in a cast for seven years now. An iron brace. He played professional football and they broke his neck for him."

Darling smiled. That, at least, had turned out well.

"Our suits are an easy product to sell, Mr. Darling," Rosenberg said. "We have a handsome, custom-made garment. What has Brooks Brothers got that we haven't got? A name. No more."

"I can make fifty-sixty dollars a week," Darling said to Louise that night. "And expenses. I can save some money and then come back to New York and really get started here."

"Yes, Baby," Louise said.

"As it is," Darling said carefully, "I can make it back here once a month, and holidays and the summer. We can see each other often."

"Yes, Baby." He looked at her face, lovelier now at thirty-five than it had ever been before, but fogged over now as it had been for five years with a kind of patient, kindly, remote boredom.

"What do you say?" he asked. "Should I take it?" Deep within him he hoped fiercely, longingly, for her to say, "No, Baby, you stay right here," but she said, as he knew she'd say, "I think you'd better take it."

He nodded. He had to get up and stand with his back to her, looking out the window, because there were things plain on his face that she had never seen in the fifteen years she'd known him. "Fifty dollars is a lot of money," he said. "I never thought I'd ever see fifty dollars again." He laughed. Louise laughed, too.

Christian Darling sat on the frail green grass of the practice field. The shadow of the stadium had reached out and covered him. In the distance the lights of the university shone a little mistily in the light haze of evening. Fifteen years. Flaherty even now was calling for his wife, buying her a drink, filling whatever bar they were in with that voice of his and that easy laugh. Darling half-closed his eyes, almost saw the boy fifteen years ago reach for the pass, slip the halfback, go skittering lightly down the field, his knees high and fast and graceful, smiling to himself because he knew he was going to get past the safety man. That was the high point, Darling thought, fifteen years ago, on an autumn afternoon, twenty years old and far from death, with the air coming easily into his lungs, and a deep feeling inside him that he could do anything, knock over anybody, outrun whatever had to be outrun. And the shower after and the three glasses of water and the cool night air on his damp head and Louise sitting hatless in the open car with a smile and the first kiss she ever really meant. The high point, an eighty-yard run in the practice, and a girl's kiss and everything after that a decline. Darling laughed. He had practiced the wrong thing, perhaps. He hadn't practiced for 1929 and New York City and a girl who would turn into a woman. Somewhere, he thought, there must have been a point where she moved up to me, was even with me for a moment, when I could have held her hand, if I'd known, held tight, gone with her. Well, he'd never known. Here he was on a playing field that was fifteen years away and his wife was in another city having dinner with another and better man, speaking with him a different, new language, a language nobody had ever taught him.

Darling stood up, smiled a little, because if he didn't smile he knew the tears would come. He looked around him. This was the spot. O'Connor's pass had come sliding out just to here . . . the high point. Darling put up his hands, felt all over again the flat slap of the ball. He shook his hips to throw off the halfback, cut back inside the center, picked his knees high as he ran gracefully over two men jumbled on the ground at the line of scrimmage, ran easily, gaining speed, for ten yards, holding the ball lightly in his two hands, swung away from the halfback diving at him, ran, swinging his hips in the almost girlish manner of a back in a broken field, tore into the safety man, his shoes drumming heavily on the turf, stiff-armed, elbow locked, pivoted, raced lightly and exultantly for the goal line.

It was only after he had sped over the goal line and slowed to a trot that he saw the boy and girl sitting together on the turf, looking at him wonderingly.

He stopped short, dropping his arms, "I . . ." he said, gasping a little, though his condition was fine, and the run hadn't winded him. "I—once I played here."

The boy and the girl said nothing. Darling laughed embarrassedly, looked hard at them sitting there, close to each other, shrugged, turned and went toward his hotel, the sweat breaking out on his face and running down into his collar.

GLENDON SWARTHOUT

The Ball Really Carries in the Cactus League Because the Air Is Dry

Al hit one out when they played Cleveland in Tucson on Monday. Then they flew to Palm Springs on Tuesday and played California and he hit two out. Then they played Chicago at home on Wednesday and Al was in

Originally appeared in *Esquire* (1978).

there the last five innings and felt like eighty years old and this was only March. But the Cubs sent some bean name of Hernandez to try to "pilfer second" as the sportswriters would write it and Al threw him out by two steps and, not only that, hit another. Four over the fence in three days. Off good fast balls. Thinking that over in the shower took the lead out of his legs because he knew they'd also be thinking it over upstairs.

While Al was dressing, the guy from the local Chamber of Commerce that sponsored the spring training came around with the loot you got when you hit a homer at home. He got coupons for a necktie from a clothing store, a lube job from a gas station, a car wash, a haircut, and a steak dinner for two. It was maybe a little bush-league but the donors went for it because when anybody on the ball club homered, the names of their businesses were read over the P.A. system, so the promo was probably worth the price.

Al thanked the guy and left the locker room. On the way to his car he autographed balls for some kids and a program for an old geezer who said he remembered Al from when he was catching for Detroit ten years ago.

"Detroit? I was never with Detroit."

"Hanh? You wasn't?"

"Nope. I been with this club ten years. Up and down between them and their farms. Burlington, Spokane, Valdosta—you name it, I been there."

"Up and down, hanh?"

"That's right, up and down," Al said. He gave the geezer back his program and knew he'd lost interest and would drop it in the nearest trash barrel.

Parked next to his Chev in the club lot was the Italian sportscar owned by the bonus catcher he was supposed to instruct in the fine arts of keeping the pitchers happy and base runners honest and hanging on to all five fingers of his throwing hand. And incidentally the hundred thousand he'd got for signing fresh out of high school. To Al the car was unpatriotic. Play the great American game, drive an American car. And sexy. The front end of the Ferrari reminded him of a big boob with two nipples.

As he drove to the apartment the darkness shut down over the Arizona desert like a door. But the last of the sun lay red upon the mountains in the distance. They blushed the way Babe used to blush.

He went up to the apartment and onto the balcony and just then the lights went on in the palm trees around the swimming pool and putting green and he could see Babe and the other three wives putting. What they did every day was sleep late and swim and lie around the pool and go downtown to shop and have lunch, then nap and swim and lie around the pool, then get dressed and have a drink or drinks and, while they were waiting for their husbands, putt. They never went to the games. The new wives went to the games. These were married to two outfielders and the third baseman. They were ten-year wives and would rather putt. For dough. There were nine holes in the green and they'd bet on low score. Babe usually won even though she usually had a load on by now, which he could hear she did by how loud she laughed.

Al thought of making himself a drink, but when she came up she'd want another and him to have one with her and then another and by the time they went out to eat she'd have a snootful. So he stood on the balcony and listened to her laugh and watched the stars come out in a sky like a big black mitt waiting for the ball of the world. They flashed on suddenly, like signs. One star for the fast ball, two for the curve. He still didn't think it very smart of him to let her come along in the spring. It cost. He got the apartment from the club, and $18.50 per diem for food, and they could eat on that, but the $50 a week walking-around money never covered her buying clothes and crap and his salary didn't start till opening day. No, she should be at home where she could booze it up just as good as here, maybe better, but cheaper. Al's legs were lead again. Oh, Babe, Babe, he thought, where the hell we going when the party's over?

When she came in from putting he was making them a drink.

"Hi," he said. "Steak tonight."

"Whoopee."

"Listen, that's four in three days. They'll think that over upstairs."

"Sure they will. Then they'll send you down anyways and go with their hunderd thousand."

"Maybe not."

"Then when the bonus baby starts cutting out paper dolls they'll bring you up again. Up an' down, up an' down, like every year."

"You have a nice day?"

"Only maybe he won't start cutting out paper dolls. Maybe he'll stick. Then where are you?"

"He's not ready."

"Famous last words."

"Upstairs they know he's not."

"He's nineteen an' you're thirty-six."

"They're not going with a catcher can't throw."

"Leave us pray."

"Here." Al gave her her drink and touched his glass to hers. "Here's mud."

"Here's t'his broken leg."

They drank.

"Give us a kiss." Al said.

She laid limp lips on him reluctantly. "He can hit, though."

"So can this chicken. Four in three days."

"Sure you can. In the spring. How many'd you hit last spring?"

"Twelve."

"An' how many on the season?"

"You know how many."

"No I don't."

"You should. A guy plays ball his wife oughta know his record."

"You get a record I'll know it. How many last season?"

Al sat down. "Ten."

Babe didn't. "Ten. About what I thought. Ten. My God. Twelve in four weeks in the spring an' ten on the whole damn season, when they count, an' what I wanta know is why."

"I told you."

"Tell me again. In plain English."

"Because the ball carries a lot farther out here because the air's dry. I mean, back home with the muggy air you hit one just as good it's a long out. So out here I hit twelve in four weeks and back there ten on the season and about twenty long outs."

"You mean," she said, drinking and thinking, "you mean there was a major-league club in Arizona an' you was on it you'd hit thirty a year an' we'd be in the bucks on account of dry air?"

"That's right."

She had a piece of ice in her mouth and spat it back into her glass, *thoo*. "If that ain't the dumbest, damnest alibi I ever heard. You expect me t'buy that?"

"Christ," Al said.

She turned her back on him and made herself another drink. "What'd the kid do t'day?"

"Up twice, singled twice."

"Ah-ha."

"And also threw into center field and two runs score. I told you, he can't throw yet. They steal him blind. I keep telling him, you gotta feel like you stretch out your arm and touch the guy on second's glove or the guy on first's and once you feel that you never miss. It's all in your mind, not your arm."

She turned. "Quit tellin' 'im."

"That's my job."

"That's your job t'talk yourself out of a job?"

"Somebody showed me once."

Babe blew on that one. "Showed you? Showed you what? How t'get a hunderd thousand out of high school? How t'pay off a mortgage? How t'knock up your wife? How t'be an up-an'-down second-string dumb-damn catcher hits two two nine for ten years?"

"Two three one," Al said.

"My ass," Babe said.

"Let's go eat," Al said.

"Steak," Babe said.

"Free," Al said.

"Free my ass," Babe said.

He drove them past the ball park about three miles out of Scottsdale in the desert to the OK Steak Corral and parked and they went in. Babe had to stop first to see the grave of the gunfighter in front, a mound of earth with plastic flowers and a Stetson at the head of the mound and boots protruding from the dirt at the foot. There was also a headboard that said HERE LIES LESTER MOORE, KILLED BY A SLUG FROM A .44, NO LES NO MORE.

"Al," Babe said.

"What."

"There ain't actually anybody actually dead under there, is there?" She asked him every time.

"No. It's for the tourists." It was what he told her every time but he wasn't actually sure himself.

Al gave the waitress his freebie dinner ticket and they had another drink and ordered.

"You bastard," Babe said.

"Who, me?"

"Lookin' at that girl that way."

"Not me," Al said. "Not with the best-looking broad in the place with me."

"You bastard."

They didn't talk much while waiting because there was so much to see. The restaurant was full of winter tourists and the ceilings were hung with thousands of neckties cut off at the knot by the waitresses if you wore a tie to dinner here and the walls were covered with thousands of business cards from all over the country. Everyone said the OK Steak Corral had a lot of color. Al found one card on the wall behind him that cracked him up. "Cooney Plumbing, Dover, N.J.," the card said. "Your Sewers Bring Our Bread and Butter."

The girl brought the meal and they ate like from starvation. The only dinner served was a two-pound cowboy T-bone steak, pinto beans, salad, and bread and butter. They started getting along better right away. There were three things, Al had learned, that sobered Babe up fast when she had a load on: (1) steak, (2) compliments, (3) death.

Then they had coffee and she smoked. "Okay, okay," she said. "So what's gonna happen to us?"

"They'll keep me up," Al said. "Most of the year they will. They'll break the kid in easy. I'll work the tail end of double-headers and teach him. We got a knuckleballer over from Milwaukee, for instance, and he wouldn't know a knuckle ball from his sister. Anyway, they'll keep me up. We're good for this year. One more."

"One more," Babe said. She sucked smoke like a vacuum cleaner. "Tell me the pension thing again."

"Again?"

"You want your piece tonight?"

Al groaned. "Okay. I start drawing at forty-five. Nine years to go. They figure it on how many days you been in the bigs. You're up there four years and you draw two hundred a month. For life. That's minimum. They keep books on you, and outa my ten years I been up with the big club nearly five. Or will be by fall."

"So how much is that?"

"As close as I can figure, three twenty a month."

"Three twenty," Babe said. "God."

"Let's go, huh," Al said.

"Three twenty," Babe said. "Jesus."

"Let's go, huh," Al said.

He left a dollar for the girl and they left the OK Steak Corral and walked by the gunfighter's grave and got in the Chev and started back toward town.

"'Your sewers bring our bread and butter,'" Al said. "Ain't that something though?"

"You sure we're set for this year?"

"Sure I'm sure. We're ahead in the late innings and they need defense they'll yank the kid and use me. I got a great arm. There's no better throw to second than mine in the league. They don't get cute on me, ever, they don't even lean the wrong way. I don't scare when they come in from third. I'm a rock."

"Okay, they keep you. After this year what? We got nine to go before the pension."

"Well, Ray's been after me to sell cars for him, you know."

"You selling cars," Babe said bitterly. "The best throw to second in the league selling cars."

"Why not?" Al said. "I'm not in no Hall of Fame. What else do I do?"

"Three twenty a month. God."

"Not only do I sell cars, we get a cat."

"A cat?"

"I like cats."

"I can just see it—me sewing buttons or some damn thing and you playing with a cat."

"Home sweet home."

"Home sweet sheeeit."

"Not only that, I want us to adopt a kid."

Al drove half a mile before Babe said anything. Then she said, slowly, "Not having a kid of your own can be the man's fault, not the woman's. I read that somewhere."

"I didn't say it was your fault."

"No but that's what you think."

"No I don't."

"You and your great arm, ha."

Al drove half a mile before he said anything. Then he said, slowly, "Let's bury the bone, huh. I love you. I'd like us to adopt a kid. Boy or girl, it don't matter to me. Whichever you say. Stay off the sauce you'd make a helluva mother."

Babe was silent, wrestling with the concepts of temperance and motherhood. The night was cold. Finally she snuggled up and put her head on his shoulder.

"You have a nice day?" Al asked.

"So-so. I bought some beads. On sale. Indian."

"That's nice. You win putting?"

"A buck. I never lose."

"You did with me. Marrying me."

"No I didn't."

"I bet you thought you snagged yourself a three-hundred hitter."

"I didn't know from nothing about things like that. All's I knew I was marrying a ballplayer. Going where it's warm in the spring, your name in the papers, things like that. You know, glamoor."

"Two three one's not a bad average, lifetime."

"You're not kidding."

"Four in three days outa there—that's not exactly chopping wood neither."

"I don't believe it, Al. I mean, about the dry air."

"It's a fact."

"Unh-hunh. Get a violin."

"Hey," Al said.

"Hey what."

"I'll prove it."

"What?"

"I'll prove it. I got an idea."

They were passing the ball park. Al braked and pulled in the entrance and up behind the stands and stopped in the club lot.

"We gonna neck?"

"C'mon," he said, opening her door. "C'mon, I'll prove it."

"You freaked out or something?"

"I just got one hell of an idea."

He took her by the arm to a gate in the chain link fence, opened the gate with a key, and led her along the stands.

"I can't see. Al, what is this?"

"Your eyes'll adjust. Anyway, stand right here and I'll turn on the lights. Then you go on up the stairs and sit behind home plate."

"Al, you outa your mind?"

"Babe, I got one hell of an idea. Give it a try, huh? Just stand here."

He felt for another key on his ring, unlocked a door under the stands, and went in. On a wall to the right were the switches. He pulled every switch he could find. They played semipro in this park in the summer, at night. Then he went into the locker room, turned on another light, grabbed one of his bats from the rack and a bag of fungo balls, and climbed the ramp from the locker room into the dugout and stepped up onto the field.

They had a good system. The park was bright as afternoon except for shadows in the outfield corners. In right center on top of the wall was the beer-ad scoreboard and above the wall in left center were the fans of palm trees and beyond the wall, beyond the light, out there scouting in the night, were the mountains. First he checked to see if Babe was behind home plate, which she was, standing and hugging herself against the cold and waiting on him like a mother on her adopted child.

"Write me every week," she said.

"From where?"

"The funny farm."

He frowned at her, then checked to make sure nobody else was around. Nobody was. Leaving the bat at the plate he trotted out to the bullpen beyond third, located the cord, and plugged it into the outlet. Then, as the cord unreeled, he pushed the Lambert-St. Louis pitching machine out to the mound. It was a big rig but it rolled easily on rubber wheels. He placed it carefully and trod the spikes into the ground for stability. The club used the machine a lot in the spring as an alternative to a lot of sore arms and usually stationed a rook or the bat boy behind the netting to feed it. It would throw strikes or breaking balls and he set it for strikes. Taking six balls from the bag he fed them into the V-tube, flicked the switch and heard the thing hum and ran around the protective netting for the plate. He had twenty seconds. It fired at twenty-second intervals.

He grabbed the bat and some dirt and wiped his hands on his sport shirt, but before he could dig in, the first ball came through the hole in the netting like a cube of ice spat into a glass. *Thoo.* Past him to the screen.

He looked back at Babe and dug in and waggled the bat and cocked it. *Thoo.* It was low and away but he swung and topped it foul down the first-base line.

He dug in deeper. *Thoo*. Low and away again but he swung from the heels and missed and nearly ruptured a disk.

He stepped away from the plate and walked back to the stands. Babe was sitting now and leaning back and pretending to eat peanuts.

"Oh and two," she said.

Thoo.

"Two and oh," Al said. "It's supposed to throw strikes."

"They look good to me," Babe said.

"They're low and away," Al said.

Thoo.

"Busher," Babe said.

"Goddammit," Al said, turned, dropped the bat at the plate, and headed for the machine.

Thoo.

He let the damn thing go on humming and took his time resetting it, raising the spikes, pushing the machine a hair higher on the mound, and aiming through the hole in the netting to line it up dead center of the strike zone. From here his wife looked very small in the empty stands behind the screen and he thought, Oh, Babe, Babe, what'll we do when we have to pay to get in a park? Then he stomped the spikes down, fed another six balls into the V-tube, sprinted for the plate, grabbed the bat, for the fun of it pointed at the center-field wall the way Ruth did that series in Chicago in the old days, and dug in deep. He was sweating. He could see his breath in the cold and hear his heart chant.

Thoo.

Down the pipe. He swung and got good wood on it and the ball sprang off the bat like something alive and soared on up through the light and over the center-field wall between two palm trees right where he'd pointed.

He didn't even look back at the stands. He cocked his wrists and waited.

Thoo.

Down the pipe and he was loose now and had his timing and hit it over the wall in left center.

Thoo.

Like a white bird winging through the light and close to the left-field foul line but fair, fair, and out of there.

Al quit while he was ahead. Three out of five. She had to be a believer now.

He dragged the Lambert-St. Louis back to the bullpen and put away the bat and fungo balls and cut the park lights and got Babe and they got in the car and drove to the apartment and were in the living room with a light on before she opened her mouth. She sat down and looked at him like a long putt.

"You conned me," she said.

"What about?"

"The dry air. That show you put on, three out of five. You just lucked out."

Her putt dropped.

"That's right," Al said.

"You oughtn't do that to me, Al."

"I know it. But I ain't really a rock. I get scared sometimes."

"But why'd you con me?"

He sat down.

"Listen," Al said. "We been married fourteen years. It's about time we find out if it's for real. If we're gonna make it. I told you, Babe, I love you. The way you are. Even when you're in the bag. And I'll do any goddamn thing to make you love me the way I am. Even selling cars."

He waited.

"A kid," she said.

"A kid," he said.

"A cat," she said.

"A cat," he said.

She looked away like at the mountains.

Al went in the bedroom hoping she'd follow him but she turned on the ten-o'clock news. He sat on the bed in the dark and after a while shut the door and turned on the lights and stripped down to the raw. Then out of the closet he got the cowboy hat and cowboy boots he wore in the parade opening day each spring and under the bed found one of her dress boxes and tore it apart and using one of her lipsticks printed a sign on the white bottom. Then he put on the boots, lay down on the bed on his back, put the sign on his chest, and covered his face with the hat.

Babe came in. First she saw him bare-assed and out on the bed like dead and second the sign printed in purple lipstick that said HERE LIES AL, YOUR LOVING COOKIE, DYING FOR A LITTLE NOOKY.

He thought she'd laugh. Instead she cried. Babe cried taking off his boots and hat and sign and her clothes and cried lying down beside him and cried she swore to God she loved him the way he was and would be no matter what and even with the lights on they played the longest, strongest, most beautiful doubleheader of their entire married life. True love had a lot to do with it. So did the protein probably.

DAVID HILTON

The Poet Tries to
Turn in His Jock

*"The way I see it, is that when
I step out on that court and feel
inside that I can't make the plays,
it'll be time to call it quits."*

—Elgin Baylor

Going up for the jump shot,
Giving the kid the head-fakes and all
'Til he's jocked right out the door of the gym
And I'm free at the top with the ball and my touch,
Lofting the arc off my fingertips,
I feel my left calf turn to stone
And my ankle warp inward to form when I land
A neat right angle with my leg,
And I'm on the floor,
A pile of sweat and sick muscles,
Saying,
Hilton,
You're 29, getting fat,
Can't drive to your right anymore,
You can think of better things to do
On Saturday afternoons than be a chump
For a bunch of sophomore third-stringers;
Join the Y, steam and martinis and muscletone.
But, shit,
The shot goes in.

From *Huladance* (1976).

WILLIAM HARRISON

Roller Ball Murder

The game, the game: here we go again. All glory to it, all things I am and own because of Roller Ball Murder.

Our team stands in a row, twenty of us in salute as the corporation hymn is played by the band. We view the hardwood oval track which offers us the bumps and rewards of mayhem: fifty yards long, thirty yards across the ends, high banked, and at the top of the walls the cannons which fire those frenzied twenty-pound balls—similar to bowling balls, made of ebonite—at velocities over three hundred miles an hour. The balls career around the track, eventually slowing and falling with diminishing centrifugal force, and as they go to ground or strike a player another volley fires. Here we are, our team: ten roller skaters, five motorbike riders, five runners (or clubbers). As the hymn plays, we stand erect and tough; eighty thousand sit watching in the stands and another two billion viewers around the world inspect the set of our jaws on multivision.

The runners, those bastards, slip into their heavy leather gloves and shoulder their lacrosselike paddles—with which they either catch the whizzing balls or bash the rest of us. The bikers ride high on the walls (beware, mates, that's where the cannon shots are too hot to handle) and swoop down to help the runners at opportune times. The skaters, those of us with the juice for it, protest: we clog the way, try to keep the runners from passing us and scoring points, and become the fodder in the brawl. So two teams of us, forty in all, go skating and running and biking around the track while the big balls are fired in the same direction as we move—always coming up behind us to scatter and maim us—and the object of the game, fans, as if you didn't know, is for the runners to pass all skaters on the opposing team, field a ball, and pass it to a biker for one point. Those bikers, by the way, may give the runners a lift—in which case those of us on skates have our hands full overturning 175cc motorbikes.

No rest periods, no substitute players. If you lose a man, your team plays short.

Today I turn my best side to the cameras. I'm Jonathan E, none other, and nobody passes me on the track. I'm the core of the Houston team and for the

---

From *Roller Ball Murder* (1974). Originally appeared in *Esquire* (1973).

two hours of play—no rules, no penalties once the first cannon fires—I'll level any bastard runner who raises a paddle at me.

We move: immediately there are pileups of bikes, skaters, referees, and runners, all tangled and punching and scrambling when one of the balls zooms around the corner and belts us. I pick up momentum and heave an opposing skater into the infield at center ring; I'm brute speed today, driving, pushing up on the track, dodging a ball, hurtling downward beyond those bastard runners. Two runners do hand-to-hand combat and one gets his helmet knocked off in a blow which tears away half his face; the victor stands there too long admiring his work and gets wiped out by a biker who swoops down and flattens him. The crowd screams and I know the cameramen have it on an isolated shot and that viewers in Melbourne, Berlin, Rio, and L.A. are heaving with excitement in their easy chairs.

When an hour is gone I'm still wheeling along, naturally, though we have four team members out with broken parts, one rookie maybe dead, two bikes demolished. The other team, good old London, is worse off.

One of their motorbikes roars out of control, takes a hit from one of the balls, and bursts into flame. Wild cheering.

Cruising up next to their famous Jackie Magee, I time my punch. He turns in my direction, exposes the ugly snarl inside his helmet, and I take him out of action. In that tiniest instant, I feel his teeth and bone give way and the crowd screams approval. We have them now, we really have them, we do, and the score ends 7–2.

The years pass and the rules alter—always in favor of a greater crowd-pleasing carnage. I've been at this more than fifteen years, amazing, with only broken arms and collarbones to slow me down, and I'm not as spry as ever, but meaner—and no rookie, no matter how much in shape, can learn this slaughter unless he comes out and takes me on in the real thing.

But the rules. I hear of games in Manila, now, or in Barcelona with no time limits, men bashing each other until there are no more runners left, no way of scoring points. That's the coming thing. I hear of Roller Ball Murder played with mixed teams, men and women, wearing tear-away jerseys which add a little tit and vulnerable exposure to the action. Everything will happen. They'll change the rules until we skate on a slick of blood, we all know that.

Before this century began, before the Great Asian war of the 1990s, before the corporations replaced nationalism and the corporate police forces supplanted the world's armies, in the last days of American football and the World Cup in Europe, I was a tough young rookie who knew all the rewards of this game. Women: I had them all—even, pity, a good marriage once. I had so much money after my first trophies that I could buy houses and land and lakes beyond the huge cities where only the executive class was allowed. My photo, then, as now, was on the covers of magazines, so that my name and the name of the sport were one, and I was Jonathan E, no other, a survivor and much more in the bloodiest sport.

At the beginning I played for Oil Conglomerates, then those corporations became known as ENERGY; I've always played for the team here in Houston, they've given me everything.

"How're you feeling?" Mr. Bartholemew asks me. He's taking the head of ENERGY, one of the most powerful men in the world, and he talks to me like I'm his son.

"Feeling mean," I answer, so that he smiles.

He tells me they want to do a special on multivision about my career, lots of shots on the side screens showing my greatest plays, and the story of my life, how ENERGY takes in such orphans, gives them work and protection, and makes careers possible.

"Really feel mean, eh?" Mr. Bartholemew asks again, and I answer the same, not telling him all that's inside me because he would possibly misunderstand; not telling him that I'm tired of the long season, that I'm lonely and miss my wife, that I yearn for high, lost, important thoughts, and that maybe, just maybe, I've got a deep rupture in the soul.

An old buddy, Jim Cletus, comes by the ranch for the weekend. Mackie, my present girl, takes our dinners out of the freezer and turns the rays on them; not so domestic, that Mackie, but she has enormous breasts and a waist smaller than my thigh.

Cletus works as a judge now. At every game there are two referees—clowns, whose job it is to see nothing amiss—and the judge who records the points scored. Cletus is also on the International Rules Committee and tells me they are still considering several changes.

"A penalty for being lapped by your own team, for one thing," he tells us. "A damned simple penalty, too: they'll take off your helmet."

Mackie, bless her bosom, makes an O with her lips.

Cletus, once a runner for Toronto, fills up my oversized furniture and rests his hands on his bad knees.

"What else?" I ask him. "Or can you tell me?"

"Oh, just financial things. More bonuses for superior attacks. Bigger bonuses for being named World All-Star—which ought to be good news for you again. And, yeah, talk of reducing the two-month off-season. The viewers want more."

After dinner Cletus walks around the ranch with me. We trudge up the path of a hillside and the Texas countryside stretches before us. Pavilions of clouds.

"Did you ever think about death in your playing days?" I ask, knowing I'm a bit too pensive for old Clete.

"Never in the game itself," he answers proudly. "Off the track—yeah, sometimes I never thought about anything else."

We pause and take a good long look at the horizon.

"There's another thing going in the Rules Committee," he finally admits. "They're considering dropping the time limit—at least, god help us, Johnny, the suggestion has come up officially."

I like a place with rolling hills. Another of my houses is near Lyons in France, the hills similar to these although more lush, and I take my evening strolls there over an ancient battleground. The cities are too much, so large and uninhabitable that one has to have a business passport to enter such immensities as New York.

"Naturally I'm holding out for the time limit," Cletus goes on. "I've played, so I know a man's limits. Sometimes in that committee, Johnny, I feel like I'm the last moral man on earth sitting there and insisting that there should be a few rules."

The statistical nuances of Roller Ball Murder entertain the multitudes as much as any other aspect of the game. The greatest number of points scored in a single game: 81. The highest velocity of a ball when actually caught by a runner: 176 mph. Highest number of players put out of action in a single game by a single skater: 13—world's record by yours truly. Most deaths in a single contest: 9—Rome vs. Chicago, December 4, 2012.

The giant lighted boards circling above the track monitor our pace, record each separate fact of the slaughter, and we have millions of fans—strange, it always seemed to me—who never look directly at the action, but just study those statistics.

A multivision survey established this.

Before going to the stadium in Paris for our evening game, I stroll under the archways and along the Seine.

Some of the French fans call to me, waving and talking to my bodyguards as well, so I become oddly conscious of myself, conscious of my size and clothes and the way I walk. A curious moment.

I'm six-foot three inches and weigh 255 pounds. My neck is 18½ inches. Fingers like a pianist. I wear my conservative pinstriped jump suit and the famous flat Spanish hat. I am 34 years old now, and when I grow old, I think, I'll look a lot like the poet Robert Graves.

The most powerful men in the world are the executives. They run the major corporations which fix prices, wages, and the general economy, and we all know they're crooked, and they have almost unlimited power and money, but I have considerable power and money myself and I'm still anxious. What can I possibly want, I ask myself, except, possibly, more knowledge?

I consider recent history—which is virtually all anyone remembers—and how the corporate wars ended, so that we settled into the Six Majors: ENERGY, TRANSPORT, FOOD, HOUSING, SERVICES, and LUXURY. Sometimes I forget who runs what—for instance, now that the universities are operated by the Majors (and provide the farm system for Roller Ball Murder), which Major runs them? SERVICES or LUXURY? Music is one of our biggest industries, but I can't remember who administers it. Narcotic research is now under FOOD, I know, though it used to be under LUXURY.

Anyway, I think I'll ask Mr. Bartholemew about knowledge. He's a man with a big view of the world, with values, with memory. My team flings itself into the void while his team harnesses the sun, taps the sea, finds new alloys, and is clearly just a hell of a lot more serious.

.   .   .

The Mexico City game has a new wrinkle: they've changed the shape of the ball on us.

Cletus didn't even warn me—perhaps he couldn't—but here we are playing with a ball not quite round, its center of gravity altered, so that it rumbles around the track in irregular patterns.

This particular game is bad enough because the bikers down here are getting wise to me; for years, since my reputation was established, bikers have always tried to take me out of a game early. But early in the game I'm wary and strong and I'll always gladly take on a biker—even since they put shields on the motorbikes so that we can't grab the handlebars. Now, though, these bastards know I'm getting older—still mean, but slowing down, as the sports pages say about me—so they let me bash it out with the skaters and runners for as long as possible before sending the bikers after me. Knock out Jonathan E, they say, and you've beaten Houston; and that's right enough, but they haven't done it yet.

The fans down here, all low-class FOOD workers mostly, boil over as I manage to keep my cool—and the oblong ball, zigzagging around at lurching speeds, hopping two feet off the track at times, knocks out virtually their whole team. Finally, some of us catch their last runner/clubber and beat him to a pulp, so that's it: no runners, no points. Those dumb FOOD workers file out of the stadium while we show off and score a few fancy and uncontested points. The score 37—4. I feel wonderful, like pure brute speed.

Mackie is gone—her mouth no longer makes an O around my villa or ranch—and in her place is the new one, Daphne. My Daphne is tall and English and likes photos—always wants to pose for me. Sometimes we get out our boxes of old pictures (mine as a player, mostly, and hers as a model) and look at ourselves, and it occurs to me that the photos spread out on the rug are the real us, our public and performing true selves, and the two of us here in the sitting room, Gaelic gray winter outside our window, aren't too real at all.

"Look at the muscles in your back!" Daphne says in amazement as she studies a shot of me at the California beach—and it's as though she never before noticed.

After the photos, I stroll out beyond the garden. The brown waving grass of the fields reminds me of Ella, my only wife, and of her soft long hair which made a tent over my face when we kissed.

I lecture to the ENERGY-sponsored rookie camp and tell them they can't possibly comprehend anything until they're out on the track getting belted.

My talk tonight concerns how to stop a biker who wants to run you down. "You can throw a shoulder right into the shield," I begin. "And that way it's you or him."

The rookies look at me as though I'm crazy.

"Or you can hit the deck, cover yourself, tense up, and let the bastard flip over your body," I go on, counting on my fingers for them and doing my best not to laugh. "Or you can feint, sidestep up hill, and kick him off the track—which takes some practice and timing."

None of them knows what to say. We're sitting in the infield grass, the track lighted, the stands empty, and their faces are filled with stupid awe. "Or if a biker comes at you with good speed and balance," I continue, "then naturally let the bastard by—even if he carries a runner. That runner, remember, has to dismount and field one of the new odd-shaped balls which isn't easy—and you can usually catch up."

The rookies begin to get a smug look on their faces when a biker bears down on me in the demonstration period.

Brute speed. I jump to one side, dodge the shield, grab the bastard's arm and separate him from his machine in one movement. The bike skids away. The poor biker's shoulder is out of socket.

"Oh yeah," I say, getting back to my feet. "I forgot about that move."

Toward midseason when I see Mr. Bartholemew again he has been deposed as the chief executive at ENERGY. He is still very important, but lacks some of the old certainty; his mood is reflective, so that I decide to take this opportunity to talk about what's bothering me.

We lunch in Houston Tower, viewing an expanse of city. A nice Beef Well-ington and Burgundy. Daphne sits there like a stone, probably imagining that she's in a movie.

"Knowledge, ah, I see," Mr. Bartholemew replies in response to my topic. "What're you interested in, Jonathan? History? The arts?"

"Can I be personal with you?"

This makes him slightly uncomfortable. "Sure, naturally," he answers easily, and although Mr. Bartholemew isn't especially one to inspire confes-sion I decide to blunder along.

"I began in the university," I remind him. "That was—let's see—more than seventeen years ago. In those days we still had books and I read some, quite a few, because I thought I might make an executive."

"Jonathan, believe me, I can guess what you're going to say," Mr. Barthole-mew sighs, sipping the Burgundy and glancing at Daphne. "I'm one of the few with real regrets about what happened to the books. Everything is still on tapes, but it just isn't the same, is it? Nowadays only the computer specialists read the tapes and we're right back in the Middle Ages when only the monks could read the Latin script."

"Exactly," I answer, letting my beef go cold.

"Would you like me to assign you a specialist?"

"No, that's not exactly it."

"We have the great film libraries: you could get a permit to see anything you want. The Renaissance. Greek philosophers. I saw a nice summary film on the life and thought of Plato once."

"All I know," I say with hesitation, "is Roller Ball Murder."

"You don't want out of the game?" he asks warily.

"No, not at all. It's just that I want—god, Mr. Bartholemew, I don't know how to say it: I want *more*."

He offers a blank look.

"But not things in the world," I add. "More for *me*."

He heaves a great sigh, leans back, and allows the steward to refill his glass. Curiously, I know that he understands; he is a man of sixty, enormously wealthy, powerful in our most powerful executive class, and behind his eyes is the deep, weary, undeniable comprehension of the life he has lived.

"Knowledge," he tells me, "either converts to power or it converts to mel-ancholy. Which could you possibly want, Jonathan? You *have* power. You have status and skill and the whole masculine dream many of us would like to have. And in Roller Ball Murder there's no room for melancholy, is there? In the game the mind exists for the body, to make a harmony of havoc, right? Do you want to change that? Do you want the mind to exist for itself alone? I don't think you actually want that, do you?"

"I really don't know," I admit.

"I'll get you some permits, Jonathan. You can see video films, learn something about reading tapes, if you want."

"I don't think I really *have* any power," I say, still groping.

"Oh, come on. What do *you* say about that?" he asks, turning to Daphne.

"He definitely has power," she answers with a wan smile.

Somehow the conversation drifts away from me; Daphne, on cue, like the good spy for the corporation she probably is, begins feeding Mr. Bartholemew lines and soon, oddly enough, we're discussing my upcoming game with Stockholm.

A hollow space begins to grow inside me, as though fire is eating out a hole. The conversation concerns the end of the season, the All-Star Game, records being set this year, but my disappointment—in what, exactly, I don't even know—begins to sicken me.

Mr. Bartholemew eventually asks what's wrong.

"The food," I answer. "Usually I have good digestion, but maybe not today."

In the locker room the dreary late-season pall takes us. We hardly speak among ourselves, now, and like soldiers or gladiators sensing what lies ahead, we move around in these sickening surgical odors of the locker room.

Our last training and instruction this year concerns the delivery of death-blows to opposing players; no time now for the tolerant shoving and bumping of yesteryear. I consider that I possess two good weapons: because of my unusually good balance on skates, I can often shatter my opponent's knee with a kick; also, I have a good backhand blow to the ribs and heart, if, wheeling along side by side with some bastard, he raises an arm against me. If the new rules change removes a player's helmet, of course, that's death; as it is right now (there are rumors, rumors every day about what new version of RBM we'll have next) you go for the windpipe, the ribs or heart, the diaphragm, or anyplace you don't break your hand.

Our instructors are a pair of giddy Oriental gentlemen who have all sorts of anatomical solutions for us and show drawings of the human figure with nerve centers painted in pink.

"What you do is this," says Moonpie, in parody of these two. Moonpie is a fine skater in his fourth season and fancies himself an old-fashioned drawling Texan. "What you do is hit 'em on the jawbone and drive it up into their ganglia."

"Their *what?*" I ask, giving Moonpie a grin.

"Their goddamned *ganglia*. Bunch of nerves right here underneath the ear. Drive their jawbones into that mess of nerves and it'll ring their bells sure."

Daphne is gone now, too, and in this interim before another companion arrives, courtesy of all my friends and employers at ENERGY, Ella floats back into my dreams and daylight fantasies.

I was a corporation child, some executive's bastard boy, I always preferred to think, brought up in the Galveston section of the city. A big kid, naturally, athletic and strong—and this, according to my theory, gave me healthy mental genes, too, because I take it now that strong in body is strong in mind: a man with brute speed surely also has the capacity to mull over his life. Anyway, I married at age fifteen while I worked on the docks for Oil Conglomerates. Ella was a secretary, slim with long brown hair, and we managed to get permits to both marry and enter the university together. Her fellowship was in General Electronics—she was clever, give her that—and mine was in Roller Ball Murder. She fed me well that first year, so I put on thirty hard pounds and at night she soothed my bruises (was she a spy, too, I've sometimes wondered, whose job it was to prime the bull for the charge?) and perhaps it was because she was my first woman ever, eighteen years old, lovely, that I've never properly forgotten.

She left me for an executive, just packed up and went to Europe with him. Six years ago I saw them at a sports banquet where I was presented an award: there they were, smiling and being nice, and I asked them only one question, just one, "You two ever had children?" It gave me odd satisfaction that they had applied for a permit, but had been denied.

Ella, love: one does consider: did you beef me up and break my heart in some great design of corporate society?

There I was, whatever, angry and hurt. Beyond repair, I thought at the time. And the hand which stroked Ella soon dropped all the foes of Houston.

I take sad stock of myself in this quiet period before another woman arrives; I'm smart enough, I know that: I had to be to survive. Yet, I seem to know nothing—and can feel the hollow spaces in my own heart. Like one of those computer specialists, I have my own brutal technical know-how; I know what today means, what tomorrow likely holds, but maybe it's because the books are gone—Mr. Bartholemew was right, it's a shame they're transformed—that I feel so vacant. If I didn't remember my Ella—this I realize—I wouldn't even *want* to remember because it's love I'm recollecting as well as those old university days.

Recollect, sure: I read quite a few books that year with Ella and afterward, too, before turning professional in the game. Apart from all the volumes about how to get along in business, I read the history of the kings of England, that pillars of wisdom book by T. E. Lawrence, all the forlorn novels, some Rousseau, a bio of Thomas Jefferson, and other odd bits. On tapes now, all that, whirring away in a cool basement someplace.

The rules crumble once more.

At the Tokyo game, we discover that there will be three oblong balls in play at all times.

Some of our most experienced players are afraid to go out on the track. Then, after they're coaxed and threatened and finally consent to join the flow, they fake injury whenever they can and sprawl in the infield like rabbits. As for me, I play with greater abandon than ever and give the crowd its money's worth. The Tokyo skaters are either peering over their shoulders looking for approaching balls when I smash them, or, poor devils, they're looking for me when a ball takes them out of action.

One little bastard with a broken back flaps around for a moment like a fish, then shudders and dies.

Balls jump at us as though they have brains.

But fate carries me, as I somehow know it will; I'm a force field, a destroyer. I kick a biker into the path of a ball going at least two hundred miles an hour. I swerve around a pileup of bikes and skaters, ride high on the track, zoom down, and find a runner/clubber who panics and misses with a roundhouse swing of his paddle; without much ado, I belt him out of play with the almost certain knowledge—I've felt it before—that he's dead before he hits the infield.

One ball flips out of play soon after being fired from the cannon, jumps the railing, sails high, and plows into the spectators. Beautiful.

I take a hit from a ball, one of the three or four times I've ever been belted. The ball is riding low on the track when it catches me and I sprawl like a baby. One bastard runner comes after me, but one of our bikers chases him off. Then one of their skaters glides by and takes a shot at me, but I dig him in the groin and discourage him, too.

Down and hurting, I see Moonpie killed. They take off his helmet, working slowly—it's like slow motion and I'm writhing and cursing and unable to help—and open his mouth on the toe of some bastard skater's boot. Then they kick the back of his head and knock out all his teeth—which rattle downhill on the track. Then kick again and stomp; his brains this time. He drawls a last groaning good-bye while the cameras record it.

And later I'm up, pushing along once more, feeling bad, but knowing everyone else feels the same; I have that last surge of energy, the one I always get when I'm going good, and near the closing gun I manage a nice move; grabbing one of their runners with a headlock, I skate him off to limbo, bashing his face with my free fist, picking up speed until he drags behind like a dropped flag, and disposing of him in front of a ball which carries him off in a comic flop. Oh, god, god.

Before the All-Star game, Cletus comes to me with the news I expect: this one will be a no-time-limit extravaganza in New York, every multivision set in the world tuned in. The bikes will be more high-powered, four oblong balls will be in play simultaneously, and the referees will blow the whistle on any sluggish player and remove his helmet as a penalty.

Cletus is apologetic.

"With those rules, no worry," I tell him. "It'll go no more than an hour and we'll all be dead."

We're at the Houston ranch on a Saturday afternoon, riding around in my electrocart viewing the Santa Gertrudis stock. This is probably the ultimate spectacle of my wealth: my own beef cattle in a day when only a few special members of the executive class have any meat to eat with the exception of mass-produced fish. Cletus is so impressed with my cattle that he keeps going on this afternoon and seems so pathetic to me, a judge who doesn't judge, the pawn of a committee, another feeble hulk of an old RBM player.

"You owe me a favor, Clete," I tell him.

"Anything," he answers, not looking me in the eyes.

I turn the cart up a lane beside my rustic rail fence, an archway of oak trees overhead and the early spring bluebonnets and daffodils sending up fragrances from the nearby fields. Far back in my thoughts is the awareness that I can't possibly last and that I'd like to be buried out here—burial is seldom allowed anymore, everyone just incinerated and scattered—to become the mulch of flowers.

"I want you to bring Ella to me," I tell him. "After all these years, yeah: that's what I want. You arrange it and don't give me any excuses, okay?"

We meet at the villa near Lyons in early June, only a week before the All-Star Game in New York, and I think she immediately reads something in my eyes which helps her to love me again. Of course I love her: I realize, seeing her, that I have only a vague recollection of being alive at all, and that was a long time ago, in another century of the heart when I had no identity except my name, when I was a simple dock worker, before I ever saw all the world's places or moved in the rumbling nightmares of Roller Ball Murder.

She kisses my fingers. "Oh," she says softly, and her face is filled with true wonder, "What's happened to you, Johnny?"

A few soft days. When our bodies aren't entwined in lovemaking, we try to remember and tell each other everything: the way we used to hold hands, how we fretted about receiving a marriage permit, how the books looked on our shelves in the old apartment in River Oaks. We strain, at times, trying to recollect the impossible; it's true that history is really gone, that we have no families or touchstones, that our short personal lives alone judge us, and I want to hear about her husband, the places they've lived, the furniture in her house, anything. I tell her, in turn, about all the women, about Mr. Bartholemew and Jim Cletus, about the ranch in the hills outside Houston.

Come to me, Ella. If I can remember us, I can recollect meaning and time.

It would be nice, I think, once, to imagine that she was taken away from me by some malevolent force in this awful age, but I know the truth of that: she went away, simply, because I wasn't enough back then, because those were the days before I yearned for anything, when I was beginning to live to play the game. But no matter. For a few days she sits on my bed and I touch her skin like a blind man groping back over the years.

On our last morning together she comes out in her traveling suit with her hair pulled up underneath a fur cap. The softness has faded from her voice and she smiles with efficiency, as if she has just come back to the practical world; I recall, briefly, this scene played out a thousand years ago when she explained that she was going away with her executive.

She plays like a biker, I decide; she rides up there high above the turmoil, decides when to swoop down, and makes a clean kill.

"Good-bye, Ella," I say, and she turns her head slightly away from my kiss so that I touch her fur cap with my lips.

"I'm glad I came," she says politely. "Good luck, Johnny."

New York is frenzied with what is about to happen.

The crowds throng into Energy Plaza, swarm the ticket offices at the stadium, and wherever I go people are reaching for my hands, pushing my bodyguards away, trying to touch my sleeve as though I'm some ancient religious figure, a seer or prophet.

Before the game begins I stand with my team as the corporation hymns are played. I'm brute speed today, I tell myself, trying to rev myself up; yet, adream in my thoughts, I'm a bit unconvinced.

A chorus of voices joins the band now as the music swells.

The game, the game, all glory to it, the music rings, and I can feel my lips move with the words, singing.

ERNEST HEMINGWAY

Fifty Grand

"How are you going yourself, Jack?" I asked him.
"You seen this Walcott?" he says.
"Just in the gym."
"Well," Jack says, "I'm going to need a lot of luck with that boy."
"He can't hit you, Jack," Soldier said.
"I wish to hell he couldn't."
"He couldn't hit you with a handful of bird-shot."
"Bird-shot'd be all right," Jack says. "I wouldn't mind bird-shot any."
"He looks easy to hit," I said.
"Sure," Jack says, "he ain't going to last long. He ain't going to last like you and me, Jerry. But right now he's got everything."
"You'll left-hand him to death."
"Maybe," Jack says. "Sure. I got a chance to."
"Handle him like you handled Kid Lewis."
"Kid Lewis," Jack said. "That kike!"
The three of us, Jack Brennan, Soldier Bartlett, and I were in Hanley's. There were a couple of broads sitting at the next table to us. They had been drinking.
"What do you mean, kike?" one of the broads says. "What do you mean, kike, you big Irish bum?"
"Sure," Jack says. "That's it."
"Kikes," this broad goes on. "They're always talking about kikes, these big Irishmen. What do you mean, kikes?"
"Come on. Let's get out of here."
"Kikes," this broad goes on. "Whoever saw you ever buy a drink? Your wife sews your pockets up every morning. These Irishmen and their kikes! Ted Lewis could lick you too."
"Sure," Jack says. "And you give away a lot of things free too, don't you?"
We went out. That was Jack. He could say what he wanted to when he wanted to say it.
Jack started training out at Danny Hogan's health farm over in Jersey. It was nice out there but Jack didn't like it much. He didn't like being away from his wife and the kids, and he was sore and grouchy most of the time. He

From *The Snows of Kilimanjaro and Other Stories* (1927).

liked me and we got along fine together; and he liked Hogan, but after a while Soldier Bartlett commenced to get on his nerves. A kidder gets to be an awful thing around a camp if his stuff goes sort of sour. Soldier was always kidding Jack, just sort of kidding him all the time. It wasn't very funny and it wasn't very good, and it began to get to Jack. It was sort of stuff like this. Jack would finish up with the weights and the bag and pull on the gloves.

"You want to work?" he'd say to Soldier.

"Sure. How you want me to work?" Soldier would ask. "Want me to treat you rough like Walcott? Want me to knock you down a few times?"

"That's it," Jack would say. He didn't like it any, though.

One morning we were all out on the road. We'd been out quite a way and now we were coming back. We'd go along fast for three minutes and then walk a minute, and then go fast for three minutes again. Jack wasn't ever what you would call a sprinter. He'd move around fast enough in the ring if he had to, but he wasn't any too fast on the road. All the time we were walking Soldier was kidding him. We came up the hill to the farmhouse.

"Well," says Jack, "you better go back to town, Soldier."

"What do you mean?"

"You better go back to town and stay there."

"What's the matter?"

"I'm sick of hearing you talk."

"Yes?" says Soldier.

"Yes," says Jack.

"You'll be a damn sight sicker when Walcott gets through with you."

"Sure," says Jack, "Maybe I will. But I know I'm sick of you."

So Soldier went off on the train to town that same morning. I went down with him to the train. He was good and sore.

"I was just kidding him," he said. We were waiting on the platform. "He can't pull that stuff with me, Jerry."

"He's nervous and crabby," I said. "He's a good fellow, Soldier."

"The hell he is. The hell he's ever been a good fellow."

"Well," I said, "so long, Soldier."

The train had come in. He climbed up with his bag.

"So long, Jerry," he says. "You be in town before the fight?"

"I don't think so."

"See you then."

He went in and the conductor swung up and the train went out. I rode back to the farm in the cart. Jack was on the porch writing a letter to his wife. The mail had come and I got the papers and went over on the other side of the porch and sat down to read. Hogan came out the door and walked over to me.

"Did he have a jam with Soldier?"

"Not a jam," I said. "He just told him to go back to town."

"I could see it coming," Hogan said. "He never liked Soldier much."

"No. He don't like many people."

"He's a pretty cold one," Hogan said.

"Well, he's always been fine to me."

"Me too," Hogan said. "I got no kick on him. He's a cold one, though."

Hogan went in through the screen door and I sat there on the porch and read the papers. It was just starting to get fall weather and it's nice country there in Jersey, up in the hills, and after I read the paper through I sat there and looked out at the country and the road down below against the woods with cars going along it, lifting the dust up. It was fine weather and pretty nice-looking country. Hogan came to the door and I said, "Say, Hogan, haven't you got anything to shoot out here?"

"No," Hogan said. "Only sparrows."

"Seen the paper?" I said to Hogan.

"What's in it?"

"Sande booted three of them in yesterday."

"I got that on the telephone last night."

"You follow them pretty close, Hogan?" I asked.

"Oh, I keep in touch with them," Hogan said.

"How about Jack?" I says. "Does he still play them?"

"Him?" said Hogan. "Can you see him doing it?"

Just then Jack came around the corner with the letter in his hand. He's wearing a sweater and an old pair of pants and boxing shoes.

"Got a stamp, Hogan?" he asks.

"Give me the letter," Hogan said. "I'll mail it for you."

"Say, Jack," I said, "didn't you used to play the ponies?"

"Sure."

"I knew you did. I knew I used to see you out at Sheepshead."

"What did you lay off them for?" Hogan asked.

"Lost money."

Jack sat down on the porch by me. He leaned back against a post. He shut his eyes in the sun.

"Want a chair?" Hogan asked.

"No," said Jack. "This is fine."

"It's a nice day," I said. "It's pretty nice out in the country."

"I'd a damn sight rather be in town with the wife."

"Well, you only got another week."

"Yes," Jack says. "That's so."

We sat there on the porch. Hogan was inside at the office.

"What do you think about the shape I'm in?" Jack asked me.

"Well, you can't tell," I said. "You got a week to get around into form."

"Don't stall me."

"Well," I said, "you're not right."

"I'm not sleeping," Jack said.

"You'll be all right in a couple of days."

"No," says Jack, "I got the insomnia."

"What's on your mind?"

"I miss the wife."

"Have her come out."

"No. I'm too old for that."

"We'll take a long walk before you turn in and get you good and tired."

"Tired!" Jack says. "I'm tired all the time."

He was that way all week. He wouldn't sleep at night and he'd get up in the morning feeling that way, you know, when you can't shut your hands.

"He's stale as poorhouse cake," Hogan said. "He's nothing."

"I never seen Walcott," I said.

"He'll kill him," said Hogan. "He'll tear him in two."

"Well," I said, "everybody's got to get it sometime."

"Not like this, though," Hogan said. "They'll think he never trained. It gives the farm a black eye."

"You hear what the reporters said about him?"

"Didn't I! They said he was awful. They said they oughtn't to let him fight."

"Well," I said, "they're always wrong, ain't they?"

"Yes," said Hogan. "But this time they're right."

"What the hell do they know about whether a man's right or not?"

"Well," said Hogan, "they're not such fools."

"All they did was pick Willard at Toledo. This Lardner, he's so wise now, ask him about when he picked Willard at Toledo."

"Aw, he wasn't out," Hogan said. "He only writes the big fights."

"I don't care who they are," I said. "What the hell do they know? They can write maybe, but what the hell do they know?"

"You don't think Jack's in any shape, do you?" Hogan asked.

"No. He's through. All he needs is to have Corbett pick him to win for it to be all over."

"Well, Corbett'll pick him," Hogan says.

"Sure. He'll pick him."

That night Jack didn't sleep any either. The next morning was the last day before the fight. After breakfast we were out on the porch again.

"What do you think about, Jack, when you can't sleep?" I said.

"Oh, I worry," Jack says. "I worry about property I got up in the Bronx, I worry about property I got in Florida. I worry about the kids. I worry about the wife. Sometimes I think about fights. I think about that kike Ted Lewis and I get sore. I got some stocks and I worry about them. What the hell don't I think about?"

"Well," I said, "tomorrow night it'll all be over."

"Sure," said Jack. "That always helps a lot, don't it? That just fixes everything all up, I suppose. Sure."

He was sore all day. We didn't do any work. Jack just moved around a little to loosen up. He shadow-boxed a few rounds. He didn't even look good doing that. He skipped the rope a little while. He couldn't sweat.

"He'd be better not to do any work at all," Hogan said. We were standing watching him skip rope. "Don't he ever sweat at all any more?"

"He can't sweat."

"Do you suppose he's got the con? He never had any trouble making weight, did he?"

"No, he hasn't got any con. He just hasn't got anything inside any more."

"He ought to sweat," said Hogan.

Jack came over, skipping the rope. He was skipping up and down in front of us, forward and back, crossing his arms every third time.

"Well," he says. "What are you buzzards talking about?"

"I don't think you ought to work any more," Hogan says. "You'll be stale."

"Wouldn't that be awful?" Jack says and skips away down the floor, slapping the rope hard.

That afternoon John Collins showed up out at the farm. Jack was up in his room. John came out in a car from town. He had a couple of friends with him. The car stopped and they all got out.

"Where's Jack?" John asked me.

"Up in his room, lying down."

"Lying down?"

"Yes," I said.

"How is he?"

I looked at the two fellows that were with John.

"They're friends of his," John said.

"He's pretty bad," I said.

"What's the matter with him?"

"He don't sleep."

"Hell," said John. "That Irishman could never sleep."

"He isn't right," I said.

"Hell," John said. "He's never right. I've had him for ten years and he's never been right yet."

The fellows who were with him laughed.

"I want you to shake hands with Mr. Morgan and Mr. Steinfelt," John said. "This is Mr. Doyle. He's been training Jack."

"Glad to meet you," I said.

"Let's go up and see the boy," the fellow called Morgan said.

"Let's have a look at him," Steinfelt said.

We all went upstairs.

"Where's Hogan?" John asked.

"He's out in the barn with a couple of his customers," I said.

"He got many people out here now?" John asked.

"Just two."

"Pretty quiet, ain't it?" Morgan said.

"Yes," I said. "It's pretty quiet."

We were outside Jack's room. John knocked on the door. There wasn't any answer.

"Maybe he's asleep," I said.

"What the hell's he sleeping in the daytime for?"

John turned the handle and we all went in. Jack was lying asleep on the bed. He was face down and his face was in the pillow. Both his arms were around the pillow.

"Hey, Jack!" John said to him.

Jack's head moved a little on the pillow. "Jack!" John says, leaning over him. Jack just dug a little deeper in the pillow. John touched him on the shoulder. Jack sat up and looked at us. He hadn't shaved and he was wearing an old sweater.

"Christ! Why can't you let me sleep?" he says to John.

"Don't be sore," John says. "I didn't mean to wake you up."

"Oh no," Jack says. "Of course not."

"You know Morgan and Steinfelt," John said.

"Glad to see you," Jack says.

"How do you feel, Jack," Morgan asks him.

"Fine," Jack says. "How the hell would I feel?"

"You look fine," Steinfelt says.

"Yes, don't I," says Jack. "Say," he says to John. "You're my manager. You get a big enough cut. Why the hell don't you come out here when the reporters was out! You want Jerry and me to talk to them?"

"I had Lew fighting in Philadelphia," John said.

"What the hell's that to me?" Jack says. "You're my manager. You get a big enough cut, don't you? You aren't making me any money in Philadelphia, are you? Why the hell aren't you out here when I ought to have you?"

"Hogan was here."

"Hogan," Jack says. "Hogan's as dumb as I am."

"Soldier Bahtlett was out here wukking with you for a while, wasn't he?" Steinfelt said to change the subject.

"Yes, he was out here," Jack says. "He was out here all right."

"Say, Jerry," John said to me. "Would you go and find Hogan and tell him we want to see him in about half an hour?"

"Sure," I said.

"Why the hell can't he stick around?" Jack says. "Stick around, Jerry."

Morgan and Steinfelt looked at each other.

"Quiet down, Jack," John said to him.

"I better go find Hogan," I said.

"All right, if you want to go," Jack says. "None of these guys are going to send you away, though."

"I'll go find Hogan," I said.

Hogan was out in the gym in the barn. He had a couple of his health-farm patients with the gloves on. They neither one wanted to hit the other, for fear the other would come back and hit him.

"That'll do," Hogan said when he saw me come in. "You can stop the slaughter. You gentlemen take a shower and Bruce will rub you down."

They climbed out through the ropes and Hogan came over to me.

"John Collins is out with a couple of friends to see Jack," I said.

"I saw them come up in the car."

"Who are the two fellows with John?"

"They're what you call wise boys," Hogan said. "Don't you know them two?"

"No," I said.

"That's Happy Steinfelt and Lew Morgan. They got a poolroom."

"I been away a long time," I said.

"Sure," said Hogan. "That Happy Steinfelt's a big operator."

"I've heard his name," I said.

"He's a pretty smooth boy," Hogan said. "They're a couple of sharpshooters."

"Well," I said. "They want to see us in half an hour."

"You mean they don't want to see us until a half an hour?"

"That's it."

"Come on in the office," Hogan said. "To hell with those sharpshooters."

After about thirty minutes or so Hogan and I went upstairs. We knocked on Jack's door. They were talking inside the room.

"Wait a minute," somebody said.

"To hell with that stuff," Hogan said. "When you want to see me I'm down in the office."

We heard the door unlock. Steinfelt opened it.

"Come on in, Hogan," he says. "We're all going to have a drink."

"Well," says Hogan. "That's something."

We went in. Jack was sitting on the bed. John and Morgan were sitting on a couple of chairs. Steinfelt was standing up.

"You're a pretty mysterious lot of boys," Hogan said.

"Hello, Danny," John says.

"Hello, Danny," Morgan says and shakes hands.

Jack doesn't say anything. He just sits there on the bed. He ain't with the others. He's all by himself. He was wearing an old blue jersey and pants and had on boxing shoes. He needed a shave. Steinfelt and Morgan were dressers. John was quite a dresser too. Jack sat there looking Irish and tough.

Steinfelt brought out a bottle and Hogan brought in some glasses and everybody had a drink. Jack and I took one and the rest of them went on and had two or three each.

"Better save some for your ride back," Hogan said.

"Don't you worry. We got plenty," Morgan said.

Jack hadn't drunk anything since the one drink. He was standing up and looking at them. Morgan was sitting on the bed where Jack had sat.

"Have a drink, Jack," John said and handed him the glass and the bottle.

"No," Jack said, "I never liked to go to these wakes."

They all laughed. Jack didn't laugh.

They were all feeling pretty good when they left. Jack stood on the porch when they got into the car. They waved to him.

"So long," Jack said.

We had supper. Jack didn't say anything all during the meal except, "Will you pass me this?" or "Will you pass me that?" The two health-farm patients ate at the same table with us. They were pretty nice fellows. After we finished eating we went out on the porch. It was dark early.

"Like to take a walk, Jerry?" Jack asked.

"Sure," I said.

We put on our coats and started out. It was quite a way down to the main road and then we walked along the main road about a mile and a half. Cars kept going by and we would pull out to the side until they were past. Jack didn't say anything. After we had stepped out into the bushes to let a big car go by Jack said, "To hell with this walking. Come on back to Hogan's."

We went along a side road that cut up over the hill and cut across the fields back to Hogan's. We could see the lights of the house up on the hill. We came around to the front of the house and there standing in the doorway was Hogan.

"Have a good walk?" Hogan asked.

"Oh, fine," Jack said. "Listen, Hogan. Have you got any liquor?"

"Sure," says Hogan. "What's the idea?"

"Send it up to the room," Jack says. "I'm going to sleep tonight."

"You're the doctor," Hogan says.

"Come on up to the room, Jerry," Jack says.

Upstairs Jack sat on the bed with his head in his hands.

"Ain't it a life?" Jacks says.

Hogan brought in a quart of liquor and two glasses.

"Want some ginger ale?"

"What do you think I want to do, get sick?"

"I just asked you," said Hogan.

"Have a drink?" said Jack.

"No, thanks," said Hogan. He went out.

"How about you, Jerry?"

"I'll have one with you," I said.

Jack poured out a couple of drinks. "Now," he said, "I want to take it slow and easy."

"Put some water in it," I said.

"Yes," Jack said. "I guess that's better."

We had a couple of drinks without saying anything. Jack started to pour me another.

"No," I said, "that's all I want."

"All right," Jack said. He poured himself out another big shot and put water in it. He was lighting up a little.

"That was a fine bunch out here this afternoon," he said. "They don't take any chances, those two."

Then a little later, "Well," he says, "they're right. What the hell's the good in taking chances?"

"Don't you want another, Jerry?" he said. "Come on, drink along with me."

"I don't need it, Jack," I said. "I feel all right."

"Just have one more," Jack said. It was softening him up.

"All right," I said.

Jack poured one for me and another big one for himself.

"You know," he said, "I like liquor pretty well. If I hadn't been boxing I would have drunk quite a lot."

"Sure," I said.

"You know," he said, "I missed a lot, boxing."

"You made plenty of money."

"Sure, that's what I'm after. You know I miss a lot, Jerry."

"How do you mean?"

"Well," he says, "like about the wife. And being away from home so much. It don't do my girls any good. 'Who's your old man?' some of those society kids 'll say to them. 'My old man's Jack Brennan.' That don't do them any good."

"Hell," I said, "all that makes a difference is if they got dough."

"Well," says Jack, "I got the dough for them all right."

He poured out another drink. The bottle was about empty.

"Put some water in it," I said. Jack poured in some water.

"You know," he says, "you ain't got any idea how I miss the wife."

"Sure."

"You ain't got any idea. You can't have an idea what it's like."

"It ought to be better out in the country than in town."

"With me now," Jack said, "it don't make any difference where I am. You can't have an idea what it's like."

"Have another drink."

"Am I getting soused? Do I talk funny?"

"You're coming on all right."

"You can't have an idea what it's like. They ain't anybody can have an idea what it's like."

"Except the wife," I said.

"She knows," Jack said. "She knows all right. She knows. You bet she knows."

"Put some water in that," I said.

"Jerry," says Jack, "you can't have an idea what it gets to be like."

He was good and drunk. He was looking at me steady. His eyes were sort of too steady.

"You'll sleep all right," I said.

"Listen, Jerry," Jack says. "You want to make some money? Get some money down on Walcott."

"Yes?"

"Listen, Jerry," Jack put down the glass. "I'm not drunk now, see? You know what I'm betting on him? Fifty grand."

"That's a lot of dough."

"Fifty grand," Jack says, "at two to one. I'll get twenty-five thousand bucks. Get some money on him, Jerry."

"It sounds good," I said.

"How can I beat him?" Jack says. "It ain't crooked. How can I beat him? Why not make money on it?"

"Put some water in that," I said.

"I'm through after this fight," Jack says. "I'm through with it. I got to take a beating. Why shouldn't I make money on it?"

"Sure."

"I ain't slept for a week," Jack says. "All night I lay awake and worry my can off. I can't sleep, Jerry. You ain't got an idea what it's like when you can't sleep."

"Sure."

"I can't sleep. That's all. I just can't sleep. What's the use of taking care of yourself all these years when you can't sleep?"

"It's bad."

"You ain't got an idea what it's like, Jerry, when you can't sleep."

"Put some water in that," I said.

Well, about eleven o'clock Jack passes out and I put him to bed. Finally he's so he can't keep from sleeping. I helped him get his clothes off and got him into bed.

"You'll sleep all right, Jack," I said.

"Sure," Jack says, "I'll sleep now."

"Good night, Jack," I said.

"Good night, Jerry," Jack says. "You're the only friend I got."

"Oh, hell," I said.

"You're the only friend I got," Jack says, "the only friend I got."

"Go to sleep," I said.

"I'll sleep," Jack says.

Downstairs Hogan was sitting at the desk in the office reading the papers. He looked up. "Well, you get your boy friend to sleep?" he asks.

"He's off."

"It's better for him than not sleeping," Hogan said.

"Sure."

"You'd have a hell of a time explaining that to these sport writers though," Hogan said.

"Well, I'm going to bed myself," I said.

"Good night," said Hogan.

In the morning I came downstairs about eight o'clock and got some breakfast. Hogan had his two customers out in the barn doing exercises. I went out and watched them.

"One! Two! Three! Four!" Hogan was counting for them. "Hello, Jerry," he said. "Is Jack up yet?"

"No. He's still sleeping."

I went back to my room and packed up to go in to town. About nine-thirty I heard Jack getting up in the next room. When I heard him go downstairs I went down after him. Jack was sitting at the breakfast table. Hogan had come in and was standing beside the table.

"How do you feel, Jack?" I asked him.

"Not so bad."

"Sleep well?" Hogan asked.

"I slept all right," Jack said. "I got a thick tongue but I ain't got a head."

"Good," said Hogan. "That was good liquor."

"Put it on the bill," Jack says.

"What time you want to go into town?" Hogan asked.

"Before lunch," Jack says. "The eleven o'clock train."

"Sit down, Jerry," Jack said. Hogan went out.

I sat down at the table. Jack was eating a grapefruit. When he'd find a seed he'd spit it out in the spoon and dump it on the plate.

"I guess I was pretty stewed last night," he started.

"You drank some liquor."

"I guess I said a lot of fool things."

"You weren't bad."

"Where's Hogan?" he asked. He was through with the grapefruit.

"He's out in front in the office."

"What did I say about betting on the fight?" Jack asked. He was holding the spoon and sort of poking at the grapefruit with it.

The girl came in with some ham and eggs and took away the grapefruit.

"Bring me another glass of milk," Jack said to her. She went out.

"You said you had fifty grand on Walcott," I said.

"That's right," Jack said.

"That's a lot of money."

"I don't feel too good about it," Jack said.

"Something might happen."

"No," Jack said. "He wants the title bad. They'll be shooting with him all right."

"You can't ever tell."

"No. He wants the title. It's worth a lot of money to him."

"Fifty grand is a lot of money," I said.

"It's business," said Jack. "I can't win. You know I can't win anyway."

"As long as you're in there you got a chance."

"No," Jack says. "I'm all through. It's just business."

"How do you feel?"

"Pretty good," Jack said. "The sleep was what I needed."

"You might do good."

"I'll give them a good show," Jack said.

After breakfast Jack called up his wife on the long-distance. He was inside the booth telephoning.

"That's the first time he's called her up since he's out here," Hogan said.

"He writes her every day."

"Sure," Hogan says, "a letter only costs two cents."

Hogan said good-by to us and Bruce, the nigger rubber, drove us down to the train in the cart.

"Good-by, Mr. Brennan," Bruce said at the train, "I sure hope you knock his can off."

"So long," Jack said. He gave Bruce two dollars. Bruce had worked on him a lot. He looked kind of disappointed. Jack saw me looking at Bruce holding the two dollars.

"It's all in the bill," he said. "Hogan charged me for the rubbing."

On the train going into town Jack didn't talk. He sat in the corner of the seat with his ticket in his hat-band and looked out of the window. Once he turned and spoke to me.

"I told the wife I'd take a room at the Shelby tonight," he said. "It's just around the corner from the Garden. I can go up to the house tomorrow morning."

"That's a good idea," I said. "Your wife ever see you fight, Jack?"

"No," Jack says. "She never seen me fight."

I thought he must be figuring on taking an awful beating if he doesn't want to go home afterward. In town we took a taxi up to the Shelby. A boy came out and took our bags and we went in to the desk.

"How much are the rooms?" Jack asked.

"We only have double rooms," the clerk says. "I can give you a nice double room for ten dollars."

"That's too steep."

"I can give you a double room for seven dollars."

"With a bath?"

"Certainly."

"You might as well bunk with me, Jerry," Jack says.

"Oh," I said, "I'll sleep down at my brother-in-law's."

"I don't mean for you to pay it," Jack says. "I just want to get my money's worth."

"Will you register, please?" the clerk says. He looked at the names. "Number 238, Mister Brennan."

We went up in the elevator. It was a nice big room with two beds and a door opening into a bath-room.

"This is pretty good," Jack says.

The boy who brought us up pulled up the curtains and brought in our bags. Jack didn't make any move, so I gave the boy a quarter. We washed up and Jack said we better go out and get something to eat.

We ate a lunch at Jimmy Hanley's place. Quite a lot of the boys were there. When we were about half through eating, John came in and sat down with us. Jack didn't talk much.

"How are you on the weight, Jack?" John asked him. Jack was putting away a pretty good lunch.

"I could make it with my clothes on," Jack said. He never had to worry about taking off weight. He was a natural welterweight and he'd never gotten fat. He'd lost weight out at Hogan's.

"Well, that's one thing you never had to worry about," John said.

"That's one thing," Jack says.

We went around to the Garden to weigh in after lunch. The match was made at a hundred forty-seven pounds at three o'clock. Jack stepped on the scales with a towel around him. The bar didn't move. Walcott had just weighed and was standing with a lot of people around him.

"Let's see what you weigh, Jack," Freedman, Walcott's manager said.

"All right, weigh *him* then," Jack jerked his head toward Walcott.

"Drop the towel," Freedman said.

"What do you make it?" Jack asked the fellows who were weighing.

"One hundred and forty-three pounds," the fat man who was weighing said.

"You're down fine, Jack," Freedman says.

"Weigh *him*," Jack says.

Walcott came over. He was a blond with wide shoulders and arms like a heavyweight. He didn't have much legs. Jack stood about half a head taller than he did.

"Hello, Jack," he said. His face was plenty marked up.

"Hello," said Jack. "How you feel?"

"Good," Walcott says. He dropped the towel from around his waist and stood on the scales. He had the widest shoulders and back you ever saw.

"One hundred and forty-six pounds and twelve ounces."

Walcott stepped off and grinned at Jack.

"Well," John says to him, "Jack's spotting you about four pounds."

"More than that when I come in, kid," Walcott says. "I'm going to go and eat now."

We went back and Jack got dressed. "He's a pretty tough-looking boy," Jack says to me.

"He looks as though he'd been hit plenty of times."

"Oh, yes," Jack says. "He ain't hard to hit."

"Where are you going?" John asked when Jack was dressed.

"Back to the hotel," Jack says. "You looked after everything?"

"Yes," John says. "It's all looked after."

"I'm going to lie down a while," Jack says.

"I'll come around for you about a quarter to seven and we'll go and eat."

"All right."

Up at the hotel Jack took off his shoes and his coat and lay down for a while. I wrote a letter. I looked over a couple of times and Jack wasn't sleeping. He was lying perfectly still but every once in a while his eyes would open. Finally he sits up.

"Want to play some cribbage, Jerry?" he says.

"Sure," I said.

He went over to his suitcase and got out the cards and the cribbage board. He played cribbage and he won three dollars off me. John knocked at the door and came in.

"Want to play some cribbage, John?" Jack asked him.

John put his hat down on the table. It was all wet. His coat was wet too.

"Is it raining?" Jack asks.

"It's pouring," John says. "The taxi I had got tied up in the traffic and I got out and walked."

"Come on, play some cribbage," Jack says.

"You ought to go and eat."

"No," says Jack. "I don't want to eat yet."

So they played cribbage for about half an hour and Jack won a dollar and a half off him.

"Well, I suppose we got to go eat," Jack says. He went to the window and looked out.

"Is it still raining?"

"Yes."

"Let's eat in the hotel," John says.

"All right," Jack says, "I'll play you once more to see who pays for the meal."

After a little while Jack gets up and says, "You buy the meal, John," and we went downstairs and ate in the big dining-room.

After we ate we went upstairs and Jack played cribbage with John again and won two dollars and a half off him. Jack was feeling pretty good. John had a bag with him with all his stuff in it. Jack took off his shirt and collar and put on a jersey and a sweater, so he wouldn't catch cold when he came out, and put his ring clothes and his bathrobe in a bag.

"You all ready?" John asks him. "I'll call up and have them get a taxi."

Pretty soon the telephone rang and they said the taxi was waiting.

We rode down in the elevator and went out through the lobby, and got in a taxi and rode around to the Garden. It was raining hard but there was a lot of people outside on the streets. The Garden was sold out. As we came in on our way to the dressing-room I saw how full it was. It looked like half a mile down to the ring. It was all dark. Just the lights over the ring.

"It's a good thing, with this rain, they didn't try and pull this fight in the ball park," John said.

"They got a good crowd," Jack says.

"This is a fight that would draw a lot more than the Garden could hold."

"You can't tell about the weather," Jack says.

John came to the door of the dressing-room and poked his head in. Jack was sitting there with his bathrobe on, he had his arms folded and was looking at the floor. John had a couple of handlers with him. They looked over his shoulder. Jack looked up.

"Is he in?" he asked.

"He's just gone down," John said.

We started down. Walcott was just getting into the ring. The crowd gave him a big hand. He climbed through between the ropes and put his two fists together and smiled, and shook them at the crowd, first at one side of the ring, then at the other, and then sat down. Jack got a good hand coming down through the crowd. Jack is Irish and the Irish always get a pretty good hand. An Irishman don't draw in New York like a Jew or an Italian but they always get a good hand. Jack climbed up and bent down to go through the ropes and Walcott came over from his corner and pushed the rope down for Jack to go through. The crowd thought that was wonderful. Walcott put his hand on Jack's shoulder and they stood there just for a second.

"So you're going to be one of these popular champions," Jack says to him. "Take your goddam hand off my shoulder."

"Be yourself," Walcott says.

This is all great for the crowd. How gentlemanly the boys are before the fight. How they wish each other luck.

Solly Freedman came over to our corner while Jack is bandaging his hands and John is over in Walcott's corner. Jack puts his thumb through the slit in the bandage and then wrapped his hand nice and smooth. I taped it around the wrist and twice across the knuckles.

"Hey," Freedman says. "Where do you get all that tape?"

"Feel of it," Jack says. "It's soft, ain't it? Don't be a hick."

Freedman stands there all the time while Jack bandages the other hand, and one of the boys that's going to handle him brings the gloves and I pull them on and work them around.

"Say, Freedman," Jack asks, "what nationality is this Walcott?"

"I don't know," Solly says. "He's some sort of a Dane."

"He's a Bohemian," the lad who brought the gloves said.

The referee called them out to the center of the ring and Jack walks out.

Walcott comes out smiling. They met and the referee put his arm on each of their shoulders.

"Hello, popularity," Jack says to Walcott.

"Be yourself."

"What do you call yourself 'Walcott' for?" Jack says. "Didn't you know he was a nigger?"

"Listen—" says the referee, and he gives them the same old line. Once Walcott interrupts him. He grabs Jack's arm and says, "Can I hit when he's got me like this?"

"Keep your hands off me," Jack says. "There ain't no moving-pictures of this."

They went back to their corners. I lifted the bathrobe off Jack and he leaned on the ropes and flexed his knees a couple of times and scuffed his shoes in the rosin. The gong rang and Jack turned quick and went out. Walcott came toward him and they touched gloves and as soon as Walcott dropped his hands Jack jumped his left into his face twice. There wasn't anybody ever boxed better than Jack. Walcott was after him, going forward all the time with his chin on his chest. He's a hooker and he carries his hands pretty low. All he knows is to get in there and sock. But every time he gets in there close, Jack has the left hand in his face. It's just as though it's automatic. Jack just raises the left hand up and it's in Walcott's face. Three or four times Jack brings the right over but Walcott gets it on the shoulder or high up on the head. He's just like all these hookers. The only thing he's afraid of is another one of the same kind. He's covered everywhere you can hurt him. He don't care about a left-hand in his face.

After about four rounds Jack has him bleeding bad and his face all cut up, but every time Walcott's got in close he's socked so hard he's got two big red patches on both sides just below Jack's ribs. Every time he gets in close, Jack ties him up, then gets one hand loose and uppercuts him, but when Walcott gets his hands loose he socks Jack in the body so they can hear it outside in the street. He's a socker.

It goes along like that for three rounds more. They don't talk any. They're working all the time. We worked over Jack plenty too, in between the rounds. He don't look good at all but he never does much work in the ring. He don't move around much and that left-hand is just automatic. It's just like it was connected with Walcott's face and Jack just had to wish it in every time. Jack is always calm in close and he doesn't waste any juice. He knows everything about working in close too and he's getting away with a lot of stuff. While they were in our corner I watched him tie Walcott up, get his right hand loose, turn it and come up with an uppercut that got Walcott's nose with the heel of the glove. Walcott was bleeding bad and leaned his nose on Jack's shoulder so as to give Jack some of it too, and Jack sort of lifted his shoulder sharp and caught him against the nose, and then brought down the right hand and did the same thing again.

Walcott was sore as hell. By the time they'd gone five rounds he hated Jack's guts. Jack wasn't sore; that is, he wasn't any sorer than he always was. He certainly did used to make the fellows he fought hate boxing. That was why he hated Kid Lewis so. He never got the Kid's goat. Kid Lewis always had about three new dirty things Jack couldn't do. Jack was as safe as a church all the time he was in there, as long as he was strong. He certainly was treating Walcott rough. The funny thing was it looked as though Jack was an open classic boxer. That was because he had all that stuff too.

After the seventh round Jack says, "My left's getting heavy."

From then he started to take a beating. It didn't show at first. But instead of him running the fight it was Walcott was running it, instead of being safe all the time now he was in trouble. He couldn't keep him out with the left hand now. It looked as though it was the same as ever, only now instead of Walcott's punches just missing him they were just hitting him. He took an awful beating in the body.

"What's the round?" Jack asked.

"The eleventh."

"I can't stay," Jack says. "My legs are going bad."

Walcott had been just hitting him for a long time. It was like a baseball catcher pulls the ball and takes some of the shock off. From now on Walcott commenced to land solid. He certainly was a socking-machine. Jack was just trying to block everything now. It didn't show what an awful beating he was taking. In between the rounds I worked on his legs. The muscles would flutter under my hands all the time I was rubbing them. He was sick as hell.

"How's it go?" he asked John, turning around, his face all swollen.

"It's his fight."

"I think I can last," Jack says. "I don't want this bohunk to stop me."

It was going just the way he thought it would. He knew he couldn't beat Walcott. He wasn't strong any more. He was all right though. His money was all right and now he wanted to finish it off right to please himself. He didn't want to be knocked out.

The gong rang and we pushed him out. He went out slow. Walcott came right out after him. Jack put the left in his face and Walcott took it, came in under it and started working on Jack's body. Jack tried to tie him up and it was just like trying to hold on to a buzz-saw. Jack broke away from it and missed with the right. Walcott clipped him with a left-hook and Jack went down. He went down on his hands and knees and looked at us. The referee started counting. Jack was watching us and shaking his head. At eight John motioned to him. You couldn't hear on account of the crowd. Jack got up. The referee had been holding Walcott back with one arm while he counted.

When Jack was on his feet Walcott started toward him.

"Watch yourself, Jimmy," I heard Solly Freedman yell to him.

Walcott came up to Jack looking at him. Jack stuck the left hand at him. Walcott just shook his head. He backed Jack up against the ropes, measured him and then hooked the left very light to the side of Jack's head and socked the right into the body as hard as he could sock, just as low as he could get it. He must have hit him five inches below the belt. I thought the eyes would come out of Jack's head. They stuck way out. His mouth come open.

The referee grabbed Walcott. Jack stepped forward. If he went down there went fifty thousand bucks. He walked as though all his insides were going to fall out.

"It wasn't low," he said. "It was a accident."

The crowd were yelling so you couldn't hear anything.

"I'm all right," Jack says. They were right in front of us. The referee looks at John and then he shakes his head.

"Come on, you polak son-of-a-bitch," Jack says to Walcott.

John was hanging onto the ropes. He had the towel ready to chuck in. Jack was standing just a little way out from the ropes. He took a step forward. I saw the sweat come out on his face like somebody had squeezed it and a big drop went down his nose.

"Come on and fight," Jack says to Walcott.

The referee looked at John and waved Walcott on.

"Go in there, you slob," he says.

Walcott went in. He didn't know what to do either. He never thought Jack could have stood it. Jack put the left in his face. There was such a hell of a lot of yelling going on. They were right in front of us. Walcott hit him twice. Jack's face was the worst thing I ever saw—the look on it! He was holding himself and all his body together and it all showed on his face. All the time he was thinking and holding his body in where it was busted.

Then he started to sock. His face looked awful all the time. He started to sock with his hands low down by his side, swinging at Walcott. Walcott covered up and Jack was swinging wild at Walcott's head. Then he swung the left and it hit Walcott in the groin and the right hit Walcott right bang where he'd hit Jack. Way low below the belt. Walcott went down and grabbed himself there and rolled and twisted around.

The referee grabbed Jack and pushed him toward his corner. John jumps into the ring. There was all this yelling going on. The referee was talking with the judges and then the announcer got into the ring with the megaphone and says, "Walcott on a foul."

The referee is talking to John and he says, "What could I do? Jack wouldn't take the foul. Then when he's groggy he fouls him."

"He'd lost it anyway," John says.

Jack's sitting on the chair. I've got his gloves off and he's holding himself in down there with both hands. When he's got something supporting it his face doesn't look so bad.

"Go over and say you're sorry," John says into his ear. "It'll look good."

Jack stands up and the sweat comes out all over his face. I put the bathrobe around him and he holds himself in with one hand under the bathrobe and goes across the ring. They've picked Walcott up and they're working on him. There're a lot of people in Walcott's corner. Nobody speaks to Jack. He leans over Walcott.

"I'm sorry," Jack says. "I didn't mean to foul you."

Walcott doesn't say anything. He looks too damned sick.

"Well, you're the champion now," Jack says to him. "I hope you get a hell of a lot of fun out of it."

"Leave the kid alone," Solly Freedman says.

"Hello, Solly," Jack says. "I'm sorry I fouled your boy."

Freedman just looks at him.

Jack went to his corner walking that funny jerky way and we got him down through the ropes and through the reporters' tables and out down the aisle. A lot of people want to slap Jack on the back. He goes out through all that mob in his bathrobe to the dressing-room. It's a popular win for Walcott. That's the way the money was bet in the Garden.

Once we got inside the dressing-room Jack lay down and shut his eyes.

"We want to get to the hotel and get a doctor," John says.

"I'm all busted inside," Jack says.

"I'm sorry as hell, Jack," John says.

"It's all right," Jack says.

He lies there with his eyes shut.

"They certainly tried a nice double-cross," John said.

"Your friends Morgan and Steinfelt," Jack said. "You got nice friends."

He lies there, his eyes are open now. His face has still got that awful drawn look.

"It's funny how fast you can think when it means that much money," Jack says.

"You're some boy, Jack," John says.

"No," Jack says. "It was nothing."

ADAM SMITH

"Sport Is a Western Yoga"

QUARTERBACKING IN AN ALTERED STATE

Murphy, the great mystic, alumnus of Stanford and the Sri Aurobindo ashram, founder of Esalen, Murphy has been Rolfed and Alexandered and grouped and Zenned and yogaed and *gestalted* and God knows what, there is no trip he hasn't been on, every one that wants to surface has to check in with him, and serious, too, shelves of books on mystics and philosophers, lots of meditation every day, marvelous enthusiasm, and what is Murphy into? Jogging. No, not jogging, *running*, jogging is only eight minutes to the mile, Murphy wants to run a mile in five minutes, five miles in thirty-five minutes, the mystical long-distance runner. The aikido black belt has checked his centering and Murphy is out there on the running track, what's-his-name the middle-distance runner who almost made the Olympics is running alongside of him, three miles, four miles, here comes the pain, pain is a cultural attitude it says in *Principles of Psycho-physiology*, it is only as real as we make it, the Italians and Jews make it more than the Yankees it says, hello pain—Murphy is in his mid-forties, bound to be pain, hello pain, go into the pain, don't fight, see if you can come out the other side and—

"Five minutes and seventeen seconds!" Down the coast in Murphy's own famous ashram, Esalen, the gurus are guruing and the *gestalters* are *gestalting* and Bob and Carol and Ted and Alice are sorting out their hang-ups, people are screaming screams, letting it all hang out, getting out of all that linear crap, sitting on cushions listening to the residents with M.A.'s in psychology—academic market a little tight these days, no jobs there—rap on what it's all about, and where is Murphy? On the golf course, and since there is no golf course at Esalen that means the president of the ashram is far away, teeing off with John Brodie, the quarterback, because golf is a kind of meditation too—

—it is? And tennis? And bowling? Hunting? Swimming? Hey, this is going to be easier than sitting and staring at the wall, hi-tot-tsu, hu-tot-tsu, mi-it-tsu—how can I attain the mortgage if the taxes go up?

I should have known Murphy would bring East to West through sports, his

From *Powers of Mind* (1975). Appeared in earlier form in *Psychology Today* (1975).

imperatives are all from sports. "We *have* to go to Pebble Beach tomorrow." "Why do we have to go to Pebble Beach tomorrow, Mr. Bones?" "*Nicklaus* is playing, we have to follow Nicklaus around the course."

Who am I talking to, that Good Ol' Boy my junior-year roommate, or the great ashram leader? Murphy is in awe of Nicklaus not because of the money he wins or how far he hits the ball or any of that; Nicklaus has the *greatest powers of concentration* in golf. "I've followed him around the course lots," Murphy says. "Nicklaus *plays in a trance.* He and the club and the ball are all the same thing, and there isn't anything else. He can lock right in, real one-pointedness. I think he can influence the flight of the ball after it's hit, even."

Murphy has been into this in his book, *Golf and the Kingdom,* which is a mystic book about golf, or a golf book about mysticism, same thing.

"What Nicklaus needs now is a challenger, somebody to keep his concentration on the absolute razor's edge, the way he was to Arnold Palmer."

So Murphy cancels all his appointments to walk behind Nicklaus, where he can pick up the right vibes. And vibes there are, let me tell you, "energy streamers" that the golf ball rides toward the hole. When the golfer can visualize and execute his shot in a moment of high clarity, the ball rides the energy streamer right up to the green.

John Brodie, ex-Stanford star, seventeen-year quarterback for the 49ers, most valuable player NFL 1970, second most all-time yards gained passing, and so on, is not one to dispute the energy streamers.

"I would have to say that such things seem to exist." Brodie's white teeth flash into a perfect smile. "It's happened to me dozens of times. An intention carries a force, a thought connected with an energy that can stretch itself out in a pass play or a golf shot or a base hit or a thirty-foot jump shot in basketball. I've seen it happen too many times to deny it."

Murphy: "Can you develop this? Practice it? Can you learn to develop clarity and strengthen your intentions?"

Brodie: "Yes."

Brodie is six three, two fifteen, big shoulders, moves gracefully, and as far as I know does not know a Zen master from a rubber duck, but he is about to sound like one:

"The player can't be worrying about the past or the future or the crowd or some other extraneous event. He must be able to respond in the here and now, I believe we all have this naturally, maybe we lose it as we grow up. Sometimes in the heat of the game a player's perception and coordination improve dramatically. At times, I experience a kind of clarity that I've never seen described in any football story, sometimes time seems to slow way down, as if everyone were moving in slow motion. It seems as if I have all the time in the world to watch the receivers run their patterns, and yet I know the defensive line is coming at me just as fast as ever, and yet the whole thing seems like a movie or a dance in slow motion. It's beautiful."

Stoned John Brodie. The defensive line is coming at him in slow motion, like a ballet, the crowd is screaming for twelve hundred pounds of linemen to gobble him up and spit out his white, bleached bones, and he is dancing along, the ball in one very large but somehow dainty hand, in this altered state, stoned on all the vibrations of the moment, seventeen years is a long time to have those tackles coming at you but Brodie stays with it because it's so beautiful—

—Murphy's Esalen has gathered a lot of jocks and coaches together in San Francisco for a sports seminar, Murphy suspects these moments in sport are all unarticulated but similar to the awareness of the Zen master staring at the guy in the sword fight—

—the NBC man nudges me at the seminar. "I heard Brodie was getting a little wiggy," he whispers.

Clot, I think, you do not know Zen from a rubber duck.

Brodie is telling how he has four chances on every play to communicate a pattern to Gene Washington, his wide receiver. First, the play itself, in the huddle. Brodie comes up to the line, the defense shifts, he has a second chance, an audible, a shouted signal. Somebody moves in the enemy back-field, he has a third chance, a quick hand signal. And fourth—"Sometimes I let the ball fly before Gene has made his final move, *without* a pass route ex-actly, it's sort of intuition and communication, Gene and I are good friends, of course, then you don't know what the cornerbacks and safety men will do, that's part of the fun, you don't know where those guys are going to be a sec-ond before something happens, you have to be ready for the sudden glim-mer—"

"The pass pattern is from your collective unconscious," Murphy suggests.

Brodie doesn't know about that. "I know the *feeling*," he says. "You can get into another order of reality when you're playing that doesn't fit the grids and coordinates most people lay across life."

I am getting a little worried for Brodie. I am adding to my list of altered states: you can take a chemical, you can run balam balam balam through your head, you can just sit, and you can stand with a football in your hand and twelve hundred pounds of linemen coming at you while you look for your receivers. They all work.

But will the fans understand? The telepathic pass pattern, won't the fans say, *yuhh bum, yuh goddam yogi* if he misses? And then he will end up a well-paid TV commentator, that was a real fine play, just a super play, let's take another look at it from the end zone camera.

"If I were an effect of the fans it would affect me, but I am not an effect."

Scientology talk, Big John could only lift his arm to *here* and then Scientology rearranged his perception and he could lift it to *here*.

I asked Murphy why Esalen was getting involved in sports. The Esalen track team, for God's sake, here is Esalen on the frontier supposedly and what are they doing? Sending their own track team to AAU events for seniors. That has to be where they lose all the psychiatrists who don't hate them already. Thank you, Dr. Freud, but could you give us your times in the 220 and 440?

"Isn't this exciting?" Murphy says. "Sport anticipates what the Divine Essence is. Sport is a Western yoga. The Dance of Shiva. Pure play, the delight in the moment, the Now. We need a more balanced and evolutionary culture. We already have physical mobility, why shouldn't we have psychic mobility, the ability to move psychically into different states?"

Sure enough, the athletes are beginning to talk to each other about funny spaces which they have trouble describing. "There isn't any language." It's all a bit ambiguous, but it seems they are talking about sports equivalents of the "peak experience" described by Abe Maslow, the late psychologist who hung out at Esalen. Moments of exhilaration and clarity and awareness, the click that tells you the shot is good before you know the shot is good.

We don't have long hours of meditation like they did in the exotic East, and we don't have martial arts, kung fu and judo, but when you're preparing for the Olympics and swimming six hours a day, thousands of miles a year, you get yourself to something of the same state, only you have no roshi or guru to tell you what's happening while your times are getting faster.

The California track coach tells how he does it. First he gets all these sprinters out there, every one of them can travel ten yards in less than a second, a hundred yards splitting somewhere between the ninth and tenth second, all of them straining at the leash. Now he has them run the middle part of the sprint, a running start, then forty or fifty yards that "count," then they keep on another thirty or forty. "Okay," he says, "now do it with four-fifths effort." Really? Cut the effort back? *The times get faster.* "Okay, now run at four-fifths speed and relax your jaw." The sprinters don't believe it, they think the timer's thumb has slipped on the stop watch, four-fifths is faster than five-fifths.

Funny spaces. We're all sitting around the room, coaches, athletes, some of the athletes feel a bit strange, they wouldn't want anybody to hear them talking this way, so it helps to have a big quarterback like Brodie saying it's a ballet, the linemen coming at you in slow motion.

A gentleman gets up who is a well-known diver, deep diver, not fancy diver. He has set up a "surfing and diving ashram." No breathing in and out and looking at the wall, you put your scuba gear on, *then* you can count your breaths. "I had a diver who was skeptical, and then one day, in just thirty feet of water, something happened, and he said that suddenly he felt absolutely at one with the ocean, and *he could hear grains of sand on the bottom*. He spent almost an hour listening to the grains of sand, and his life has been changed ever since."

Nitrogen narcosis, I suggested. Not in thirty feet of water, everybody said angrily.

What is the click that tells you the shot is good before you know it's good? Maybe that isn't so mysterious. Maybe it's right-brained information that usually gets suppressed by the left brain, but sometimes it gets through before it stops to be translated into words.

And that total concentration, some psychologists say we crave it almost instinctively, damping down and focusing, and then opening up with a new state of concentration, that's why people take on activities that demand *total attention*, mountain climbing and tobogganing and skiing and car racing, where the penalties for non-concentration are so great that even the language-using mind shuts up for a minute because it understands that at least for a few minutes it better get out of the way. (The language-using mind gets to come back and write the whole thing up for the Sierra Club journal, how time slows down, and the climber is suddenly aware of all the crystals in the rocks—)

We all may crave that sort of focusing, but a lot of us pay our dues to the feeling by watching the crazies toboggan down the mountain on TV, while we have a beer can in hand.

ZEN AND THE CROSS-COURT BACKHAND

I signed up for "yoga tennis." Yoga tennis surfaced at Esalen, and then I pursued it other places. *Sports Illustrated* wanted to know about it, and secretly I hoped to fix my serve while exploring this new frontier. I had one yoga tennis teacher who wore a blue jogging suit and a Sikh beard and a turban; he was a former business-forms salesman who talked a lot about *ki*, energy. And there was another yoga tennis instructor who hoped to have "a tennis ashram."

But Tim Gallwey did not wear a beard or a turban. Gallwey had been the captain of the Harvard tennis team, and he had been brooding about tennis while following the Guru Maharaj Ji. He was very articulate, and eventually I took him to see my publisher, and Gallwey wrote *The Inner Game of Tennis*.

"We learn tennis element by element," Gallwey said, standing on a tennis court at the California junior college where Esalen was having a sports seminar. "If we learned it as totality, we could learn it in one-hundredth the time.

Our biggest problem is Ego, is trying too hard. We know how to play perfect tennis. Perfect tennis is in us all. Everyone knows how to ride a bicycle, and just before we really ride for the first time, we know we know. The problem with Ego is that it has to achieve; we are not sure who we are until by achieving we become. So we hit the ball out and the Ego says, 'Ugh, out.' Then it starts to give commands, 'Do it right.' We shouldn't have a judgment. The ball goes *there*, not out. Ninety percent of the bad things students do are intentional corrections of something else they are doing. We have to let the body experiment and by-pass the mind. The mind acts like a sergeant with the body a private. How can anybody play as a duality?"

I recognized the sergeant's voice right away; in my mind, it says, "Move your feet, dummy," and "Watch the ball." What to do about the sergeant?

"You have to check the mind, to preoccupy it, stop it from fretting. Look at the ball. Look at the *seams* on the ball, watch the pattern, get preoccupied so the mind can't judge. In between points put your mind on your breathing. In, out. In, out. A quiet mind is the secret of yoga tennis. Most people think concentration is fierce effort. Watch your facial muscles after you hit the ball. Are they tensed or relaxed? Concentration is effortless effort, is *not trying*. The body is sophisticated; its computer commands hundreds of muscles instantly; it is wise about itself; the Ego isn't. Higher consciousness is not a mystical term. You see more when all of your energy runs in the same direction. Concentration produces joy, so we look for things that will quiet the mind."

I could see that parking the mind would be essential. I sat next to Jascha Heifetz once at a dinner party and asked him what he thought about when he was giving a concert. He said if the concert was, say, on a Saturday night he thought about the smoked salmon and the marvelous bagel he was going to have on Sunday morning. If he was thinking about the bagel, then who was thinking about the concerto? His hands.

Don't you have to know the right form before you park the mind?

The body seeks out the right form if the mind doesn't get in the way, Gallwey said. No teenager could do a monkey or a locomotive or whatever teenage dance is now rampant from a set of instructions, but he can do it in one night by observing.

Ah, observing. You didn't say observing.

"You have to talk to the body in its native language," said the tennis guru. "Its native language is not English, it is sight and feel, mostly sight. The stream of instructions most students get are verbal and have to be translated by the body before they are understood. If you are taking a tennis lesson, let the pro show you, don't let him tell you. If you want the ball to go to a cross-court corner, get an image of where you want the ball to go and let the body take it over. Say: 'Body, cross-court corner, please.'"

"Let the serve serve itself," Gallway said. "When I first used this technique my serve got hot. Then I thought, wow, I've mastered the serve and immediately it got cold because it was me, not the serve, serving itself."

This imagining the ball into the corner, was this the power of positive thinking, Norman Vincent Peale?

"Oh, no. Positive thinking is negative thinking in disguise. If you double-fault six times in a row your positive thinking will flip to negative. So I try not to pay compliments because the compliment can always be withheld on the next show. What we are talking about is *no thinking*."

It seemed a marvelously Rousseauistic philosophy. Man is born with a perfect tennis game and he is everywhere in chains. Rousseau was influenced by the sunny Polynesians brought to Europe by the eighteenth-century sailors; what if they had sailed a little further over, and brought back fierce and aggressive Melanesians? You don't need a tennis pro with negative instructions, you need a movie of each shot and a ball machine to drill with. It was hard for me to see the difference between the instruction "Be aware of your racket head," from the tennis guru, and "Follow through, where is your racket head?" from the ordinary pro.

"The distinction is, the pro says, good shot, bad shot," Gallwey said. "I just want to focus awareness, not make a judgment."

It occurred to me that yoga tennis was a misnomer. Hatha yoga has breathing and movement, but what the "yoga tennis" pros had come up with was a version of the Japanese and Chinese martial arts. *Zen in the Art of Archery* would be closer. The student was a middle-aged German philosophy professor in Japan, Eugen Herrigel, and he suffered through the same agonies as a yoga tennis student. He tried to tell his right hand to release the bowstring properly with his sergeant mind. The Zen master never coached him at all. The master said, "The right shot at the right moment does not come because you do not let go of yourself . . . the right art is purposeless, aimless! What stands in your way is that you have a much too willful will. You think that what you do not do yourself does not happen." The breathing exercises were to detach the student from the world, to increase a concentration that would be comparable to "the jolt that a man who has stayed up all night gives himself when he knows that his life depends on all his senses being alert." Nothing more is required of the student than that he copy the teacher: "The teacher does not harass and the pupil does not overtax himself."

One day the Zen student of archery Herr Professor Doktor Herrigel loosed a shot and the master bowed and said, "Just then It shot," and the Herr Professor Doktor gave a whoop of delight and the Zen master got so mad he wouldn't talk to him, because this wasn't the student's achievement and there he was thinking he had done it and taking the credit.

There are some pros playing, said my Zen tennis teachers, who are well into these forms of concentration without articulating them, just as Jack Nicklaus may never have gone hi-tot-tsu hu-tot-tsu mi-it-tsu. Billie Jean King, it is said, meditates upon a tennis ball. Ken Rosewall gets mentioned all the time, a perfectly balanced, classical game. And Stan Smith—if you asked Stan Smith what he was thinking about during one of those booming serves he would say the bagel he had for breakfast. (Nobody would be foolish enough to ask Jimmy Connors.) A grooved game means you can play without your head.

I told some friends about watching the patterns on the ball. One of them said later: "I tried that. It worked, it really worked. But I got so much into watching the patterns on the ball that I didn't get to play tennis, it was like a lot of work, I'd rather be lousy and not watch the patterns on the ball."

There was no immediate impact on my game, but then, the Zen archery student got restless in his fourth year of instruction, when he still had met with no success. Depressed, he said to the master that he hadn't managed yet to get one single arrow off right—four years, and not one single arrow off right—or It had not appeared to loose the arrow—and his stay in Japan was limited and four years he'd been at it.

The master got cross with him. "The way to the goal is not to be measured!" he said. "Of what importance are weeks, months, years?"

Zen has gotten to be a good word now, the true thing, the thing itself. We have *Zen and the Art of Running*, and *Zen and the Art of Seeing*, and an autobiography, *Zen and the Art of Motorcycle Maintenance*. We still have to go through *Zen and Turning Your Spares into Strikes*, and *Zen Your Way to Higher Earnings*; the Zen books are getting shorter and more flowery, with any luck they will soon be mostly soupy photographs and we can be done with it.

I went back to my tennis guru. My requirements were simple: I wanted a serve, that's all, with the power of a rocket, accurate to within six inches, one that would zing into the corner of the service court and spin away with such a dizzying kick that the opponent would retire nauseated.

We went out to the court with a basket of balls. I hit a couple. The Zen master didn't say anything. Some went in, some went out. The Zen master didn't say anything. I hit some more.

"Okay," he said. "Breathe in with your racket back, and out when it moves."

That was easy.

"Okay, now, where should the ball go over the net? And where should it land?"

I pointed.

"Okay, ask your body to send it there, and get out of the way."

"Please, body, send it there."

A miss.

"It's not listening."

"Slow it down. Visualize the whole shot before you hit it. Listen to the sound the ball makes against the string."

It's amazing, but if you really visualize, and you really listen to the sound, you can't go ratcheta ratcheta with your mind, which is very uncomfortable, mutiny in the enlisted men's quarters.

We set up an empty tennis ball can in the corner of the service court. I know, those fierce kids in California and Florida who are out hitting three hundred sixty days a year, who hit five hundred serves a day for practice, can knock over the empty can a couple of times a day, but weekend players can't even get the ball in the court.

"Slow it down more. More. Please, body, send the ball—"

"Please, body, send the ball—"

"Slower. Slower. Make time stand still. No time."

"Please, body, send the ball—"

Zank! The empty tennis ball can went up into the air and bounced metallically.

"Who did that?" I said.

The tennis guru said nothing. He handed me another ball. It went into the corner of the service court, on roughly the same spot. So did the next one.

I began to giggle wildly. I danced around a little, the scarecrow had a brain, the cowardly lion had courage, I had a serve. "I did it! I did it!" I said.

Immediately it went away.

The next five balls went into the net.

"I shouldn't have said that," I said. "That sonofabitch is sure sensitive."

"Please, body, send the ball—"

"Please, body, send the ball—"

"Visualize. Don't use words. Don't think. Use images. In between shots, count your breath."

Now the afternoon began to take on a very eerie quality indeed, an underwater, slow-motion quality. Who-o-o-ck went the ball to its accustomed place in the service court; I had to consciously fight the exhilaration. It went away. My breathing sounded like the breathing in scuba gear. The ball was going into the service court, into the corner, but I wasn't feeling anything, no joy, no sorrow, and this was so uncomfortable I came up for air. I felt greed.

"It's going in, but it isn't going in very *hard*," I said. "I want power, more power."

"Power comes from the snap of the wrist. Ask your wrist to snap at the top of the arc, and don't try. Use images: please, wrist, snap at the top—"

The serve began to pick up speed.

"I don't know what this is," I said, "but it isn't tennis and it isn't me."

I didn't feel at all well. The next afternoon I went out alone at a tennis club. A guy came up and asked me if I wanted to hit some. We rallied. He was very strong. He asked me if I wanted to play. I thought: he doesn't even know my name, I can lose six-love, six-love, and no one will ever know. I put on my mental scuba gear. I wasn't very nice to play with, because you can't say "Oh, nice shot" when you are breathing into your scuba mask. I watched the pattern on the ball, the serve went in, and far, far away I could hear my opponent talking to himself: "Oh, watch the ball, stupid! Don't hit it out! Don't double-fault! Move your feet, idiot!" He began to hit the ball harder and harder. Some of his hard shots were winners, but more of them began to go out. He began to get better at the end. Six-love, six-two.

"I don't know what was the matter with me today," said my opponent.

I was afraid to say anything, but I shouldn't have been afraid—the serve packed its bags and went away as soon as I got back to playing with people I knew. Sometimes it would reappear for a flash, like a tiny acid rerun. Once, on the court, I shouted, sounding like a madman: "I know you're in there, you bastid, come on out!" Please, body, send it there, please, body—and nothing. Nothing. It is on Its vacation. If I wanted It, It wouldn't come, and if I didn't want It, it might, but then who cared? And gradually it began to seem like there was tennis and Something Else, very difficult to do both at the same time even if Something Else has one hell of a serve.

And this was a bit spooky: It was living in there with me; It could bring the music back on with a thumb twitch, without telling me; It could make the biofeedback machine switch from beep beep to boop boop without letting me know; It wasn't taking any orders from me, and, in fact, It would go away if I even pretended to notice, sensitive bastid, It had a much better serve than I did but wouldn't play with any of my friends, It could take over but only if I would go do some idiot-child task like breath-counting; why does It only like me if I will play idiot? It was actually a bit frightening, was It.

THE SWEET MUSIC OF THE STRINGS

"The siddhi is a by-product of the process, not the process," said Torben. "That's what the yogis say."

Siddhis are powers, odd powers, spooky things yogis can do, or people can do, that are sort of impossible: materialize objects, read minds, knock over empty tennis ball cans at the corner of the court.

"But what does that mean?"

"We-l-l, it doesn't mean anything, does it? It's what the yogis say."

Somehow, I was always asking Torben what does that mean? and Torben would say, it doesn't mean anything, does it? which would make me feel as though the question had been the wrong question.

Torben Ulrich is described as a Danish touring pro, a member of a Danish family that always played the Davis Cup for Denmark—that's not who Torben is. I don't know who Torben is, I get a feeling—very hard to stuff into words—well—

Torben walked into the seminar, the one where the guy was talking about listening to the grains of sand on the bottom of the ocean, and I thought who is *that* because here is this character with the Old Testament beard and lines around the eyes and all the tennis pros stir and ruffle a bit, Torben is also described as a blithe spirit and not like anybody else, that is, I suppose, because he has this ponytail down to his waist tied with a blue ribbon and he is out playing Newcombe and Laver and Smith and—

I wish I could capture that Danish lilt, Torben can bend "no" over three syllables, $_{nooo}{}^{ooo\,oo}{}_{ooooo}$ —

Torben wasn't part of the weekend, but he belonged. He stopped by with Jeff Borowiak, former NCAA singles and doubles champion, ex-UCLA captain, top-twenty ranking, haircut like a tall Renaissance prince, Torben is in his mid-forties, these young players pick him up as a guru sometimes—

Torben said: "The egoless game goes further than the ego game. 'I would like to become a better tennis player' really has nothing to do with winning. The Western world is so oriented to winning that the temptation of winning is there almost always. The tennis court, seen as a mandala—"

A mandala, you already know, is an object of meditation, a geometric figure, a representation of the cosmos—*the tennis court is a mandala?*

"What does that mean?" I said for the first of a hundred times. "What does that mean, the tennis court is a mandala?"

"It doesn't mean anything," said the soft lilting voice. "It is a mandala if you choose to see it as a mandala, a confined space made an object of activity. If we are centered around the court as an object, the court is a mandala."

"You mean if you're in it or if you look at it?"

Wrong question again.

"Noo$^{oooo}_{\;\;\;oooo}$," Torben said, "it doesn't mean anything because you can see the court as anything you like. No$^{ooo}_{\;\;ooo}$, I don't think it has much meaning. But if you take it very far, sooner or later you have to see the court as a mandala, sooner or later."

"But what does that mean?" I said, for the third of a hundred times.

Borowiak had gone to Denmark to hang out with Torben. They got up at four in the afternoon—Torben likes to get up at four in the afternoon, and everybody in Denmark likes Torben—one wonders about Mrs. Torben's schedule, after all they have a kid who gets up and goes to school and plays soccer—and every other day they would jog a little, twelve miles or so, through forests that Torben named Forest #1, Forest #2, Forest #3, running through the snow, two-foot drifts sometimes, and then to the saunas and whirlpools of the public baths, and then they would come home and play tapes, Torben is an accomplished musician and a jazz critic for a Copenhagen paper, music with strange instruments like the Indian veena, hours of ragas, or Tibetan monks singing—and have dark bread and cheese, Torben eats a lot of cheese—then they'd play their flutes along with the records, Borowiak's father was a musician, Borowiak had years of music, Torben can play all the reeds—and then, from three to six in the morning they would play indoor tennis—that's three to six in the morning, must be easy to get on the courts then—and then talk—

"Torben would delve into long discussions on such things as light producing waves in the air creating noises that the ear is not sensitive enough to decipher, certain lights give off sour notes. Or he might wander into his feelings about the longer muscles, he'd demonstrate with diagrams and pencils with rubber hands."

Torben tries these things out—say, twenty-five minutes to open a door—so he can make a map of his muscles, his fingers go onto the doorknob and slowly, slowly, twenty-five minutes later—

—it blew Borowiak's mind. "An explosion of horizons," he said. "There are few people in sports who have this quality, this sense of unification—"

Torben was in the Eastern U.S. to play a couple of tournaments and then Forest Hills—it wasn't easy. I would call up—

"Can we get together today?"

"Hey, hey. We might get together today. Would that be a good idea? Maybe we won't. I wonder if we will."

"Sure we will. We just make up our minds to do it, that's all. We say, we'll meet each other at such-and-such a time, at such-and-such a place—"

"Y-e-es, ye-e-es, that would be nice, if we could both be at the same place, then we could get together, we could say ten o'clock, or four o'clock, or nine o'clock, or no time at all—"

"Noon?" A little early for Torben, but he has a match that afternoon—

"Noon," said Torben, testing the wood, "noon, no-o-o-o-oon, noo$^{ooo}_{ooo}$ooon. A very nice quality, noon."

Torben practically never made a date, so I would go out to where he was playing, or where he was staying, and appear— "Hey, hey," Torben would say, without surprise. One time in Torben's room, the books were *Asian Journey*, Thomas Merton, a book on acupuncture, and *Buddhist Wisdom*. Another time it was the Tibetan *Book of the Dead*.

Torben Story #21:

Torben has made it to the semifinals of the National Indoor, playing Ismail El Shafei, the Egyptian. Torben beat El Shafei's *father* in the 1948 Davis Cup.

The reporters gather in the press trailer, Torben enters, his hair down past his shoulders, really an Old Testament prophet now, in a gown, his tone lilting and saintly:

"How old are you, really, Torben? Forty-one? Forty-four?"

"How old is old?" says Torben. "What is age? Am I forty-one or twenty-one or sixty-one? Who knows?"

"Do you think you will win tomorrow?"

"No, noo$^{ooo°}$ooo, I will not win. What is winning?"

Torben Story #36:

"Torben, you are playing Pancho Gonzalez tomorrow, how do you feel about his fast serve?"

"What is speed?" says Torben. "Is speed fast or slow? Speed is relative to observation. A big serve can come in slow motion."

"Pancho is very hot right now. Will you have trouble with his serve?"

"Pancho's serve is a thing of beauty. How can a thing of beauty be trouble?"

Torben Story #51:

"Torben, you are playing at an age when most players are teaching or running something else, how long will you play? What are your plans when you stop?"

"I could play or I could stop. That assumes a structure to the future. I hate getting involved in schedules and specifics. If we don't eat, we will get hungry. Then we will eat."

"How do you stay so young?"

"Young? How young you are depends on when you died last. If you die every minute, you can last a long time. If you don't establish a past . . . then when you lie down to sleep and journey into night, you can wake up as a new person or whatever you are in the morning. But you're not dragging the day before you along so that you're staggering under this bag of yesterdays: scores, bad shots, rankings. I don't always succeed."

Torben story #62: (the classic)

Torben is at Forest Hills in the fourth round, leading the great Australian, John Newcombe, two sets to none. On a vital point a butterfly flutters into his face and forces a weak volley. Newcombe goes on to win in five sets.

"Did the butterfly bother you on the crucial point?"

Torben quotes the ancient *Tao*, Chuang-tzu:

"Was I then a man dreaming I was a butterfly, or am I now a butterfly dreaming I am a man?"

"They sure ask about your age a lot," I said. I really wanted to know, myself, why Torben continued to tour the world. In the hotel lobby, the players—they seemed like such kids—would stop him—are you going to play in the Australian Open, Torben? Will you be in India this year? Why did Torben keep it up, all these hotel rooms, all these plane flights, Buenos Aires and Melbourne and London and Calcutta, when he could be running through the snow to the sauna in Denmark, or whatever?

"Well, we will have to change the idea of aging," Torben said. "A fifty-year-old musician is not out of it, why should an athlete be, if we learn not to burn up our bodies?"

We went to dinner with Tomas Koch, a left-handed Brazilian pro who also wears his long hair in a ponytail. Koch wanted to know if Torben would come and play in a tournament in Brazil. Tomas seemed a little down.

Tomas pushed the glass of water in a circle, in the restaurant, an Indian place which Vijay Amritraj, the lanky Indian, had found.

"Torben, tell me the part again about how there is no opponent."

"No opponent, only the ball."

"No opponent, only the ball."

"The ball moves to you and the ball moves away from you, no opponent. Even when you think you watch the ball, you don't watch it all the time, you see like, in a movie, only the fourth frame and the fifteenth frame and the twenty-sixth frame—when the play goes well, it is a better performance than each actor."

"Is that the click that tells you?" Tomas said.

I kept thinking I had missed a line.

"Are you talking about playing in some sort of altered state?" I asked.

"Oh, Western athletes only get into this for a few seconds, in a crude way," Torben said.

"The grass," Tomas said.

"Very bald and spotty," I volunteered. "I understand they're going to phase it out."

"The grass in Calcutta opens like a flower, you can put your face on it, so many groundskeepers for each blade, the grass in Wimbledon is very lush, such professionals, and each place has a sound," Torben said.

Now I will collapse several conversations, because I stopped asking Torben direct questions, you can't really have much of a conversation with Torben anyway, I was just there, *each place has a sound*, "All the movement can only be best if it is in harmony with the tonic, the keynote sound of the chord. So I don't think, this is music and this is tennis because everything is, traveling, tennis, music, theater, dance, if I am on a plane then this is part of the music, the sound of the engines and the pilot's voice, some tournaments it is hard to find the sound, in the Indoor the air conditioning and the crowd did not make the right sound together—"

"They talk about the home court advantage in basketball," I said, "the vibrations are part of that."

Torben stopped and was staring far away—

"They asked me, you know, to endorse a steel racket, a French company, but I tried it and I couldn't make it work because I couldn't find the sound, the sound of the ball against the racket has to be—"

Torben's voice trailed off, and it was some minutes before he spoke again.

"In music I try to let the sound take over and consume my concentration, and the same in tennis."

In the humid, ninety-degree atmosphere at Forest Hills, a Czech called Vladimir Zednik, all shoulders, looking like a draft choice for the Chicago Bears, overpowered Torben. Overpowered may not be right, because Torben was never out of it, full of deft touches and spins and surprising bursts of power. He did not seem at all upset.

"I could not find my song today," he said.

Laver was playing well.

"Rod is over his trouble," Torben said. "He is so goal-oriented, remember, after the Grand Slam, he won everything in the world that year and then he couldn't play well because he had lost the reason for playing. Poor Rod."

"Poor Rod is right up there," I said. "I don't feel a bit sorry for him."

"The goal is to be free of a goal," Torben said. "Who is that who is playing? Who is that who is making the stroke? Who is that who is making the next stroke? Until they all disappear. If you succeed at tennis then you hang up the racket because you are beyond all that, everything like that."

I had a glimmer of what Torben was talking about, but it did not make me feel at all secure. It would be playing; It would be gliding into Its perfect shots, and I would be out counting daisies somewhere. But maybe this is just the savage irony of I, fighting a potential threat, or an illusory threat.

"Once," Torben said, "Louis Armstrong was in Sweden."

Crinkly lines in the weathered, tanned Torben face, spaces between the big front teeth—

"And," Torben said, "he was going to come to Denmark. And we went to meet him in Göteborg, and we took our instruments, and we played on the ferry with Louis Armstrong all the way across, like the ferry was a Mississippi riverboat with those great jazz musicians, and the *sound* went out over the water and over the freighters and over the ferryboats, and the *sound* came back again, and that was a *wonderful* day."

Torben lost to Pancho Gonzalez in the finals of the seniors'; somebody is always winning and somebody is always losing. And my curiosity—why? why?—had long since dissolved, for obviously if you are alive you are out amidst these textures and these sounds, the sweet music of the strings, and if the music is there then you are the music while the music lasts.

MARGARET STEEL

What We Know When We Know a Game

Paul Ziff points out in "A Fine Forehand" (7) that there are significant epistemological problems in connection with sports. It is to some of these that I will address myself in this paper. I am asking the basic question: "What kind of knowledge is required to engage in a game or sport?" It is a question that deserves to be answered for itself, and we will find that the answers have implications for other areas of knowledge.

In "The Nature of Sport: a Definitional Effort" (4:pp. 48,49), John W.

Originally appeared in *Journal of the Philosophy of Sport* (1977).

Loy, Jr. classified knowledge as one of the technological aspects of games. What he has in mind is our knowledge of the rules and strategies and so on involved in playing the game, or participating in the sport. This is related to the statement that "What we know about a game is how to play it," and "how to play it" is characterized in terms of the rules and strategies. In fact, as I shall show, this is a much too simple view of the matter. A good deal more is involved in knowing a game.

I will begin by characterizing two kinds of learning, both of which are involved in learning how to play a game. This is a good place to begin, as knowledge is what we have learned. The first kind of learning is inductive, which is best described as forming expectations about future experience on the basis of past instances. It is the method by which we acquire many habits. It is also the method by which we make generalizations about the world in our every day lives, and in science. Clearly, it is an important mode of learning. Much of what we call "factual" or "propositional" knowledge is acquired in this way. The simplest version of this is stimulus-response, but inductive learning can obviously be a good deal more complex than the simple level.

The second mode is one I will call "learning by exemplars." This is most clearly characterized in T. S. Kuhn's (1, 2, 3) writings on the philosophy of science, so I will first give a brief summary of his views. Kuhn's view of science is developed in relation to the notion of a paradigm. He distinguishes two major senses of this term. The first is the paradigm as "disciplinary matrix." The second is the paradigm as "exemplar." A disciplinary matrix is a whole world view. It determines what kinds of things there are, what counts as a problem and as a solution, what the values are, what kinds of action and experimentation are acceptable and which are not. That is, it tells what the world is like, what our relationship with it is and what our attitude to it should be. This notion was intended to explain both the ongoing enterprise of science, "normal science" and to account for scientific revolutions. Normal science is the practice of science within the framework of the accepted disciplinary matrix. When the latter begins to break down and become unsatisfactory, a revolution may occur, and the old disciplinary matrix be replaced by a new one. When the revolution is completed, normal science goes on with a new world view and new problems.

This account of science as a world view is supported and strengthened by Kuhn's account of the paradigm as exemplar. An exemplar, or shared example, is a standard scientific experiment or problem that the student has to work through. The theories of science are merely formal theories until they are given content in experimental situations. By performing the classic experiments, the student begins to see how the theory is realized in the world in terms of what there is, and what we can do with it. He learns what counts as an entity, and what counts as a legitimate problem, by learning how problems are like each other. This likeness is not in terms of specific criteria, but rather in terms of what Kuhn calls "similarity classes." Kuhn claims that the student acquires a "learned ability to group objects and situations into similarity classes which are primitive in the sense that the grouping is done without an answer to the question 'similar with respect to what'" (2 : p. 275). By acquiring this skill, the student can solve new problems in ways analogous to the ways he solved old ones. He can recognize new entities by seeing analogies between them and others. Science thus becomes something that can be extended, rather than a rigid body of fact and procedure.

Kuhn suggests that when we acquire a scientific education, we acquire a disciplinary matrix, and in doing so we enter into a new world and acquire a new language, the language of science, at the same time. A particular way of seeing nature is embedded in the language. The new world and the new language are acquired largely through the exemplars. Now the point is that the student in learning science is learning how to *do* something. In becoming a scientist, he acquires specific skills, and specific ways of perceiving. He learns to see the world in a new way, and this is in itself a skill acquired by doing. We cannot learn to see the world the way the scientist sees it without trying and practising seeing it in this way. This trying and practising is embodied in the exemplars. In learning science we *do* science by working through the exemplars, the problems and classical experiments. Once the science is learned we can go on to new discoveries.

Note also that in learning science we learn something we cannot say. If we could explain, if we could say exactly what is to be learned, there would be no need for exemplars. As is clear from the quote from Kuhn above, we cannot answer the question "similar with respect to what?", when we recognize that problems are analogous. We do not know how it is that we recognize similarities and dissimilarities because we do not do it in terms of specific criteria. We learn to perceive and to judge in a particular way, yet we do not know precisely how we do it. For some time we are learners, trying to assimilate the unfamiliar. Then at some point the unfamiliar becomes our own world, within which we move easily.

I will now go on to show that this account of the learning of science can be extended to account for the learning of all skills, from simple bodily skills such as an infant's hand-waving, to games such as tennis, and to sophisticated philosophical argumentation. These skills are not equally creative, nor are they equally sophisticated, but I think it will be clear that they are all learned in the same way.

In turning to the learning of games and sports, the first thing to be noticed is that there are two levels of learning involved. There is the level of the game as a whole, involving the rules and the strategies, the moves and the tactics. The other level is that of the particular physical skills that must be acquired; some examples would be such skills as dribbling or heading the ball in soccer, or serving or volleying in tennis. It is clear that if you are unable to dribble or head the ball in soccer, or serve or volley in tennis you will not be able to play these games properly. Even if the word "play" is stretched as far as possible, you will only be, at best, a marginal player. The particular physical skills, therefore, are necessary in order to play the game. It is with this level of learning that I will deal first.

To begin with, learning a physical skill is not an inductive process. We do not learn to play tennis by generalization from past instances. Once the player has "caught on," he knows how it feels to do it right, he knows from past experience that he *is* doing it right, but this is not how he learned. A player may serve incorrectly twenty times, then do it correctly. Those twenty incorrect performances do not teach him how to do it right, nor do they even teach him how to avoid doing it incorrectly. In order to perform correctly, the student must in fact perform correctly. He is not learning a belief or forming an expectation about the future (although I do not deny that these play a part, for instance in estimating the angle and velocity of a tennis return). Rather he is learning how to do something. It is in this sense that what the tennis player knows can be said to be "knowing how" rather than "knowing that."

How *do* we learn a physical skill? First of all we have to know what it is we want to be able to do. We have to be shown the skill by another person, or a picture or diagram. In other words we have to have an exemplar. In order to learn a physical skill we have to try to do it, and practise doing it. To do this we have to know what we want to do, and to want to be able to do it. The instructor demonstrates a serve to a beginner, who attempts to copy him. He tries, by imitating the actions of the instructor, to duplicate the whole physical act, the whole *gestalt* of serving. He must throw the ball up a certain distance, must bring down the racket on it, and direct it to a certain specified area. All this requires a complex and sophisticated muscular control. The beginner can be helped by verbal instructions, such as "Throw the ball higher" or "Bring down the racket at an angle," but these will not tell him what to do. They merely function as clues in his search for the correct performance.

The beginner practises until the instructor says "Now you have it." At this point he has learned something. This is what it *feels like* to perform the serve correctly. He knows how to move his body in order to serve the ball into the opposite side. He knows how much effort to put into his movements, and how to swing and follow through. Of course, he must still practise, and even with practise will not always be successful, but this is because tennis serving is a very complex skill, requiring more muscular control than many others. But the learner now knows how to serve. He can show someone else how to do it. As with science, he has been led through a series of models, and the movements, from being strange and unfamiliar, have become natural and familiar.

Here it is important to consider what the learner does *not* know. He does not as a rule know how his muscles make his body move in the required way. He *does* know what it *feels* like for the muscles to move correctly, but he is not directing this movement, nor is he aware of it. This will be true even when the learner knows physiology, and can give an account of the muscle movements that take place in a tennis serve. Knowing the muscular movements, that is, knowing how the action takes place on the level of anatomy, is not the same as knowing how to perform the action in person. Teaching someone how the muscles move does not teach him how to serve. In fact, thinking about the muscle movements when trying to serve would inhibit, even paralyze action. We are not learning a series of muscle movements, but a whole flowing action. We do not see the forest when we look only at the trees. We do not see the action when we look only at the muscle movements.

There are several important things to notice here. The first is that the student is trying to learn a whole integrated movement. As he cannot "see" himself or what he is doing, he must learn what it *feels* like to do it right. This feeling is in fact a whole bodily *gestalt*. It comprises a new perception of the body's interaction with the world, in terms of balance, sight and so on. There is a particular set of perceptions and sensations that go along with a correct performance, and the student must learn to recognize these. This is learning what it feels like to do it right. This is particularly important, because feelings cannot be described, nor can they be taught. We must learn how to achieve a particular feeling, with our particular body, without knowing in advance what this feeling is. This is why the action must be learned by trial and error, following a model, and why knowledge of anatomy will not substitute.

Note also, that while the learning must be conscious, that is, we must be aware of what we are trying to do in order to attempt it, what we learn is also, in a certain sense, unconscious. We know how to serve, but we do not know how we do it. Our bodies must learn how to perform the actions, without our minds being aware of the movements on more than a surface level. It is on this point that Polanyi has some important points to make. He says that in the performance of a skill "we are attending *from* these elementary movements *to* the achievement of their joint purpose, and hence are usually unable to specify these elementary acts" (5: p. 10). In "The Logic of Tacit Inference" he says:

If I know how to ride a bicycle or how to swim, this does not mean that I can tell how I manage to keep my balance on a bicycle, or keep afloat when swimming. I may not have the slightest idea of how I do this, or even an entirely wrong or grossly imperfect idea of it, and yet go on cycling or swimming merrily. Nor can it be said that I know how to bicycle or swim and yet do *not* know how to coordinate the complex pattern of muscular acts by which I do my cycling or swimming. I both know how to carry out these performances as a whole and also know how to carry out the elementary acts which constitute them though I cannot tell what these acts are. (6: p. 223)

It is the whole integrated action that we are aware of in the performance of these physical skills. The individual muscle movements are below the level of awareness. It is for this reason that Polanyi calls the knowledge we have when we know a physical skill "tacit knowing." This of course is not the only kind of tacit knowing, but it is an elementary and indeed important kind. There are a great many things we know how to do with our bodies (walking and talking are two of them) and in all of these the knowing is tacit.

Let us turn now to the other level of learning that is involved in games. The tennis player must not only know how to serve, and how to volley, but must know when and where to perform these actions. He must know when and where he is allowed or forbidden to do them. This involves knowledge of the rules and procedures of the game. Knowledge of this kind is at least initially explicit. We have to memorize the rules, and keep them in mind while playing. However, it is interesting to note that this is the kind of learning that can be "internalized" as moral rules are "internalized." That is, in Polanyi's terms, our knowledge of them becomes tacit rather than explicit, and we follow them in a natural and familiar way, without having to think much about them, rather than in a conscious and forced way. Playing tennis is, however, more than following rules and procedures. The aim of the game is to score points over one's opponent, and this involves strategy and tactics, movements and intelligence.

How does the player learn these? He does not learn every possible strategy in learning the game. He may learn some from his coach, and from watching the play of others. However, the good player develops his own strategies and moves, within the parameters of the rules. The rules do not specify every possible move. The player may invent his own. In this way games are to some extent creative endeavors. The player becomes creative by performing new moves and strategies by analogy to the ones he has seen performed by others. The new moves are similar in unspecifiable ways to the old moves. This skill also cannot be taught. The player must learn by himself to extend his repertoire of moves in terms of similarity criteria. This is clearly analogous to the way in which a scientist extends the field covered by a theory, and discovers new entities to be like old ones.

We should also notice that when playing the game, the player's mind is less on his strokes than on the ball and on his opponent. Here we have another instance of Polanyi's "attending away from something toward something else." The player attends away from his service to the trajectory of the ball. He attends away from his own movements to the attempt to force movements on his opponent. Just as in practising service, the player knows only tacitly his own muscle movements, so in playing the game, he knows tacitly the strokes that he makes. This is perhaps less true of serving than of the other strokes, but even here, the mind is on the effect of the service, rather than on the service itself. The strokes are subsidiary to the game as a whole. One could perfectly execute strokes technically, yet be a poor player, if they are not used to further the game. The player must have in mind the game as a whole as he executes strokes, just as he must have in mind the total action as he performs muscle movements. Clearly, he is more conscious of his strokes than he is of his muscle movements, but the principle is the same.

What I have been claiming is that sports and games are acquired by demonstration, and not by teaching in the sense of being told. But there seems to be a problem with this. What is the role of the coach? Surely he teaches players. And often the best coaches are not good players. For instance some swimming coaches do not even swim. They therefore cannot function as exemplars or models for their students. They surely must be *telling* their students what to do, how to perform better, which would seem to contradict my thesis. This contradiction is only apparent, however, as I shall show.

Let us take two kinds of case. The first is the one in which the player or athlete already knows how to perform, but he is not proficient, or there is room for improvement. Here the athlete does not need any demonstration. He has had that at an earlier level, and already knows what it feels like to perform reasonably successfully. What he needs is more proficiency. The role of the coach in this case is to tell the student when he is close to a perfect action and when he is further from it. He then acts as a feedback, or mirror, so that the student knows what and how he is doing. The coach can also give hints. He can make suggestions such as "Raise your elbow higher" or "Follow through with your body." These do not tell the student "how to do it," rather they are ways in which he can adjust his body so that he can discover the most proficient *gestalt*. The student, in fact, is being helped to adjust his model, and to come closer to it. This does not mean that he will always be able to attain perfection in the future, but that he has a better idea of how to attain it, and thus a higher chance of succeeding.

The other kind of case is that in which one learns to do something without being shown by the teacher. For instance, I went to swimming lessons where I learned to swim, but the teacher never entered the water. But I knew that what I wanted to do was to float. I had seen objects and other people floating. I had models, exemplars, for what I wanted to do. What the instructor did was to give me clues. She demonstrated and suggested leg and arm movements, and told me when I was performing incorrectly. In this way she acted both as a partial model and as a feedback. But the actual learning to swim, to float on the surface of the water, was something I had to do myself with only demonstrations of floating to help me. Once learned, I could not say how I did it, but could do it any time I wanted to. The instructor could provide a great deal of helpful information, and act as a mirror to record my achievement, but I had to learn the crucial muscle movements myself.

Does this mean that physical instructors and coaches are unnecessary? By no means. But they are not teaching a set of facts. Rather they are leading their students through a series of movements in order to facilitate the student's learning something for himself. The student is not being spoon-fed with information. He is being helped to discover for himself. And this discovery is one of how it feels to do certain things, and one of similarities, and how to extend them by analogy to other situations. The coach, by telling the student how he is doing, helps him to see how close he is coming to a perfect execution of the movement, and by making suggestions, helps him to come closer to his ideal, or, one might say, to his model. This is why it is easier to improve with a coach than without one. On the level of the game as a whole, the coach helps the student to develop an ability to see how new strategies and moves are permissible, and are likely to be successful. By studying old moves, the student learns to recognize new ones as similar. Coaches thus function as facilitators in the student's own process of discovery.

What I have been claiming is that sports and games are acquired by demonstration, and by the player being "led through" the movements at both levels of the game. He learns what it is like to execute certain physical movements by copying the demonstration, and by being monitored and given feedback by his instructor. He learns strategies and tactics by watching other games, and develops new ones by analogy to those he has observed. This parallels Kuhn's account of learning in science. As we have seen, Kuhn claims that we learn science by being led through a series of classic experiments and problems, and by learning to extend what we have learned to new situations by means of recognizing similarities. Clearly, the kind of learning is the same.

Does this mean that physical educators are doing something different in their teaching from the teachers of other subjects? As I have been arguing, they are at least not doing something so very different from that done by teachers of science. I believe that much of what is called academic learning is in fact of this kind. The so-called "learning of facts" is of relatively minor importance. As a philosophy teacher, I am aware that I teach philosophy as a skill, rather than as a body of propositions to be memorized by the student. I lead my students through the work of a philosopher, explaining and criticizing. I show them how the philosophy is developed and integrated. I show them good arguments and bad arguments. Gradually, by reading, they learn how to read philosophy, and how to recognize important points. By observing, and by trying to argue themselves, they learn how to distinguish good arguments from bad ones. I do not *tell* them how to do these things. I show them, and hope that they will follow and begin to internalize what they begin to see. This is the same general method as is followed in physical education. In fact, the more advanced the level of the student the more like a coach a philosophy teacher becomes. This has always been the way in philosophy. A beautiful example is seen in Socrates, who taught philosophy by doing it, and in fact is still teaching philosophers by his example.

I began this paper with the question "What knowledge is required to play a game?" The answer has taken us beyond physical activities to science and philosophy. This is a significant discovery. Knowledge of physical activities is of the same kind as knowledge of those more intellectual areas. This is something we might expect. However, what is interesting is that any kind of knowledge and learning is seen more clearly in connection with physical activities. It may be that a study of learning in this area will be illuminating for the areas of science and philosophy, and many others.

BIBLIOGRAPHY

1. Kuhn, T. S. *The Structure of Scientific Revolutions*. 2d ed. Chicago: University of Chicago Press, 1970.
2. Kuhn, T. S. "Reflections on My Critics." *Criticism and the Growth of Knowledge*. Edited by I. Lakatos and A. Musgrave. Cambridge: Cambridge University Press, 1970.
3. Kuhn, T. S. "Second Thoughts on Paradigms." *The Structure of Scientific Theories*. Edited by F. Suppe. Urbana: University of Illinois Press, 1974.
4. Loy, J. W., Jr. "The Nature of Sport: a Definitional Effort." *Sport and the Body: A Philosophical Symposium*. Edited by Ellen W. Gerber. Philadelphia: Lea & Febiger, 1972.
5. Polanyi, M. *The Tacit Dimension*. Garden City, N.Y.: Doubleday & Company, 1967.
6. Polanyi, M. "The Logic of Tacit Inference." *Human and Artificial Intelligence*. Edited by Frederick J. Crosson. New York: Appleton-Century-Crofts, 1970.
7. Ziff, Paul. "A Fine Forehand." *Journal of the Philosophy of Sport* 1 (1974), 92–109.

R. SCOTT KRETCHMAR

"Distancing": An Essay on Abstract Thinking in Sport Performances

The notion of "distancing" oneself from the world has come up in many discussions on what is required for uniquely human behavior. Merleau-Ponty (6: p. 174), for example, indicated that the "human order" is entered when one "ceases to adhere immediately to his milieu." Polanyi (7: p. 121) noted that human thought involves "daring speculation, transcending *all* observable objects and extending imagination far beyond any possible experienced horizon." More recently Zaner (9: p. 176), following Goldstein's earlier work, argued that the "core of human freedom [involves] being able to free-oneself-from the actual, and thus being able to free-oneself-for the possibly-otherwise."

In this paper I will argue that athletes commonly achieve a uniquely human distance from their sport environments by reason of the abstract thinking engaged in by these performers during play. I will attempt to show that such distancing is dependent neither upon acts of reflection nor upon verbal manipulations. I hope to describe the consciousness of abstraction as it is lived during performance. It should become apparent, as a result of these discussions, that much athletic ideation is quite good and otherwise "powerful" thinking.

Distancing and fully human behavior seem to go hand-in-hand. To be at a distance from some object allows persons to circumspect and behold it, to interact with it, perhaps to influence its course in nature, to retain an individual sphere of influence, and to remain (if need be) disentangled. Those who radically lack distance are engulfed, subsumed, assimilated, or inexorably drawn to certain conclusions. Even in the realm of personal relationship, distancing seems to remain an important factor. Buber, for instance, argued that distancing is actually a presupposition for the I-thou relationship.[1] Perhaps, in some fundamental sense, to be "at a distance" from the surrounding milieu is to be humanly powerful and free.

Of course, individuals cannot literally distance themselves from their world *per se*. To leave one part of the environment is to move closer to another. To avoid poison ivy is, perhaps, to live amidst dandelions. Persons are

---

Originally appeared in *Journal of the Philosophy of Sport* (1982).

rooted, stuck, implanted, thrown into a world which can be modified but which cannot be entirely avoided. As Arendt once remarked, "The earth is the very quintessence of the human condition" (1: p. 2). In one sense then, human beings cannot gain distance from their world. Rather, they are irrevocably immersed in it.

However, selective physical distancing still seems to be an important activity. For instance, it is prudent to keep at a safe distance from certain dangerous animals, steep cliffs, and erupting volcanoes. Adversaries are to be kept "at arm's length," if not further away. Reminders of unsettling experiences are to be kept out of sight as well as out of mind. The contagious are quarantined or ghettoed, always at a safe distance.

By wearing high-heeled shoes women literally and figuratively put themselves at a distance from the earth. "The ground is not only what I take my stand on (the underground of me)," wrote Griffith (8: p. 277), "but the background against which as human I may be perceived the most sharply. I am the earth; from dust becometh, to dust returneth. But only *against* the earth in opposition to it, do I exist as human. I must maintain my separation from the earth." By building towers of Babel, donning wings, putting on sandals and forever attempting to "reach new heights," individuals actually and metaphorically gain precious distance from the earth.

Early Greeks, as is well known, attempted to distance themselves from various kinds of activities, not just certain places. Human dignity and value, they felt, came from doing some things and avoiding others. Thus, they tried to distance themselves from labor, from the appetitive process, from all activities designed merely or primarily to preserve life itself.[2] The activities of leisure, on the other hand, were to be pursued and embraced. Involvement in dialogue, politics, music, dance, debate and contemplation showed humans at their best. And not incidentally, it showed them to be quite a distance from the world of labor.

Even the upright posture, according to Straus, symbolizes a kind of distancing from control by various animal instincts and tendencies. Straus'(8: p. 341) wrote that

Man looks and moves in a direction perpendicular to the length axis of his body. In the upright posture the skull becomes head, upheld by the trunk. The muzzle, turned mouth, has receded beneath the line of sight; in the human "face" the eyes are directed at the things themselves, no longer exclusively devoted to in-corporation, desire and aversion, approach and withdrawal.

Upright, individuals stand against the objects of appetite. They are capable of beholding them, not simply pointing toward them or living under their irrevocable spell.

Therefore, while being human is unavoidably to be immersed in the physical world and its curtailed temporo-spatial activities, it is also to gain, in selective fashion, a distance from this milieu. Curiously then, with the well known potentiality for becoming aloof, "out of range," or ineffectual by being too distant, there is somehow the possibility for uniquely human involvement. While this particular tension will not be explored in this paper, it is important to note in passing that distancing, whether thought of literally or figuratively, is not a panacea for effective behavior. Indeed, it carries with it its own dangers.

It should be quite evident that there is much ambiguity in this talk about distancing, for some of it refers to an actual physical separation from parts of the world, some to a temporal separation, and some to an avoidance of certain realms of action. In addition, there are distinctive values associated with these diverse senses of distancing—safety, human affirmation, dignity, power, leisure, and rational observation, to name but a few.

There is, however, a very specific sense of distancing which is associated with abstract thinking. Clearly, this notion of distancing is metaphorical in nature. The separation here is one which exists between individuals and their objects of consciousness—some of these objects being physical things such as chairs, tables, and alligators and some not, such as truth, hope, or a specific purpose.

All sentient beings, of course, stand in relationship to some sort of regularly shifting milieu. Consciousness, for animals and persons, is always "of something." But those who are capable of *distancing* themselves from this world are able to deal with it in a particularly nimble and graceful fashion. In a sense, they can "dance" with their world; they can manage it in any number of unusual and creative, but still "right," ways. This distancing requires neither the use of words, nor acts of formal reflection, nor significant periods of time for circumspection. Distancing, it seems, is present every bit as much in some intuitive insight as it is in the acquisition, for instance, of scientific knowledge.[3] This, of course, will have to be demonstrated later in the paper.

Distancing in human behavior can be described further in terms of poles or extremes. The relative absence of distance would be evident in the consciousness of pure reflex behavior. Wherever (and admittedly, it is difficult to find this) there is a one-to-one correlation between a raw stimulus and some response, there is little or no behavioral distance between self and world. Here, as Merleau-Ponty described it, the stimulus and the reflex circuitry are wholly exterior to one another. They effect and respond, respectively, in ways which are required by their separate natures and which are quite predictable, given sufficient information.

Dostoevsky (5: p. 75), in his inimitable way, once remarked that individuals who "reside" at this pole have become like piano keys. He noted too that this fate could be avoided:

> It is just his fantastic dreams, his vulgar folly that he will desire to retain, simply in order to prove to himself—as though that were so necessary— that men still are men and not the keys of a piano, which the laws of nature threaten to control so completely that soon one will be able to desire nothing but by the calendar.

Dostoevsky's fears notwithstanding, Merleau-Ponty argued that the classical reflex theory cannot successfully account for any animate behavior.[4] If this is correct, there can be no *pure* absence of distance in human and subhuman behavior. There is no pure exteriority between stimulus and responding organism. However, in degrees, there can be "domination" by the stimulus event, predictable responses, elements of exterior influence in human-world interaction and thus, a relative lack of behavioral distancing.

The opposite pole—that of maximal distancing—requires conscious, intentional adaptation. Raw stimulation becomes an occasion for various behaviors, not a dominating cause. Stimulus objects are intended as meaningful, and responses in relation to that meaning are varied, unpredictable, sometimes creative. The predominantly external relationship between stimulus and responding organism which was posited under the classical reflex theory is exchanged for one of inherent mutual influence among numerous items, some of which are present to consciousness and some of which are not.

Objects of consciousness, under the mode of maximal distancing, become themes proper which can be "seen" in limitless ways through any number of different intentional acts. Human consciousness displays a nimbleness of adjustment by intending various objects first, perhaps, through acts of judgment, then through acts of valuation, then acts of doubt, and so on—each time uncovering different aspects of the objects in question, each time opening up possibilities for new or different acts which would be consistent with the themes intended.

"Maximal distancing" seems to be a good metaphor to describe this type of thinking. To have such diversity of access to the objects of consciousness is to be at an "intentional distance" from them. Indistinct or unrecognizable objects (say, unfamiliar sign languages) lack such distance. They cannot be intended in a variety of right ways; they cannot be "held at bay" by the clever mind. (I cannot do much of anything, let alone anything consistent with the meaning of sign languages, when confronted with these "strange" actions.) Unrecognizable objects engulf the thinker and confound further dealings with them.

ATHLETIC DISTANCING

For several reasons, sport would seem to be a poor place to look for examples (let alone models) of intentional distancing. Good athletes, for instance, have a repertoire of firmly ingrained habits which exhibit themselves regularly in their play. In addition, in many sports, athletes rely on a variety of reflex actions. There is not time to think things over; the response must "be there," and it must be automatic!

It is also widely known that athletes generally cannot reflect on their skill and play at the same time. A basketball player who begins to meditate on the mechanics of shooting the ball probably will lose his touch, as long as that distracting rumination continues. In a similar vein, coaches will frequently remind an overly tentative performer that he is "thinking too much." Less thought and more spontaneous reaction are needed.

Yet, there is nothing inherently incompatible between spontaneous, "thought-less" play and distancing. I will attempt to show that athletes distance themselves from their sport milieu (in the specific sense that they achieve the abstract attitude) by analyzing four features of performance cognition: 1. multiplicity of "invitations"; 2. frequency of junctures for adaptation; 3. degree of apparent incompatibility between ends and means; and 4. durability of this same incongruence.

As noted by Zaner and Gurwitsch[5] all coherent intendings presuppose a discrete theme. The theme "stands out" from a thematic field or context from which it emerges. The theme is what is directly attended to—say, driving around some basketball opponent in order to score two points. The context against which this act stands out could be: "attempting to win a one-on-one basketball game." Obviously, there is a relationship of relevancy here between theme and thematic field (context). Presumably, this relationship would hold throughout any game. If, however, the context changed (e.g., if I were called home to dinner), old themes would become irrelevant to this new "field" and thus slip to what is called the "perceptual margin."

Nearly all performers—both athletes who think well and those who do not, both beginners and accomplished players—know what they are about. They have a clear context for their impending activity. They understand what the "object" of the game is, how the score is kept, how individuals win and lose. But not all performers enjoy the same richness and variety of theme. Here those athletes who think more powerfully and, generally, those players who are more skilled have an insightful access to their world which cannot be fully appreciated or understood by others who lack such capability.[6]

A MULTIPLICITY OF INVITATIONS

An advanced performer, in particular, usually receives multiple invitations to act when he faces his athletic dilemmas. There is rarely a single avenue, one solution, or only one strategy which can be engaged. Rather, the theme is rich with possibility, with potential for substitution.

In the game of basketball, the proficient athlete senses, with varying degrees of clarity and force, invitations say, to drive left, to start left and pull up for the jump shot, to go straight up, and so on in the attempt to score a basket. Though none of these invitations normally will become an object for reflection, and though the group of possibilities as a whole may never be formally known, still each one may be intuited to have a comparable "functional significance" (9: pp. 77–78). In principle, each distinct invitation is sensible or coherent relative to the context. Each such invitation is well received, though some will be accepted and others not. The good athlete, then, basks in the security which comes with encountering multiple invitations. This diverse "encouragement" will ultimately allow the performer to "body forth" in ways which not even he can say or predict beforehand.

Of course, not all invitations carry the same "weight" even though they may have a comparable significance or meaning. In other words, though "driving to the right" and "driving to the left," for instance, may be intuited to be possible ways to score a basket (they have a like functional significance), they still may not be intuited to have the same concrete invitational "weight" or "pull." In this case, for example, it could be that the opening to the right is sensed to offer the better avenue to the basket. The skilled player instantaneously accepts the invitation and initiates a drive in that direction.

It is a delightful occasion when an athlete receives multiple invitations which carry a comparable functional significance *and* which have good invitational weight. "Everything" seems to work. It is possible, however, for a number of functionally comparable invitations to be received where only one (or a small number) carry good "weight" or "pull." The athlete senses that there is only one or a small number of things to do.

In situations where "good defense" or other circumstances in the game repeatedly frustrate the athlete's intentions, there may be no invitations which carry good weight. Such is often the case in mismatches where any number of comparable possibilities are intuited but where none of these are particularly attractive. Driving left may be the right *kind* of thing to do (it is sensed to be compatible with the context), but still that space has a foreboding quality to it.

There are also occasions when intuited possibilities for action diminish in number, even to the point of extinguishing themselves altogether. As the end of the game approaches, for instance, there often are fewer and fewer options left for the performer. Gradually the athlete reaches the point in a contest (whether winner or loser) where "nothing more can be done." Of course, a multitude of factors—rules of the particular game being played, the experience and talents of the athlete, the actions of the opposition, among many others—influence the number of possibilities encountered at any concrete moment of play as well as the invitational weight of these opportunities. But regardless of type of influence at work, the number of possibilities for action sensed by athletes is never fixed. The expanse of opportunity in sport waxes and wanes with the moment-to-moment ebb and flow of the contest.

The number of invitations extended, for instance, by a basketball milieu and which carry a comparable functional significance increases as the performer's foundation of good habits and right tendencies grows. Paradoxically, as elements of behavior become relatively stereotypic (habits play themselves out in much the same way time after time), behavior as a whole can be infinitely more creative and thus, less stereotypic. Good habits allow the focus of attention to rest "out there," *at* the basketball world, precisely where significant invitations are offered. Not having to be concerned with various mechanics of good movement, the skilled athlete is in a position to sense subtle or unusual possibilities. Phenomenally, as portions of behavior become more "locked in" and "automatic," possibilities for action usually increase.

The problem with a lesser athlete is that issues which should be kept at the perceptual margin (perhaps, concerns for keeping a dribbled basketball at hand) repeatedly call for specific attention. As skilled movement breaks down, what was part of the margin becomes a new theme. The old theme, in turn, becomes its "thematic field" or context. To be sure, a number of possibilities can now be intuited relative to dribbling a basketball (the new theme), but this can have unfortunate consequences relative to the original project of winning a one-on-one basketball game. With this shift in theme, opportunity in relationship to the original project is severely curtailed. Not unexpectedly then, novices are frequently observed to be engaged in irrelevant or marginally relevant movement.

The good performer is not explicitly aware of the number of functionally equivalent avenues open to him at any specific "performance moment." This athlete may live one moment of his project in a kind of giddy openness, where invitations cascade into consciousness from every side. During another slice of time, the world of possibility may narrow or, as noted, close itself off altogether. But regardless, the athlete lives discrete possibilities tacitly. During play there is never a counting up of opportunities nor a reflecting on the merits of one possibility over another. The accomplished basketball player does not live a discrete "move" as "one of twelve or fourteen things which could have been done." (Sport *theorists* encounter basketball in that fashion.) Rather, a given action is taken because it "seems right at this moment." On a subsequent like occasion, a different option might "seem right" and still accomplish the same end.

In sum, an athlete can distance himself from his world by encountering multiple, functionally equivalent possibilities in it. He cannot say beforehand how many he will meet; during the process he is not objectively aware of why one option was selected over another; even after a contest often he cannot tell why he performed in a certain fashion.[7] Yet the freedom experienced at a multitude of "sport moments" is quite real and unmistakable for the performing athlete. While some elements of society (and a good portion of academe) may ignore or denigrate this form of distinctly human behavior because it does not usually produce formal knowledge and because it is not normally "put into words," it nonetheless shows a rather full encounter with the "possibly otherwise." To utilize an image once employed by Frankena (3: p. 177), the athlete is far more a bus than a tram.

FREQUENCY OF JUNCTURES FOR CHANGE

Distancing, as conceived of here, is not the sort of thing which when once won is always won. It is rather an ongoing process, a continuous reclamation of choice from automatic patterning, of making claims on unfolding situations rather than being "claimed" by them.

Consequently, while an athlete may receive multiple invitations to perform in functionally equivalent ways, it could be that the same invitation (or a small number of them) is accepted time after time. Behavior remains repetitive and stereotypic. Or it could be that different invitations are accepted on both like and different occasions, but once the initial choice is made the athlete plays out this option in some preset pattern to a temporally distant conclusion. The possibly otherwise is confronted once, but then a mold for behavior is cast for an indefinite period.

The former concern is one which speaks to the issue of "invitational weight." Could it be that an accomplished performer receives multiple, functionally equivalent invitations, while only one (or a small number) of these opportunities, time after time, is experienced as attractive? There certainly are occasions during which inept opponents allow a player to succeed with the "same move" repeatedly. But barring this circumstance, the weight or pull of different opportunities regularly shifts, often in dramatic fashion. For one, the history preceding each discrete act is forever different. Thus, while external conditions may approximately repeat themselves—an opponent positions himself in the same way, game conditions are much the same—preceding events to any two points of decision-making are never the same. Curiously then, although a panorama may be virtually identical on any two occasions, it is likely that a very different invitational pull will be experienced at each point in time.

In addition, there seems to be no formula which might explain this rather constant shift in the attractiveness of different equivalent opportunities. It is not simply a case where unsuccessful thrusts show up as unattractive possibilities on all future occasions. Nor is it a case where successful avenues retain their pull. In fact, a good performer *can* be plagued by a kind of siren-call-of-the-untried from time to time. A successful gesture *will not be repeated*; it has lost some of its original charm or intrigue; or the opponent could be waiting for it. Whatever the reason for this largely unpredictable flux in invitational weight, its presence is unmistakable. An athlete can hardly become an automaton, acting as if his world had somehow gained a solidified significance.

The latter concern identified earlier in this section raises questions about opportunities for changing or modifying behavior once a course of action has been initiated. Once again, the accomplished athlete finds himself in an advantageous position. It seems that, as skill increases, junctures for change and modification are encountered more frequently.

The advanced basketball player, for instance, may initiate a drive to the right with the intent to proceed to the basket for a lay-up shot. However, if his skill is developed well enough and if he remains peacefully attentive to the constantly shifting sense of his world en route to the basket, he will live through countless opportunities to modify his course of action or abort the mission altogether. With each bounce of the ball, each step, each shift in position, junctures for change are encountered. A shift in pace, a new rhythm, a modified direction, a head movement, a fake with the shoulders, a shot, a pass off—all may be consistent with the overall context of the action, though they are not a part of the initial project to drive to the basket straightaway.

Once again, the athlete is not objectively aware of the number of junctures for change encountered in any discrete project. He cannot count them beforehand, nor is he aware of how many were met after some performance. Junctures may be lived as nothing more than an intuition of expanded opportunity. At a given moment in a gesture, a unique place, a different timing, an unanticipated kinesthetic "feel" may show themselves as attractive or "right."

Such experiences do not always occur at the same "places" in a movement, though there are physical constraints which limit such invitations.[8] On one occasion at a given point in a drive to the basket, the performer might sense a rich opportunity for adjustment. On a subsequent attempt at precisely the same "place," the athlete might be irrevocably committed to his initial project. Sensed junctures for change shift. They can surprise the performer, showing up where they had never been noticed before. They can be strangely scarce upon occasion, as an athlete blunders ahead, forcing his gestures upon his world.

Habits play an ambiguous role with regard to finely tuned athletic adjustment or change. On the one hand, habits have a life of their own. They "carry" the athlete to some conclusion, occasionally *whether or not* the performer desires it. A habitualized group of faking movements in basketball might carry a player to some predestined endpoint time after time. The habit will, it seems, have its way. The behavior pattern will run its course. The athlete, in a sense, is unredeemable. Junctures for change remain hidden.

On the other hand, of course, habits allow the athlete to pay attention to the larger sport picture rather than finite movements which contribute to an overall effect. In this sense, as indicated earlier, creative movement is actually grounded in or dependent upon habitualized action.

There is clearly a tension here between habit as an unavoidable pattern for behavior and as a precondition for high-level creativity. The athlete constantly lives this tension by way of a regularly shifting sense of cohesion among simultaneous and sequential physical gestures. Where cohesion is experienced as significant or great, the athlete is compelled to couple, for instance, given arm movements with certain changes in stance. Or he is compelled to follow one gesture with a specific sequel. Where cohesion is experienced as insignificant or slight, the performer experiences an "openness" with regard to which gestures must accompany other movements and which actions must follow preceding behavior.

It could be, for example, that a fine basketball player has a highly habitualized dribbling pattern and does it much the same way time after time, paying it little heed. Even if he wanted to, he could hardly intervene in this set of movements. The sequence of body movements utilized in the dribble are lived as strongly cohesive both with regard to simultaneous and sequential actions. In a way, this athlete belongs to his pattern of dribbling a basketball. In a sense, he is at *its* mercy—as beneficiary, victim, or both.

However, the cohesion between this habitualized dribbling pattern and *other* simultaneous and sequential actions might be very modest. Thus, on the foundation of this habit any number of other gestures could be built. There can be, to put it another way, a "loose connection" between given habits and other specified behavior patterns which themselves may or may not be highly habitualized. Under these conditions habits become a foundation and springboard for unpredictable, adaptive behavior. Partly on the basis of a habitualized dribbling pattern, the athlete may be free to vary the tempo of movement, subtly shift direction, cleverly avoid a trapping defense. Dribbling habits then, no matter how "controlling" they might be, do not necessarily bring with them other dominating habits.

Behavior elements which comprise a single athletic gesture and which can be, in varying degrees, habitualized are both mutually referencing and referenced.[9] A subtle shift in direction, for example, is referencing with regard to the highly habitualized activity of dribbling. This bit of creativity "gives" the act of dribbling a slightly different significance, a slightly different "place" in the total scheme of things. This habit is referenced by the modification of the project.

Likewise, the habit of dribbling is referencing with regard, for instance, to the very invitations to modify behavior received. This habit affects the way the basketball world is seen, the kinds of opportunities which present themselves, the places that appear attractive. The unique fabric of the basketball world is referenced, in part, by this one habit.

Consciousness does not invade some mechanistic world from the outside, as it were, but rather grows, sees new aspects of reality, intuits different possibilities, senses a novel strategy, in part, by virtue of such mundane phenomena as a habitualized head fake, the power in a calf muscle, the size of a forearm, and an ingrained pattern of dribbling. Thus, both the multitude of invitations received by good performers and the frequent junctures for change which are experienced are inherently related to the athlete's habits, as well as such things as his health, his state of rest or fatigue, and his sheer physical qualities.

Athletic distancing, then, is very much colored by a myriad of factors which normally remain in the performer's perceptual margin. The athlete need not focus on his habits, nor on his weight, nor upon parts of his body. But still they all play a role in what is seen as possible, what is regarded as true or right, what is seen as dangerous or wrongheaded.

A fine athlete can be marvelously unpredictable. He can act toward his world in any number of surprising, equivalent, and right ways. Yet his unpredictability is grounded in the peculiar features of this one individual. When an athlete achieves distance from his sport milieu, he does not become impersonal; neither are his intuitions impersonally abstract. Rather, he experiences the world *vis-a-vis his* distinctiveness ever more sharply. And intuited truth is honed to the unique person that *he* is ever more completely.

DEGREE OF APPARENT INCOMPATIBILITY

By examining the phenomena of "multiple invitations which are sensed to be functionally equivalent" and "junctures for change or modification," two important bases for human distancing were identified. But the *kind* of invitations received and the *kind* of adjustments made were not specifically analyzed, and this has much to do with uniquely human distancing in sporting activity. It could be claimed, for instance, that lower animals operate on the basis of functional equivalents and demonstrate finely tuned adaptive behavior. A deer bounding through the woods is not predestined to take but one path nor is it unable, once this project is underway, to make wonderfully coordinated, global body adjustments to changing circumstances.

The athlete, however, can do more. He is capable of adopting what Goldstein (4) has called the "abstract attitude." The performer who adopts such a posture toward his world can see connections between two or more phenomena which do not belong intrinsically together. He can grasp the essence of a theme and a context, break up wholes, isolate parts and recombine them into new wholes. He can also plan ahead "ideationally," acting on the basis of what is "merely possible."

There is something, in short, about a capacity to create, make new connections, and see old realities in new ways which is critical in specifically human distancing as engendered by the abstract attitude. Merleau-Ponty (6: p. 175) once put it, "What defines man is not the capacity to create a second nature—economic, social or cultural—beyond biological nature; it is rather the capacity of going beyond created structures in order to create others."

Polanyi argued that "invention" and "creativity" are two distinct levels for human behavior. Inventive activity, according to Polanyi, requires the use of two specific intellectual capacities. First, the power of imagination can turn a world of rather common invitations and standard possibilities for modification into one of rich, provocative, and varied opportunity. Unconventional places on a basketball court, for instance, unusual tempos, strange postures, and so on may announce themselves (with varying degrees of clarity and force) as possibilities and as live invitations for modification for an athlete who is imaginative.

The second "moment" in inventive activity involves the power to integrate apparent incompatibles. For any gesture to be sensible, a particular set of unfolding experiences must be intended as compatible with the context of the activity. Their meaning must be consistent with the sense of the project itself. For example, a set of shifting kinesthetic, visual, and auditory cues in the sport environment must be continuously intuited as "right," "appropriate," "compatible" with regard to the intent of the performer—say, winning a basketball game. The athlete is forever attempting to sense whether this particular location, this "feel" of force, this hesitation on some visual field means "offensive advantage gained."

In the degree to which the theme/margin and context appear to be incompatible with one another, the resultant invention is noteworthy and the performer is acknowledged to be genuinely insightful or clever. As incompatibility is lessened, the "invention" appears more commonplace.

Undoubtedly, nearly all athletes are inventors to one extent or another. Each performer brings with him a unique set of physical capabilities, a unique history, a distinct set of hopes and desires. Technically then, no athlete who intends to be successful can afford to play his game *entirely* by tried and true methods. He has his own assets and liabilities, and no textbook on how to play some game can hope to take all of these issues into account. Each athlete, if only in relatively insignificant ways, must invent ways of accomplishing his ends which suit him—in terms both of who he is and what he is capable of doing. To say that an athlete, over time, develops his own style is to notice, in part, that each performer must invent his own ways to succeed.

Sport inventiveness, however, does not necessarily take place before the game begins or during any other period of time which allows for meditation. Some of the invitations to try certain "avenues" in a contest are themselves invitations to invention. Sometimes, perhaps when a game is well in hand or when an athlete is desperate to find "anything" that will work, such invitations carry more weight. But in degrees, there seems to be some "tug" or "pull" to try out a new stance, get the feel of a new grip, check on the rightness of a new location, or apply a new force to some object, regardless of situation. The invitations may not always (or even normally) be accepted, but they remain a part of the athlete's lived experience. They play a part in the composition of the world that each athlete encounters.

So too at the many junctures for change experienced by the athlete, opportunities for inventiveness present themselves. Sometimes the more spectacular inventions occur when the player is already in the "middle of a move." Such a gesture, like a fastbreak drive to the basket, has its own normal sequence of motions. Partly for physical reasons (e.g., gravity *will* limit the time that the leaping ball player can be in the air) and partly by press of habit, attempts at inventiveness "in mid-air" would seem to be difficult, if not entirely misguided. But inventive possibilities present themselves even here. Consciousness is still able to intuit right pathways and fully monitor an unfolding invention in reflex time. The "drawing boards" of invention for the athlete frequently are the changing vistas of his sport world. The time for invention may be the next moment.

Inventiveness fully requires abstract thinking. Except for the accidental "invention" which is the product of blind trial and error, inventiveness requires the athlete to abstract a new sense or meaning from a generally familiar situation. A certain location on the basketball court, for instance, has usually been lived as "dead space." Could it become "live or relevant space"? What new things can that space mean? How many different ways can that identical place be sensibly intended? The highly inventive athlete can neither count nor exhaust them. His capacity to extract still new meanings leaves his sport and his ways of acting toward it constantly uncertain, in a very positive, exciting sense.

APPARENT INCOMPATIBILITY: A MATTER OF DURABILITY

However impressive the intuitively monitored inventive activities are, the original incompatibles "melt away" once the gesture has been successfully performed. Polanyi noted that inventive acts can be repeated indefinitely once the true coherence between a given theme and context is noted. For instance, the inventions of the basketball jumpshot or Fosbury's "flop" were rather easily duplicated once the new connections between sport means and ends were made. In fact, these rather clever inventions are now part of the highly habitualized skill patterns of countless basketball and track athletes.

The abstract attitude which allows the reconciliation of apparent incompatibles is not taxed once that reconciliation is made. The new invention is studied, produced, practiced, and worked, in some cases, into the common fabric of day-to-day life.

Such is not the case with what Polanyi calls creativity. Here the incompatibles involved endure as incompatibles when viewed objectively, as it were, from the outside. Imaginative vision is needed to resolve the incompatibles into a meaningful whole, and when that vision is relaxed, the contraries reemerge.

A rather common enigma in sport is the notion of the effortless performance. What seems incompatible here is a very difficult, effort-filled action, on the one hand, and the ideal of effortlessness on the other. The two do not seem to be well suited for one another.

Yet, there are occasions when a literally effort-filled movement can be encountered by the athlete as effortless, smooth, easy. There are occasions too when an arrow in archery "shoots itself," a basketball feels feather-light, a distance runner feels full of energy after running 15 miles, a victory is experienced as profoundly sad. Though there have been scientific attempts to explain these perplexing phenomena, this cannot erase the enigma in lived experience. The athlete who tries again and again to perform effortlessly is not helped with explanations about chemical reactions in the body. Nor when this individual achieves the desired experience will such analyses allow him to hold onto the result any better or any longer.

The resilient enigmas of sport do not usually lend themselves to easy and quick solutions. Just as it is difficult to be "moved" or "carried away" by paintings, poetry, prose literature, or music by dealing with them skeptically or half-heartedly, so too sport does not normally render up its full charm and meaning to the occasional or distracted participant. The athlete has to *give* himself to the contest, become committed to the game, fully live the activity, if he desires to understand some things about himself and his sport world which are most difficult to grasp.

SOME SPORTING CONCLUSIONS

I have attempted to highlight the fact that a number of fundamental and significant aspects of specifically human behavior are related to various features of abstract thinking. Much of human capability comes, it seems, from this "intentional distancing" and the inventiveness and creativity such distancing permits. Sport performers, particularly good athletes, were described as participating frequently in this kind of activity.

Distancing, it was shown, does not necessarily produce knowledge. Nor does it inherently beg for the use of language. The "medium of exchange" in sport is "feel," and meaningful distinctions in this realm typically outrun any verbal ability to refer to them. Athletes cannot adequately recollect past lived experiences both because of their complexity and by reason of the fact that much of what goes into such activity is not present to consciousness. Also, sensed distinctions are countless. They surpass the capability of any vocabulary to adequately point them out.

Can, then, behavior which does not culminate in knowledge proper (at least it need not so terminate), and which does not require the utilization of language be esteemed? If *distancing* is a significant activity of mankind, then it may be proper, if not long overdue, to praise some athletes for their brand of thinking.

NOTES

1. See Buber, *The Knowledge of Man* (2). In chapter 2, entitled "Distance and Relation," Buber contrasts the animal "realm" from the distinctively human "world." "It is only the realm which is removed, lifted out from sheer presence, withdrawn from the operation of needs and wants, set at a distance and thereby given over to itself, which is more than a realm. Only when a structure of being is independently over against a living being . . . , an independent opposite, does a world exist" (p. 61).

2. Arendt in *The Human Condition* (1) presents a provocative trichotomy of human behavior. Labor, the least valued of the three, is repeatedly associated with physical survival endeavors such as "working" the land. One of Arendt's recommendations is that persons should not become enmeshed in such cyclical, temporary, and ultimately futile activity.

3. This is one of Polanyi and Prosch's major points in their volume entitled *Meaning*. They argue that there are common features to all knowing. Both scientific and artistic procedures, they claim, require "personal acts of tacit verification." Distancing attaches itself to tacit thinking which, in turn, is unavoidable.

4. For instance, Merleau-Ponty took pains to show that even actions of an insect are intricately coordinated and open to modification in tremendously complex ways. He pointed out that even for such "simple" activity, the classical reflex theory—forced by such evidence to posit an ever increasing number of neural pathways—shows itself as highly implausible. See, for example, *The Structure of Behavior*, pp. 22–28.

5. Zaner in his new volume entitled *The Context of Self* (9) is influenced heavily by Gurwitsch, particularly by his work *The Field of Consciousness*. Zaner largely adopts Gurwitsch's descriptions of human consciousness which emerge from the Gestalt tradition.

6. Polanyi, for example, has argued that tacit knowing is irreducible. In short, it is one thing to *have* a tacit insight as a skilled performer. It is quite another to talk about it or otherwise "point" to it. In many ways then, the realms of insight enjoyed by all skilled individuals (scientists, athletes, and artists alike) are closed off to those who do not have the integrative "tools" needed to appreciate them.

7. An athlete normally has a very difficult time in talking accurately about a past performance. Many subtle aspects of his actions are forgotten; others are not formally noticed. Frequently, a performer is driven by the media, for instance, to invent a story about his play. The athlete truly cannot accurately say how or why he succeeded in doing some feat. But the "public" demands some account, anyway.

8. For example, an athlete cannot change direction once he has left the ground. Thus, opportunities for change in this regard are not experienced constantly.

9. For further information on this notion, see 9: pp. 67–86.

BIBLIOGRAPHY

1. Arendt, Hannah. *The Human Condition*. Chicago: The University of Chicago Press, 1958.

2. Buber, Martin, *The Knowledge of Man: A Philosophy of the Interhuman*. Translated by Maurice Friedman and Ronald Gregor Smith. New York: Harper and Row, 1965.

3. Frankena, William. *Ethics*. 2nd ed. Englewood Cliffs, NJ: Prentice-Hall, 1973.

4. Goldstein, Kurt. *Language and Language Disturbances*. New York: Grune and Stratton, 1948.

5. Kaufmann, Walter (ed.). *Existentialism from Dostoevsky to Sartre*. Cleveland: World Publishing, 1956.

6. Merleau-Ponty, Maurice. *The Structure of Behavior.* Translated by Alden R. Fisher. Boston: Beacon Press, 1963.

7. Polanyi, Michael, and Harry Prosch. *Meaning.* Chicago: University of Chicago Press, 1975.

8. Spicker, Stuart F. (ed.). *The Philosophy of the Body: Rejections of Cartesian Dualism.* Chicago: Quadrangle Books, 1970.

9. Zaner, Richard. *The Context of Self.* Athens, OH: Ohio University Press, 1981.

A Guide for Further Study

Several sports literature anthologies provide ample material from the participant's viewpoint. Among these are Henry Chapin, *Sports in Literature*; Tom Dodge, *A Literature of Sports*; and Robert J. Higgs and Neil Isaacs, *The Sporting Spirit: Athletes in Literature and Life.* Dodge's collection contains much more poetry than the others. Two excellent fiction collections are Robert B. Gold, *The Roar of the Sneakers* and Jerome Holtzman, *Fielder's Choice: An Anthology of Baseball Fiction.* The most useful anthology of poetry is P. K. Ebert and R. R. Knudson, *Sports Poems.*

Of the myriad novels, we suggest James Whitehead, *Joiner*; Peter Gent, *North Dallas Forty*; and Mark Harris, *It Looked Like For Ever*—all dealing with the athlete in transition. Good non-fiction chronicles are Jim Brosnan, *The Long Season* and Pat Jordan, *A False Spring.*

Some of the best philosophical work comes from the pen of Drew A. Hyland. See his "Athletic Angst: Reflections on the Philosophical Relevance of Play," in *Sport and the Body: A Philosophical Symposium*, edited by Ellen W. Gerber; and his "The Stance on Play," *Journal of the Philosophy of Sport* 7 (1980). Patsy E. Neal's *Sport and Identity* is worth examining, too. From the Oriental viewpoint, and for those who wish to read further about the ideas explored by Adam Smith, consult Eugen Herrigel, *Zen in the Art of Archery*; Allan Bäck and Daeshik Kim, "Towards a Western Philosophy of the Eastern Martial Arts," *Journal of the Philosophy of Sport* 6 (1979); and Carl B. Becker, "Philosophical Perspectives on the Martial Arts in America," *Journal of the Philosophy of Sport* 9 (1982).

Section II: The Spectator

DON DELILLO

The Exemplary Spectator

The special teams collided, swarm and thud of interchangeable bodies, small wars commencing here and there, exaltation and firstblood, a helmet bouncing brightly on the splendid grass, the breathless impact of two destructive masses, quite pretty to watch.

(The spectator, at this point, is certain to wonder whether he must now endure a football game in print—the author's way of adding his own neat quarter-notch to the scarred bluesteel of combat writing. The game, after all, is known for its assault-technology motif, and numerous commentators have been willing to risk death by analogy in their public discussions of the resemblance between football and war. But this sort of thing is of little interest to the exemplary spectator. As Alan Zapalac says later on: "I reject the notion of football as warfare. Warfare is warfare. We don't need substitutes because we've got the real thing." The exemplary spectator is the person who understands that sport is a benign illusion, the illusion that order is possible. It's a form of society that is rat-free and without harm to the unborn; that is organized so that everyone follows precisely the same rules; that is electronically controlled, thus reducing human error and benefiting industry; that roots out the inefficient and penalizes the guilty; that tends always to move toward perfection. The exemplary spectator has his occasional lusts, but not for warfare, hardly at all for that. No, it's details he needs—impressions, colors, statistics, patterns, mysteries, numbers, idioms, symbols. Football, more than other sports, fulfills this need. It is the one sport guided by language, by the word signal, the snap number, the color code, the play name. The spectator's pleasure, when not derived from the action itself, evolves from a notion of the game's unique organic nature. Here is not just order but civilization. And part of the spectator's need is to sort the many levels of material: to allot, to

---

From *End Zone* (1972). Title supplied by the editors.

compress, to catalogue. This need leaps from season to season, devouring much of what is passionate and serene in the spectator. He tries not to panic at the final game's final gun. He knows he must retain something, squirrel some food for summer's winter. He feels the tender need to survive the termination of the replay. So maybe what follows is a form of sustenance, a game on paper to be scanned when there are stale days between events; to be propped up and looked at—the book as television set—for whatever is in here of terminology, pattern, numbering. But maybe not. It's possible there are deeper reasons to attempt a play-by-play. The best course is for the spectator to continue forward, reading himself into the very middle of that benign illusion. The author, always somewhat corrupt in his inventions and vanities, has tried to reduce the contest to basic units of language and action. Every beginning, it is assumed, must have a neon twinkle of danger about it, and so grandmothers, sissies, lepidopterists and others are warned that the nomenclature that follows is often indecipherable. This is not the pity it may seem. Much of the appeal of sport derives from its dependence on elegant gibberish. And of course it remains the author's permanent duty to unbox the lexicon for all eyes to see—a cryptic ticking mechanism in search of a revolution.)

JAMES DICKEY

For the Death of Vince Lombardi

I never played for you. You'd have thrown
Me off the team on my best day—
No guts, maybe   not enough speed.
Yet running in my mind
As Paul Hornung, I made it here
With the others, sprinting down railroad tracks,
Hurdling bushes and backyard Cyclone
Fences, through city after city, to stand, at last, around you,
Exhausted, exalted, pale
As though you'd said "Nice going": pale
As a hospital wall. You are holding us

Originally appeared in *Esquire* (1971).

Millions together: those who played for you,
And those who entered the bodies
Of Bart Starr, Donny Anderson, Ray Nitschke, Jerry Kramer
Through the snowing tube on Sunday afternoon.
Warm, playing painlessly,
In the snows of Green Bay Stadium, some of us drunk
On much-advertised beer   some old   some in other
Hospitals—most, middle-aged
And at home. Here you summon us, lying under
The surgical snows. Coach, look up: we are here:
We are held in this room
Like cancer.
The Crab has you, and to him
And to us you whisper
Drive, *Drive*. Jerry Kramer's face floats near—real, pale—
We others dream ourselves
Around you, and far away in the mountains, driving hard
Through the drifts, Marshall of the Vikings, plunging, burning
Twenty-dollar bills to stay alive, says, still
Alive, "I wouldn't be here
If it weren't for the lessons of football." Vince, they've told us;
When the surgeons got themselves
Together and cut loose
Two feet of your large intestine,
The Crab whirled up,   whirled out
Of the lost gut and caught you again
Higher up. Everyone's helpless
But cancer. Around your bed
The knocked-out teeth like hail-pebbles
Rattle down miles of adhesive tape from hands and ankles
Writhe in the room like vines   gallons of sweat
Blaze in buckets
In the corners   the blue and yellow of bruises
Make one vast sunset around you. No one understands you.
Coach, don't you know that some of us were ruined
For life? Everybody can't win. What of almost all
Of us, Vince? We lost.
And our greatest loss was that we could not survive
Football. Paul Hornung has withdrawn
From me, and I am middle-aged and grey like these others.
What holds us here?

It is that you are dying by the code you made us
What we are by. Yes, Coach, it is true: love-hate is stronger
Than either love or hate. Into the weekly, inescapable dance
Of speed, deception, and pain
You led us, and brought us here weeping,
But as men. Or, you who created us as George
Patton created armies, did you discover the worst
In us: aggression, meanness, deception, delight in giving
Pain to others, for money? Did you make of us, indeed,
Figments   overspecialized, brutal ghosts
Who could have been real
Men in a better sense? Have you driven us mad
Over nothing? Does your death set us free?

Too late. We stand here among
Discarded TV commercials
Among beer cans and razor blades and hair tonic bottles,
Stinking with male deodorants: we stand here
Among teeth and filthy miles
Of unwound tapes, novocaine needles, contracts, champagne
Mixed with shower water,
Unraveling elastic, bloody face guards,
And the Crab, in his new, high position
Works soundlessly. In dying
You give us no choice, Coach,
Either. We've got to believe there's such a thing
As winning. The Sunday spirit-screen
Comes on   the bruise-colors brighten   deepen
On the wall   the last tooth spits itself free
Of a linebacker's aging head   knee cartilage cracks,
A boy wraps his face in a red jersey and crams it into
A rusty locker to sob, and we're with you
We're with you all the way
You're going forever, Vince.

ROLFE HUMPHRIES

Night Game

Only bores are bored,—wrote William Saroyan—
And I was a bore, and so I went to the ball game;
But there was a pest who insisted on going with me.
I thought I could shake him if I bought one ticket,
But he must have come in on a pass. I couldn't see him,
But I knew he was there, back of third, in the row behind me,
His knees in my back, and his breath coming over my shoulder,
The loud-mouthed fool, the sickly nervous ego,
Repeating his silly questions, like a child
Or a girl at the first game ever. *Shut up,* I told him,
For Christ's sake, shut up, and watch the ball game.
He didn't want to, but finally subsided,
And my attention found an outward focus,
Visible, pure, objective, inning by inning,
A well-played game, with no particular features,—
Feldman pitched well, and Ott hit a couple of homers.

And after the ninth, with the crowd in the bleachers thinning,
And the lights in the grandstand dimming out behind us,
And a full moon hung before us, over the clubhouse,
I drifted out with the crowd across the diamond,
Over the infield brown and the smooth green outfield,
So wonderful underfoot, so right, so perfect,
That each of us was a player for a moment,
The men my age, and the soldiers and the sailors,
Their girls, and the running kids, and the plodding old men,
Taking it easy, the same unhurried tempo,
In the mellow light and air, in the mild cool weather,
Moving together, moving out together,
Oh, this is good, I felt, to be part of this movement,
This mood, this music, part of the human race,
Alike and different, after the game is over,
Streaming away to the exit, and underground.

From *Collected Poems of Rolfe Humphries* (1965).

JOSEPH EPSTEIN

Obsessed with Sport

On the interpretation of a fan's dreams

I cannot remember when I was not surrounded by sports, when talk of sports was not in the air, when I did not care passionately about sports. As a boy in Chicago in the late Forties, I lived in the same building as the sister and brother-in-law of Barney Ross, the welterweight champion. Half a block away, down near the lake the Sullivan High School football team worked out in the spring and autumn. Summers the same field was given over to baseball and men's softball on Sundays. A few blocks to the north was the Touhy Avenue Fieldhouse, where basketball was played, and lifeguards trained, and behind which, in a softball field frozen over in winter, crack-the-whip, hockey, and speed skating took over. To the west, a block or so up Morse Avenue, was the Morse Avenue "L" Recreations, a combined pool hall and bowling alley. Life, in short, was games.

My father had no interest in sports. He had grown up, one of the ten children of Russian Jewish immigrant parents, on tough Notre Dame Street in Montreal, where the major sports were craps, poker, and petty larceny. He left Montreal at seventeen to come to Chicago, where he worked hard and successfully so that his sons might play. Two of his boyhood friends from Notre Dame Street, who had the comic-book names of Sammy and Danny Spunt, had also come to Chicago, where they bought the Ringside Gym on Dearborn Street in the Loop. All the big names worked out at Ringside for their Chicago fights: Willie Pep, Tony Zale, Joe Louis. At eight or nine I would take the El downtown to the Ringside, be introduced around by Danny Spunt ("Tony Zale, I'd like you to meet the son of an old friend of mine. Kid, I'd like you to meet the middleweight champion of the world"), and return home with an envelope filled with autographed 8-by-10 glossies of Gus Lesnevich, Tammy Mauriello, Kid Gavilan, and the wondrous Sugar Ray.

I lived on, off, and in sports. Sport magazine had recently begun publication, and I gobbled up its issues cover to cover, soon becoming knowledgeable not only about the major sports—baseball, football, and basketball— but about golf, hockey, tennis, and horse racing, so that I scored reputably on the Sport Quiz, a regular department at the front of the magazine. Another

Originally appeared in *Harper's* (1976).

regular department was the Sport Classic, which featured longish profiles of the legendary figures in the history of sports: Ty Cobb, Jim Thorpe, Bobby Jones, Big Bill Tilden, Red Grange, Man o' War. I next moved on to the sports novels of John R. Tunis—All-American, The Iron Duke, The Kid from Tomkinsville, The Kid Comes Back, World Series, the lot—which I read with as much excitement as any books I have read since.

The time was, as is now apparent, a splendid era in sports. Ted Williams, Joe DiMaggio and Stan Musial were afield; first Jack Kramer, then Pancho Gonzales, dominated tennis; George Mikan led the Minneapolis Lakers, and the Harlem Globetrotters could still be taken seriously; Doc Blanchard and Glen Davis, Mr. Inside and Mr. Outside, were playing for Army, Johnny Lujack was at Notre Dame; in the pros Sammy Baugh, Bob Waterfield, and Sid Luckman were the major T-formation quarterbacks; Joe Louis and Sugar Ray Robinson fought frequently; the two Willies, Mosconi and Hoppe, put in regular appearances at Bensinger's in the Loop; Eddie Arcaro seemed to ride three, four winners a day. Giants, it truly seemed, walked the earth.

All learning of craft—which sport, like writing, most assuredly is—involves imitation, especially in the early stages; and I was an excellent mimic. By the time I was ten years old I had mastery over all the big-time moves; the spit in the mitt, the fluid infield chatter, the knocking of dirt from the spikes; the rhythmic barking out of signals, hands high under the center's crotch to take the ball; the three bounces and deep breath before shooting the free throw (on this last, I regretted not being a Catholic, so that I might be able to make the sign of the cross before shooting, as was then the fashion among Catholic high-school and college players). I went in for athletic haberdashery in a big way, often going beyond mimicry to the point of flat-out phoniness—wearing, for example, a knee pad while playing basketball, though my knees were always, exasperatingly, intact.

I always looked good, which was important, because form is intrinsic to sports; but in my case it was doubly important, because the truth is that I wasn't really very good. Or at any rate not good enough. Two factors accounted for this. The first was that, without being shy about body contact, I lacked a certain indispensable aggressiveness; the second, connected closely to the first, was that, when it came right down to it, I did not care enough about winning. I would rather lose a point attempting a slashing cross-court backhand than play for an easier winner down the side; the long jump shot always had more allure for me than the safer drive to the basket. Given a choice between the vanities of winning and looking good, I almost always preferred looking good.

I shall never forget the afternoon, sometime along about my thirteenth year, when, shooting baskets alone, I came upon a technique for shooting the hook. Although today it has nowhere near the consequence of the jump shot—an innovation that has been to basketball what the jet has been to air travel—the hook is still the single most beautiful shot in the game. The rhythm and grace of it, the sway of the body off the pivot, the release of the ball behind the head and off the fingertips, the touch and instinct involved in its execution, make the hook altogether a balletic thing, and to achieve it is to feel one of the most delectable sensations in sports. That afternoon, on a deserted side street, shooting on a rickety wooden backboard and a black rim without a net, I felt it and grew nearly drunk on the feeling. Rain came down, dirt washed in the gutters, flecks of it spattering my clothes and arms and face, but, soaked and cold though I was, I do not think I would have left that basket on that afternoon for anything. I threw hook after hook, from every angle from farther and farther out, off the board, without the board, and hook after hook went in. Only pitch darkness drove me home.

I do not say that not to have shot the hook is never to have lived, but only that, once having done so, the pleasure it gives is not easily forgotten. Every sport offers similar pleasures, the pleasures taken differing in temperament; the canter into the end zone to meet a floating touchdown pass, or the clear crisp feeling of a perfect block or tackle; the long straight drive or the precisely played approach shot to the green; the solid overhead; the pick-up on the tricky short hop or the long ball down one of the power alleys. Different sports, different pleasures. But so keen are these pleasures—pleasures of execution, of craft completed—that, along with being unforgettable, they are also worth recapturing in any available way, and the most available way, when reflexes have slowed, when muscle no longer responds so readily to brain, is from the grandstand or, perhaps more often nowadays, from the chair before the television.

PLEASURES OF THE SPECTATOR

I have put in days on the bench, but years in my chair before the television set. Recently it has occurred to me that over the years I have heard more hours of talk from the announcer Curt Gowdy than from my own father, who is not a reticent man. I have been thoroughly Schenkeled, Mussbergered, Summeralled, Cosselled, DeRogotissed and Garagiolaed. How many hundreds—thousands?—of hours have I spent watching sports of all sorts, either at parks or stadiums or over television? I am glad I shall never have a precise answer. Yet neither apparently can I get enough. What is the fascination? Why is it that, with the prospect of a game to watch in the evening or on the weekend, the day seems lighter and brighter? What do I get out of it?

What I get out of it, according to one fairly prominent view, is an outlet for my violent emotions. Knee-wrenching, rib-cracking, head-busting, this has it, is what sports are really about, with sports fans being essentially sadists, and cowardly sadists at that, for they take their violence not firsthand but at second remove. Enthusiasm for sports among Americans is little more than a reflection of the national penchant for violence. Military men talk about game plans; the long touchdown pass is called the bomb. The average pro-football fan, seeing a quarterback writhing on the ground at midfield as a result of the ministrations of Joe Green, Carl Eller or Lyle Alzado, twitters with glee, finds his ultimate reward, and declares a little holiday in the blackest corner of his heart.

But this is a criticism that comes at sports by way of politics. To believe it one has to believe that the history of the United States is chiefly one of rape, expropriation, and aggressive imperialism. To dismiss it, however, one need only know something about sports. Violence is indubitably a part of some sports; in some—hockey is an example—it sometimes comes close to being featured. But in no sport—not even boxing, that most rudimentary of sports—is it the main item, and in so many other sports it plays no part at all. A distinction worth insisting on is that between violence and roughness. Roughness, a willingness to mix it up, to take if need be an elbow in the jaw, is part of rebounding in basketball, yet violence is not. Even in pro football, most maligned of modern American sports, more of roughness than of violence is involved. Roughness raises the stakes, provides the pressure, behind execution. A splendid because true phrase has come about in pro football to cover the situation in which a pass receiver, certain that he will be tackled upon the instant he makes his reception, drops a ball he should otherwise have caught easily—the phrase, best delivered in a Southern accent such as Don Meredith's, is "He heard footsteps on that one, Howard." Although a part of the attraction, it is not so much those footsteps that fill the stands and the den chairs on Sunday afternoons as it is the men who elude them: the Lynn Swanns, the Fran Tarkentons, the O. J. Simpsons. The American love of violence theory really will not wash. Dick Butkus did not get us into Vietnam.

Many who would not argue that sports reflect American violence nevertheless claim that they imbue one with the competitive spirit. In some who are already amply endowed with it, sports doubtless do tend to refine (or possibly brutalize) the desire to win. Yet sports also teach a serious respect for craft. Competition, though it flourishes as always, is in bad odor nowadays; but craft, officially respected, does not flourish greatly outside the boutique.

If the love of violence or the competitive urge does not put me in my chair for the countless games I watch, is it, then, nostalgia, a yearning to regain the more glowing moments of adolescence? Many argue that this is precisely so, that American men exist in a state of perpetual immaturity, suspended between boy- and manhood. "The difference between men and boys," says Liberace, "is the price of their toys." (I have paid more than $300 for two half-season tickets to the Chicago Bulls games, parking fees not included.) Such unending enthusiasm for games may have something to do with adolescence, but little, I suspect, with regaining anything whatever. Instead, it has more to do with watching men do regularly and surpassingly what, as an adolescent, one did often bumblingly though with an occasional flash of genius. To have played these games oneself as a boy or a young man helps immeasurably the appreciation that in watching a sport played at professional caliber one is witnessing the extraordinary made to look ordinary. That a game may have no consequence outside itself—no effect on history, on one's own life, on anything really—does not make it trivial but only makes the enjoyment of it all the purer.

The notion that men watch sports to regain their adolescence pictures them sitting in the stands or at home watching a game and, within their psyches, muttering, "There, but for the lack of the Grace of God, go I." And it is true that a number of contemporary authors who are taken seriously have indeed written about sports with a strong overlay of yearning. In the men's softball games described in the fiction of Philip Roth, center field is a place akin to Arcady. Arcadian, too, is the outfield in Willie Morris's memoir of growing up in the South, *North Toward Home*. In the first half of *Rabbit, Run* John Updike takes up the life of a man whose days are downhill all the way after hitting his peak as a high-school basketball star—and in the writing Updike himself evinces a nice soft touch of undisguised longing. In *A Fan's Notes*, a book combining yearning and self-disgust in roughly equal measures, Frederick Exley makes plain that he would much prefer to have been born into the skin of Frank Gifford rather than into his own.

But most men who are enraptured by sports do not think any such thing. I should like to have Kareem Abdul-Jabbar's sky hook, but not, especially for civilian life, the excessive height that is necessary to its execution. I should like to have Jimmy Connors's ground strokes, but no part of his mind. These are men born with certain gifts, gifts honed by practice and determination, that I, and millions along with me, enjoy seeing on display. But the reality principle is too deeply ingrained, at least in a man of my years, for me to even imagine exchanging places with them. One might as well imagine oneself in the winner's circle at Churchill Downs as the horse.

Fantasy is an element in sports when they are played in adolescence—an alley basket becomes the glass backboard at Madison Square Garden, a concrete park district tennis court with grass creeping out of the service line becomes center court at Wimbledon—but fantasy of this kind is hard to come by. Part of this has to do with age; but as large a part has to do with the age in which we live. Sport has always been a business but never more so than currently, and nothing lends itself less to fantasy than business. Reading the sports section has become rather like reading the business section—mergers, trades, salary negotiations, contract disputes, options, and strikes fill the columns. Along with the details of business, those of the psychological and social problems of athletes have come to the fore. The old *Sport* magazine concentrated on play on the field, with only an occasional digressive reference to personal life. ("Yogi likes plenty of pizza in the off-season and spends a lot of time at his teammate Phil Rizzuto's bowling alley," is a rough facsimile of a sentence from its pages that I recall.) But the magazine in its current version, as well as the now more popular *Sports Illustrated*, expends much space on the private lives of athletes—their divorces, hang-ups, race relations, need for approval, concern for security, potted philosophies—with the result that the grand is made to seem small.

On the other side of the ledger there is a view that finds a shimmering significance in everything having to do with sports. Literary men in general are notoriously to be distrusted on the subject. They dig around everywhere, and can be depended upon to find much treasure where none is buried. Norman Mailer mining metaphysical ore in every jab of Muhammad Ali's, an existential nugget in each of his various and profuse utterances, is a particularly horrendous example. Even the sensible William Carlos Williams was not above this sort of temptation. In a poem entitled "At the Ball Game," we find the lines "It is the Inquisition, the / Revolution." Dr. Williams could not have been much fun at the ball park.

THE REAL THING

If enthusiasm for sports has little to do with providing an outlet for violent emotions, regaining adolescence, discovering metaphysical truths, the Inquisition or the Revolution, then what, I ask myself, am I doing past midnight, when I have to be up at 5:30 the next morning, watching on television what will turn out to be a seventeen-inning game between the New York Mets and the St. Louis Cardinals? The conversation coming out of my television set is of a very low grade, even for sports announcing. But even the dreary talk cannot put me off—the rehash of statistics, the advice to youngsters to keep their gloves low when in the field, the thin jokes. Neither the Mets nor the Cards figure to be contenders this year. The only possible effect that this game can have on my life is to make me dog-tired the next day. Yet I cannot pull myself away. I want to know how it is going to end. True, the score will be available in the morning paper. But that is not the same thing. What is going on here?

One thing that is going on is the practice of craft of a very high order, which is intrinsically interesting. But something as important is involved, something rare in contemporary life, the spectacle of which gives enormous satisfaction. To define this satisfaction negatively, it is the absence of fraudulence and fakery. No small item, this, when one stops to think that in nearly every realm of contemporary life fraud and fakery have an established—some would say a preponderant—place. Advertising, politics, business, and journalism are only the most obvious examples. Fraud seems similarly pervasive in modern art: in painters whose reputations rest on press agentry; in writers who write one way and live quite another; in composers who are taken seriously but whose work cannot be seriously listened to. At a time when *image* is one of the most frequently used words in American speech and writing, one does not too often come upon the real thing.

Sport may be the toy department of life, but one of its abiding compensations is that, at least on the field, it is the real thing. Much has been done in recent years in the attempt to ruin sport—the ruthlessness of owners, the greed of players, the general exploitation of fans. But even all this cannot destroy it. On the court, down on the field, sport is fraud-free and fakeproof. With a full count, two men on, his team down by one run in the last of the eighth, a batter (as well as a pitcher) is beyond the aid of public relations. At match point at Forest Hills a player's press clippings are of no help. Last year's earnings will not sink a twelve-foot putt on the eighteenth at Augusta. Alan Page, galloping up along a quarterback's blind side, figures to be neglectful of that quarterback's image as a swinger. He is alone out there, naked but for his ability, which counts for everything. Something there is that is elemental about this, and something greatly satisfying.

Another part of the satisfaction to be got from sports—from playing them, but also from watching them being played—derives from their special clarity. Sports offers clarity of a kind sufficient to engage the most serious minds. That the Cambridge mathematician G. H. Hardy closely followed cricket and avidly read cricket scores is not altogether surprising. Numbers in sports are ubiquitous. Scores, standings, averages, times, records—comfort is found in such numbers. ERA, RBIs, FGP, pass completions, turnovers, category upon category of statistics are kept for nearly every aspect of athletic activity. (Why, I recently heard someone ask, are records not kept for catchers throwing out runners attempting to steal? Because, the answer is, often runners steal on pitchers, and so it would be unfair to charge these stolen bases against catchers.) As perhaps in no other sphere, numbers in sports tell one where things stand. No loopholes here, where figures, for once, do not lie. Nowhere else is such specificity of result available.

Clarity about character is also available in sports. "You Americans hold to the proposition that it is self-evident that all men are created equal," I not long ago heard an Englishman say, adding, "it had better be self-evident, for no other evidence for it exists." Sport coldly demonstrates physical ine-qualities—there are the larger, the faster, the stronger, the more graceful ath-letes—but it also throws up human types who have devised ways to redress these inequalities. One such type is the hustler. In every realm but that of sports the word *hustle* is pejorative, whereas in sports it is approbative. Two of the hustler breed, Pete Rose of the Cincinnati Reds and Jerry Sloan of the Chicago Bulls, are men who supplement reasonably high levels of ability with unreasonably high levels of courage and desire. Other athletes—Joe Morgan and Oscar Robertson come to mind—bring superior athletic intelligence to bear upon their play. And Bill Russell, late of the Boston Celtics, who if the truth be known was not an inherently superior athlete, blended hustle and intelligence with what abilities he did have and through force of character established supremacy.

Whence do hustle, intelligence, and character in sports derive, especially since they apparently do not necessarily carry over into life? Joe DiMaggio and Sugar Ray Robinson, two of the most instinctively intelligent and physi-cally elegant athletes, brought little of either of these qualities over into their business or personal activities. Some athletes can do all but one important thing well: Wilt Chamberlain at the free-throw line, for those who recall his misery there, leaves a permanent picture of a mental block in action. Other athletes—Connie Hawkins, Ilie Nastase, Dick Allen—have all the physical gifts in superabundance, yet, because of some insufficiency of character, some searing flaw, never come near to fulfilling their promise. Coaches supply yet another gallery of human types, from the fanatical Vince Lombardi to the comical Casey Stengel to the measured and aptly named John Wooden. The cast of characters in sport, the variety of situations, the complexity of be-havior it puts on display, the overall human exhibit it offers—together these supply an enjoyment akin to that once provided by reading interminably long but inexhaustibly rich nineteenth-century novels.

In a wider sense, sport is culture. For many American men it represents a common background, a shared interest. It has a binding power that tran-scends social class and education. Some years ago I found myself working in the South among men with whom I shared nothing in the way of region, religion, education, politics, or general views; we shared nothing, in fact, but sports, which was enough for us to get along and grow to become friends, in the process of showing how superficial all the things that might have kept us apart in fact were. More recently, in Chicago, at a time when race relations were in a particularly jagged state, I recall emerging from an NBA game, in which the Chicago Bulls in overtime beat the Milwaukee Bucks, into a snowy night and an aura of common good feeling that, for a time, submerged the enmity between races; laughing, throwing snowballs, exuberant generally, the crowd leaving the Chicago Stadium that night was not divided by being black and white but unified by being Bull fans. Last year's Boston-Cincinnati World Series, one of the most gratifying in memory, coming hard upon a year of extreme political divisiveness, performed, however briefly, something of the same function. How much better it felt to agree about the mastery of Luis Tiant than to argue about the wretchedness of Richard Nixon.

In sports as in life, character does not much change. I have recently begun to play a game called racquetball, and I find I would still rather look good than win, which is what I usually do: look good and lose. I beat the rumdums but go down before quality players. I get compliments in defeat. Men who beat me admire the whip of my strokes, my wrist action, my anticipation, the power I get behind the ball. When this occurs I feel like a woman who is complimented for the shape of her bottom when it is her mind she craves admiration for, though of course she will take what praise she can get.

R. H. Tawney, the great historian of religion and capitalism, once remarked that the only progress he could note during the course of his lifetime was in the deportment of dogs. For myself, I would say that the chief progress in the course of my lifetime has been in the quality and variety of athletic gear. Racquets made of metal, aluminum, wood, and fiberglass, balls of different colors, sneakers of all materials and designs, posh warm-up suits, tube socks, sweatbands for the head and wrist in various colors and pipings; only the athletic supporter, the old jockstrap, remains unornamented, but perhaps Vera or Peter Max is at the drawing board. In any event, with all this elegant plumage available, it is a nice time to be playing ball again.

Sports can be impervious to age. My father-in-law, a man of style, seriousness, and great good humor who died a year ago in his late sixties, was born in South Bend, Indiana, and in his early manhood left the Catholic Church—two facts that conjoined to give him an intense interest in the fortunes of the teams from Notre Dame. He loved to see them lose. The torch has been passed on. I now love to see Notre Dame lose, and when it does I think of him and remember his smile.

When I was a boy I had a neighbor, a man who, after retirement, had a number of strokes. An old man and a young boy, we had in common a love of sports, which, when we met on the street, was our only topic of conversation. He once inspected a new glove of mine, and instructed me to rub it down with neat's-foot oil, place a ball firmly in the pocket, wrap string tightly around the glove, and leave it like that for the winter. I did, and it worked. After his last stroke but one, he seldom left his house. Afternoons he spent in a chair in his bedroom, a blanket over his lap, listening to Cub games over the radio. It was while listening to a ball game that he quietly died. I cannot imagine a better way.

FREDERICK EXLEY

Frank Gifford and Me

It seems amazing to me now that while at USC, where Gifford and I were contemporaries, I never saw him play football; that I had to come three thousand miles from the low, white, smog-enshrouded sun that hung perpetually over the Los Angeles Coliseum to the cold, damp, and dismal Polo Grounds to see him perform for the first time; and that I might never have had the urge that long-ago Sunday had I not once on campus had a strange, unnerving confrontation with him. The confrontation was caused by a girl, though at the time of the encounter I did not understand *what* girl. I had transferred from Hobart College, a small, undistinguished liberal arts college in Geneva, New York, where I was a predental student, to USC, a large, undistinguished university in Los Angeles, where I became an English major. The transition was not unnatural. I went out there because I had been rejected by a girl, my first love, whom I loved beyond the redeeming force of anything save time. Accepting the theory of distance as time, I put as much of it between the girl and myself as I could. Once there, though, the prospect of spending my days gouging at people's teeth and whiffing the intense, acidic odor of decay—a profession I had chosen with no stronger motive than keeping that very girl in swimming suits and tennis shorts: she had (and this, sadly, is the precise extent of my memory of her) the most breath-taking legs I had ever seen—seemed hideous, and I quite naturally became an English major with a view to reading The Books, The Novels and The Poems, those pat

---

From *A Fan's Notes* (1968). Title supplied by the editors.

reassurances that other men had experienced rejection and pain and loss. Moreover, I accepted the myth of California the benevolent and believed that beneath her warm skies I would find surcease from my pain in the person of some lithe, fresh-skinned, and incredibly lovely blond coed. Bearing my rejection like a disease, and like a man with a frightfully repugnant and contagious leprosy, I was unable to attract anything as healthy as the girl I had in mind.

Whenever I think of the man I was in those days, cutting across the neat-cropped grass of the campus, burdened down by the weight of the books in which I sought the consolation of other men's grief, and burdened further by the large weight of my own bitterness, the whole vision seems a nightmare. There were girls all around me, so near and yet so out of reach, a pastel nightmare of honey-blond, pink-lipped, golden-legged, lemon-sweatered girls. And always in this horror, this gaggle of femininity, there comes the vision of another girl, now only a little less featureless than all the rest. I saw her first on one stunning spring day when the smog had momentarily lifted, and all the world seemed hard bright blue and green. She came across the campus straight at me, and though I had her in the range of my vision for perhaps a hundred feet, I was only able, for the fury of my heart, to give her five or six frantic glances. She had the kind of comeliness—soft, shoulder-length chestnut hair; a sharp beauty mark right on her sensual mouth; and a figure that was like a swift, unexpected blow to the diaphragm—that to linger on makes the beholder feel obscene. I wanted to look. I couldn't look. I had to look. I could give her only the most gaspingly quick glances. Then she was by me. Waiting as long as I dared, I turned and she was gone.

From that day forward I moved about the campus in a kind of vertigo, with my right eye watching the sidewalk come up to meet my anxious feet, and my left eye clacking in a wild orbit, all over and around its socket, trying to take in the entire campus in frantic split seconds, terrified that I might miss her. On the same day that I found out who she was I saw her again. I was standing in front of Founders' Hall talking with T., a gleaming-toothed, hand-pumping fraternity man with whom I had, my first semester out there, shared a room. We had since gone our separate ways; but whenever we met we always passed the time, being bound together by the contempt with which we viewed each other's world and by the sorrow we felt at really rather liking each other, a condition T. found more difficult to forgive in himself than I did.

"*That?*" he asked in profound astonishment to my query about the girl. "*That?*" he repeated dumbly, as if this time—for I was much given to teasing T.—I had really gone too far. "*That,*" he proclaimed with menacing impatience, "*just happens to be Frank Gifford's girl!*"

Never will I forget the contempt he showered on me for asking what to him, and I suppose to the rest of fraternity row, was not only a rhetorical but a dazzlingly asinine question. Nor will I forget that he never did give me the girl's name; the information that she was Gifford's girl was, he assumed, quite enough to prevent the likes of me from pursuing the matter further. My first impulse was to laugh and twit his chin with my finger. But the truth was I was getting a little weary of T. His monumental sense of the rightness of things was beginning to grate on me; shrugging, I decided to end it forever. It required the best piece of acting I've ever been called upon to do; but I carried it off, I think, perfectly.

Letting my mouth droop open and fixing on my face a look of serene vacuousness, I said, "Who's Frank Gifford?"

My first thought was that T. was going to strike me. His hands tensed into fists, his face went the color of fire, and he thrust his head defiantly toward me. He didn't strike, though. Either his sense of the propriety of things overcame him, or he guessed, quite accurately, that I would have knocked him on his ass. All he said, between furiously clenched teeth, was: "*Oh, really, Exley, this has gone too far.*" Turning hysterically away from me, he thundered off. It had indeed gone too far, and I laughed all the way to the saloon I frequented on Jefferson Boulevard, sadly glad to have seen the last of T.

Frank Gifford was an All-America at USC, and I know of no way of describing this phenomenon short of equating it with being the Pope in the Vatican. Our local *L' Osservatore Romano, The Daily Trojan,* was a moderately well-written college newspaper except on the subject of football, when the tone of the writing rose to an hysterical screech. It reported daily on Gifford's health, one time even imposing upon us the news that he was suffering an upset stomach, leading an irreverent acquaintance of mine to wonder aloud whether the athletic department had heard about "milk of magnesia, for Christ's sake." We were, it seems to me in retrospect, treated daily to such breathless items as the variations in his weight, his method of conditioning, the knowledge that he neither smoked nor drank, the humbleness of his beginnings, and once we were even told the number of fan letters he received daily from pimply high school girls in the Los Angeles area. The USC publicity man, perhaps influenced by the proximity of Hollywood press agents, seemed overly fond of releasing a head-and-shoulder print showing him the apparently proud possessor of long, black, perfectly ambrosial locks that came down to caress an alabaster, colossally beauteous face, one that would have aroused envy in Tony Curtis. Gifford was, in effect, overwhelmingly present in the consciousness of the campus, even though my crowd—the literati— never once to my knowledge mentioned him. We never mentioned him because his being permitted to exist at the very university where we were apprenticing ourselves for Nobel Prizes would have detracted from our environment and been an admission that we might be better off at an academe more sympathetic with our hopes. Still, the act of not mentioning him made him somehow more present than if, like the pathetic nincompoops on fraternity row, we spent all our idle hours singing his praises. Our silence made him, in our family, a kind of retarded child about whom we had tacitly and selfishly agreed not to speak. It seems the only thing of Gifford's we were spared—and it is at this point we leave his equation with the Bishop of Rome—was his opinion of the spiritual state of the USC campus. But I am being unkind now; something occurred between Gifford and me which led me to conclude that he was not an immodest man.

Unlike most athletes out there, who could be seen swaggering about the campus with *Property of USC* (did they never see the ironic, touching servility of this?) stamped indelibly every place but on their foreheads, Gifford made himself extremely scarce, so scarce that I only saw him once for but a few brief moments, so scarce that prior to this encounter I had begun to wonder if he wasn't some myth created by the administration to appease the highly vocal and moronic alumni who were incessantly clamoring for USC's Return to Greatness in, as the sportswriters say, "the football wars." Sitting at the counter of one of the campus hamburger joints, I was having a cup of chicken noodle soup and a cheeseburger when it occurred to me that he was one of a party of three men seated a few stools away from me. I knew without looking because the other two men were directing all their remarks to him: "Hey, Frank, how about that?" "Hey, Frank, cha ever hear the one about . . ." It was the kind of given-name familiarity one likes to have with the biggest man on the block. My eyes on my soup, I listened to this sycophancy, smiling rather bitterly, for what seemed an eternity; when I finally did look up, it was he—ambrosial locks and all. He was dressed in blue denims and a terry-cloth sweater, and though I saw no evidence of USC stamped anyplace, still I had an overwhelming desire to insult him in some way. How this would be accomplished with any subtlety I had no idea; I certainly didn't want to fight with him. I did, however, want to shout, "Listen, you son of a bitch, life isn't all a goddam football game! You won't always get the girl! Life is rejection and pain and loss"—all those things I so cherishingly cuddled in my self-pitying bosom. I didn't, of course, say any such thing; almost immediately he was up and standing right next to me, waiting to pay the cashier. Unable to let the moment go by, I snapped my head up to face him. When he looked at me, I smiled—a hard, mocking, so-you're-the-big-shit? smile. What I expected him to do, I can't imagine—say, "What's your trouble, buddy?" or what—but what he did do was the least of my expectations. He only looked quizzically at me for a moment, as though he were having difficulty placing me; then he smiled a most ingratiating smile, gave me a most amiable hello, and walked out the door, followed by his buddies who were saying in unison, "Hey, Frank, what'll we do now?"

My first feeling was one of utter rage. I wanted to jump up and throw my water glass through the plate-glass window. Then almost immediately a kind of sullenness set in, then shame. Unless I had read that smile and that salutation incorrectly, there was a note of genuine apology and modesty in them. Even in the close world of the university Gifford must have come to realize that he was having a fantastic success, and that success somewhat embarrassed him. Perhaps he took me for some student acquaintance he had had long before that success, and took my hateful smile as a reproach for his having failed to speak to me on other occasions, his smile being the apology for that neglect. Perhaps he was only saying he was sorry I was a miserable son of a bitch, but that he was hardly going to fight me for it. These speculations, as I found out drinking beer late into that evening, could have gone on forever. I drank eight, nine, ten, drifting between speculations on the nature of that smile and bitter, sexually colored memories of the girl with the breath-taking legs back east, when it suddenly occurred to me that she and not the girl with the chestnut hair was the cause of all my anger, and that I was for perhaps a very long time going to have to live with that anger. Gifford gave me that. With that smile, whatever he meant by it, a smile that he doubtlessly wouldn't remember, he impressed upon me, in the rigidity of my embarrassment, that it is unmanly to burden others with one's grief. Even though it is man's particularly unhappy aptitude to see to it that his fate is shared.

GEORGE VECSEY

Fans

D on Decker was mad at himself. Here he was, surrounded by New York Rangers fans bearing signs like "GET SCHULTZ" or "FUCK THE FLYERS," and he was without a banner.

"Aw, I was going to make a sign," said Decker, a fireman from New Jersey. "I had two ideas—'SCHULTZ'S MOTHER HATES HIM' or 'SCHULTZ IS REALLY MARTIN BORMANN.' But I didn't get around to it."

Well, it was too late now. Somewhere down below the cigar haze and the

Originally appeared in *Esquire* (1974).

poor sight lines of Madison Square Garden, the Philadelphia Flyers and the Rangers were slugging each other around in the Stanley Cup semifinals—a rivalry matched only by the fans of their respective cities.

In New York, adoring fans would squeal, "Eddie, Eddie, Eddie," like bobby-soxers for Frank Sinatra, whenever the grey-haired goalie, Giacomin, made a save. When the series switched to Philadelphia, every time the puck got past Giacomin, the fans would sneer, "Eddie, Eddie, Eddie." Back in New York, the fans yelled so much abuse that Philly goalie Bernie Parent rammed his stick against the protective glass, like a kid at the zoo taunting the hyenas.

Also in New York, rugged Dave Schultz didn't like being called a "scab" so he whipped the puck into the offending fan's section. In past years, the fans might have dumped garbage on Schultz as he left the ice between periods. But it's not that easy since the Garden erected a thick canopy over the ramp to the dressing room—to protect the players from the fans, officials say. (Actually, it went up after a visiting team stomped a fan who had infiltrated the players' ramp.)

Sports fans have always been part of the action, leading to home-court advantages that players (and bettors) acknowledge. But in recent years, fans seem to be establishing a kind of participatory democracy:

—Last fall, after Pete Rose of the Cincinnati Reds had punched little Bud Harrelson of the Mets, some fans in Shea Stadium threw everything they could pry loose at Rose. A few fans even harassed the Reds' club officials and their wives, until the Reds' players rescued them, bats in hand.

—In Cincinnati this past season, Houston outfielder Bob Watson hit the wall and fell, nearly unconscious, prompting several fans to pour beer on him. Sparky Anderson, the decent guy who manages the Reds, raced out to admonish his hometown followers. Another day, somebody conked umpire Satch Davidson with a beer can.

—In North Carolina last season, coach Kevin Loughery of the New York Nets got into a hassle on the court. But he never expected to get slugged by a fan who raced out of the crowd to help the home team. The Nets did not arouse many passions in their own suburban Nassau County until the night they clinched the title. Then some young louts shattered a glass backboard, sending the celebrating players scurrying to the locker room in fear for their heads.

Things haven't gotten to the point where sports arenas need moats or wire fences to keep the fans from the field, as in soccer fields around the world. But some sports people think the tempo is getting a little too rough.

"Maybe it's just me, but it seems there are more bad fans now," says Jim Bouton, the former Yankee pitcher, now a television sportscaster, who spent much of his youth in the Polo Grounds grandstands.

"I still see kids like myself," Bouton says, "with their brown-bag lunches, yelling to get the players' attention, checking the scoreboard to see who the new players are. But I also see more people throwing hot pennies on the ice at hockey games, or tossing beer on the guys in the bullpen. I didn't see that when I was a kid—maybe because I wasn't looking for it.

"There are more troublemakers today," Bouton continues. "For instance: the booing of Walt Frazier in the Garden. It's nothing personal. The fans don't care about his personal life. The only thing they care about is points. If he gets forty-five, he's a hero. If he gets twenty-five, he's a bum. There's more of that today."

If the fans are more nasty, more critical, today, one could make some weighty pronouncement about "the mood of the times." But more likely the fans are more involved because they are inundated with so much sports on television. After hearing all the technical jargon, the tell-it-like-it-is hyperbole, they become consumers—they consider themselves "professional" fans, as knowledgeable and tough as the players. Many men (and not a few women) are never more authoritative at social gatherings than when they launch into their smooth-voiced rap about what's *really* wrong with the Knicks.

"People want to talk about my business more than I do," says Steve Jacobson, who helps give *Newsday* of Long Island one of the best sports sections in the country. "I'll meet somebody at a party and he'll assume there's more to a story than I wrote. It's fine if I run into friends who understand sports. But with some fans . . . it's hard."

Superfans are everywhere. Remember the morning at the Lincoln Memorial, when the young people wanted to discuss invading Cambodia but the President of the United States wanted to prove he knew the sports nicknames of the youngsters' colleges? (Syracuse? Ah, yes, the Orangemen.) And while the hordes demonstrated outside, the President was watching some athletic-scholarship Hessians performing on television. Sports keep people's minds off their troubles. They also allow fans to practice vicarious brotherhood—admiring Reggie Jackson's courage on the field is better than living next door to him.

Sometimes fans seem interchangeable, with the ever-present chants of "We're Number One" or "DEEEE-fense" ringing from coast to coast. But there is no such thing as "the sports fan," according to Leonard Koppett, The New York *Times*'s sports man in California.

"There are probably twenty identifiable subgroups," says Koppett. "There are people where I live, in Palo Alto, seriously dedicated to Stanford athletics, who couldn't care less about the San Francisco Giants or Oakland Raiders. You couldn't say they're the same as a die-hard pro fan.

"Audiences here cover a broader social range than back East," continues

Koppett, who was raised in New York. "In New York, there are people who never go to games. Here, the same person could go to a symphony concert and a Giant game."

Northern California is not one of the great spectator-sport areas in the U.S. anyway. The two-time baseball champions, the Oakland A's, drew a dismal 158,230 fans for their first twenty-five games in 1974, and the Giants across the bay weren't doing much better, drawing all of 22,526 fans for a Sunday game with the hated Los Angeles Dodgers.

Harry Jupiter, once a sportswriter, now a news reporter for the *Chronicle*, thinks he knows why fans stay away in Northern California:

"With Patty Hearst and the Zebra killings on the six o'clock news, who's going to get excited over a ball game?" he asks. "Also, the weather is so great out here, adults play golf or kids play baseball or the whole family goes camping. People are outdoors all year instead of waiting six months for spring, like they do back East.

"You know why team sports, particularly baseball, are big back East? Life is so dreary in those old cities like New York, Philadelphia, Pittsburgh, that people become attached to teams at an early age. If the baseball team wins, at least the day isn't a total loss. Out here, who needs it? People would rather get off their asses and go fishing."

It is possible that the lack of space that makes people so tense in the Northeastern cities also creates the superfans. Most athletes agree that the roughest fans are in Boston, New York and Philadelphia (although the huge throng that celebrated Philly's Stanley Cup title may hurt Philly's image as a city of sore losers). Fans also vary from sport to sport.

There are fans who root for their money (horse racing, obviously, but team sports as well); there are fans who root for players of their favorite leisure sport (golf, tennis); then there are fans who root for some measure of violence—pro wrestling and roller derby being theatre; automobile racing being for real.

"Are auto-racing fans really sadists?" muses Don Ballinger, a sports buff who plays rhythm guitar for country singer Loretta Lynn. "Let me put it this way. If you guaranteed a good clean race, with absolutely no chance of an accident, attendance would drop at auto racing. I'm sure of it."

John Christensen, who has written about auto racing for the *Louisville Times*, does not see much "bloodlust" at Indianapolis or other tracks he visits.

"We all drive cars," Christensen says. "You drive through this part of the country, you see cars up on concrete blocks where people are working on them. Sure, Indy fans know if there's a wreck, somebody is liable to get killed. But I don't think they go for accidents."

Christensen also gets to view Kentucky Derby fans, a huge once-a-year breed all its own: "You get two different crowds," he says. "One crowd has box seats and celebrates in the old Southern tradition. The other crowd goes to the infield. It got so bad this year that people backed up into the tunnel under the track." The infield is where the "People's Derby" is held—Frisbee-catches, tossing girls in the air from a taut blanket, fried chicken underfoot, smuggling Boone's Farm Apple Wine onto the grounds, away from the prying fingers of the security guards, standing in line for an hour at the portable toilets, occasionally seeing a glimpse of horse. This may not exactly be a sports event; rather, it's the old pagan rites of spring drawing license plates from two dozen states.

In the Southern and Central portions of the country, college football is a tangible way to appreciate one's region, one's state, one's church, one's roots. When Texas fans stick up their index and pinkie fingers and scream, "Hook 'em, Horns" they are, in fact, cheering themselves. Those good old boys on the field are brave Texas Longhorns. But so are the fans who braved monstrous traffic jams, monstrous hangovers, monstrous weekend rates at the motel.

"I think college football is big here because professional sports were slow to move south of the Mason-Dixon line," says Mickey Herskowitz, writer and television commentator in Houston. "It was the only entertainment the people had."

Herskowitz says the wildest college stadium is Tiger Stadium in Baton Rouge, Louisiana: "The fans come at noon and start screaming before the teams warm up," he says. "This can upset a young visiting team. Also, they had this little trick of placing their mascot, a real tiger, right by the visiting team's locker room. The coach would be talking and the players could hear this tiger roaring. Oh, he wasn't real dangerous, I guess, but nobody wanted to test him out."

Herskowitz also tells of the hazards of driving in the Ozarks while an Arkansas-Texas football game is being broadcast: "People drive miles out of their way just to get better reception through the mountains," he says. "You see some dizzy things on the highways."

Houston football fans are vociferous, he notes, but he finds a strain of sarcasm in Dallas fans. He recalls Southern Methodist University fans, spoiled by the Doak Walker-Kyle Rote glories of the 1940s, grown sour on the team in the 1960s. The college had the slogan "Excitement '68," but the fans weren't fooled. They made jokes about "Excitement 68, SMU 0," "Highway 66, SMU 0," or "Temperature 88, SMU 0."

In professional sports, enthusiasm is great when the home team is winning. But when the home team slips, most pro fans treat the players with as much respect as they would a Roto-Rooter man whose work backfires. This can be explained partially by the players who jump clubs—and the huge salaries going around.

"The Rangers are fat cats," says Bob Bernstein, who sits next to Don Decker in the upper reaches of the Garden. "I've heard some Rangers say they don't want to win the Stanley Cup for the money—just for the pride. I say that's not healthy. If an athlete isn't hungry, he doesn't fight. Here I'm getting an upset stomach—and they *ain't!*"

Bernstein does indeed risk an upset stomach the way he howls for Giacomin's scalp each game. But he keeps coming back, paying over three hundred dollars for a season ticket. In his spare time, Bernstein coaches a roller-hockey team in Brooklyn. His seatmates stay up late listening to hockey broadcasts from Chicago and St. Louis.

Hockey officials claim hockey fans have the highest income and education of all pro-sports fans. Certainly Bernstein and Decker and Bill Applegate, up in the rafters, are pleasant men. But Ranger crowds seem to be getting more vicious each year.

"Ranger fans have a loser syndrome," says Jerry Eskenazi, hockey writer for The *Times*. "It really got bad last year when they kept calling Derek Sanderson dirty names. There's one girl who balls some of the players, then curses them during a game. Hockey fans like violence. They defend the fights as part of the game."

Eskenazi says the most knowledgeable hockey fans are in northern cities like Boston, Montreal and Minnesota, where fans have played the game and save their applause for the truly good play.

New York used to have that reputation, too. A Stan Musial could get six hits in a doubleheader at Ebbets Field but Dodger fans would cheer his boyish enthusiasm and nickname him "Stan the Man."

While New York fans think of themselves as the hippest of fans—wearing their finest dungaree suits or superfly costumes to Knickerbocker basketball games—they have gotten into the habit of jeering certain abrasive visiting stars like Rick Barry or Dave Cowens, while applauding a John Havlicek or a Jerry West.

"Oh, there is still some admiration for a great play," says Steve Jacobson of *Newsday*. "But I believe there is less appreciation for a Jerry West than there used to be for a Bobby Davies."

Certain towns, like Seattle and San Antonio, have a reputation for polite, knowledgeable basketball fans while Indianapolis has been known to stage a fight or two. In Louisville, the two Thomas brothers sit at opposite ends of the looming Freedom Hall and loudly heckle referees and visiting American Basketball Association players. But most Midwestern fans appreciate the best players.

"At a play-off game over in Lexington," reports John Christensen of Louisville, "the fans were rooting for the Colonels but they cheered every move by Doctor J [Julius Erving of New York]. Fans in this area know their basketball and they'll boo the Colonels if they're having a bad night. But this is the Midwest. People are reasonably patient."

More and more women have been appearing at basketball games in recent years, either by themselves or as eager dates. One former Iowa schoolgirl player, now a career woman in New York, says she finds basketball "so intellectual. Those plays, the back-door play, are choreographed, just like ballet."

Then she really gets down to it:

"Some of my friends tease me that I watch basketball because I like to watch the men's bodies. Well, that's true. Basketball players are in great shape. They look nice in those short uniforms. Walt Frazier has the best body I've ever seen. Bob Lanier, he's too fat; Oscar Robertson is usually overweight early in the season. Most of them, though, are very handsome."

Football fans have their own world, fashioned by the once-a-week intensity. Grim football writers and zealots like Vince Lombardi have created a gloomy world where there is only one winner each year—the Super Bowl champion—and fans in twenty-five other cities must penitently sulk all winter. In New York, for almost a decade Giant fans have been yowling for the scalps of quarterbacks and coaches, because the fans believed they had the divine right to an annual championship.

"Say you've had tickets for a long time," says Norman Papazian, a Giant fan from Fairfield, Connecticut. "You can remember when the Giants were good. Now if the Giants make a slight gain, you hear mocking cheers. It's half humorous—and half real."

Rita Papazian, once a college journalist, likes football because it is "fast-moving." She also says she relates better to football players because "deep down, you feel they've gone to college, just like you, whereas the baseball player probably signed out of high school."

It would do little good to suggest that many pro football players acquired only a college *veneer* when they lived on a campus playing football. Maybe pro football players look intellectual because they carry their play books in attaché cases. Anyway, the important thing is that pro football has been packaged, like white bread or Detroit cars, and has been accepted by many success-oriented people as "our sport."

Baseball, on the other hand, is a Depression sport. It is a great sport for hooky players, for the unemployed, or for anybody else with a clear mind and lots of time. And the fans don't care if a player is a nuclear physicist or a dropout. Even with the new remote stadiums, the floating franchises, baseball is still a great fan game—action every day from March through October, something always happening. In baseball, no manager can duck the issue by saying, "I'll have to check the films to see who missed the block." When the shortstop fumbles the grounder, he is naked to the world. He must stand there and scuff at the dirt while the fans give him advice. But even there, fans differ from town to town.

In one of the few long conversations we ever had, Mickey Mantle told how he loved to play in Minnesota and Kansas City because the fans were so friendly. Even when Mantle and the Yankees faded in the late Sixties, he could return to his hotel in Kansas City after a game and find dozens of families in Bermuda shorts and funny straw hats politely taking pictures and asking for autographs.

Not so on the East Coast.

"I hate going to Boston," Mantle said. "I don't know why. They just don't act like baseball fans up there. They get on me for everything. They say silly things."

Bob Sales, a former sportswriter, now an urban reporter for *The Boston Globe*, says he finds a melting pot in the jammed bleachers of Fenway Park:

"You get all the college kids from Harvard and M.I.T.," Sales says. "Then you get the older fans from South Boston, where Louise Day Hicks is from. At home, they probably say 'Kill the hippies'—who knows? But in the bleachers, everybody talks about the Sox."

Jim Bouton recalls the friendly fans in Minnesota: "The most threatening statement they'd ever make was, 'Boy, you guys are gonna have trouble with our Twins tonight.'" But Bouton admits he got more of a thrill from pitching in Boston.

"There's nothing like being heckled in a foreign tongue," Bouton says lapsing into a Boston accent, which is something like a crow talking out of the side of its mouth: "'Hey, Bouton, you're gawna get yaw blawk knawcked awf. Yaz is gawna hit two awfa you, Bouton!'

"The fans in Boston are very knowledgeable. Somebody would make a play in one inning and you'd hear fans buzzing about it for innings after. Boston fans yell strategy right into the dugout. The players listen, whether they admit it or not."

Bouton remembers other ball parks he pitched in:

"In Houston, the management puts fans down by telling them what to do," he says. "Fans would sit on their hands until the scoreboard told them to applaud. If the scoreboard was late, they wouldn't know enough to applaud. But in Fenway Paaahk, if they tried that 'applaud' stuff, the fans would shout, 'Screw you, scoreboard.'"

Mickey Herskowitz, who covered Houston baseball when Houston entered the major leagues in 1962, remembers the "eerie silences" when the fans weren't told what to do. He also remembers the early years in the Astrodome, when the wealthy Houston citizens attended in fur coats and suits—"just like the opera"—while in the next box, a farmer might be sticking his manure-caked boots up on the railing. Herskowitz says the fans now dress and yell more like fans everywhere else.

Another strange place for baseball is Los Angeles, where Jim Bouton remembers all the "Hollywood types" coming out for a game.

"Sometimes you'd be out on the field in uniform thinking you were just another interestingly dressed person at a party," he recalls.

Baseball fans have their own subgroups: intense and knowledgeable in Detroit; still relying on Vin Scully on the transistor radio in laid-back pastel Dodger Stadium; hip matrons keeping score and sipping from a flask at sun-swept day games in San Francisco; tourists, numbed by Disneyland, eyes reddened from pool chlorine, sleeping in the cool night air at Anaheim Stadium; Chicago Cubs "bleacher bums" heaving rivets or live mice at visiting left fielders; leaden Atlanta fans, barely able to appreciate Henry Aaron; Oakland, with its prison-concrete decor, attracting only hard-core fans for a championship team.

And Mets fans. The stuffy Mets management didn't know how to cope when those maniacs came out of the closet in 1962, carrying bed-sheet banners that said: "BRING BACK BUTTERBALL BOB BOTZ," in memory of a pitcher who couldn't make it in spring training. Encouraged by the press, the Met management was holding a "Banner Day" by the end of 1962, and has enjoyed huge attendances ever since.

"Mets fans are still the hippest in sports," says Steve Jacobson. "I'll give you an example. Late in 1973, they brought up a pitcher named Bob Apodaca. In his first major-league appearance, he was probably nervous and he walked two batters and was removed. All right. Now it's early 1974. Apodaca comes into his first game and throws a strike—one strike—and an awful lot of fans start cheering. They remembered some minor incident that happened *six months before!*"

But there is another side to the self-expression of the Mets fans—the indulgent rampages when the Mets won pennants in 1969 and 1973, leaving Shea Stadium looking like a battlefield. Following the Rose-Harrelson fight in the 1973 play-offs, some fans threatened to stop the game, almost forcing a forfeit.

It was the kind of unchecked exuberance left over from pioneer days—the notion that the country is so big that there is room for any ripsnorting behavior, like suburbanites who let their big dogs run loose or smokers who foul up other people's air. But fans like to get involved in the game, from shouting "DEEEE-fense" to heckling the opposition. And come to think of it, Don Decker and his buddies in the upper reaches of Madison Square Garden pay nine dollars for their play-off seats. At those prices, who is to say a fan doesn't have the right to get into the act?

BIL GILBERT

AND

LISA TWYMAN

Violence: Out of Hand in the Stands

Perhaps because we're so heavily bombarded with dire news and doomsday prophecies, there's a temptation for those concerned with a problem— whether it be viral skin disorders, reading deficiencies of youth or the drying up of swamps—to call attention to it by stridently suggesting that if it isn't immediately solved the Republic will crumble. This is an especially suspect and ludicrous practice when applied to sports. The difficulties of junky jocks, sneaky coaches or greedy promoters are seldom related in any significant way to the substantial ills of society. This should be kept in mind as we consider the subject of this report, fan violence.

Through the ages sporting spectators have been notorious for hooliganism. The original Olympics were suspended because of belligerent crowd behavior. In one three-day period in 532 A.D., during the reign of the Emperor Justinian, 30,000 Romans died in riots at the chariot races. In year 1314 Edward II of England banned "that dreadful game, football," because it touched off such bloody brawls among 14th-century fans. The worst recent outburst of this sort occurred in Lima, Peru, where at a soccer match in 1964, 300 people were killed and 500 injured. There have always been incidents of this kind, but their number and seriousness fluctuate, reflecting, some theorize, disorders in the real world. (The hypothesis that behavior at sports events may serve as a barometer for measuring pressures and tension in society is probably the most thought-provoking aspect of this phenomenon.)

Originally appeared in *Sports Illustrated* (1983).

Currently, nearly all knowledgeable sources think there is a rising level of fan violence in the U.S. The consensus is that, in comparison to 20 or even 10 years ago, it's more difficult and expensive to control sports crowds; that they cause more personal injury and property damage and are uglier in manner and mood. Now, this is bad news for sport, but it hardly constitutes a grave threat to public order, health and morals. In any general discussion of violence, that which occurs at sports events is little more than an aside. During the past year, on any number of days in the Middle East or Central America there was more violence than has occurred in all of modern sports history. Spending an evening at Yankee Stadium now may be more risky than going to the zoo or staying at home, but it's still safer than walking for three hours in the neighborhood around Yankee Stadium. What fan violence amounts to may be suggested by the following sampler of happenings in recent years:

•After the WBC California State Junior Lightweight Boxing Championship in Sacramento last summer, a brawl broke out and eventually involved, police estimated, 75 to 100 fans. Before it was over, seven spectators had been stabbed, four requiring hospitalization.

•At a Friday night of boxing in Madison Square Garden in 1978, two men were stabbed, another man was shot (by an off-duty corrections officer) and a woman was treated for a severe head laceration after being struck by a bottle. While the police were carrying the gunshot victim from the Garden, someone lobbed an exploding cherry bomb at them.

•At New York's Shea Stadium during a 1978 Jets-Steelers game, spectators overpowered a security guard and dropped him over a railing to a concrete walkway 15 feet below. He suffered a fractured skull, along with a concussion and various neck injuries.

•At a 1981 Rams-Bears game in Chicago's Soldier Field there were 31 arrests, the principal charges being battery, disorderly conduct and possession of drugs. Two security men and several ushers were attacked by fans, one of whom dropped his pants and shot a moon for the benefit of the Honey Bears, the Chicago cheerleaders, and the ABC television cameras.

•In 1980 the Detroit Tigers temporarily closed the bleacher section in their stadium to retake it, so to speak, from chronically violent spectators. For the same reason, in May, 1981 the Cincinnati Reds asked their players and the opposing players, the Pittsburgh Pirates, to leave the field at Riverfront Stadium until the rowdy crowd could be brought under control.

•During a 1981 American League playoff game at Yankee Stadium, a fan carrying a blackjack ran onto the field and charged and knocked down the third-base umpire, who was saved from injury by the quick intervention of the Yankees' Graig Nettles and Dave Winfield.

•Pittsburgh outfielder Dave Parker claims to be the No. 1 target of fan violence in America because he's black, highly paid, hasn't performed well the
last couple of seasons and is proud, perhaps even a bit arrogant. He has been
pelted with apple cores, hundreds of paper beer cups, jawbreakers, transistor-
radio batteries and bullets (thrown not fired), as well as obscenities and racial
slurs. "You ain't nothin' but a stinkin', lousy nigger" is a printable example of
the latter. Once, in his hotel room in Philadelphia, Parker received a telephone call from a man who informed him that if he came down to the lobby
he would be killed. Parker did and wasn't. He's among the growing number of
sports figures who have received death threats during the past five years.

The list of such happenings isn't endless, but it's very long. Beyond those
that draw public attention there are innumerable violent acts that go unre-
ported. It's fair to say that on game day in every major sporting facility there
are a few fights and several minor assaults and a dozen or so spectators are
ejected because of bad conduct.

"This crowd violence thing has been in the dark for so long," says David M.
Schaffer, director of park operations (including security) for the Chicago
White Sox, a team that recently has made notable efforts to face up to its
problems. "Hell, just go anywhere and there will be a fight of one kind or
another."

Traditionally, the sporting establishment has been mum on the subject, believing that a certain amount of crowd misbehavior is part of the game and
one which, like the legs of a Victorian lady, gentlemen speak of euphemistically; that talking about violence would focus attention on it and stimulate others to commit it; that the subject is bad for business. "We prefer to
talk about crowd involvement rather than violence," said a Philadelphia
Flyers official several years ago. "Violence has such an ugly connotation."

However, the fact that buying a ticket to a game markedly increases a customer's chances of getting a punch in the snoot, doused with beer, an earful
of X-rated language or a vandalized car makes it difficult to sustain former
traditions and illusions. By their actions, if not their words, most sports executives indicate that they regard fan violence as a large problem, one that's
going to get larger, more expensive and more embarrassing if something isn't
done about it soon. As never before, leagues and teams are trying to find out
why their fans have grown so difficult to handle, and in making such assessments, sports executives are calling in "violence experts," a new breed of
consultant.

Some of the observations, theories and conclusions of these violence experts are:

•Sports crowds generally follow some vague rules of order—for example, people don't usually stand and block the view of other spectators—but can become unstable, erratic and edgy human organizations. Within a crowd there are many low-level sources of tension—close, involuntary contact with strangers, abnormal physical discomforts, competition for territory, goods, services and information—that frustrate individuals and make them more irritable and belligerent than they are when alone or in smaller groups. Crowds provide anonymity and encourage miscreants to act more irresponsibly than they might in situations where they can be easily identified and punished. Simple, primitive emotions, such as elation, anger, panic and vengeance, are contagious within a crowd and create so-called mass hysteria. Sports events regularly draw the largest crowds of any public events, but sports facilities, compared to those offered to other crowds, are often among the most inefficient, uncomfortable and unattractive. If the environment were as grim and aggravating at art galleries, lecture halls and movie theaters as it is at Schaefer Stadium, there probably would be more disturbances at those places.

•Sports events are exhibitions of skill, grace, strength, coordination and other attractive human properties. They're also contrived, dramatic charades, of which violence is an intrinsic element or, at least, violence is not too far below the surface. In some sports, such as boxing, football and hockey, the scripts are explicitly violent. Even in those sports where the participants are not called upon to push, shove and beat each other the action is confrontational, with one individual or team trying to demolish, as the scribes say, an opponent—or crush, roll over, thump, trample, pulverize, stick it to and kill him, as they also say. The underlying themes of competitive games are strikingly similar to those of war, and the language of the two activities has become almost identical.

Our newspapers, magazines, books, TV shows, movies, theater, music and advertisements testify to our fascination with violence, that it rates not far behind sex in its vicarious attraction. One explanation for this is that many people would like to be more violent than they are. They find the idea of taking arms against their enemies—or people who merely frustrate or cause them trouble—and flattening them, so to speak, by direct physical action to be very appealing. Most people don't act on such impulses because of the law, ethics or the fear of getting hurt. Stymied by reality, they take deep satisfaction in watching and identifying with others who seem to be acting in this bold way. As a group, athletes are encouraged and rewarded for being violent while on-stage, and sport has become one of our most successful devices for providing fantasy relief.

Sports crowds are encouraged to respond freely to the action of the game. Cheering, booing, hissing, stamping feet, waving fists and screaming criticisms and threats are considered normal at games, though those activities would be treated as aberrant and unruly in other circumstances. As tragedies can bring their audiences to tears and comedies can provoke laughter, sport can make its crowds a bit more violent. And as in other forms of show business, the assumption is that the more powerful the production the more pronounced the reaction of the audience.

Michael Smith, a former football and hockey player and hockey coach, is a Canadian sociologist interested in such matters. He says, "I believe that violence in sport contributes to violence in the crowd, as opposed to the notion of catharsis, that viewing violent acts results in draining away feelings of violence. I have looked at newspaper accounts of 68 episodes of collective violence or riots among spectators during or after sporting events, and in three-quarters of those the precipitating event was violence in the game. Yet for decades and decades eminent scholars wrote without a shred of evidence that acts of violence in sport are cathartic or therapeutic for spectators." Indeed, the catharsis theory is still advanced occasionally but, as Smith suggests, has been largely discredited by social scientists simply because nobody can find cases where this saltpeter-like effect has been produced.

The association between sport and violence isn't aberrant. However, it's supposedly understood by everyone involved that what's going on is just a game, a staged conflict. That this is frequently forgotten is testimony to the power of sports. Even participants who have long rehearsals and the rules of the game and referees to remind them that they are actors in a play get carried away by the make-believe battle. Losing one's grip on reality happens more often in the stands. Spectators have few restraints on their behavior, and it isn't surprising that some of them give vent to their own fantasies by responding physically to the fictitious battle being played out by the athletes. "The crowd is going crazy" is an instructive sporting cliché.

Dr. John Cheffers, a former Australian football player and international track athlete and coach, is a professor of education at Boston University. For a decade he has been professionally interested in fan violence and now offers his services to sports organizations, among them the New England Patriots. For some time Cheffers and an associate, a sociologist named Dr. Jay Meehan, have been using video equipment and graduate students to observe spectators at football, hockey, soccer and baseball games in order to identify types and causes of what they call "incongruous behavior."

Cheffers and Meehan have been investigating whether "unwarranted" actions by athletes, *i.e.*, fights, elicit exceptional responses from fans. Here their findings have been surprising. In soccer, fights among the players have triggered violence in the stands in 57% of the cases the researchers have observed. For football and baseball the percentages are 49 and 34, respectively. However, in hockey only 8.5% of the on-ice fights touched off acts of fan violence. Cheffers speculates that hockey customers see so many fights that they have become a bit blasé about them. He suggests that hockey may be moving in the direction of what he calls the "giggle sports," professional wrestling and Roller Derby. At these attractions, ostensibly illegal and violent acts by the participants are so common and highly stylized that they are largely regarded as phony and have lost much of their impact.

Such information as Cheffers and a few others have collected tends to confirm the commonsense observation that the rougher the game the rougher the crowd. Cheffers believes that "If it [violence] is on the field it will be in the stands." Contact sports provide most of the examples of fan violence, while in golf, tennis and track they are rare. But if this is the rule, there are many exceptions and anomalies. Outside the U.S., soccer, not a contact sport, has the most dangerous and destructive fans. This may be because of social and economic factors. There's a strong tradition in Europe, and particularly in the British Isles, that soccer is a workingman's game, and the rowdyism of the spectators may be, Cheffers speculates, a kind of class statement, a means of showing contempt for polite society and cocking a snoot at the well-behaved gentry.

Boxing is the most violent of all sports, but its crowds are not exceptionally disorderly. However, when something does stir them, they often become more vicious than other fans. In the U.S. during the past 10 years, *all* of the disturbances in which spectators have had at each other with knives and guns, with the intent to kill and maim, have occured in boxing crowds. Apparently, the nature of the sport enables its fans to deal sanely with a lot of violence, but when they lose control, it's with great ferocity. Baseball may demonstrate the opposite side of the hockey-boxing coin. Small, fairly tame acts of violence on a baseball field may appear to be much worse than they really are because the game generally lacks physical contact. Also at the heart of baseball is one of the most explicitly warlike charades in all sport: the repeated and possibly fatal confrontation between pitcher and batter.

In many cases the players' unwarranted (illegal, according to the rules) acts, which Cheffers finds are likely to stir up fans, are unintentional or accidental. When an athlete makes mistakes in judgment—say, commits a dumb foul—he sometimes becomes so aroused that he begins fighting or throwing a tantrum. In other cases such displays are a matter of design and are performed for inspirational reasons or in the hope of achieving competitive advantage. Baiting umpires is a traditional baseball tactic that also incites spectators, whose calls of kill the ump or throw the bum out are often followed by fisticuffs in the stands and objects thrown out of them. Jack Dunn III, the vice-president for stadium operations of the Baltimore Orioles, says that the most fights he ever saw in the stands occurred on a day when former Oriole

Manager Earl Weaver argued with an umpire and was ejected from the game. Last summer Sam Rutigliano, coach of the Cleveland Browns, in effect came down on the side of unnecessary roughness in the NFL. He said that while officials might still penalize his players for such infractions of league rules, he wasn't going to reinforce the refs' authority by fining, as he had the year before, Browns who drew unnecessary roughness calls. He said that he thought worrying about being assessed such fines might interfere with the concentration of his players and lower their morale.

Perhaps more regularly than any other sporting figures, basketball coaches attempt to incite and exploit crowd reaction by means of histrionic displays. "There's no question about it," says Shelby Metcalf, the basketball coach at Texas A&M. "Some coaches—we have a couple here in the Southwest Conference—try to get their home crowds fired up and use them to intimidate opposing players and officials. I think it works less often than these coaches and the press think it does because the players and officials are more sophisticated than they used to be. But it works often enough that there are coaches who continue to use the technique to try to get an edge. It is a danger and a disgrace to the game. We ought to be doing more than we are to stop it."

Metcalf is an unusual and unusually well-qualified authority on fan violence. In addition to having coached the Aggies for 19 seasons, he has a Ph.D. from A&M in philosophy. For his doctoral dissertation on crowd behavior and control, Metcalf selected 84 variables, ranging from the deportment of cheerleaders to the size of arena, that he thought might influence crowd actions. His list was sent to the Southwest Conference office. After each of the 112 basketball games used in the survey, referees, coaches and sports information directors on the scene were asked to check the factors that seemed to have most influenced the fans. Tabulating the results, Metcalf found, again to the surprise of no one, that the behavior of coaches, players and officials had the most effect, good and bad, on the spectators. Commenting tangentially, Metcalf says, "It's sad but true. If there's a good fight, one that gets a lot of attention in the press, attendance is going to be up for two or three weeks afterward for games of the teams involved."

Though sports entrepreneurs may not deliberately set out to pump up their customers to the point of belting each other or trashing stadiums, many team officials are inclined to stimulate frenzy and emphasize the wilder aspects of the entertainment being offered. Touting mayhem has been the principal promotional thrust of wrestling and Roller Derby. There are chronic suspicions that hockey moguls, despite repeated pious protests to the contrary, are inclined to regard brawls as good for business. The late and unlamented professional box-lacrosse league advertised itself as putting on happenings that Attila the Hun and anybody with a taste for blood and battle would love.

There are a good many sporting hypes—provocative cheerleaders, drums, horns, organs, posters, cartoons, effigy burnings, pep rallies, exploding and smart-aleck scoreboards—that have become so common that nobody thinks much about their subliminal messages and influence anymore. For example, like many other major league baseball teams, the Baltimore Orioles have an official mascot, in this case a guy in bird drag who hops around Memorial Stadium to entertain and exhort the home crowd. Among other stunts of the Baltimore bird: Between innings he dons boxing gloves and goes a few rounds with someone dressed to represent the opponents, say the Detroit Tigers, before scoring a KO, to the delight of the fans.

Pat Sullivan's family operates the Patriots, and he's the club officer concerned with crowd control. Having listened to various theories about why spectators are so unruly, Sullivan says in effect that while the ideas are interesting, "the main thing is so many of the fans are drunk."

Many other sports officials have made the same observation. Buffalo's Don Guenther, the manager of Rich Stadium, home of the Bills, says he thinks 99% of the arrests at games are related to alcohol.

Dick Vertlieb now is an entertainment and financial consultant in Seattle but in the past has been the general manager of three NBA teams, the Warriors, Pacers and Sonics, and of baseball's Seattle Mariners. "The problem," says Vertlieb, speaking of fan violence, is the "goddamn beer. All the teams do is push beer and push beer, and then when someone gets out of line, they send the cops after the guy. When I was with the Sonics there was no beer in the Coliseum and it was a family event. Now it's difficult even to take your wife. It's an outrage."

The connection between guzzling and fan violence needs very little explanation. Nobody has ever suggested that a good way to calm down a crowd is to fill it to the gills with strong drink. To a greater degree than at any other assemblies, except perhaps stag conventions, alcohol is made available to sports spectators, and they are encouraged to use it freely. There are 63 stadiums and arenas in the U.S. that serve major pro teams. Beer is sold in 61 of them and hard liquor in 24. (Only a handful of colleges sell beer at their games. This is almost universally accepted as a principal reason why collegiate crowds, despite their youth and exuberance, present fewer serious security problems than do professional ones.)

Why beer and booze, despite being named by many executives as a main cause of fan violence, are so readily available is also fairly obvious. They are profitable. How profitable can't be precisely determined, because teams and concessionaires don't routinely divulge sales figures. However, it seems likely that where beer is sold it accounts for about half of the overall concession take. This would work out to about $500,000 a season generated by a team such as the Sonics.

Beyond the retail income, the alcohol business is profitable for sports organizations in many other ways. Radio and TV broadcasts of virtually every major league game are sponsored in whole or part by breweries. According to a 1982 survey conducted by Simmons Market Research Bureau, the heavy beer-drinker is a sports lover. Male heavy beer-drinkers represent 30% of the total beer-drinking public and are responsible for nearly 80% of the total volume of beer sales.

The relationship of beer and booze to sports is so profitable that managerial types are loath to finger in-park sales as a contributing cause of fan violence. Invariably, they say the real problem is with contraband stuff, *i.e.*, alcohol that's brought to the ball park by fans in coolers, brown bags or their bloodstreams.

Joe McDermott, the Boston Red Sox executive in charge of security at Fenway Park, says that most of the Sox spectator trouble occurs in the first few innings of a game and is caused by people who were soused on arrival. "Let's face it," says McDermott, his righteous instincts overcoming his commercial caution, "it's pretty hard to get loaded on the beer sold here—it's mostly froth." Like many other teams, the Red Sox have and exercise the right to search incoming customers, confiscate containers and refuse entry to those who seem likely to make trouble.

Though, again, it's not much talked about for obvious reasons, spectator use of drugs, notably marijuana, cocaine and Quaaludes, seems to be increasing more rapidly than alcohol consumption. "Get yourself a Coke with whatever you smoke," chants a Schaefer Stadium soft-drink vendor. "Get your hot pretzels, ludes and joints," responds a mocking fan. In many arenas particular ramps and rest rooms are favored by the heads and dealers. The dangers and morality of drug use can be debated elsewhere, but there's no reason to believe that numbers of people with rolling eyeballs or runny noses make a constructive contribution to the good behavior of sports crowds.

To improve crowd control in 1976, the Red Sox began employing 20 football players from local colleges. During games they roam Fenway with the aim of soothing potentially troublesome fans or unobtrusively giving the heave-ho to those—sometimes 30 a game—who are beyond pacifying. Sox management has been pleased with the footballers, whose size gives them respect as well as clout and whose youth gives them rapport with the sort of spectators most likely to be difficult. Security people everywhere single out 20-to-30-year-old males as the most likely to create disturbances. The general opinion is that they are especially vulnerable to macho fantasies and to acting them out when stirred up by sporting events.

Wayne Thornton, a 6′ 3″, 230-pound Holy Cross graduate, was a member of the Fenway patrol last summer and says of his routine activities, "We look for drunks, of course, and very loud belligerent types. Every couple of innings we check out some of the rest rooms and ramps for people smoking and snorting dope. Also, we watch for guys who aren't paying much attention to the game, just waiting around and hanging out."

It's perhaps arbitrary to say that hangers-out come to an event with the intention of being violent. But there's reason to believe that the possibility of bashing heads is on their minds and an attraction in itself. Dr. Arnold R. Beisser, a Los Angeles psychiatrist with an interest in sports, has commented, "We're seeing a new use of violence. It's being used not as a means to an end but for recreational purposes, for pleasure. It's an end in itself."

A 24-year-old man—let's call him Tim—is a hanger-out type. (He won't be better identified because there's a suspicion that he might regard any public mention as a feather in his cap, a glorification of his deeds.) Tim has a better than average blue-collar job and a decent apartment in the suburbs of a Midwestern metropolis that supports franchises in all major professional sports. He has no dependents, only temporary girl friends and, therefore, a considerable amount of disposable income. Even so, he says that he doesn't regard his life as being all that good. As to ambitions? "I don't know," he says. "Livin', I guess. I got a lot of things I want to do: One, get rich. How? I don't know. I wish I knew."

Tim is a wispy 5′ 6″ and weighs 120 or so pounds. But there's an indefinable quality about him—insolence, sullenness, rebelliousness—that suggests he could be trouble. "Tim," says an acquaintance, "is the kind of person that a cop will pick out of a crowd when there's a disturbance, or somebody will come up to and slug for no real reason. Maybe he looks like a loser."

Tim wasn't a high school athlete and isn't a rabid sports fan in the sense of being particularly knowledgeable or attached to a given team. However, he goes to a number of events to pass his time. At the moment, his favorite sport is hydroplane racing. He will drive long distances to attend regattas with groups of friends. "We'll get a hotel or room someplace," he says. "No showers. You know. Usually girls go, just to have fun, wherever there is a race. It's just mostly, I don't know, unreal the way those things [boats] aren't even in the water. I don't know, they just look so excellent in the water, all the spray and everything."

Last April, Tim and a dozen or so male cronies went to a hockey playoff game. Some of the gang allegedly had been to a baseball game earlier in the afternoon and had amused themselves and provoked security men by throwing snowballs at the players on the field. Tim wasn't with them and wasn't, he says, drunk before leaving for the hockey game. "I'm not saying I haven't gone like that to the races and stuff," he says. "I'll drink and stuff, but I don't get obliviated [sic] where it's not going to be worth it to me if I can't know what's going on when I leave."

Tim said he had a couple of beers before arriving and only one at the game. His version of what went on there is as follows. He says that toward the end of the game some trouble started in the section where he was sitting; he thinks maybe people started pouring beer on each other after a fight broke out on the ice. He and his friends edged into the melee to see the action. Then, he says, spectators and cops started grabbing people. The next thing he knew he woke up in a hospital with five broken teeth. According to security men on the scene and police records, Tim and his pals were the instigators of the brawl, dumping beer on people, threatening those around them and throwing whatever was at hand on the ice. (The players on the ice actually stopped skating to watch the fight in the stands, but not before one player tripped over some of the debris, separated his shoulder and was sidelined for the rest of the playoffs.) Tim himself imprudently attacked a very large, bearded customer, who was the one who cold-cocked him, literally driving his teeth down his throat. Tim was arrested, and pleaded guilty to charges of assault and battery and mob action. He was fined and barred by the stadium management from attending any games there for a year. Nevertheless, he thinks that the whole thing was a mistake, that he got a bum rap. He pleaded guilty, he says, only because he didn't know what really happened. "I know what I am, and that ain't it," he says. "You know what was said? It was all turned around so I came out being troublemaker Tim, you know, and that ain't true, but that's me against the world. Whoever believes it and whoever don't."

"I believe the incidences of violence are way up," says Dr. Irving Goldaber, a sociologist who is the director and founder of the Center for Study of Crowd and Spectator Behavior, a Miami-based research and consulting firm. "My file of current incidents gets larger and larger every year. Where about 10 years ago I had one folder, now every year I do another file drawer."

Goldaber, who has advised the NFL, major league baseball and the International Association of Chiefs of Police, among others, is perhaps the country's best-known expert on fan violence. He says that five years ago he was receiving about three requests a year to appear as an expert witness in court actions having to do with incidents involving sporting crowds. Now he's getting about one every two weeks.

During the 1950s and '60s, Goldaber, who says, "Human conflict was always my field," instructed law-enforcement groups in dealing with street disturbances, protesters, terrorists and hostage takers. In the mid '70s, he says, he detected the emergence of a new form of violence in this country. He terms it "violence for vicarious power" and finds it's most openly manifested in sporting crowds, whose behavior is now one of his principal professional interests. Like many other experts Goldaber believes that the problems of sport reflect larger ones in society. Specifically, he says, "More and more people aren't making it. You work hard, you exist, but you haven't got much to show for it. There are increasing numbers of people who are deeply frustrated because they feel they have very little power over their lives. They come to sporting events to experience, vicariously, a sense of power."

In a stadium, the power trippers are even more vulnerable to ordinary crowd stimuli and irritations than more traditional fans. "They respond to the violence on the field," says Goldaber. "They respond to the hype and hoopla of the event, to the beer, cheerleaders, scoreboards and bands. When you have a crowd that is anticipating a physical experience, it will have a physical experience."

Goldaber believes that several characteristics distinguish the vicarious power-seekers. They're very prone to overidentify with a team or individuals. "They're dressed in the numbers and the letters and the names and the colors, with the jackets, the sweaters, the scarves and the pennants," he says. "They're part of the team and they're in the game." They aren't particularly concerned or knowledgeable about how games are played and take little pleasure in stylish athletic performances. "The reason they come to sporting events isn't so much to watch the game as to be in the game and especially to experience winning through their team or hero. In this world, where so many individuals are diminished, it's pretty important to matter, to win, to be No. 1. When their team wins, they have a sense of being important: 'I won.'

"Because they overidentify and think they're in the game, they feel they have a right to affect the outcome of the game, in the old ways by cheering and booing, but also with new violent forms of threatening and intimidating action. Because winning, being No. 1, is everything, they're likely to be very ferocious if they—their team—are thwarted and they vent their frustrations physically against players, officials or other spectators. That's the nub of the problem."

Goldaber feels that a vicious cycle has been created. Sensing the obsessive mood, sports management has tended to pander to it, overpromoting fan identification. Goldaber has developed this theme perhaps more fully than others, but that there's a connection between fan violence and win-at-all-cost attitudes has occurred to many. Lennie Wirtz, a veteran basketball referee who has had visions of an enraged spectator coming at him with an ice pick, says he thinks the most important reason for the worsening of behavior of coaches and players—and because of them, crowds—is the enormous pressure to win that's now at work on the participants.

Bill Veeck, a shrewd and iconoclastic baseball entrepreneur and observer for more than half a century, agrees with Wirtz. "Unfortunately, like Dr. Frankenstein, people in baseball have created a monster," Veeck says. "They think only a winning club is any good. People forget that we're in the entertainment business. Look what you get then, a George Steinbrenner. What more horrible fate could possibly happen, unless you get two?"

Many authorities say there's evidence that things could get worse. Based on information provided by police departments from around the nation, Goldaber makes the ominous estimate that in any large pro sports crowd somewhere between 0.5% and 2% of the spectators are now carrying concealed weapons. This works out to 250 to 1,000 fans packing guns, lethal knives or Wirtz's ice pick in a crowd of 50,000. Goldaber believes it's likely that we will shortly have a sports assassination, carried out by a demented fan who will rise up with, say, a 30-30 and take out a quarterback or power forward. "And when it happens once," he says, "there will be enormous publicity and this will trigger more of it. Years ago, if somebody said that we would have weapons checks before boarding airplanes it would have been thought absurd, but that's normal now and may well become normal at sporting events. Hostage-seizing at games is also a possibility. In a sense, we have already had it. Death threats are really hostage situations in which an athlete is told not to play in a certain way or be killed."

Neither Goldaber's facts nor predictions much surprise other crowd-control professionals. As to the 30-30 scenario, Cheffers remarks, "Actually, it's surprising it hasn't happened. In this country athletes are at least as celebrated as rock stars or politicians. There are a lot of Hinckleys out there who have strong feelings about sport."

Cheffers finds it easy to imagine that because of such a disaster, or in an attempt to prevent one, high-security measures might alter sport as drastically as the violence itself. "We could reach a point where major sporting events are staged in shielded areas before 5,000 or so spectators who pay several hundred dollars each for safe, luxurious accommodations," Cheffers says. "Attending live sporting events could disappear as a popular entertainment."

All of this is prophecy, but events that have occurred suggest that such possibilities should be taken seriously. The almost reflexive response of sports promoters to bad crowd situations is to lay on more cops of one sort or another. Following an ugly Monday-night football game, Sullivan said that to prevent further outbursts he would "bring in the National Guard if we have to to make things safe." Attack dogs were used for crowd control in a 1980

World Series game in Philadelphia and in 1982 in St. Louis. This prompted Goldaber to quip, "If dogs aren't effective [he thinks they are], maybe they'll bring out attack lions next." Both the Patriots and Red Sox are converting sections of their stands into posh, heavily guarded apartment-like boxes that lease for $20,000 to $36,000 a year. Most other stadiums have, or are planning, similar facilities. Elsewhere, the ultimate crowd-control technique has already been employed. Because of reasonable fears about the conduct of supporters of rival teams, soccer games in England and American high school football and basketball games have been played in facilities from which all fans have been barred.

If we evolve into a Brave New World society, we'll no doubt have Rollerball games and Orwellian crowds—or none of either—because sport cannot be maintained in splendid isolation. Furthermore, given the nature of crowds and sport, there are probably no steps that can, or should, be taken to make spectators as pacific as Quakers at meeting. However, with these basic reservations, students of crowd behavior believe that there are steps that can be taken to improve the present situation and that the apparent trend isn't irreversible. Consultants such as Cheffers, Meehan and Goldaber have remarkably similar ideas about corrective and preventive actions. Though they use different terminology, they have developed similar models describing various states of crowd psychology. These range from controlled to explosive. When by reason of panic, anger or exuberance a crowd comes to this latter condition, it's so dangerous and destructive that nothing much can be done beyond calling riot police or troops to quell the violence. Therefore, the aim of controllers should be to keep things below the explosive level, and if the atmosphere approaches that, to make use of what Goldaber calls "defusing mechanisms."

The most commonly recommended measure is to improve facilities to lessen environmental irritations in crowd situations. Places that are clean, comfortable and convenient tend to promote good behavior. Even the illusion that management is concerned with the amenities seems to have a good effect. Goldaber advises clients, not entirely facetiously, that if they have only $50 for crowd-control innovations, they should employ two men, dress them in immaculate white coats, give them brooms and set them to furiously and conspicuously sweeping. Whether they sweep up any dirt is beside the point.

Last fall, Cheffers attended a Monday-night Patriots game at Schaefer Stadium. He's a big, beefy man, but even so found himself uneasy in the midst of bands of drunken, truculent, orgiastic fans roaming about in shadowy parking lots, reeking corridors and grimy stands. Following his field trip he submitted a detailed report to the Patriots, with suggestions for improvements. He thought "animalistic behavior" could be reduced if the joint—he called the parking lot Grub City—was cleaned up, smelled sweeter and was better lit. He felt there was great need to improve access to the parking and concession areas to cut down on jostling and long, frustrating lines. Hundreds of fans gathered hours before the game in parking lot "wastelands," where they had little to do but mill about, drink and start trouble. He thought that prettifying the lots, putting in some picnic and play areas, with room to throw Frisbees and balls around, might be worth a try. Among other things, Cheffers is very big on flowers as crowd controllers. "We will jump over ropes, knock down barricades, tear up lawns," he says, "but it takes a lot to make us walk through a flower bed." Cheffers believes that judiciously planted hardy annuals can do much to keep crowds where they are wanted and subliminally to remind them of their manners.

The Patriots, with the benefit of advice from both Cheffers and Goldaber, are now in the process of spending $5.8 million to upgrade Schaefer Stadium. "Generally, we want to make it an attractive place. We want good fans," says Sullivan. "Security and crowd control are not the only factors, but they are important ones."

Today, the idea of staging a major sporting event without dozens of law-and-order officers on hand is unthinkable. (On game day at Schaefer Stadium the security force, in or out of uniform, numbers more than 250.) However, security forces are often part of the fan-violence problem, not the solution to it. By tradition there is a certain anti-authoritarian spirit in sporting crowds, and this can be inflamed by rude, belligerent or even overly conspicuous cops. "When a guard ejects a fan, who is getting booed?" Goldaber asks. "Invariably, it's the guard." Goldaber thinks there's a need, not necessarily for larger security forces, but for those that are better trained and more inclined to calm spectators by means other than busting them. Employing the 20 unarmed, ununiformed, fairly cool football players to patrol Fenway is seen as a step in the right direction.

Like everyone else, unruly spectators buy tickets, and promoters not wanting to offend them are inclined to tolerate behavior that wouldn't be permitted outside the stadium. Cheffers feels this is shortsighted. He thinks crowd controllers should be trained to spot troublemakers before they reach the explosive stage and to remove them quickly. Fans who are repeat offenders should be suspended for misconduct, as players are, and barred from attending games for a period of time. He agrees that the ejection should be accomplished as gently and unobtrusively as possible so as not to rile other spectators, but that the policy should be publicized and firmly carried out. Some customers might be lost, he admits, but their loss would be more than compensated for because new and better fans would be attracted by the improved conditions.

The link between hooliganism and alcohol consumption is as obvious as the reasons that sporting entrepreneurs have been loath to face up to this problem. Perhaps one of the best indications of serious concern about fan misbehavior is the new willingness to cut down on the beer and booze trade. In the last several years a dozen or so major stadiums and arenas have taken steps to halt sales before the latter part of a game and to restrict sales in certain particularly rowdy sections or the amounts individual fans can buy. There's even occasional talk of eliminating beer concessions entirely. For example, Sullivan says the Patriots "had considered" such a drastic move at Schaefer Stadium, even though it's named for a brewery, which reportedly paid a million dollars for the honor.

Perhaps the boldest action of this sort has been taken by the Chicago White Sox. According to Schaffer, the Comiskey Park security chief, when new ownership acquired the Sox in 1981, it was alarmed at the amount of violence in the park and Comiskey's steadily deteriorating reputation. In an effort to improve things, all hard-liquor sales were banned inside the stadium. The Sox estimate this cost them about $100,000 but that it has had a calming effect on crowd behavior and made security enforcement, for which the White Sox now pay about $300,000 a season, much easier.

Sports have been successful in developing techniques that move spectators toward rather than away from explosive states. Again, nobody wants them actually to blow up, just to come close to the exhilarating flash point. "It's good business for the teams to psych up a crowd," says Goldaber. "We talk about killer instincts, rivalries. You give the wrong guy a rivalry, give him people around him who are raucous, contributing to the steam-up, and you may well have a dangerous problem."

The statement of the problem more or less indicates the solution. What Goldaber calls the hype and hoopla needs to be toned down, and reality— that these are games, not genuine confrontations of world-shaking significance—must be emphasized. The participants, from management to coaches to players, are in the best position to deliver this message and make it believable in the stands. "Unwarranted behaviors"—such as on-the-field fights, tantrums and the like, which Cheffers has found are so likely to incite spectators—need to be eliminated, not just mildly rebuked or penalized. Goldaber also believes players should be instructed and encouraged to display pacific behavior and to make more gestures of what used to be referred to as sportsmanship—pre-game handshakes, etc.

"When a lineman hits the quarterback," says Goldaber, "the crowd is going to yell for a roughing-the-passer call. But if the lineman reaches down and yanks up the guy he just hit and pats him on the back, and they both run back to their huddles, that's something I call a sociological signal to the crowd that this is just a game. Those fans who feel they're in a war will be calmed by the gesture."

Cheffers also feels that efforts must be made to educate or reeducate fans. "I care about this," he says, "because I'm one of those who think that sport can and should have a very constructive influence on society. I would say that the greatest value of sporting competition is that it teaches us how to handle winning and losing without becoming antisocial. When what's achieved predominates over how it's achieved, then a disrespect for the entire game, the entire sport, ensues. Violence follows disrespect. The fearful thing is that what we are now being taught to respect is violence. Sport is making it fashionable."

ROGER ANGELL

The Interior Stadium

Sports are too much with us. Late and soon, sitting and watching—mostly watching on television—we lay waste our powers of identification and enthusiasm and, in time, attention as more and more closing rallies and crucial putts and late field goals and final playoffs and sudden deaths and world records and world championships unreel themselves ceaselessly before our half-lidded eyes. Professional leagues expand like bubble gum, ever larger and thinner, and the extended sporting seasons, now bunching and overlapping at the ends, conclude in exhaustion and the wrong weather. So, too, goes the secondary business of sports—the news or non-news off the field. Sports announcers (ex-halfbacks in Mod hairdos) bring us another live, exclusive interview in depth with the twitchy coach of some as yet undefeated basketball team, or with a weeping (for joy) fourteen-year-old champion female backstroker, and the sports pages, now almost the largest single part of the newspaper, brim with salary disputes, medical bulletins, franchise maneuverings, all-star ballots, drug scandals, close-up biogs, after-dinner tributes, union tac-

From *The Summer Game* (1972). Originally appeared in *The New Yorker* (1971).

tics, weekend wrapups, wire-service polls, draft-choice trades, clubhouse gossip, and the latest odds. The American obsession with sports is not a new phenomenon, of course, except in its current dimensions, its excessive excessiveness. What *is* new, and what must at times unsettle even the most devout and unselective fan, is a curious sense of loss. In the midst of all these successive spectacles and instant replays and endless reportings and recapitulations, we seem to have forgotten what we came for. More and more, each sport resembles all sports; the flavor, the special joys of place and season, the unique displays of courage and strength and style that once isolated each game and fixed it in our affections have disappeared somewhere in the noise and crush.

Of all sports, none has been so buffeted about by this unselective proliferation, so maligned by contemporary cant, or so indifferently defended as baseball. Yet the game somehow remains the same, obdurately unaltered and comparable only with itself. Baseball has one saving grace that distinguishes it—for me, at any rate—from every other sport. Because of its pace, and thus the perfectly observed balance, both physical and psychological, between opposing forces, its clean lines can be restored in retrospect. This inner game—baseball in the mind—has no season, but it is best played in the winter, without the distraction of other baseball news. At first, it is a game of recollections, recapturings, and visions. Figures and occasions return, enormous sounds rise and swell, and the interior stadium fills with light and yields up the sight of a young ballplayer—some hero perfectly memorized—just completing his own unique swing and now racing toward first. See the way he runs? Yes, that's him! Unmistakable, he leans in, still following the distant flight of the ball with his eyes, and takes his big turn at the base. Yet this is only the beginning, for baseball in the mind is not a mere returning. In time, this easy summoning up of restored players, winning hits, and famous rallies gives way to reconsiderations and reflections about the sport itself. By thinking about baseball like this—by playing it over, keeping it warm in a cold season—we begin to make discoveries. With luck, we may even penetrate some of its mysteries. One of those mysteries is its vividness—the absolutely distinct inner vision we retain of that hitter, that eager base-runner, of however long ago. My father was talking the other day about some of the ballplayers he remembered. He grew up in Cleveland, and the Indians were his team. Still are. "We had Nap Lajoie at second," he said. "You've heard of him. A great big broad-shouldered fellow, but a beautiful fielder. He was a rough customer. If he didn't like an umpire's call, he'd give him a faceful of tobacco juice. The shortstop was Terry Turner—a smaller man, and blond. I can still see Lajoie picking up a grounder and wheeling and floating the ball over to Turner. Oh, he was quick on his feet! In right field we had Elmer

Flick, now in the Hall of Fame. I liked the center fielder, too. His name was Harry Bay, and he wasn't a heavy hitter, but he was very fast and covered a lot of ground. They said he could circle the bases in twelve seconds flat. I saw him get a home run inside the park—the ball hit on the infield and went right past the second baseman and out to the wall, and Bay beat the relay. I remember Addie Joss, our great right-hander. Tall, and an elegant pitcher. I once saw him pitch a perfect game. He died young."

My father has been a fan all his life, and he has pretty well seen them all. He has told me about the famous last game of the 1912 World Series, in Boston, and seeing Fred Snodgrass drop that fly ball in the tenth inning, when the Red Sox scored twice and beat the Giants. I looked up Harry Bay and those other Indians in the *Baseball Encyclopedia*, and I think my father must have seen that inside-the-park homer in the summer of 1904. Lajoie batted .376 that year, and Addie Joss led the American League with an earned-run average of 1.59, but the Indians finished in fourth place. 1904. . . . Sixty-seven years have gone by, yet Nap Lajoie is in plain view, and the ball still floats over to Terry Turner. Well, my father is eighty-one now, and old men are great rememberers of the distant past. But I am fifty, and I can also bring things back: Lefty Gomez, skinny-necked and frighteningly wild, pitching his first game at Yankee Stadium, against the White Sox and Red Faber in 1930. Old John McGraw, in a business suit and a white fedora, sitting lumpily in a dark corner of the dugout at the Polo Grounds and glowering out at the field. Babe Ruth, wearing a new, bright yellow glove, trotting out to right field—a swollen ballet dancer, with those delicate, almost feminine feet and ankles. Ruth at the plate, upper-cutting and missing, staggering with the force of his swing. Ruth and Gehrig hitting back-to-back homers. Gehrig, in the summer of 1933, running bases with a bad leg in a key game against the Senators; hobbling, he rounds third, closely followed by young Dixie Walker, then a Yankee. The throw comes in to the plate, and the Washington catcher—it must have been Luke Sewell—tags out the sliding Gehrig and, in the same motion, the sliding Dixie Walker. A double play at the plate. The Yankees lose the game; the Senators go on to a pennant. And, back across the river again, Carl Hubbell. My own great pitcher, a southpaw, tall and elegant. Hub pitching: the loose motion; two slow, formal bows from the waist, glove and hands held almost in front of his face as he pivots, the long right leg (in long, peculiar pants) striding; and the ball, angling oddly, shooting past the batter. Hubbell walks gravely back to the bench, his pitching arm, as always, turned the wrong way round, with the palm out. Screwballer.

Any fan, as I say, can play this private game, extending it to extraordinary varieties and possibilities in his mind. Ruth bats against Sandy Koufax or Sam McDowell. . . . Hubbell pitches to Ted Williams, and the Kid, grinding the bat in his fists, twitches and blocks his hips with the pitch; he holds off but still follows the ball, leaning over and studying it like some curator as it leaps in just under his hands. Why this vividness, even from an imaginary confrontation? I have watched many other sports, and I have followed some— football, hockey, tennis—with eagerness, but none of them yields these permanent interior pictures, these ancient and precise excitements. Baseball, I must conclude, is intensely remembered because only baseball is so intensely watched. The game forces intensity upon us. In the ballpark, scattered across an immense green, each player is isolated in our attention, utterly visible. Watch that fielder just below us. Little seems to be expected of him. He waits in easy composure, his hands on his knees; when the ball at last soars or bounces out to him, he seizes it and dispatches it with swift, haughty ease. It all looks easy, slow, and, above all, safe. Yet we know better, for what is certain in baseball is that someone, perhaps several people, will fail. They will be searched out, caught in the open, and defeated, and there will be no confusion about it or sharing of the blame. This is sure to happen, because what baseball requires of its athletes, of course, is nothing less than perfection, and perfection cannot be eased or divided. Every movement of every game, from first pitch to last out, is measured and recorded against an absolute standard, and thus each success is also a failure. Credit that strikeout to the pitcher, but also count it against the batter's average; mark his run unearned, because the left fielder bobbled the ball for an instant and a runner moved up. Yet, faced with this sudden and repeated presence of danger, the big-league player defends himself with such courage and skill that the illusion of safety is sustained. Tension is screwed tighter and tighter as the certain downfall is postponed again and again, so that when disaster does come—a half-topped infield hit, a walk on a close three-and-two call, a low drive up the middle that just eludes the diving shortstop—we rise and cry out. It is a spontaneous, inevitable, irresistible reaction.

Televised baseball, I must add, does not seem capable of transmitting this emotion. Most baseball is seen on the tube now, and it is presented faithfully and with great technical skill. But the medium is irrevocably two-dimensional; even with several cameras, television cannot bring us the essential distances of the game—the simultaneous flight of a batted ball and its pursuit by the racing, straining outfielders, the swift convergence of runner and ball at a base. Foreshortened on our screen, the players on the field appear to be squashed together, almost touching each other, and, watching them, we lose the sense of their separateness and lonesome waiting.

This is a difficult game. It is so demanding that the best teams and the weakest teams can meet on almost even terms, with no assurance about the result of any one game. In March 1962, in St. Petersburg, the World Cham-

pion Yankees played for the first time against the newborn New York Mets—
one of the worst teams of all time—in a game that each badly wanted to win;
the winner, to nobody's real surprise, was the Mets. In 1970, the World
Champion Orioles won a hundred and eight games and lost fifty-four; the
lowest cellar team, the White Sox, won fifty-six games and lost a hundred
and six. This looks like an enormous disparity, but what it truly means is that
the Orioles managed to win two out of every three games they played, while
the White Sox won one out of every three. That third game made the difference—and a kind of difference that can be appreciated when one notes that
the winning margin given up by the White Sox to all their opponents during
the season averaged 1.1 runs per game. Team form is harder to establish in
baseball than in any other sport, and the hundred-and-sixty-two-game season
not uncommonly comes down to October with two or three teams locked together at the top of the standings on the final weekend. Each inning of baseball's slow, searching time span, each game of its long season is essential to
the disclosure of its truths.

Form is the imposition of a regular pattern upon varying and unpredictable
circumstances, but the patterns of baseball, for all the game's tautness and
neatness, are never regular. Who can predict the winner and shape of today's
game? Will it be a brisk, neat two-hour shutout? A languid, error-filled 12-3
laugher? A riveting three-hour, fourteen-inning deadlock? What other sport
produces these manic swings? For the players, too, form often undergoes terrible reversals; in no other sport is a champion athlete so often humiliated or
a journeyman so easily exalted. The surprise, the upset, the total turn-about
of expectations and reputations—these are delightful commonplaces of baseball. Al Gionfriddo, a part-time Dodger outfielder, stole second base in the
ninth inning of the fourth game of the 1947 World Series to help set up La-
vagetto's game-winning double (and the only Dodger hit of the game) off the
Yankees' Bill Bevens. Two days later, Gionfriddo robbed Joe DiMaggio with a
famous game-saving catch of a four-hundred-and-fifteen-foot drive in deepest
left field at Yankee Stadium. Gionfriddo never made it back to the big leagues
after that season. Another irregular, the Mets' Al Weis, homered in the fifth
and last game of the 1969 World Series, tying up the game that the Mets won
in the next inning; it was Weis's third homer of the year and his first ever at
Shea Stadium. And so forth. Who remembers the second game of the 1956
World Series—an appallingly bad afternoon of baseball in which the Yankees'
starter, Don Larsen, was yanked after giving up a single and four walks in less
than two innings? It was Larsen's *next* start, the fifth game, when he pitched
his perfect game.

There is always a heavy splash of luck in these reversals. Luck, indeed,
plays an almost predictable part in the game; we have all seen the enormous

enemy clout into the bleachers that just hooks foul at the last instant, and the half-checked swing that produces a game-winning blooper over second. Everyone complains about baseball luck, but I think it adds something to the game that is nearly essential. Without it, such a rigorous and unforgiving pastime would be almost too painful to enjoy.

No one, it becomes clear, can conquer this impossible and unpredictable game. Yet every player tries, and now and again—very rarely—we see a man who seems to have met all the demands, challenged all the implacable averages, spurned the mere luck. He has defied baseball, even altered it, and for a time at least the game is truly his. One thinks of Willie Mays, in the best of his youth, batting at the Polo Grounds, his whole body seeming to leap at the ball as he swings in an explosion of exuberance. Or Mays in center field, playing in so close that he appears at times to be watching the game from over the second baseman's shoulder, and then that same joyful leap as he takes off after a long, deep drive and runs it down, running so hard and so far that the ball itself seems to stop in the air and wait for him. One thinks of Jackie Robinson in a close game—any close game—playing the infield and glaring in at the enemy hitter, hating him and daring him, refusing to be beaten. And Sandy Koufax pitching in the last summers before he was disabled, in that time when he pitched a no-hitter every year for four years. Kicking swiftly, hiding the ball until the last instant, Koufax throws in a blur of motion, coming over the top, and the fast ball, appearing suddenly in the strike zone, sometimes jumps up so immoderately that his catcher has to take it with his glove shooting upward, like an infielder stabbing at a bad-hop grounder. I remember some batter taking a strike like that and then stepping out of the box and staring back at the pitcher with a look of utter incredulity—as if Koufax had just thrown an Easter egg past him.

Joe DiMaggio batting sometimes gave the same impression—the suggestion that the old rules and dimensions of baseball no longer applied to him, and that the game had at last grown unfairly easy. I saw DiMaggio once during his famous hitting streak in 1941; I'm not sure of the other team or the pitcher—perhaps it was the Tigers and Bobo Newsom—but I'm sure of DiMaggio pulling a line shot to left that collided preposterously with the bag at third base and ricocheted halfway out to center field. That record of hitting safely in fifty-six straight games seems as secure as any in baseball, but it does not awe me as much as the fact that DiMadge's old teammates claim they *never* saw him commit an error of judgment in a ball game. Thirteen years, and never a wrong throw, a cutoff man missed, an extra base passed up. Well, there was one time when he stretched a single against the Red Sox and was called out at second, but the umpire is said to have admitted later that he blew the call.

And one more for the pantheon: Carl Yastrzemski. To be precise, Yaz in September of the 1967 season, as his team, the Red Sox, fought and clawed against the White Sox and the Twins and the Tigers in the last two weeks of the closest and most vivid pennant race of our time. The presiding memory of that late summer is of Yastrzemski approaching the plate, once again in a situation where all hope rests on him, and settling himself in the batter's box—touching his helmet, tugging at his belt, and just touching the tip of the bat to the ground, in precisely the same set of gestures—and then, in a storm of noise and pleading, swinging violently and perfectly . . . and hitting. In the last two weeks of that season, Yaz batted .522—twenty-three hits for forty-four appearances: four doubles, five home runs, sixteen runs batted in. In the final two games, against the Twins, both of which the Red Sox *had* to win for the pennant, he went seven for eight, won the first game with a homer, and saved the second with a brilliant, rally-killing throw to second base from deep left field. (He cooled off a little in the World Series, batting only .400 for seven games and hitting three homers.) Since then, the game and the averages have caught up with Yastrzemski, and he has never again approached that kind of performance. But then, of course, neither has anyone else.

Only baseball, with its statistics and isolated fragments of time, permits so precise a reconstruction from box score and memory. Take another date—October 7, 1968, at Detroit, the fifth game of the World Series. The fans are here, and an immense noise—a cheerful, 53,634-man vociferosity—utterly fills the green, steep, high-walled box of Tiger Stadium. This is a good baseball town, and the cries have an anxious edge, for the Tigers are facing almost sure extinction. They trail the Cardinals by three games to one, and never for a moment have they looked the equal of these defending World Champions. Denny McLain, the Tigers' thirty-one-game winner, was humiliated in the opener by the Cardinals' Bob Gibson, who set an all-time Series record by striking out seventeen Detroit batters. The Tigers came back the next day, winning rather easily behind their capable left-hander Mickey Lolich, but the Cardinals demolished them in the next two games, scoring a total of seventeen runs and again brushing McLain aside; Gibson has now struck out twenty-seven Tigers, and he will be ready to pitch again in the Series if needed. Even more disheartening is Lou Brock, the Cards' left fielder, who has already lashed out eight hits in the first four games and has stolen seven bases in eight tries; Bill Freehan, the Tigers' catcher, has a sore arm. And here, in the very top of the first, Brock leads off against Lolich and doubles to left; a moment later, Curt Flood singles, and Orlando Cepeda homers into the left-field stands. The Tigers are down, 3–0, and the fans are wholly stilled.

In the third inning, Brock leads off with another hit—a single—and there is a bitter overtone to the home-town cheers when Freehan, on a pitchout, at last throws him out, stealing, at second. There is no way for anyone to know, of course, that this is a profound omen; Brock has done his last damage to the Tigers in this Series. Now it is the fourth, and hope and shouting return. Mickey Stanley leads off the Detroit half with a triple that lands, two inches fair, in the right-field corner. He scores on a fly. Willie Horton also triples. With two out, Jim Northrup smashes a hard grounder directly at the Cardinal second baseman, Javier, and at the last instant the ball strikes something on the infield and leaps up and over Javier's head, and Horton scores. Luck! Luck twice over, if you remember how close Stanley's drive came to falling foul. But never mind; it's 3−2 now, and a game again.

But Brock is up, leading off once again, and an instant later he has driven a Lolich pitch off the left-field wall for a double. Now Javier singles to left, and Brock streaks around third base toward home. Bill Freehan braces himself in front of the plate, waiting for the throw; he has had a miserable Series, going hitless in fourteen at-bats so far, and undergoing those repeated humiliations by the man who is now racing at him full speed—the man who must surely be counted, along with Gibson, as the Series hero. The throw comes in chest-high on the fly from Willie Horton in left; ball and baserunner arrive together; Brock does not slide. Brock does not slide, and his left foot, just descending on the plate, is banged away as he collides with Freehan. Umpire Doug Harvey shoots up his fist: Out! It is a great play. Nothing has changed, the score is still 3−2, but everything has changed; something has shifted irrevocably in this game.

In the seventh inning, with one out and the Tigers still one run shy, Tiger manager Mayo Smith allows Lolich to bat for himself. Mickey Lolich has hit .114 for the season, and Smith has a pinch-hitter on the bench named Gates Brown, who hit .370. But Lolich got two hits in his other Series start, including the first homer of his ten years in baseball. Mayo, sensing something that he will not be able to defend later if he is wrong, lets Lolich bat for himself, and Mickey pops a foolish little fly to right that falls in for a single. Now there is another single. A walk loads the bases, and Al Kaline comes to the plate. The noise in the stadium is insupportable. Kaline singles, and the Tigers go ahead by a run. Norm Cash drives in another. The Tigers win this searching, turned-about, lucky, marvelous game by 5−3.

Two days later, back in St. Louis, form shows its other face as the Tigers rack up ten runs in the third inning and win by 13−1. McLain at last has his Series win. So it is Lolich against Gibson in the finale, of course. Nothing happens. Inning after inning goes by, zeros accumulate on the scoreboard, and anxiety and silence lengthen like shadows. In the sixth, Lou Brock singles. Daring Lolich, daring the Tiger infielders' nerves, openly forcing his luck, hoping perhaps to settle these enormous tensions and difficulties with one more act of bravado, he takes an excessive lead off first, draws the throw from Lolich, breaks for second, and is erased, just barely, by Cash's throw. A bit later, Curt Flood singles, and, weirdly, he too is picked off first and caught in a rundown. Still no score. Gibson and Lolich, both exhausted, pitch on. With two out in the seventh, Cash singles for the Tigers' second hit of the day. Horton is safe on a slow bouncer that *just* gets through the left side of the infield. Jim Northrup hits the next pitch deep and high but straight at Flood, who is the best center fielder in the National League. Flood starts in and then halts, stopping so quickly that his spikes churn up a green flap of turf; he turns and races back madly, but the ball sails over his head for a triple. Disaster. Suddenly, irreversibly, it has happened. Two runs are in, Freehan doubles in another, and, two innings later, the Tigers are Champions of the World.

I think I will always remember those two games—the fifth and the seventh—perfectly. And I remember something else about the 1968 Series when it was over—a feeling that almost everyone seemed to share: that Bob Gibson had not lost that last game, and the Cardinals had not lost the Series. Certainly no one wanted to say that the Tigers had not won it, but there seemed to be something more that remained to be said. It was something about the levels and demands of the sport we had seen—as if the baseball itself had somehow surpassed the players and the results. It was the baseball that won.

Always, it seems, there is something more to be discovered about this game. Sit quietly in the upper stand and look at the field. Half close your eyes against the sun, so that the players recede a little, and watch the movements of baseball. The pitcher, immobile on the mound, holds the inert white ball, his little lump of physics. Now, with abrupt gestures, he gives it enormous speed and direction, converting it suddenly into a line, a moving line. The batter, wielding a plane, attempts to intercept the line and acutely alter it, but he fails; the ball, a line again, is redrawn to the pitcher, in the center of this square, the diamond. Again the pitcher studies his task—the projection of his next line through the smallest possible segment of an invisible seven-sided solid (the strike zone has depth as well as height and width) sixty feet and six inches away; again the batter considers his even more difficult proposition, which is to reverse this imminent white speck, to redirect its energy not in a soft parabola or a series of diminishing squiggles but into a beautiful and dangerous new force, of perfect straightness and immense distance. In time, these and other lines are drawn on the field; the batter and the fielders are also transformed into fluidity, moving and converging, and we see now that all movement in baseball is a convergence toward fixed points—the pitched ball toward the plate, the thrown ball toward the right angles of the bases, the batted ball toward the as yet undrawn but already visible point of congruence with either the ground or a glove. Simultaneously, the fielders hasten toward that same point of meeting with the ball, and both the base-runner and the ball, now redirected, toward their encounter at the base. From our perch, we can sometimes see three or four or more such geometries appearing at the same instant on the green board below us, and, mathematicians that we are, can sense their solution even before they are fully drawn. It is neat, it is pretty, it is satisfying. Scientists speak of the profoundly moving aesthetic beauty of mathematics, and perhaps the baseball field is one of the few places where the rest of us can glimpse this mystery.

The last dimension is time. Within the ballpark, time moves differently, marked by no clock except the events of the game. This is the unique, un-changeable feature of baseball, and perhaps explains why this sport, for all the enormous changes it has undergone in the past decade or two, remains somehow rustic, unviolent, and introspective. Baseball's time is seamless and invisible, a bubble within which players move at exactly the same pace and rhythms as all their predecessors. This is the way the game was played in our youth and in our fathers' youth, and even back then—back in the country days—there must have been the same feeling that time could be stopped. Since baseball time is measured only in outs, all you have to do is succeed utterly; keep hitting, keep the rally alive, and you have defeated time. You remain forever young. Sitting in the stands, we sense this, if only dimly. The players below us—Mays, DiMaggio, Ruth, Snodgrass—swim and blur in memory, the ball floats over to Terry Turner, and the end of this game may never come.

A. JAMES MEMMOTT

Wordsworth in the Bleachers: The Baseball Essays of Roger Angell

Since 1962 Roger Angell has written more than thirty essays on baseball for *The New Yorker* magazine, and these essays have been gathered into two collections: *The Summer Game* (1972) and *Five Seasons: A Baseball Companion* (1977). Angell, a fiction writer and editor, is not a sports reporter, and *The New Yorker* is hardly *The Sporting News*, but Angell's essays are, without question, the best writing on baseball that has been produced in recent years.

Explaining his discovery of baseball's mystery and beauty, Angell writes in the introduction to *The Summer Game*, "how could I have guessed . . . that baseball, of all team sports anywhere, should turn out to be so complex, so rich and various in structure and aesthetics and emotion, as to convince me, after ten years as a [baseball] writer and forty years as a fan, that I have not yet come close to its heart."[1] This statement neatly categorizes Angell's interest in baseball. Structure, aesthetics and emotion—how the game works, appears and feels—form the themes of his baseball writings; they are, in a sense, the three bases which lead toward home plate, the mysterious heart of the game itself.

To get near to home plate Angell uses a method quite different from that of the typical baseball writer. He notes that he writes "at length for a leisurely and most generous weekly magazine" (SG, p. x), and that he is not hard pressed by deadline or by space limitation. While the sports writer for a daily newspaper must strike his lead and fix his view of the game before the fans have left the stadium, Angell has the time to sit and think awhile, to replay the game within his mind until its telling images fix themselves upon his memory. These images in turn become the lyrical passages within the essays, spots of inspiration amidst the reportage. They seem to stop and bring back not only the game but time itself and to achieve, fleetingly, the victory of time which Angell finds latent in the structure of baseball itself.

Roger Angell's prefatory account of his themes and his methods in *The Summer Game* echoes another introduction, the landmark "Preface to the Second Edition of Lyrical Ballads" (1800) of William Wordsworth. The Lake Country would seem a long way from Shea Stadium, and Wordsworth an un-

Originally appeared in *Journal of American Culture* (1982).

likely denizen of the press box, but the resemblance is too clear to be ignored. Like Wordsworth, Angell finds emblematic images, "spots of time," which break down the distinction between the present and the past and restore the feeling that had been lost. And like Wordsworth, Angell achieves this resto-ration of emotion by the paradoxical technique of getting away from the event in order that he can bring the event back. In the "Preface" Wordsworth outlines his theory and his method: "poetry is the spontaneous overflow of powerful emotions: it takes its origin from emotion recollected in tranquility: the emotion is contemplated till, by a species of re-action, the tranquility gradually disappears, and an emotion, kindred to that which was before the subject of contemplation, is gradually produced, and does itself actually exist in the mind."[2] As outlined by Wordsworth, the movement is from event, to tranquil contemplation of the emotional reaction to the event, to the appear-ance of an emotion similar to the original emotion. Upon the page, within the poem, the recalled experience stands as what Wordsworth called a "spot of time" in which the past is recalled as if it were present. The spot of time records not so much the details of the experience as the feeling felt during the experience. In *The Prelude* (1850) Wordsworth distinguishes between "mere memory," the intellectual recollection of what happened, and the soul's memory, the recollection of what was felt: "the soul / Remembering how she felt, but what she felt / Remembering not."[3] Like Wordsworth, Angell seeks to recall and recreate emotions; he writes, "my main job, as I conceived it, was to continue to give the feel of things—to explain the baseball as it hap-pened to me, at a distance and in retrospect" (SG, p. x.).

It can be seen that Angell imitates Wordsworth's technique of getting away in time and space from the experience in order to understand it, as he seeks to recreate his emotional response, what he calls "the feel of things." Angell does not attempt to describe how the player felt while playing, though often he will let the players do this themselves, and he will record their comments. Many sportswriters do try to see the game through the player's eye, or at least they imply that they are on the field and not in the press box. But Angell makes his vantage point clear; he stresses the fact that he sees the game from the stands at a self-imposed distance. Watching the game from afar and then recollecting it in tranquility, Angell achieves a sense of the whole process. Steve Blass, the former Pittsburgh pitcher, endorses Angell's perspective, telling him, "'Hey, you really see how it *works* from here, can't you? . . . Down there, you've got to look at it all in pieces. No wonder it's so hard to play this game right.'"[4]

How baseball works, its structure, can be perceived from afar with the help of an optical trick. In the last two paragraphs of "The Interior Stadium," the concluding essay of *The Summer Game*, Angell instructs the reader to "sit quietly in the upper stand and look at the field. Half close your eyes against the sun, so that the players recede a little, and watch the movements of baseball. The pitcher, immobile on the mound, holds the inert white ball, his little lump of physics. Now, with abrupt gestures, he gives it enormous speed and direction, converting it suddenly into a line, a moving line. The batter, wielding a plane, attempts to intercept the line and acutely alter it, but he fails; the ball, a line again, is redrawn to the pitcher, in the center of this square, the diamond" (SG, p. 302).

The trick of half closing the eyes offers one a view of baseball's substructure, the permanent forces and immutable laws which govern it. But the structure is only the first part of Angell's trinity of structure, aesthetics and emotions, and the game as seen through half-closed eyes is not the whole game, for it is baseball rendered abstract and dehumanized; it resembles a Saul Steinberg drawing such as the one which accompanied "The Interior Stadium" in its *New Yorker* publication. The half-closed eye views a game which is, in Angell's words, "neat, pretty and satisfying" (SG, p. 303), something akin to a mathematical equation, but the fully-opened eye allows one to see players upon the field and to witness the game in three dimensions. It is this game which Angell recalls in his soul's memory, which he recreates in arrested images which are to his essays what the "spots of time" are to Wordsworth's poetry.

In "The Interior Stadium" Angell recalls moments which have remained in his father's memory and his own memory: "Sixty-seven years have gone by, yet Nap Lajoie is in plain view, and the ball still floats over to Terry Turner. Well, my father is eighty-one now, and old men are great rememberers of the distant past. But I am fifty and I also bring things back: Lefty Gomez, skinny-necked and frighteningly wild, pitching his first game at Yankee Stadium. . . . Old John McGraw, in a business suit and a white fedora, sitting lumpily in a dark corner of the dugout at the Polo Grounds and glowering out at the field. Babe Ruth, wearing a new, bright yellow glove, trotting out to right field—a swollen ballet dancer, with those delicate, almost feminine feet and ankles" (SG, pp. 293–294). One cannot read this and similar passages without appreciating Angell's ability to strike the right phrase and his ability to add humanizing details, not to bring heroes down to size but rather to give them their individual and unique attributes. McGraw sits "lumpily"; Ruth trots to right field, almost preening with his "new, bright yellow glove." If one read these descriptions in a novel, he would conclude that the details served as indexes of character, signs of the inner self of the individual described. And it seems safe to argue that Angell, like the novelist, intends these descriptions as economical explanations of McGraw and Ruth. As in these images, Angell's spots of time often show the player on the brink of play or immediately after the action has taken place. Consequently, Angell's suspended spots of time, his verbal images, are themselves images of suspended or potential moments.

But if the image captures the player's inner character, his potential, the description of the action itself is technically redundant for, at least in Angell's essays, character predicts action. Consequently, Angell, in his reports on the World Series, will often condense the historical elements of the game—who won, who lost—and enlarge what might be called the peripheral moments. It is as if to say that Roberto Clemente could be understood by closely watching him take batting practice, as Angell did come to understand Clemente in 1971.

Angell's verbal spots of time are often images of men alone, players on a team who are separated from their teammates by the literal space of the playing field and by the game's existential requirements that the player act alone, that he hit by himself and catch the ball in his own hand. Angell writes: "what is certain in baseball is that someone, perhaps several people, will fail. They will be searched out, caught in the open, and defeated, and there will be no confusion about it or sharing of the blame. This is sure to happen, because what baseball requires of its athletes, of course, is nothing less than perfection, and perfection cannot be eased or divided. Every movement of every game, from first pitch to last out, is measured and recorded against an absolute standard, and thus each success is also a failure" (SG, p. 296). Angell seldom speaks to baseball's social lessons, perhaps because he sees the game as an individual and not a communal experience, an exercise which tests the player and not the team. Other sports, especially football, lend themselves more easily to sociology because they demand that the team act as a unit. The baseball player is forever in an existential predicament; he is vulnerable, exposed and alone, and his prior good deeds and great plays do not help him much at all in meeting the demands of the present. As Gilbert Sorrentino argues, baseball is essentially unfair: "No matter how good the pitcher has been, he must get the last out. . . . What he *has done* has no effect on the batter he must face next. The eight men who assist him can only assist him after the ball is released."[5]

Angell's images of solitary men at play contain implicit assumptions about human nature and the human predicament. They suggest that the baseball player is to be admired because he faces difficult tasks with courage, a courage which he often disguises with the very grace with which he performs his role. And though player and spectator are separated by space and by task, both are alike in their essential isolation and in their vulnerability to change, their susceptibility to accident. Though the spectator cannot feel *with* the player he can feel *for* the player, especially because the player's act can take the spectator outside of the "real" world for a few minutes. The spectator can extend sympathy to the player for he understands the difficulty of the player's tasks, and watching the game can involve a sympathetic, imaginative connection between spectator and player. Consequently, though the very space and nature of baseball reinforce the view that men are isolated from one another, the game also provides the opportunity for men to be brought together through shared feelings, feelings which are irresistible and spontaneous and potentially recollectable.

Angell implies that while watching and playing a sport are inevitably different actions, they are similar experiences in that they temporarily liberate man from reality and place him in a different kind of space and time. As Angell points out, baseball's time is different from clock time; the action is measured by outs and not by minutes. Conceivably the game could go on forever: "Since baseball time is measured only in outs, all you have to do is succeed utterly; keep hitting, keep the rally alive, and you have defeated time. You remain forever young. The players below us—Mays, DiMaggio, Ruth, Snodgrass—swim and blur in memory, the ball floats over to Terry Turner, and the end of this game may never come" (SG, p. 303).

Of course the other side of the coin is that the end of the game must come if the game is to have an existence separate from ordinary reality. Roger Caillois recognizes this when he argues that games are separate, "circumscribed within limits of space and time which are precise and fixed in advance."[6] The end of a baseball game—the last out—is a fixed and inflexible end, however long it may be in coming. But here I am speaking of the real game, and Angell may refer to the game of baseball in the mind, the game in which Mays and Snodgrass can take the field at once. It is this game which seems to break down history and connect the present with the past. Significantly, it joins Angell with his father, as the father's memories are passed on like a legacy to the son.

The virtues of the mental game are shown forth in another of Angell's essays, an article on Steve Blass, a former major league pitcher who inexplicably lost his control. Angell begins his account of Blass's fall from glory with a detailed description of a photograph. The description of the picture is a microcosm of Angell's themes and techniques:

The photograph shows a perfectly arrested moment of joy. On one side—the left, as you look at the picture—the catcher is running toward the camera at full speed, with his upraised arms spread wide, his body is tilting toward the center of the picture, his mask is held in his right hand, his big glove is still on his left hand, and his mouth is open in a gigantic shout of pleasure. Over on the right, another player, the pitcher, is just past the apex of an astonishing leap that has brought his knees up to his chest and his feet well up off the ground. Both of his arms are flung wide, and he, too, is shouting. His hunched, airborne posture makes him look like a man who has just made a running leap over a sizable object—a kitchen table, say. By luck, two of the outreaching hands have overlapped exactly in the middle of the photograph, so that the pitcher's bare right palm and fingers are silhouetted against the catcher's glove, and as a result the two men are linked and seemed to be executing a figure in a manic and difficult dance. There is a further marvel—a touch of pure fortune—in the background, where a spectator in dark glasses, wearing a dark suit, has risen from his seat in the grandstand and is lifting his arms in triumph. This, the third and central Y in the picture, is immobile. It is directly behind the overlapping hand and glove of the dancers, and it binds and recapitulates the lines of force and the movements and the themes of the work, creating a composition as serene and well ordered as a Giotto. The subject of the picture, of course, is classical—the celebration of the last out of the seventh game of the World Series. (FS, pp. 223–224)

Angell appreciates the picture because it shows a "perfectly arrested moment of joy"; as a maker of verbal images which attempt to capture a moment and arrest time, he praises the camera's ability to stop the action at a perfectly emblematic moment. And while Angell did not take the picture of Sanguillen and Blass running, leaping toward each other, the picture becomes his as he interprets it and stresses those elements which he finds important. He is, first of all, taken by its aesthetic, structural qualities. The catcher's outspread arms are reflected by the pitcher's arms, and both figures are recapitulated and bound by the spectator in the middle of the frame whose upraised and immobile arms form the Central Y. The Roger Angell who discovers this internal symmetry within the picture is the same man who squints his eyes and discovers the interweaving lines of force upon the baseball field. But, as always, structure is only part of the story, and it is not the picture's arrangement which captures Angell's heart. He writes: "I am not a Pittsburgher, but looking at this photograph never fails to give me pleasure, not just because of its aesthetic qualities but because its high-bounding happiness so perfectly brings back that eventful World Series and that particular gray autumn afternoon in Baltimore and the wonderful and inexpungible expression of joy that remained on Steve Blass's face after the game ended" (FS, p. 224). Consequently, the image brings back a moment of joy, an inexpungible expression that Angell witnessed and shared. In a sense, Angell becomes the spectator in the center of the picture who reflects the players' motions and emotions.

But while the union between Sanguillen, Blass and the spectator is re-corded and recalled, Angell suggests in his description that the union is also a physical illusion, though it may have been, and may still be, a spiritual real-ity. The camera's elimination of spatial distance brings the background and foreground of the picture together so that Sanguillen and Blass *seem* to touch and dance, though the reality is that they are apart. The spectator, too, is further away from the players than he seems to be. Furthermore, Angell finds embedded within the picture a suggestion that the moment of joy is lost as soon as it is gained. The picture catches Blass just after the moment of his greatest triumph and at the beginning of his decline. He is "just past the apex" of his astonishing leap, and he will never reach such a height again. But the fact of the decline was not known at the time of the victory, and Angell or I may impose the present upon the past by looking at the picture as a premonition of Blass's fall. The picture's primary message is not that Blass is about to go down but that he has succeeded and that he has reacted to his success with a joyous leap. The leap reveals Blass's open, responsive tempera-ment, a temperament which will remain unchanged throughout the testing times that are to follow the World Series victory. The point of "Down the Drain" becomes not that Blass has lost his control but that he has reacted with grace and humility to the loss of his control.

To prove that Blass's decline is unusual, even extraordinary, Angell offers extensive statistical data to establish how good Blass was and how bad he be-came. Angell writes, "of all the mysteries that surround the Steve Blass story, perhaps the most mysterious is the fact that his collapse is unique. There is no other player in recent baseball history—at least none with Blass's record and credentials—who has lost his form in such a sudden and devastating fashion and been totally unable to recover" (FS, p. 249). Having made this gener-alization, Angell turns to case histories, dismissing the ever wild Rex Barney as a man who had no control to lose and the suddenly wild Dick Radatz as a player who let himself get out of shape. The case histories are supplemented by oral testimonies to Blass's control and loss of control from his teammates, coaches and friends. Everyone seems to have a theory about the decline of Steve Blass, but the most convincing of the explanations is that which Blass offers himself: "'There's one possibility nobody has brought up. . . . I don't think anybody's ever said that maybe I just lost my control. Maybe your con-trol is something that can just go. It's no big thing, but suddenly it's gone'" (FS, p. 256). Again we are given a non-rational, but convincing testimony to baseball's complexity and difficulty. Blass and Angell imply that statistics and science will only carry one so far, that there are some things that one cannot know and probably should not even question.

But if Blass's control is lost on the real playing field it is not gone for good upon the imaginary turf of the interior stadium; it can be recreated just as Angell can call back his remembrances of baseball past. Angell tells how he used Blass to pitch an imaginary game against the Cincinnati Reds. Warmed to the task, Blass narrates his pitches and Angell calls the balls and strikes. The imaginary game then shifts parks and Blass is once again pitching against the 1971 Baltimore Orioles. Sanguillen catching; Angell umpiring; in full control Blass strikes out Boog Powell; the ball floats toward the plate and the end of the game may never come.

But retreats into the interior stadium are more and more difficult for Angell because baseball itself seems more and more threatened by the real world. In his introduction to *Five Seasons*, Angell writes, "we have begun to understand at last that baseball is most of all an enormous and cold-blooded corporate enterprise, and as such is probably a much more revelatory and disturbing part of our national psyche than we had supposed. . . . Most grown-ups, I believe, will find little pleasure now if they try to isolate the game—simply to sit in the stands as before and smile upon the familiar patterns and adventures on the bright lawns below" (*FS*, p. 8). Discussions of free agent negotiations, players' strikes and owners' lockouts weigh down an essay and a heart, but they also serve to set off and make more special the times when the patterns and adventures on the field are exhilarating and joyous. If rarer, the spots of time in *Five Seasons* seem brighter than those in *The Summer Game*, and perhaps the brightest of them is Angell's account of Carlton Fisk's winning home run in the sixth game of the 1975 World Series.

Again, as in the case of Steve Blass's marvelous leap, Angell has to describe something he did not see, for while he was in the park watching the ball, the television cameras caught Fisk "waving wildly, weaving and writhing and gyrating along the first-base line, as he wished the ball fair, *forced* it fair with his entire body." But if he did not see Fisk's dance, the home run did lead Angell to think of other dancers, Boston fans throughout New England, "jumping up and down in their bedrooms and kitchens and living rooms, and in bars, trailers, and even in boats here and there, I suppose, on the back-country roads (a lone driver getting the news over the radio and blowing his horn over and over, and finally pulling up and getting out and leaping up and down on the cold macadam, yelling into the night), and all of them, for once at least, utterly joyful and believing in that joy—alight with it" (*FS*, p. 305). Here Angell creates an image of something he did not see; at this moment he may be more Milton than Wordsworth, though a cheerful Milton to be sure. The image of the lone driver leaping up and down on the cold macadam connected in joy with Carlton Fisk, with Roger Angell, and with the reader of the essay recreates and affirms the joy that was felt and, for a moment, comes close to the heart of baseball and to the heart itself.

NOTES

1. New York: Viking, 1972, p. x. Subsequent references to *The Summer Game (SG)* will be cited in the text. The final essay of this book is reprinted in this anthology, pp. 147–156.
2. *The Poetical Works of William Wordsworth*, ed. Ernest De Selincourt (Oxford: Clarendon, 1944), pp. 400–401.
3. *The Prelude*, ed. Ernest De Selincourt (London: Oxford, 1928), II, 315–17.
4. Roger Angell, *Five Seasons: A Baseball Companion* (New York: Simon and Schuster, 1977), p. 240. Subsequent references to *Five Seasons (FS)* will be cited in the text.
5. "Baseball," in *IQ: Baseball Issue*, 10, p. 94.
6. As quoted in "Homo Ludens Revisited," by Jacques Ehrmann, in *Game, Play and Literature*, edited by Ehrmann (Boston: Beacon, 1968), p. 35.

HAROLD J. VANDERZWAAG

The Interior Stadium: Enhancing the Illusion

In *Sports Illusion, Sports Reality* (1981), the noted sportswriter, Leonard Koppett, explicates the two diverse dimensions of the sport enterprise as seen from his perspective. That perspective is one which leads him to define sport as "the commercialized segment of athletic games aimed at a large audience" (p. 5). The title of his work reveals the two diverse dimensions of that enterprise—the illusion and the reality.

The reality side of sport probably is no surprise to most readers of Koppett's book. It is the kind of information which is typically brought to attention by the news media. For instance, there is a chapter on "Cutting Up the Pie," which is basically a description of the financial situation in professional sports. He also presents the legal issues in sport as well as discussing the alliances and conflicts which are inherent in the sport enterprise. Reflecting his journalistic background, there is also an extended analysis of the news media.

The other dimension, the illusion, is that which really provides the pro-

---

Published for the first time in this anthology.

vocative aspect of Koppett's work. The illusion is the bottom line for without it the realities could not exist. What is this illusion? According to Koppett, the essence of the illusion can be found in the idea that the outcome of a game really matters to the fan. He begins his work by telling a story about Jonathan Schwartz, a sophisticated and highly regarded novelist and musician, who also happened to be an avid Boston Red Sox fan. A specific incident demonstrates how strongly Schwartz was caught up in the illusion. During a two-month period from August to October of 1978 the Red Sox lost a big lead which they held on the New York Yankees. Koppett notes that the entire two-month experience was a "nightmare" as described by Schwartz. The culminating blow was when the Red Sox lost the single playoff game for first place.

> Jonathan watched that series, with increasing agitation, on cable television in his apartment in upper Manhattan. In the seventh inning of the final game, unable to bear it any longer, he walked out of the house with nothing in his pockets but fifty dollars and a Visa card, went to the airport, flew to Los Angeles, rented a car, and started driving into the desert toward Palm Springs. Only when he was about halfway there, did he bring himself to stop at a phone booth and call back to New York (where it was past midnight) to apologize to his girl friend for his abrupt and unannounced departure. (Koppett, p. 12)

Koppett uses this example to demonstrate that this kind of illusion is the commodity which is at the heart of sport promotion. The bottom line in the promotion is to attract the fan. The primary way of doing that is to convince the fan that the outcome of a game or series of games is really very important to all concerned. There is no doubt about the fact that the outcome actually is important to the players, coaches, managers, and promoters, including those who bet on the game. But, what about the fan?

> Nor does the outcome of a Red Sox game—any Red Sox game—have any effect whatsoever on Jonathan Schwartz's job, earning power, writing talent, living conditions, health, or personal relationships, except to the extent that his voluntary emotional commitment allows it to have an indirect effect.
>
> That commitment is to an illusion—an illusion so strong and so long ingrained that beyond a certain point the attachment is no longer entirely voluntary. And the sports business consists of finding ways to create and maintain this illusion. (p. 13)

This is the kind of illusion which is shared by millions of sport fans. It is easy to see why Koppett selected the Jonathan Schwartz example. One might suspect that the latter, being a highly educated man, would be immune from this kind of attachment. But certainly when he boarded the plane for Los Angeles he demonstrated a commitment to an illusion wherein the attachment was no longer voluntary. Koppett presents a formula for what takes place in this regard, and this is what makes sport a most marketable form of entertainment.

> The illusion engages our emotions.
> The suspense engages our intellect.
> The identification engages our spirit. (p. 15)

The illusion, with its occupying results, is also reflected in the work of Michael Novak (1976). He writes:

> That hot September night, the Dodgers lost. I was three days shy of forty, and their loss depressed me. . . . They were going to blow first place, lose the pennant—and later in the month that's exactly what they did. I was angry at the Dodgers; blowing it. . . .
> How could I be forty years old and still care what happens to the Dodgers? How could I have thrown away three hours of an evaporating life, watching a ritual, an inferior dance, a competition without a socially redeeming point? About the age of forty, almost everything about one's life comes into question. . . . (pp. x-xi)

Novak wrote the book in an attempt to answer that question. *The Joy of Sports* is actually a celebration, a glorified explanation of the appeal of sports to the sport fan. However, it is also a splendid example of the illusion. Novak, too, was caught up in an attachment which was no longer entirely voluntary. Jonathan Schwartz, Michael Novak, the millions of other fans (including the author) have much in common.

"WORDSWORTH IN THE BLEACHERS"

The purpose of this paper is to respond to James Memmott's "Wordsworth in the Bleachers: The Baseball Essays of Roger Angell." So, one might ask: what does the foregoing discussion about the illusion have to do with this particular article? What I hope to make clear is that Angell and Memmott have also provided testimony to the significance of the illusion. Beyond that they have done much to enhance the illusion, to make it seem as though there is even a larger significance to the sport event. To begin with, the very comparison between Angell and Wordsworth is illusory in itself. Memmott admits that Wordsworth's "Lake Country would seem a long way from Shea Stadium" (p. 52), but he proceeds with the comparison. However, there is good reason to believe that this opening reference to Wordsworth is merely "the frosting on the cake." The "interior stadium" is the key concept in Memmott's critique because it represents the idea that Angell has an understanding and appreciation for the game of baseball which extends far beyond the attachment to the illusion.

This enhancement of the illusion is in marked similarity to the approach taken by Novak. In "Part Two" of his book he explicates "The Seven Seals" which "lock the inner life of sports." In other words, Novak has also probed "the interior stadium." The seals are "sacred space, sacred time, bond of brothers, rooting, agon, competing, and self-discovery." His prefatory comments reveal much about the intent:

> There are priests who mumble through the Mass, lovers who read letters over a naked shoulder in love's embrace, teachers who detest students, pedants who shrink from original ideas. So also there are athletes, fans, and sportswriters who never grasp the beauty of the treasure entrusted them. It must not be imagined that the mysteries of sport are directly penetrated. Much depends on the qualities of heart of the pursuer. . . (p. 121)

These same seven seals are either explicitly or implicitly found in Memmott's account of Roger Angell's essays. Collectively, they provide the basis for "the interior stadium" and the enhancement of the illusion.

Sacred Space
With direct reference to "The Interior Stadium" from *The Summer Game*, Memmott notes:

> Angell instructs the reader to "sit quietly in the upper stand and look at the field. Half close your eyes against the sun, so that the players recede a little, and watch the movements of baseball. The pitcher, immobile on the mound, holds the inert white ball, his little lump of physics. Now, with abrupt gestures, he gives it enormous speed and direction, converting it suddenly into a line, a moving line. The batter, wielding a plane, attempts to intercept the line and acutely alter it, but he fails; the ball, a

line again, is redrawn to the pitcher, in the center of this square, the diamond." . . . but the fully-opened eye allows one to see players upon the field and to witness the game in three dimensions. (p. 53)

Although, as Novak points out, there are various aspects of sacred space in sports, the above reference to the baseball field fits the criteria very well.

Sacred Time

Among all seven seals, sacred time is the one which comes through most clearly and repeatedly in "Wordsworth in the Bleachers." We begin with that which is used as basis of comparison between Wordsworth and Angell: "Like Wordsworth, Angell finds emblematic images, spots of time which break down the distinction between the present and the past and restore the feeling that had been lost" (p. 52). However, the "spot of time" is a more abstract sense of "sacred time." We note more concrete references to sacred time as we read on in Memmott's article.

As Angell points out, baseball's time is different from clock time; the action is measured by outs and not by minutes. Conceivably the game could go on forever: "Since baseball time is measured only in outs, all you have to do is succeed utterly; keep hitting, keep the rally alive, and you have defeated time. You remain forever young. . . ."

Of course the other side of the coin is that the end of the game must come if the game is to have an existence separate from ordinary reality. Roger Caillois recognizes this when he argues that games are separate, "circumscribed within limits of space and time which are precise and fixed in advance." The end of a baseball game—the last out—is a fixed and inflexible end, however long it may be in coming. (p. 54)

Bond of Brothers

Here it is important to note that the "bond of brothers" is the least distinguishable seal in Memmott's assessment of Angell's essays. In fact, Memmott initially stresses the polarity, the focus on the individual:

Angell seldom speaks to baseball's social lessons, perhaps because he sees the game as an individual and not a communal experience, an exercise which tests the player and not the team. Other sports, especially football, lend themselves more easily to sociology because they demand that the team act as a unit. The baseball player is forever in an existential predicament; he is vulnerable, exposed, and alone . . . (p. 53)

However, one does not have to read much further to observe that Novak's "bond of brothers" also emerges in "Wordsworth in the Bleachers":

> Though the spectator cannot feel *with* the player he can feel *for* the player, especially because the player's act can take the spectator outside of the "real" world for a few minutes. The spectator can extend sympathy to the player for he understands the difficulty of the player's tasks, and watching the game can involve a sympathetic, imaginative connection between spectator and player. Consequently, though the very space and nature of baseball reinforce the view that men are isolated from one another, the game also provides the opportunity for men to be brought together through shared feelings, feelings which are irresistible and spontaneous and potentially recollectable. (p. 54)

Agon

Before continuing with Memmott on Angell, agon probably requires some explanation from the Novak perspective. The latter writes:

> If I had to give one single reason for my love of sports it would be this: I love the tests of the human spirit. I love to see the incredible grace lavished on simple plays—the simple flashing beauty of perfect form—but, even more, I love to see the heart that refuses to give in . . . (p. 150)

When we return to Memmott's exposition, we once again find a very similar theme:

> Angell's images of solitary men at play contain implicit assumptions about human nature and the human predicament. They suggest that the baseball player is to be admired because he faces difficult tasks with courage, a courage which he often disguises with the very grace with which he performs his role. (p. 53)

Competing

Competing is perhaps the most pervasive concept in any treatise on sport. That is not at all surprising for to play the game is to compete. Although Novak presents competing as his "sixth seal," it is an enduring theme throughout his book. Somewhat by contrast, Memmott begins by low-keying Angell's interest in the competitive feature of baseball. But eventually, the competitive aspect also emerges:

Angell writes: "what is certain in baseball is that someone, perhaps several people, will fail. They will be searched out, caught in the open, and defeated, and there will be no confusion about it or sharing of the blame. This is sure to happen, because what baseball requires of its athletes, of course, is nothing less than perfection, and perfection cannot be eased or divided. Every moment of every game, from first pitch to last out, is measured and recorded against an absolute standard, and thus each success is also a failure." (p. 53)

Self-Discovery

Next to sacred space and sacred time, self-discovery may well be the most prominent seal in "Wordsworth in the Bleachers." For a frame of reference here, Novak's conception of self-discovery includes both extreme dimensions of this complicated concept. The one aspect of self-discovery is the feeling to be derived from achieving one's potential. This is the glorious moment in sport when everything seems to come together. On the other hand, self-discovery can also be manifested in the recognition of one's limitations. Every athlete at some point in time must face up to the fact that he or she can only achieve up to a point, which could be far short of expectations. Memmott's entire analysis of Angell's essay on Steve Blass is replete with the seal or concept of self-discovery. The essay covers both dimensions of self-discovery. First, we note the joy which accompanied Blass's top achievement:

> The picture catches Blass just after the moment of his greatest triumph and at the beginning of his decline. He is "just past the apex" of his astonishing leap, and he will never reach such a height again. But the fact of the decline was not known at the time of the victory, and Angell or I may impose the present upon the past by looking at the picture as a premonition of Blass's fall. (p. 55)

Then we have the other side of self-discovery, the recognition that one no longer has it or is not about to achieve greater heights:

> Everyone seems to have a theory about the decline of Steve Blass, but the most convincing of the explanations is that which Blass offers himself: "There's one possibility nobody has brought up. . . . I don't think anybody's ever said that maybe I just lost my control. Maybe your control is something that can just go. It's no big thing, but suddenly it's gone." (p. 55)

THE KEY: THE ILLUSION

The reader who has carefully followed this progression of ideas will note that there is still one missing seal: rooting. It has been reserved for the concluding discussion because therein we find the key which unlocks the principal message of "Wordsworth in the Bleachers." Angell and Memmott have vividly reinforced the significance of the illusion as set forth by Leonard Koppett. One has to wait for the last paragraph of Memmott's article to find out that all the previous discussion was there to enhance that illusion. This is where the seventh seal, rooting, also enters into the picture:

But if he did not see Fisk dance, the home run did lead Angell to think of other dancers, Boston fans throughout New England "jumping up and down in their bedrooms and kitchens and living rooms, and in bars, trailers, and even in boats here and there, I suppose, on the back-country roads (a lone driver getting the news over the radio and blowing his horn over and over, and finally pulling up and getting out and leaping up and down on the cold macadam, yelling into the night), and all of them, for once at least, utterly joyful and believing in that joy, alight with it." (p. 55)

What this portrays is a reaction to having "rooted" for a team. More importantly here, whether so intended or not, Memmott, through these words of Angell, provides dramatic testimony to what baseball or any other sport is really all about from the spectator's point of view: "an illusion so strong and so long ingrained that beyond a certain point the attachment is no longer entirely voluntary" (Koppett, p. 13). The Boston fans, as described by Angell, certainly must have had a commitment to such an illusion.

Earlier in this critique I suggested that Memmott's comparison of Angell and Wordsworth is the "frosting on the cake." In the final analysis one would conclude that "the interior stadium" is just a deeper layer of that same frosting. The similarity with the work of Michael Novak is most evident. He used "the seven seals" to enhance "The Joy of Sports." Memmott probed "The Interior Stadium" and other essays of Angell to enhance a similar joy—the illusion. The bottom line is found in the concluding words of "Wordsworth in the Bleachers":

The image of the lone driver leaping up and down on the cold macadam connected in joy with Carlton Fisk, with Roger Angell, and with the reader of the essay recreates and affirms the joy that was felt and, for a moment, comes close to the heart of baseball and to the heart itself. (p. 55)

So, what does this all mean? Is this critique designed to cast a negative light on the works of Angell, Memmott, Novak, and others who have enhanced the illusion? Of course not. They have served admirably in providing an enrichment of the basic treasure of spectator sports. It can be said that much of life is an illusion as well as a reality. The world's literature contributes much to the enhancement of life's illusion. The sport literature reflects that condition.

BIBLIOGRAPHY

Koppett, Leonard. *Sports Illusion, Sports Reality.* Boston: Houghton Mifflin Company, 1981.
Memmott, A. James. "Wordsworth in the Bleachers: The Baseball Essays of Roger Angell." *Journal of American Culture* 5, No. 4 (1982). Reprinted in this anthology, pp. 157–165.
Novak, Michael. *The Joy of Sports.* New York: Basic Books, 1976.

A Guide for Further Study

No better work exists than the whole of Frederick Exley's *A Fan's Notes: A Fictional Memoir* for investigating the complex bond between spectator and player. The most celebratory book on the spectator is, of course, Michael Novak, *The Joy of Sports,* especially his chapter on "Rooting." Considerably less positive assessments of fans are to be found in Arnold R. Beisser, *The Madness in Sport;* Robert Lipsyte, *SportsWorld: An American Dreamland;* and Howard Cosell's chapter "The Myth of the Fan" from his *Cosell.* On the speculative side, see Paul Weiss, *Sport: A Philosophic Inquiry,* and Lawrence Meredith, "Of Super Bowls and Sisyphus: Why Do We Care Who Wins Any Contest?" *Arete: The Journal of Sport Literature* 1 (Spring 1984).

Section III: The Community

GARY GAY

Ishmael in Arlis

Know what it's like to be a heretic? I do. I do, because I live in Arlis, Texas, and don't play football. At least, not any more. I quit.

"Whatever you do," Daddy said when I told him I guessed I'd go out, "don't quit." Not, ". . . don't break your neck," or ". . . put out an eye," but ". . . don't quit." After school Monday when I came in and told him, he seemed hurt. You know, you could tell he was real disappointed. I felt about this tall. Tried to explain. He already knew about Friday night and my mouth ulcers, so I told him about Coach Rhiney, Friday-before-last, and those three commodes in the john across from study hall. But, instead of understanding, he got mad. So mad, that I was glad I quit. I mean, I can't count the times he's come in off a rig carrying his hard hat and safety shoes. Says to Mother, "I told 'em to cram it." But me . . . if I do a headstand, that's it. I'm supposed to stay like that till the Social Security checks start rolling in, then I can get down and go fish or something till I die.

You wouldn't believe how many people have come up to me since Monday and asked why I quit football. It kind of chaps me. You know, it's the *way* they ask. I quit football, I didn't rob a bank. Some of them remind me that I won't get a letter jacket. The ones who say that say it like I won't get air to breathe. The red-headed lady who checks groceries at Arlis Food said, "Isn't it a shame you won't get to go on the El Paso trip?" She was talking about the Sun Bowl. That's where the Arlis football team goes every year, to El Paso to see the Sun Bowl. Don't ever ask any of them the score, though. Of course, all of them get around to asking if I quit because of Friday night. That's the main thing they want; they want to hear what I've got to say about Friday night. But I cool it. Tell them, "No, me quitting football doesn't have anything to do with *that*. Besides," I say, "you probably don't even know what *really* happened Friday night. But it doesn't make any difference if you do,

Originally appeared in *The Bi-centennial Collection of Texas Short Stories* (1974).

because Friday night was just the straw that broke the camel's back. I quit football for a million reasons."

And I did, too. Nine reasons are these little ulcers in my mouth. When I get hit in the mouth, I always get a little ulcer where the scratch was. They like to never go away, my mouth swells up, and I just have to barely get bumped for it to bring tears to my eyes. A couple of weeks ago, I heard old Rhiney—that's Coach Walker's first assistant, Coach Rhiney—I heard Rhiney telling Calvin Upshaw that salt tablets would help his shin splints. I told Rhiney about these ulcers and asked did he know of anything that'd make them go away.

"Naahhh," he told me, "Sores are good for you. Make you tough."

The ulcers are nine reasons I quit football and Coach Rhiney makes it an even ten. He thinks I'm an atheist or something. Not last Friday, but the Friday before, the night of the Fort Conners game is when it happened. Before a game, after we've warmed up and go back into the fieldhouse, Coach Walker calls on someone to lead the team in prayer. I knew he'd call on me sooner or later, and had I ever been dreading it. I answered him just like I'd told myself I would, though, loud and clear. Maybe a little *too* loud. And, I couldn't help it—I tried not to let it happen—but my voice trembled and sounded high pitched.

"Coach, would you mind calling on someone else?"

When he asked me, everyone was whooping and whistling and pounding each other on the shoulder pads. But right after I said that about would he mind calling on someone else, you could hear a pin drop. I was looking right at Coach Walker when I said it—like I'd told myself I would—and he did raise his eyebrows. Just for a second, though. Then he sort of shrugged his shoulders. You know, like, "Well, okay. If that's the way you feel about it . . ." Only he didn't say anything. He didn't get a chance to say anything.

"What!"

It was Rhiney. He was standing by the door when I asked Coach Walker to call on someone else, but in no time he was next to Coach. "What'd he say?" he asked, but the way he said it, you could tell old Rhiney knew good and well what I said.

Someone behind me answered him anyway:

"Said he wudn't gonna pray."

"Lupe," Coach Walker said, and I knew he was about to ask Lupe Valdez to say the prayer.

"Fifty-eight'll pray," Rhiney said. On Friday night, Coach Rhiney is all business. That's why he said it that way, referring to me by my number. He was a second team linebacker at Sul Ross, but the way he's all business on Friday night, you'd think old Rhiney was Sam Huff.

"I don't mind," Lupe Valdez said.

"That's all right, thirty-two, fifty-eight'll pray," old Rhiney told him and folded his arms the way he does while he's strutting up and down the sideline on Friday night. "Fifty-eight," he said to me like, "We're waiting."

"Our Father who art in heaven, Hallowed be thy name . . ."

Everyone looked at Coach Walker. His head was bowed and he was praying. We all bowed our heads and joined in. When we finished, Coach Walker said, "Let's go." I don't know if Rhiney would have tried to push it any more after that; all I know is he didn't get a chance. ". . . Amen. Let's go," that's the way Coach Walker said it. We clanked down the hall and ran out onto the field behind the cheerleaders. Everyone on the Arlis side stood up and cheered. I sure could have used a cigarette about then. I was about to die for a cigarette.

It's not what Rhiney thinks. I'm not an atheist or anything. I may not know *what* I am, but it's not an atheist. What it is, is those guys, the guys on the team. I wouldn't pray in front of them. No way. Not when all they ever talk about is parking by a pumpjack and playing with some dumb little freshman's tits.

Fort Conners is a hundred and nineteen miles from Arlis and during the way back on the bus, not one person said a word to me. A hundred and nineteen miles and not one goddam word. I mean, I sat up straight in my seat plenty long for anyone to say something if they wanted to, but no one did. After the bus got warm, I folded my sweater and put it between my head and the window. Just pretended to sleep all the way to Arlis. I did doze some. I know I dozed some, but I was awake just about all the way. I was awake when we turned off Interstate to take the short cut to Arlis. That was when I heard some guys talking up front. Coach Walker and Rhiney were talking. Rhiney was driving and Coach Walker was talking. Rhiney was driving and Coach Walker was sitting in the seat right behind him, but *they* were talking about the game. *This* was someone else. I was pretty sure it was Mark Powell and Randy Owens. I mean, I'm still not sure about Powell, but the other one was Randy Owens. Old Owens and I ran around together our first year in P.O.N.Y. League. That was before he started spending every summer at his uncle's marina on Possum Kingdom. I still know him pretty well, though. Every once in a while we go get a coke and drag main or shoot eight-ball at the Youth Center.

Anyway, him and Mark Powell, they weren't whispering, but they were talking low, and I couldn't make out what they were saying, except I was positive I heard my name three or four times.

Where you exit Interstate at the Wrangston cutoff, you have to stop at this stop sign. There weren't any headlights, though, so Rhiney didn't stop all the way, just slowed down enough to get the bus in low gear. But while he was doing that, I could make out what Mark Powell and Randy Owens were saying. Just two or three sentences, but it was enough for me to be sure they were talking about me.

Powell or whoever it was said, ". . . could get expelled, because everyone in school is *supposed* to go to the pep rallies."

And Randy Owens said, "I don't care what he's *supposed* to do. He plays on the team. He should *want* to go to them."

That chapped me good. I didn't care whether I ever went to a pep rally, on Friday night I gave everything I had. From the opening kickoff till the final horn—everything. There were others who did, too; I wasn't the only one. But Owens. If you ever saw our uniforms, I wouldn't have to explain. They're gold. They start off *light* gold. But by the end of the game, they're dark gold. Dark gold, because they're soaked with sweat. Not old Owens's uniform, though. He's light gold from start to finish. And I've never seen him play all of a game without getting helped off the field. Says it's the cramps. *Cramps* my eye. Randy Owens doesn't lose any salt. While Rhiney and Andrew— that's our manager, Andrew Phillips—help Owens off the field, the Rattler- ettes clap their white gloves and chant, "He's a Rattler, a *real* Rattler," and old Owens eats that jazz up.

Rhiney gunned the bus and we swung onto the Wrangston highway. With him gunning it like that, I wasn't able to hear any more. I must have dozed, because when I opened my eyes again, Randy Owens was curled up asleep in the seat across from me. I knew it was Owens, because I could make out his Tony Lamas in the aisle. I didn't doze after that, though, because you could see the lights of Arlis. I sat up in the seat and watched the lights of Arlis get closer and closer until we were finally there.

On Friday morning everybody files into the gym at ten-thirty. About the time they all get set down, the band comes in. Not in their uniforms, but they've got their instruments. That's why everyone in the band is always a little late, because they have to go across the street to the band hall and get their instruments. Then the cheerleaders lead some yells and maybe do a skit. Teachers usually get in on the skits, usually men teachers dressed up like women to be funny. And it is funny. Sometimes funny as hell. When I was a freshman, Arlis got into the state play-offs, and *those* pep rallies were some- thing. Black and gold signs hung all over the gym, signs that said, "GO BIG RATTLERS," and "ALL THE WAY TO STATE!" Half the town jammed the gym and everyone yelled until they were hoarse. The band would play "Prai- rie Jump" over and over and everyone just kept right on yelling maybe fifteen minutes into third period.

I went to a pep rally this year—the first one. Marched down onto the basketball court with the team while the band played "Prairie Jump." Stood there facing the stands with my hands in my back pockets while they played "Good Ol' Arlis High." It really made my heart pound, too. Made me proud I was playing football for Arlis. Then that night West Sands waxed our ass. It was forty-two to nothing. And we were lucky that's all it was, because they had thirty-five at the half. I couldn't sleep that night. All the things that happened in the game kept going through my head. Over and over I thought about that fumble rolling around right in front of me and somebody getting on it before I could. That big tackle for West Sands, he got it. Then I thought about the way I felt at the pep rally. Standing out there like I was a stud. I mean, we hadn't even played a game. Instant stud, that's what I was. And I swore I couldn't let myself feel like that again, wouldn't let my heart pound with pride. Not till we got out there and did good, did something to be proud of, I swore I wouldn't.

What I did was, that next Friday when the bell rang ending second period, instead of going to pep rally, I went to the john.

I like to died that first time I stayed in there, the morning before the Ratliff game. I mean, ever since I was little, I had one ambition and that was to play football for the Arlis Rattlers. That's the way it is in Arlis, all the kids want to play for the Rattlers. And so there I was, starting on the A-team and all, but not going to the pep rally made it sort of like I didn't even play. Funny, I wanted to go and didn't want to go for the same reason. It was sort of a vicious circle. After I heard the first cheer and knew the band was there and pep rally had begun, I almost went ahead on. Only, I didn't. I just thought about it, that's all. I decided to study my English assignment. Only I never got past the sentries in *Julius Caesar*. I could tell they were doing "Stomp-Clap" in the gym. You couldn't hear the clap, just the stomp. And the stomp sounded weak and far away like something in a dream. Or like someone shutting a car door in a dust storm. It's kind of like a train whistle, I know you've heard that, a train whistle from somewhere a long way off. It makes you feel sad about everything, even the happy things in your life. I tried not to listen. I tried reading *Julius Caesar* again, but even *that* depressed me. I mean, he'd only been dead two thousand years. What I did, I went into the first stall, the one nearest the door, and flushed the commode. You know how loud that is. I couldn't hear anything coming from the gym. When all the water swirled down that commode and it was about to get quiet again, I flushed the one in the next stall. And after that, the one in the third stall.

Even after we lost our first four games, nobody was worried about going "0" and ten. Nobody was worried because our fifth game was with Spiller. Spiller *never* beats Arlis. That's what everyone was saying after Fort Conners racked us up, "Thank God Spiller's next." We would beat Spiller and we would be one and "0" in district. After all, that's what it's really all about, district. Only we lost. That was just last Friday night. We lost to Spiller and everyone blames me.

Late in the fourth quarter they had us twenty to nineteen. Up to then we'd fumbled eight times and Spiller'd got six of them. But it looked like things were finally going to go our way. What happened was, a cold front hit. I mean, *hit*. I bet the wind was blowing seventy-five miles an hour. Seventy-five miles an hour and right into Spiller's face. Just after it hit, we had to punt. Calvin Upshaw kicked a low spiral that sailed over Spiller's safety. The ball bounced and rolled eighty yards before it finally blew out of bounds on their four yard line. When they lined up on first down, the wind was blowing so hard the Spiller quarterback sounded like he was calling signals from six blocks away. He gave off on a quick dive to his right halfback. We were in a *six-three* and I was head up on the guard. It was one of those deals where the quarterback goes on down the line faking. I just knew he still had it, but the dive was my responsibility. I was really surprised when I got up off that halfback and saw the ball. Everybody on the team ran up and patted me and banged me on the shoulder pads and it felt great having them do that just a week after the Fort Conners game.

On second and ten Spiller swept the side away from me. It was like watching a game film. Bodies were colliding in open field, but you didn't hear a thing—just a constant roar of the wind past the holes in your headgear. They picked up eight yards. That killed me, them getting so much. I had just about caught up to the play and it was all I could do to keep from piling on.

In the stands, the Rattlerettes began clapping their white gloves. Third down, two for Spiller from their twelve. We showed them a *five-four*, see, but fell into a gap eight right before they snapped the ball. Only the ball went between the quarterback's legs to the fullback for another sweep. Our end got a shot at him but he spun loose. Spun loose and for a second my heart stopped. Looked like clear sailing for thirty-three. Then it was like Lupe Valdez came out of nowhere and caught him on the twenty-five.

We broke our defensive huddle and I looked at the clock. The lighted orange bulbs showed two minutes and thirty-one seconds. Randy Owens tapped me on the shoulder pad. In a *five-four* Owens is an inside linebacker, and I was the middle guard. That's what Upshaw called in the huddle, a *five-four*, and I figured Owens wanted to stunt. We'd done it several times already and I figured he wanted to again.

He hollered into the hole of my headgear, "Going to the dance?"

I looked at his uniform. If there had been just a *patch* of dark gold. Anywhere, I didn't care where. He took hold of my face bar and turned my head away from him.

"After the game," he yelled into my ear, "you going to the dance?"

I don't know if Spiller had broken huddle yet or not. In fact, I don't remember much at all. Just first a ref, then two of them, and finally Coach
Walker and old Rhiney pulling me off Owens and dragging me to the sideline.
I don't remember, but the way everyone talks I got his helmet off and was
really pounding him good. I do remember the ref trotting back onto the field,
remember him picking up the ball like he was Jesus Christ. Everyone thought
it'd just be five for "Delay of Game" or something, but that ref kept on going
for fifteen and signalled "Unsportsmanlike Conduct." Rhiney was out on the
field screaming that he couldn't do that, but the ref just swept his arm around
and round for the clock to start. When I saw him do that, when I saw that ref
set the ball down on the forty yard line and sweep his arm around and round,
I couldn't help it, I knew I was going to cry. I bit my bottom lip as hard as I
could, but it didn't do any good. I turned and trotted toward the fieldhouse.

It was like an oven in the fieldhouse. I was sweating to start with, and it
was so hot in there I thought I would throw up. I just piled my pads and stuff
on the floor. I dressed in nothing flat and hauled. When I choked the pickup
and it started, I didn't think about where I was going.

I had already passed the cattleguard where you turn off to go to the watertower when I decided to go up there. When I pulled off in the bar ditch to
make a u-turn, I really didn't have anything more in mind than just driving
by the thing.

I didn't realize how tired I was until I was standing there shivering in the
wind and reading that stuff kids had painted on the watertower. It's not the
regular Arlis watertower I'm talking about. It's the old one that Tideland Oil
built for the people who lived in a camp they had there during the boom.
And I was cotton-mouthed. That's when your mouth ulcers really get to hurting, when you're cotton-mouthed. The ones inside my bottom lip where I bit
myself were killing me. I put my tongue against them and turned to look at
Arlis. Just as I did, the stadium lights went out. I saw the Youth Center all lit
up. After a Rattler home game, they always have a dance at the Youth Center. I didn't want to see things like that, so I made my way around the catwalk.

I don't know exactly when I decided to quit, but I know while I was standing up there, it was already cut and dried in my mind. Maybe my mind was
made up as soon as I hit Randy Owens, I don't know. Anyway, I leaned on
the handrail and tried to light a cigarette. The wind kept blowing the matches
out. I stood there watching the string of red taillights on the Spiller highway
and wondered what it'd be like not being a football player any more.

ROGER KAHN

Lines on the Transpontine Madness

At a point in life when one is through with boyhood, but has not yet discovered how to be a man, it was my fortune to travel with the most marvelously appealing of teams. During the early 1950s the Jackie Robinson
Brooklyn Dodgers were outspoken, opinionated, bigoted, tolerant, black,
white, open, passionate: in short, a fascinating mix of vigorous men. They
were not, however, the most successful team in baseball.

During four consecutive years they entered autumn full of hope and found
catastrophe. Twice they lost pennants in the concluding inning of the concluding game of a season. Twice they won pennants and lost the World Series
to the New York Yankees. These narrow setbacks did not proceed, as some
suggested, from failings of courage or of character. The Dodgers were simply
unfortunate—it is dreamstuff that luck plays everyone the same—and, not to
become obsessively technical, they lacked the kind of pitching that makes
victory sure. In the next decade, a weaker Dodger team, rallying around
Sandy Koufax, won the World Series twice.

But I mean to be less concerned with curve balls than with the lure of the
team. Ebbets Field was a narrow cockpit, built of brick and iron and concrete,
alongside a steep cobblestone slope of Bedford Avenue. Two tiers of grandstand pressed the playing area from three sides, and in thousands of seats fans
could hear a ball player's chatter, notice details of a ball player's gait and, at a
time when television had not yet assaulted illusion with the Zoomar lens, you
could see, you could actually see, the actual expression on the actual face of
an actual major leaguer as he played. *You could know what he was like!*

"I start in toward the bench, holding the ball now with the five fingers of
my bare left hand, and when I get to the infield—having come down hard
with one foot on the bag at second base—I shoot it, with just a flick of the
wrist, gently at the opposing team's shortstop as he comes trotting out onto
the field, and without breaking stride, go loping in all the way, shoulders
shifting, head hanging, a touch pigeon-toed, my knees coming slowly up and
down in an altogether brilliant imitation of The Duke." Philip Roth as Alex-
ander Portnoy as Duke Snider. In the intimacy of Ebbets Field it was a short
trip from the grandstand to the fantasy that you were in the game.

My years with the Dodgers were 1952 and 1953, two seasons in which they

---

Preface to *The Boys of Summer* (1972).

lost the World Series to the Yankees. You may glory in a team triumphant, but you fall in love with a team in defeat. Losing after great striving is the story of man, who was born to sorrow, whose sweetest songs tell of saddest thought, and who, if he is a hero, does nothing in life as becomingly as leaving it. A whole country was stirred by the high deeds and thwarted longings of The Duke, Preacher, Pee Wee, Skoonj and the rest. The team was awesomely good and yet defeated. Their skills lifted everyman's spirit and their defeat joined them with everyman's existence, a national team, with a country in thrall, irresistible and unable to beat the Yankees.

"Baseball writers develop a great attachment for the Brooklyn club if long exposed," Stanley Woodward, an extraordinary sports editor, complained in 1949.

This was so in the days of Uncle Wilbert Robinson [1920] and it is so now. We found it advisable [on the New York *Herald Tribune*] to shift Brooklyn writers frequently. If we hadn't, we would have had on our hands a member of the Brooklyn baseball club, rather than a newspaper reporter. The transpontine madness seems to affect all baseball writers, no matter how sensible they outwardly seem. You must watch a Brooklyn writer for symptoms and, before they become virulent, shift him to the Yankees or to tennis or golf.

By the time Woodward was writing, the concept of the Dodgers as appealing incompetents—"Dem Bums" in a persistent poor joke—was dying. Research suggests that when they were incompetent, the Dodgers appealed as a conversation piece, but not as an entertainment. I remember a succession of mots about a shortstop named Lonny Frey, *fl. c.* 1935, who made more than fifty errors in one season. People said, "There's an infielder with only one weakness. Batted balls." Everyone laughed, but few chose to pay to see Frey fumble. Attendance was so poor that by the late 1930s the Dodgers, "a chronic second division team," to quote the sportswriters, had passed from family ownership to the Brooklyn Trust Company. It took a succession of winning teams, with dependable shortstops named Durocher and Reese, to rescue the franchise from receivership.

Accents echo in the phrase "Brooklyn Dodgers." The words strike each other pleasantly, if not poetically, suggesting a good-humored bumping about. You get an altogether different sense from other nicknames. The Brooklyn Astros would skate in the Roller Derby. The Brooklyn Tigers would play football in a stony sandlot. The Brooklyn Braves would be an all-black schoolyard basketball team in 1945. The Brooklyn Yankees will not penetrate the consciousness. It is an antiphrase, like the Roman Greeks.

As far as anyone knows, the nickname proceeded from benign absurdity. Brooklyn, being flat, extensive and populous, was an early stronghold of the trolley car. Enter absurdity. To survive in Brooklyn one had to be a dodger of trolleys. After several unfortunate experiments in nomenclature, the Brooklyn National League Baseball Team became the Dodgers during the 1920s, and the nickname endured after polluting buses had come and the last Brooklyn trolley had been shipped from Vanderbilt Avenue to Karachi.

Brooklyn is not an inherently funny word, although the old Brooklyn accent, in which one pronounced "oil" as "earl" and "earl" as "oil," was amusing. The native ground might be enunciated "Bvooklyn" and "thirty" was a phonetist's Armageddon. It could be "tirdy," "toidy," "dirty," "doity," "tirty," "toity," "dirdy" or "doidy." But dialect, all dialect, Brooklyn, Boston, German, Jewish, British, Russian, Italian dialect, is the stuff of easy rough humor. Have you ever heard a Georgia belle insert four question marks into a declarative paragraph? "Ah went to Rollins? That's in Florida? South of heah? An' real pretty?" When a Georgia girl says *no*, she asks a question.

The lingering sense of Brooklyn as a land of boundless mirth with baseball obbligato was the creation of certain screen writers and comedians. Working for a living, they synthesized *that* Brooklyn. In one old patriotic movie, Bing Crosby defends the American flag against a cynic by asking others "to say what Old Glory stands for." A Southerner talks of red clay and pine trees. A Westerner describes sunset in the Rocky Mountains. But it is a Brooklynite who carries the back lot at Paramount Pictures. His speech begins with the apothegm, "Hey, Mac. Ever see steam comin' out a sewer in Flatbush?" As if that were not enough, can anyone forget William Bendix dying happy in a mangrove swamp? Just before a Japanese machine gunner cut him in two, Bendix had heard by shortwave that the Dodgers scored four in the ninth. *Requiescat in pace.* Winning Pitcher: Gregg (7 and 5).

The Brooklyn of reality, where one Harold Dana Gregg pitched inconsistently for five seasons, suffered a wartime disaffection from baseball. Selective Service hit the Dodgers particularly hard and the 1944 team finished seventh. At about the time screenwriters were conceiving other, yet more heroic deaths for Baseball Bill Bendix, genuine Dodger fans sang parodies of the soldier's song, "Bless 'Em All." In Brooklyn, the words went, "Lose 'em all." That was the darkness before the sunburst of peace and the great Jackie Robinson team.

After World War II, Brooklyn, like most urban settlements, began a struggle to adjust which presently turned and became a struggle to survive. Brooklyn had been a heterogeneous, dominantly middle-class community, with remarkable schools, good libraries and not only major league baseball, but extensive concert series, second-run movie houses, expensive neighborhoods and a lovely rolling stretch of acreage called Prospect Park. For all the out-siders' jokes, middle-brow Brooklyn was reasonably sure of its cosmic place, and safe.

Then, with postwar prosperity came new highways and the conqueror au-tomobile. Families whose wanderings had not extended beyond the route of the New Lots Avenue subway at last were able to liberate themselves. For $300 down one could buy a Ford, a Studebaker or a Kaiser, after which one could drive anywhere. California. Canada. *Anywhere.* Whole families left their blocks for outings. California was a little far and Canada was said to be cold, but there was Jones Beach on the south shore to the east and Kiamesha Lake in the Catskill Mountains to the northwest. Soon families began to leave their blocks for good. They had been overwhelmed by the appeal of a split-level house (nothing down to qualified Vets) on a treeless sixty-by-ninety foot corner of an old Long Island potato farm. What did it matter about no trees? A tree could always come later, like a television.

Exodus worked on the ethnic patterns and economic structure and so at the very nature of Brooklyn. As old families, mostly white, moved out, new groups, many black and Puerto Rican, moved in. The flux terrified people on both sides. Could Brooklyn continue as a suitable place for the middle class to live? That was what the Irish, Italian and Jewish families asked themselves. Are we doomed? wondered blacks, up from Carolina dirt farms and shacks in the West Indies. Was black life always to be poverty, degradation, rotgut? The answers, like the American urb itself, are still in doubt.

Against this uncertain backdrop, the dominant truth of the Jackie Robin-son Dodgers was integration. They were the first integrated major league baseball team and so the most consciously integrated team and, perhaps, the most intensely integrated team. All of them, black and white, became targets for the intolerance in which baseball has been rich.

As many ball players, officials, umpires and journalists envisioned it, the entity of baseball rose in alabaster, a temple of white supremacy. To them, the Robinson presence was a defilement and the whites who consented to play at his side were whores. Opposing pitchers forever threw fast balls at Dodger heads. Opposing bench jockeys forever shouted "black bastard," "nigger lover" and "monkey-fucker." Hate was always threatening the team. But the Dodgers, the dozen or so athletes who were at the core of the team, and are at the core of this book, stood together in purpose and for the most part in cama-raderie. They respected one another as competitors and they knew that they were set apart. No one prattled about team spirit. No one made speeches on the Rights of Man. No one sang "Let My People Go." But without pretense or visible fear these men marched unevenly against the sin of bigotry.

That spirit leaped from the field into the surrounding two-tiered grandstand. A man felt it; it became part of him, quite painlessly. You rooted for the team, didn't you? You'd rooted for the team all your life. All right. They got this black guy now, and he can run and he can bunt, but can he hit?

Below, Robinson lines a double into the left-field corner. He steals third. He scores on a short passed ball, sliding clear around the catcher, Del Rice.

The stands erupt. The Dodgers win. We beat the *Cardinals*. That colored guy's got *balls*, I tell you that.

By applauding Robinson, a man did not feel that he was taking a stand on school integration, or on open housing. But for an instant he had accepted Robinson simply as a hometown ball player. To disregard color, even for an instant, is to step away from the old prejudices, the old hatred. That is not a path on which many double back.

The struggle seems modest now. What, after all, did Robinson ask? At first, a chance to play. Then the right to sleep in a good hotel and to eat in a clean dining room. Later to fight with umpires and dispute the press. But each step drew great whoops of protest. The Robinson experience developed as an epic and now, not only a national team, the Dodgers were a national issue. Everywhere, in New England drawing rooms and on porches in the South, in California, which had no major league baseball teams and in New York City, which had three, men and women talked about the Jackie Robinson Dodgers, and as they talked they confronted themselves and American racism. That confrontation was, I believe, as important as *Brown* vs. *Board of Education of Topeka*, in creating the racially troubled hopeful present.

One did not go to Ebbets Field for sociology. Exciting baseball was the attraction, and a wonder of the sociological Dodgers was the excitement of their play. It is not simply that they won frequently, brawled with umpires, got into bean-ball fights and endlessly thrashed in the headwaters of a pennant race. The team possessed an astonishing variety of eclectic skills.

One never knew when a powerful visiting batter, "one o' them big, hairy-assed bastards" in manager Charlie Dressen's fond phrase, would drive a terrific smash up the third-base line. There, squinting in a crouch, Billy Cox, a wiry, horse-faced man with little blacksmith's arms, waited to spring. He subdued hard grounders by slapping his glove downward and imprisoning the ball between glove and earth. The glove was small and black and ancient. Someone accused Cox of having purchased it during a drugstore closeout. With the Whelan glove, Cox was a phenomenon.

Drives to right field activated stolid Carl Furillo. A powerful monolithic man, Furillo possessed an astonishing throwing arm and a prescient sense of how a ball would carom off the barrier. The grandstands did not extend behind right field. Between the outfield and the sidewalk of Bedford Avenue, a cement wall rose sloping outward. It straightened at about ten feet and then fifteen feet higher gave way to a stiff screen of wire-mesh. In straightaway right a scoreboard jutted, offering another surface and describing new angles. Furillo reigned here with an arm that, in Bugs Baer's phrase, could have thrown a lamb chop past a wolf.

Center field belonged to Snider, rangy and gifted and supple. Duke could get his glove thirteen feet into the air. The centerfield wall was cushioned with foam rubber, and Snider, in pursuit of high drives, ran at the wall, dug a spiked shoe into the rubber and hurled his body upward. Pictures of him in low orbit survive.

But Robinson was the cynosure of all eyes. For a long time he shocked people seeing him for the first time simply by the fact of his color: uncompromising ebony. All the baseball heroes had been white men. Ty Cobb and Christy Mathewson and John McGraw and Honus Wagner and Babe Ruth and Dizzy Dean were white. Kenesaw Mountain Landis and Bill Klem and Connie Mack were white. Every coach, every manager, every umpire, every batting practice pitcher, every human being one had ever seen in uniform on a major league field was white. Without realizing it, one had become conditioned. The grass was green, the dirt was brown and the ball players were white. Suddenly in Ebbets Field, under a white home uniform, two muscled arms extended like black hawsers. *Black*. Like the arms of a janitor. The new color jolted the consciousness, in a profound and not quite definable way. *Amid twenty snowy mountains, the only moving thing was the eye of a blackbird.*

Robinson could hit and bunt and steal and run. He had intimidating skills, and he burned with a dark fire. He wanted passionately to win. He charged at ball games. He calculated his rivals' weaknesses and measured his own strengths and knew—as only a very few have ever known—the precise move to make at precisely the moment of maximum effect. His bunts, his steals, and his fake bunts and fake steals humiliated a legion of visiting players. He bore the burden of a pioneer and the weight made him more strong. If one can be certain of anything in baseball, it is that we shall not look upon his like again.

As a young newspaperman covering the team in 1952 and 1953, I enjoyed the assignment, without realizing what I had. Particularly during one's youth, it is difficult to distinguish trivia from what is worthy. The days are crowded with deadlines, with other people's petty scoops and your own, bickering and fantasies and train rides and amiable beers. The present, as Frost put it,

Is too much for the senses,
Too crowded, too confusing—
Too present to imagine.

The team grew old. The Dodgers deserted Brooklyn. Wreckers swarmed into Ebbets Field and leveled the stands. Soil that had felt the spikes of Robinson and Reese was washed from the faces of mewling children. The New York *Herald Tribune* writhed, changed its face and collapsed. I covered a team that no longer exists in a demolished ball park for a newspaper that is dead.

Remembering and appreciating the time, which was not so very long ago, I have found myself wondering more and more about the ball players. They are retired athletes now, but not old. They are scattered wide, but joined by a common memory. How are the years with them? What past do they remember? Have they come at length to realize what they had?

Unlike most, a ball player must confront two deaths. First, between the ages of thirty and forty he perishes as an athlete. Although he looks trim and feels vigorous and retains unusual coordination, the superlative reflexes, the *major league* reflexes, pass on. At a point when many of his classmates are newly confident and rising in other fields, he finds that he can no longer hit a very good fast ball or reach a grounder four strides to his right. At thirty-five he is experiencing the truth of finality. As his major league career is ending, all things will end. However he sprang, he was always earthbound. Mortality embraces him. The golden age has passed as in a moment. So will all things. So will all moments. *Memento mori.*

What, then, of the names that rang like chords: Erskine and Robinson, Labine and Shuba, Furillo and Cox. One evening, for no useful reason, I telephoned Billy Cox at his home in Newport, near Harrisburg, Pennsylvania, and said I'd like to drive out for a drink. I hadn't seen him for fourteen years.

"You come all the way out here to visit me?" Cox sounded surprised. "It's hard to get to now. The commuter train from Harrisburg, it's discontinued."

"I'll find my way."

"I'm tending bar at the American Legion Club. You know, it's at the top of the hill. How do you like that, they discontinued the Harrisburg train."

Cox, the third baseman, was above all lithe. Now, at the Legion bar in Newport, he was a fat man. His hair was still black but before him he carried Falstaff's belly. "Hey," he cried when I came in. "Here's a fella seen me play. He'll tell you some of the plays I made. He'll tell you." Three stone-faced old trainmen glared from the bar, where they were drinking beer.

"Billy, you were the best damn glove I ever saw."

"See," Cox said to the trainmen. "See. An' this man's a writer from *New York.*"

It was as if New York were a light-year distant, as if Cox himself had never played in Brooklyn. The experience had so diffused that it became real now only when someone else confirmed it. Most of the time there was no one.

"What do you do now, Bill?" I said. "What is it you like to do?"

"Watch kids," he said. His eyes gazed cavernous and blank. "Watch little kids play third. They make some plays."

One thing a writer has, if he is fortunate, and I have been fortunate, is a partnership with the years. In the 1970s, our own confusing, crowded present, I have been able to seek out the 1950s, to find these heroic Dodgers who are forty-five and fifty, in lairs from Southern California to New England, and to consider them not only as old athletes but as fathers and as men, dead as ball players to be sure, but still battling, as strong men always battle, the implacable enemy, time.

Already time has dealt some fiercely. Roy Campanella, the cheerful, talkative catcher, is condemned to a wheelchair; he has been through a divorce like something out of *Lady Chatterley*. Gil Hodges, the strongest Dodger, and Jackie Robinson have suffered heart attacks. Duke Snider, who dreamed of raising avocados, has had to sell his farm. Carl Erskine, the most compassionate of men, is occupied at home with his youngest son. Jimmy Erskine is an affectionate child. Most mongoloid children are said to be affectionate.

"Sooner or later," the author Ed Linn observes, "society beats down the man of muscle and sweat." Surely these fine athletes, these boys of summer, have found their measure of ruin. But one does not come away from visits with them, from long nights remembering the past and considering the present, full of sorrow. In the end, quite the other way, one is renewed. Yes, it is fiercely difficult for the athlete to grow old, but to age with dignity and with courage cuts close to what it is to be a man. And most of them have aged that way, with dignity, with courage and with hope.

"Now entertain conjecture of a time."

MICHAEL NOVAK

Regional Religions

Christianity has many denominations, and Judaism many traditions. Sports, too, awaken different symbolic echoes in different areas of the

From *The Joy of Sports* (1976).

nation. Not all lovers of sports love hunting. A few count demolition derbies as a sport; many fewer think dog shows are a sport; and others train dogs for savage, bloody dogfights. Tennis is the sport of a social class not likely to appreciate the grease, dust, roar, and danger of auto racing. The kingdom of sports has many mansions. The nation's three major sports have regional variants.

Football was born in western Pennsylvania, and it remains basic and well loved throughout the region. The rivalry between Johnstown and Altoona high schools was so fierce in the 1930s and 1940s that I never got to see them play. The annual riots after every game were too destructive; competition between the schools was banned for twenty years. For decades, one could predict the national championship from year to year by which college the best players from the region agreed to attend. The Southern schools—Louisville, Alabama, Miami, Kentucky—began wooing them to warmer climes just after World War II. Yet it would be difficult to say that football was a mania in the region. The predominant local cultures are mainly Eastern and Southern European, Irish, German, and black. The style was hard, calculating, driving, tough. One fullback from Windber, a mining town of fewer than 6,000 souls that specialized in defeating (or at least beating up) the major schools of the area, was famous for having sent six opponents to hospitals for a night of observation; his knees drove into opposing lines as though he were a locomotive rather than a lad of seventeen. The earliest amateur and professional clubs began with scions who had attended Rutgers or Princeton, but soon recruited the sons of miners and steelworkers. In a region of little upward mobility, young men played with a ferocity tutored by knowledge that, however violent football might be, the mines and mills were more violent still.

The passion feeding football in western Pennsylvania was the passion of chargers and hitters who gloried in their endurance of pain and punishment. There is a strain of masochism in the western Pennsylvanian character, almost a need to absorb punishment in order to prove oneself. In any case, endurance is perhaps the most highly prized characteristic—playing both ways, on offense and defense, as Johnny Lujack did with the Chicago Bears; going on forever like George Blanda; being "durable" like John Unitas; coming back operation after operation like Joe Namath; carrying four or five men with him before falling to the ground, as Leon Hart did; refusing to go down, as little Jim Mutscheller, not big for an end, used to do at Notre Dame. Not that Pennsylvania football lacked excitement. Daring passers and runners abounded. But the essence of the Pennsylvania game was physical aggression. Each team was trained to hit hard; desperate line play was the rule. Jack Ham and Pete Duranko are recent alumni of this school. Even the most explosive and brilliant players had to conquer that defensive fierceness first. The top passers specialized in quick release and long, flat bullets. The formations usually were basic, punchy, organized for power rather than flash.

A football game there, as liturgy, is not primarily a celebration of the state of Pennsylvania or of the regional culture; the larger social identity is not so highly developed. Penn State has little of the statewide glory Ohio State carries. Pitt does not glamorize the city of Pittsburgh. Loyalties tend to be diffuse and local. Notre Dame is probably more powerful symbolically than any team within the state (which is not to suggest that Pittsburghers don't feel delight when Pitt beats, or even threatens, Notre Dame, as Carnegie Tech did in the 1930s). A football game in western Pennsylvania is a celebration of local fighting spirit rather than of local institutions.

It is said that Southern and Eastern Europeans, having learned over centuries to distrust governmental or non-familial institutions, are not so civic-minded as Anglo-Americans; they do not react to the symbols of the state with unalloyed attachment. In any case, the liturgies of sports in western Pennsylvania tend to celebrate the sports and the athletes rather than a regional or civic jurisdiction. Fans were loyal to the Pirates and Steelers through long years of drought; the glory of the city was hardly to be celebrated. (Pittsburgh? Glory? The concepts hardly fit.) If there is madness and riot nowadays when the Pirates clinch the World Series or the Steelers take the Super Bowl, it is not exactly chauvinism that is celebrated; rather, a sort of vindication, surprise, astonishment, and the unfamiliar sense of being number one. The sports of the region are rugged, violent, and aggressive; so, too, are the victory celebrations. It is certainly true that labor in the mines and mills has seethed with suffered violence for generations. For generations, men have endured the worst industrialism could do to them: chopped-off fingers, broken knees, poison-coated lungs, bent backs, blackened hands, and mangled death. Sports are, comparatively, an easy way to make a living. What people there respect in athletes—and politicians—is learned from their own lives.

In Alabama, Arkansas, and Mississippi, by contrast, college football is a statewide religion; it *does* celebrate the state and the region. The poor boys of the South, white as well as black, also hit hard, glory in aggression, and value toughness; it is for them, too, a form of populism and assault on the unseen establishments that govern their lives. Bear Bryant, in particular, loves speed and wit and complex strategy. His teams play a wide-open brand of football. They run, it seems, from dozens of formations, and his recent staple, the wishbone, is remarkable for its swiftness, multiple options, and ability to open up the defense. The football of the Deep South is a rugged kind of football, but it is best described as fleet, explosive, difficult to contain. It is almost the reverse image of Pennsylvania football.

Somehow, in the South, to play a good game is to honor one's state, one's university, the South, and the true spirit of the American nation. The dominant churches, Baptist and Methodist, doctrinally so explicit about the separation of church and state, actually have forged a new *tertium quid* with the regnant society: a unity of religious values and national values that makes every liturgy of one simultaneously a liturgy of the other. A victory by Alabama is celebrated by virtually the entire state. The rivalry between Auburn and Alabama is a contest to decide who, for the year, is the established institution of the state religion. A loss by Alabama is carefully dissected by the state newspapers, the key plays diagramed for all to see, so that the "bugs" that somehow got into the healthy organism can be diagnosed and medically destroyed in time for next week's return to health. The young men are taught to play with heart, with concentration, with dedication, to be worthy of university and state and nation—and themselves. All these are grasped as a kind of unity, within a holistic culture. The liturgy of a football game is, indeed, a communal and statewide worship service, within a unitary cosmic scheme. (In professional football, Miami and Dallas most closely approach this collegiate symbolism; at a Southern Super Bowl, even national football "gets religion" in the classic style of the region.)

Football in the Big Ten is, undoubtedly, a focal point of passional religion every centimeter as deep as in the Deep South. But the style and manner are as different as a Baptist from a Lutheran liturgy. The Baptist and Methodist churches are in the "free church" tradition, and they cherish emotion, inspiration, charismatic speaking in tongues, the surges of personal conversion and sudden seizure. The churches of the Midwest—even the Midwestern Methodists—are filled by far more orderly and sober folk. They believe in orders, institutions, fixities; they distrust sudden conversions, too much talk, and flashy "show." Their faith is guarded in traditions, forms, and authorities, not left to the spontaneous spirit of the revival. In Alabama and Mississippi, the whole state is enthralled every spring by the photographs in their local papers: Bear Bryant presiding behind the kitchen table as yet another local lad chooses to accept a scholarship to 'Bama and signs, under the beaming faces of his parents, a letter of intent in the sanctity of yet another humble home. In the Midwest, Woody Hayes may refuse to buy so much as a single gallon of gas in Michigan, but everyone expects him to recruit every great athlete in Canton, Massillon, and throughout the state. A testimonial ceremony isn't necessary; you just show up in church in September.

"Three yards and a cloud of dust," they say of Ohio State football, and everyone makes fun of Woody Hayes's aversion to the pass. The forward pass was, of course, perfected in the Midwest, at Notre Dame, and Fran Tarkenton at Minnesota, Bart Starr at Green Bay, and Sid Luckman and Johnny Lujack with the Chicago Bears have thrown as well as any passers in the game. (Tarkenton and Starr were, of course, imported Southerners.) Still, the Packers, Vikings, and Bears—like Michigan, Ohio State, and Minnesota—have played essentially Midwestern football: hard, orderly, cleanly executed, disciplined, tight. The "black and blue" conference, they call it. The Midwestern spirit does not easily accept the flashy, the glamorous, the shortcut, the easy way. The fans come to cheer, and they take enormous pride in their favorites; they fill some of the most enormous stadia in the nation with the regularity of the seasons. Their form of exaltation, however, is not the intoxicating, spirit-beseeching revivalism of the cheering sections, nor the dazzling card-section displays of California; it is the large, disciplined, soul-stirring marching band. Legions of girls in cowboy boots are not the style, nor platoons of beach girls with pom-poms; a single "golden girl" from Purdue is nightclub act enough. The cheerleaders are male as well as female; they perform with spirited decorum rather than with frenzy. In the Midwest, football is businesslike. The celebrity culture of East and West passes over the plains nonstop by air. Let Texas and Alabama give the nation passers and shifty-footed halfbacks; the Midwest supplies the linebackers and the hard runners who believe in power. "Hopalong" Cassady, Red Grange, Bob Griese, and others make these symbolic statements lies, of course. Football teams in every region absorb all sorts of talents and take talent where they find it. But the style of play—and celebration—in the great Midwest is built on character, solidity, and dependability.

Nowhere, they say, is football more passional and single-minded than in Texas (around Dallas) and Oklahoma. A Notre Dame fan can hardly help being aware that Notre Dame's past encounters with Southern Methodist, Texas, and Oklahoma have brought Notre Dame into a wholly different sort of world. In the Southwest, the great runners have the speed of halfbacks and the power of fullbacks. The passers fill the air with footballs. The mythic spirit there is not of miners and millworkers, nor farm boys, nor rebels, but of cowboys. In Texas they play football as though the constricted field were wide open spaces, and they seem to shoot their way in and out of times of possession. It is as though the culture of the region were pressing in on them, pulverizing them with the gentle terror of the huge sky; they are fixing to explode. There is a charged-up energy in the Southwest that resists fencing in. They play the game in order to break away.

When I was young and saw early telecasts from Dallas, El Paso, and Norman, I could hardly believe the rapid exchanges of touchdowns. Down there, it seemed, no one respected order, patience, hard work; down there, they went for broke all the time. They seemed to look beyond the humble first-down markers; all they saw were goal lines. Perhaps my image of the South-west is colored by the great confrontation of Notre Dame and Doak Walker of Southern Methodist in 1947. Walker, "perhaps the greatest player the game has ever known," according to *Esquire*, was too injured to play. (We Notre Dame kids, in the arrogant wisdom of our fourteen years, had early predicted that "Choo Choo" Justice of North Carolina and Doak Walker of SMU would "conveniently" be unable to face Notre Dame when the day came; and they were indeed injured.) Yet Kyle Rote, unheralded, taking the ball in shotgun formation and firing it all over the field, ripped the greatest Notre Dame team of all to shreds, firing touchdown after sudden touchdown, and until the final gun it was impossible to believe Notre Dame could halt his unorthodox, intensely spirited, and brilliant play. Notre Dame finally won, in a game of heart attacks.

Southwestern football combines the speed of the Deep South and the power of the Midwest. The teams seem built to race toward game totals of 40 points, to see who gets there first. Big scores for big states. And Okies and small-town Texans seem to have a psychology parallel to that of northern white ethnics, with one exception. Like northern workers, they know the yoke of being looked down upon—"rednecks"—and being given society's dirty jobs and low esteem; and they play as though their egos depended on it. The one exception is the attitude of obedience and social rectitude that gov-erns the Southwest, as opposed to the cynicism and sullen hostility to au-thority that infuses the northern working classes. Vince Lombardi, coach of the Green Bay Packers, commanded obedience and bullied people to attain it; the players of Texas and the Dallas Cowboys speak of coaches Darrell Royal and Tom Landry as softspoken but ruthless machines. In the South-west, the power of the establishment is almost unchallengeable. In northern cities, Lombardi was no establishment; he had to earn his authority by the force of personality. Players complain that the Texas coaches are aloof and impersonal; no such complaint was registered against Lombardi, hate his guts as some players did. "He treats us all equally," said one. "Like dogs." A foot-ball coach in the Southwest becomes an institution and joins the oil men; a football coach up North still faces establishments that he will never enter.

In California, football, like everything else, seems to be more fun. The weather is so good, not even rain and snow toughen character. Social repres-sion and industrialization were never so cruel as elsewhere in the country. Chiefly settled in the last fifty years, California does not have the same entrenched ruling class as elsewhere. Blacks and chicanos have undergone the sort of humiliation rednecks and ethnics have known elsewhere; but everyone else seems to have been born above the snapping jaws of poverty. The Chinese and Japanese, so cruelly regarded on their arrival, have been spectacularly successful in business and the professions. The social order of California is easier than elsewhere. California is not a fertile soil for the rebellions of football. When restless Americans shook the dust of stiff eastern societies from their boots, they sought liberty ever westward—until, at Berkeley, the Pacific hemmed them in and there they gathered. When California radicals protest against establishments, it is not for the bare exigencies of survival but for the pleasures of a full and "liberated" hedonism. California is America's Mediterranean. California is for the history-stricken easterner what Oran was for Camus: maroon bodies in the sun, at one with the shimmering sea, just beyond the hovels of disease and poverty that history has never changed.

In California, football is the exuberance of the healthy body delighting in its talents. If one hears of a Bartkowski, one does not imagine a factory worker but a handsome beachboy. A young socialite like John Brodie can move from Stanford to the 49'ers as one would expect few wealthy easterners to do. Football elsewhere is a game of the oppressed, fed by inner rage and anger, bursting for daylight. In California, the entire game is sunny, and a pagan delight in physical contact replaces anger. Jack Snow is competitive and spirited, but it is hard to think of him as full of pent-up rage. O. J. Simpson, Anthony Davis, and John McKay, Jr., play with every ounce of energy imaginable, but they do so, it seems, from enjoyment rather than from meanness. Lew Alcindor, changing his name to Kareem Abdul-Jabbar, betrayed his New York origins in the sullenness and anger of his presence. Bill Walton, the tall, red-haired, California-born radical, did not play in order to escape a harsher fate; not knowing the system of mines, mills, and prairie towns, he found the system of *sports* oppressive. He explains that his love for the game and his inability to find suitable competition outside its organization keep him playing, not a fierce desire to find a better life.

Both John Wooden, the great basketball coach at UCLA, now retired, and John McKay, the former football coach at USC, spoke often of making the game "fun" for their players. They recruited widely and well. Who would not like to go to school in California? The sun soaks enmity out. The social structure is uniquely open, fluid. The soft morality of the cinema lingers in the background. Flowers grow in abundance; the air is sweet. A football game televised from California is uniquely festive. Nature makes pretty girls prettier. The fans participate in elaborate and lovely card signals. The pom-pom girls dance with western Indian steps never practiced elsewhere. Fans arrive in shirt-sleeves and Bermudas. The athletes on the field seem, on the average, taller and handsomer than elsewhere, of a distinctly higher social class. Football in California is a civilized game, however grueling. Spirit rather than inherent toughness seems to play a greater role in the surging scores and quick excitement of California football.

In the Ivy League, sports are a very important symbol—but it is not considered sophisticated there to say so. Students in the Ivy League are in a very difficult emotional position. They are supposed to be "above" the rest of the population, including the cleaning ladies, janitors, and policemen from Cambridge, Ithaca, and the other Ivy towns who serve them. They are supposed to be more critical, sophisticated, and self-aware than, say, students at Ohio State. So even when they enjoy a game—like the magnificent last-minute Harvard "miracles" over Yale in recent years—they have to be slightly self-mocking and guarded. Once they have become successful alumni, of course, and can come back in camel's-hair topcoats, with silver liquor flasks and shiny family station wagons, it is all right for them to delight in a school victory and buzz about it for weeks. While they are students, enthusiasm of that sort is déclassé.

It is not that the Ivy League does not recruit seriously and hard, or that the athletes are not superb. Calvin Hill, Ed Marinaro, Chuck Bednarik, Harvard's Pat MacInally, Bill Bradley, and many others have moved quickly into stardom in the pros. It is, of course, difficult to find many young Americans able to carry the heavy load of verbal skills required of students in the Ivy League. Yet athletics are taken seriously in the Ivy League—and on the front page of the New York *Times*—and seem to arouse just as much passion in their fans as in virtually any other schools their size. In the old English upper-class tradition, of course, it is bad form to be *seen* trying too hard. (If you must study late, do it with a flashlight under covers.) Enthusiasm is all right in the free churches; in the cultural traditions of the Ivy League, it is repressed.

The Ivy religion is cool, like a clean white Unitarian church. Its passions are cerebral, like those of Brook Farm, the transcendentalists, and William James. The proper treatment to inflict on the defeated is mock mockery—the waving of white handkerchiefs from Harvard's side to Yalies across the way. The athletic event is put in "proper perspective": an excuse for a date, a drink, a fireplace, a room. It is not the athletic contest that dominates the weekend. As little as possible of life and death are invested in the game, or in anything. Detachment is the central tenet of the Ivy faith.

Moreover, the *true* life-or-death conflict in the Ivy schools is the grade point. It is, of course, bad form to wish too earnestly for an athletic team to be number one in the Ivy League or in the nation (God forbid!). It is also bad form *not* to be, perennially, as near to the top of the class as possible, *not* to be accepted in the best graduate schools, *not* to be offered the most prestigious job opportunities after graduation. True faith requires, not disbelief in the competition to be number one, but disbelief in the view that athletics is the chief avenue of competition. The Ivy League is the only league in the country in which acceptance of a professional athletic contract is silently regarded as a step *down* in social power. The scholars of the Ivy League have rarely been astute commentators on the mythic life. Cold analysis is their speciality. Power, not sports, is their religion.

In the Ivy League, a truly superb football game has the added excitement of participation in an almost forbidden passion. One should not care; one really *ought* to be above winning or losing; a truly incompetent performance by the athletes of both teams would give reassurance that one's own kind of people really aren't very good as jocks. The Ivy League style was once devoutly Puritan, and now is devoutly given to detachment. Yet every creed has its forbidden pleasures. At Harvard, Yale, Cornell, Princeton, and the rest, it is sinful to care. Nowhere else is secret caring more delicious.

The beating of the Crimson's drums outside my window on an October afternoon, as the band marched in maroon jackets and dark pants (none of those Midwestern braids or high bobbing caps), reminded me with pleasurable surprise during each year of my years of graduate school that the world was still alive. I wanted to see Harvard *cream* Yale. This secret feeling tasted almost as sweet as sin. "A sign of lower-class origins," one Professor clucked at me when he caught me waiting for a meeting with my *Times* open to the sports page.

Nevertheless, when Harvard twice in a row surprised supposedly superior Yale in the last minute—in true Frank Merriwell finishes (Merriwell having been a Yalie)—it is difficult to believe that in at least 10,000 sinful hearts a little lust for victory did not slyly creep. If Hester Prynne could not resist adultery, can all of Harvard have resisted secret consent to the delights of total triumph? I have played squash with Harvard men, and watched others, even in their fifties, playing tennis; believe me, they will *kill* opponents as pleasurably as any monster man of Michigan's front four. Being number one is the deepest of the Ivy League traditions, which other athletes imitate only from afar.

EDWIN H. CADY

Pop Art and the American Dream

But no matter what Huizinga and all his followers declare, I cannot feel, cannot intellectually perceive, that the Big Game really is religious. I think I do not believe in the real existence of what is sometimes called "the secular religion." The Big Game is not in fact sacramental. It only feels that way at some of its highest moments—as every successful art does. It is not at last even "ritual" in a final sense—only, in the pop phrase which catches the situation just right, "sort of" ritual. It is, simply, one of the best, most potent popular art forms.

The best party in American life, the Big Game enacts itself as the most vitally folkloristic event in our culture. Nothing about it, then, seems more extraordinary than the fact that it is also an academic festival, organic to institutions of higher education and learning. It expresses their character and the qualities of their accumulated experience. Perhaps sharing in the lives of colleges and universities permits the people who celebrate it to feel free, licensed, protected. The Big Game is franchised by its place near the heart of alma mater. Who will condemn it? Who would reduce it by hostile analysis to dead components? Only perhaps that fraction of the faculties who happen to hate it. Some of them also despise modern, postindustrial culture for having cut its roots to myth, the rituals of earth's rhythms, the naturalness of the folk. Might it be true that, while folkloristic ways celebrate themselves, alive and well in the stadium, some of the faculty sit sequestered in their library carrels, weeping anew the century-old tears of William Morris?

At what point of complexity organized human behavior crosses the line between "primitive culture" and "civilization"—like ours—it is fortunately no part of my responsibility to define. But it would seem to me that in a brilliant essay by Clifford Geertz called "Deep Play: Notes on the Balinese Cockfight" he had crossed the line and provided a drama of insights both bridging our condition with that of the Kurelu or Kwakiutl and indispensably balancing what their "primitive" gambling cultures appear to say. Dominantly, the culture of Bali is Apollonian as can be. Poise and balance, harmony, detachment, and coolness are everything. Yet Balinese men are obsessive breeders, petters, and trainers, experts about, and gamblers upon fighting cocks. Investigating, Geertz found that the fights and betting functioned as "a dramatiza-

From *The Big Game: College Sports and American Life* (1978).

tion of status concerns" central to the culture. "Fighting cocks," the Balinese peasants in sum told Geertz, "is like playing with fire only not getting burned. You activate village and kingroup rivalries and hostilities, but in 'play' form." The theme runs deep in folktale: "Along with everything else that the Balinese see in fighting cocks—themselves, their social order, abstract hatred, masculinity, demonic power—they also see the archetype of status virtue, the arrogant, resolute, humor-mad player with real fire, the Ksatria prince."

Somewhere, then, at the core of that Apollonian culture lies hidden a Kwakiutl with a Dionysian myth celebrated by participant gamblers "allegorically humiliated by one another, day after day." We are dealing, Geertz says, with an art form.

> The cockfight renders ordinary, everyday experience comprehensible by presenting it in terms of acts and objects which have had their practical consequences removed and have been reduced (or, if you prefer, raised) to the level of sheer appearances, where their meaning can be more powerfully articulated and more exactly perceived. The cockfight is "really real" only to the cocks—it does not kill anyone, castrate anyone, reduce anyone to animal status, alter the hierarchical relations among people, nor refashion the hierarchy; it does not even redistribute income in any significant way. What it does is what, for other peoples with other temperaments and other conventions, *Lear* and *Crime and Punishment* do; it catches up these themes—death, masculinity, rage, pride, loss, beneficence, chance—and, ordering them into an encompassing structure, presents them in such a way as to throw into relief a particular view of their essential nature.

Making an important effort to carry esthetic insights into culturally expressive modes, Geertz pointed out that, essentially, what their cockfight presents to the Balinese imagination and sensibility is tragic, "life as the Balinese most do not want it." Using "emotion for cognitive ends," the cockfight talks "in a vocabulary of sentiment—the thrill of risk, the despair of loss, the pleasure of triumph." It provides for the Balinese a "sentimental education" in "what his culture's ethos and his private sensibility (or, anyway, certain aspects of them) look like when spelled out externally in a collective text." Geertz has made a brilliant advance over difficult terrain:

> Every people, the proverb has it, loves its own form of violence. The cockfight is the Balinese reflection on theirs: on its look, its uses, its force, its fascination. . . . If, to quote Northrop Frye again, we go to see *Macbeth* to learn what a man feels like after he has gained a kingdom and

lost his soul, Balinese go to cockfights to find out what a man, usually composed, aloof, almost obsessively self-absorbed, a kind of moral auto-cosm, feels like when, attacked, tormented, challenged, insulted, and driven in result to the extremes of fury, he has totally triumphed or been brought totally low.

The very fact, Geertz concluded, that "the cockfight is not the master key to Balinese life" but only one among many "cultural texts" and not even one pitched in an affirmative key, suggests that a "culture is an ensemble of texts" (dare you say an anthology?) which only "close" and wary reading can make available to the reader. So it is with our Big Game.

Though it is often argued from the example of Shakespeare that high art may be found in undeniably popular culture, popular art tends to make up in breadth for what it lacks in height or depth. Its appeal is actuarial, so to speak; like the true odds in life or fire insurance, it can be relied upon to cover the majority of cases. It is "Coke," not caviar, to the general. Whether its effects resonate or endure is not so important as immediacy. Nevertheless, when there is art in pop it works like the rest of the arts.

Daniel Boorstin includes an interesting analysis of the broad problem in *Democracy and Its Discontents*. Looking to the "distinction between the great tradition and the little tradition, between the high culture and the folk culture," he says, you see odd discontinuities between the European and the American ways of treating them. European custom generalized the folk culture but kept it powerless; it centralized the high culture and associated it with power and privilege. But with us "high culture is one of the least centralized" aspects of the national life. "And our universities express the atomistic, diffused, chaotic, and individualistic aspect." Our popular culture, on the other hand, comes to us from powerfully centralized advertising agencies. Because it is in business, "the advertising folk culture" is subject to constant "self-liquidation and erasure"; it is "discontinuous, ephemeral, and self-destructive"; it "attenuates and is always dissolving before our very eyes."

These truths hold for most pop art and culture but not football and basketball. Though the games change, they neither dissolve nor erase. Their continuities are striking, and Wallace Wade and Clair Bee remain trenchant analysts of sports they have not played nor even coached for decades. The games unfold in patterns of repetition, variation, and novelty rich in fascination. And the Big Game—party within party from the pep rally through the Monday Quarterback Club Luncheon—reveals the Americans, stripped of feasts by modern history, strenuous at reinventing the folk-festive heritage of the human race.

Arguably, there may be a linked progression in which materials, themes, ideas, impulses move from folk art to popular art, thence to public "high" art and in turn to high "private" art—and thence back to folk art again. At the Big Game festivities the folkloristic elements have become pop; perhaps they sometimes wash up the beaches of public "high" art. At any rate, the continuities of tradition and forms in student life and the institutions supportive of the Big Game lend the college festivities immense affective advantage. You have only to contrast the dull pathos of halftime activities at a professional game or the stale, faintly sordid activities of the professional auxiliaries recruited from the night club circuit to lend color and cheer to their sidelines. Without forms or vital tradition, the fan at the pro game remains pathetic even when some promotion makes him seem creative. An Associated Press story in 1975 tells it all: "A new fad is sweeping through Baltimore. . . . Thousands of kazoos will toot the Colt fight song when Baltimore takes on the Miami Dolphins Sunday." The mass fad was started by "Hymie the Kazoo Guru," said the account, and "Hymie estimates more than 1,500 kazoos are in circulation for Sunday's game." Fifteen hundred?

On the other hand, the vitality and color of the Big Game are such that everybody wants a piece of that action. Though it can and does profit from shrewd promotion, it is so far from being a creature of the advertising industry that the industry is always alert and vigorous to hook on to Big Game popular momentum. Promoters and politicians tirelessly angle to get the band, get a picture with the quarterback or the coach, use the stadium or arena for a backdrop. Whole media professions live on it.

No small part of the common academic rejection of the Big Game stems from an understandable rejection of its emotional prominence. It takes its rise from resentment of the festival, the party, and can reflect feelings like those Macaulay named when he said that the Puritans abolished bear-baiting in England not because it gave pain to the bear but because it gave pleasure to the spectators. Another fount of resentment is the applause, the attention, that communal and public enthusiasm which indeed create the Big Game. The difficulty is not unreal, as a master of the violin told me once:

"I find myself really concerned," he said, "about something which is both wrong and right. I can't help it. I never had to worry about it before I joined the University. And it upsets me."

"What do you mean?"

"It's the applause at concerts. I look out at the audience, and there sit Roe, who won a Nobel Prize, and Doe who wrote the best book in his field. I'm surrounded by first-class minds and very gifted people who work hard at really important things, and nobody ever claps for them. And I come out and play a little music and there are storms of applause every time. It's not right."

And so, comparatively, it is not. In the best of all possible worlds the emotional, psychic support of applause, cheers, festival would uplift intellectual achievement even more powerfully than it rewards acting or music or athletic success. But it does not, partly because the natures of the cases differ so radically: the musician plays to a rapt and ardent community what the composer imagined in a loneliness which only fortitude prevented from crushing him. Nothing is more competitive than intellectual work. You fight the self with all its defects and limitations. You fight the discipline, with all its accumulations of genius, famous or forgotten. You fight the other practitioners, to get ahead and beat them out, to impress them and force not only them but their and your successors to dance a measure to your tune. No good professor dare think himself not a competitor, not a gambler. It is hazardous duty, and you have to risk laying yourself on the line and risk humiliation, even crippling injury to those most precious powers of spirit and ego which must be spent in the service of creativity.

And you have to know that in the common life nobody will care. Personally I cannot believe that these facts of life are tragic. But if they were, why not take the loss with good grace? As Loren Eiseley says of man's fate as all our past reveals it, the best response is to know and accept it. "Only so can we learn our limitations and come in time to suffer life with compassion."

Why might the professors not much better settle gladly for the community available to them in academe, with all its constituencies? Should they think to look, they would find them, communally festive, at the Big Game as nowhere else.

Not to repeat what the cultural anthropologists say, a chorus of impressive voices joins in what really are our times to urge us toward community. Democracy, says Boorstin, "depends on the communication which is sharing, not on that which is purely self-expressive, explosive, or vituperative." Aidan Kavanaugh, Professor of Liturgics at Yale, sets as one of the footings for a strong essay the point that "a people whose festivals atrophy will not long remain a people, much less a culture." And Beisser, in his sober but incisive way, sums them up. "The masses of Americans" in the stands or on the fields or floors of sport are not to be thought psychiatrically disordered. On the contrary, they are engaged in "performing rituals which in every respect constitute an integral part of American life and are in no way deviant. In fact, . . . one might conclude that the non-participant in sports is more likely to be disordered than is the participant." Analysis of "life processes," he continues, has often fatally changed them; and it has killed most of the festivals on which our culture once depended, leaving the skulls to be inhabited by advertising.

For whatever reasons, Beisser concludes, cultural vitality survives in athletics: "Sports events . . . have defied analysis and have retained the appeal of excitement and commitment formerly associated with holiday rituals. The magnitude of sports interest has grown in proportion to the loss of involvement by Americans in other rituals." He hopes, as a last word, that "America's intense interest in games may . . . represent a transition from the vestiges of the past to the birth of a new vitality." Academe need not raise its sights to levels at which the fate of nations is decided to see that the virtues of identity, loyalty, and communitas available in the Big Game ought to be cherished. The advantages of "exposure" and identification from the academic community to the populace at large ought to be exploited, if only for the good of all those, from freshmen to distinguished professors, for whom no applause will ever ring out.

Games might even be thought the true business of the university. And what is there in a democratic culture which might arrogate to itself the condemnation of mass dreams and of those dreams which connect the professional and apprentice professional dreamers to the common? The realities of the situation have turned the seeking mind not back but beneath the crust of fatal appearances toward the sources of human vitality. With something like a practical infinity of resounding titles, prerational and extrarational ways of thinking have become "intellectually" popular in the academy. Though definitionally elusive, they provide instruments for locating and explaining ranges of human experience not available to other means. What is centrally human but rationally inexplicable demands to be studied with postrational as well as rational tools. How striking that, emerging through the debris on the other side of "analysis," the almost necessarily nonreligious psychiatrists and ethnologists should find themselves nearly at one with, for instance, Roman Catholic scholars like Kavanaugh.

> Of all the American games that small boys play and adults take seriously, football has been the most heavily romanticized in print. There is always the suspicion that this is because no one—except coaches, scouts and intellectually gifted players—really understands the game; that those who write about it are forced to lean on fancy rather than fact. But granted the complexities of modern football and the average person's inability to understand them, there is much in the nature of the game that has a distinctly romantic appeal.

So says Jack Newcombe in the best of football anthologies. Take "in print" from that first sentence and it covers most photography, painting, printmaking, and sculpture concerned with football, leaving only the cartoon.

And football cartooning, mostly devoted to satire on romantic themes, presents only the other side of the one coin. Basketball, too, like football, is "heavily romanticized."

On the other hand, people will insist on taking popular culture into their own hands, letting one man's lie be another man's authentic experience and leaving the recorder of folly to shake his puzzled head. Back to culture theory and its new frontier where ethnology and esthetics, as in Clifford Geertz, interface. Where Geertz found illumination in the esthetic ideas of Northrop Frye, a different light dawned on Gertrude Jaeger and Philip Selznick. Working the standard line from the ethnography of Emil Durkheim to the philosophy of Emil Cassirer and the esthetics of Susanne Langer, they arrived at a definition: "Culture consists of everything that is produced by, and is capable of sustaining, shared experience." Then they turned to the ideas of an esthetician of another stripe: John Dewey.

Dewey's point, American as can be, speaks from his title, *Art As Experience*. He erased the lines between "art" and "life," between "high" and "popular" culture, asking of them all only one question: how authentic is the experience it arouses in persons, whether taken individually or in groups? He thought common experience esthetic and esthetic experience common when either was real. He could not be more democratic. Jaeger and Selznick noted that in proportion as culture is authentic and vital, then, it "strains toward the esthetic." Not quarreling in the last analysis with Geertz, that approach through Dewey makes it easy to see how the Big Game is art.

Though all work and no play will indeed make Jack and Jill dull types, the distinction rigidly applied tends to fog in the topic. Sport and play are not "recreation" conducted during "leisure" from "work." All really productive work is play. Persons successful within themselves play at work and play at life. They turn life and work into art by playing at them and winning. Full creativity expresses life, but it achieves, too. Sport is art, as Santayana said (following Friedrich Schiller); and art, as Picasso said, is the lie that tells the truth about life. But it is a prime truism of esthetics that art comes from struggle. Freedom, inspiration, innocence, love and frenzy fight against convention, medium, craft, discipline, and knowledge to produce form. No fight, no art. No victory, no art. But, no victory being perfect, defeat counts too.

A great deal of true and eloquent testimony shows that his game is art and a life of art to the athlete. But, though they would make a shelf of first-rate books, the formal esthetics of the sports themselves have been little treated. Football and basketball in particular cry out for study as American arts. Though any one of those temptations represents another of the books this one cannot be, however, I think it may be necessary in fairness to say something about the esthetic assumptions upon which this book cannot help proceeding.

As applied to any kind of art, the esthetics which make sense to me are transactional. I can understand the human experience of art best as a series of transactions. The first is a deal made inside the artist between his conscious and preconscious minds.

Watching a painter at work one day, I saw that he worked out a powerful design by combining in one perspective three radically different views, photographically impossible, of his big scene. I could understand that, but I wondered,

> "We have traveled hundreds of miles in the landscape and seen thousands of views. How do you know which ones to make a picture of?"
>
> "All I know," he answered, "is that every once in a while I see a picture."

Transactional translation: as an artist of forty years' practice, he had, preconsciously, a reservoir of creative impulse which, not controllably, boiled up like a geyser from the depths with its "vision of a picture." He stoked the geyser, so to speak, with incessant stimulation from his trained eye and appreciating mind. But when the impulse rose, the process became reversed. Now his powers, long trained, to capture and fix and meditate upon his "vision" were tested, especially by the challenge: "Can you make a picture of me?" His power to respond depended on his capacity to transact the necessary subjective business, transferring his vision to a craftsman's conception without losing it. The next transaction would be expressive—getting the vision on paper.

> "How do you know how to start?"
> "I am a professional. But as soon as I make the first dot on the paper a struggle begins among my vision, my power to express it, and the laws of art."

Transactionally, all of this went into the production of the work of art. The art experience, which is not at all the experience of the artist in producing the work, can only be a transaction, or a series of transactions, between the work of art, the object, and its consumer—be he hearer, viewer, reader, receiver, or whatnot, alone or in a group. Art happens to consumers as experience. It takes place, transactionally, in the imagination of the consumer. Only through the object can the artist communicate to his audience, and the object is what the audience can know esthetically about the artist. All the rest, I am convinced, is folly.

A sports contest provides an unrivaled analog by which to understand all this. To take an example that really happened. I sat at one of the most hotly contested and beautifully realized games I ever saw alongside a man who, as it unfolded, forgot himself and began to root wholeheartedly for the other team. By that I mean that he had come, as usual, to his seat in a section of fervent home team supporters and found himself swept away by the game into unabashed support for the visitors. Perhaps he was a recent graduate of Red Raider U, who had become a graduate student at Siwash. It became a basketball game where Siwash could not stop the Red Raiders inside but the Raiders could do nothing with the brilliant outside shooting of the Siwash guards, particularly one who sank long swisher after heart-stopping bomb, shattering scoring records. Basket matched basket for forty minutes to a tie, and then through one overtime period after another. My neighbor shouted himself hoarse and limp.

Then came the closing second of the fifth overtime, score tied, and one more of those long shots arching through the air as the buzzer sounded. It is worth remarking that until that point my friend (as by then he was) and I had witnessed exactly the same events, seen the same object. Indeed, everything about the situation depended on the events, however controlled by rule and artifice, being objective, the same to us both. And that ball in the air must either, with entire objectivity and as the same event to us both, swish through the cords or not.

It swished. Were our experiences, his and mine, the same? In a sense not in the least. Mine were victorious, ecstatic. His were defeated, frustrated. But the events were exactly the same. What determined the experiences? Orientation, preparation, commitment—many things, but the chief was imagination. The experience was, as Emily Dickinson said of art, "internal difference, / Where the Meanings, are. . . ."

But in another sense the experiences were deeply the same. They rose from the same events, the same frame and form of things, the same assumptions, the same perceptions and preparations. Winning and losing are really only, esthetically, the inevitable outcomes of the one art. And that is one reason the game is only to the player as the poem to the poet. Neither poet nor player is a consumer, and the consumer need never bother to ask either "What is it like?" Let the player live his own life and we ours. Youth's a stuff will not endure. He will join us in the stands soon enough.

The commerce between the player and the game is one thing, belonging to the athlete as person—of whom more later. But the commerce between the game and the congregation, the audience, the constituencies, the fans, is something else and the heart of the matter. Like most performances of music, drama, dance, the Big Game exists only while it is being played to and within its beholders. As art experience it happens "of within" individuals; but the crowd at an artistically successful game achieves a collective life, too. Its responses can be awesome. Ohio Stadium at Columbus talks back to the game like a great, gruff beast. I heard Texas Stadium turn a game around with one long, disgusted growl at what it thought a cheap shot, lifting Texas and depressing the other team visibly, decisively. The great team games are, then, instant and collective art forms. Hence they are, though Walt Whitman never saw one, ideally Whitmanian—democratic, organic.

They are in type arts of time. Along with the aforementioned audience arts, reading is a different art of time; and it can be argued that the demands of perception, moving from one point of view to another, burning up the energy you have available for concentration and realization, turn painting, sculpture, and architecture into arts of time for the consumer.

The time of play for the game itself and the time during which the fans participate, are "in the game," will vary both as to clock time and the intensities of internal response which often carry players in their way and spectators in theirs into ecstatic orbits where time almost has a stop, elongates blissfully. In any case a most important factor is flow. Dancelike the figures flow on the field or floor, weaving their patterns. Symphonically the progressions of play flow, back and forth, in and out, up and down, punctuated by the clock and scoreboard. Dramatic suspense builds as skill and fortune flow to and fro. The forms of fortune which will become, altogether, the ultimate shape of the game flow into architectonics.

Because all seems freedom, choice, and chance, limits mean everything. No bounds of space or play or time, no game. Plan and training, character and giftedness, devotion, discipline, sacrifice, all flow into equations of tension. And then chance takes a hand. "A football is an oblate spheroid. It takes funny bounces." And who has not seen a basketball balance delicately, impossibly on the rim, rotating gently or dead still, seeming to meditate whether it will lazily roll left to victory or right to defeat? Extemporization can become so decisive and so beautiful in the Big Game that you can understand what Lukas Foss is getting at in music.

The arts of time are like a fire, which is a process, not a substance, but achieves substantial results for good or ill. When it is over the fire is out, dead and gone. It leaves the lovers, vows consummated, abed, or the beans baked on the hearth. Or the pride of the House of Priam dead in the ashes of Troy. So with music or dance or the Big Game. When they are all over they leave behind only the experience, which is what we have made of them but can not get any other way. The theme's intrinsically human. As old as poetry, it asks,

"*Ubi Sunt?*" Where are they—the snows of yesteryear? the flowers of spring? the golden lads and lasses? Gone to dust.

The wisdom of the human ages has been that the one thing you can do about that is to shine where your candle is lighted. If the theme is transience, life, as Robinson Jeffers wrote, nevertheless "is good, be it stubbornly long or suddenly / A mortal splendor: meteors are not needed less than / mountains." One way to make meteors is in the brief glory of a human performance that burns incandescent, transcendent, and is over forever—in the dance, the song, the play, the game, the festival—in human life. The wisdom of the game is at once the wisdom of the body and of Ecclesiastes, the sage of this present world, mind, and body. It is also the mystery of humanity: how can mere fragile humankind burn so nobly? die so quickly? A fine Eskimo poet, Orpingalik, got at it exactly for artist, player, and common consumer of life or art:

A wonderful occupation
Hunting caribou!
But all too rarely we
Excel at it
So that we stand
Like a bright flame
Over the plain.

There seems, regrettably, to be no way to escape the ugliness of the language in which esthetics, the theory of beauty, must be discussed. So perhaps it is best to say that, although you can do interesting things with the esthetics of sport by using Aristotle's ideas about imitation and catharsis, the ideas of Susanne Langer about "presentational symbolism" provide a necessary corrective. Her point, which she applies to all art, works beautifully for sport. In brief, it is that the most direct, most powerful, perhaps most original modes of human contact communicate emotion and experience without the use of words. They "present" themselves, nonverbally, not "discursively," requiring only direct apprehension and no translation by sender or receiver. Sports are by nature visible and kinesthetic, at least as immediate and primordial as music.

PETER S. WENZ

Human Equality in Sports

I ssues of social justice are among the most intellectually challenging to both the ethicist and philosopher of law, especially when there appear to be permanent, biologically determined differences of ability and potential among the people and between the groups for whom justice is sought. Such is the case between men and women in the realm of sports. The problem of providing justice in this area has been the topic of popular magazine articles,[1] federal[2] and state[3] legislation, adjudication[4] and philosophical contemplation.[5] But the heart of the matter has yet to be discussed. I will attempt to do this by first reviewing some of the current issues in this area, then exploring the relationship between the use and exchange values of athletic participation, and finally proposing a radical solution which is defended on utilitarian, egalitarian and Rawlsian ethical grounds. The result will be an approach to promoting social justice and equality amongst biologically diverse groups which may be applicable beyond the area of sports.

CONTEMPORARY ISSUES

One of the first issues concerning sex equality in sports was, and still is, monetary. Traditionally, schools have spent much more money on men's than on women's athletic programs. Schools tended to fund a greater number of men's sports in the first place. They also went to the expense of entering more men's than women's teams in interscholastic competition, and gave members of these teams such extra benefits as free laundry service and enlarged coaching staffs. Finally, "men's" sports—those traditionally reserved for male competition, especially football—are the most capital intensive in terms of both the equipment needed to play the game and the facilities needed to accommodate spectator interest. The unsurprising result of these disparities is that women and men were not, and for the most part still are not, afforded equal athletic opportunities at school.

One response to this situation is to attack the monetary issue directly, insist that women's athletic programs be funded at levels equal to men's. But it is unclear what this might mean. If it means that all of the same sports are to be funded for both men and women, and at the same level, there is a prob-

Originally appeared in *The Philosophical Forum* (1981).

lem. One result of sex discrimination in the past is that women have been convinced to take less seriously the desirability and even the possibility of developing their own athletic abilities. One of the worst aspects of social inequality is the internalization of their inferior status on the part of disadvantaged people. The problem this poses for the equal funding of athletics is that there are at present likely to be fewer women than men interested in spending many after-school hours engaged in athletics. So, equal funding of women and men would likely result in greater per capita expenditures for women than men. This may be viewed as unjust.

Also, women and men have been tracked into many different sports, women into field hockey and softball and men into football and baseball, for example. This, too, is most likely reflected in current patterns of participation preferences among men and women so that even if men's and women's programs were funded equally, whether on a per-team or per-capita basis (it's not obvious which it should be), the sports funded would still not be identical. This would cause three difficulties for effecting sex equality in sports. First, the traditionally male sports are more capital intensive, especially when you include the facilities needed to accommodate spectator interest. One might try to circumvent this problem by claiming that because the school stadium is used by women for field hockey as well as by men for football, it is not a football stadium. The capital investment it represents should not, therefore, be attributed to men's as opposed to women's athletics. But this is a sham. The stands could be much smaller and cheaper if designed to accommodate only the number of spectators wanting to see women's field hockey.

The second problem is also a result of disproportionate spectator interest in men's rather than women's athletic competition. If funding is the issue, and that was the issue with which we began, spectator interest in men's athletics can be translated into gate receipts which, it might be argued, could justifiably be spent disproportionately on those sports generating the funds. Rawls's theory of justice might be invoked, improperly I hope later to show, in support of such a position. The disadvantaged—women's field hockey—are treated justly when the advantaged make additional gains, so long as the disadvantaged also gain in the process. So, increased funding of the football program in response to its gate receipts would seem justified, if this was a device used to generate more money for athletics generally, including women's field hockey.

However, further emphasis on traditionally popular men's athletic programs exacerbates the problem of disproportionate spectator interest in men's athletics generally. This is troublesome not only because it allows the gate receipt argument to be used to justify even greater funding for football (a second round of the same reasoning), but also because it reinforces the pressure in our culture for women to discount their athletic abilities. If the rest of society is interested primarily in men's athletics, perhaps women athletes and potential athletes should be also. Thus, the rich get richer and the poor get pom-poms. For this reason, Rawls, who values self-respect preeminently, would probably abjure the view that increased funding of men's sports is justified when some of the increased gate receipts are given to women's athletics.

In sum, fostering sex equality in sports through changed funding patterns is problematic at best. In some cases it is not clear which changes would be just and which unjust. Finally, funding alone cannot address the problems of motivation, self-concept and self-respect among women that are the legacy of past injustices. This is apparent from the fact that equal funding of men's and women's athletic programs is a "separate but equal" position. It is now normally considered unjustified when applied to different races because separate is considered inherently unequal when applied to groups between whom there is a history in the dominant culture of invidious contrast. Because there is just such a history in the dominant culture concerning men and women's athletics, separate athletic programs for men and women might be inherently unequal. This is illustrated concretely and poignantly by cases of women wanting to compete on men's athletic teams for the increased prestige and competition this would allow.[6]

It might appear, then, that altered funding patterns could be supplemented or replaced altogether by the integration of athletics. The difficulty is that for many sports, including most of those popular in the United States, the biological differences between men and women give men a statistical advantage. These sports include strength and speed and often height and weight among the traits helpful for successful competition. Although some women are stronger, faster, taller and heavier than some men, on the average men are stronger, faster, taller and heavier than women. So some proponents of women's athletics fear that sex-integrated athletic programs will result in even fewer women participants and less funding for and concentration upon the development of women athletes.[7]

In short, given all the variables present in the current situation, the optimal course of action is neither obvious nor agreed upon.

USE VALUE AND EXCHANGE VALUE IN SPORTS

One philosophic strategy for approaching such situations is the elaboration of an ideal state of affairs which, were it to be realized, would constitute a solution to the problem. The solution is often ideal in the sense that no one knows how its realization might be effectively promoted; aspects of the society which create the problem in the first place might render impractical even *attempts* to directly effect the ideal's realization. Nevertheless, the ideal has an important function. As various policies which are amenable to practical implementation are reviewed and considered, those which would move the society toward the ideal might be preferred to those with an opposite or neutral tendency.

The ideal in this case can be explained by applying to sports Adam Smith's distinction between value in use and value in exchange.[8] The exchange value of a sport to an individual is the fame and fortune he or she derives from participating in that sport. Such rewards result from, but are extrinsic to the athletic activity in question. The activity itself, the rules in accordance with which it is carried out, the physical qualities and interpersonal cooperation it calls for and so forth, could all be exactly the same whether or not the rewards of fame and fortune are offered for participation. This is because fame and fortune result not from the activity itself, but from the interest others show in one's participation. This interest results in admiration for the participant and a willingness to monetarily compensate him or her for participating. Someone deriving fame and fortune by participating in a sport under these conditions exchanges his or her participation for these other goods. Thus, they constitute the exchange value for that individual of participating in that sport.

The use value of a sport to an individual, by contrast, is the value to that individual which is intrinsic to his or her participation in that sport. It is dependent on the formal rules of the game, the mores in accordance with which it is played, the qualities of physical coordination and interpersonal cooperation it calls for, and its competitive nature. The values resulting from participation normally include development of motor skills and improvement of bodily health, as well as the enhancement of self-esteem which results from overcoming difficulties. In addition, participation can be character building, teaching the individual to accept criticism, be a good winner and a good loser and, in team sports, a cooperative person. Finally, participation can be fun. Because these goods, which constitute the use value of a sport to a given individual, do not depend on rewards offered by others, they are intrinsic rather than extrinsic to the athletic endeavor.

Though there are exceptions, it will be assumed here that the use value of most sports for most people who voluntarily participate in them is positive. Possible exceptions might include an extremely dangerous sport, like hang-gliding, or moto-cross competition for an epileptic. Generally, however, the use value of voluntary participation is positive.

The aggregate use value of a sport is the total use value of that sport to individuals in a society over a given period of time, such as a year. It is the sum of the sport's use values to all individuals in that society who participated

in that sport during that time period. Since the use value of athletics is assumed to be generally positive, the aggregate use value is positively related to
the number of people and the time spent by those people participating in that
sport during that time period.

The aggregate exchange value of a sport is the total fame and fortune accruing to participating individuals due to this participation. It is positively
related to the spectator interest in that sport, because fame and fortune ac-
crue to participants only when others care enough to witness the sport being
played that they offer these rewards to participants.

The relationship between the aggregate use and aggregate exchange values
of a sport, that is, between the population's interest in playing and watching
it, is the topic of the remainder of this section. Generally, people who enjoy
participating in a sport come to enjoy watching others play. Having played
the sport themselves they can empathize, kinesthetically in some cases, with
the players they are watching. Spectators can appreciate, admire and enjoy the
players' skills when they have, by playing the sport themselves, attempted to
develop and exercise those same skills. They can also better understand and
therefore appreciate player strategy and team cooperation if they have played
the sport themselves. For all these reasons, it is more likely that someone
who has played basketball but not hockey will prefer watching basketball to
hockey on television when both are available. Thus, it seems that participation in a sport, its (aggregate) use value in a given population, increases spectator interest and therewith the (aggregate) exchange value of the services of
excellent players.

It is doubtful, however, that watching and playing a sport are mutually supporting. I shall argue in the remainder of the section that whereas playing
increases watching, watching tends to depress rather than increase the level
of participation. I call this the inverse relationship thesis (IRT). Stated fully
the thesis is that, all other things being equal, an increase in the use value of
a sport causes an increase in its exchange value. But its increased exchange
value tends to depress its use value. In this causal direction the use and exchange values are inversely relational. This means that any conditions which
cause an increase in the use value of a sport will cause a greater such increase
if other conditions operate to prevent the exchange value from increasing as
well. More important, it also means that any conditions which cause a decrease in a sport exchange value will, other things being equal, cause an increase in its use value.

This inverse relationship thesis (IRT) is central to the argument of this
paper. Nevertheless, I will not claim to have demonstrated its truth in the
arguments which follow. Considerable investigation by social scientists is required for its refutation or confirmation. I do claim, however, that the argu-

ments which follow in this section make the IRT exceedingly plausible, and that subsequent arguments from it to further conclusions demonstrate its importance to any consideration of equality in sports.

The first argument for the IRT is that watching can serve as a vicarious outlet for urges to participate, thereby dissipating those urges before they can reach the level at which they would be acted upon. Thus, someone who sometimes plays basketball may find it easier to forego playing if he or she can watch others play. This is analogous to the claim made by those who argue against legal restrictions on the availability of pornography for adults. They claim that watching pornography, rather than inciting people to sex crimes, dissipates the urge to commit such crimes, because it affords people vicarious sexual involvement which serves to replace actual involvement. The evidence gathered to support this claim indirectly favors the view that watching a sport decreases the level of participation.

The same view is supported by a very different consideration. The exchange value of an individual's athletic endeavors is generally directly related to his or her level of proficiency. The function is not linear, of course, but it is generally true that the exchange value increases with proficiency. A society in which the exchange value of participation for those who are proficient is very high is a society in which there is greater spectator interest in that sport. It is also one in which the level of proficiency that becomes normative is very high. As people increasingly watch something done with great proficiency, they tend to think it normal that the activity in question be carried on at that level of proficiency. But as the normative level of proficiency increases beyond what most people are capable of attaining, people are discouraged from participating. Lacking respect for the level of their own attainment, participation is ego-damaging. Conversely, as the norms of proficiency are increasingly established by an individual for himself or herself, or by that individual's peers, participation is encouraged and can be expected to increase. Thus, the exchange value of participating in a given sport in a given society probably varies inversely with its use value.

Another consideration is that as the exchange value, and so the level of spectator interest in a sport increases, the organization of participation in that sport tends to become increasingly institutionalized. The reason for this is not hard to find. Spectator interest can be translated into a market demand. In a profit-minded society, people tend to organize themselves and others so as to meet the market demand and gain monetary rewards. What is more, the institutional organization of the sport does not stay at the professional level. It is replicated at lower levels. Professional baseball results ultimately in Little League. Football and basketball are played interscholastically in organized leagues at the grade school level.

It might seem that such organization and institutionalization of a sport might increase its aggregate use value in society as schools and other organizations prompt children to join athletic institutions (organized teams and leagues). The predominant tendency, however, is probably just the opposite. Institutionalized sports notoriously discriminate in favor of the most athletically talented individuals. Development of skills of the less talented is often ignored. The norms of performance of the more talented become normative for the group as a whole, with the consequence that the less talented are not only ignored but dispirited. The net effect of the institutionalization of sports that results from emphasis on its exchange value is therefore predominantly to discourage rather than encourage widespread participation, to decrease rather than increase its aggregate use value in society.

In sum, three reasons have been advanced to support the inverse relationship thesis, the contention that the aggregate use value of a sport ordinarily decreases with an increase in its aggregate exchange value. (1) Watching a sport can serve as a vicarious outlet which dissipates urges to participate. (2) The norms of excellence increase with a sport's exchange value, discouraging the participation of the less talented. And, (3) as the exchange value increases the sport is increasingly institutionalized, which also puts a premium on talent and discourages the participation of others.

Some examples may be helpful at this point. It is commonly thought, and I have no reason to doubt, that a larger percentage of the American population played baseball in the earlier part of the century than at present. Its professionalization and institutionalization have increased its aggregate exchange value while decreasing its aggregate use value. Jogging, by contrast, is not very institutionalized and has very little exchange value at present. It is not much of a spectator sport. People set norms of proficiency for themselves and engage in the activity informally. Its exchange value is low and its use value high. It is what might be called a folk-sport.

Sports that might seem to constitute counter-examples are golf and tennis. Their use and exchange values have increased simultaneously in recent years, in direct rather than inverse relation to one another. These are sports in which participation is found particularly enjoyable by a large percentage of the people in our culture who are introduced to them. But until recently participation in them was reserved for the relatively wealthy primarily because of the expense, much as is still the case with equestrian events. A major proximate cause of their increased use value, I submit, has been the decreased expense of participating in them.

Since World War II, the percentage of the average family's income spent on food and housing has declined somewhat, leaving more disposable income for recreation of all sorts. More important, the expansion of the public sector beginning with the New Deal has manifested itself in public works projects which include public recreation facilities, among them tennis courts and golf courses. People are paying for these facilities with their taxes, diminishing considerably the differential cost of participation versus non-participation. In addition, tennis was first played on grass, which is very difficult to maintain at the required quality level, then on clay, which also requires considerable maintenance. Now, most people play on asphalt, which is much cheaper to maintain. The developing technology of lawn care has made golf course maintenance less expensive also, though the change is less dramatic here. Those developments, I believe, are primarily responsible for the increased use value of golf and tennis. The availability of tennis and golf as spectator sports, especially on television, is a consequence, not a cause of their increased use value. This is consistent with the IRT.

To see this, let us conduct a thought experiment. Imagine a dramatic increase of television time devoted to equestrian events. If the cost of participating remained about the same, so, I believe, would participation. Now imagine instead a dramatic decrease in that cost. Participation would increase dramatically even in the absence of increased television coverage. Then, of course, responding to increased participation, television coverage would follow suit. This kind of media response is currently occurring in the case of racquet ball. In sum, just as media coverage would not be necessary for people to increase their participation in equestrian events were their expense dramatically reduced, so media coverage was not necessary for the increased use values of tennis and golf.

Finally, consider the case of soccer. It is not a folk-sport in this country, so its use value is so low that its professionalization and institutionalization can increase that value. (Goodness knows why this is happening. Perhaps it is spurred on by the same folks who want us to think metric, namely, multinational corporations. I suppose they want us to play soccer so that everyone will be able to get along at international-employee picnics. These are only conjectures, of course.) The point is that the use value of sports is great only in folk-sports anyway. Institutionalization holds the level of participation in any sport below that of a folk-sport. So high use value cannot be attained through institutionalization. High use value in a sport occurs only when the culture is allowed to take up its own folk-sports, spurred on by the usual forces involved in cultural evolution. In our country this does involve commercialism, and producers of jogging shoes and racquet ball racquets have been doing an excellent job of late.

I hope at this point to have made the IRT very plausible. The important part of the thesis is that, other things being equal, a decrease in exchange value will *ordinarily* cause an increase in use value. The qualification "ordinarily" is included because absolute universality is not essential. Only the strong predominance of the tendency for decreased exchange values to increase use values is necessary. The usefulness of the IRT for subsequent arguments will not be diminished if an exceptional sport is found not to conform to it. Having made the qualification, I will neglect its reiteration.

ETHICAL ARGUMENTS

Because the exchange value of athletic participation includes esteem from others, it can probably never be reduced to zero. Nor would it be desirable to do so. I will argue, however, that eliminating the *major* source of exchange value, financial rewards for athletic participation, is desirable. What is more, the desirability can be deduced from egalitarianism, John Rawls's theory of justice and the most popular forms of utilitarianism when they are combined with the IRT.

Consider first the ethical view that average utility ought to be maximized. Imagine a society in which, like our own at this time, the monetary aspect of the exchange value of athletic participation is very great for the exceptionally gifted athlete. Because those who reap these scarce benefits are very few, a matter of thousands in a society of millions, these benefits do not constitute much of the utility in the society as a whole. This is especially the case because those exchanging their participation in athletics for really large monetary rewards constitute only a small fraction of those thousands receiving any monetary rewards at all. Consequently, the loss of this aspect of the exchange value of sports in society would, taken by itself, have a minute effect upon the average level of utility in the society as a whole. More important from the perspective of average utility would be the effect on spectators. People are spectators, presumably, because they enjoy watching sports. If people are prevented from reaping monetary rewards from athletic participation, it would seem that there would be less athletic competition for would-be spectators to watch, hence a considerable drop in average utility.

If the exchange and use values of athletic participation are inversely related, however, such a drop in average utility would almost surely not occur. The general level of proficiency among athletes whose play is being watched would, on the whole, be drastically reduced. But it is not at all clear that one's enjoyment as a spectator is primarily or even very largely a function of the level of proficiency of the athletes being watched. A close contest, personal acquaintance with the contestants and personal presence at the site of competition are each as significant a determinant of spectator enjoyment as is the level of the contestants' proficiency. And two of these would be increased, for those who chose to be spectators, if athletes were not paid for their participation. By drastically reducing the exchange value of sports, the use value would be greatly increased. This means that many more people would be playing more of the time in more locations. Those who chose to be spectators would more often be able to witness athletic events in person because such events would more often be taking place nearby and the cost of admission would be little (to cover maintenance of the grounds, for example) if anything. And since more people would be participating in athletics, it would more often be possible to view contests among people with whom the spectator is personally acquainted. So there is no reason to suppose that the enjoyment of those who chose to be spectators would be diminished if athletes were not paid.

It is the aggregate of spectator enjoyment which would be reduced, not the average. It would be reduced because fewer people would be spectators as more, if use value is inversely related to exchange value, voluntarily eschew watching in favor of participating. But if, as I have argued, sporting events would be as available and enjoyable for spectators as at present, the predominance of participation would signal that people gain even more enjoyment from participation. This would represent a broad based net gain in utility that would, because it affects so many people, have a greater effect on average utility than all of the preceding considerations.

In sum, the loss of utility to professional athletes would be more than compensated for by the gain in utility on the part of the large proportion of the population who would voluntarily exchange watching for participating.[9] Those who continued to watch would at worst be affected neutrally. So, if the inverse proportionality thesis is correct, the proponent of maximizing average utility should adopt the ideal of a society in which athletes are debarred from being paid for their athletic participation.

Those who, like Richard Brandt and Nicholas Rescher, believe that utilitarian considerations should be combined with egalitarian considerations have a stronger reason for reaching the same conclusion. For this is a case in which utility and equality go hand-in-hand. The gain in utility is broad-based. It accrues to the large number of people who voluntarily exchange watching for participating. The loss in utility, besides being smaller than the gain, includes the loss to those making substantial sums from their athletic participation. There is thus a leveling effect. The relative have-nots gain and the haves lose.

Rawls has an even stronger reason for adopting the ideal of a society in which athletics is de-professionalized. An example will make this clear. Rawls is interested in maximizing the level of welfare of the representative individual from society's least advantaged group. Welfare is gauged in terms of what he calls primary goods, wealth, power, liberty and, importantly, self-respect. Suppose, then, that we group people by sex. (We could get the same results grouping people by age, size or weight.) Suppose, further, that the aggregate of use value and of exchange value accruing to women from sports is less than the corresponding values accruing to men. Finally, suppose that the exchange value of athletic participation for exceptionally gifted individuals in the society is great. These suggestions probably accord well with the actual situation in our society at this time. But this is not essential since the same conclusion can be drawn from plausible alternate assumptions.

On these suppositions women are the worse off group. De-professionalizing sports would result in a greater loss of wealth to men than to women because men have more to lose. But if the inverse relationship thesis, and the accompanying utilitarian calculations presented above are correct, utility would be increased by de-professionalization, even for men. The loss to male professional athletes would be more than compensated for by the gain to many more other men in terms of the use value of sports. Rawls's particular emphasis on the primary good of self-respect and his employment of what he calls the Aristotelian Principle both serve to strengthen this conclusion. For the loss among men would be primarily financial, whereas the gain would be, through greater athletic participation, in the realms of self-confidence and self-respect, as these come, in accordance with the Aristotelian Principle, from progressive mastery of skills and development of talents.

A *fortiori*, the position of women would be improved by the de-professionalization of athletics. They have less to lose financially and more to gain in terms of self-confidence and self-respect. So if Rawls advocates maximizing primary values among the most deprived group, and women are the most deprived group (when we group by sex), then he should advocate the de-professionalization of athletics.

The same conclusion would follow were the aggregate exchange value of women's athletic participation equal to that of men. In such a case women would have as much to lose financially as men from de-professionalization. But they would still have more to gain than men in terms of the self-respect that comes from the use value of sports. And even men gain more than they lose by de-professionalization. So women would still be the most deprived group whose accumulation of primary goods would be maximized by banning financial rewards for athletic participation. Like men, they would gain more in self-respect than they lost financially. Such a ban would, therefore, still follow from Rawls's theory when combined with the inverse relationship thesis.

CONCLUSION

In sum, if the inverse relationship thesis is correct, the de-professionalization of sports is ethically mandatory from the utilitarian, egalitarian and Rawlsian ethical perspectives. Two conclusions follow from this. First, empirical, social scientific research designed to test the IRT is in order. Second, if the IRT is correct, sex equality in sports is a by-product of and impossible without the more general human equality in sports that results from an emphasis on use over exchange values. This prompts, without in any way confirming, the following conjectural generalization concerning social equality between members of groups which are, as groups, biologically unequal. The equality of the groups can be approached only as a general egalitarianism among individuals, taken as individuals, is approached through a concentration on use rather than exchange values.

ADDENDUM—THE FINE ARTS OBJECTION

In my discussions with colleagues and students, one objection to the ideas in this paper recurs. There is also a common misunderstanding. I will deal first with the misunderstanding, and then with the objection.

Many people have supposed that if professionalism in sports is disallowed, there could be no professional *teachers* of sports. This is not what I mean, and does not follow from the reasoning that I present in the paper. De-professionalizing sports, as I understand it, involves disallowing anyone from accepting money for his or her participation as a *player* or *contestant*. It does not disallow payment for providing instruction in sports. For example, teachers may still be paid for providing instruction in physical education. Professional instruction in sports, as in other areas, like reading, writing, arithmetic and the fine arts, can broaden participation and improve not only the quality of performance, but also the quality of experience of participation. Aggregate use value is thus increased. If the instruction is inexpensive and widely available, the increase in use value will satisfy egalitarian and Rawlsian, as well as utilitarian principles. So the argument in the paper does not imply that *instruction* in sports, or in any other area, should be de-professionalized.

Now for the objection. It is objected that if it is ethically mandatory that sports be de-professionalized, the same should follow for the fine arts. The objector maintains that painters, sculptors, singers, actors and other practitioners of the fine arts should be debarred from receiving payment for the practice of their art. As in the case of sports, de-professionalization would result in a steep decline in the quality of performance. Are we really willing, the objector asks, to have the quality of our fine arts decline precipitously? The objector believes that we should not be willing to experience such a decline. Thus, de-professionalization in the arts is unacceptable. This casts doubt upon the cogency of any reasoning that leads to the view that such de-professionalization is ethically mandatory. The reasoning that leads to the view that *sports* should be de-professionalized is problematic, because it is the same reasoning that is used to show that the arts should be de-professionalized. If the reasoning is suspect when applied to the arts, it is suspect when applied to sports.

The reply to this objection is that sports and fine arts are so fundamentally different from one another that the argument about sports does not suggest that the fine arts be de-professionalized. The arts, unlike sports, are attempts to examine, illustrate and illuminate various aspects of the human condition. They attempt to foster individual and social self-understanding. The quality of fine arts productions are therefore of great importance. A general lowering of quality in the fine arts could easily impede self-understanding and promote alienation on the part of all concerned, artists and non-artists alike. In sum, unlike sports, the benefit that spectators derive from the arts is crucially affected by the quality of the artists' products. If, as seems likely, disallowing payment for such products were to depress their quality (even when professional instruction is allowed) the loss to society would be great. Assuming that this loss would outweigh any gains from de-professionalization, such as increased numbers of participants in the arts, de-professionalization does not satisfy the utilitarian criterion of maximizing the good. If access to the products of professional artists is widespread, there would be no egalitarian or Rawlsian objections to professionalism in the fine arts. In fact, Rawls's view suggests that people with talent in the fine arts be encouraged by the promise of personal reward to develop and employ their talents fully. Everyone, including those who are least well-off, can benefit from the esthetic experience and improved self-understanding that artists make possible.

The argument against professionalism in sports is, therefore, not open to the objection that it leads to the unacceptable conclusion that the fine arts, too, should be de-professionalized.

NOTES

1. Rose De Wolf, "The Battle for Good Teams," *Women Sports* 1 (July 1974), pp. 61–63; in *Sex Equality* ed. Jane English (Prentice-Hall, 1977), pp. 231–238. Ellen Weber, "Boys and Girls Together: The Coed Team Controversy," *Women Sports* 1 (September, 1974), pp. 53–55. Brenda Fasteau, "Giving Women a Sporting Chance," *Ms. Maga-*

zine, July, 1973. Ann Crittenden Scott, "Closing the Muscle Gap," Ms. Magazine, September, 1974, pp. 49–55, 89. Mariann Pogge, "From Cheerleader to Competitor," Update, Fall, 1978, pp. 15–18.

2. Title IX of the 1964 Civil Rights Act as amended 42 U.S.

3. Michigan, Connecticut, New Jersey, Indiana, Minnesota and Nebraska have statutes providing for the integration of non-contact sports at the high school level.

4. Hollander v. Connecticut Interstate Athletic Conference, Superior Court of New Haven Co., Conn., March 29, 1971. Haas v. South Bend Community School Corp., 289 N.E. 2d 495 (Ind. 1972). Bucha v. Illinois High School Association, 351 F. Supp. 69 (N.D. Ill. 1972). N.O.W. Essex County Chapter v. Little League Baseball, 127 N.J. Superior, 22, 318A. 2d, 33 (1974).

5. Jane English, "Sex Equality in Sports," Philosophy and Public Affairs 8 (Spring, 1978).

6. De Wolf, pp. 232 ff.

7. De Wolf, p. 235.

8. This is similar but not identical to Jane English's distinction between the basic and scarce benefits of sports.

9. More remote effects can be ignored because they are so problematic and might, for that reason, as likely favor one side as another. Also, those which can be counted on, like the losses to promoters of professional athletics, lawyers for professional athletes and others dependent on professional athletics for a living, will largely be matched by gains for those who produce the athletic equipment used by increasing numbers of participants.

A Guide for Further Study

A long with Novak and Cady, a vast number of writers have addressed the issue of sport and community. Among the most insightful and provocative are Richard Lipsky, How We Play the Game: Why Sports Dominate American Life; Jerry Izenberg, How Many Miles to Camelot: The All-American Sport Myth; Neil D. Isaacs, Jock Culture, U.S.A.; Don Atyeo, Blood & Guts: Violence in Sports; and Dan Jenkins, Saturday's America. From a Marxist point of view, see Paul Hoch, Rip Off The Big Game. And predominantly from a historian's perspective, see Johan Huizinga's classic study, Homo Ludens: A Study of the Play Element in Culture. Soccer Madness by Janet Lever analyzes the sport and its effect on Brazil's society, yielding a fascinating study of people and culture in the twentieth century—the Age of Sport.

Part II:

Sport and Society

Introduction

WHEN THE GOING GETS TOUGH, THE TOUGH GET GOING.
WINNERS NEVER QUIT; QUITTERS NEVER WIN.
WHAT HAVE YOU DONE TODAY FOR YOUR TEAM, YOUR COUNTRY,
   AND YOUR GOD?

Slogans like these, pinned to the bulletin boards of America's dressing rooms, assume as a self-evident truth that a nation's sports and its deepest beliefs about itself complement and reinforce one another. Part II: Sport and Society explores the notion that football and baseball mirror everyday American life and our country's living social mythology. In the following readings, great diversity of both approach and perspective characterizes the exploration.

As he details the exploits of Dallas players on their day off, Peter Gent clearly reveals his conviction that the NFL and American life are one and the same. The topics offered in the excerpt from "Monday," the opening chapter of *North Dallas Forty*, to support Gent's contention spread like one of O. W. Meadows' shotgun shells used in the drunken indiscriminate killing of the opening dove hunt sequence: personal and political violence, drug abuse, traffic madness, phony religious piety, bigotry and intolerance, alienation, aimlessness, sexual exploitation—you name it. In Gent's vision, America in the late Sixties has become simply a psychotic wasteland for which pro football is the perfect metaphor. While pro football styles itself as an incorruptible moral island that reflects the best in the American character, Phil Elliott experiences the Dallas franchise as just another military-industrial complex, the players merely equipment.

In contrast to Gent's graphic indictment of warped values, Alex Michalos offers up an argument that football can transcend American life in "The Unreality and Moral Superiority of Football." This piece tries to establish that football qualifies as *play* because it is unlike our daily routines, or distinctly better from a moral point of view, in five important respects. The distinguishing features are: that football gives the other team a chance to score when it is behind (a principle of fairness is built into the game); that it is not a game of territorial acquisition; that the game is played in the open for everyone to see and judge (a principle of non-concealment or openness); that money does not give an advantage in football; and that you can't fake it in football (a non-feigning activity)—sooner or later you've got to *do* something.

John McMurtry—pro-football player turned philosopher—counters in his essay, showing that the reasons Michalos offers are not good ones for believing that football is above life. For McMurtry, football is "not just a reflection of our society's capitalist order, but . . . is a re-enforcer of this order." Society's ills and perversions are causally enhanced (and celebrated) by the game. McMurtry sees what Gent sees.

Millions assent to the proposition that American mythology—the stories, ideas, and values that explain us to ourselves—can be discerned with crystal clarity in American sport. This proposition comes under review in Section II: Sport and Social Myths. The very title of Gerald Ford's "In Defense of the Competitive Urge" encodes his premise: sport builds those peculiarly American qualities of character that made us great and will keep us great in perpetuity. Using himself as his own exhibit A, the former President and Michigan center flatly asserts that the "experience of playing the game can be applied to the rest of your life, and drawn from freely." The piece nearly implies that not to have played a sport is to be an incomplete American. Indeed, the "vanguard of our young leadership" are athletes.

According to Dan Jenkins, if the jocks have not inherited the earth, they have inherited a prime spot in America's civil religion whereby Super Bowl Sunday is nearly on a par with the Fourth of July. In the selection reprinted from *Semi-Tough*, Coach Cooper tells the Giants about the "patriotic flavor" of the pre-game and halftime festivities. Not only will 2000 crippled soldiers sing the national anthem, but thousands of painted birds will fly overhead forming the image of Vince Lombardi. Of course, Jenkins is attempting to spoof such excess, but we have seen enough Orange Bowl and Super Bowl spectaculars that would seem to have adopted Jenkins' parody as working script. Jenkins' satiric point is that to be a football fan is to be a patriotic American, an equation Jenkins finds dubious.

However, that being a baseball fan is synonymous with being an authentic American is for George Grella a sensible, legitimate, profoundly aware linkage, since "baseball responds to some of the deepest yearnings of the American soul." Grella's strident, celebratory essay, "Baseball and the American Dream," claims that "this most American of sports speaks as few other human activities can to our country's sense of itself." Like Roger Angell's "The Interior Stadium," Grella's essay develops the spatial and temporal uniqueness of baseball along with its pastoral associations, rich heritage, legendary figures, and seasonal symbolism. In addition, Grella believes that as an illustration of our social mythos, baseball's deepest significance lies in the way the game "allows us to sense that old American yearning for pure, unbounded possibility."

Certainly sport as a context in which to identify and evaluate a cultural ideal of manhood cannot be ignored. Consider the respect accorded the athlete who "plays with pain," a phenomenon examined by Drew Hyland's piece, "Playing to Win: How Much Should It Hurt?" Athletes who continue to play while injured may be attracted by several qualities of American machismo: the willingness to take risks, the impetuous pursuit of excellence, the desire for the fame and money of big time athletics. Ethical dilemmas emerge when the physician's commitment to healing conflicts with the athlete's desire to win, and are compounded when he is employed as a team doctor. As Hyland concludes, "In all these ethical dilemmas—playing with pain, disclosure of injuries, use of drugs—the values of prudence, autonomy, confidentiality, and fairness are often overridden by another, more compelling value: the desire to win at all costs."

Section I: Sport and Life

PETER GENT

Monday

I was freezing my ass in the back of the pickup when O. W. Meadows finally turned off the blacktop and pulled to a stop alongside an oat field. We had been driving west about forty-five minutes from Fort Worth on the old Weatherford Highway. Meadows, Seth Maxwell, and Jo Bob Williams were crowded in the cab. I had been elected to ride in the back, owing more to my smaller size, milder demeanor, and lesser status than to my desire to do so. Occasionally Seth passed me the bottle of Wild Turkey bourbon and it helped cut the cold some, but mostly I just huddled behind the back of the cab against the damp wind.

As the truck bounced to a halt, Jo Bob stumbled out laughing and fell in the ditch. He was clutching the bottle of Wild Turkey. There was about an inch of the amber fluid left. He tossed it at me.

"Here, motherfucker," he growled. "Finish off the birdbigger and let's un-load them guns."

I complied, grimacing as the heat burned my throat and boiled up into my sinuses.

It was a drizzling, cold autumn day. Everything was either gray or yellow brown. It was the kind of day I like to watch from the warmth and security of my bed. Instead, I was with three drunken madmen on a Texas dove hunt. I told myself it was for the good of the team.

"Goddam, lookit that." O. W. Meadows had scrambled from behind the wheel. He was standing in the road pissing and pointing at several mourning doves coasting lazily into the oat patch. "Jeeeeesus. Gimme my gun."

"They're out of range," I protested.

"Gimme my gun!" he screamed.

I handed him his square-backed Browning 12-gauge automatic with the gold trigger. He blazed away, the shot raining into the oats about halfway between the pickup and the doves.

From *North Dallas Forty* (1973).

"Jesus Christ," I yelled. "That fucking gun was loaded!"

Several more doves flew out of the field and away from us. The three men scrambled to the back of the truck for their shotguns and shells and then headed into the low brown oats. I grabbed my Sears 20-gauge and followed a few yards behind, trying to load and walk at the same time.

"The wet'll keep 'em down," Jo Bob said. "All we gotta do is put the phantom stalk on 'em and they'll start comin' in with their hands up."

"As soon as they know we're here," Meadows added, "I 'spect they'll just surrender."

A field lark jumped about ten yards in front and headed away from us. Meadows' Browning and Jo Bob's Winchester over-and-under roared simultaneously, and the tiny speckled bird exploded into feathers.

"Still got the ol' eye," Jo Bob laughed. Meadows slid another shell into the bottom of the Browning.

Seth Maxwell looked back at me and grinned. I had come on the hunt at Maxwell's insistence. He thought it would be good therapy. I had been on the same football team with Jo Bob and Meadows for several years and, at best, we had reached an uneasy truce. They disliked me and I was terrified of them. Naked in the locker room they were awesome enough, but drunk and armed, walking through a Parker County oat field, they were specters. I was depending on Maxwell to protect me from severe physical harm. There was no protection against emotional damage. That was an occupational hazard.

Jo Bob and Meadows moved a few yards ahead of Maxwell. Jo Bob picked up the shambles that had been the field lark and threw it back in my direction. I ducked; the gore fell several feet short. The two giant linemen, walking side by side, shotguns over their arms, were an anxious sight and I wanted only to please them. The problem was to figure out how. Maxwell dropped back and fell in step with me.

"Hey poot," he asked, "what's the trouble?"

I eyed him curiously. "This is like a long weekend in the DMZ."

"Relax." Maxwell soothed with the manner that made him one of professional football's better leaders. "Ain't nobody gonna get hurt."

"Mention that to the scalp hunters," I suggested.

"Just stay behind 'em," he instructed. "That's what I always do."

"That's comforting."

Our conversation was cut off by the roar of shotguns. Jo Bob and Meadows had brought down three doves between them.

"I got a double," Jo Bob hollered.

"Double my ass," Meadows argued. "I shot two of them birds myself. That leaves you only one. And I think he died of fright." Meadows howled with laughter.

"Bullshit," Jo Bob argued, breaking his gun and jamming in two more shells. He reached down and picked up the first bird, which was still flopping, its wing shattered. Jo Bob caught the bird's head between his thumb and fore-finger and jerked it off. The wings flapped spasmodically and then the be-headed dove went limp. Jo Bob tossed the head back at me. I caught it and threw it back at him; it left my hand covered with blood. I wiped my palm on my Levi's but the blood had quickly coagulated and I couldn't rub it all off. When I clenched my fist the skin stuck together.

Meadows moved ahead and picked up another of the birds. It too was still alive.

"Here," Meadows said, tossing the cripple at Jo Bob. "Pop its head. I'll find the other." The wounded bird sailed through the air like a baseball. At the top of the arc it suddenly came alive and began to fly toward us.

"Son of a bitch," Meadows screamed, raising his gun, aiming at the bird.

"Hold it, O. W.," Maxwell yelled, already ducking.

We hit the ground as the Browning roared twice more and the bird fell out of the sky, dropping next to me. I pounced on the dove like a loose fumble for fear it would start to crawl toward me and Meadows would open up again.

We continued on through the oat field, getting five doves. Maxwell and I scored one apiece. Jo Bob shot two more doves and demolished an owl asleep in a tree along the fence line. Meadows hit two doves, finding only one, and produced another bottle of Wild Turkey. When we reached the opposite edge of the field we stood around taking pulls out of the bottle and considering our next move. Finally we decided to hike about a mile to a cattle tank, where Meadows said there were some duck blinds. At least we could sit and drink out of the wind.

At the tank, we slipped up on five careless mallards. Jo Bob and Meadows killed four before the ducks got off the water. Maxwell brought down the fifth when it circled back over the tank, looking for its pals.

"Did you see that?" Meadows laughed. "I got two with one shot."

"Shit," Maxwell argued. "You shot 'em on the water."

"Did not," Meadows said, grinning and holding his arms askew, his left foot off the ground. "They had one foot up." He broke into peals of laughter.

"How do we get 'em?" I asked.

"You can swim after 'em for all I care," Jo Bob said. "I don't want 'em. Just have to clean 'em. Besides, I don't have a duck stamp."

The pond was about five acres in all, with small blinds on each side. Maxwell and I positioned on one side, Jo Bob and Meadows on the other.

"What am I doing here?" I said, after a cold, silent wait. The lonesome sounds of the wind picking up and the water lapping against the side of the blind were depressing.

"Calm down," Maxwell said. "It'll do you good."

I watched a hawk drift overhead, its wings outstretched, soaring on the currents of the barren west Texas sky.

The two shotguns on the other side roared. I scanned the sky. It was empty. The guns boomed again and something rattled on the outside of our blind.

"Jesus Christ," I yelled. "They're shooting at us."

We dropped to the floor of the blind as the two men blazed away from the other side of the tank. Pellets rained off the side of the blind. After every shot, I could hear Jo Bob laughing like a loon.

"Goddammit, Jo Bob," Maxwell screamed. "You two cocksuckers better cut the shit or I swear to God I'll have your asses." The shooting stopped, but Meadows and Jo Bob continued to giggle.

I peered over the side of the blind. The ambushed mallards floated limply in the water. A dying green head flapped weakly. Jo Bob and Meadows both shot it again. After a half hour of empty sky, we moved back through the oat field to the truck. I got two more doves as we reached the road. Maxwell had bagged one just as we left the tank. That made a total of eleven.

The second bottle of Wild Turkey was dead. We stood at the truck again trying to decide what to do next.

"Look out, Jo Bob." Meadows had slipped two dead doves from his pocket and had thrown them into the air. "Shoot 'em quick. . . . shoot 'em."

Jo Bob quickly shouldered his gun and fired twice, hitting one of the birds. When they struck the ground Meadows emptied his shotgun into them, blowing the birds to shreds. Jo Bob and Meadows left them where they fell and clambered onto the fenders of the truck.

The decision was made to road hunt. I was elected to drive. Maxwell sat next to me. The two assassins remained on the fenders.

As we drove slowly along the gravel road, Maxwell ferreted another bottle of bourbon from beneath the seat. We passed it back and forth. The warmth of the liquor was relaxing me. I tried to settle back and enjoy the day. It was Monday, our day off. The day before we had beaten St. Louis—through no small effort on my part. There was no reason why I shouldn't be having fun.

As I reached for the hundred-proof bourbon the booming shotguns turned my attention back to the road.

"You got him, O. W.," Jo Bob laughed, barely keeping his balance on the fender. "Right in the ass."

"Goddammit," Meadows howled, "I spoiled the meat." They both laughed insanely, beating their thighs with open hands.

A gray-striped cat was trying to pull itself off the road with its forepaws, its hindquarters shredded by a double load of number six shot. I stopped the truck and Maxwell grabbed his shotgun.

"Jesus Christ, you two." Maxwell was angry. He raised his gun and shot the tortured animal again. The force of the shot slammed the cat limply into the ground and made it skid several feet. A hind foot kicked out twice, stiffly. The animal twisted its head up and died. Maxwell looked at the dead cat, then back at his smirking teammates. He shook his head and crawled back into the cab.

"They're fucking crazy," I said.

"Naw," Maxwell disagreed. "Just tryin' to relax and have a good time."

I grabbed the bottle and took a long, stinging swig.

"Well, I can't relax as long as they got the guns."

"We'll head back to Fort Worth in a bit."

"Do I have to ride in the back again?"

Maxwell looked at me and shrugged.

I had to and by the time we reached the Big Boy Restaurant where we had left our cars, I was numb. We returned cold, tired, drunk, and empty-handed. Jo Bob had thrown the remaining doves at passing cars.

"Jo Bob, you take my car," Maxwell ordered. "I'll ride with Phil. We'll catch you at Crawford's place."

Jo Bob and Meadows looked quizzically at each other. They didn't understand Maxwell's desire to hunt or drink with me. His riding all the way back to Dallas in my car was pure bedevilment. I enjoyed their confusion.

It was late afternoon. In a last gasp the sun had burned away the gray sky and had disappeared into the Panhandle. The air had warmed some and the best part of the day remained. Being in Texas is a skin feeling, strongest this time of day. There is a softness to the twilight. The days could be overpowering in their sun-soaked brightness, not so much now since the smog, but still incredibly vibrant. This afternoon, it was the predark peace that I needed, a quiet power I had never felt in the changing gray of the Midwest or the choking paranoia of New York.

I love Texas, but she drives her people crazy. I've wondered whether it's the heat, or the money, or maybe both. A republic of outlaws loosely allied with the United States, Texas survives, and survives quite well by breaking the rules. Now there is a new generation of Texans who want to do away with the rules. The old resist violently, unable to conceive of the dream of wealth, devoid of any rules to break.

I took out my keys and bent to unlock my car, a brand-new honey-beige Buick Riviera with all the extras, an embarrassing car. Maxwell had sent me to the Buick dealer who sponsors his television show. He swore the guy would give me a great deal. I had wanted a used Opel.

In one hour, the sales manager (the dealer had been too busy to talk to me) showed me how "for practically the same money" I could own a new Riviera and all the accompanying good feelings.

A good salesman knows the purchaser is totally without sense—why else would anyone ask a salesman anything? Once you speak to a salesman you have shown your hole card. I not only spoke, but shook his hand and hoped deeply that we could become friends.

On the other side of the lot Jo Bob was getting into Maxwell's blue-on-blue Cadillac convertible.

"Say er ah babee." Maxwell fell into a black dialect, which he often did when asking for or talking about drugs. "Ah, let's have some of what you call your grassss." He hissed out the last word purposely.

"Hey man, just say grass."

"Can't, babee. Gots to get in de mood. Now where's dat killer weed?"

"There's some in the glove compartment."

I picked through the cartridge tapes scattered on the floor beneath my feet. I pushed the Sir Douglas Quintet *Together After Five* into the deck, adjusted the eight-position steering wheel, and pulled out of the lot. Doug Sahm sang about the ill-fated love of two kids in Dallas.

"Seems her father didn't approve
Of his long hair and far-out groove . . ."

Maxwell lit the joint and took a long drag, making the familiar hissing sound that could only come from someone inhaling cannabis.

"So . . . that there is what you call yer killer weed." Maxwell held the joint up for inspection. "Well, it ain't Cutty and water, but it'll do." He passed me the joint, and I sucked on it in short soft puffs, a habit acquired from turning on in airplanes, public restrooms, and dark back yards at straight parties. All getting pretty risky what with the current dope publicity and universal vigilance for peculiar smells.

Three years ago, on the team plane from Washington, Maxwell and I had kept sneaking to the john to smoke dope. The stewardess noticed the smell and thought the galley wiring was smoldering. There was a five-minute panic, both for those who were scared the plane was afire, and for Maxwell and me, who were terrified that it wasn't. We weren't caught but we swore a blood oath to never smoke on the team plane again. It was a promise we kept until the next road game.

The lights from the toll plaza appeared up ahead. I eased off the gas and rolled down my window. A fat man, about forty-five, in a sweat-stained gray uniform, stood at the door of the booth. One hand held out the toll ticket, the other was stuffing what appeared to be a peanut butter and lizard sandwich into his face. I slowly coasted the car through the gate, neatly picking the ticket from the outstretched hand. A name tag stenciled BILLY WAYNE ROBINSON hung from his shirt-pocket flap.

"Hey, Billy Wayne." Maxwell leaned toward the open window. "How's yer mom and them?"

The attendant looked startled, then confused, then, recognized the famous smiling face. Like a true Texas football fan he went completely berserk. Waving and trying to speak as we glided through, he spat half his sandwich on the trunk.

"Did you know that guy?"

"Naw, just a little of the ol' instant humble. I shoulda offered him some of this here maryjawana."

"Show 'em you can straddle the old generation gap," I said.

I accelerated into the main lanes of the Dallas-Fort Worth Turnpike, heading for Dallas at about ninety miles an hour, a high-speed island of increased awareness and stereophonic sound heading back to the future. The turnpike was twenty-eight straight miles of concrete laid on rolling hills, connecting the two cities for anyone with sixty cents and a Class A automobile. Factories, warehouses, and two medium cities smother the land the length of the highway. Back in the early sixties, five minutes past the toll gate, heading for either end, you were out in the West. That was when Braniff's planes were gray. Jack Ruby ran a burlesque house. And the School Book Depository was a place they kept schoolbooks.

"Smoke will rise
In the Dallas skies
Comin' back to you
Dallas Alice . . ."

"Here."

"Huh?"

"Here!" Maxwell was thrusting the joint at me. His eyes and cheeks and neck were bulging. He was trying to stifle a cough. His face was crimson. I took the joint. Maxwell exhaled, coughing and clearing his throat. He looked and sounded like a four-pack-a-day man getting out of bed in the morning.

"B. A. wants me in his office at ten tomorrow morning," I said, remembering.

"He's probably gonna tell you you're starting Sunday."

"I doubt it." I frowned. "If he was gonna do that he'd just call in Gill and tell him he wasn't starting. No, I think B. A. just wants to make certain I understand the nonprejudicial, technically flawless way he arrived at the opinion I should sit on the bench."

"I dunno." Maxwell gazed out the windshield. "That was a big catch you made yesterday. It put us ahead to stay."

"Yeah maybe, but it was the only pass I caught."

"You only played the last quarter. Besides, it was the only one I threw at you."

"He'll want to know why you don't throw at me more." It frustrated me to use the coach's logic. I paused. "By the way," I turned my face from the windshield and frowned at Maxwell, "why don't you throw to me more?"

"Cause you ain't been playing that much, asshole."

"I suppose. After that truly amazing catch, you'll surely want me as the special guest on your television show. Gimme the opportunity to snuggle my way into the heart of Dallas-Fort Worth. It's the least you could do."

"It's also the most," Maxwell said. "Besides, I'm having Jo Bob on the show this week."

"How about a remote interview?" I suggested, smiling widely. "I could tell how I overcame a truly Middlewest upbringing and a childhood case of paralytic ringworm. Maybe they could do some closeup shots of my hands doing something—like picking my nose."

"Listen, man," Maxwell interrupted, "it's a family show."

I shook my head. "Why can't there be a football show for the hard-core pervert?"

There was no response from Maxwell. He seemed lost in thought.

"What do you think of the SCA?" Maxwell said finally.

"What?"

"The Society of Christian Athletes." His voice was deep and halting as he tried to keep the marijuana smoke down in his lungs. "B. A. asked me to make an appearance at the national rally they're having in May. At the Cotton Bowl."

"You don't believe that shit, do you?"

"Sort of." Maxwell's voice became submissive. "I mean, when you have a chance to influence people you oughta do some good."

"Who says that's good?" I asked. "Besides B. A."

"What's wrong with him? For God's sake, the man's a Christian. That's a helluva lot more than you are."

"Sure, our coach has money, success, his life planned down to the minutest detail. Everything going off like clockwork. He must have God on his side."

"You sure are bitter," Maxwell said. "What harm can it do?"

"I don't care, man. Go ahead, influence people." I deepened my voice to affect an imitation. "Hi kids. Seth Maxwell here to give you a little good influence. Don't get your kicks doping. Get out on the ol' gridiron and hurt somebody. It's cleaner and more fun."

Maxwell stared silently through the windshield. I turned my attention back to the road.

Six Flags Amusement Park flashed by on the right. In all the years I'd lived in Dallas, I'd been to this "Disneyland of the Southwest" only once. I'd spent the entire time, stoned on mescaline, in the Petting Zoo caressing a baby llama. I considered screwing the furry little bugger as a protest against captivity, his and mine. But I decided even if the llama understood, the guards wouldn't, so I chalked up another sexual and sociological frustration and went home.

Flailing arms and loud coughing brought me out of my thoughts.

"Goddam. Goddam." Maxwell's voice was raspy and he was gagging. "Goddam. I swallowed the roach." He shook his head. "It burned the livin' shit outta me."

"I warned you about suckin' so hard."

"Fuck," he said. He leaned over and spit on my floor. "You got another?"

"In the glove compartment."

Maxwell pulled out a joint rolled in a replica of a one-hundred-dollar bill.

"Shit." He held the joint out in front of him. "I'll bet the guy that came up with that made a killing."

Sir Douglas started into "Seguin." I pushed the reject button and replaced the tape with the Rolling Stones. They started somewhere in the middle of "Honky Tonk Women."

"You know," Maxwell said, staring vacantly at the road, "I've always wanted to take about six months and just travel around Texas, going from one honky-tonk to another. Find the best jukeboxes and the women with the saddest stories."

"The people in honky-tonks," he continued, "are just like a good country-music jukebox. Full of stories about people who just lost somethin', or never had anything to start with." He clasped his hands behind his head and leaned back in the seat. The joint dropped from his lips. "We'd go to a different one ever' night. Just drink, fuck, eat pussy, and listen to country music. You could learn a lot, podnah."

"Maybe. But we could get the shit beat outta us in a lotta those places. Like the Jacksboro Highway."

The Jacksboro Highway was a honky-tonk-lined road leading from Fort Worth to Jacksboro. The Old West still lived in the bars along this particular stretch and there were shootings and knifings every night.

Maxwell thought for a moment, then turned slowly to look at me. "What are you so scared of?" he asked.

"Pain, man. Nothing flashy or existential. Just plain old pain. I don't like it, never have. I can't even stand the thought of my skin splitting open and my bodily fluids spilling onto the Astroturf in front of millions of screaming fans—for money. Do you think I wanna do it for free? Alone? And in the dark?"

"But it's all part of being alive, man. The pleasure and the pain. You can't have one without the other."

"It's an age of specialists."

We were both silent. I was reminded of another car trip we had made back in the early spring. On a dull Wednesday in March we had gotten high, filled the car with gasoline, whiskey, speed, and grass and driven to Sante Fe non-stop. We spent two nights at an old hotel, until at 3 A.M. the second morning Maxwell finally seduced the night clerk on a brown leather couch in the lobby. I alternated between standing guard and watching them fuck. She was a heavyset woman, about forty-five, and all the time Maxwell humped away at her, she babbled endlessly about him being her son's favorite football star, and how pleased the boy would be to learn she and Maxwell had met and become friends.

The return took eighteen hours. All the way back we took speed, smoked dope, drank Pepsi, and ate pork rinds. Beginning ten minutes outside of Sante Fe and continuing to the outskirts of Dallas, Maxwell described in detail every sex act he had ever committed. Except for gas and piss, we stopped only once, in Odessa, to see the World's Largest Statue of a Jackrabbit.

"You know," Maxwell began talking, "I'm actually getting to where I don't think I mind pain. You know what I mean? Remember when I dislocated my elbow? For a minute there it hurt so bad I thought I'd go crazy. There was no way I could stand it. Then all of a sudden . . . Well, I can't explain it." His face screwed up in an attempt to find words. "Except that it hurt. And it didn't hurt. I mean, it still really hurt bad, but I could stand it and actually sort of liked it, in a different sort of way."

"I'm not sure I get it," I said, nonetheless feeling a nebulous sense of identity with the feelings he was trying to describe.

"Well, it's sorta like pain makes me think I'm doin' something. Nothing occupies my mind but the pain, it's all I care about. I feel secure in it. When the pain is the worst I'm the most relaxed. Weird, isn't it?"

"I don't know if *weird* is a strong enough word."

I gripped the wheel tighter and looked ahead to the approaching Dallas toll plaza. The Dallas skyline was directly ahead. I paid the toll and headed for the Trinity River Bridge and I35 beyond. Crossing Commerce, Main, and Elm of the I35 overpass, I read the giant Hertz sign atop the Schoolbook Depository. I looked to the spot on Elm Street where Kennedy was shot. I had seen the historic place hundreds of times, but I still couldn't actually picture it happening. Now the country had another President who liked guys like me and football and attended the Washington practices to call screen passes. What was more perfect? A President who liked deceptive plays. He was B. A.'s favorite.

I turned into the Motor Street exit, followed Motor past the hospital that had received the mangled Kennedy and onto Maple, then right again to The Apartments. The parking lot was jammed. The only open spot was adjacent to a fire hydrant. I parked there.

"Lock your door, Seth," I said. "If they can't take a joke, fuck 'em."

Maxwell stepped out, leaned over and took the last drag on the joint. Taking long, slow strides and throwing his arms and head back, he broke into song.

"Turn out the lights, the party's over."

He walked around the hedge into the passageway that led down a flight of stairs to the pool. The song faded off.

I leaned back, hands on my hips, and stretched, looking up at the sky, wishing I would witness a supernova. No such luck.

ALEX C. MICHALOS

The Unreality and Moral Superiority of Football

A few years ago my friend, John McMurtry, showed us several similarities between football and society. His general thesis was that the sport and the society in which it is played are mirror images of each other, and that both are pretty sick, violent and fascist.

Since at least half the people in our philosophy department are ex-athletes

Originally appeared in *Journal of the Philosophy of Sport* (1976).

of one sort or another, we spent a number of lunch hours and coffee breaks mulling over John's thesis. Some of us turned off our TV sets for a while, a short while to be sure. Still, McMurtry had his point. Indeed, it would perhaps be more remarkable if football, or any sport for that matter, bore no resemblance to the society in which it or they are played. People can hardly be expected to turn their personalities inside out when they participate in sports.

Nevertheless, stretched out on my sofa a couple weeks ago relishing O. J. Simpson's zipping hither and yon through somebody's helpless defensive squad, it just seemed to me that what was going on was too good to be on balance bad. There's something admirable about the performance of an excellent running back, a scrambling quarterback or a defensive player with the knack of being in the right place at the right time. Anyone who has tried to match such performances must admire them.

The more I thought about football, the amount of my life spent watching others play and playing it myself, the more its virtues became apparent. Generally speaking, it is because the nature of football departs significantly in a morally superior direction from the nature of our everyday lives that it constitutes a worthwhile sport. Granted that it has unattractive features, insofar as football gives us a glimpse of a moral order and a just society, it merits all the attention it receives.

I present some of the features that distinguish the world of football from the ordinary world in which we live. In the first place, with the exception of the point after a touchdown, as soon as one team scores points on the other, it must surrender the ball. That is, the team that has just scored typically gives the other team a chance to score. That is not like the real world. People are not obliged to give others an advantage after taking them to the cleaners. Think of what a change it would make in our world if they were. What a blow it would strike against avarice and greed!

Second, contrary to McMurtry and others, the aim of the game is not territorial acquisition. It's not Monopoly! The aim of the game is to score more points than the other side, and when you get those points, you are not taking anything away from the other side. If gaining yards to get a touchdown makes football a game of territorial acquisition, then gaining bases to get a run makes baseball another game of territorial acquisition, and shooting baskets to get a higher score makes basketball another one. Unlike the real world where people do go after other people's property and there is a definite advantage in having more property, in football the aim is to cross over the property to score points. Whatever property is taken is never kept. No one ever intends to keep it, unlike the real world.

Third, most of the game of football is played in the open under the watchful eyes of referees and spectators. The bigger the play, the more thoroughly it is inspected. In the real world big plays often go on under the table, behind closed doors, in the corner in the dark. The real operators tend to have a low profile—in more ways than one. They don't stand there in the open on crippled knees like Joe Namath taking their lumps from Eller and Greene. Imagine the difference it would make to our world if everyone had to bare the risks and costs of his own actions. Imagine the change in our economy if businessmen would behave as if there were no "externalities," if they all paid their own pollution costs.

Fourth, rich people don't have an advantage on the field. In the game of life, people with money do have an advantage. Even the richest backers can only put eleven or twelve men on the field at a time. They know the other team will play the same number and all the money in the world can't throw a touchdown pass.

Fifth, in football it's difficult to fake it. Sooner or later you have to put up or shut up. You have to kick a ball or catch it or block someone or tackle someone or do something worthwhile. In the real world pretense can be a way of life. One can fake it in school, fake it on the job, fake it in bed, fake it just about all the way. In football, sooner or later the real you has to stand up and take your lumps. In fact, as we become increasingly technologically sophisticated, it is likely that your standing or failing to stand will be captured on film. For better or worse, your performance can be run and rerun ad nauseum. Imagine the consequences of that!

When all these features are taken together, it seems to me that the unreality and moral superiority of the game of football compared to the game of life is beyond dispute. Because football is in important respects unlike our daily routines and distinctly better from a moral point of view, it can qualify as play. It makes sense to teach young people how to play football, as much sense as it makes to teach anyone the principles of fair play. Being a good sport in football is much more than being willing cannon fodder for the varsity or a willing pawn in the hands of frustrated old generals or would-be generals. Unfortunately, too often it has these undesirable features as well as the virtues described above. But that should not be allowed to disguise all that is decent and worthwhile in the sport. Some people eat turkey just for the fun of wringing its neck, but that doesn't make Thanksgiving a bad idea.

JOHN MCMURTRY

The Illusions of a Football Fan: A Reply to Michalos

Some years ago, I proposed the thesis that the major spectator sports of a society are paradigms of it: the underlying principles of such games being, I suggested, pure-type versions of the underlying principle of the social game. It was not just a reflectionist thesis I proposed, but a causal one. That is, I held that the logic of major spectator sports does not merely *mirror* the social order in which they occur, but more importantly, *causes this order to be maintained intact* by evangelizing in popular form its essential structure of action. Thus, for instance, I pointed to the competitive territorial-acquisition principle of North American football as not just a *reflection* of our society's capitalist order, but as a *re-enforcer* of this order, in the idolized terms of which not only young males model their lives on and off the field, but even Presidents of the United States formulate their country's foreign policy (e.g. Richard Nixon's remark on Vietnam War strategy: "It's like football. You run a play and it fails. Then you turn around and call the same play again because they aren't expecting it"). [1]

In his "Unreality and Moral Superiority of Football," [2] my friend Alex Michalos takes the reflectionist aspect of my thesis as the whole of it and, thereby, misrepresents it. But, misrepresentation or not, the five arguments he proposes in objection to that part of my thesis to which he attends, deserve reply.

Objection 1: "The team that has just scored [in football] typically gives the other team a chance to score. That is not like the real world. People are not obliged to give others an advantage after taking them to the cleaners" (pp. 22–3).

Reply: Michalos acknowledges, it seems, that racking up a score [3] on the opposing team *is* analogous to "taking them to the cleaners" in the real world. So far, then, he unwittingly argues from my thesis, by identifying a symmetry of principle between football and real life.

However, even the less significant asymmetry of principle Michalos claims here—return of possession to the scored-upon team—does not stand up to examination. For the scoring team kicks off from the *advantaged position of*

Originally appeared in *Journal of the Philosophy of Sport* (1977).

owning a point-accumulation at the expense of the other team. It then typically attempts to use its kickoff from this advantaged position to push the opposing team back as far as it can into its own end and, from there, it further attempts to seize new possession as quickly as possible.

The logic of football is not, then, different from the logic of the "real world." Rather, it exemplifies it.

Objection 2: "The aim of the game [of football] is not territorial acquisition. It's not Monopoly! . . . the aim is to cross over the property to score points. Whatever property is taken is never kept. No one ever intends to keep it, unlike the real world" (p. 23).

Reply: There are a number of confusions here: about football, about the "real world," and plain logical confusion.

First of all, "to cross over the property" of the football field *is*, unless there is no game on, to "get yards," "to penetrate the territory of the opposition," to—more pointedly—"rip off a big gain." To redescribe the process here as "crossing over the property" of the field is merely to generate a distinction where there is none, by the imprecision of euphemism.

Secondly, the territory thus gained *is* kept, so long as "the line holds." Then by a rule-governed contest of power it is added to ("yardage gained"), or subtracted from ("yardage lost"), until such time as one or other team is able to press its territorial gains to "pay-dirt": at which juncture, there being no more territory left to be seized, the team in question gains abstract assets called "points," which are football's homologue to money.[4] As in the "real world," territorial gains are ultimately geared towards a maximum accumulation of these abstract assets, and the minimum allowance to others of the same.

Finally, the aim of the game *is*, very much, monopoly. Football teams standardly set as their basic objective "total possession" and "monopolization of the ball," as anyone familiar with their workings will readily testify.

Objection 3: "Most of the game of football is played in the open under the watchful eyes of referees and spectators. The bigger the play, the more thoroughly it is inspected. In the real world big plays often go on under the table, behind closed doors, in the corner in the dark" (p. 23).

Reply: The contrast here between football and "real world" again does not stand up to scrutiny.

Plans of action are indeed regularly made "behind closed doors" in the real world, but they are *always* so made in the game of football: via the top-secret playbook, the closed practice session, and the strictly secluded huddle before every play of the game.

As for the action itself on the field, it is true that, on game-day, it is exposed to referee and public view. But so too is the action of "the real world."

The football stadium is no more open than the political arena; referees are no more watchful than other law-enforcement agencies; and football spectators have no more privileged access to what's occurring on the field than citizen spectators have to what's occurring on the public stage. Most citizens, of course, do not witness the secret deals and dirty moves of "the real operators," but then most football fans do not either. Indeed, in football as much as in the real world, mechanisms of "deception" and "fake" typically veil even that which the public can see.

Objection 4: "Rich people don't have an advantage on the field. In the game of life, people with money do have an advantage" (p. 23).

Reply: Rich people have an advantage in "the game of life" because they can buy goods and services which others cannot. Precisely the same advantage falls to rich football teams.

As for individual players, wealth does not secure them an advantage on the field, barring bribery. But then wealth does not secure an advantage in publicly-witnessed skill performances anywhere else either, barring bribery. In football and in the game of life, in short, riches have similar advantages, similar limitations.

Objection 5: "In football, it's difficult to fake it. . . . In the real world pretense can be a way of life. One can fake it in school, fake it on the job, fake it in bed, fake it just about all the way" (p. 23).

Reply: Again, the contrast between our game of football and our social game is contrived. There is nothing at all inherent in the logic of football that makes it easier, or harder, to "fake" than scholarship, vocational skill, or physical love. What makes a put-on difficult in any of these forms of activity is the other participants' expertise at the activity in question. If they are skilled at it, football or fucking, someone else cannot pretend that he or she is too, when he or she is not. Michalos has given us an illicit comparison— between an activity *pursued in the company of experts* (i.e. pro football), and other activities *not pursued in the company of experts* (i.e. school, job, and bed routines); and then he has derived from this illicit comparison the unwarranted conclusion that football specially precludes phonies. It does not. I have played next to mass-watched football pros faking it as much as, say, guild-watched academic pros. There is nothing, in this regard, romantically peculiar about football. It is no more, and no less, subject to participant pretense than any other activity: though, as with any other activity, the opportunity for faking it doubtless declines in direct proportion to the excellence of the company.

In summary, then, none of Michalos's five counter-arguments stands up to examination.

But is there, then, *nothing* about spectator football which makes it substantively unlike, or morally superior to, "real life"? Leaving aside its sheerly athletic requirements (unusual power, acceleration, co-ordination), I would say that it is distinctive—even "unreal" and "morally superior" compared to our social game—in the extraordinary physical courage, and instant system-analysis ability, it requires of its participants. In these respects, it truly does require an altogether higher order of being than our social game and, depending on one's values, might properly be celebrated as a special and elevated form of activity on these accounts. However it may ironically be precisely these "higher" norms of spectator football which enable it to be so effective as a glorified model of our social order: endowing thereby this social order—of which it is ultimately a dramatic exemplum—with the *couleur de rose*, the false *Schein*, of heroic-mindedness.

NOTES

1. Cited in: "Philosophy of a Corner Linebacker," *The Nation* 212, No. 3 (Jan. 18, 1971), p. 84. Some other places in which my thesis of sport as social paradigm is argued are: "Smash Thy Neighbour," *The Atlantic* 229, No. 1 (Jan. 1972); "Sport or Athletics: A North American Dilemma," *Proceedings of the 15th Annual Canadian-American Seminar*, Windsor, 1973; and "A Case for Killing the Olympics," *Macleans* 86, No. 1 (January, 1973).

2. *Journal of the Philosophy of Sport* 3 (1976), pp. 22–24; reprinted in this anthology, pp. 238–240.

3. The concept of "racking up a score" deserves pause. What it designates is the placement on a publicly prominent "rack" of a point-accumulation of one team at the expense of another team. In this way, an extrinsic, exclusive benefit (i.e. a publicly-recognized registration of score-ownership) is accorded one team at the expense of the other, and it is here, in my judgment, that the deformation of football (or indeed, any other sort of play) begins. Mimicing our social order, instead of, as true play does, transcending it, "racking up" scores is the necessary, and perhaps sufficient, condition for the transmogrification of sport into business.

4. Quarterback/coach of the Saskatchewan Roughriders, Ron Lancaster, made this homologue clear when asked to comment on the upcoming Western Football League finals in November, 1976: "Edmonton has the same sort of defence we do. They'll try to establish a running game, throw short, and not attempt to get rich in a hurry."

A Guide for Further Study

A good starting point for the analysis of American sport and American life is Robert Boyle, *Sport—Mirror of American Life*. James A. Michener's *Sports in America* has its uses, most especially in Michener's account of heartland America. Although a bit dated, Frederick W. Cozens' *Sports in American Life* provides excellent background reading on the Thirties and Forties. For those who want more historical grounding, see Herbert Manchester, *Four Centuries of Sport in America, 1490–1890*. A broad-based collection of contemporary studies is *Sport and Play in American Life: A Textbook in the Sociology of Sport*, compiled by Stephen K. Figler. For a continuation of the arguments concerning sport and life, see Duane L. Thomas, "A Definitional Context for some Socio-Moral Characteristics of Sport," *Journal of the Philosophy of Sport* 6 (Fall 1979).

Section II: Sport and Social Myths

GERALD R. FORD
WITH JOHN UNDERWOOD

In Defense of the Competitive Urge

One lesson to be learned in reaching an age where you are both a viable politician and a washed-up lineman is that past glories are not negotiable in the open market. When you stop winning they not only start booing, they start forgetting.

I used to think of myself as a pretty dashing figure on the ski slopes of the East and in northern Michigan, and could at least count on outstripping my children on the various runs we tried. Nowadays, when the family gets together at Vail for our annual Christmas ski reunion, my sons and my daughter go zooming by, usually with just the encouragement to make me boil. Such as "Hurry up, Dad." They see themselves getting faster and faster as I get slower and slower. They forget all the times I picked them out of the snowbank.

When I was House Minority Leader and a regular adversary of Lyndon Johnson's, he once said—with minimum affection—"There's nothing wrong with Jerry Ford except that he played football too long without his helmet." Lyndon got a lot of mileage out of that quote, and I used it myself one year when I addressed the Gridiron Club in Washington. I said he was wrong, that I always wore my helmet on any gridiron, and I picked up my old leather bonnet and put it on, right on top of my white tie and tails. It had been a while, though. I had a hard time getting it down over my ears. Of course, heads do have a tendency to swell here in Washington.

My playing days at Michigan are now a standard introduction in magazine stories such as this, usually accompanied by a picture of a rugged-looking hairy young man (me) hunched over a ball in the center's position, and the notation that Ford was "the most valuable player on a losing Michigan team." I always feel damned with faint praise when I read that. I'd much rather have been the "least valuable player on a winning Michigan team," the kind we

Originally appeared in *Sports Illustrated* (1974).

had my sophomore and junior years when we were undefeated and won national championships.

Those were what sportswriters up on their clichés would call my "halcyon days." Certainly they offer brighter memories than my efforts to stay competitive—and fit—since. Today I am a habitual exerciser—a 15-minute swim twice a day in the backyard pool, slower-and-slower skiing near our place in Vail, and an occasional round of golf with fellow hackers around Washington.

The reason I make reference to those winning seasons at Michigan is that we have been asked to swallow a lot of home-cooked psychology in recent years that winning isn't all that important anymore, whether on the athletic field or in any other field, national and international. I don't buy that for a minute. It is not enough to just compete. Winning is very important. Maybe more important than ever.

Don't misunderstand. I am not low-rating the value of informal participation. Competing is always preferable to not competing, whether you win or not, and one reason is as good as another for getting involved. Swimming laps, for example, is preferable to doubling your waistline. As a young man I took up skiing in order to get to know a certain young lady better. She happened to be a devotee, and I an eager beginner. I lost the girl but I learned to ski. The subject used to be a sensitive one with my wife, who came along afterward, but I have reminded her that that was instructive athletics, not competitive athletics. The important thing was I learned to ski.

If you don't win elections you don't play, so the importance of winning is more drastic in that field. In athletics and in most other worthwhile pursuits first place is the manifestation of the desire to excel, and how else can you achieve anything? I certainly do not feel we achieved very much as a Michigan football team in 1934. And I can assure you we had more fun on those championship teams in 1932–33.

Broadly speaking, outside of a national character and an educated society, there are few things more important to a country's growth and well-being than competitive athletics. If it is a cliché to say athletics build character as well as muscle, then I subscribe to the cliché. It has been said, too, that we are losing our competitive spirit in this country, the thing that made us great, the guts of the free-enterprise system. I don't agree with that; the competitive urge is deep-rooted in the American character. I do wonder sometimes if we are adjusting to the times, or if we have been spoiled by them.

For one, do we realize how important it is to compete successfully with other nations? Not just the Russians, but many nations that are growing and challenging. Being a leader, the U.S. has an obligation to set high standards. I don't know of a better advertisement for a nation's good health than a healthy athletic representation. Athletics happens to be an extraordinarily swift avenue of communication. The broader the achievement the greater the impact. There is much to be said for Ping-Pong diplomacy.

With communications what they are, a sports triumph can be as uplifting to a nation's spirit as, well, a battlefield victory. And surely no one will argue that it is not more healthful. The Africans were terrific in the last two Olympics, and their stars have become national heroes. These countries were tasting the first fruits of international achievement, and their pride was justified. In a wink of the eye they caught us in some areas, passed us in others.

When I was in China a few years ago I was astounded by the number of basketball courts. They were everywhere—in school yards, outside factories and farms. Boys and girls were playing basketball at age three and four, with miniature balls and undersized baskets. The sizes and heights were graded to coincide with the age group, something we might consider here, even up to the professional level. The agricultural and factory communes were alive with competition, in conjunction with their mandatory calisthenics.

In 1972, when I received the college Football Hall of Fame award at the Waldorf in New York, I remarked on this new Chinese passion for the old American game, and I said that one day soon we would have to cope with a seven-foot Chinese Wilt Chamberlain. Sure enough, last year the Chinese had a touring team that featured some real giants, and they did all right. In five years they will be competitive. Of course, the Chinese do things we would never find acceptable in a free society. Completely regimented, state-supported, state-manipulated athletic programs are not for us. It is a matter of style as well as philosophy. But if we want to remain competitive, and I think we do, we owe it to ourselves to reassess our priorities, to broaden our base of achievement so that we again present our best in the world's arenas. From a purely political viewpoint, I don't know of anything more beneficial in diplomacy and prestige. I don't think we really want to be booed or forgotten.

For that reason I am in favor of doing all we can, as quickly as we can, to resolve the jurisdictional differences which hurt our Olympic effort, which hinder at the grass-roots level the development of athletes. It is a disgrace in this country for anyone not to realize his or her potential in any sport. The petty conflict between the NCAA and the AAU is, as Mike Harrigan of the President's Council on Physical Fitness outlined recently, just the most visible symptom of an overall organizational problem.

I leave the details to Congressman Bob Mathias, the former decathlon champion, and those more acquainted with the specific difficulties, but certain things proposed in the recent flurry of congressional activity have my support. No one will deny that the United States Olympic Committee, a federally chartered organization and therefore a legitimate area of federal concern, needs to be restructured. The Administration has under advisement a plan—Mr. Harrigan's—to accomplish this with minimal federal involvement and control, and therefore at minimal cost to the taxpayer. This would include the creation of a President's Commission on Olympic Sports, composed of prominent interested Americans who are not partisan to either of the conflicting organizations. Two members of the Senate and two of the House would serve on the commission and it would have a fixed life of 15 months—eight to examine the USOC and report, and seven to make proposals and iron out the problems in time for the 1976 Olympics, and beyond.

The Amateur Athletic Act of 1974, sponsored by Senator Jim Pearson, is anathema to most governing athletic bodies because it implies too much federal control, including the formation of a permanent sanctioning federal amateur sports body. Congressman Mathias' amendment to the federal Olympic charter would remove some of the onus by providing that the American Arbitration Association act as a binding arbiter in settling disputes. But regardless of how it is achieved, something should be achieved—and soon—to improve the systems for developing our athletes.

Even if there were no other nations to impress, even if there were no international events to prepare for, the value of competitive athletics in this country would still be boundless. Consider what an athletic field does for a depressed neighborhood, or a successful sports program for a college—the spirit it breeds on campus and the moneys it generates to provide a broader intramural base. The whole school benefits. I don't know anything that gave a greater boost to Michigan than our football teams in 1932 and 1933 (but not necessarily 1934).

A winning pro football team like the Dolphins can galvanize an entire metropolitan area. Washington rallies around the Redskins. I found myself identifying with their success. George Allen's principles are consistent with mine (his dedication to hard work, his personal habits), and the Redskins were extraordinarily unified. The man holding an end-zone season ticket—or, if he is like me, the three-game-a-Sunday armchair quarterback watching at home while trying to get some work done (at about 50% capacity)—not only identifies, he feels a part of the effort.

I am beginning to wonder, however, if that vital relationship might not have taken a turn for the worse in recent months. Or been given a shove in the wrong direction. I refer to what seems to be a growing appetite—an apparently insatiable one—for money in sports, a preoccupation with "how much" instead of "how good," with cost instead of value. If I read my sports pages correctly, and I read them every day, the age of benevolent ownership is over. The emerging super figures of the '70s are the dollar-oriented athlete and the profit-oriented owner, usually in conflict. Neither side trusts the other. And neither is particularly attractive. The sports news is glutted with salary disputes and threats of strike, of demands and contractual harangues, of players jumping from one league to another or owners threatening to pull their franchises out of this or that city unless demands are met or profits improve.

I have mixed emotions about much of this. On the one hand I would not deny an athlete his opportunity for maximum compensation. A professional athletic career is short-lived at best, and in the free enterprise system a man should be able to realize his worth. By the same token, management can handle just so much. Professional sport has a history of failing ownerships, of bankrupt franchises. The balance is often delicate and Congress has, in the past, been very sympathetic with its anti-trust legislation.

I take neither side. But I do pose a few questions on behalf of the man in the middle: the fan. I'm one myself, and what scares me is that the fan may ultimately be abused, if he has not been already. The money has to come from somewhere. Traditionally, the somewhere is the fan's pocketbook—and in the electronic age in which we live, the advertiser's. At what point will the fan become disillusioned? When he comes to the conclusion that the team he is supporting has no reciprocal interest in his affection, I think there will be a withdrawal of support. It might not come today, or this season, but it will surely come.

It will be interesting to see how the fans react to the players who are now jumping to the new World Football League. It will be interesting to see how the Miami fans react this season to Csonka, Kiick and Warfield, who are committed to the Memphis franchise in 1975. I personally wish them well, because they are fine athletes who are fun to watch. From the rival Redskins' point of view, goodby will no doubt be good riddance.

I wonder, too, what the preoccupation with money is doing to the athletes themselves. When a pitcher throws a no-hitter and is quoted that from the fifth inning on he was thinking about the bonus he would get, how does this affect the young athlete reading the story? When a college basketball senior drafted by the NBA in the first round talks about being worth "at least three million," what clicks in the mind of the freshman on that team?

There must be some serious clicking going on because I am told that the colleges are experiencing the worst run of recruiting violations since World War II. Whether or not the super-paid athlete begets the super-paid-under-the-table athlete I would not venture to say, but I was shocked when I heard that. I was under the impression the colleges were in a saner period, were better controlled, with safeguards at both conference and national levels.

When honesty and integrity suffer nationally, they no doubt suffer in athletics. And vice versa. It would be difficult to measure what effect scandalous behavior in sport has on the nation as a whole, but I do not doubt there is one. The last thing we need is to be cynical about it.

I don't think the fan is unaware. In their rush to get his money promoters have often tried to sell him labels rather than contents, figures rather than pedigrees, and as often as not he turns up his nose. It will be interesting to see how the World Football League fares in that respect. It will not be the NFL's equal for some time, but it is going to ask the fan to consider it major league. If it *is* major league, the fan will recognize it as such and support it.

I have my doubts about the advisability of the WFL telecasting games on week nights, in effect invading the time and territory of the high schools. We already have legislation preventing Friday night NFL telecasts. I don't know if the Congress will sit still for Thursday night telecasts that might cut the revenue of high school sports.

I have to admit to a certain empathetic thrill in reading about all the money being tossed around today in sports. It takes me back to the time I was offered a big-money deal to play for the Green Bay Packers: $200 a game, with a 14-game schedule and a 10-day contract cancellation provision.

There was a lot happening to me then to turn my head. In 1931, when I was being recruited out of South High in Grand Rapids, Harry Kipke himself, the famous Michigan coach, brought me to Ann Arbor for a visit. I had made two All-State teams—one of which I captained—and must have been worth rushing because Michigan State, Northwestern and Harvard also expressed interest, and in those days recruiting wasn't as widespread as it is today.

The Kipkes took me to their home for the weekend, and to several sports events, and then to the bus on Sunday night. I had to be impressed by the personal attention.

So the hotshot center from Grand Rapids came to live at Michigan, in a third-floor 10-by-10 room way in the back of the cheapest rooming house I could find. I shared the rent ($4 a week) with a basketball player from my hometown. We each had a desk and a bed, which pretty much exhausted the floor space, and there was one small window between us.

The Big Ten did not give athletic scholarships then. My tuition was paid by a scholarship from South High, and Coach Kipke got me a job waiting on tables in the interns' dining room at University Hospital and cleaning up in the nurses' cafeteria. My aunt and uncle sent me $2 a week for Depression-day extravagances. My father's paint factory was going through a depression of its own, and since there were three other Fords to raise he couldn't send anything.

When I pledged Delta Kappa Epsilon my sophomore year, I moved into the fraternity house and got a job washing dishes. There were four of us at the sink, including Herman Everhardus, an outstanding Michigan football player. As dishwashers I would say we showed good early foot but uncertain technique. I doubt we would pass today's sanitation codes.

I know I am guilty of leaning heavily on football jargon in speeches and off-the-cuff remarks, but for two reasons I think this is understandable. First, there is obviously a deep American involvement in and a great social significance to the game. No game is like football in that respect. It has so many special qualities, among them the combination of teamwork involving a large number of people, with precise strategies and coordination that are essential if anyone is going to benefit. The athletes are highly skilled, but subservient to the team. Yet if they do their job, they give an individual an opportunity for stardom. I know of no other sport that demands so much, and returns so much.

The experience of playing the game can be applied to the rest of your life, and drawn from freely. I know it is easy to find similarities in politics. How you can't make it in either field without teamwork and great leadership. How you attract grandstand quarterbacks by the droves. In football you hear them during and after the game. In politics we hear them 30 seconds after our last speech. Or during it. Most grandstand quarterbacks have never played either game, yet are the loudest and most knowledgeable critics. The thick skin developed in football pays off.

The second reason is that I truly enjoyed my football experience, and just don't want to forget it. Under Harry Kipke, Michigan used the short-punt formation, which was popular then, and as the center I fancied myself the second-best passer in the lineup. If I'm dating you, the center in the short punt or single wing is not just a guy who sticks the ball in the quarterback's hands. Every center snap must truly be a pass (between the legs), often leading the tailback who is in motion and in full stride when he takes the ball. I don't mean to be critical, but I think that is why you now see so many bad passes from center on punts and field goals. They don't have to do it enough. I must have centered the ball 500,000 times in high school and college.

Football was probably more enjoyable for us then because the pressures were not as great as they seem to be now. What made it *less* enjoyable was that we labored under limited-substitution rules, which reads out as total exhaustion after every game. In a close one no more than 15 or 16 men would play. If you left the game at any point during either half you couldn't go back during that half. The rule was modified my senior year to allow you to return to play in the next period. It didn't help much.

I averaged about a fourth of a game my first two years. Kipke had superb teams, so a lot of guys played. I got the "best prospect" award after the 1932 season, but the next fall I hurt a knee and was out of the running early. Chuck Bernard not only kept the job at center but made All-America.

My senior year, when I played regularly and was voted Most Valuable, the team, as I've mentioned, was not as good, and we didn't run up any scores. We were too busy trying to keep them from being run up on us. The starters were usually the finishers. We held Minnesota, the Big Ten champion that year with such stars as Pug Lund, Phil Bengtson and Bud Wilkinson, scoreless in the first half, and missed two good scoring opportunities ourselves. Then we ran down and were overwhelmed 34–0. (Having been worn out once too often, I would say that today's unlimited substitution is better. More people get to play, and the game is less a test of stamina and more of skill.)

But though we weren't very good, we weren't very exciting, either. Kipke's style was written up in *The Saturday Evening Post* under the headline "A Punt, A Pass and A Prayer." As far as I know that was the origin of the phrase and it bespoke the Michigan system: Play tough defense. Punt when in doubt. Force the other guy into mistakes. Then score on a pass. And pray for deliverance. We *always* kicked off. We *always* punted on third down inside our own 25, unless we had about a yard to go. We played tough defense—a straight 6-2-2-1, with none of the sliding and stunting you see today. We ran the short punt to death. We were dull.

That last year we had an excellent passer named Bill Renner, who broke his leg before the season started. Our punter was the best I ever saw in pro or college, John Regeczi, and he got hurt in the third game. If your system depends on a punt, a pass and a prayer, and all you have left is a prayer—well, that might put you in good hands, but you better not count on any favors. We lost seven out of eight.

Despite our humble record I was invited to play in the East-West Shrine Game in San Francisco on Jan. 1, 1935, primarily on the recommendation of Dick Hanley, the Northwestern coach. I had had a pretty good day against his star guard, Rip Whalen. According to Hanley, when he asked Whalen why Michigan made so much ground up the middle that day, Whalen said, "Ford was the best blocking center I ever played against." I still cherish that remark.

The Shrine signed two centers for the East, a boy from Colgate named George Akerstrom, and me. On the train ride from Chicago to California, Curly Lambeau, the coach of the Packers, went from player to player, plying the good ones about their pro football interest. He ignored me. Then in the first two minutes of the game Akerstrom got hurt. I played the rest of the way— 58 minutes, offense and defense. After the game a group of us were given the option of a train ride home or a free trip to Los Angeles to see the movie studios. Being a conservative Midwesterner unacquainted with glamour, I naturally chose Hollywood.

On the train from San Francisco to Los Angeles, Curly Lambeau sat with me the whole way. He suddenly knew my name. And he asked me to sign with the Packers. I told him I'd think about it.

That August I played in the All-Star game in Chicago, the second in which the college stars played a pro team. We had Don Hutson and a number of outstanding players, but the Bears beat us 5–0. Shortly after that I got Curly's offer in writing: $200 a game for the 14 games. Potsy Clark of the Lions matched the bid.

But pro football did not have the allure it has now, and though my interest was piqued I didn't lose any sleep over my decision. When Ducky Pond, the Yale coach, came to Ann Arbor at Kipke's bidding to ask me to be on his staff at New Haven, I saw the chance to realize two dreams at once—to stay in football and to pursue a long-nurtured aspiration for law school. Pond's offer was $2,400 for the full 12 months, as his assistant line coach, jayvee coach and scout—and to coach the boxing team in the winter. Of boxing I knew next to nothing. No, that's not right. I knew absolutely nothing.

So that summer while working in my father's paint factory I slipped off to the YMCA three times a week to get punched around by the Y's boxing coach. I didn't get good, but I got good enough to fool the Yale freshmen, one of whom was Bill Proxmire.

I coached at Yale for six football seasons, from 1935 through 1940. My scholastic advisers were convinced I couldn't handle law school and a full-time job, so they wouldn't let me try until 1938 when, with reluctance, they relented for two courses. I was warned that of the 125 students entering law school that year, 98 were Phi Beta Kappa, and that was clearly another league from the one I had been in. Somehow I got by, and that spring, without telling Ducky Pond, I began taking a full load of law courses.

In the fall of 1938 Pond made me head jayvee coach in charge of scouting and raised my pay to a fabulous $3,600 a year. One of the teams I scouted that year was my alma mater, Michigan, starring the great Tom Harmon. Michigan beat Yale, but barely—15–13.

The Yale staff was excellent. Greasy Neale was on it, and Ivy Williamson, who had played at Michigan before me and was my roommate one summer when I took a couple of law courses there. He was going for his master's in education. Williamson later became a winning head coach at Wisconsin.

By January of 1941 I had completed my law requirements and I received my degree in June. World War II ended my football career. I was in Tom Hamilton's V-5 program for two years, working as athletic officer with responsibilities as an assistant ship's navigator on an aircraft carrier in the Pacific, but I never went back to coaching, except vicariously on Sunday afternoons at RFK Stadium. I doubt George Allen notices.

I spoke earlier of the lessons to be learned from football. The reverse is also true: football learns. Or at least its practitioners do. Of all our sports I think football best reflects the nation's tastes, and is constantly adjusting to meet them. I know of none that changes as often, or as radically.

I don't think anyone—except the coaches and the placekickers—would argue that the changes in the pro game that were adopted this winter were not in answer to public taste. There had been a growing conservatism in pro football, and by nature Americans are not conservative—at least not in sports. The last several Super Bowl games were played by highly competent teams, maybe the best ever, but they were so competent within the framework of their own restrictions that the Super Bowl lost the spontaneity and the sparkle the public likes. They were almost too good for their own good, if that's possible. The fan likes to see an error as a very real threat, as a possible sudden turn to rev up a game. Right or wrong he likes his heroes to take gambles now and then, to make mistakes. Interestingly enough, the impact of the new rules brings the pro game closer to the college game, and as far as I'm concerned that's for the better. The colleges have had that spontaneity. Their coaches have been more daring. Two or three of the most recent college bowl games were far more interesting than the Super Bowl.

As I think back on my own football days, I find myself marveling at today's athletes—in all sports. They are better in every respect; bigger, stronger, faster and better cared for. I think it is true that they have had much to divert their attention from the drive to excel—affluence can be disconcerting, and there was the war in Vietnam. But these are hardly insurmountable handicaps. Affluence should be an asset. It helps provide the facilities that broaden the base we need now. And, of course, all wars end.

The fact remains that these athletes *do* excel. And together with our international programs, I would like to see our national institutions reflect that excellence. I would prefer, to mention one example, that the service academies be in the forefront of college football instead of in the rear. Or at least be above average.

The reason for their current slump is obvious and forgivable: the five-year service commitment a cadet or midshipman has after graduation. Proposals have been made to get around that commitment, to balance the need for good intercollegiate representation by the academies against the requirements of the services. One idea is to allow academy graduates who have a chance for a professional athletic career to postpone their military duty for X number of years. The argument is that they will wind up being more valuable to the service at an older, more settled age, when they will be looking for the post-athletic career so many pros fail to establish. And, of course, they would still be young men.

My surface judgment is that it might be workable for an athlete to spend, say, five years after his academy class graduates in a reservist's role, meeting once a week for training and two weeks a year on active duty, and then fulfill his service obligation. There well may be an Arnold Tucker or a Doc Blanchard or a Pete Dawkins out there waiting for such a chance. All three were All-Americas, and all became outstanding career military men.

I think this, too: that our better athletes today, despite the times and all the terrible crises, are really the vanguard of our young leadership. I know that in terms of spiritual awareness they are way out in front.

A friend of mine from my old Congressional District, Billy Zeoli, does a lot of ministerial work for the Dallas Cowboys, and over the years—at various group meetings and breakfasts and banquets—I have come to know men like Norm Evans, Bobby Richardson, Stan Smith and Bill Glass, and each time I meet another one like them I am reassured.

Three years ago Billy took me to his services for the Cowboys when they were in Washington to play the Redskins. I can't tell you how impressed I was. But my son Jack was really impressed. Jack got to sit next to Jethro Pugh. He didn't tell his old man to hurry up that day.

DAN JENKINS

Game-Face

I may have to dough-pop Cissy Walford before I ever get around to the dog-ass Jets.

What she has done is semi-unforgivable and a rotten thing to do to somebody that she is supposed to be about half-crazy about, which is me.

I am hotter than a pot of butter beans right now, as you might can guess. Shit, I'm hot.

What Cissy did was go squirt off her mouth to Boke Kellum, our friendly neighborhood fag Western hero, about this book I am writing.

From *Semi-Tough* (1972). Title supplied by the editors.

And what Boke Kellum did was go squirt off his mouth to the newspapers about it, and here it all is, right here in my hand in the Saturday morning Los Angeles *Times*.

The dog-ass headline says:

PUCKETT TURNS AUTHOR FOR SUPER BOWL.

The story says:

All-Pro Running Back Billy Clyde Puckett, who may hold the key to the New York Giants' chances in tomorrow's Super Bowl, will be taking notes on the sidelines throughout the game.

The *Times* has learned that Puckett is keeping a diary of Super Bowl Week and will turn it into a hard-cover book for a major publishing house next fall.

Puckett's book will be most revealing, according to reliable sources.

It is understood that Puckett is delving into many personalities involved in the Super Bowl attraction, and will present some of the darker sides of the game of pro football itself.

Much of the book, the *Times* has learned, will be devoted by Puckett to describing exactly how the Giants prepared for the contest.

It is also believed that Puckett will describe how he developed his rip-roaring running style, a style which has made him the leading rusher in the NFL.

Parts of the book will also touch on some of Puckett's close friends, such as Boke Kellum, the handsome star of the hit TV series, *McGill of Santa Fe*.

There's some more but mainly it's quotes from some of the dog-ass Jets, like Dreamer Tatum, about me being so talented as to be able to prepare for a big game and write a book at the same time.

Boy, I am so hot right now that I could turn into some kind of T. J. Lambert.

If there was ever a bad time for something like this to come out, it is the day before the Super Bowl.

Cissy Walford has already cried a few times this morning and tried to make everything all right by grabbing me in the crotch but it hasn't helped.

I've told her that if I lay my eyes on Boke Kellum again I was gonna leave him every way but alone.

Man, I'm still hot. And all of this hit me more than an hour ago when I got up. I don't usually get hot like this for anything other than a football game. But I am hot.

Shake says that I shouldn't be so hot because a lot of other stud athletes have written books and everybody just figures that it's what a stud athlete does for money these days.

Barbara Jane said she didn't think it was anything to be bothered about.

"It's not as if we've just lost to Spring Branch." She smiled.

Barb said the best way to look at it was that the dog-ass Jets wouldn't know what to do, going up against a real live intellectual book writer.

I said what bothered me most was having to go to a squad meeting pretty soon and take a lot of shit from my pals.

But it's something I've got to do. And right away, in fact.

See you in a little while, gang. If there's anything left of me after T. J. Lambert gets through.

If not, I'd like my ashes pitched out of a taxi at the northeast corner of Fifty-fifth and Third.

That's where P. J. Clarke's is, of course.

It's probably asking too much of the owner, Danny Lavezzo, to hang my photo on the wall, back there in the back room where all the celebs hang out; back there with the checkered tablecloths and the Irish waiters.

There wouldn't be much status in having it hanging in the middle room, behind the front bar—the room where everybody stands in line, hoping and praying for a table in the back. There's nothing in the middle room but too much light, and some drunks standing around a garbage pail.

I guess I don't know of anybody who ever got his picture up on the wall in Clarke's, without dying. Not even a Greek ship owner or a columnist. If Frank Gifford or Charley Conerly or Kyle Rote couldn't do it from the old Giant glory days, I don't know how I could expect it.

Maybe my only chance is if T. J. Lambert turns me into a tragic legend.

"Oh, what could have been," they'll say in Clarke's.

And hang my picture.

Feelin' you is feelin' like a wound that's opened wide,
Feelin' you means troubles by my side.
Feelin' you ain't easy,
Don't know how much I can take.
Feelin' someone gone is feelin' nuthin' but an ache.

When you took my credit cards and headed north across the bay,
When you piled up all my clothes there in the hall,
When your anger made you laugh at all the bills I'd have to pay,
I could hear you laughin' louder while I kicked and beat the wall.

You ain't nuthin' but a servin' wench, it's true.
Serve it up and grab a tip or two.
Eggs fried greasy, coffee dark,
Donuts hard as sycamore bark,
But you'll trap another fool like you know who.

I just hope you'll keep on movin' down the road.
Movin' faster than I'm drivin' this old load.
Much more heartache I ain't needin',
Though your looks have got me bleedin',
I'm just about to get your memory throwed.

But feelin' you is feelin' like a wound that's opened wide,
Feelin' you means troubles by my side.
Feelin' you ain't easy,
Don't know how much I can take.
Feelin' someone gone is feelin' nuthin' but an ache.

Nothing helps trouble and woe, I think, like listening to music. I've been listening to some Elroy Blunt tunes here on the portable stereo we brought with us to our palatial suite.

One of my favorites among his new songs is "Feelin' You," which is those words I've just recited, in a semi-tuneful way.

It's late in the afternoon upon this Saturday in January. I've been back from the squad meeting for quite a while and had lunch up here in the suite.

Some of the Giant fans who have flown out for the game are having a party down around the cabanas by one of the swimming pools. That's where Barbara Jane and Cissy are. Shake Tiller and Hose Manning have gone over to the Beverly Wilshire to talk to some *Sports Illustrated* writers and editors and reporters and photographers.

We'll be heading out to Elroy Blunt's mansion for his party in a while. He drew up directions for our rented car on how to get there.

This hasn't been too good a day for the stud hoss, unfortunately.

All of my teammates had read that story in the Los Angeles *Times*, and of course they all clapped when I walked into the squad meeting.

I caught a whole bunch of heat.

Varnell Swist said, "Say, baby, you ain't gonna write anything about what a cat does on the road, are you?"

Puddin Patterson said, "Tell us about that rip-roarin' runnin' style. Do you just jive it on in there for six by your own self?"

Puddin said, "Er, uh, say, baby. Do you rip first, or do you roar first?"

There was lots of giggling among my pals.

Euger Franklin said, "If me and Puddin ain't blockin' nobody's ass, he just lay down, baby."

Varnell Swist said, "What you gonna say about the road, baby? Some wives is gonna read that mother you writin', you dig what I'm sayin'?"

Puddin Patterson said to the squad, "Lookie here, cats. Lookie here at the cat who holds the key to the whole jivin' tomorrow. Ain't he a dandy? He just gonna go out there tomorrow by his own self and win his self a Super Bowl."

I was trying to grin while I blushed.

Puddin said, "Cat gonna put that rip-roarin' jive on them other cats and they just gonna say, 'Oooo, he hit har-rud,' Cat just goes shuckin' and jivin' out there with nobody but his own self. Lookie here at this mean cat."

Jimmy Keith Joy said, "Say, baby. That *dark* side of pro football you gonna jive about. You ain't talkin' about brothers, are you?"

Euger Franklin said, "Show us that key you holdin' to the game, baby."

"It's them moves," said Puddin Patterson. "Say. Say, lookie here. The key is in them big old strong legs that lets this cat go rippin' and roarin'."

"Make my hat hum he hit so har-rud," said Euger Franklin.

Puddin said, "Everybody get down and cat say hup. Cat say hup-hup. Cat say hup-hup-hup. And old Billy Clyde go jivin' for six. Crowd say oooo-weee, he run so har-rud because he's a-rippin' and roarin'."

O.K., I said. Go ahead on.

Puddin said, "Everybody get down and cat say hup again. Cat say hup-hup. And Billy Clyde go hummin' for six. And crowd say oooo-weee, he run so har-rud and he writin' a book while he rip-roarin'."

T. J. Lambert hadn't spoke until he finished the sack of chili cheeseburgers he brought to the squad meeting.

He finally stood up and licked his fingers and bent over, with his butt toward me, and he cut one that must have been the color of a Christmas package.

"That's all I got for tootie fruities what write books," he groaned.

In the serious part of the squad meeting, Shoat Cooper explained to us what the drill would be for Sunday, in terms of what time everything would occur.

Shoat said we would start getting our ankles taped at eight o'clock tomorrow morning. Those that needed special braces and pads taped on, he said, ought to get to the taping room thirty minutes earlier.

He said he hoped everybody on the team could have breakfast together at nine in the Señor Sombrero Café on the second floor.

He said we would leave for the Los Angeles Coliseum about ten-thirty. It would be about eleven-fifteen when we got there, he said, and that would give us plenty of time. "To get frisky for them piss ants," he said.

The kickoff wasn't until one-fifteen, he pointed out. It had been set back fifteen minutes by CBS, he said, in order for the network to finish up a news special it was doing on some kind of earthquake that wiped out several thousand chinks somewhere yesterday.

It was news to me and Shake and we shared some kind of look which had to do with Big Ed Bookman. News about the earthquake, I mean. Not about the kickoff.

Shoat said that both the offense *and* the defense would be introduced, on both teams, for television before the game. He said we should line up under the goal post that would be appointed to us and carry our hats under our arms when we trotted out to our own forty-five yard line and faced the dog-ass Jets and stood there for the "Star-Spangled Banner."

That would be the last thing we would do before the kickoff, Shoat said. Therefore, he said, this would come after we had warmed up and then gone back into the dressing room and crapped and peed and drank some more Dexi-coffee. Them what needed it, like the interior linemen.

"A little spiked coffee never hurt nobody's incentive," Shoat said. "Especially them lard butts who have to play down in that trench where the men are."

Shoat said we might have a long time to lay around the dressing room after we warmed up because the National Football League had a fairly lavish pregame show planned.

Shoat said he understood that both the pregame show and the halftime show would have a patriotic flavor.

"That can't be anything but good for football," he said.

According to Shoat, here's what was going to happen before the game:

Several hundred trained birds—all painted red, white and blue—would be released from cages somewhere and they would fly over the coliseum in the formation of an American flag.

As the red, white and blue birds flew over, Boke Kellum, the Western TV star, would recite the Declaration of Independence.

Next would be somebody dressed up like Mickey Mouse and somebody else dressed up like Donald Duck joining the actress Camille Virl in singing "God Bless America."

And right in the middle of the singing, here would come this Air Force cargo plane to let loose fifty sky divers who would come dropping into the coliseum.

Each sky diver would be dressed up in the regional costume of a state, and

he would land in the coliseum in the order in which his state became a
United State.

When all this got cleaned up, Shoat said, United States Senator Pete
Rozelle, the ex-commissioner of the NFL who invented the Super Bowl,
would be driven around the stadium in the car that won last year's Indianapolis 500. At the wheel would be Lt. Commander Flip Slammer, the
fifteenth astronaut to walk on the moon.

Riding along behind the Indy car, Shoat said, would be two men on horses.
One would be Commissioner Bob Cameron on Lurking Funk, the thoroughbred which won last year's Kentucky Derby. And on the other horse,
Podna (the horse Boke Kellum pretends to ride in his TV series), would be
the current president of CBS, a guy named Woody Snider.

Finally, Shoat said, the teams would be introduced and two thousand
crippled and maimed soldiers on crutches and in wheel chairs and on stretchers
would render the "Star-Spangled Banner."

Shoat told us the halftime was likely to run forty-five minutes. It would be
a long one, at any rate, "which might be a good thing if we got some scabs to
heal up," he said.

The length of the halftime, Shoat said, would depend on whether CBS
would decide to interrupt the Super Bowl telecast with a special news report
on the earthquake, which might still be killing chinks with its fires and floods
and tidal waves.

"I never knowed a dead chink, more or less, to be more important than a
football game," Shoat said. "But maybe if a whole gunnysack of 'em get wiped
out, it's news."

Shoat said it was too bad we would all have to miss it but the Super Bowl
halftime show was going to be even more spectacular than the pregame show.

He said there would be a water ballet in the world's largest inflatable swimming pool, a Spanish fiesta, a Hawaiian luau, a parade stressing the history
of the armored tank, a sing-off between the glee clubs of all the military
academies, and an actual World War I dogfight in the sky with the Red
Baron's plane getting blown to pieces.

The final event of the halftime, he said, would be an induction into the
pro football hall of fame of about twenty stud hosses out of the past, including
our own Tucker Frederickson, the vice-president of DDD and F. United
States Senator Pete Rozelle would preside, Shoat said, along with Camille
Virl, the actress, and Jack Whitaker, the CBS announcer. When the induc-
tion ceremony was over, Shoat said, then Rozelle and Whitaker and Camille
Virl would lead the inductees in singing a parody on the "Battle Hymn of the
Republic," which was written by somebody in the league office. The title of

it, he said, was "The Game Goes Marching On," and he understood it might make some people cry.

Shoat said CBS hoped the whole stadium would join in the singing, since all 92,000 people would have been given a printed copy of the lyrics.

The last thing in the halftime would be some more birds. While the stadium was singing this song, Shoat said, several thousand more painted-up birds would be released and they would fly in such a way overhead that the likeness of Vince Lombardi, the great old coach, would appear.

This was about all that was discussed at the meeting.

Shoat said for all of us to start getting our game-face on.

"When we take that field," he said, "I want you pine knots to be in a mood to stand them piss ants ever way but up."

I got a collect long-distance call from Fort Worth a while ago and of course it was from my Uncle Kenneth.

He just called up to thank me for the fifty-yard line seat I sent him along with a first-class round-trip plane ticket.

Uncle Kenneth said that as much as he wanted to be out here, he didn't rightly see how he could go off and leave an acquaintance he had made with an old boy who thought he knew all about how to play gin.

I said I understood. That when a good business opportunity presented itself, a man had to act on it.

Uncle Kenneth said he would certainly be watching the game on color TV, however. He said he had four large bet on it—at pick—and how did I feel?

Perfect, I said.

I told him he could cash that plane ticket in for some whip-out, if he wanted to.

Uncle Kenneth said he had done that, already. But he said he was going to keep the game ticket as a souvenir, if I didn't mind.

"How's old Shake 'Em Up, Shake Loose?" he said. "He fit and all?"

Sure was, I said.

"And old Barber Jane?" he said. "Still prettier'n a crocheted afghan, I guess."

You bet, I said.

"Well, Billy, you have a good ball game now," Uncle Kenneth said. "Remember what I've always said to you. A lot of first downs'll take you to that land of six."

That's right, I said.

"First downs, Billy," he said.

O.K., I said.

"Comin' second ain't nuthin'," he said.

You got that right, I said.

"The YMCAs are full of all 'em that come second," he said.

Sure are, I said. Take care now.

"First downs, Billy," said Uncle Kenneth, hanging up.

.   .   .

All I wanted to do just now was clean up and be ready to go to Elroy Blunt's party. That's sure all I wanted to do but of course I didn't get to do that because I had me some visitors.

Burt Danby, the head of DDD and F (and therefore the head of the Giants) stuck his self in the door of our palatial suite and held up his hand.

"Got five?" he said. "I can come back."

I said he might as well come on in and get a seat before the Communist army got here.

"I just wanted you to meet a *super* guy," said Burt, who was wearing his go-to-southern-California outfit. His pink sports coat and pink scarf with white pants and white shoes that were tight and soft like little old white and soft gloves.

It was just my own self at home, I said. Shake Tiller was still over at *Sports Illustrated*'s penthouse in the Beverly Wilshire, and the girls were down at the swimming pool.

"Saw the girls, saw the girls," said Burt. "They're in splendid hands down at the cabanas. *Hell* of a party going on down there. Christ, it looks like Manuche's at Monday noon after we've won a biggie. My God, it's like Shor's in the old days down there. Jesus, it looks like Weston's when Sinatra used to drop by. Fantastic! It looks like Elaine's when the King of Morocco's in town. The place is crawling with top guys. *Crawling*."

I said there wasn't any party going on up here unless somebody cared to watch me take a shower. I had on my shorts.

Burt Danby came on in and behind him he brought in this tall, sunburned fellow who had a drink in his hand and was dolled up in such a way that nobody could ever have guessed that he came from Madison Avenue and had to be one of those Eastern, lockjaw motherfuckers who wouldn't know shit from tunafish.

Burt's friend had on some light-gray pants and a navy blue coat and some shiny buckled loafers and the last of the Brooks Brothers white button-downs and a green-and-gold striped tie. He also had on a big button, pinned to his coat, which said: ALCOHOLICS UNANIMOUS.

It only took me an instant to figure out that I had seen the guy before. He was that empty suit from the *Sports Illustrated* party that Shake Tiller had made sport of.

Burt Danby said, "Stud hoss, say hello to a *hell* of a guy. Put it in the vise with Strooby McMackin, the *president* of Kentuckian Cigarettes."

I said hidy.

"*President*," Burt Danby said. "As in *who* runs the store. As in how do I love thee, *let* me count the ads."

I said hidy again.

Strooby McMackin had a voice no louder than your average lift-off at Cape Kennedy. He said, "I met the stud the other night. Unfortunately—heh, heh—I was shit-faced and don't remember much. Hello again."

Burt Danby said Strooby McMackin was a *hell* of a good guy and a *super* client of DDD and F, even if he was sort of a sentimental Jet rooter.

"Oh, I like all football," said Strooby McMackin. "I guess I became a Jet fan a few years ago before I took over this company. You have to be Jesus Christ to get a Giant ticket."

Burt Danby said, "You've got 'em now, fellow. For next year. As many as you need."

Burt laughed heartily and patted Strooby McMackin on the arm.

"Get you a pop?" Burt said to his friend. "Another tightener? Just down the hall. Won't take a second. How about another train-misser? Want a little see-through?"

Strooby McMackin said no, he was fine.

He said, "Puckett, I saw those young ladies you were with at the SI party. They're down around the cabanas with your whole New York Giant gang. Mike was down there a while ago, and Jerry and Felix and Stanley. All the die-hards I see around midtown."

Good, I said.

"The whole goddamn gang," he said, "Danny's there, Susan, Norm, Jimmy, Teddy, Eloise, Jack, Crease. Goddamn place looks like the back room at Clarke's."

Burt Danby said, "Strooby walked up and said, 'Can Frankie get a table here?' *Christ*, that was funny, Stroob."

I tried to smile.

Strooby McMackin said, "Anyhow, I apologized to your girl friends for all the language the other night. *Dynamite* girls, by the way."

Sure are, I said.

Burt Danby said, "By gosh, we'll convert Strooby yet. You *ought* to be in the Giant camp, Stroob. You *really* should."

Burt looked at me and said, "He'd better go with a winner, hadn't he?"

I said, "It's gonna be semi-tough, but we're lookin' forward to it."

Burt Danby said, "Hey, Stud. Listen. Strooby here has a couple of the niftiest damn teen-age boys you'll ever meet. Really a nifty couple of kids. Chip and Clipper. Thirteen and fourteen. *Terrific* sailors and *plenty good* at paddle tennis."

That was good, I said.

"Oh, hell, they're sports fans, all right," said Strooby McMackin. "They read *Sports Illustrated* from cover to cover every month, and of course they don't miss a Colgate game. I was Colgate 'Fifty-one."

No kidding, I said.

Burt Danby said, "Stud, I know you want to relax, and we're leaving. But take just a minute here and write something to Chip and Clipper on this menu from the Señor Sombrero Café. Just anything. 'Hi, Chip and Clipper, all the best, from the All-Pro himself, Billy Clyde Puckett.' Anything at all."

Strooby McMackin said, "Hell, they'll put that right up on their wall with the poster of Robert Redford."

Then he said, "Puckett, I really do feel badly about being so shit-faced the other night. I was totaled, believe me. And Burt knows that I can usually outdrink anybody at the Creek or Twenty-One or the Frog, or anywhere."

I wrote something fast on the menu to Clip and Chipper, or maybe it was the other way around.

"*Super*," said Burt Danby, slapping me on the bare back. It stung, as a matter of fuckin' fact.

I couldn't resist asking the president of Kentuckian Cigarettes, since he hadn't mentioned it, if he recognized that girl with Shake Tiller the other night, the one down at the cabanas. Barbara Jane Bookman.

"Yeah," he said. "That was, uh, who was that?"

I took considerable delight in telling him that she was the girl in all of his Kentuckian ads right now, on all of the signboards and on the backs of magazines.

"The hell she is," he said. "Well, that just goes to show you how much a president knows."

"*Plenty* good-looking girl," said Burt Danby. "And the ad's a real winner, Stroob. Our creative guys just did a *super* job."

I said she worked a lot at what she does and that she might be the most familiar girl in advertising. I said she had been the Ford Fatigue Girl and the Chrysler Catastrophe Girl and the Mercury Malaria Girl.

Strooby McMackin said, "Well, I'll have to keep an eye out for her. Say, Burt. If this girl's working for me and she's a Giant fan, I guess I'll have to cheer a little for your guys tomorrow."

Burt Danby looked at me and said, "Is he a *top* guy? You're too much, Stroob. You *really* are."

They said they had to go.

"Have a good game, Puckett," said Strooby McMackin. "And may the best team win."

"As long as it's us." I smiled.

Burt Danby whooped. "Is that something, Stroob? Is that *positive* enough?"

As they left Burt Danby turned back toward me and gritted his teeth and made a gesture with his doubled-up fist like he was hitting somebody in the stomach.

"Let's get 'em *good*," he said.

I said O.K. I'd get 'em if he would.

I think I've just heard Shake and Barbara Jane and Cissy come in. So I guess this is all the news for now from Walter Cronkite.

I'll try to get up early enough tomorrow morning to share a few experiences from Elroy's party with you before I go to get taped and eat breakfast with the team.

Might help me calm down some to get up early and do that.

Don't know as though I'll be able to sleep much anyhow.

As Shoat Cooper says about big games, "I believe I see in the papers where we got us a damned old formal dance comin' up."

We sure do, if there is any truth in all captivity.

And old Billy Clyde is gonna be asked to dance ever dance.

GEORGE GRELLA

Baseball and the American Dream

Despite Howard Cosell, Pete Rozelle, and other purveyors of fashionable despair, baseball, not football, will always be our National Pastime, the Great American Game. Occupying a unique place in our national heritage,

Originally appeared in *Massachusetts Review* (1975).

this most American of sports speaks as few other human activities can to our country's sense of itself. It is a game of manifold delights, many of which have been detailed by chroniclers both attentive and inspired; few, however, have pondered its meanings and metaphors, its ethics and aesthetics. The game is as instructive, as beautiful, and as profound as the most significant aspects of American culture. It should be compared not only with other sports, but with our other indigenous arts—our painting, music, dance, and literature. In its theory and practice baseball embodies some of the central preoccupations of that cultural fantasy we like to think of as the American Dream. Anyone who does not understand the game cannot hope to understand the country. A subtle and complex activity, it rewards not mere brute strength, but agility, intelligence, imagination, and daring. It quite naturally requires similar qualities of its students: imbued with ritual, magic, myth, and intimations of immortality, baseball is a game for poets and priests, philosophers and scholars, worthy of contemplation and rich in wonder.

Historians and anthropologists generally agree that all ball games played by teams originate in Egyptian fertility rituals, which were transmitted to many other cultures throughout the Western world. With their characteristic penchant for dualities, the Egyptians combined sport with their Spring ceremonies, splitting up a group of priests into two teams which fought to move a ball across a designated line or through the doorway of a temple. The game was a symbolic contest between the forces of good and evil, light and darkness, summer and winter. Some scholars believe the ball was intended to represent the head of the dismembered and decapitated Horus, son of Osiris, the god of fertility; others think it was meant to be the head of Osiris; still others see it as a sun symbol. Whatever it represented, the ball clearly was related to some symbol of a lifegiving power, and the game was a ceremonial celebration of Spring, life, and fertility. (Some cultures, by the way, used an actual head in their games; perhaps the maturity of a civilization can be dated from the time a symbolic head replaced the genuine article.) Ritual ball games of one sort or another appear in most cultures since ancient Egypt; the contests were even amalgamated into the Spring festival of the medieval Church—Easter—reinforcing the Christian doctrine of the Resurrection. The fertility rites that inspire ball games also provide the source for drama as we know it; the *agon* or contest is the ritual conflict from which Greek drama grew and flourished. Sports, religion, and art are therefore intimately connected in their origins; baseball has never relinquished this important connection to other modes of human creativity.

It requires no giant leap of logic or intuition to recognize that the magical qualities of primitive religion also exist in baseball. The sport is the nearest thing to a national Rite of Spring that all Americans can celebrate and enjoy;

no other activity in our country is so closely linked to ritual and myth. It is, as we have been recently reminded, the Summer Game, played by the Boys of Summer, an ongoing celebratory dance in the golden season. Its limits in time are April and October, including our happiest months. Even in cold climates we know that if Opening Day has come, Spring cannot be far behind. In most human communities a holy or exalted personage blesses his people or their implements, prays for successful crops or business, weds his city to the sea, or celebrates some religious rite to mark or even to guarantee the coming of warm weather; in America some honored person—perhaps even whoever is currently impersonating the President—throws out the first ball. We know then that the weather will moderate, crops will be planted, and life will renew itself. Baseball is obviously life-centered and lifegiving, a game of youth and its attendant virtues—grace, growth, joy, and love.

Although the life-enhancing functions of baseball are undeniable, serious questions inevitably arise. It must be a sunlit game, despite the high incidence of night baseball (the Chicago Cubs are the only major league team who intransigently decline to perform the deed of darkness), yet the Spring, as any fan knows, is invariably marked by large numbers of rained-out contests. If baseball brings the sunshine, why is there so much rain? The apparent contradiction is easily resolved by remembering that the coming of the rain in Spring is also a sign of the renewal of life; the game, paradoxically, in the early season is played precisely so that it will be rained out. Its inception causes the beneficial rain to fall and, in Chaucer's phrase, pierce the drought of March. Conversely, when the players went on strike in 1972, the whole country suffered a very cold and late Spring; as soon as the strike was settled, so was the weather. Because its long season extends into the Fall, baseball not only introduces the fine weather but also holds off the forces of death, darkness, and sterility until its World Series is over. It guarantees, then, both the sowing and the reaping, the planting and the harvest; it begins in seedtime and ends with the golden haze of Autumn. When it ends its season we must prepare for the long nights of winter darkness, the death of the year, the maimed and maiming rites of football, the death-centered game. We endure as well as we can this season of blight until late February, when the teams, mixing memory and desire, go South once more to welcome and initiate their Spring Training, and the annual cycle is renewed.

In perfect accord with its agricultural and life-sustaining functions, baseball possesses the power to unite its particular community around itself, endowing huge groups with pride, spirit, and harmony. In the latter stages of the season its magical effects—called pennant fever—can draw spectators from widespread locations who urge their team onward to success and participate vicariously in its triumph; the city glows with exuberance, power, and a kind of happy madness. The whole nation pauses to participate in the World Series. The pennant race of 1969 demonstrates baseball's *mana*, its super-natural powers of approbation and benediction, to full effect. Mayor Lindsay of New York, caught up in a tight race of his own, took pains to be seen at the games of the New York Mets, not only for the public exposure but undoubt-edly to be inspired by the team, to drink at the fount of charisma. When the miracle of '69 occurred and the Mets won the National League pennant and the World Series, Lindsay was baptized by the joyous Mets in their victory champagne—the drink of heroes—and was a sure winner in his own contest. Although his race was difficult, any scholar of the game could have con-fidently predicted Lindsay's win, ignoring the nonsense of polls and ballots. Although he honored the team, the Mayor never fully credited their efforts for his triumph; but he owed it all to that spilt-over charisma.

In addition to its relationships with the historic rites of antiquity, baseball's development continually demonstrates other connections with the magic realms of myth. Like mysticism, in Cardinal Newman's brilliant pun, baseball begins in mist and ends in schism. Quite properly for a sport that partakes of the divine and the transcendent, its origins are shrouded in mystery, obscured by the dark backward and abysm of time, hidden in claims and counter-claims, theories, dreams, and fantasies. One of the most persistent of its many falsehoods is the Abner Doubleday legend, a bit of folklore perhaps in-spired by Abner's perfect baseball name. The game actually seems to have descended from the English game of rounders, but nothing so prosaic as normal evolutionary development marked its real coming of age. The first recorded instance of a game played under more or less recognizable rules (mostly, forbidding the throwing of the ball at the runner, which permitted a hard and hittable ball to be used and changed the game immeasurably from a children's sport to an artistic endeavor) was on a June day in 1846. It is suffi-cient proof of the essential rightness of things and of the existence of a benevo-lent divinity that this immortal contest took place in an area of Hoboken, New Jersey known as the Elysian Fields. From its beginnings, then, the sport enjoyed sanctity by association; not even the most ardent fan could have in-vented the fortuitous conjunction of the abode of the blessed, the playground of the gods, with the grand and godlike game.

Even the demonstrable falsehood of the Doubleday story has created fur-ther happy implausibilities. Because of the legendary Abner, baseball estab-lished its Valhalla, the Hall of Fame, in the bucolic hamlet of Cooperstown, New York, a central location in the country of the American imagination. It is the spot where the most important American literary hero, James Fenimore Cooper's archetypal frontiersman, Natty Bumppo (a great baseball name), roamed the woods and hills. Also known as Hawkeye, Deerslayer, Pathfinder,

and Leatherstocking, Natty would have been a remarkable ballplayer: his un-
erring eye, his speed afoot, his stealthy tread would have made him one of the
game's immortals. But his spirit still patrols the vast and rolling outfield
around Cooper's Lake Glimmerglass, where two major national myths can
forever harmoniously commingle. The close connection between two pastoral visions of America has occasionally surfaced in other places. Zane Grey,
whose novels depend upon Cooper's frontier myth, also wrote baseball stories.
A recent movie, *The Great Northfield, Minnesota Raid* has a lovely comic sequence showing Jesse James and his gang attending a small town baseball game,
a rare moment of homage to the nexus of two important American traditions.
In living memory, the marriage of Joe DiMaggio and Marilyn Monroe represents an astonishing celebration of two interpenetrating mythologies. The
coupling of star athlete and movie queen was not only the usual celebrity
wedding, but a magical fulfillment: the best ball-player in the world was rewarded with the love of the dream goddess of Hollywood's illusions; the silent, solitary, superbly gifted American hero possessed the Golden Girl of the
West, the acknowledged avatar of the Perfect Blonde of our national fantasy.
A consummation so perfect was destined to be ephemeral. Even our literature
has only hinted at and yearned towards such a match; it has never permitted
itself more than the dream of such completion. (Some years ago a magazine
story on DiMaggio beautifully capsulized the equality of the relationship.
Monroe had made a morale building trip to entertain the troops in Korea
which was an enormous success. She told her husband, "Joe, you never heard
such cheering." He replied, "Yes, I have." And indeed he had.)

Along with its happy connections with other aspects of the divine in
America, baseball provides us with a daily reminder of our rapidly disappearing past. In the age of future shock, where in many neighborhoods the oldest
house may be a trailer with a flat tire, baseball recollects an earlier and calmer
time, forming an organic and unbroken continuum back to those days when
men played the game on the Elysian Fields. It is one of the few forms of creative endeavor where as much knowledge seems to reside in men as in documents, books, and records. Because a ballplayer's athletic life is so short and
the game so difficult, he is usually continually under the tutelage of retired
ballplayers who learned the subtleties of the game from still older ballplayers
in a solid line going back to the past. These men, like Nestor and Mentor and
the sages of myth, impart their lessons, their advice, and their tales to aspi-
rants, preserving a living heritage. Thus many generations have already
passed through the hundred or so years since the game reached its first full
blossoming. It flourished, of course, in a very different America from our
own, yet retains an aura of nineteenth-century innocence in some of its
quaintly unfunctional equipment. There is an appealing naivete about the

odd uniform, with its high stockings and knickers, the collarless shirts, the boys' caps, all of it not very far removed from the uniforms of the Currier and Ives illustrations, a vestigial survival of what must have been gentlemen's leisure wear a century ago.

The very textures of the sport, which today we would probably call organic, not only present a pleasing spectacle, but also recall a lost America of endless pastures and widening vistas, when potential ball fields spread out toward the horizon in all directions. Those horizons have become so constricted that today the baseball stadium in some cities may be the only spot of greensward larger than a front lawn—and then, alas, it may turn out to be made of the detestable plastic turf, a merely symbolic field. But the greenness of the park, the tan dirt of the infield, the white of the lines and uniforms (though, again, some teams are now clothed in what look like rejects from the dye vats of a pajama factory), the shining ash or hickory bats, the natural ingredients of wood and leather and horsehide remind us of our agricultural heritage, of the homely handcrafts of the past, when the land was the entire source for all the needed implements of the game. It is fashionable among students of the sport to see it as an essentially rural pastime, brought into the city in order that we may vicariously repeat and recreate an illusionary ideal of our agrarian heritage. The pastoral associations of the game certainly reinforce the rural nature of baseball, but I think the game is neither wholly rural nor urban. It is instead a game of the small towns and villages, of a place appropriately between the poles of the American experience. The middle ground of the towns suits the democratic nature of the sport, its Jeffersonian quality; every player toils in solitude, temporarily relinquishing his independence to join in the loose confederation of the team, united with other men in struggle by the flight of the ball. Certainly it seems likely that only a village of at least a modest size could supply enough players to make up a team and enough spectators to guarantee regular play; the rural areas, after all, were underpopulated, the fields cultivated or stubbled, lacking the necessary community to support a group of men playing together on a smooth parkland. The game was generally played on the ubiquitous village greens; the earliest known representation of the sport in America shows a group of boys playing on Boston Common in 1834, using the existing footpaths for baselines. In some of its earlier variations the game was even called "Town Ball."

The great difficulty of the sport, ignored by its detractors and neglected by its defenders, further contributes to its democratic implications. As in the best of American institutions—with the current exception of the presidency—individual freedom means individual accountability. Every player is potentially responsible for victory or defeat; just as his triumphs are visible to all, so are his mistakes. He cannot hide an error in a mass of struggling bodies or commit it in some obscure corner of the field, for it is there in the open for everyone to see. The complex variety of skills the game demands—hitting, throwing, fielding, running, and, above all, thinking—make it impossible for anyone to attain perfection (always excepting the pitcher: with a rare combination of great ability and good luck he can conceivably pitch a perfect game; there have been, in fact, eight in regular season play since 1900; the chances of pitching one are something like one in 75,000). As Ted Williams has pointed out, baseball is the only field of endeavor where a man can succeed only three times out of ten and be considered an outstanding performer. The difficulty and the presence of luck in the game further ensure its democracy; on any given day the worst team in the league can defeat the best. If the teams all played once a week for fourteen or fifteen weeks, as they do in the winter game, nothing at all would be proved. A team that can win 65% of its games is almost assured of a pennant, so far as anything is assured in this most chancy of sports. But it takes a long season of struggle and tenacity to determine the winner; the baseball season tests, over and over, the skill, the courage, the character of the players. The possibility of a team winning all of its games or a player batting 1.000 may exist in theory, but has something of the likelihood of the earth falling into the sun or a politician telling the truth.

Perhaps because they must learn to live with failure as an essential ingredient of their pursuit of success, baseball players have always seemed a special breed of men with personalities as striking and memorable as their abilities. Americans have always responded to imperfect glory or glorious imperfection; at least since Captain Ahab, we have preferred our heroes to be not only superhuman but also maimed, wounded, somehow incomplete. Amid its myriad legends—zany, pathetic, or inspiring—the flaws, the failures, the defeats of baseball live the longest. Merkle's boner, Snodgrass's muff, Mickey Owens' dropped third strike will endure forever in the memory of the fans and the unforgiving history of the game; the good such men have done is interred with their bones. The injuries and accidents that shortened or reduced otherwise remarkable careers instruct us in courage and sustain endless speculation about what might have been: the stoic suffering of DiMaggio, crippled by a bone spur, led Hemingway to immortalize him all over again in *The Old Man and the Sea*; we wonder what glories Sandy Koufax would have achieved with a healthy arm or Mickey Mantle with healthy legs. How many games would Dizzy Dean or Denny McLain have won had one of them not had a freak injury and the other a freak personality? What would Pete Reiser's future have been if he had not played with such courage and abandon that he broke his body and its gifts against a dozen outfield walls? Perhaps when they bestow great talents the gods of baseball exact some harsh demands.

Some baseball players simply seem bewildered by their abilities. The game abounds with drunks and suicides, with players who burned as brightly, briefly, and mysteriously as comets, with strange, doomed men who systematically abused and destroyed their skills, great athletes who were inept custodians of their genius. Shoeless Joe Jackson, with a lifetime batting average of .356, hit .375 in the 1919 World Series without even trying, but was banished from the sport for his part in the fix. Ty Cobb, the Georgia Peach, was one of the nastiest men who ever played; perhaps the game's greatest hitter, his absolute need to win tormented him into an obsessed and driven man. He played the game cruelly and ruthlessly, behaving like a spoiled boy when things didn't go his way: on many occasions he simply walked out of a ballgame when piqued by an umpire's call or a manager's remark. If Cobb was driven by Furies like Orestes, Ted Williams was the petulant Achilles of the game, sulking and pouting in his tent if the sportswriters criticized or the fans mocked him; his unyielding pride made him the least loved superstar in baseball. In 1968 Denny McLain won an incredible 31 games; after squandering his talent as if it were inexhaustible, he was last heard from pitching in some obscure hinterland from whose dark bourne few right-handers return.

The inherent craziness of baseball's history redeems some of its darker side. Baseball fact rivals folklore: its true stories read like tall tales out of the legendary American past. Its eccentric characters and bizarre events probably evolve from the inherent magic of the game; certainly not even the most daring and fertile creative genius could dream up some of the zany improbabilities of baseball history. Three Dodgers winding up at third base on the same play; Germany Schaefer stealing second base on a pitch, then stealing first base back again on the next; Smoky Joe Wood and Rogers Hornsby initiating their distinguished careers by playing for the Bloomer Girls: it all happened. Shoeless Joe Jackson, the illiterate country boy who was a Shakespeare at the bat, playing the outfield barefoot; Bill Veeck sending a midget up to the plate; Wilbert Robinson circling under an airplane trying to catch a grapefruit tossed out by one of his players: as Casey Stengel says, you could look it up. The hardheaded John McGraw once hired a total incompetent (and kept him for three years) because the man informed him that a fortune teller had predicted the Giants couldn't win the pennant without him; with the nonplaying Charles Victory Faust warming up before every game the Giants won three pennants in a row. Despite the dubious wonders of jet travel, television, and Astroturf, baseball retains its magic. Every season has its crazy plays—in a game at Pittsburgh this year Davey Lopes of the Dodgers had to slide in to home plate from the dugout side in a botched play. Detroit slugger Willie Horton took one of his tremendous swings at Fenway Park in April and lofted a high foul, which killed a pigeon on the wing; the bird landed dead at home plate, perhaps an ill omen for Red Sox pennant aspirations.

No legend in or out of baseball compares with the real life and exploits of the game's most famous player, Babe Ruth. A ringtailed roarer off the field, a Bunyanesque batter on it, Ruth dominated the game as no man before or since could; if history is the lengthened shadow of a man, baseball still lives in the shade of that awesome slugger. His deeds and life are an American epic; none of the singers of his fame has been so far the Homer that the man deserves. More than any individual, Ruth saved baseball and America's faith in itself by introducing a new heroic age in our national game; after the Black Sox Scandal of 1919, which may have been more important than World War I in educating the nation in the dubious lessons of disenchantment, Ruth's powerful bat and personality revived public interest in the sport. His extravagant life style, his joy and abandon both on and off the field, his expansive triumphs in one of the great ages of expansion in our history, made him the perfect man for his time. He hit his 60 home runs in 1927, the boom year in which Lindbergh flew the Atlantic, giving the country two heroes totally suited to the public imagination.

With the properly obscure origins of the mythic hero, Ruth came out of a background of poverty and trouble with the law, was introduced to baseball at some sort of reform school, and rose to be a player of unparalleled gifts, an immortal legend while still an active ballplayer. Everyone, even those who know nothing of the game, has heard the stories—Ruth saving a dying child by hitting a home run, Ruth picking his spot in the stands and hitting a ball right to it, Ruth hitting baseballs farther than anyone had before. Appropriate for our culture, Ruth was a life-enhancing phenomenon, a hero whose deeds demanded constant attention. Gifts were showered on him, children mobbed him, a cigar and a candy bar used his name, his extracurricular activities earned him the biggest fine in baseball history. A lovable grotesque, a comic giant, he was America's eternal child; he never knew his teammates' names, lived only for the moment, possessed an infant's prodigious orality, eating himself into a mammoth stomachache that crippled him for most of a season. His name was right—he was always the Babe. His presence still lives in the game because he became its most extraordinary personality, its most completely heroic figure, entering almost immediately into the realm of myth. The greatest wonder of Ruth's life may be that he really lived: it still seems hard to believe that he wasn't evolved from the brave hopes of the nation.

In addition to its richness of ritual and history, its fascination of character and event, baseball offers ample material for philosophical speculation. The true fan is not only a spectator, enthusiast, and historian, but also must be a student of the ethics, aesthetics, and ontology of the game. The thoughtful fan investigates more than simply the obvious lore; he pursues the essence of baseball, its shape and meaning, its resonant possibilities. One of the most fundamental and significant truths of the game derives from the peculiar shape of its playing area. With the exception of cricket (which you have to be English to understand) baseball is the only team sport played with a ball that does not use a rectangular field. All other ball games are territorial and circumscribed; all play occurs within a box, where a team defends one end and attempts to penetrate the other. In such games success is measured by the number of penetrations a team perpetrates and/or permits; football is so territorial that one of its hallowed statistics deals with land acquisition, i.e., yardage gained and lost. Territorial games rely upon time, depending always upon a predetermined duration of the clock. Baseball, on the other hand, virtually denies the limitations of space and time.

Like all sports, baseball must, of course, accede to the authority of lines. Without boundaries, a game is merely chaotic free play: it may even be true that a culture whose games have no boundaries is anarchic, while a culture whose games are rigidly circumscribed is tyrannical. (It is probably no accident that professional football, with all its associations with war and death and its tightly limited playing area, rose to its greatest popularity during the Vietnam War; notice, too, that a recent occupant of the White House proclaimed himself an ardent football fan.) Baseball, however, submits to the fewest lines of any sport, and is the game of the libertarian, of the free and the brave. Although the field is commonly called a diamond, the term is incorrect: only the infield basepaths constitute a diamond, while the full playing area occupies a large, ever-expanding angle whose apex is home plate.

The winning team in baseball, because of the shape of its field, cannot acquire territory, operating instead in a realm beyond mere spatial measurement. The play advances and runs score through the cyclical actions of the players leaving and returning to home, in the one arena of American life where you can go home again. A player may make this long and arduous journey with a single gesture—a home run, quite properly dubbed a roundtripper or a circuit clout—but more often he progresses in stages, dependent on the performance of his teammates following him. The diamond, then, is merely an arrangement of bases, small islands of security in the perilous avenues leading from and toward home; most of that diamond is dangerous territory, with only three small spots where a man can be safe. The left and right field foul lines constitute the game's only boundary; the space they limit can expand outward beautifully and indefinitely. As a result, the state of being in or out of bounds is expressed in the terms "fair" and "foul," the criteria of aesthetic judgment; the men who play and umpire the game obviously recognize its potential as art, appreciating as they do the varying distances, sometimes awesome, sometimes minuscule, between the fair and the foul. No other game opens rather than encloses space. If the stands were removed from the football field, the game would still be conducted within its dreary box; if baseball's outfield bleachers were removed (they exist only for the convenience of the spectator and the profit of the owner) the game could continue its space across the land, widening ever outward over the prairies and pastures of the Republic. The nation then becomes one grand ballfield. The importance of baseball's potential for infinity cannot be ignored; as Thoreau remarks after measuring the depth of Walden Pond, "I am thankful that this pond was made deep and pure for a symbol. While men believe in the infinite some ponds will be thought to be bottomless." So baseball's space endows us with the opportunity for our imaginations to romp, untrammeled, with the gods.

Baseball not only extends space to infinity, but also suspends and dissolves time. With no clock, no regulation of seconds, minutes, and hours, baseball need not submit to the inexorability of temporal limitation. Naturally, time passes as the innings progress and the grandstand shadow lengthens across the field: Yogi Berra, who often speaks with the perception of a Zen master, described for all the ages the problem of the outfield penumbra in the late innings—"Out there," he said, "it gets late early." Baseball's unique freedom from any external time imposes great challenges along with great joys: the team cannot stall, or run the ball into the line to kill the clock, or manipulate the clock in order to score. A tie game does not exist—all games must end in a victory and a defeat, and a tied game could conceivably go on forever. The game succeeds in creating a temporary timelessness perfectly appropriate to its richly cyclical nature.

The usual length of a game, as everyone knows, is nine innings; the structural unit is, presumably, the inning, which is further subdivided into the three outs that make it up. Notice that any number of runs or hits can occur in an inning, but it must always have three outs. Like hits or runs, outs can be accomplished in an extraordinary number of ways. Since an inning, like a game, exists free of time, its result and length depend only on the factors that cause outs; games seem, therefore, to be lost rather than won. Pressure is exerted most strongly on the team in the field rather than the team batting. Since pitching is usually considered 75 percent of the game, and since the ball must beat the runner to the base rather than vice versa, much of the burden of winning ball games seems to be placed on getting the other team out, on performing defensive tasks perfectly, on making as few mistakes as possible. In the terrible realities, the excruciating tensions of pennant races, it is axiomatic that the team that makes the fewest mistakes will win: this suggests that the inning and the game—and, for that matter, the entire season—possess a moral or ethical quality. If a player does something wrong—commits an error, hangs a curve, throws to the wrong base, forgets to back up a play, swings at a bad pitch—he may cause the downfall of his team. Since baseball denies players perfection, and luck plays so large a part in the game, no one can escape being wrong many times throughout the season. The game teaches a humbling lesson: one must approach as nearly as possible to perfection, but will always fail. Sooner or later even the best players will err, the fastest pitchers will be maltreated, the cellardwellers will beat the first-place club, the superlative hitter will strike out with the bases loaded. Baseball teaches character, courage, fortitude, and patience; it tests men and teams as no other sport can. No mistake can be forgiven; it will always turn up in the box score, which accounts for every run, fixing the blame indelibly. Thus, for all its celebratory qualities, there is a tragic side to the game. There must always be a loser as well as a winner, and every team loses, without hope of equality, since there cannot be a tie; often the difference between winning and losing is tragically small—a bit of shoe polish on a white ball, a minute foul tip instead of a clean strike, a pebble in the infield to give a crazy hop, a dropped ball, a dumb play, a missed sign—but since every team must lose, even the haughtiest clubs can be instructed in humility. (The once mighty Yankees have received plenty of such instruction in the last decade.) In every game someone must falter so that someone will win, somehow, somewhere, some time.

It should by now be obvious that those observers who constantly complain about the static nature of the game are sado-masochistic types who feed on a steady diet of violence and action and enjoy mindless repetition. (Despite the propaganda which asserts that an offensive lineman must have the intellectual capabilities of a nuclear physicist to play football, the pro teams appear to use about five or six basic plays—the better the team the fewer and less imaginative the plays—which is what makes the so-called Super Bowl so tremendously boring.) More charitably, they may be suffering from a mere lack of proper instruction in the riches of the game. The true fan knows that no two games are ever alike, that the hero of one game may be the goat of the next, that one day's overwhelming triumph turns into another's bitter defeat, that the proud can be brought low and the humble exalted on any given day of the long season. Like any rite, baseball is necessarily repetitive, yet constantly changing; though every game is different, all share the structure of the inning, and participate in the great design of the season. Like any work of art, the game is both static and dynamic, temporal and timeless, a thing constantly moving and always in repose. Its much criticized pauses and its irregular rhythms provide for both player and spectator moments of real time within its timeless world—periods for memory and dream, for introspection, exhortation, communion, and prayer. (One of the reasons soccer will never be fully successful in this country lies in its inattention to the reflective pause: it has no timeouts of any kind.) In the interruptions of quiet we live, learn, and grow, while the game pauses momentarily in its defiance of time and space and stands utterly still.

So baseball responds to some of the deepest yearnings of the American soul. It develops its ritual around the summer season, beginning in Spring rain and ending in mists and mellow fruitfulness. Along the way it celebrates the significant American holidays—Memorial Day, Independence Day, Labor Day—by making them the subject of doubleheaders, and uses its All Star Game to observe Midsummer Eve. Suggesting a pastoral vision of peace and harmony, it feeds both our memories and our dreams, our sense of the past and our awareness of the future. The game reveals to us an unending drama, both comic and tragic, of thwarted hope and vain ambition, of glorious fulfillment and sublime achievement, of the necessary contests between cities, regions, and generations; it combines this drama with a fabulous narrative of a thousand extraordinary tales. Learning to accept both victory and defeat, the random hand of fate, the endless possibility of reparation and improvement, we are daily instructed in the conduct of our lives. Like the greatest works of art, the game suggests to man his godlike potential: it reveals to him in form and metaphor the transcendent capabilities within his life, his spark of divinity. The game, expanding space and dissolving time, allows us to sense that old American yearning for pure, unbounded possibility, that marvel of infinity and eternity. Baseball should clearly be considered *sub specie aeternitatis* and its chroniclers—who should be not only reporters but aestheticians—must be ever mindful of their duty to the essence of the game. The thoughtful student of the art comprehends its subtleties and its grand metaphors, its texture and its structure, its space and time. More simply, like any player or any fan, he responds to a game unlike any other in its place in our culture and its peculiar hold upon the men who play it and watch it: all who know the game love it beyond logic or reason.

The golden season rolls all too quickly onward and the summer game flourishes rhythmically with it. The teams rise and fall, winning and losing, gaining courage from suffering and joy from triumph. The pitcher coils and throws, the batter swings, the runners start, the fielders trace their intricate patterns—grown men move gracefully about a huge green vista, poised against an infinity of space in a timeless moment of eternal youth. They all celebrate something older and younger than most human activities: a game, a rite, a myth, a dream: a vision of green pastures and the Elysian Fields. All lovers of baseball, when they speak of the game, end, like Falstaff, babbling of green fields.

DREW A. HYLAND

Playing to Win: How Much Should It Hurt?

When quarterback Dan Pastorini of the Houston Oilers severely injured his knee, elbow, and ribs during the 1978 football season, yet continued to play—with a knee brace, heavily bandaged elbow, and flak jacket— he gained new-found respect from many fans for his great courage. But when basketball star Bill Walton of the Portland Trailblazers objected to taking pain killers for his injured foot and adamantly refused to play, his strength of character was questioned.

These two incidents suggest the seriousness with which sports is viewed by the American public. In fact, what used to be considered just "fun and games" has attained a certain academic respectability among sociologists, psychologists, historians, and even a few philosophers;[1] and a new subspecialty, "sports medicine," has appeared within medicine. In both academia and medicine, it is not that play or sports present peculiar problems (or injuries); rather play and sports highlight certain disciplinary or medical issues in a new way. For the psychologist, an individual's choice of a specific sport and mode of participating can offer revealing insights into personality and temperament.[2] And it is fairly clear that the orthopedic treatment of knee or foot injuries would not have advanced so rapidly if surgeons had not been called upon to treat an increasing number of athletic injuries, particularly for college and professional teams. Both professors and physicians have been forced to look at sports in a new way and to join in focusing on an important set of ethical and, more generally, "value" questions raised by athletic injuries, their treatment, and the ensuing problems of "playing with pain."

The reactions of typical sportswriters and fans to the behavior of Pastorini and Walton were predictable, and reflect the common tendency to assess a person's willingness to continue playing when injured in terms of courage and cowardice. There are others—not highly thought of by sports fans—who regard Pastorini, and those who play in his condition, as "stupid" and even "insane," while seeing in Walton an "intelligent" person who was smart enough to refuse to risk further injury for what was, after all, only a game.

Bill Russell, the former Celtic basketball star, reflected yet a third perspec-

---

Originally appeared in *The Hastings Center Report* (1979).

tive. In an interview on a late-night talk show, the host commented favorably on the courage exhibited by professional athletes who play when injured. Russell laughed and replied that it had nothing to do with courage; professional athletes tend to have high pain thresholds! They don't always feel the pain. Sedentary spectators may project their own anticipated feelings of pain onto injured athletes for whom the injuries simply do not hurt that much.

Still another consideration must be taken into account, that is, the context in which an injury may take place. Suppose, for example, I am out jogging one afternoon and sprain my ankle. I stop running and limp home. Now change the context: I am running on the last leg of a relay which might win the championship for my college team, and the same accident occurs. Now change the context still again: I am hiking with a friend who has diabetes and discovers to his horror that he has forgotten his insulin. I am racing to get the medication when the same accident occurs.

Obviously these examples change the context within which the injury occurs and will alter our assessment of the injured party's response. Who would call me a coward for refusing to continue jogging after a sprain? But, if while racing to get insulin for my friend I cease running because I have sprained my ankle, will I not be a coward, indeed a villain, and perhaps even stupid? The relay team example is more ambiguous, but also highlights the issue. Our assessment of people's responses to injury, and especially their willingness to continue the activity, depends in large measure on the nature of the activity and the value we place on it. Those inclined to ascribe courage to athletes who play when injured and cowardice to those who refuse obviously place a high value on sports and continued participation even when injured. Why?

RISK-TAKING, EXCELLENCE, & FAME

Risk-taking is one of the major appeals of play. Most of the play situations we create involve some element of risk, especially in competitive sports. There we incur the psychological risk of losing, as well as the ever-present risk that what begins as friendly competition may degenerate into hostility. In assuming these risks, we thus test ourselves in the hope that we will both affirm who we are and become more than what we are.[3]

The most obvious form of risk-taking in many sports is the risk of injury. In sports such as sky-diving, deep sea diving, rock climbing, and to a certain extent contact sports such as football or hockey, life itself may be placed at risk. Almost all sports involve greater risk of physical injury than everyday living. Indeed, such risks, far from inclining us to avoid such sports, are part of their very appeal. This same appeal leads athletes, once injured, to be more willing than nonathletes to continue playing and so risk further injury.

This "athletic syndrome" may be a "natural" tendency of those inclined to choose risky activities in the first place.

Nonetheless, three different issues ought to be distinguished: first, the willingness to risk injury; second, the willingness, once injured, to risk further injury by continuing to play; and third, the willingness to play while injured and thus endure the pain, quite apart from the risk of further injury. Almost all serious athletes express willingness to risk injury (to the extent that a specific sport involves this risk), but it is the willingness or unwillingness, once injured, to incur the risk of further injury that distinguishes the Dan Pastorinis from the Bill Waltons. Finally, certain injuries are exquisitely painful although playing with those injuries does not increase the risk of further injury. And some players do display a willingness to endure pain under those conditions.

The pursuit of excellence is a second factor in playing with pain. In *Sport: A Philosophic Inquiry*, Paul Weiss makes the pursuit of excellence the foundation of the significance of play.[4] Most of us, once we become involved in a given sport, are strongly motivated to improve our performance. Moreover, once that impetus is in motion, we may become considerably more willing to play while injured. Often, for example, athletes are more willing, indeed anxious, to play while injured in a "big" game than in a game with a lesser opponent. Why? One factor may be the sense of a greater challenge in the contest.

A third factor, and perhaps the most obvious one, is the desire for fame and glory, or in its more material manifestation, financial gain. If a national championship, an athletic scholarship to college, recognition as an all-American, or next year's salary is at stake, an athlete may exhibit considerably more willingness to play when injured than without these or similar incentives.

Desire for fame or reward may be a self-conscious motive for playing with pain. The other factors, however, such as the appeal of risk-taking or the pursuit of excellence, may not function so much as explicitly recognized motives but as "background conditions" that encourage an athlete to play while injured.

Surely a fourth factor in the "background" category is sheer fun. I may love tennis, or running, so much that my enjoyment encourages me to continue playing though injured, even though I may not list that as one of my explicit motives for continuing.

DECISION MAKING IN SPORTS INJURIES

Factors such as these lead to two situations that cause genuine ethical dilemmas regarding athletic injuries: situations where the *athlete's* desire to play while injured conflicts with what others may think is best for him or her, and situations where the desire of *others* to have an athlete play with injuries conflicts with the individual's own assessment. Because freedom is considered the essence of play and play is precisely something that we *freely choose* to do, the athlete should be the final arbiter of whether or not he or she should play with a given injury. The burden of proof, therefore, should always be on those claiming to supercede the prima facie authority of the athlete over his or her own playing status. What might be some of the limitations on that authority? Under what conditions should we prohibit athletes from playing despite their desire to do so?

Suppose the athlete happens to be my nine-year-old son, desperate, despite a severely wrenched knee, to play in tonight's Little League game. Obviously age and, more important, maturity and responsibility are limiting factors. We are more inclined to give a college or professional athlete the authority to decide than a high school student, a high school student than an elementary school youngster, and so on. It is difficult to state more specific principles than this and it is not a problem limited to sports. Arbitrary age stipulations (the age of majority, post-high-school) are notoriously suspect. I have read that Jerry Kramer, the former star lineman of the Green Bay Packers, once played a game with a detached retina; another severe blow could have blinded him for life. If this is true, then age is obviously no guarantor of rational decisions on this issue any more than on others. Still, age and maturity are factors to which we sometimes legitimately appeal in limiting an athlete's "right" to decide for himself or herself whether an injury should preclude playing.

A second and closely related issue is that of "paternalism," both on the part of parents and coaches. Parents sometimes refuse to allow their children to play this or that sport (usually football) because of the risk of injury. When is such refusal legitimate? Grade school? Most would agree. High school? This is probably the locus of the controversy. College? Here it begins to seem inappropriate.

What of the coach? Suppose the athlete who has an injured knee is one of the team's best players. The player insists that he is able to play; but the coach, knowing the player's excessive enthusiasm and dedication, decides not to put him in the game (this may strain the credulity of some cynics, but it happens). On the one hand, the prima facie authority here rests with the athlete. On the other hand, the coach has responsibility and authority to choose the starting team and to substitute according to his best judgment. Does that authority hold in this instance, or is that an affront to the athlete's authority to decide for himself whether his physical condition warrants playing?

Suppose the team *physician* has advised the coach that it would be detrimental to the athlete to play. Does the physician have the authority to override a player's right to decide whether or not to play? Here is the threshold of a host of ethical dilemmas surrounding the physician's relation to a player, to the coach, team, school, or parents. Suppose that the physician is not directly associated with a team or school. The athlete is, say, a runner who comes to a private physician for treatment. Presumably the traditional relationship between physician and patient applies. Perhaps the physician knows of the athlete's commitment and status as an athlete and may tend to be more "liberal" in his or her advice. The physician will make the diagnosis and offer the best advice possible. The patient is of course free to take it or leave it (even if the athlete is unconscious, there are standard proxies for consent: parents, guardians, or, as a last resort, courts). Suppose the physician advises the athlete to stop running for a month and the patient decides to ignore this recommendation. In that case, the physician is free to withdraw from the case.

Although this situation may seem legally straightforward, it is morally complex. Suppose, for example, that the case involves a runner with a weak heart. In the physician's judgment, continued running involves increased risk of a severe heart attack and even death. The physician fully informs the patient of the diagnosis and the dangers; yet the patient tells the physician he intends to run anyway. We might think that morally the physician ought to take further steps—perhaps speak to the patient's family or employer, explaining the situation and urging support. Still, and finally, it seems that the physician's authority here is limited to offering the best information and advice in the strongest possible terms.

The situation becomes considerably more complex if the physician works with a team, say, a college or professional team. Inevitably, a conflict of interest arises. But one might think not. After all why should this change things? The physician still has the health of the patient as his or her primary responsibility. It is the player who should be the first (and perhaps only) recipient of information and advice regarding injuries. In fact, the situation is considerably more complicated, as is nicely indicated by a selection of quotes from an article in *The Physician and Sports Medicine* entitled "Legal, Moral, and Ethical Questions In Sports Medicine."[5] The article records a panel discussion between several team physicians, a lawyer, a player, and an owner of a professional basketball team. Early in the article, one physician clearly states the traditional version of the issue: "This is a field where the ground rules haven't been completely mapped out, but the physician has an obligation, first and foremost, to the player." The question is complicated almost immediately by the following: "The physician also has an obligation to the coaches, or in professional teams, the owners, because he must help obtain the maximum function of an athlete." Clearly a coach's or owner's assessment of the "maximum function" of an athlete may conflict with the long-term welfare of the athlete.

In a curiously colorful blending of these two positions, one doctor later adds, "And remember that the athlete is the prime consideration here. This means that the athlete is property, and the physician is trying to keep the property at its highest value." By the conclusion of the article, the relative weight of the two considerations seems to have changed: "The professional sports team physician is responsible to management, but he has an *equal* responsibility to the athlete who is his patient"[6] (emphasis added).

Therein lies the problem. Why has the responsibility of the physician shifted to, or at least been complicated by, responsibility to the team? Because the team pays his salary? Because the physician works closely with the trainers and coaches? I believe the concluding quote accurately describes the real relation that exists between many if not most team physicians and the players, coaches, and trainers. But I have yet to see an ethical argument over why the physician's position *ought* to have ever shifted from the first and fundamental position, that "the physician has an obligation, first and foremost, to the player." A tension exists here between the physician's ethical, moral, and professional responsibilities *qua* physician, and other considerations, many of them ultimately economic, created by the intensity and importance of "big time" athletics.

DISCLOSURE OF INJURY

Other important ethical issues arise with special force within the realm of sports medicine: the traditional problem of the patient's right to know and the issue of public disclosure of injury. Again it would seem that an athlete has the same rights and expectations as any patient, namely, to get as thorough and complete an explanation of his or her injury as possible, a careful delineation of alternative treatments, and an honest evaluaton from the physician of the relative merits and dangers of continuing to play with the injury.

What complicates this relatively pristine situation is the physician's association with a team or school. Once a physician begins to perceive himself or herself as having "equal" responsibility to the team and the athlete, conflicts easily emerge. For example, it may seem advantageous to the team *not* to have the physician disclose the extent of the injury to the athlete in the hope that the player will not "panic" and will continue to play. Unethical as this may appear, numerous accusations have been made against physicians whose primary loyalties have seemed to belong not to the athlete but the team; perhaps the most well-publicized recent case is that of Bill Walton, who became so upset over the issue that he refused to play for the rest of the season.

The converse of this issue is the problem of public disclosure. Again, standard practice seems relatively clear: a physician should only make public disclosure of a person's illness or injury with the patient's consent. But the nature of sports, especially "big-time" sports, makes the issue more complex. Consider the following examples: a high school basketball star hoping for an athletic scholarship to college seriously injures his knee. He informs the physician that he intends to hide the extent of his injury, out of fear that it will affect his chances for a scholarship. Representatives of the team contact the physician, inquiring about the status of the player's knee. Is it not unethical to disclose this information without the consent of the player? On the other hand, would it not be equally unethical *not* to inform the team that they are about to give a scholarship to an athlete whose career is precarious at best?

Take a second example: a team physician discovers that an athlete has epilepsy or sickle cell trait, which involve certain dangers for the athlete who continues playing, but which can be reasonably controlled with proper medication and/or careful observation and quick treatment. The athlete wishes to keep the information secret, fearing that it will be "held against him" by the coach. Should the physician honor the athlete's request, or does his "equal" responsibility to the team and the player demand that he disclose the information to the coach?

Finally, an athlete is the star of a professional team, and gets hurt so severely in practice that he will not be able to play in next week's big game. At the same time thousands of spectators are purchasing expensive tickets for the game, primarily to see him play. Both the player and the team owner request that the injury not be disclosed, so that ticket sales for the game will not decrease. Should the physician honor the request, or does he have a responsibility to the public to disclose the extent of the injury so that they know what they are paying for? (Bookies and big-time gamblers value such "secret" information highly.)

Although general guidelines for such situations have been suggested (professional athletes must expect to have their injuries become public knowledge, injuries or illnesses not relating to the athlete's performance should be kept confidential, and so on), I submit again that the burden of proof should always fall on those who wish to deviate from the standard practice, which is that physician/patient confidentiality demands that disclosures of injury or illness be at the patient's discretion.

DRUG USE IN ATHLETICS

A final issue in sports medicine is the use of drugs by athletes. Two fundamental ethical problems are: the problem of fairness, and that of risking further injury. The recent uproar over "blood-doping" in long-distance running
is a case in point. "Blood-doping" is a technique of withdrawing an individual's blood, storing it (either whole or the red blood cells) and later, when the
individual's hemoglobin level has returned to a previous level, reinjecting it
into the original donor. The extra hemoglobin theoretically increases the
blood's oxygen-carrying capacity, and hence, the body's endurance. Notwithstanding the name, one might argue that the procedure actually does not involve drugs, since it is the athlete's own blood that is reinjected before an
event.

As a second example, consider the recent accusation that the Russians and
Rumanians are giving their young female gymnasts drugs which inhibit their
maturation, thereby retarding their physiological development but enhancing
their gymnastic abilities. Suppose that in both cases the drugs are harmless
but there is a clear advantage to the participant. (In the gymnasts' case the
evidence is as yet too sketchy to decide; in the case of blood-doping, recent
evidence suggests that it does not give any advantage.[7])

The case against drug use in these situations is that it gives an unfair advantage to those able, willing, and sufficiently knowledgeable to employ the
procedure. It thus apparently violates the spirit of fairness that is supposed to
characterize sport competition.[8] But what constitutes unfair advantage? Does
not the fact that an aspiring cross-country ski racer happens to have been
raised in northern Vermont rather than northern Florida constitute an "advantage" at least as great as would be gained by blood-doping? Or is not a 5-
foot 9-inch basketball player facing opponents 7 feet tall playing under a
grossly unfair advantage?

In order to enhance fairness, there are weight categories in some sports
(wrestling, boxing, crew) but not in others where the advantage seems as distinct (basketball, football, or shot-put). Clearly, what constitutes "unfair advantages" in sports is ambiguous. Should we then legalize *all* drugs and techniques which give advantage, hoping to alleviate the situation by making the
drugs "fairly" available to everyone?[9] But we would then risk legalizing grossly
unfair practices simply because of our inability to resolve the more ambiguous ones.

Moreover, this leads us directly to the second problem. Many of the drugs
which are supposedly advantageous to the performance of the athlete are also
potentially harmful. The dangers of anabolic steroids, used by many athletes

who want to build weight and muscle, are now well-documented.[10] Pain killers such as novocaine and xylocaine may not be directly harmful but often are
indirectly so, since they inhibit one of the body's most important monitoring
systems for injury, the sensation of pain.

What about dangerous drugs? Alcohol and tobacco are substances that are
or may be dangerous; yet we allow their general use for those who have
reached some arbitrary age of majority. Shall we then allow the use of potentially dangerous drugs for athletes out of high school? Or out of college? Or
over 21? Should we outlaw the use of potentially dangerous drugs for athletes
altogether? We would then be faced with the problem of which drugs are dangerous and which not, a problem as sticky as the problem of unfair advantage.
The problem here, as in the case of unfair advantage, seems to rest, on the
one hand, on our desire to *limit* the use of drugs and artificial supports in
the name of fairness and/or safety, yet on the other hand on the difficulty, if
not impossibility, of making nonarbitrary decisions about these matters.

CONCLUSION

In all these ethical dilemmas—playing with pain, disclosure of injuries, use
of drugs—the values of prudence, autonomy, confidentiality, and fairness are
often overridden by another, more compelling value: the desire to win at all
costs. Ambitious parents, coaches whose jobs are on the line, school officials,
and owners aware of the larger revenues produced by winning teams sometimes value winning more than the welfare of the player. It is tempting to join
those who have deplored the attitude that "winning isn't everything, it's the
only thing," which has led to so many abuses of individual athletes.

But far-reaching reforms would be needed, even to moderate the preva-
lence of this attitude, much less eliminate it. Begin with the coaches. How
might they be encouraged to stop placing winning above the welfare of their
players? Minimally, school administrations or team owners have to stop *firing*
them simply for having losing seasons, or in some cases for failing to have
undefeated seasons. Then, how might the administrators and owners be
stopped from firing coaches simply for not winning enough? By eliminating
the basis of *their* pressure: with few exceptions only winning teams get financial support from alumni and spectators. Ultimately, the attitude of spectators who only want to support winning teams would have to be changed.
Some of those spectators, of course, are the parents who put such pressures
directly on their own children. In short, this situation would only be genuinely alleviated if our entire society modified its excessive emphasis on winning in sports.

Even though such major change is unlikely to occur, individual athletes ought to be encouraged to assess carefully the risks they are undertaking and to assert their rights as patients against the desire of others when the two conflict. In some cases this may take more courage than playing with pain, but the athlete—not the coach, the physician, or the fan—must live with the consequences, long after the game is over.

NOTES

1. In addition to the increasing number of books on the subject, there is now an organization, The Philosophic Society for the Study of Sport, with its own journal, the *Journal of the Philosophy of Sport*.

2. See Arnold Beisser, *The Madness in Sport* (Bowie, Md.: Charles Press Publishers, 1977).

3. For extended discussion of these topics, see Drew Hyland, "Competition and Friendship," *Journal of the Philosophy of Sport* 5 (1979), and "Living Dangerously: Reflection on the Risk-taking Element in Play," presented to the Philosophic Society for the Study of Sport, Ft. Worth, Texas, October 6, 1978.

4. Paul Weiss, *Sport: A Philosophic Inquiry* (Carbondale, Illinois: Southern Illinois University Press, 1969).

5. "Legal, Moral and Ethical Questions in Sports Medicine," *The Physician and Sports Medicine* (March 1975), pp. 71–84.

6. "Legal, Moral and Ethical Questions in Sports Medicine," p. 84.

7. American College of Sports Medicine, "Position Statement on the Use and Abuse of Anabolic-Androgenic Steroids in Sports," pp. 11–12.

8. One of the best discussions of the complexities of this issue is in an unpublished paper by Miller Brown, Trinity College, Hartford, Connecticut, entitled "Boundaries of Victory: Running and Doping."

9. This is Brown's proposal in the above article.

10. American College of Sports Medicine, "Position Statement on the Use and Abuse of Anabolic-Androgenic Steroids in Sports," pp. 11–12.

A Guide for Further Study

The material available on sport and social myths in America is absolutely staggering. Consult Chapter 6, "Sports, Money, and Social Values," in Robert Higgs, *Sports: A Reference Guide* for an introduction to the more important readings. Jason Miller's drama, *That Championship Season*, is a veritable catalogue of sport and social mythology. A pioneering analysis debunking sport as a character builder is Bruce C. Ogilvie and Thomas A. Tutko,

"Sports: If You Want to Build Character, Try Something Else," *Psychology Today* 5 (October, 1971), 61–63. For a piece supportive of character building, a document of the Sixties, see Max Rafferty, "Interscholastic Athletics: The Gathering Storm," in Tom Dodge, ed., *A Literature of Sports*; and John Talamini and Charles H. Page, eds., *Sport and Society: An Anthology*. On defining manhood in sport, try Donald F. Sabo, *Jock: Sports and Male Identity*. For critiques of gender issues, see volumes six through eight of the *Journal of the Philosophy of Sport* which contain articles on these issues by R. A. Belliotti, B. C. Postow, Mary Vetterling-Braggin, and Patrick Grim.

Part III:

The Meanings of Sport

Introduction

Part III: The Meanings of Sport takes up the mighty and controversial subjects of what sport has to do with religion, myth, philosophy, and artistic creation—the human imagination's greatest concerns. Are the poets being facetious or outrageous in claiming that God is a baseball or that baseball is like writing or that The Way can be discerned in the bleachers at Yankee Stadium? The following readings invite us to look more deeply into the play world, to search for ourselves.

Section I: Sport and the Religious ponders what it means to say that sport in America is a religion, or at least a quasi-religious activity. Jack Spicer's startling metaphor, "God is a big white baseball," implies that sport is a self-contained cosmos with its own immutable and merciless laws. Allen Guttmann reminds us in his excerpt, "The Sacred and the Secular," from *From Ritual to Record: The Nature of Modern Sports*, that sport originated as religious ritual in the Greek Olympics, as well as in the ancient ball games in the Americas. Guttmann argues that a process of secularization has taken place in human history whereby modern sport is fully divorced from the concept of "worship of the gods by means of an athletic festival." Also drawing upon anthropology, Edwin H. Cady echoes Guttmann in "The Sort of Sacred, Sometimes Ritual," a selection from *The Big Game*. However, for Cady, the Big Game is an American cultural text wherein the American Dream is represented. And the Big Game has ritualistic effects in its ability to create community. The attempt to create community through the yoking of orthodox Christianity and sport comes under scrutiny by Frank Deford in his three-part series, "Religion in Sport." Contemporary "Sportianity," in Deford's phrase, grew from the muscular Christianity of Victorian times through a Catholic phase to today's fundamentalist Protestant ascendancy with groups such as the Fellowship of Christian Athletes. While the grafting of a specific Christian sectarianism onto sport may be suspect, Michael Novak maintains that sport is a "natural religion." In his chapter by that title, Novak demonstrates that sport contains the same qualities manifested in religion: "an impulse of freedom, respect for ritual limits, a zest for symbolic meaning, and a longing for perfection." Alan Drengson, in "Wilderness Travel as an Art and as a Paradigm for Outdoor Education," foresees and extends the spiritual aspects of hiking. Wilderness Travel, for him, is a form of *Rasa Yoga*, the Yoga which leads to unity of self through an aesthetic appreciation of the natural world and the human being's place in it. In learning the art of mountaineering, one becomes more deeply aware of the source of life and its creative capacities. Such journeys can teach us important lessons about daily life, such as, for example, learning to pace oneself in work.

It is a commonplace that the modern age has no heroes, no extraordinary feats nor larger than life figures. The gods are dead; the pygmies prevail. Neil Armstrong's first step on the moon in 1969 had considerably less public impact than Charles A. Lindbergh's first transatlantic flight to Paris in 1927. Yet America's creative writers find in the sportsworld a realm of heroic achievement, tragic failure, and symbolic meaning—America's equivalent to Homer, Virgil, King Arthur, and El Cid. In Section II: Sport and the Mythic, several writers clarify the mythic dimensions inherent in sport.

Baseball, because of its relatively "ancient" history in our culture and its eccentricity in both players and anecdotes (Dave Winfield beaning a seagull?), lends itself most readily to mythic interpretation. Indeed, the shelf-space for baseball-centered writing triples that of all other sports put together. Most fiction, and much of the poetry, on baseball is written in modes of the bizarre, the surreal, and the supernatural. Very little "straight," meaning realistic, writing can be found. Even the cultural classic, "Casey at the Bat," imagines a magnified and gigantic drama. "Pre-game," from Bernard Malamud's first novel, *The Natural*, recounts the story of Roy Hobbs within an allusive context of Greek myth, King Arthur's knights of the round table, and baseball legend. Each plot action in the excerpt has a built-in mythic level. In the duel between Roy and Whammer, the young hero displaces the elder. In Sam's death via an organ rupture from a Hobbs fastball, the son slays the father. In the shooting of Roy, we see Fate punishing man's overweening pride in his talent. All this occurs on a train ride, a symbolic quest journey by a young man seeking initiation into adulthood and finding his place in society. Malamud's strategy admirably illuminates the mythic power of sport. Tom Meschery's ode to Wilt Chamberlain also speaks forth the mythic proportions of an already colossal human being. The man who once scored 100 points in an NBA game is certainly a "giant Cimmerian statue," larger than life, an incarnate myth. Finally, John Updike's bittersweet and moving account of

Ted Williams' last time up, "Hub Fans Bid Kid Adieu," celebrates another athlete of superhuman ability. Like a Hollywood script, like a fairytale—like a myth—Williams jacked one into the bullpen in Fenway Park in the eighth, then retired. Despite the clamoring crowd, Williams refused to make a curtain call. For Updike, Williams' disdain was perfectly fitting since "Gods do not answer letters."

Lynne Belaief and Hans Lenk offer philosophical analyses of these mythic structures attributed to sport. Their interpretations, like those of the above literary writers, offer new sets of living symbols and archetypes for our culture. Belaief traces the negative views of the body through much of Western thinking and concludes optimistically that "sport clearly expresses a new living myth for a new society, namely, that individual human power can be positive rather than destructive." Belaief's optimism is tempered by Lenk's discussion of the Herculean myth aspects of sport. Lenk sees these myth aspects as something which are in need of being exposed for what they are and perhaps checked. He encourages others to develop "mythological" interpretations of sport (as he has done), since "the social significance of top level sport in mass media societies is growing even larger."

The philosopher in the playground is no longer an unusual sight. Although the ancients, Plato in particular, commented on sport, only in the last forty years or so has sport become a respectable subject for philosophical attention. Indeed, the discipline flourishes, complete with an international society devoted to the study of play, game, and sport. The pieces in the third section, Sport and the Philosophic, are a small, selective, varied, yet representative sample of contemporary thinking about homo ludens, man the player.

As a preface to the several analyses, John Updike's "Tao in the Yankee Stadium Bleachers" proves that sport invites meditation. The poem's Eastern quotations and images applied to a most Western sport move the poem to the level of the universal—the harmony of opposites, proportion, order, unity, peace—the desires of human consciousness itself. William Harper introduces us to philosophy with a little piece entitled "The Philosopher in Us." All of us, Harper contends, have an extraordinary capacity or urge to philosophize. We all *wonder* about things we cannot connect with things we know, including the realm of sport. In asking questions, we come to the point where we cannot answer all the questions we raise: the world appears differently to us. The world at this point is immensely more interesting, and the riddles and mysteries which abide in us and the world can be appreciated. However, this appreciation only comes from sharpening or cultivating our philosophical capacities. Peter Heinegg raises questions about the meaning of sport. Sport, for him, is utopian, comic, sexless, an escape from life, and in the end, a pointless partisan struggle. Heinegg's essay is contemplative and speculative, and invites us to be the same.

The other kind of philosophical activity—the discursive or analytical—is represented by an ongoing discussion concerning deception and cheating in sport. Kathleen Pearson develops a rule for deciding when an act is unethical in sport: "an act must be designed to deliberately interfere with the purpose of the activity in order for that act to be labeled unethical." So Pearson and Warren Fraleigh conclude that the intentional commission of a foul in athletics is an unethical or unsportsmanlike act. A compulsory corollary of this conclusion is that it is logically impossible to win, or even compete, in a game while at the same time breaking one of its rules (intentionally, at least). Craig Lehman questions the logical incompatibility of cheating and competing by examining several arguments offered on its behalf. These fail to stand up to careful scrutiny. So he concludes that there are no good reasons for believing that offensive linemen, if they hold, are generally regarded as poor sports by their peers or the fans: "On the contrary, it seems likely that many of them are regarded as displaying all the essentials of good sportsmanship. Sportsmanship seems to transcend the rulebook, not only in the sense of sometimes requiring more than adherence to the rules, but also in the sense of sometimes permitting less."

The two companion pieces remaining in this section represent the latest application of analytic philosophy to the field. Hans Lenk gives us a feel for what this new area of philosophy is like by focusing in on issues pertaining to definitions (like "sports" and "competition") and action theory. In the last essay, Lenk shows that analytical philosophy of action has a definite bearing on social scientific approaches to the analysis of sport. His methodological considerations lead him to conclude that a necessary integration of the different branches of sport sciences including analytic philosophy is desirable if long range productiveness is to be achieved in understanding sport.

Our philosophical journey through sport begins with speculation, proceeds with analysis, and ends with recommendation.

The readings in Section IV: Sport and the Aesthetic give credibility to the cliché that Ozzie Smith turning two or Dr. J. slamming a 360 is "poetry in motion." Sport as a form of art seems an inevitable and valid comparison. Certainly the poets and essayists in this section have been compelled to aesthetic contemplation by the dance on the field.

For Marianne Moore, baseball is—purely and simply—like writing poetry. How? Her poem provides several answers: the sense of open-ended possibility, the unexpected that can delight or dismay, risk, deception, improvisation, yet containing rhythm and pattern. The metrics of poetry are standard while the word choices are infinite, just as the structure of baseball's innings, strikes, balls, and outs remains constant while no two games are identical in nature. If the tight form of baseball were a sonnet, then 162 sonnets are written between April and October. For Moore, "the Stadium is an adastrium," both fixed and fluid.

Norman Mailer once said that American writers have always seen themselves as athletes. Some are both. Tom Meschery for one, and James Dickey for another, the subject of Peter Meinke's "To an Athlete Turned Poet." In Meinke's playful vision, the same emotions Dickey brought to linebacking converge in his poetry, only now Dickey red-dogs words on poetic lines, not running backs across scrimmage lines. But, clearly, Dickey is a performing artist in both endeavors. That sport has similarities with performing arts is the message of Robert Wallace's "The Double Play." Drawing imagery from ballet, Wallace takes us through all the dance steps from the pitch, the bouncer to short, the feed to the pivoting second baseman, the relay throw, and the stretch at first. Then the defense trots off "in the space where the poem has happened," and we as readers stand convinced that we have surely experienced poetry in motion.

In "Aesthetics Applies to Sports as Well as to the Arts," Paul Kuntz defends the literary intuition voiced in this section that sport is an art form. Wertz and Galvin continue the same line of argument in different ways. Wertz examines figure-skating and discusses artistic creativity in sport. Galvin suggests that we look at the ugly in addition to the beautiful in sport, and examines the problematic nature of appeals to intentionality in attempting to establish a sport performance as an artistic one. For an argument which uses the contrary thesis, that sport is not an art form, see Peter Wenz's appendix to his above contribution, "Human Equality in Sports," in Part I, Section III.

Section I: Sport and the Religious

JACK SPICER

God is a big white baseball

God is a big white baseball that has nothing to do but go in a curve or a
straight line. I studied geometry in highschool and know that this is
true.
Given these facts the pitcher, the batter, and the catcher all look pretty
silly. No Hail Marys
Are going to get you out of a position with the bases loaded and no outs,
or when you're 0 and 2, or when the ball bounces out to the screen
wildly. Off seasons
I often thought of praying to him but could not stand the thought of that
big, white, round, omnipotent bastard.
Yet he's there. As the game follows rules he makes them.
I know
I was not the only one who felt these things.

From *The Collected Books of Jack Spicer* (1975).

ALLEN GUTTMANN

The Sacred and the Secular

Primitive cultures rarely have a word for sport in our sense.[1] If we hold
strictly to our definition of sport as a nonutilitarian physical contest, we
may be tempted to say that primitive men had no sports at all. Carl Diem's

From *From Ritual to Record: The Nature of Modern Sports* (1978).

monumental world history of sports begins with the bold assertion, "All physical exercises were originally cultic."[2] Plentiful evidence exists to document the claim that primitive societies frequently incorporated running, jumping, throwing, wrestling, and even ball playing in their religious rituals and ceremonies.

Ethnographers have done a great deal of work on the games of the American Indians, especially of the Plains Indians who were the last to fall under the cultural influence of their conquerors. In his enormous compendium, Stewart Culin writes:[3]

> Children have a variety of other amusements, such as top spinning, mimic fights, and similar imitative sports, but the games first described are played only by men and women, or youths and maidens, not by children, and usually at fixed seasons as the accompaniment of certain festivals or religious rites. . . . In general, games appear to be played ceremonially, as pleasing to the gods, with the object of securing fertility, causing rain, giving and prolonging life, expelling demons, or curing sickness.

Culin's collection of ethnographic information does not, with rare exceptions, actually elucidate the religious nature of the games, but an excellent example is available from a later account.

The Jicarilla Apaches of the Southwest used "sports" in conjunction with solar-lunar symbolism as part of a yearly fertility rite. Apache myth dramatizes the delicate balance between the two main sources of food among Plains Indians. Animal sources were associated with the sun, vegetable sources with the moon. "The sun is connected with the animal and the moon with the fruit because the sun is a man and the moon is a woman."[4] This dualistic conception of natural order is one that Claude Lévi-Strauss and many other anthropologists posit as an inevitable facet of la pensée sauvage. Writing about the Timbira Indians of Brazil, Käthe Hye-Kerkdal emphasizes the connection between the sport and the world-view: "Athletic contests and the dualistic social organization of primitive peoples can be characterized as two different representations of a polarized picture of the world (eines polaren Weltbildes)."[5] The enactment of the dualistic myth which interests us at present is a kind of relay race in which all males participated at least once between puberty and marriage. One side represented the sun, the other side the moon. The race was governed by complicated rituals. Abstinence from meat and from sexual intercourse was required prior to the race. The track was called "the Milky Way" after the heavenly path over which the sun and the moon had originally raced. The "Milky Way" connected two circles around whose circumference small holes were dug, clockwise, into which the leaders of the two sides, praying all the while, dropped pollen. Trees were then planted in the holes. This and other rituals were accompanied by drums representing the sun and the moon, by flags, dances, songs, a feast. The race itself was on the third day of the festival, at which time a fire was ignited in the center of each circle. The boys were painted, pollened, adorned with feathers, and led to their circles by two young girls carrying an ear of corn in one hand, an eagle feather in the other (symbolizing the two sources of food). Four old men paced out the track, then came the race itself. The ceremony was clearly more important than the question of winning or losing. The leaders ran first, followed by the others in no particular order. Some ran four or five times, but everyone ran at least once. Dances and another feast followed the conclusion of the race.[6]

A second example of cultic sport is not, strictly speaking, drawn from a primitive society, because the Zulu soccer players of Durban, South Africa, are members of a transitional culture between tribal and modern social organization. Their game, soccer, is the most widespread of modern ballgames, but their perception of the game assimilates it to a way of life anything but modern. Zulu soccer teams play by the rules of the International Football Association and the desire to perform well can lead to behavior which directly violates Zulu custom. A coach or trainer, for instance, may strike an older player—a clear instance of an imperative of modern sport overriding a traditional tabu. Other aspects of the "soccer culture" are contributions of the Zulus themselves. There is a preseason and a postseason sacrifice of a goat. Pregame ritual requires that players, coaches, and dedicated supporters of the team spend the night before a game together—sleeping in a huge group around a camp fire. All are naked, but there are no sexual relations. A witch doctor, called an "Inyanga," makes incisions in the knees, elbows, and other joints of the players (very much like the medicine man in the ritual ball game of the Cherokee Indians). The players are also given a purifying emetic. On the day of the game, there is a procession, a movement in tight formation with each man touching those adjacent to him. The Inyanga administers magic potions. When the team is unsuccessful, it is the Inyanga, rather than the coach or manager, who is replaced.[7]

My examples demonstrate the concurrence of sport and religious cult, but Carl Diem's comment implies not merely the possibility but also the inevitability of this concurrence. His generalization forces an implied question upon us. Is sport among primitive peoples invariably a part of religion or is there an independent sector where sports are simply a part of secular life? The question supposes that primitive people have a secular life, which some authorities deny, arguing instead that primitive religious life was coterminous

with culture. The question has a special significance in light of our preliminary paradigm of play–games–contests–sports. If we decide that sports
among primitive peoples were always sacred, always part of cult, then we are
forced to the somewhat curious conclusion that they had no sports at all in
our sense because their physical contests were religious in nature and thus in
an extended sense utilitarian. They were for an ulterior purpose—like assuring the earth's fertility—rather than for the sheer pleasure of the activity
itself.

But is Diem right? I think not. From ethnographic reports we can document many instances of cultic sports, but we cannot meaningfully stretch the
term "religion" to the point where all human behavior falls within the sphere
of the sacred. Children wrestling or casting spears at a target? It is difficult to
think of their actions as part of a cult. Although Käthe Hye-Kerkdal's account of the arduous "log-races" of the Timbira Indians of Brazil makes clear
the cultic significance of many of the races, *some* of them seem to have been
secular activities pursued for their own sake.[8] Dogmatic proclamations of
negative universals ("Primitive peoples have *no* secular sports") are unwise.
Nonetheless, Diem's overstatement contains an important truth—sports, as
opposed to "physical exercises," may indeed have entered the lives of primitive adults primarily in conjunction with some form of religious significance.
It is a fault of our own pervasive secularism that we tend to underestimate the
cultic aspects of primitive sports.

Among the most thoroughly documented and intensively studied of all religious sports was the ball game of the Mayans and Aztecs, whose complex
civilization we can classify as ancient rather than primitive. Although my
subsequent discussions of ancient sports will concentrate on classical antiquity
rather than on the distant pasts of China, India, and other "non-Western" cultures, the prominent place of the Mayan-Aztec ball-court game in anthro-
pological literature, plus the intrinsic interest of the activity, justify the use of
this example.

Behind the game itself was the myth of twin brothers whose names appear
in various transliterations. The brothers left their mother's house in order to
challenge the gods of the underworld in a game of football (actually soccer of
sorts). They lost and paid the mythically predictable price of defeat—death.
The head of one brother was placed in a tree, where a young girl happened
upon it. From the mouth of the head spurted a stream of seeds which impregnated the girl, who removed to the house of the twins' mother, where she
bore children. They grew to youthful manhood and challenged the gods at
football and, again predictably, won. Whereupon the heads of the twins rose
to the heavens and became the sun and the moon.[9]

The archeological evidence for this sun-moon myth can be found in the more than forty ball courts which have been located in an area stretching from Arizona to Guatemala and Honduras. Considered as symbols of the heavens, the ball courts are invariably within a temple complex, the best preserved of which is at Chichén Itzá in Yucatán. In Aztec times, the game itself was under the protection of the goddess Xochiquetzal, but the stone rings through which the ball seems to have been propelled were carved with the symbols of Quetzalcoatl, the famed plumed serpent. To these and other gods, thousands of human sacrifices were offered annually, some of them in direct connection with the ball game. Whether the losing players or the winning ones were sacrificed is unclear, but we can safely assume that the requirements of the contest *qua* contest doomed the losers rather than the winners. In either event, the archeological evidence indicates clearly that the game was quite literally for life or death. Each of the six reliefs at the great ball court of Chichén Itzá shows the decapitation of a player. On the whole, details about the actual playing of the game are meager and much disputed, but Spanish observers of the sixteenth century clearly saw the religious nature of the activity and one of them noted, "Every tennis-court was a temple." [10] The Spanish authorities banned the game—if game it was. [11]

Although Greek sports may be conceived of as the ancestors of modern sports, the physical contests of Olympia and Delphi were culturally closer to those of primitive peoples than to our own Olympics. The relative familiarity of Greek culture and the revival of specific track and field sports in our own time act to obscure fundamental similarities between the sports of the Athenians and those of the Apaches and Aztecs. The problem is only in part a lack of information. Book XXIII of the *Iliad*, containing the funeral games celebrated in honor of the slain Patroclus, is merely the first, and most important, of numerous literary texts which are the heritage of every educated person. Athletic encounters depicted on Greek vases remain a part of the aesthetic experience of Western man and Myron's *Discus Thrower* must rank among the best known statues ever sculpted. Although our knowledge of Greek sports is marked by many lacunae, the problem is less one of information than of interpretation.

The Olympic games, like the Pythian, the Isthmian, the Nemean, and the Athenaic, were sacred festivals, integral aspects of the religious life of the ancient Hellenes. In the words of one scholar, "The Olympic games were sacred games, staged in a sacred place and at a sacred festival; they were a religious act in honor of the deity. Those who took part did so in order to serve the god and the prizes which they won came from the god. . . . The Olympic games had their roots in religion." [12] The games at Olympia were in homage to Zeus. Those of Corinth—the Isthmian games—were sacred to Poseidon,

Table 1
Greek Athletic Festivals

Festival	Place	God Honored	Branch or Wreath	Intervals (years)	Founded (B.C.)
Olympic	Olympia	Zeus	olive	4	776
Pythian	Delphi	Apollo	bay	4	582
Isthmian	Corinth	Poseidon	pine	2	582
Nemean	Nemea	Apollo	parsley	2	573

while Apollo was worshipped by the runners and wrestlers of Delphi and Nemea. (See table 1.) [13]

The exact history of the origins of the Olympic games is unknown and in all likelihood never will be known. It is thought that Olympia was first sacred to Gea, goddess of the earth. Greek legend told also of Pelops ("producer of abundance") and of his suitor's victory in the chariot-race against Oenomaus, father of Hippodamia. It was said that Herakles inaugurated the games at the tomb of Pelops, who was considered to have been brought back to life by the sacrifice of a boy. Defeat in an athletic contest was thus the symbolic substitute for sacrificial death. (Contemporary football coaches who liken defeat to death are better anthropologists than they realize.) Since Herakles had been a Minoan fertility god whom the conquering Greeks demoted to a demigod and hero, the fertility myth is the common thread of every version of the founding of the games. By classical times the games were marked by a kind of syncretism—the altar of Gea remained as one of the four at Olympia, the funeral rites of Pelops were celebrated on the second day of the games, and the great sacrifice to Zeus took place on the third day. The purpose of the games remained cultic, religious. The athletic events were "held in order to persuade the god to return from the dead, to reappear in the form of a new shoot emerging from the dark womb of the earth into the light of day." [14]

The time of the games was as sacred to the Greeks as the place. The games occurred at the time of the second or third full moon after the summer solstice, and three heralds went forth to announce an Olympic truce. The athletes gathered at the nearby town of Elis and spent thirty days in final preparation for their exertions, after which came a two-day procession with much religious ceremony to the actual site on the river Eurotas. Because of the sacred nature of the games, women were excluded even as spectators, except for the priestess of Demeter. The games expanded over time from the simple stade race (one length of the stadium) in 776 B.C. to an elaborate program of foot races, chariot races, boxing, wrestling, a combination of boxing and wrestling known as the *pankration*, discus and javelin throwing. There were contests for boys as well as men and, from 396 B.C., contests for trumpeters and heralds. According to most accounts, the fifth and last day was devoted entirely to religious ceremony. There was a banquet, the gods were solemnly thanked for their sponsorship of the games, the winners were awarded olive branches cut from the sacred grove of Zeus by a boy whose two parents were still alive. The religious character of the Olympic games was never in doubt, nor was that of the other "crown" games (thus named because the victors were crowned with olive, bay, pine, or parsley wreaths).

With this information in mind we can return to the contention of Frayssinet that sports are forms of artistic expression. "The study of various Greek religious ceremonies teaches us that one can always please the gods by offering them . . . music, dance, poetry, drama and athletic contests." [15] The "crown" games, and many hundreds of local games, were indeed a way to please the gods, but this fact should not incline us to the conclusion that sports are one with music, dance, poetry, drama, and the other arts. The relationship of sport and art among the Greeks was the opposite of that suggested by Frayssinet. To the degree that Greek athletic festivals were religious ritual and artistic expression, they had a purpose beyond themselves and ceased to be sports in our strictest definition of the term. The closer the contests came to the status of art, the further they departed from that of sport.

The Olympic and other "crown" games were sacred festivals, and athletic events were often endowed with religious significance; but we can nonetheless detect among the Greeks the emergence of sports as a more or less secular phenomenon too. The remark of a German scholar is relevant. "When one speaks in this context of 'secularization,' one does not mean that an originally religious phenomenon becomes worldly but rather that an athletic game (*sportliches Spiel*), originally laden with religious significance, concentrated itself upon its own essential elements—play, exercise, competition." [16] This is what happened. Sports gradually became a part of the ordinary life of the *polis* as well as a means of worship. That Greek society generally valued physical excellence is obvious from any examination of Hellenic civilization. Cities gloried in the athletic victories of their citizens, rewarded the victors materially with large pensions and other benefits, honored them in legend, in the form of statues, and in some of the greatest poetry ever written (the Olympic odes of Pindar, for instance). Socrates, who had participated in the Isthmian games, admired physical excellence and scorned those who took no pride in their bodies. Even Plato, who never wavered from his conviction that the world of pure ideas was of a higher order than the sphere of the corporeal, had been a wrestler in his youth and had won prizes at the Pythian,

Nemean, and Isthmian games. And in *The Republic* he insisted upon the importance of gymnastic exercises for both men and women. Ordinary citizens emulated the achievements of the most gifted and no city was without its athletic facilities. We can be sure that those who exercised in the gymnasium did not neglect to offer libations to the gods, but we can nonetheless detect the secularization of sport.

Roman society continued and accelerated the tendency. The Romans were given neither to athletic competitions nor to athletic festivals. They believed in physical fitness for the ulterior end of warfare. In his classic study of sports in antiquity, E. Norman Gardiner wrote, "The only athletic events which interested them at all were the fighting events, wrestling, boxing, and the pankration." [17] Roman moralists tended to mock the degeneracy of those who revealed an interest in Greek athletics. "The Greek principle of a harmonious development of the body, and a striving for bodily beauty and grace, was considered effeminate." [18] Not even Scipio Africanus, the famous conqueror of Hannibal in the Third Punic War, was immune from the verbal darts of his fellow citizens when he appeared at the gymnasium in Greek clothing. Not even the imperial prestige of Augustus was sufficient for him to establish "isolympic" games patterned on the Greek model. Such festivals as existed were usually occasions for Roman spectators to watch Greek athletes from Pergamon, Antioch, or Alexandria. More typical for Roman tastes than races or the discus were the gladiatorial combats which date from the funeral celebrations for the father of Marcus and Decimus Brutus in 264 B.C. It is common knowledge that gladiatorial spectacles reached bestial enormity by imperial times. Whatever religious significance remained was apparently overshadowed in the eyes of the mob accustomed to bread and circuses and blood.

In their secularism as in most of their other characteristics, modern sports are closer to the Roman than to the Greek model. It is, indeed, precisely this pervasive secularism which made modern sports suspect in the view of many religious leaders of the seventeenth through the nineteenth centuries. After long and stubborn opposition to the allegedly misplaced emphasis on the body symbolized in Greek athletics, both Catholicism and Protestantism have worked out a *modus vivendi*, a kind of concordat, with modern sports. Theologians now repudiate the harsh condemnations of earlier generations and blame Platonism and Neo-Platonism for the ascetic strain in traditional Christianity. Churchmen now seek eagerly to establish the harmony of modern sports and Christian doctrine. [19] The Cathedral of St. John the Divine in New York has a stained-glass window depicting baseball and other modern sports, the Fellowship of Christian Athletes endeavors to leaven the hard ethos of football and basketball and hockey with the words of Jesus, and in a popular song of the 1970s, the singer asks, in a refrain, that Jesus drop kick him "through the goal-posts of life."[20]

There is, however, a fundamental difference between obligatory pregame lockerroom prayers and the worship of the gods by means of an athletic festival. For the Jicarilla Apache running between the circles of the sun and the moon or the Athenian youth racing in the stadium built above the sacred way at Delphi, the contest was in itself a religious act. For most contemporary athletes, even for those who ask for divine assistance in the game, the contest is a secular event. The Sermon on the Mount does not interfere with hard blocking and determined tackling. Religion remains on the sidelines.

Unless sports themselves take on a religious significance of their own. One of the strangest turns in the long, devious route that leads from primitive ritual to the World Series and the *Fußballweltmeisterschaft* is the proclivity of modern sports to become a kind of secular faith. Young men, and many no longer young, seem quite literally to worship the heroes of modern sports. Journalists, referring to the passion of the Welsh for rugby or the devotion of Texans to football, speak of sports as the "religion" of the populace. "Sport," says an Australian authority, "is the ultimate Australian super-religion, the one thing every Australian believes in passionately."[21] Pierre de Coubertin, founder of the modern Olympic games, spoke reverently of the "religio athletae" and the French version of Leni Riefenstahl's monumental documentary film of the 1936 Olympics was entitled *Les Dieux du stade*. Michael Novak's ecstatic homage to the joy of sports contains a reference to baseball, football, and basketball as a "holy trinity." He goes on to maintain that sports are "secular religions, civil religions. . . . The athlete may of course be pagan, but sports are, as it were, natural religions."[22] If we shift our attention from philosophic ecstasy to sophomoric irony, we can consider the name given by the students of Notre Dame University to their library's mosaic of Christ with upraised arms: "Six Points."[23]

Whether or not one considers the passions, the rituals, and the myths of modern sports as a secular religion, the fundamental contrast with primitive and ancient sports remains. The bond between the secular and the sacred has been broken, the attachment to the realm of the transcendent has been severed.[24] Modern sports are activities partly pursued for their own sake, partly for other ends which are equally secular. We do not run in order that the earth be more fertile. We till the earth, or work in our factories and offices, so that we can have time to play.

NOTES

1. See Hans Damm, "The So-Called Sport Activities of Primitive People," *The Cross-Cultural Analysis of Sport and Games*, ed. Günther Lüschen (Champaign, Illinois: Stipes, 1970), pp. 52–69. Many anthropologists deplore the term "primitive" because of its ethnocentric connotations. Unfortunately, none of their suggested alternatives seems wholly satisfactory and I fall back upon the layman's term, although I do not use it in order to make moral judgments.

2. *Weltgeschichte des Sports*, 3rd ed., 2 vols. (Frankfurt: Cotta, 1971), 1:3.

3. *Games of the North American Indians* (Washington: U.S. Government Printing Office, 1907), pp. 31, 34.

4. Quoted in Morris Edward Opler, "A Jicarilla Apache Ceremonial Relay Race," *American Anthropologist* 46 (1944), 78n.

5. "Wettkampfspiel und Dualorganisation bei den Timbira Brasiliens," *Die Wiener Schule der Völkerkunde Festschrift*, ed. A. Haekel, A. Hohenwart-Gerlachstein, and A. Slawik (Vienna: Verlag Ferdinand Berger, 1956), p. 509.

6. Opler, "A Jicarilla Apache Ceremonial Relay Race," 75–97.

7. N. A. Scotch, "Magic, Sorcery and Football among the Urban Zulu," *Journal of Conflict Resolution* 5 (1961), 70–74. Scotch's experiences among the Zulu seem to have led to conclusions about baseball; see William A. Gamson and N. A. Scotch, "Scapegoating in Baseball," *American Journal of Sociology* 70 (1964), 69–72. For other examples of the blend of primitive and modern, see J. R. Fox, "Pueblo Baseball: A New Use for Old Witchcraft," *Journal of American Folklore* 74 (1961), 9–16; Eugene H. Freund, "The Transition of a Fertility Rite to an Indigenous Spectator Sport," *Quest Monograph* no. 16 (June 1971), 37–41; "Orioles in 'Spirited' Race," *New York Times*, September 16, 1975.

8. "Wettkampfspiel und Dualorganisation," pp. 504–33.

9. Walter Umminger, *Supermen, Heroes and Gods*, trans. James Clark (New York: McGraw-Hill, 1963), pp. 71–72.

10. Quoted in W. A. Goellner, "The Court Ball Game of the Aboriginal Mayas," *RQ* 24 (May 1953), 164.

11. The best studies of the game are Goellner, *ibid.* pp. 147–68; Walter Krickeberg, "Das mittelamerikanische Ballspiel und seine religiöse Symbolik," *Paideuma* 3 (1948), 118–90; Theodore Stern, *The Rubber-Ball Games of the Americas* (Seattle: University of Washington Press, 1949), pp. 34–45, 50–71; Kurt Weis, "Die Funktion des Ballspiels bei den alten Maya," *Die Soziologie des Sports*, ed. Günther Lüschen and Kurt Weis (Darmstadt: Luchterhand, 1976), pp. 115–129.

12. Ludwig Deubner, quoted by Ludwig Drees, *Olympia: Gods, Artists, and Athletes*, trans. Gerald Onn (New York: Praeger, 1968), p. 24. A contrary view appears in E. Norman Gardiner, *Athletics of the Ancient World* (Oxford: Clarendon Press, 1930), pp. 32–33.

13. Data for the table were derived from Gardiner, *Athletics of the Ancient World*, pp. 33–37; H. A. Harris, *Greek Athletes and Athletics* (London: Hutchinson, 1964), p. 36.

14. Drees, *Olympia*, p. 31.

15. Pierre Frayssinet, *Le Sport parmi les beaux-arts* (Paris: Arts et Voyages, 1968), p. 27.

16. Hans Kamphausen, "Traditionelle Leibesübungen bei autochthonen Völkern," *Geschichte der Leibesübungen*, ed. Horst Überhorst, 6 vols. (Berlin: Verlag Bartels und Wernitz, 1972–   ), 1:69.

17. *Athletics of the Ancient World*, p. 49.

18. Peter L. Lindsay, "Attitudes towards Physical Exercise Reflected in the Literature of Ancient Rome," *History of Sport and Physical Education to 1900*, ed. Earle F. Zeigler (Champaign, Illinois: Stipes, 1973), p. 179.

19. See Alois Koch, *Die Leibeserziehung im Urteil der antiken und frühchristlichen Anthropologie* (Schorndorf: Karl Hofmann, 1965); Ralph B. Ballou, Jr., "An Analysis of the Writings of Selected Church Fathers to A.D. 394 to Reveal Attitudes Regarding Physical Activity," *History of Sport and Physical Education*, ed. Zeigler, pp. 187–99; Georg Söll, "Sport in der katholischen Theologie des 20. Jahrhunderts," *Sport im Blickpunkt der Wissenschaft*, ed. Helmut Baitsch (Heidelberg: Springer Verlag, 1972), pp. 43–63; Rüdiger Schloz, "Probleme und Ansätze in der protestantischen Theologie," *Sport im Blickpunkt der Wissenschaft*, pp. 64–83.

20. See Frank Deford, "Religion in Sport," *Sports Illustrated* 44 (April 19, April 26, and May 3, 1976); reprinted in this anthology, pp. 319–350.

21. Keith Dunstan, *Sports* (North Melbourne: Cassell Australia, 1973), p. 1.

22. *The Joy of Sports* (New York: Basic Books, 1976), pp. xiv, 18–19, 34.

23. Dan Jenkins, *Saturday's America* (Boston: Little, Brown, 1970), p. 88.

24. See Martin Hörrmann, *Religion der Athleten* (Stuttgart: Kreuz Verlag, 1968).

EDWIN H. CADY

The Sort of Sacred, Sometimes Ritual

If the Big Game is, then, seriously a popular art form is it also, seriously, "ritual"? About half, I think, "sort of." But let's not wax too serious about all that. Kavanaugh, for instance, helps if we see him squarely. "e.e. cummings's line, 'damn everything but the circus,' contains a truth so true as to be scary," he observes. "Ritual, symbol and feasts are scary because of the power they release." Of liturgical worship, he continues, "Sports are an example.

From *The Big Game: College Sports and American Life* (1978). This selection continues the discussion reprinted on pp. 197–207 of this anthology.

Football is largely ritualized combat." Without "its regular discipline, rhythm and formality," it is merely "a riot," no longer "an event which can bring thousands to their feet as one body in a shared experience of enormous psychic and social intensity."

Talking like that, a liturgist has used football as a successful metaphor for ritual. Turning the relationship around brings interesting questions into view. Is the Big Game a ritual? Or is ritual a good metaphor for the game? About half, I should guess, each way: fifty-fifty. And it pays, by the way, in dealing with "ritual" to take some pains to try to be sure you know what you are talking about. That it is easy to get silly has been demonstrated by T. H. Ferril in "Freud on the 50-Yard Line," a bit of humor worthy of Mark Twain. A wild mix of keen, deadpan observation with arbitrary assignment of "Freudian" meanings, Ferril's essay is funny but mordant. It has earned its popularity, its power as a fool-killer, and ought to have sobered up some of us commentators.

Irony aside, the soberest observer would see at the Big Game all the patterned actions of the teams, the auxiliaries, the crowds. He could hardly fail to feel the rapture of the crowd and, if he knew enough, would glimpse something of that of the players. People become rapt, are "carried away," some in a rapture of fierceness, but some sweetly, in a rapture of identification, of love. Many have it both ways. If our observer could not sense these emotions, he would see and hear them dramatized, even liturgically, during typical "half-time ceremonies." Then suddenly the band comes to attention in solemn array, the bouncy, funny, exhibitionistic mood changes, and a hush falls over the crowd as people rise to their feet. Music in sonorities appropriate to a mass announces the "alma mater" and people begin to sing together a "credo," a "confessio," proclaiming their love and loyalty, everlasting devotion. Sometimes they join in united gesture or salute as well. At Wisconsin they sing the last bar to the words of a cheer, thousands of people swaying in unison as far as they can to left together and then right together with each successive syllable: "U! Rah! Rah! Wis! Con! Sin!" It is liturgical to a degree of intensity not exceeded in St. Peter's in Rome when the Pope appears, to say nothing of what happens in most American churches. Is it not somehow, and other things with it at the Big Game, ritual?

But if you say it is ritual you come up against the demand to say what that means without exposing yourself to Mr. Ferril. Perhaps the best way to begin is to say that ritual means a pattern of established behavior repeated in form to serve a symbolic function. Where some process of cultural evolution has produced particular rituals in specific cultures, what happens then? It is helpful to discover a large degree of agreement among analysts of different stripes. To say nothing of thinkers like Father Kavanaugh, the coincidence between an esthetician and literary "myth-critic" like Philip Wheelwright and a behavioristic ethnologist like Roy A. Rappaport suggests that there may really exist middle ground upon which almost any enquirer might safely stand.

In a fine study of primitive gardening ritual in New Guinea, Rappaport argues that ritual may be objectively as well as psychically functional, as when it makes an ecological difference in the relations between a people and their environment. He visualizes ritual metaphorically as a "mechanism" analogous to such technological devices as a thermostat, or a photoelectric cell, converting one kind of energy (religion) into another (agriculture). The sacred aspect of ritual, says Rappaport, not only lends it credibility but authority, the force of "a functional alternative to political power." Finally, he points out that ritual may be understood from the points of view of two realms of discourse: the realm of the culture in which it functions as "a cognized model"; the realm of the observer who sees from the outside that the ritual may function well in ways not perceivable from inside the culture, functioning as an "operational model." He falls at last into the almost inevitable trap of identifying the "operational model" with "the real world," the normal ethnocentric slip from which not even ethnographers are safe. But it permits him to observe that it is desirable, perhaps even essential, that the two models not be identical, that ritual not "conform in all respects to the real world."

From an altogether different angle of approach, Philip Wheelwright undertook "to inquire into the character of both language and existence" and explore "the semantic characteristics which enable the language of religion and myth and poetry, at their best, to speak in a way that truly 'mounts to the dwelling-place of the gods,' and testify to the reality of that dwelling." It was a work of high seriousness, devoted to what seemed to him the best and highest in contemporary civilization and climaxing in explication of T. S. Eliot's *Four Quartets* as "the most fully pertinent single poem of our moment in History." In short, Wheelwright represents the long line of "myth and ritual" critics whose ideas have moved contemporary culture vigorously.

He sees "ceremonies" of "four main types: the coercive, the contractual, the assimilative, and the confrontative." The first two are forms of magic. "Assimilative ritual" affirms and seeks "to intensify man's continuity and partial oneness with nature, or with the mysterious creative force behind nature." It operates, Wheelwright says, according to the principles of primitive logic which Lucien Lévy-Bruhl called "the law of participation." Ignoring the literalness of post-Hellenic logics, the law of participation makes no difficulty over "contradiction." It seeks images and symbolic patterns which speak intensely to the group, not the individual. They are "collective representations" valued for communal effectiveness rather than consistency.

"Confrontation" ritual, explicitly religious, seeks the living presence of that which is beyond us.

Since Wheelwright also recognizes the significance of personal ritual and the sorts of group "secular ritual" which provide the fun and solace of a felt "wehood," it would not be difficult to translate his terms into those of Huizinga. In fact, the points about ritual upon which decidedly different students agree seem more striking than their differences. All agree that ritual serves not only to represent something, or to present something esthetically, to affect people inwardly: ritual wields genuine power; it makes a difference; it makes things happen in the ordinary sensible and outward worlds.

If, then, the Big Game is, among other things, sometimes ritual, what does it do? what does it make happen? That there may be a difference between the way art works affectively and effectively and the way ritual works depends, I suppose, on faith. An extreme way of putting it would be to say that "ritual" is what they do who worship false gods, and its power is esthetic; what we who possess the truth do is "sacrament," and its power is real. Since in the Big Game we are talking not about the primitive but about forms used in a culture complex huge beyond all human imagining past or present, it pays to recognize that classifications taken from the primitive can be supposed to hold only relatively. They are the best we have but not to be presumed upon.

If you could apply Rappaport's distinction between "cognized" and "operational" models of ritual to the Big Game, for instance, it would clear up our perceptions. But I have yet to see a description of the events which seemed to me even to bring all of the Big Game into one field of reference, one mode of discourse sufficiently sophisticated to take it all in. When you cannot describe the "cognized" except by radical misrepresentation, what are you to do with the "operational"? It's a ritual, all right, functional as Rappaport says, coercive and contractual and assimilative as Wheelwright says, potent even to the point of the "scary" as Kavanaugh says. Part of the difficulty the Big Game presents may rise from the fact that, like everything in its context, it is a specialization. It began and still functions as specialized to the colleges and their constituencies. So far as it reaches out to the great tumultuous galaxy of the larger culture, it performs increasingly tenuous functions.

In theory, I propose, the Big Game as one combined, dramatic whole may be taken for a ritual, "collective representation" of the American Dream. For reasons not always flattering to the reasoners, The American Dream has often been drastically reduced in analytic discourse. It is, however, inherently complex and many valued, always flowing into new forms. At base it rests on two ideas which, united, compose a vital paradox, as Walt Whitman said in a characteristic poem: "One's self I sing, a simple separate person / Yet utter the word Democratic, the word En-Masse." To treat the American Dream as a unitary generalization concerned only with the "isolato," as Melville called him, the separate person in frantic pursuit of Franklin's "The Way to Wealth," is to miss most of the actuality. Not only does it miss the searching irony of Franklin's little masterpiece and ignore the service-minded and religious aspects of American personal ethics, it fails to see the other, global half, the dream of that nation Lincoln called "the last, best hope of earth." It cannot hear "the word Democratic, the word En-Masse."

From the start the American Dream stood on twin hopes: self-realization, national success. The Puritans, with their Bible Commonwealth, need not have come to the wilderness to seek "election," personal salvation. Of those they had achieved conviction in England. They came to light a communal candle in the wilderness, to be "the city set on a hill" as an example to wicked Europe of what God's community should be. Alexis de Tocqueville, that French aristocrat, thought he saw the American democrat walking naked in the world, without institutions. He saw wrong. To him the covert, Protestant institutions of the word—the anti-institutional institutions—stood invisible. *The American Democrat*, as Cooper called him, went warmly clad by faith. He possessed, as young Emerson put it, "a Land without history, . . . A land without nobility or wigs or debt, / No castles no Cathedrals and no kings— / Land of the forest." It was his answer to Tocqueville.

For castle and cathedral expressed as they symbolized and celebrated faith. When the feudal faiths went, where were the princes of the blood and the church? The American believer in the Dream expected to be saved, under Providence, personally and by his own faith and works. But that he equally expected to be saved nationally, by the national faith and works, will appear plainly in the briefest perusal of the national scriptures from the Mayflower Compact forward. Not to know this is not to have read or merely to discount the documents. Had the American democrat been any such cynic there would long since have ceased to be a nation.

It is among the complex functions of the Big Game to serve for what Geertz calls a "cultural text" which, specialized, speaks to the condition of the academic constituencies in their specialized relations and, generalized, speaks to the condition of citizens in their relations to the multiple components of the American Dream, the American Idea. The dream perceives freedom, equality, and community positively, not negatively, as a set of achievements, not immunities. To return to its foundation, it rests on two pillars: the idea of self-realization; the idea of the supremacy of the common. It supposes these two ideas, articles of faith, to be life-enhancing, mutually supporting, thrust meeting and balancing thrust. To realize the self requires struggle— agonism relieved and lubricated by fraternity. To realize the fraternal supremacy of the common requires achieved selves: "Produce great persons," said Whitman. "All the rest follows."

Putting it with stark, necessary brevity, the dream of self-realization assumes pluralism as a condition of individual probation. It assumes that the person proved itself by attaining the prize of competency—economic, political, psychic, moral, spiritual. Poor Richard's proverb goes straight to the point: "It is hard for an empty bag to stand upright." The supremacy of the common, on the other hand, rests as an article of faith on an innate ambiguity of the word, all language, as Emerson said, being "fossil poetry." The "common" is average, ordinary, vulgar. But it is also shared, harmonious, normative, general, universal, perhaps divine. The trick of seeing the common as double made democrats out of both American platonists and American realists.

Those ambiguities permit the supremacy of the common to function like a governor or self-compensating mechanism upon American fierceness. Where pluralism opens the door to competitiveness and where probation ("prove yourself") compels it, the common asserts equality, fraternity, community, and tends to balance winning with losing and check the spirit of fierceness back to the satisfactions of competency. Politically, it can finally bear an LBJ no better than a Nixon. It wants its heroes incidental to common victory and benefit, and it wants them temporary. Cincinnatus and not the Order of the Cincinnati, heroes for whom success is a journey are its style. Its furthest dream conceives a people's culture, where art and ritual and faith have become at once great and common. Said Whitman, concluding "Song of Myself," "I bequeath myself to the dirt to grow from the grass I love, / If you want me again look for me under your boot-soles." Melville had his Ishmael, considering his Polynesian pal Queequeg, who had just plunged into a wintry sea to save the life of a fool, reflect that, silently, Queequeg "seemed to be saying to himself—'It's a mutual, joint-stock world in all meridians. We cannibals must help these Christians.'"

And so the oft-despised cannibals down on the field or floor undertake to help those—Christians or Pharisees—in the stands. They dance ritually round the magic ring of play, weaving the American text. Team against team, individual with team, person against person, person with person, team against individual: unity in diversity, diversity in unity, agonism and fraternity. The new start, the chance for "the hungry"; democracy by competency; self-realization and respect in cooperation, in victory but yet in loss; risk and fierce competition and catharsis, yet decorum—and all surrounded and buoyed up by the atmosphere and communal joy of the great party: this is the Big Game's gift of a ritual text to participants near and far.

What does it make happen? Two things: first, the presentation with es-

thetic power of community realized, all conflicts and multiplicities reconciled, the ideal of organic unity glimpsed and faith in its possibility restored.
Has this the liability of esthetic experience, its being an only momentary stay
against confusion? Yes, but so have all rituals, all human acts. And it can be
almost indefinitely repeated. In a democracy there can be no authority wielding the powers of sanctity and unchallenged status; everything depends at last
on the piety of the people. So the second function of the Big Game as ritual is
renewal. It is "assimilative" in Wheelwright's sense, calling up from the
depths not of nature but of the people the powers of piety renewed. It enacts
democratic roles and fates, the process of the culture with its relative openness, its myths of risk and chance, the joy of the journey, the tragic sense of
life, the festival that reassures. It says, much better to the people, what the
democratic poet, for instance Carl Sandburg, kept trying all his life to say,
"the people, yes."

Supposing such a theory of the Big Game to be true, or potentially true, to
what degree it might be actually operative must depend on two sets of variables, one of them being, for practical purposes, the same as infinite. Only
the occasion reaching heights of intensity and near perfection in itself and
inducing trances of rapture in participants could attain really ritual altitudes.
Only the committed, the free and susceptible, the innocent or the believing
among those present could be supposed relatively able to rise to the opportunity. And yet—such games occur; such crowds of the participant devout
may be seen; there are that hunger, that thirst, that insistent quest: all to
testify that, yes, it is sometimes there. The Big Game may so function, when
it is successful, just so far as it is in fact a ritual expressing and communicating
a secular religion of the American Dream—about half, I say. For the other
half, as ritual it is a metaphor. As religion it is altogether a metaphor. For
Kavanaugh as for others, the game works better as a metaphor for religion
than religion works as a metaphor for the game. The festival is, at best, sort
of sacred.

Beyond that the point has, I think, been perfectly put by Father Hugo
Rahner: "we cannot truly grasp the secret of *Homo ludens* unless we first, in all
reverence, consider the matter of *Deus ludens*." As soon as you begin considerations like that, you run the danger of being shriveled by the terrible ironies
of the comparison. Says Rahner:

Life then . . . has this dual character. It is gay because secure in God, it
is tragic because our freedom continually imperils it, and so the man
who truly plays must be both gay and serious at the same time; we must
find him both smiling and in tears. His portion, if I may here bring in
the profound synthesis of the Fathers, will be both joy and perseverance.

With its stronger connection to an Augustinian, if not Calvinistic, feeling, Reinhold Niebuhr's way of handling the same observation is tougher-minded. In a Christian view, he says, "the whole drama of human history is under the scrutiny of a divine judge who laughs at human pretensions without being hostile to human aspirations. . . . The judgment is transmuted into mercy if it results in . . . prompting men to a contrite recognition of the vanity of their imagination." In all seriousness, when you have carried the metaphor to this sort of point, you are out of the ball park whether you believe or not. As Huizinga quietly concluded, "The human mind can only disengage itself from the magic circle of play by turning towards the ultimate."

To keep ourselves only a little deserving of the laughing derision of the *Deus ludens*, then, it is well for us to deal as truly as we can with realities and to keep our realities as clean as we can. In dealing with the Big Game we can, with a little care, set our feet solidly on the realities of the games as art, as American culture, popular culture, student life, and institutions. In all five realms, people, however subject to error and perversion, can keep it clean. "Corruption never has been compulsory," said Robinson Jeffers. And if in our times you should feel compelled to suppose that this ethic too might be situational, in those five situations Jeffers was right about college sport.

It is when you remember that the Big Game is a mass affair, public, a big market, entertainment, and plugged into the industry that high wind warnings begin to fly on your moral halyards. Though everybody feels at least unhappy and many of us feel guilty or even indignant about the facts, it cannot be denied that the Big Game sports define themselves, are defined by circumstances, as two. Not even the slightly patronizing distinction between "revenue" and "nonrevenue" sports represents the realities. College hockey makes money, occasionally as much as basketball, where they play it. But as a national phenomenon it is as peripheral as lacrosse—though both are great and greatly deserving games. The relations of Olympic sports in general to the colleges have become a perplex.

Football makes and spends for NCAA Division I athletic programs in general. Its one rival, which often talks as if it felt like a younger brother, is basketball. Born just as football emerged from its lyric period, basketball swept the country with striking speed. It quenched the thirst for a first-rate game to play indoors, out of the mud and sleet, when baseball was impossible and football not much fun. Exactly why it triumphed over its rivals and became queen of the games played on boards it would not be easy to say. But that it recapitulated the evolution of football, swiftly overtook it, and in some ways surpassed it could not be denied.

Everything true about football as an expression of student life, as a form of culture and popular culture, as entertainment, and as art, holds for basketball. Though it makes less money because it does not lift people to the same ecstatic heights as football, its peaks are surpassed only by those of football. And what basketball lacks in height it makes up in breadth. Where once little boys played baseball and football in the fallow fields, the pastures, the vacant lots, now they play basketball, indoors or out. Anywhere there is a wall or a post and a bit of paved surface and a boy appear a backboard and a hoop. On city playgrounds basketball is the game supreme, but so it is in farm yards where the hoop may be nailed to the barn and the floor be nothing but smooth-trampled dirt. Where do the best players come from? Ah, to decide that, at least for one year, is the good excuse for playing the far-flung national tournaments.

No game surpasses basketball in beauty, and no fan is crazier than its *aficionado*. As its public base spreads wider than football's into the pool of potential participants, it has a far greater number of school, college, industrial league, and club teams competing. Year by year its players' skills grow, and it spreads internationally with a power of appeal outdistancing other new games. It bids fair to become a substantial American contribution to world culture.

Though television cannot in fact capture anything like the experience of being at the basketball game and near the physical, three-dimensional action with its true rhythms, basketball lends itself better to the tube than football. Pursuing football, the lens never comes close to registering the essential action, and the fabled "instant replay" is a snare and a delusion. Why, then, the continued supremacy of football? The height of its appeal rests on its reach into preconscious and culturally primitive associations deep among the roots of American experience. It is these which entice and romanticize. Basketball is of course not devoid of such associations. Both create the "Big Game." Both supply their participants, active and spectatorial, with intense esthetic experience: the esthetics of winning; the equal and opposite, but finally reconciled, esthetics of losing. Both sometimes achieve the power of American ritual.

By a practically infinite margin of advantage in numbers, the public audience for the Big Game watches television. Not only are they not at the game but, alien from the communal experience of the stands and bedeviled by frantically intrusive "personalities," television watchers never see it. The cameras and directors fragment, skew, and impoverish the potential esthetic experience. The almost entire loss of depth perception on the flat screen, the loss of the whole field or floor and thus of the frame and ground of action and flow, become the loss of almost everything. Much of what the camera eye, the replay, and the commentators' explications insist "occurred" is subtly, sometimes blatantly, false. All the patterns of tension, relation, and rhythm, everything pictorial, balletic, and musical—and much that is simply athletic—are diminished if not lost. The television fan does not know the game; he has never seen it.

Yet he does encounter esthetic experiences, and the power of the television game as entertainment cannot be denied—by many millions of dollars' worth. As popular culture, of course, entertainment is people's culture and absolutely OK as long as you keep it clean, and "clean" in this case has to mean "nontoxic to the consumer." It should not screw up his life. Its effects should be life-enhancing, or at least not life-degrading. The consumer has a right to feel that he can trust his entertainment, the popular culture, to console and relieve him, make him laugh, make him cry, make him sing or dance and feel happy a while but not rob him of his self-respect and leave him cheated, disillusioned, sorry he came and hating himself for a cheap sucker.

To pick up that word again, the problem defines itself as Dionysian—the OK and true versus the phony and toxic. For the constituents at the Big Game the esthetics are as Dionysian as for a Kurelu warrior, a Kwakiutl potlatcher, a Balinese cockfighter. And there is nothing wrong with that in the stands so long as it is true. The problem is hokum, or commercial perversion. Careful observers at least since Melville and Clemens, Howells and Crane, have registered the poisonous vices of American culture as springing from faked romanticism. It makes fools of folks. Dying to wallow in Dionysian dreams of the ideal, the heroic, we degrade the common "ordinary," which we are, to "ornery."

The constituencies want their Big Game esthetics, comic or tragic, outsized and romantic. We yearn from the realities, which are common, toward the metaphors, exaggerating, overintensifying them because they are not real. Just to list those metaphors, as many as I can think of at the moment, stirs my capacity for romance. What is a Big Game? Why chivalry, a knightly tournament; it's communal, a family, tribal reunion; it's drama, but a folk festival, too; it's a gladiatorial combat or Thermopylae, Greek; it's youthful initiation into manhood, an ordeal; it's the heart of the law, adversary conflict; or of democratic politics, the contest; it's religion and ritual, sacred fest; it's war by surrogate. Romantic? Oh, wow!

But for the players and their coaches, and for the institutional servants of the whole grand process, the Big Game and all it involves are realistic. And, absurdly but typically, it is that ordinariness which the constituencies and, oddly, the media cannot seem to abide. They insist on being disillusioned about realities because they want it all Disneyland—Disneyland out front, that is. And among the most dangerous perverters are those who, carried away by its esthetic power but dazzled by their illusions, lose the power to see that it is art and insist on trying to transpose it into the familiar "reality," which they themselves think intrinsically dirty, of American business.

Northrop Frye put the right, opposite point exactly in discussing "the principle that the transmutation of act into mime, the advance from acting out a rite to playing at the rite, is one of the central features of the development from savagery into culture." He continued:

> It is easy to see a mimesis of conflict in tennis and football, but, precisely for that very reason, tennis and football players represent a culture superior to the culture of student duellists and gladiators. The turning of literal act into play is a fundamental form of the liberalizing of life which appears in more intellectual levels as liberal education, the release of fact into imagination.

Perhaps to perform just such acts of the imagination was the triumph of student *virtu* in creating the games and the Big Game as arts and ornaments of college life and popular culture.

On field or floor the teams enact American culture, in play releasing fact into imagination. The people in the stands, responding, play their various games, all different from those of the teams. And in their ways they enact American culture too. The several symbolic dramas speak to the condition of a culture in which, much liberalized, the presences, in vibrant performance, of *homo agonistes* and *ludens* and *aleator* often dominate. The lives of imaginative business and political careers, of divinity, law, medicine, public service, and teaching as professions, of the creation of arts or of knowledge, have become long, patient fights and games and gambles in that culture. The games symbolize and support and provide release from the pains and discontents consequent on lives and careers like ours. And, shape-shifting toward *homo fraternalis*, they not only enact but create community. It would be expensive to pervert or abolish them. They would prove vexingly difficult to replace. If they present us difficulties, and they do, in controlling and channeling them, the one way to respond which will not do is the way Milton condemned: the way of a "fugitive and cloistered virtue" seeking the deathliness of nothing in preference to the challenge of a moral life.

FRANK DEFORD

Religion in Sport

The young lions roar after their prey, and seek their meat from God.

—Psalms 104:21

I t seems just like any other college basketball game. The gym is well filled with students and alumni, and a pep band is accompanying some pretty cheerleaders who wear pleated skirts and saddle shoes and wave pompons for the home team. The visitors are not well represented. They have taken the date for a guarantee of only $350, a fifth of what another team would demand. They are accompanied only by a handful of rooters and the word of God. The visitors have come to play and preach.

They are down four at the half. The home team, Loyola Marymount University of Los Angeles, departs for its locker room, there to rest and to drink in new strategies. The visitors, Athletes In Action, do not leave the floor. Instead, they retire to their bench and put on snappy sweat suits of immaculate white, with red and blue trim, the name of the organization embroidered above the numbers, USA below them. Athletes In Action stands for Christ and country alike, and its founder, Dave Hannah, not only desires that the players represent a God-fearing America but that they become the finest amateur team upon the earth. It is Hannah's view, and the prevailing one in these Christian precincts, that infidels will not listen to losers. The AIA wrestling team was the 1975 national champion. The most powerful AIA basketball unit, the one playing Loyola, beat one Top Ten college team last season and played others to the wire. It finished the year 30-7-8, all road games, and won the national AAU title. It hardly matters that God in His wisdom has not seen fit to bless AIA with any good big guards.

In a moment, four of the AIA players arise, and with their coach, Bill Oates, move to a microphone set up at the far end of the gym. Oates explains that his men will tell the crowd about "the most fantastic Individual the world has ever known." Dave Lower, a skinny substitute, leads off. The theme of his two-minute talk is that "God loves and accepts us just as we are." The fans—those who have not already shuffled out for Cokes—listen in grudging silence at first, but quickly grow dubious or bored with the pitch and

---

Originally appeared in *Sports Illustrated* (1976).

begin to chatter among themselves. Soon, it is difficult to hear the message. Irv Kiffin, the best Athletes In Action player this evening, speaks next, reminding the listeners of Romans 6:23—"The wages of sin is death."

Tim Hall, a 6' 8" forward who played at Colorado State, follows, but over the rising crowd murmurs his words are almost lost, and when the Loyola team comes back onto the floor, the first player dribbles right past the speakers and shoots a practice layup before, embarrassed, he realizes that he is intruding on something. Nonplussed, Hall goes on, informing the crowd that he has seen a goodly number of collegians "turn to alcohol, to hard drugs or simply to a carefree way of life." He says that he found Jesus Christ instead.

John Sears is the clean-up speaker. Each game a different set of AIA players "disciple," the most forceful and articulate being saved for last. Sears is in his third year with Athletes In Action. He is 26, married, and has two small children. On the court he is a front-line reserve of little distinction, but at 6' 7", 215, he is lean and rugged, a magnificently handsome man, and at least now the women in the audience pay attention, if for the wrong reasons. Sears sums up and offers a prayer. Politely, heads are lowered, kind of. "Thank you, Jesus, for coming into my life," he says.

When the crowd looks up, Mike Gratzke, the assistant coach, has taken over the microphone. He asks the spectators to fill out comment cards. These are passed out by young volunteers who carry them (and, thoughtfully, pencils) in Kentucky Fried Chicken tubs. On the cards are boxes to check. For example, "I would like more information on how I can grow in my Christian faith." This knowledge is available and will be sent through the mail. Last year 125,000 people used these cards.

The second half begins and, despite having two starters out with ankle sprains, AIA catches Loyola and wins in the final three minutes. Maybe the fans would have listened to the message more attentively at halftime if AIA had been ahead then, too. "We need to win to command respect," John Sears says. But he goes on to emphasize that he could see some people watching him intently when he spoke; a few, he suggested, appeared so interested that he thought they might take Christ into their lives straightaway. He adds that the speakers are paid much better attention in the Midwest and South.

Dave Lower comes into the locker room and, truly excited, says that someone has just informed him that a man who watched AIA play tonight "saw Christ in every one of us." The players are obviously moved by this news. Coach Oates suggests they pray.

The men speak up, one by one; heads are bowed. The thoughts are genuine, spontaneous, even disarming. "Father," each begins. The first player thanks Him for the coach, for his guidance. Next, the coach thanks Him for the team, for its noble character. The manager asks His forgiveness for getting upset at an official's call. Another player prays that the injured ankles be quickly healed. Another prays that their halftime message was accepted. Another says, "And, Father, thank you for the win." It puts AIA at 11-4 for the year.

It is regularly said (if a bit too easily) that sport has become the religion of America. This is a glib appraisal, and probably no more accurate than Marx's equally facile assessment of religion, that it is "the opiate of the people." The claim that sport has developed into a national faith may be linked to the nagging awareness that something has happened to Sunday. With all the other cultural revolutions in the country, the Sunday revolution has been overlooked, but it has been as thoroughgoing as any.

Throughout American history, going back to Cotton Mather and beyond, Sunday was tightly structured and well defined as a day of peace: worship in the morning, then a heavy meal, leavened with the fellowship of the entire family, followed by rest and rumination. In *Ragtime*, the best-selling novel set at the turn of the century, E. L. Doctorow has selected Sunday to evoke the mood for the era. In his first paragraph, he writes, "On Sunday afternoon, after dinner, Father and Mother went upstairs and closed the bedroom door. Grandfather fell asleep on the divan in the parlor. The Little Boy in the sailor blouse sat on the screened porch and waved away the flies." Forty years later the Japanese chose Sunday as our soft underbelly. It became a Hollywood cliché to show the scene when the main characters learned of Pearl Harbor— the family was always in the living room, knitting, perusing the funny papers, playing dominoes and whatnot. Grandfather was dozing on the divan. Thus, for our first 300 years, was Sunday, the Lord's day.

If Pearl Harbor came now, in 1976, where would people learn of it? On the tennis court, at a bar watching Demolition Derby on CBS, at the arena? There is no time for the family or for lunch. Grandfather is in front of his Sony, with a take-out Whopper, French fries and a six-pack, screaming his fool head off because he gave 6½ and took the Oilers. After three centuries, Sunday changed overnight. Have we forgotten that until very recently baseball never dared play Sunday night games lest they conflict with vespers? Coincidence or not, the last great religious boom in America came in the mid-1950s, and the decline in church attendance, which set in thereafter, took place just as pro football, the Sunday game, became the passion of the land.

Now, the trip out of the house on Sunday is not to visit a church, but to see a game or to play one. At most Roman Catholic churches, where regular attendance traditionally is highest, convenient Saturday afternoon services are now featured so that communicants can get in a full 18 holes the next morning before returning home for the NBA Game of the Week. At Notre Dame these Saturday masses have become especially popular on game days, sort of the second half of a doubleheader.

So the churches have ceded Sunday to sports, to games. But we should not be deceived; that really is not a good indication of the popularity of religion or its place in the U.S. It is just that games defeated prayer in the battle for a day, and that should not come as a surprise, inasmuch as religion does not televise nearly as well as golf and only slightly better than ice hockey. It does not follow that since sport has won Sunday, we have embraced a form of temporal worship. Indeed, the more sport is proclaimed our religion, the more people in sport seem to be seeking religion. If anything, sport is less inspirational, less spiritual than ever before. Is God dead? Well, whatever His present status, the gods of sweat have definitely expired. Babe Ruth, Jack Dempsey and the others in that pantheon were the subjects of childlike idolatry.

Donald Cutler, an Episcopal rector who is also a New York literary agent, says, "Sport in America is more secular than ever. The talk is of money, contracts, litigation. How do you worship something like that? Put your faith in a team that will be in another city next year? I grew up living and dying with the Pittsburgh Pirates, listening to recreated games on the radio. Sport had stability then, and one could dare to identify with teams and players. That's gone. The innocence is gone, the glory. There is nothing in the experience to lift us up, no heroes to idolize. Hank Aaron a hero? Roger Maris? Arnold Palmer was the last epic hero in sport, I suppose. Jack Nicklaus is merely a money-winner. That is what we have left: money-winners. And you do not worship those."

And yet, as the American reverence for the saints of sport declines, religion itself has increasingly become a handmaiden to sport. Clergymen are standing in line to cater to the spiritual needs of the deprived athletic elite, and the use of athletes as amateur evangelists is so widespread that it might be fairly described as a growth industry. "Jocks for Jesus" is what *The Wittenburg Door*, an acerbic contemporary religious magazine, derisively calls the movement. "Who gives these people authority but the pagan world in which we live?" asks the magazine, its cover adorned with an athletic supporter festooned with a cross. But Jocks for Jesus is booming. It is almost as if a new denomination had been created: Sportianity. While Christian churches struggle with problems of declining attendance, falling contributions and now even reduction in membership, Sportianity appears to be taking off.

Today every major league baseball and football team—all 50 of them—holds Sunday chapel services, home and away. Many teams have their own ministers. Pat Jantomaso, a Red Sox chapel speaker, who lives in Boca Raton, Fla. but joins the team virtually every Sunday on the road, says, "many are caring for down-and-outers, but I decided to minister to up-and-outers." Sunday services are also held in sports as varied as stock-car racing and golf. In many cases, week-night Bible classes have been started up so that wives may participate.

Athletes In Action has 250 full-time staff men (domestic missionaries, really). Eight are assigned to large cities where their only job is to minister to the pro athletes. Athletes In Action deploys two proselyting basketball teams, two wrestling teams, plus squads in gymnastics, track and weight lifting. With the AIA teams, the major thrust is toward the colleges. Says Greg Hicks, a 1974 national AAU wrestling champion and an AIA assistant athletic director, "We believe in a real soft sell. As an athlete, I can get into a fraternity, a locker room, where nobody else would be permitted."

Sports Ambassadors is an overseas equivalent of the AIA. Since 1952, "in a world gone berserk with sports," it has sent basketball and baseball teams into more than 40 countries in Europe, the Orient, Africa and Central and South America, playing and preaching under the organization's name or Venture For Victory. A newcomer in the field is the basketball team known as News Release, which carries its pray-for-play ministry to Europe, even behind the Iron Curtain.

The Fellowship of Christian Athletes, which is the patriarch of Sportianity, does not subsidize teams, but uses older athletes to bring younger ones to Christ, mainly at summer sports camps ($110 a week) and in high school group sessions known as "Huddles." The FCA's annual budget is $2.2 million, and its president, John Erickson, refers to it as a "para-church."

For years, some coaches who are not members have complained that the Fellowship—which bills itself as the "muscle and action" of Christianity—operates as a powerful lobby when one of its member coaches is up against an outsider for a job. As a result, there are coaches who feel that they have to protect themselves by signing on as FCA members. "It's like getting a union card," says one. "If you don't join, some coaches in the Fellowship will bad-mouth you with kids they're recruiting, tell 'em you're a drunk or your marriage is breaking up. I know, because kids I've recruited told me."

Another substantial organization, Pro Athletes Outreach, was founded largely as an intramural peace-keeping force because the giants of Sportianity, AIA and FCA, were squabbling so indecorously over enlisting the best missionary athletes. It was an outgrowth of Sports World Chaplaincy, Inc. but is now a thriving operation with an annual budget of $250,000, and it sends phalanxes of pros off on what it calls "speaking blitzes" of the U.S. The PAO stars also entertain with flag football games, tugs-of-war, wrist-wrestling and other fun games.

The movement has grown so that it has even spawned a think tank, the

Institute for Athletic Perfection, which formulates dogma for athletic religion. Moreover, the presses of Sportianity are flooding the market with pamphlets, books, newsletters, magazines, even comic books and films (*A Man & His Men*, featuring Tom Landry. . . . "The thrill of victory, the agony of defeat, the impact of a Christian life"). Athletes In Action sends out taped vignettes and interviews that have been played on more than 150 radio stations. It established a national television network for its top basketball team this past season, with John Wooden mike-side.

Sport and religion were not total strangers before all this began. Billy Sunday, the turn-of-the-century evangelist, was a reformed weak-hitting major league outfielder. Dr. James Naismith was a seminarian before he invented basketball at the YMCA. C. T. Studd, a millionaire British missionary, was the progenitor of groups like Athletes In Action. Studd was a great cricket player who agreed to make a tour of army garrisons in India if he could preach after his innings. And remember Deacon Dan Towler? The Vaulting Vicar, Bob Richards? The House of David baseball team? Other athletes went on to the ministry when their playing days were done: Albie Pearson, Donn Moomaw, Henry Carr. Bill Glass, the former All-Pro end, is now one of the nation's top evangelists. Jerry Lucas, whose previous enterprises included fast food and magic, has opened up Memory Ministries, a nonprofit organization that will instruct the nimble-minded, for a $20 fee, in memorizing all 89 chapters of the four Gospels. Lucas' new book, *Remember The Word*, has sold almost 60,000 copies.

But religion rarely intruded into sport in the past except in the occasional instance of a player who refused to perform on a holy day—Sandy Koufax was probably the most famous and most recent. Hank Greenberg was another. But Cassius Clay's conversion to the Black Muslims provoked a *cause célèbre* in sport. Later, Kareem Abdul-Jabbar found his life endangered when he was caught in the middle of an interdenominational Muslim war. Alvin Dark— "Preacher Dark" and "Sister Dark" to Charles Finley—lost his job as manager of Finley's A's in large part for taking to a pulpit and suggesting that his boss would go to hell if he didn't let Christ enter his heart. A few Muslims claim that certain Jewish basketball owners have black-balled some of them because of the Arab-Israeli conflict. Some teams, notably the 1974 Kansas City Chiefs, have been disrupted by overzealous God Squadders trying to push hellfire and brimstone on the whole team.

That religion should suddenly be a factor in sport while its influence elsewhere is declining is not the paradox it seems. Certain members of the religious community have quite openly set out to mine athletics. The belief in these ecclesiastical pockets is that athletes need special spiritual assistance,

that they are especially vulnerable to preaching and, finally and most important, that they are ideal instruments to be used in bringing others into
the fold. Addressing the Cincinnati Reds at chapel at Fenway Park during the
World Series last October, the Rev. Billy Zeoli, the biggest individual star in
Sportianity, told the players, "I hope you have a concept of how much you
affect people, how they look up to you. Let me remind you that your national
influence on youth is greater than that of any single pastor, priest or rabbi."

Arlis Priest, the head of Pro Athletes Outreach, is convinced that athletes
can strongly influence moral and religious life in the United States. Among
the sincere, dedicated men in athletic religion, surely none is more sincere or
dedicated than Priest. Converted in a foxhole in France ("Every man I saw
die talked about mother or God"), Priest is known as Uncle Arlis to the 90 or
so NFL players who form the heart of his organization. Priest was a baseball
aspirant before World War II, good enough to merit a Double A tryout; afterward, he was a successful real estate broker before giving his life over to the
lay ministry. Now gray-haired and distinguished, he is a dead ringer for Harry
Reasoner. At PAO headquarters near Phoenix, Priest speaks evenly, almost
dispassionately, but there is conviction and emotion in what he says. He explains how athletes are crucial to saving America:

"We're losing. We've lost our perspective, turning to drugs, free sex—and
did you know there are now 26,000 suicides a year? And here we are, more
blessed than any nation in the history of the world. Do we really think we're
that much smarter that we can turn away from God? Well, professional athletes can reach the people who want to find God, who want to be Christians,
but don't know how to. Particularly the young people—they'll listen to athletes. Pros have the right background. Why, they're probably the most disciplined group of people left in this country. They're dedicated, they're taught
to play as part of a team, and they're willing to pay the price. This is what we
need in America.

"Two years from now I expect to have half the professional athletes as
Christians. Yes, half. I will be disappointed if we don't have half. And then,
as Romans 1:16 says, the power is in the Gospel, and it is the athletes in our
society who can best carry that message."

Like Priest, virtually all the leaders in the Christian athletic movement are
fundamentalist. Organizations such as the Fellowship of Christian Athletes
and Athletes In Action are studiously nondenominational, and even the individual stalwarts, ministers like Zeoli and Tom Skinner (who is associated
with the Washington Redskins), avoid mentioning their particular church
affiliation. Evangelistic Catholicism has been under steam for almost a decade, and this has helped bring Roman Catholic recruits from that wing of

the church into Sportianity—Mike McCoy of the Green Bay Packers is one Catholic invariably cited. But the sense and thrust of the movement still comes from the Bible Belt.

The Bible is to be taken literally. The message is simple, all or nothing; there is no truck with intellectualizing, the appeal is gut. It does not seem surprising that football—authoritarian, even militaristic—is the sport at the heart of the movement. The pregame football chapel services are important not so much because they take place on the Sabbath, but because they take place on a game day, when the players are sky high and emotionally exposed. A pro star who once was active in Sportianity but left in disgust says, "Why do you think this simplistic type of religion appeals to athletes? Because you're talking to people who operate primarily with their bodies, not their minds."

Ray Hildebrand was a pop singer who had one big hit (*Hey Paula*) before he gave up show business to work for the Fellowship of Christian Athletes. He has had all the spotlights he ever wanted and so is not awed by hotshot athletes. As a matter of fact, the best way to preach to athletes, to hold their limited attention, is with show-biz flypaper. "The pros have got so much flash themselves," Hildebrand says, "that the only way you're going to impress them is to throw flash at them. You got to come on strong, joking, and then you give them what we call 'three points and a poem'—No. 1, No. 2, No. 3 and a simple little rhyme to wrap it up for 'em." Hildebrand smiles and shakes his head at this foolishness. "Sometimes I'll even wear one of those silly shirts."

Being essentially fundamentalist, the movement draws its strength from the South and the rural areas of the nation where that type of theology has thrived. Despite its growth and clout, the Fellowship of Christian Athletes has failed to make inroads into the more sophisticated areas of the nation. There are now 1,600 high school Huddles in the U.S., but only a dozen of these—.8% of the total—are located in the Northeast, where 15% of the population resides. The FCA is hardly more successful in California. The bulk of the Huddles are found in the South, Southwest and Midwest, and most of the stars who participate in the program were brought up in those areas, in white, middle-class environs.

The FCA has sought to broaden its reach but has failed, in large part because in the more urban (and allegedly liberal) sections of the nation, school officials often seem intimidated by laws concerned with the separation of church and state. Because it is a religious organization, the FCA has been denied access to some schools. Those in Sportianity consider this "discriminatory" and absurd—as preposterous as viewing registered Democrats and Republicans as agents of political prejudice. There have been instances when the PAO speaking caravan has been permitted into a school auditorium and allowed to address students, but only if the players promised not to use any names. Accordingly, they say things like: "My life was changed by"—and here they offer a longing look skyward—"by someone whose name I can't mention in school."

The fundamentalist sweep into sport is relatively new. Previously, only Roman Catholics exploited athletics, using football and basketball teams to attract students and funds and attention to parochial institutions that were broke and often academically inferior as well. The classic example is Notre Dame.

Father James Riehle, the chaplain of the Notre Dame athletic department, says, "Of course Catholic schools used athletics for prestige. Notre Dame would not be the great school it is today, the great academic institution, were it not for football. But the emphases have changed here. I think that now we realize the value of sport in more ways than just the financial, whereas I'm afraid once we didn't."

The famous upset of Army by Notre Dame in 1913, when Knute Rockne (a Protestant then, but who knew?) trundled out a secret weapon known as the forward pass, had broad religious implications. Football had been an upper-class WASP sport played by the moneyed few in the Northeast. They had adapted the game from English soccer. In contrast, baseball was an American original, and urban immigrants, who were predominantly Catholic, took to it precisely because it was all-American and was not at all British. Major league baseball was limited pretty much to those large cities with heavy Catholic populations, while college football thrived and became preeminent in the more homogeneous Protestant sections of the country, particularly the South and Southwest.

So the Irish of Notre Dame used football to move up in the academic community in the same way that the lace-curtain Irish used politics to ascend in society. The Notre Dame example was followed by other Catholic schools, but in 1976 only the Irish and Boston College remain in the football big time. Because Catholic colleges were chiefly located downtown, with limited physical and financial resources, they eventually were forced to drop football and concentrate on basketball.

The Catholic emphasis on this sport continues despite a more recent phenomenon—basketball's increasing domination by blacks. Since relatively few blacks are Roman Catholic, parochial schools have had to recruit outside the faith if they wished to remain competitive. Nowadays, at many schools the student body is 90% or more Catholic but the basketball squad is virtually non-Catholic. Catholic academicians do not see any hypocrisy in this policy, equating it with a state-supported school recruiting out-of-state players.

Because of this de-Catholicization of Catholic teams, it is now rare to see a player crossing himself before shooting a free throw. It may not be frivolous to suggest that this practice was responsible for a goodly share of the anti-Catholic sentiment in the land. Jack Kennedy might have won by a landslide in 1960 but for the fact that Catholics were, at that time, still crossing themselves before shooting free throws. No matter what devout reasons Catholics had for making the sign, non-Catholics (Protestants especially) were always convinced that, deep down, the free-throw shooter was asking God to curl it in for him.

Says Father Charles Riepe, rector of the Cathedral of Mary Our Queen in Baltimore and president of John Carroll School, "It's much to the good that the practice has largely disappeared. We had one kid here a couple years ago, a very bright, sophisticated boy, too, who was crossing himself before foul shots. I took him aside and suggested, as nicely as possible, that it might be wise to drop that. If you want to cross yourself, I told him, it's the kind of thing you can do in private before a game—and really, once beforehand should be quite sufficient to cover all the eventualities in both halves. Besides, as I also told him," Father Riepe adds, laughing, "it looks awful when you do blow a free throw. Then it appears that God really does have it in for you and John Carroll."

The de-mythification of sport, leading to the demise of the hero, may be a major reason why fundamentalists have taken the ball from the Roman Catholics. In the palmy days of yore, when order reigned over innocent games, sport was uplifting and a glorious celebration, like the mass. Sport and the church both stood for authority; the reserve clause was no more to be challenged than meatless Fridays. Heroes were larger than life, canonized as athletic saints, a comfortable adjunct to the church's own hagiology. The Roman church has always been perturbed by sex, and for its male adolescents, joining a team was considered the next best thing to a vow of celibacy. As long as budding young ladies could be kept in what the sisters called "Mary-like" clothes, and growing boys could be kept shagging flies and shooting set shots, nobody would have time to think impure thoughts, much less do impure things to one another. Anyway, that was the idea.

Even today, arbitrary pregame football team rites are heavily laced with Catholic taboo and mysticism. Dr. William Arens, the anthropologist, compares these peculiar ceremonial group devotions to "the exotic rituals of a newly discovered tribe." The belief that sex should be avoided before a game, the determination to keep the players segregated (ideally, watching action movies), the participation in a final meal together (a shared communion of good red beef)—all this is highly analogous to churchly concepts.

Still, it is not football but organized baseball that has the most Roman Catholic trappings. With its grand traditions, its constancy, its statistical litany, baseball could be neatly comprehended by the church—and it was. The baseball hierarchy does not take civil government as its model, but has an ecclesiastical design, beginning with the commissioner-pope, who is elected by the owners-cardinals, right on down to the fans-parishioners—indeed, the word fan is derived from "fanatic." The Baseball Hall of Fame closely approximates a Catholic shrine, which, of course, is exactly what it is called.

However deep their involvement with athletics, Catholics have always looked upon them as a diversion, rather like Tuesday night Bingo in the parish hall. Certainly, sport was never viewed as any sort of vehicle for conversion; athletics had nothing to do with theology. Football made Notre Dame a top-notch school, but the fact that Notre Dame was Catholic was quite incidental. If an atheist wants to play on the team, fine, give him the ball and never mind what he does with his Sunday mornings; if the best coach we can get is Protestant and Ara Parseghian wants the job, hire him. To Catholics, sport might be important, but it was never churchy. The clearest embodiment of Catholic athletic philosophy was the late Father Tom Brennan of Notre Dame. A serious theologian, a man of intellect, he could also serve as pastor to young Irish athletes. He was a fine athlete himself and a whimsical man who enjoyed dry martinis, which would sometimes lead to his conducting telephone conversations (presumably imaginary) with the devil. Sport appealed to Father Brennan—its joy, its fellowship and just because it could be so exciting. He liked to sit on the Irish bench, and he did not always agree with the way officials saw matters. One night, in Evansville, he began riding a referee. He got on the poor fellow pretty hard, but the referee was reluctant to call a technical on a priest. In exasperation, he came over to Father Brennan, shook a finger at him and said, "Come on Father, you call the Mass, and I'll call the game." Catholics still roar appreciatively at this tale.

In contrast to the Catholic attitude, the Sportians, humorless and persevering, appear to be attracted to sport as an evangelical device that can be used baldly and also because, as an institution, sport is going to hell just like the rest of the country. All the talk in sport is cynical—of money, money, money, drugs and camp followers, dissension and dissatisfaction. Sin! Today's best-known white athlete is Joe Namath, whose womanizing and drinking are broadly publicized. It is said that his celebrated example provided some of the impetus for the Sportian movement.

Sportians are out to save sport by saving athletes. Once they are converted, they are cast as neo-crusaders. The field is to be an altar, the game a sacrifice. Paul Neumann, a Sports Ambassadors official who was a first-rate NBA player for several years, says, "A Christian is always keyed up before a game because he knows he is playing for his *real* coach." Alvin Dark goes further, suggesting everything he does is for the glory of Jesus Christ. In the sermon in which he revealed Charlie Finley's fiery future, Dark also said, "The more we read the Bible, the more we begin to turn our lives over to the Lord. For example, I gave the Lord my golf game. When I dedicated my life . . . one of the first things I did was turn my golf game over to the Lord."

Jesus has been transformed, emerging anew as a holler guy, a hustler, a give-it-100-percenter. While students of the new religion glumly acknowledge that his only known athletic performance was throwing the money-changers out of the temple, Jesus' sad, desperate last hours have become a kind of Super Bowl. Wes Neal, previously with AIA, left that organization to set up the Institute for Athletic Perfection in Prescott, Ariz. He has become an accepted theoretician for the movement; the pamphlets published by the institute are handed out by many Sportian groups.

The new image of Jesus, the blue-chipper, is set forth in a Neal tract entitled *Total Release Performance*, which refers to the brand of ball that Jesus played on the cross: "It was another situation that would reveal his WINNING character. . . . At any point Jesus could have turned back from his mission, but he was a WINNER!" To prove that Jesus had guts, the physical effects of being crucified are described in gory detail. Apparently, this is to shame athletes into competing more intently, whatever their injuries, their limitations or frame of mind. The crucifixion becomes an athletic sacrament, and athletes are asked to be martyrs. Without equivocation, the Institute lists as "SIN" such things as "failure to reach maximum athletic potential" and "fear of an opponent."

Clearly, the trickiest thing in mixing religion with sport is the matter of asking God for victory. It is a no-no to do so, but, unfortunately, it is quite common for athletes to get carried away and to pray precisely for that. "He's just an overly enthusiastic baby Christian," Billy Zeoli, the inspirational chapel speaker, said after a pro football player came flat-out in pregame prayers and asked Jesus to give his team a win. "Please don't get on him." Zeoli, however, felt it was unnecessary to discuss the impropriety of a victory prayer with the player. The line can be a fine one. When Kermit Zarley, one of the outspoken Christians on the PGA tour, won the Canadian Open a few years ago, he credited his success to God for having found him a new driver. Now, if that was not quite like saying that God hit tee shots for Kermit Zarley, the implication was clear that Zarley won the Canadian Open because God hung around pro shops with him when he was hunting for new clubs. Regrettably, whatever Sportianity is trying to project, the public often has another impression. Most viewers believe that teams assembling for a televised prayer after a victory are Pharisees, thanking God, paying Him off for getting them another big one in the W column. A poll of young Christian athletes, teenagers who have been specifically instructed by the movement, asked, "What does it mean to be a Christian athlete?" The response most often received was, "To have God on my side." Jesus, it seems, is coming across as the next best thing to a homecourt advantage.

At the same time, no one in the movement advises athletes to pray for victory. On the contrary, the try ethic, epitomized by Christ's Total Release Performance at Gethsemane on Maundy Thursday, is almost universally taught. The message is virtually the same all over: try your hardest, and then, win or lose, you will not be in conflict with Christian tenets. The favorite scripture comes from Paul, who is heard so regularly that he has become rather like the Curt Gowdy of Sportianity—and not only because both tend to get windy. The essence of Paul's endorsement of competition and Total Release Performance is found in 1 Corinthians 9:24, which quotes him thus in a modern paraphrase text of the New Testament: "Surely you know that in a race all the runners take part in it, but only one of them wins the prize. Run, then, in such a way as to win the prize." Also cited regularly are Paul's familiar words from 2 Timothy 4:7: "I have fought a good fight. I have finished my course, I have kept the faith." Unfortunately, Paul's most direct statement about athletics (1 Timothy 4:7–8) does not fit in Sportianity, so it is never quoted: ". . . exercise thyself rather unto godliness. For bodily exercise profiteth little."

Malcolm Boyd, Episcopal priest and author of the best-seller *Are You Running With Me, Jesus?*, replies to the try ethic, "If you're into triumphalism as a theory, then it follows that the important thing to you is to win, even if you camouflage that by saying that you're merely trying. You feel that God is on your side. You may not pray those words, but you can't tell me it's not in your heart—whether it's Vietnam we're talking about or Ohio State.

"Who was that swimmer—you know, the Olympic guy? Yes, right—Mark Spitz. Isn't that funny how quickly we've forgotten him? I'll tell you why—I'll tell you when he lost all respect: at the very instant he reached his peak, when he crawled out of the water after his last gold medal and said he never wanted to swim again.

"What is the point of swimming, of doing anything, just for the sake of trying to win? Certainly, Jesus didn't want that, and it is audacious for these guys to say it. In Gethsemane, and there hanging on the cross, Jesus didn't ask to win. In fact, his thoughts turned to the needs of others.

"Besides, I've had enough of this trying nonsense. I've seen so many kids wounded by it. It is this kind of trying, the kind that this athletic religion teaches, which is killing off so many men, leaving widows. It is very dangerous right now to be trying harder. It is making us more machinelike instead of more human. We'd do better to learn how not to try so."

The Sportians stick close to a you-and-Jesus, one-on-one theology. "Don't allow your group to stray too far off course from the Christ theme," the FCA advises its leaders (Tip No. 5). Don Cutler disagrees with the movement's lack of social concern: "If the New Testament says anything, it is that this man poured Himself out for you, and now it is your responsibility to pour yourself out for others. It is not a question of His taking care of you, whatever—your having no obligations other than signing up for the big Christian team."

Sadly, lost in the shuffle, in the competition for dotted-line converts (sign here, raise your hand, send for literature), is sport itself. In the process of dozens of interviews with people in Sportianity, not one even remotely suggested any direct effort was being considered to improve the morality of athletics. An active churchman, who has long been involved in pro sport, says, "The trouble with these people is that they worship sport as much as they do Jesus. They are so thrilled to be working with hotshot stars that they can see nothing wrong with athletics. They don't want to. I'm afraid that it is not religion that has come into sport, but athletic groupies."

More than a decade ago a deeply religious pitcher named Allan Worthington protested that he would quit the Chicago White Sox unless the club stopped stealing opponents' signals by illegal means. Since that time players in all leagues have struck righteously for more money, more benefits, more power. But not until five months ago, when Bobby Hull refused to suit up for a hockey game in protest against the violence in his sport and in fear that someone might be killed, has a single player dared put himself publicly on the line against something he considered ethically remiss.

Sportianity casts stones at players like Joe Namath for personal behavior. Dave Hannah of Athletes In Action is still angry that Lance Rentzel was doing work in Sportianity at a time when he was having deep psychological disturbances: Hannah thinks that Rentzel was inconsiderate in bringing such bad sexual publicity to the movement. But no one in the movement—much less any organization—speaks out against the cheating in sport, against dirty play; no one attacks the evils of recruiting, racism or any of the many other well-known excesses and abuses. Sport owns Sunday now, and religion is content to lease a few minutes before the big games. Religion seems to have become a support force for athletics, like broadcasters, trainers, cheerleaders and ticket-sellers. John Morley, a British statesman, wrote, "Where it is a duty to worship the sun, it is pretty sure to be a crime to examine the laws of heat." As long as it can work the territory, Sportianity seems prepared to accept athletics as is, more devoted to exploiting sport than to serving it.

THE WORD ACCORDING TO TOM

An invocation by Father Edward Rupp at the dinner before the 1976 WHA All-Star game:

"Heavenly Father, Divine Goalie, we come before You this evening to seek Your blessing. . . . We are, thanks to You, All-Stars.

"We pray tonight for Your guidance. Keep us free from actions that would put us in the Sin Bin of Hell. Inspire us to avoid the pitfalls of our profession. Help us to stay within the blue line of Your commandments and the red line of Your grace. Protect us from being injured by the puck of pride. May we be ever delivered from the high stick of dishonesty. May the wings of Your angels play at the right and left of our teammates. May You always be the Divine Center of our team, and when our summons comes for eternal retirement to the heavenly grandstand, may we find You ready to give us the everlasting bonus of a permanent seat in Your coliseum.

"Finally, grant us the courage to skate without tripping, to run without icing, and to score the goal that really counts—the one that makes each of us a winner, a champion, an All-Star in the hectic Hockey Game of Life. Amen."

Until recently, the distasteful practice of having loquacious men of the cloth deliver pregame invocations larded with sporting lingo was restricted pretty much to the South and to football. But athletic religion is not so bashful anymore. Increasingly, public team prayer and public-address entreaties to the Divine Goalie or the Head Coach in the Sky are in evidence. Sportianity, as this brand of religion might best be called, is thoroughly evangelistic, using sport as an advertising medium. The idea is simple enough: first, convert the athletes, who are among the most visible individuals in our society; then, use these stars for what is generally known in the business as "outreach," an up-to-date rendering of the old-fashioned phrase "missionary work." To put it bluntly, athletes are being used to sell religion. They endorse Jesus, much as they would a new sneaker or a graphite-shafted driver.

A classic example is an inspirational comic book, written about the life of Tom Landry, the Dallas Cowboy coach who is also chairman of the national board of trustees of the Fellowship of Christian Athletes, the best-known and most influential of the Sportian organizations. In the comic book, Landry's bald head is never shown. He always has a hat on or, indoors, his pate is cleverly obscured by well-placed lampshades and word balloons. The problem is that he became prominent in Sportianity about the time he went bald, and Spire Christian Comics apparently does not want young readers to get the impression that being a witness to Jesus causes baldness. On the other hand, children are being led to believe that religious wisdom is revealed to the

Western world through the National Football League. The comic implies that "God's Game Plan" is guaranteed—coming as it does "From the Blackboard of the Dallas Cowboys' Chapel Service." The plan is being peddled as orange drink or vitamins ("From the Training Table of the Dallas Cowboys") might be. Sportianity is a hard, clever sell.

Athletes are brought along carefully. Only natural ministers move right into the starting lineup. Dave Hannah, the president and founder of Athletes In Action, the jock arm of Campus Crusade for Christ, explains the group's redshirting of Terry Bradshaw. "We spent a long time considering whether Terry was there," Hannah says, "but now he's really coming along spiritually." The major Sportian organizations compete diligently for the best athletic outreachers, the big names that also will be hits at the religious box office.

Too often the star system becomes a numbers game. Sportianity seems mesmerized by numbers. Ben Patterson, an editor of *The Wittenburg Door*, a contemporary religious magazine, writes, "Look at the thousands who have come to Christ through the witness of a famous Christian athlete or entertainer. My reply is that if all the statistics of all the evangelistic crusades reported in just the last 10 years were accurate, then we would be living on a planet fully Christianized—several times over."

The most detailed statistics come from Baseball Chapel, which is coordinated by a retired sportswriter, Watson Spoelstra of Detroit. Spoelstra puts out a bi-weekly newsletter that provides Chapel stats every bit as detailed as those in *The Sporting News*. Chapel attendance last season soared to 6,434, which averages out to 260 a Sunday—and this without any special Bible Day or Cross Day giveaways. There were exactly 146 individuals who spoke in Baseball Chapel last season.

Pro Athletes Outreach boasts that 250,000 heard its speakers during a five-city tour in 1975. The Sports Ambassadors played before 139,400 fans last year. Athletes In Action teams packed in 700,000 spectators, with 125,000 of them filling out inquiry cards. And, from the Fellowship of Christian Athletes monthly: "Of the 70 delegates during one week, 26 indicated they found Christ as Savior and Lord, 29 made recommitments of their lives, and 22 said they would like to become involved in full-time Christian service."

While FCA rolls are expanding, especially as its roots spread—into junior high, even to girls—the group is returning more and more to its original homely precept of having young athletes support one another. The summer camps, featuring big-name players and coaches, have always provided a come-on, but the strength of the program lies in the local Huddles, where an older athlete meets with younger ones.

Ron Morris, a former SMU basketball star, is an ordained Methodist minister who has been with the Fellowship since 1956. Now vice-president in charge of fund raising, his views are representative of the growing concern within the FCA about the organization's values. "I see a danger of our being overly evangelical," Morris says. "It's important for us to understand where we stand. We're not breaking new ground. We're not even reaching the uncommitted kid. The boy we get almost always has been raised in a church, his Mom and Dad are members. We provide a strengthening process, the identification of a peer group. We get these kids to camp, we get them to play together on a team, and their trust factors go up. Through this athletic camaraderie you have an affirming process and, unfortunately, in life we don't get affirmed too often, do we? We ought to understand that what the FCA does best is affirm, not evangelize."

These sentiments have not always been a factor in FCA policy. A pro star who once was active in the Fellowship explains why he eventually was driven from it. "First of all," he says, "you can't use my name. I'll be quoted on anything else. If I were into cannibalism or polygamy, I'd come out and say it, but if you use my name here I'm going to get a thousand letters from the South telling me I'm going to hell and offering to save me again, and I just don't need it. They don't let go. Those FCA guys get their teeth in you, and they never quit. Anyway, they never quit when you're on top. Have a bad season, and they lose a lot of interest in your soul.

"I remember one time when I was playing in college and on top, and I got a telephone call from FCA headquarters asking me to go speak at a conference in Florida a couple of days later. I had an exam or something, and they're asking me to fly 6,000 miles, back and forth across the country. They wanted to show me off. I said, 'Please, not this time, I'm busy.' They said, 'What's the matter, son, aren't you a Christian anymore?' I'm 20 years old, trying to get my head on straight, and those dudes were giving me this. I didn't get that much pressure from college recruiters, or when I was drafted by the pros. They're never satisfied. No matter how good a talk you gave, afterward somebody would come up and say you only used the word 'Jesus' six times or eight times or whatever. 'Don't be afraid to come to Christ, son.' Pretty soon I began to see who the real Christians were."

FCA officials admit that athletes were unfairly pressured in the past but maintain that such practices no longer are tolerated.

Nowadays, the huge FCA breakfasts, which are held in conjunction with college and high school conventions and at various bowl games, have much the same air as an ABC cocktail party or a presentation for Converse or Wilson Sporting Goods. Sport is a big, diversified corporation, and Jesus has become a healthy part of it—and His franchise produces a nice little profit.

But the FCA has begun to serve as succor and counsel, a corporate pastor, for its weary and heavy-laden, even its fallen angels. In the old days it had no truck with losers, but Fellowship personnel now spend a significant portion of their time bolstering members who are experiencing hard times—a coach under alumni pressure, an injured player, a guy in a slump, even a coach under NCAA investigation. A call was placed to Bobby Bonds, the baseball star, after a drunk-driving arrest, asking if help could be provided.

The Fellowship has gone through several stages of development and personality. In 1947 a young Oklahoma A&M student, Don McClanen, had the idea for such an organization. He got nowhere for several years. Finally he hocked his car and bought an airplane ticket to Pittsburgh, where he went to the Pirates' office to see Branch Rickey. The Mahatma was known as a Christian gentleman of the first water, a man who honored a promise to his dead mother that he would never never desecrate the Sabbath by attending a game.

McClanen was granted a two-minute session with Rickey, but he was so convincing that the interview stretched into five hours as McClanen shared with Rickey the idea of organized athletic evangelism. On each telling of this tale, McClanen is represented as *sharing* his idea. This is the code word in Sportianity. People don't preach or evangelize, sell or push. God forbid that they should ever hustle. What they do is share. In any event, Rickey immediately took to McClanen and his ideas and shared with him some sandwiches as they discussed plans for a new type of ministry.

McClanen was eased out once the Fellowship began to take off, and his replacement died soon after his appointment. The great growth of the Fellowship came in the '60s under the aegis of a controversial Texas salesman named James Jeffrey, who could reduce an audience to tears by sharing with it a soupy story about a young football substitute who has a blind father. The kid finally gets to play—and scores the winning TD—the day after his father dies. And here comes the tearjerk finale: "It was the first time my father ever saw me play." As a ballad on 45 LP, *The Blind Man in the Bleachers* surfaced this past autumn, sung by Kenny Starr, and became No. 2 on the Country and Western charts.

Despite his prairie eloquence, Jeffrey was a haphazard administrator, and he was succeeded three years ago by 48-year-old John Erickson who, religious intensity notwithstanding, does not believe so much in hellfire and brimstone as in the bottom line. A Republican stalwart from Wisconsin, he ran for the United States Senate in 1970 and was defeated by the incumbent, William Proxmire. Prior to that, Erickson had served as basketball coach at Wisconsin and then as general manager of the Milwaukee Bucks, presiding over the team at the time when Lew Alcindor announced his conversion to Islam. As befits the man who holds the most prominent position in Sportianity, Erickson is efficient and distinguished, and even more important for the

Fellowship, which has a distinctly regional heritage and stamp, he is of sturdy Midwestern Lutheran stock.

The FCA preaches a conservative theology. Often, in fact, the movement is hung up on the petty conduct of individuals. All of Sportianity was thrown into a snit several years ago when it was revealed that Bill Bradley, an old pet, had taken to relaxing with a cold beer after a hard game. Joe Namath's love life keeps the entire movement in paroxysms of disgust. Yet Sportianity does not question the casual brutality—spearing, clothes-lining, gouging—that sends players like Namath to the hospital every year. It does not censure the intemperate behavior of coaches like Woody Hayes and Bobby Knight.

Twice, Pro Athletes Outreach has turned away a bachelor athlete who wished to check in at a conference and share hearing the Word with a girl friend. An official for Athletes In Action says that any married AIA player would be dismissed if he saw an X-rated movie, inasmuch as this would mean he had looked lustfully after a woman (albeit on celluloid) and thus, according to literal scripture, had committed adultery.

Arlis Priest of PAO is asked a hypothetical question: suppose the most exemplary man, the most Christlike man in the world, were a pro football player, but this paragon of virtue enjoyed an occasional draft beer and cigar and played some nickel-dime gin rummy with friends. Would PAO want him? Priest thinks some time before answering. "Well, I'm not saying that behavior is right or wrong, but it might offend others, so whereas we'd let him come to our meetings, he could never be a leader, he could never speak out to others." One is reminded of Jonathan Edwards, the Calvinist minister who spearheaded the Great Awakening in 18th-century America. Like Arlis Priest, Edwards was inflexible, and demanded very persuasive evidence that a petitioner had received "God's saving grace" before he would permit him communion. Edwards was known, at least until now, as "the last medieval American."

The fear of taking a stand on moral issues is acute in Sportianity. In January 1972 the FCA monthly, *The Christian Athlete*, broke away from the mainstream and ran a cover article equating sport and war—and most graphically, football and war—and the repercussions are still being felt. *The Christian Athlete*, which is put together at FCA national headquarters in Kansas City, wallows in conversion pieces but, these repetitive commercials aside, it is well written and thoughtful.

The article in question, "Sports and War," appeared at a time when Vietnam was still a national issue, when the polls showed Richard Nixon vulnerable to Edmund Muskie—in large part because of the war. The adult FCA constituency, largely conservative, Nixonian and inculcated with what the article labeled the "sports mindset," had a fit, being especially infuriated by photographs vividly juxtaposing sport and war, *e.g.*, injured player-wounded soldier. The editors well appreciated that the piece was provocative and depressing, but they felt that by examining sports morality under a harsh light, by refusing to approach athletics as "a not very subtle form of hero worship," sport could be put in better perspective—a Christian perspective. The FCA was so distressed with the article that censorship was thereafter imposed upon *The Christian Athlete* and, according to close sources, considerable thought was given to firing both the editors, two devout young Christians named Gary Warner and Skip Stogsdill. Four years later the FCA and the editors are still loth to discuss the matter.

But everyone in Sportianity is utterly candid in explaining—indeed, justifying—the concept of using athletes to preach the Gospel. John Erickson of FCA says, "If athletes can endorse products, why can't they endorse a way of life? Athletes and coaches, be it right or wrong, have a platform in this country. Athletes have power, a voice. So, simply, how can we best use this for something constructive in the faith life?"

Erickson and his colleagues take pains to emphasize that they do not believe that God thinks athletes are unique. "God is no respecter of persons, there are no stars for Him," says the Rev. Billy Zeoli, one of Sportianity's leading figures. "But the fact is that people view athletes and show-biz people as stars, and we can't change that. So we say: let's change the stars, teach them to be right and moral, and then take them to the people."

The acerbic *Wittenburg Door* took a far different view not long ago: "The word *athlete* is arrogant in a sense. It draws a line. It says here is a group of special people. [We] would like to question . . . the whole thing of the athlete. Just the word and the whole discipline involved reflects our society's values . . . the winning, the success, the achieving." At Explo '72, the evangelistic Woodstock that drew packed houses to the Cotton Bowl, the biggest hand went to Roger Staubach (whose message was that "God has given us good field position"; now we can understand why Landry sends in the plays).

Many churchmen outside the evangelical wing oppose superstar religion, in varying degrees. Malcolm Boyd, Episcopal priest and author, says, "The celebrity game is antithetical to the deepest meaning of religion. It's cynical and the misuse of a person. Sure, maybe Roger Staubach, or whoever, knows that he is being used and what for, but the practice is incorrect, the show-bizzing of religion. Religion is ego-tripping with sport.

"And don't let these guys tell me they're merely employing modern methods. Myself, I don't think it's very modern to be right back there with Herod. Some of these preachers with the hairspray are about as hip as Innocent III. Billy Graham said that we should be selling Christ like soap. I don't think so.

I think we should be trying to *act* like Christ. He never was a celebrity. Jesus Christ was the exact opposite of a superstar."

John Erickson says, "We think we've harnessed hero worship," and he states that resolutely. It is unlikely that the Fellowship, at least under Erickson, will completely renounce its star cast. The movement away from heroes and into the hinterlands is led by an FCA vice-president, Julian Dyke, who is the single most impressive individual in Sportianity. Dyke was never a big star. He went to a small college, Western Maryland, and then toiled as a high school coach and athletic administrator in Baltimore. His interest in religion came late, and like the kids themselves he was positively starry-eyed at being in the presence of big names when he first attended an FCA summer camp.

People in religion full time tend to be of great faith. They have accepted one huge absolute, and so it is natural that they accept more prosaic things completely. Simple workaday procedures can become as inviolate as belief in the divinity of Jesus. Christ is right, Huddles are right. And so on. That's the way it is. This type of man is everywhere in Sportianity, so the exception is all the more interesting. In his normal conversation Julian Dyke never says anything stronger than "my goodness," but in FCA staff meetings he deliberately inserts an occasional "hell" or "damn" to shake up the Holy Joes and bring them in touch with reality. Dyke is as devout as the next fellow in Sportianity, but he possesses an awareness and a healthy skepticism lacking in his colleagues. He doesn't confuse Jesus with football. Sadly, a lot of the others do. They worship both, it seems, and, after a time, Jesus and football become indistinguishable.

Because religion does deal in absolutes, it is attractive to athletic personnel. Sport is the converse of religion: there is nothing less absolute. You do not know whether you are going to win, lose or get rained out. The men who stay in sport, coaches who make it their career, tend to be conservative and conformist. In their most indefinite world, they seem to seek assurance and comfort in routine and order, and in religion. Marshall McLuhan suggested not long ago that athletic competition is the ultimate conformity. A game is played in an artificial atmosphere in which rules have been made, goals established, and everybody does the same thing. In effect, you win by conforming better than anyone else. It is a fascinating thesis, and one is particularly struck by it upon considering the alliance of religion and sport. Coaches— not the star players—are obviously the people in athletics best suited to share religion. Indeed, the leaders of the various groups in athletic religion sound more like coaches than executives. One always feels that it is not a calendar year for these people, as it is for everyone else, but a *season*. There is a definite feeling of competition in the air. Praise the Lord and pass the ammunition—and the ammunition is dressed in satin shorts or shoulder pads.

"For a young person," Julian Dyke says, "the star is a model who probably is irreplaceable." He pauses for emphasis, but then smiles to introduce a contradiction. "But it is the coach who has the most impact. *The coach*—more than the teacher, more than the pastor, even more than peers or parents. This is what we find. I'm afraid the negative power of a coach is incredible and too often is overlooked. All the tough-guy stuff, all the winning-is-everything, turns kids away. The toughest thing is to get the coach to tell a boy that he is important, that . . . *I love you.*

"To be perfectly honest, I'm not so sure that what we do in the Fellowship has a great deal of depth. Instead, we work with what is already there, by osmosis, showing these kids a great deal of love and concern. Evangelism is often attacked, especially by those who feel that religion should be more involved with social activism. I think we're getting into a new type of evangelism here, though, one that succeeds through fellowship."

REACHING FOR THE STARS

"Some guys who preach to teams are awed by the athletes," the Rev. Billy Zeoli says. "Some are even in it for money, for free tickets, and that doesn't do us any good. Professional athletes are the fastest guys in the world to spot a phony."

Now that religion in sport—call it Sportianity—is booming, all major league baseball and football teams have Sunday chapel services, home and away, and by any standard Zeoli is the Most Valuable Preacher. (Trivia question: Who is the only man in history to be the first outsider embraced by both a winning Super Bowl coach and a winning World Series manager? Answer: the Rev. Billy Zeoli—by Tom Landry, Dallas, 1972, and by Sparky Anderson, Cincinnati, 1975.) Zeoli is also President Ford's personal pastor, and spends a lot of his time protesting that people make too much of a fuss about his being the President's pastor. Zeoli has good anticipation and if a fuss is not made, he sees one coming and protests in advance.

One of the reasons that "Z"—as many players call him—gets along so well with the athletes is that he has many of the same ego problems they do. He is a celebrity at the height of his powers, and, like a ballplayer on top, is threatened by hotshot kids on the way up. Explaining the operation of his company, Gospel Films, Z suddenly declares, "At any moment I can reach more people around the world than any other minister alive." For emphasis, he glances at his watch. "Well, except maybe Graham. I don't know what he's doing right now." This particular Sunday morning, Z is personally going to reach only the Buffalo Bills and the New York Jets.

Many in religion do not cotton to Zeoli; some are simply jealous of his success. Players who do not attend chapel services sometimes snicker and call him Elmer Gantry behind his back. Z understands all this and accepts it. "I'm not trying to compete with anybody," he says. "I have enough problems with my personality, my chutzpah. But I pray to reach people that others aren't reaching. When I got into this, when I realized what I could do, I told God, 'Give me the chance to communicate with important people like athletes and I will promise You two things: that I will present the Gospel and that I will give You the credit. As a matter of fact, knowing me, I will give You the credit now, in advance.'"

Even though Z seems to enjoy the limelight and to relish being more controversial than humble clergy are supposed to be, his self-perspective and good humor are saving graces. Some of the most subdued, thoughtful types in Sportianity, people who should be his natural enemies, go out of their way to praise Zeoli. His methods seem to work, they say, so we must accept him at face value; everybody seems to have a favorite story of Z's converting a hard-nosed linebacker, transforming him into a veritable St. Francis of Assisi with a few well-aimed verses of Scripture. For all Zeoli's contradictions and insecurities, nobody who knows him doubts his earnestness.

Jim Hiskey, who formerly played on the golf tour along with his better-known brother Babe, helped start PGA chapel services and still organizes them, but he devotes most of his lay ministry to something called Cornerstone, near the University of Maryland campus. It is just a house where he, his wife and children and some visitors live. Young people can come for lunch or for a few weeks, to chat, to be counseled, for Bible studies or training in discipleship. Like many people in Sportianity, Hiskey sometimes seems concerned with box-office religion ("We drew 150 on the tour once when Graham spoke; we even got Palmer and Nicklaus to that service"), but he is kind and understated, and Cornerstone is a warm place, soulful, embracing—even, in the best sense, holy. Nobody is adding up names and numbers, giving out free Bibles or sign-up cards, dressing God in shoulder pads. In the summer and on winter weekends, to make some back-to-school money for his family, Hiskey works as a pro at the Hawk Valley Golf Club in Bowmansville, Pa.

"This is a decade of searching, of looking inward," Hiskey says. "In fact, there might be too much introspection. But in sport, people are less introspective. Stars especially have a high self-image. While a star's image may be distorted, he almost must feel this way about himself to have gotten where he is. I think Billy Zeoli has the kind of message that reaches those people better than most of the rest of us. He is a Christian entrepreneur, and flamboyant, that's for sure, but he has a big heart. There's no question Billy Zeoli has had an impact on some lives out there."

On the surface, Z is something of a caricature. Half Italian ("My emotional side"), half German ("My brains"), he wears long adolescent bangs that tumble in a sexy Veronica Lake lock over one eye. He dresses in flashy ensembles, the kind that *nouveau* pro athletes and guys in pick-up bars favor. This day, for the Bills and Jets, he has selected a deep open-necked shirt to go with a rust-colored three-piece suit that matches the Bible he carries (beat that, Graham).

If Zeoli has a prototype, it is not the complete, careful Graham but Dwight Moody, the 19th-century evangelist who broke through barriers to bring the message to America's industrialists. Unschooled and direct, Moody was sort of a businessmen's minister who thrived on being with fat cats, just as Zeoli plays that game with jocks. Moody indulged in food and became obese, while Zeoli, also a man of excess, has a passion for clothing and pop vernacular. Moody ate himself to death; conspicuous style could eventually do in Zeoli, professionally.

This winter morning in New York, Z's two sons are with him. Often when he travels, he takes members of his family; there are also a daughter, and a wife, Marilyn, with whom he is excruciatingly happy. Quickly, he volunteers that his and Mrs. Zeoli's spiritual life together is matched only by the physical delights they find in one another.

Z has barred photographers and a network TV crew from his service this day. He thinks the players would tab him as a phony if they saw him getting that kind of coverage. He and his coterie (some local Christians are along) go up to the assigned meeting room in the hotel where the Buffalo Bills are staying. There is excited speculation that O. J. may put in an appearance, but unfortunately only four players and a couple of assistant coaches—not a big name among them—show up, which leaves Zeoli visibly taken aback and, afterward, a bit petulant. At the service, though, he tailors his performance neatly for such an intimate group, cutting down on his more bombastic style, coming across rather like a life-insurance salesman instead of the used-car dealer that he often resembles before larger groups.

The essence of his message is the same. By his own proud admission, the Zeoli theology is brutally simple. "I am a total liberal when it comes to methods, but very conservative in theology," he says. As he tells the Bills, as he will tell the Jets, as he always says, Jesus was either the Son of God or a cuckoo—take it or leave it. God and man are separated by sin, which is labeled "The Problem." "The Answer" is to employ Jesus as the intermediary. So, there is "The Decision," and to avoid confusion Zeoli lays out the choices: "yes," "no," and "maybe." Taken as a whole, that is what Zeoli calls "God's Game Plan." The same theology appears throughout Sportianity. Zeoli considers it basic and obvious. A contrary view comes from an athlete who defected in disgust from the Fellowship of Christian Athletics; he calls God's Game Plan a "franchised religion, the McDonald's of the spirit."

But Zeoli is not a philosopher; he is a preacher, and his favorite chapels are crowded ones, especially those filled by old friends. He is something of a walking, breathing St. Christopher medal for Sparky Anderson and the Reds in the off-season, and when he is in familiar territory he is a promiscuous hugger, renewing acquaintanceships with the most generous of embraces.

At Shea Stadium, with the Jets, he is in his element. Not only is this a team he knows well, but the club's policy is to invite friends and family to chapel. There are perhaps 20 Jet players on hand, but 60 or 70 worshipers, all told, jammed into an extra locker room, and Z's eyes dance.

He uses the God's Game Plan material that he had presented at the Bills' *théâtre intime*, but for this SRO crowd he dresses it in brighter verbal fabric and provides snappy animation. Zeoli has hit upon a method of preaching in which every few minutes, cued by a kind of cyclical body-clock, he interrupts the message with a divertissement; a small humor, a studied action (he chucks his watch into the crowd at one point) or even a sudden acknowledgment of someone: "Hey, good to see you again." He breaks up any sustained thought with fluffy interludes. He says this is unintentional and, as spontaneous as he is, no doubt this is true, but the device is most effective—especially with a young audience, with that generation raised on TV, among whom commercial breaks are expected and concentration limited. Many old-time preachers bludgeoned parishioners into submission; time was no object. Apparently, modern pulpiteers must score with flicks and jabs.

Z keeps his hands moving, always the showman, never trusting just the message. He colors his speech with the street jargon he uses in conversation, and presumably even relies on it when he is counseling Betty and Jer. Jesus, the Jets are informed at one point, "cooled it." A passing mention of Plato produces this inquiry: "Is anyone here a philosophy cat?" The athletes tend to be "cats," except for blacks who are referred to as "dudes," or occasionally as "the brothers." To the casual observer, this display appears condescending, but, in fact, the cats and dudes seem to dig Z and are into his act.

Z thinks he has it all together, too. "When it comes to intensity," he says, shortly after his Jets sermon and following an obligatory courtesy call to Joe Namath, "a football team before a game gives you the most intense crowd you'll ever preach to. When I say *pray*—'Let us pray!'—you should see those cats." He drops his head like a rock to show how the players respond to his authority. "They're really up for it. Bob Hope couldn't come in there and relate to those guys in 20 minutes the way I did, could he?"

This question turns out to be not merely rhetorical, for when no direct answer is forthcoming, Z asks anxiously, "Could he? Could he?"

While most of the energy in Sportianity is devoted to using players and coaches as evangelists, an increasing amount of attention is being paid to ministering to the athletes themselves. The practice of holding chapel services originated in the late 1950s. Bill Glass, a Detroit Lions end, would assemble three or four like-minded teammates on road trips, and they would read the Bible together. Raymond Berry and Don Shinnick began a similar program with the Colts, and, in baseball, Richie Ashburn started services for the Cubs in the early '60s. Bobby Richardson of the Yankees brought chapel to the American League, and it was he who first escorted Billy Zeoli into a major league locker room.

And yet, as late as 1973, only about seven or eight baseball teams held regular chapel. The recent change has come about under the aegis of Baseball Chapel, an organization run by Watson Spoelstra of Detroit, after he retired from sportswriting and hard drinking. Baseball Chapel has a $25,000 annual budget, a big-name board of directors (including Commissioner Bowie Kuhn) and a biweekly newsletter that boasts a circulation of more than 1,000. There is no comparable pro football chapel clearinghouse (Pro Athletes Outreach is perhaps most involved), but services in the NFL are now an integral part of every team's weekly schedule.

Despite the success of Baseball Chapel, football is at the heart of the Sportian movement. Tom Landry, the Cowboys' coach who is president of the FCA national board, is the top jock in religion, and his assistant pastor, Roger Staubach, is probably the biggest name. Significantly, Pro Athletes Outreach has signed up many football players, but neither PAO nor any of the other Sportian organizations has made appreciable headway in basketball or hockey. Elvin Hayes of the Washington Bullets and Shelly Kannegiesser of the Los Angeles Kings are the best-known of a handful of converts in those two sports.

Wayne Smith, a vice-president of marketing for the Omni in Atlanta, the arena where the NBA Hawks play, is an ordained Presbyterian minister and the only NBA chaplain. It is his view, and the prevailing one in Sportianity, that pro basketball is not responsive to chapel services and religious involvement because of its frenetic schedule. Tom Skinner, the Redskins' chaplain, thinks that a football cleric could do just as well with a basketball team if he could take the job for a full season. Many basketball players, however, dispute these conclusions and maintain that it is hardly a matter of logistics. Instead, they argue that football and basketball players are distinctly different types.

Phil Jackson of the New York Knicks is the son of rural Pentecostal ministers (although with his full beard he looks rather like a Talmudic student). He is one of the few pros in any league interested in the generic subject of religion. Says Jackson, "The kind of simplistic religion that appeals to so many football players is largely based upon submission. There is no room for argument, for examination. This fits perfectly with the football mentality, where players are the cogs in a machine. Basketball players, on the other hand, are individualists, they have a higher ego sense. I don't think there are more than half a dozen fundamentalist Christians left in the NBA."

Jackson's opinion is buttressed by the Muslim population in pro sports. Virtually all are in basketball. In the NFL only Ahmad Rashad (the former Bobby Moore) is Muslim, and there are none in baseball (Willie Davis is a Buddhist). If Christians can't reach basketball players because of the schedule, why aren't Muslims similarly blocked?

The basketball players who turn to Islam offer much the same reasons other athletes do in accounting for their new devotion to Christ ("A void in my life," "Something bigger than me," etc.). Both groups are searching and/or disillusioned, young men looking for a spiritual anchor in their lives. It seems almost incidental, given their similar temperaments, that some went to Christ and others to Mohammed.

A major distinction besides doctrine is the method of indoctrination. Conversion to Islam is usually a long, thought-out move that requires a negative decision as well (renouncing Christianity). However, it is almost a point of pride with Christian athletes that they were converted quickly, in the blinding-light fashion of Saul on the way to Damascus. Moreover, Islam is more demanding, in terms of ritual and conduct. Mahdi Abdul-Rahman, who was the All-America Walt Hazzard at UCLA, the son of a Methodist minister and college president, says, "In Islam, you can't just go to church on Sunday and feel that will cool everything out. As a Muslim, I have no excuse, but these guys seem to think they're off the hook because Jesus died for them."

Muslims are required to pray five times a day, the first occasion before sunrise—but this and other requirements, such as fasting, can be adjusted for athletes when there is a conflict with their vocational responsibilities. Muslims are also obliged to tithe 2½% of their savings, but no conscious effort is made to use the famous Muslim athletes as evangelists. If only by their names, Kareem Abdul-Jabbar and the few other basketball-playing Muslims have given the impression to many whites that the Islamic religion has firmer roots in black America than in fact it does. In the public mind there also is no distinction between orthodox Muslims and the independent black Muslim sect made famous first by Malcolm X and then by Muhammad Ali. In fact, Abdul-Jabbar refers to the heavyweight champion only as Cassius Clay, believing that the Black Muslim sect holds views contrary to Islam. Those Muslims who are black—as opposed to Black Muslims—are anxious to make it clear that theirs is not a racial religion.

"We've been badly stereotyped," says Abdul-Rahman, who is now a program evaluator for a college preparatory program at UCLA. "Those blacks among us are not out to join Islam to buck the slave thing. It has nothing to do with that. It is a return to a natural way of life, not an escape from the past or anything. I'm taking my name, Hazzard, back, as Jamaal [Wilkes, of the Golden State Warriors] kept his, to show respect for my father and my past. The whole Arabic thing bothers a lot of people. We are assumed to be anti-Semitic, when in fact Arabs are a Semitic people, too, so they could hardly be anti-Semitic. But I'm afraid there are people who haven't stopped fighting the Crusades."

Abdul-Rahman stays out of the controversy, but other Muslims and black Christian players wonder why a young man of his obvious coaching ability cannot find even an assistant's job in the pros. It is darkly suggested in some quarters that Jewish executives want to keep Arab types off their teams and out of their league. Why else, it is asked, did Phoenix have so much difficulty trading the brilliant Charlie Scott, whose Muslim name is Shadid Abdul-Alim? But, in fact, it was a Jew, Red Auerbach of Boston, who finally took Scott. A Jewish NBA executive explodes at the charge. "Just tell 'em they're crazy. Does anybody seriously think I'm going to start thinking about the Gaza Strip if I can get a good shot at a guy like Scott or Wilkes?" These accusations upset Jews even more because so many of them have been active in the management of pro basketball, the sport in which blacks have obtained their greatest opportunities. Basketball has always been considered the most Jewish of games, even though the last great Jewish college player was Art Heyman 15 years ago, and the last great Jewish pro was Dolph Schayes, who also played in the early '60s. Nonetheless, Jews continue to be a substantial force in pro basketball ownership, just as preppy WASPs dominate hockey.

Despite the publicity about black athletes being converted to Islam, the truth is that Christianity is growing faster among blacks in Africa than it is anywhere else in the world. Tom Skinner, who is the best-known black in Sportianity, says, "In this country we Christians have failed in communicating our beliefs to blacks. I don't mind saying that it is the thinking blacks who have turned to Islam. But I understand them. Black people often don't relate to Jesus Christ. We are presenting Him in the wrong light. Blacks see a man who is blond and blue-eyed, yet who comes from a country halfway between Africa and Asia, and they wonder who is putting them on. Besides, Christ seems docile, soft, even effeminate in his pictures, so that you have to work full time just to overcome that. If you can just get blacks to read the

Scriptures, they'll see that He's gutsy, contemporary, radical—that He's got hair on His chest and dirt under His fingernails."

Though his father was a minister, Skinner became a homicidal gang leader in Harlem before turning to Jesus. He operates Tom Skinner Associates (Reaching Black America For Christ) out of a nicely furnished Brooklyn office. There are 36 employees and the budget now exceeds $1 million. Skinner played baseball and basketball at Wagner College, but it is to football, which he played in high school, that he has directed his sports ministry; he has been the Redskins' chaplain since 1971, and he devotes 17 long weekends each fall to being with the team. At other times he counsels city people of all classes from executives to "survivalists," those indigents just trying to get from sunup to sundown. As it does for many ministers, football holds a special fascination for Skinner. "Football is representative of what life is all about," he says. "It has goals, opposition, bad calls."

While all athletes have much the same reasons for turning to religion, football players, who live more intimately with violence and injury, seem most susceptible to the message. "I was a coach," says John Erickson, the Fellowship of Christian Athletes president. "When a player is injured, the first thing he says, every time, is: 'Coach, can I play again?' We can approach them, then, first to minister to their immediate needs, and then to talk to them about their lives."

Says Don Cutler, Episcopal rector and literary agent, "Certain kinds of religion prosper among people under stress. Of course, there's a lot of stress down on Wall Street too, but you don't see any chaplains down there. You also don't see clients physically sacking the broker. Mashing the quarterback—that doesn't bother the fans. It really is a little bit like the lions and the Christians. But for the players, people getting hurt does raise questions, because they may be the next ones injured. There is nothing in the symbolism of sports that helps them deal with that, so they turn to religion.

"The kind of religion that predominates in sport solves a personal need. There are no philosophical issues, nothing is cosmic. God is a bit larger than Pete Rozelle, and if you can just get in good with Him, then He might keep you from getting hurt and He might even get you a better contract. Anyway, what have you got to lose?"

Perhaps as important as what happens on the field is the egomania of bigtime athletes. They have been spoiled rotten since they were nine or 10. Muslim or Baptist, Catholic or Jew, virtually every player who turns to religion cites how his very success, his accomplishment at a young age, required him to look beyond for something more. The classic story is about the surfer who finally found the perfect wave, and immediately turned to God when he discovered that the ride had not made him happy. "The very reason why it is worth talking to these cats," says Billy Zeoli, "is they do have everything at age 23—money, fame, a sense of achievement, women chasing them—and yet still they're so empty."

That emptiness is most often filled with women—"stadium lizards." Any clergyman who seeks employment in the pro locker room better understand that the bulk of his counseling will involve sex. "What else is there?" asks Arlis Priest of PAO. "Even the Christian guys are promiscuous," says Ray Hildebrand of FCA. "Players are pursued by these women," says Tom Skinner. "The temptations are constant. The average man can't even conceive of how many temptations, how often. I mean, he cannot conceive."

The chaplains point out that infidelity in itself is not usually the cause of athletes' failing marriages. Promiscuity is so prevalent that many wives resign themselves to it or blot out the obvious. Instead, pros are so overpowered by stadium lizards, so spoiled by their fawning attentions, that they lose the ability to relate to their wives as individuals. It is not that a pro cheats on his wife when he is away from her, it is that he assaults her dignity when he is with her. The wife cannot cater to the pro's insufferable demands and ego.

An inordinate number of conversions are accompanied by the admission that a marriage was failing, and that new-found religion is what saved it. The guilt among athletes is great; many confess past adulterous transgressions to their wives. Often Sportianity serves as a kind of sexual Alcoholics Anonymous. To be able to tell a stadium lizard, "My religion won't let me" or "Jesus is against this"—that sort of thing—takes the athlete off the hook when he is not strong enough to say no on his own.

Once a chaplain is accepted on a team—and this may take a season or more—the players often become almost compulsive in discussing their problems, marital or otherwise. Zeoli suspects this may be another manifestation of ego—that athletes do everything larger than life, even confess. Skinner adds, "You must keep in mind that athletes need someone to talk to in confidence. So many people take athletes, use them, repeat what an athlete tells them in order to prove their close friendship to others. To be able to talk to someone who really cares and yet can keep a secret is a great release for them."

As effective as ministerial counseling may be, pregame and postgame team prayers strike many as phony and a misuse of religion. Before a game most players are fired up, single-minded, possibly even zonked out on drugs, and when they pray, many admit that they are only going through the motions. Afterward, their only thoughts are on whether they won or lost. Says Malcolm Boyd, who is an author, social critic and Episcopal priest, "This sort of slick, stage-directed prayer alienates people from religion because anybody can see that it is as shoddy as anything else in the world. The gimmick use of prayer before a game for the purpose of getting psyched up, this use of prayer as *deus ex machina*—I find it simply immoral. To use God in this way—it isn't holy. Hell isn't a bunch of fires. I think that hell is when you're using anybody, even when you're trying to use God, as in this case."

A University of West Virginia Episcopal chaplain, the Rev. Michael Paine, attacked Mountaineer football coach James Carlen (now at Texas Tech) in 1966 for forcing his players in effect to "kneel in mock piety," and team prayer was briefly an issue in the state; *The Charleston Gazette* termed it "repugnant" and "unconstitutional." But Carlen moved on to a new gridiron pulpit, and team prayer has spread to become an unchallenged part of American sport.

More and more lay people are agreeing with priests like Boyd that game-day religion has become a hypocritical farce. Even at Notre Dame, where the spiritual function is well established, the use of pregame prayer is admittedly distorted and has lost its original purpose. On a game day the team meets for Mass at 8:30, the captains say the litany and kiss the cross, and then everyone on the team is given a medal chosen especially for the occasion. Father James Riehle, the Notre Dame athletic chaplain, volunteers that the medal is "something visible" that the players can take away, because he admits there is the good likelihood, in the emotions of a game, that the religious experience of the Mass will be overcome and missed altogether. Father Riehle has no pretensions about game-day Mass. "It is somewhat religious," he says, "but only that. It is somewhat symbolic, and I'm sure that some would even say somewhat superstitious. And they may be right. Primarily, it provides unity."

Team chaplains often become talismans, good-luck charms. Zeoli seemed to serve this purpose for the Reds in their championship run. John Shumate, the former Notre Dame basketball star who is not a Catholic, once would not let the team bus depart without the priest who was scheduled to go along on the trip as chaplain. He had a good game record, and Shumate was afraid the club would be jinxed without him. It is still the custom at Notre Dame for the team chaplains to be available to bless individual players before, at half-time and after football games. Now it usually is the non-Catholics who avail themselves of these ministrations; you never know what might click for you.

Game-day religion has become a sort of security blanket, something on the order of superstitions like not stepping on the foul lines or wearing the same tie when you are on a winning streak. "All of us who read the sports pages and listen to the wisdom of color announcers are aware of the rewards of getting up for a game," says Don Cutler. "The religious contribution is largely that of enthusiasm, of morale. I would imagine that the movement is strongest in the most violent sport, where people are asked to act with the highest disregard of personal safety. Specialty teams strike me as not being appreciably different from *Kamikazes*. In football especially, you need every kind of motivation and zeal. If the religious experience is working in these locker rooms, it is working not for the best of reasons. It's merely a function of melding together, of enthusiasm and team spirit. Faith healing is a similar kind of transaction."

The increased interest by religion in sport suggests that sport is now more important in our culture than it has been. Traditionally, religion has moved to where the action is, and in that sense athletics is to be complimented by these ecclesiastical attentions. These are certainly most agreeable times for religion to find a niche in sport. In the 1960s—years of war and division— the athletic philosophy of winning-is-everything was in the ascendancy. Football, the little war, was clearly the national game. Today, sport fills a much more esthetic function, and it is common for athletes to compare their sport to art. Basketball and tennis, balletic endeavors, have advanced to positions of eminence, and baseball, the rustic game, has been restored to grandeur. There is time now for godliness on the schedule. "If winning is everything," asks John Erickson of FCA, "then why play games?"

In the final analysis, sport has had a greater impact upon religion than the other way around. While athletics does not appear to have been improved by the religious blitzkrieg, the religious people who work that side of the street seem to have been colored by some of the worst attitudes found in sport. The temper of athletic religion is competitive, full of coaches and cheerleaders, with an overriding sense of wins and losses, stars and recruiting, game plans and dugout chatter. "Remember that religion can gain the whole world and lose its soul, just like a person," says Malcolm Boyd.

It might be a good idea right now to talk to the veteran GM in the sky about the possibility of a rebuilding year.

MICHAEL NOVAK

The Natural Religion

The saga of George Blanda had further games to run. Yet its elements already exhibit the ways in which sports are a religion.

A sport is not a religion in the same way that Methodism, Presbyterianism,

---

From *The Joy of Sports* (1976).

or Catholicism is a religion. But these are not the only kinds of religion. There are secular religions, civil religions. The United States of America has sacred documents to guide and to inspire it: The Constitution, the Declaration of Independence, Washington's Farewell Address, Lincoln's Gettysburg Address, and other solemn presidential documents. The President of the United States is spoken to with respect, is expected to exert "moral leadership"; and when he walks among crowds, hands reach out to touch his garments. Citizens are expected to die for the nation, and our flag symbolizes vivid memories, from Fort Sumter to Iwo Jima, from the Indian Wars to Normandy: memories that moved hard-hats in New York to break up a march that was "desecrating" the flag. Citizens regard the American way of life as though it were somehow chosen by God, special, uniquely important to the history of the human race. "Love it or leave it," the guardians of orthodoxy say. Those on the left, who do not like the old-time patriotism, have a new kind: they evince unusual outrage when this nation is less than fully just, free, compassionate, or good—in short, when it is like all the other nations of human history. America should be *better*. Why?

The institutions of the state generate a civil religion; so do the institutions of sport. The ancient Olympic games used to be both festivals in honor of the gods and festivals in honor of the state—and that has been the classical position of sports ever since. The ceremonies of sports overlap those of the state on one side, and those of the churches on the other. At the Super Bowl in 1970, clouds of military jets flew in formation, American flags and patriotic bunting flapped in the wind, ceremonies honored prisoners of war, clergymen solemnly prayed, thousands sang the national anthem. Going to a stadium is half like going to a political rally, half like going to church. Even today, the Olympics are constructed around high ceremonies, rituals, and symbols. The Olympics are not barebones athletic events, but religion and politics as well.

Most men and women don't separate the sections of their mind. They honor their country, go to church, and also enjoy sports. All parts of their lives meld together.

Nor am I indulging in metaphor when I say that nearly every writer about sports lapses into watery religious metaphor. So do writers on politics and sex. Larry Merchant says television treated the Super Bowl "as though it were a solemn high mass." Words like *sacred, devotion, faith, ritual, immortality,* and *love* figure often in the language of sports. Cries like "You gotta believe!" and "life and death" and "sacrifice" are frequently heard.

But that is not what I mean. I am arguing a considerably stronger point. I am saying that sports flow outward into action from a deep natural impulse that is radically religious: an impulse of freedom, respect for ritual limits, a zest for symbolic meaning, and a longing for perfection. The athlete may of course be pagan, but sports are, as it were, natural religions. There are many ways to express this radical impulse: by the asceticism and dedication of preparation; by a sense of respect for the mysteries of one's own body and soul, and for powers not in one's own control; by a sense of awe for the place and time of competition; by a sense of fate; by a felt sense of comradeship and destiny; by a sense of participation in the rhythms and tides of nature itself.

Sports, in the second place, are organized and dramatized in a religious way. Not only do the origins of sports, like the origins of drama, lie in religious celebrations; not only are the rituals, vestments, and tremor of anticipation involved in sports events like those of religions. Even in our own secular age and for quite sophisticated and agnostic persons, the rituals of sports really work. They do serve a religious function: they feed a deep human hunger, place humans in touch with certain dimly perceived features of human life within this cosmos, and provide an experience of at least a pagan sense of godliness.

Among the godward signs in contemporary life, sports may be the single most powerful manifestation. I don't mean that participation in sports, as athlete or fan, makes one a believer in "God," under whatever concept, image, experience, or drive to which one attaches the name. Rather, sports drive one in some dark and generic sense "godward." In the language of Paul Tillich, sports are manifestations of concern, of will and intellect and passion. In fidelity to that concern, one submits oneself to great bodily dangers, even to the danger of death. Symbolically, too, to lose is a kind of death.

Sports are not the highest form of religion. They do not exclude other forms. Jews, Christians, and others will want to put sports in second place, within a scheme of greater ultimacy. It is quite natural and normal to envisage human life and responsibilities as falling within schedules of ultimacy. Each "world" can be ultimate of its own kind, yet subsumed within a larger circle. The family is a good in itself, not derivative from the state. It is "ultimate" in its responsibilities. Yet the individual has claims against the family. So does the common good. A sport, like the family, can be in its own sphere an ultimate concern and a good in itself, while yet being subject to other and greater claims on the part of individuals and the common good.

For some, it may require a kind of conversion to grasp the religiousness at the heart of sports. Our society has become secular, and personal advancement obliges us to become pragmatic, glib, superficial, and cynical. Our spirits often wither. Eyes cannot see; ears cannot hear. The soil of our culture is not always fertile for religious life. Americans must read religious messages in foreign languages. And so many will, at first, be tempted to read what I am saying as mere familiar metaphor. A change of perspective, and of heart, may be necessary.

Sports are religious in the sense that they are organized institutions, disciplines, and liturgies; and also in the sense that they teach religious qualities of heart and soul. In particular, they recreate symbols of cosmic struggle, in which human survival and moral courage are not assured. To this extent, they are not mere games, diversions, pastimes. Their power to exhilarate or depress is far greater than that. To say "It was only a game" is the psyche's best defense against the cosmic symbolic meaning of sports events. And it is partly true. For a game is a symbol; it is not precisely identified with what it symbolizes. To lose symbolizes death, and it certainly feels like dying; but it is not death. The same is true of religious symbols like Baptism or the Eucharist; in both, the communicants experience death, symbolically, and are reborn, symbolically. If you give your heart to the ritual, its effects upon your inner life can be far-reaching. Of course, in all religions many merely go through the motions. Yet even they, unaware, are surprised by grace. A Hunter pursues us everywhere, in churches and stadia alike, in the pews and bleachers, and occasionally in the pulpit and the press box.

Something has gone wrong in sports today. It went wrong in medieval Christendom, too. A proverb in Chaucer expresses it: *Radix malorum cupiditas* (The root of all evils is greed). True in the fourteenth century, it is as modern as television: Money corrupts. Nothing much changes down the centuries, only the props and the circumstances. With every day that passes, the "new" world recreates the "old." The ancient sources of corruption in Athens, Constantinople, Alexandria, and Rome are as vigorous in New York, Boston, and Washington as the preparations for Olympic games. Then as now, the hunger for excellence, for perfection-in-act, for form and beauty, is expressed in the straining muscles and fiercely determined wills of heroes of the spirit: of athletes, artists, and even, sometimes, political giants like a Pericles or Cicero. In the corruption of a slave state, a fleshpot, Homer wrote of deeds of beauty. Through his writing, pieces from the flames were salvaged. So it is in every age. Rise and fall are as steady as the seasons of our sports.

But Homer seems to be nodding nowadays. Larry Merchant of the New York *Post*, no Homer he, called his column "Fun and Games" and has been called the pioneer "of modern skepticism and irreverence toward sports." Merchant modestly replies to praise: "I must state for posterity that I was merely part of a broad-based movement. . . . We were irreverent, debunking heroes and myths that didn't stand up to scrutiny." Shucks, folks. Sportswriting "has changed conceptually." His own self-image isn't bad: "We were humanistic. . . . We saw ballparks as funhouses, not temples. We . . . [dug]

for the hows and whys and whos." The intellectually fearless skeptics. Sports isn't religion. It's entertainment. "A baseball game," writes Robert Lipsyte, formerly a New York *Times* sportswriter and the author of *SportsWorld*, "is a staged entertainment, and baseball players are paid performers."

Jewish and Protestant writers draw on different intellectual traditions from mine, of course, but from my point of view, Catholic that I was born, any religion worthy of the name thrives on irreverence, skepticism, and high anticlericalism. A religion without skeptics is like a bosom never noticed (which isn't entirely farfetched, since at least one writer has said that covering sports for the New York *Times* is like being Raquel Welch's elbow). When Catholicism goes sour, as periodically down the centuries it does, almost always the reason is a dearth of critics or, worse, the death of heretics. A non-prophet church decays. When things go well, it is because critics condemn what is going ill. A decent religion needs irreverence as meat needs salt.

Temples do not require whispering. Jesus knocked temple tables over, jangling metal coins on the stones. The root of the religious sense is not the stifling of questions. It lies in asking so many questions that the true dimensions of reality begin to work their own mysterious awe. No one is less religious than the pleasantly contented pragmatist after lunch. Nothing is more religious than fidelity to the drive to understand. For that drive is endless, and satisfied by nothing on earth. It is the clearest sign in our natures that our home is not here; that we are out of place; and that to be restless, and seeking, is to be what we most are.

Sports are not merely fun and games, not merely diversions, not merely entertainment. A ballpark is not a temple, but it isn't a fun house either. A baseball game is not an entertainment, and a ballplayer is considerably more than a paid performer. No one can explain the passion, commitment, discipline, and dedication involved in sports by evasions like these. Many otherwise intelligent people attempt to do so. Some sportswriters call sports the "toy department." Howard Cosell goes out of his way, when he isn't making money from them, to pronounce sports "essentially entertainment," apart from "the serious issues" of our time. A new fashion among sports journalists, like the new fashion among clergymen, is to be ashamed of their own profession and to believe that the important issues lie in social and political concerns. The dominant myth among our elites, at least since the ascension of John F. Kennedy and the evocation of Camelot, is that politics is the home of true morality. Yet politics is mainly machinery; necessary machinery, with some moral implications. "Politics begins in mysticism, and mysticism always ends in politics," Charles Péguy wrote. *Mystique* is larger than *politique*, more original, deeper, longer-lived.

The new sports journalists misunderstand their subject. They lust for politics, for *implications*; they covet power and wealth and social significance.
They seem uninterested in sports. In the modern sports pages where the new
skeptics perform, it is difficult to find coverage of actual sports events. Having
failed in their attempt to find a place on the first page, or in the financial
pages, it seems, they choose second-best by changing the nature of the sports
page. "Sportswriting has changed conceptually" seems to mean "the only
thing we will never describe is an actual sports event." From having been the
best, most lively, most significant, exciting, and revealing pages in the paper,
the new sports pages repeat the issues on page one, more boringly. Over a
third of readers buy papers chiefly for the sports; nowadays they are cheated.
(On this subject, more will be said in Chapter 14.)*

The motive for regarding sports as entertainment is to take the magic,
mystification, and falsehood out of sports. A great deal of sentimentality has
grown up around our national contests. Things are not always what they
seem. Corruptions of various sorts need to be exposed. Yet in the desire to be
honest and to tell it like it is, many of our commentators have overreacted.
They falsify the deep springs of sports. They offer a vision not deep enough
for the reality, a vision that is simply not true. They do not explain to me
the substance of my own love for sports. If they are trying to account for
me, they miss.

At a sports event, there may be spectators, just as some people come to
church to hear the music. But a participant is not a spectator merely, even if
he does not walk among the clergy. At a liturgy, elected representatives perform the formal acts, but all believers put their hearts into the ritual. It is
considered inadequate, almost blasphemous, to be a mere spectator. Fans are
not mere spectators. If they wanted no more than to pass the time, to find
diversion, there are cheaper and less internally exhausting ways. Believers in
sport do not go to sports to be entertained; to plays and dramas, maybe, but
not to sports. Sports are far more serious than the dramatic arts, much closer
to primal symbols, metaphors, and acts, much more ancient and more frightening. Sports are mysteries of youth and aging, perfect action and decay, fortune and misfortune, strategy and contingency. Sports are rituals concerning
human survival on this planet: liturgical enactments of animal perfection and
the struggles of the human spirit to prevail.

To put on a great liturgical performance, enormous funding is required.
Commerce finds its way into the temple—into its very building. Almost certainly, bribes were passed to obtain the permit for the Roman Colosseum, for

---

*Reprinted in this anthology, pp. 553–569.

the site of the Parthenon, and for the negotiation of the land on which the cathedral of Notre Dame of Paris was erected. It is naive to believe that commerce makes religion less religious. Is there an earthier religious imperative than to put up buildings?

Cynicism, skepticism, and irreverence are not only compatible with sports; without them, sports would choke us with their cloying. They are preconditions for sports. Cynicism, skepticism, and irreverence with regard to the "serious things" in life give rise to sports. Athletes and fans know that entire industries are born and obsolesce, that governments come and go, that economic cycles ebb and flow, that empires rise and fall. The British Empire has not outlived cricket, after all. Soccer will be played when China, Russia, and the United States no longer dominate the planet. A certain cynicism about the "real world" may be permitted those who live brief lives, enjoying the clear, cold taste of the combats of sports. The lessons here are eternal ones.

The news departments of our newspapers and television studios are constructed to attract consumers. Each day they give us headlines, tell of manufactured crises, and report on events created so they can report them. They pretend that in the last few hours something has happened in the world worth knowing. Like commercial sports, they are involved in selling. Buying a newspaper or a television station is a little like buying a franchise. The political myths and stories reported on the news may have less substance than the sports account of the local team's fifty-seventh loss this year. Who tells a more mythic story, the White House correspondent giving us sixty seconds on the president's day, or the local radio announcer calling the play-by-play, his sympathies clearly with the locals? The statistics of the business reporter may be less reliable than the seasonal statistics on the pitchers, hitters, fielders. Which world is more "real"?

There are difficulties for the journalist in this unique field of sports, to which a later chapter must be set aside. Here it is only necessary to assert the central proposition forcefully: Those who think sports are merely entertainment have been bemused by an entertainment culture. Television did not make sports possible—not even great, highly organized sports. College football and major league baseball thrived for decades without benefit of television. Sports made television commercially successful. No other motive is so frequently cited as a reason for shelling out money for a set. (Non-sports fans, it appears, are the least likely Americans to have sets.)

In order to be entertained, I watch television: prime-time shows. They slide effortlessly by. I am amused, or distracted, or engrossed. Good or bad, they help to pass the time pleasantly enough. Watching football on television is totally different. I don't watch football to pass the time. The outcome of the games affects me. I care. Afterward, the emotion I have lived through continues to affect me. Football is not entertainment. It is far more important than that. If you observe the passivity of television viewers being entertained, and the animation of fans watching a game on television, the difference between entertainment and involvement of spirit becomes transparent. Sports are more like religion than like entertainment. Indeed, at a contest in the stadium, the "entertainment"—the bands, singers, comedians, balloons, floats, fireworks, jets screaming overhead—pales before the impact of the contest itself, like lemonade served to ladies while the men are drinking whiskey.

Television is peculiarly suited to football, and vice versa; the case is special. But football, whether in the fresh air of the stadium, in the foul air of a sawdust tavern, or in the private corner of one's home, is far more than *Mary Tyler Moore*. The animation on the faces of the fans, the groans, the yells will show you that while televised entertainment may leave its watchers passive, football doesn't. Wives can tell, rather quickly, whether their husbands' teams have won or lost. Sports affect people, and their lives, far more deeply and for a longer time than mere diversion would.

On Monday nights, when television carries football games, police officers around the nation know that crime rates will fall to low levels otherwise reached only on Mother's Day and Christmas.

We are, as I said, too close to sports to appreciate their power. Besides, our education is rigorously pragmatic and factual: those things are real which can be counted. It teaches us nothing about play, or myth, or spirit. So we are totally unprepared to speak about the things we love the most. Our novelists write poorly of women, of love, of tragedy. Our religious sensibilities, which in some are warm with fervor, in our major publicists are chill. Grown men among us are virtually inarticulate about anything that touches our souls. Grunts, groans, and silence. Being cool. Taciturn like Bogart, Grant, Fonda, Newman, Brando, Hoffman, the American male responds to beauty by seeing, by participating, by ritual acts, but not by speaking. Our women can get nothing important out of us. Women talk one language, men another. Our nation lacks cultural institutions, rituals, and art forms that would bridge the sexes. We have no truly popular operas, or suitably complex literature, or plays in which our entire population shares. The streets of America, unlike the streets of Europe, do not involve us in stories and anecdotes rich with a thousand years of human struggle. Sports are our chief civilizing agent. Sports are our most universal art form. Sports tutor us in the basic lived experiences of the humanist tradition.

The hunger for perfection in sports cleaves closely to the driving core of the human spirit. It is the experience of this driving force that has perennially led human beings to break forth in religious language. This force is in us, it is ours. Yet we did not will its existence, nor do we command it, nor is it under our power. It is there unbidden. It is greater than we, driving us beyond our present selves. "Be ye perfect," Jesus said, "as your heavenly Father is perfect." The root of human dissatisfaction and restlessness goes as deep into the spirit as any human drive—deeper than any other drive. It *is* the human spirit. Nothing stills it. Nothing fulfills it. It is not a need like a hunger, a thirst, or an itch, for such needs are easily satisfied. It is a need even greater than sex; orgasmic satisfaction does not quiet it. "Desire" is the word by which coaches call it. A drivenness. Distorted, the drive for perfection can propel an ugly and considerably less than perfect human development. True, straight, and well targeted, it soars like an arrow toward the proper beauty of humanity. Sports nourish this drive as well as any other institution in our society. If this drive is often distorted, as it is, even its distortions testify to its power, as liars mark out the boundaries of truth.

Sports, in a word, are a form of godliness. That is why the corruptions of sports in our day, by corporations and television and glib journalism and cheap public relations, are so hateful. If sports were entertainment, why should we care? They are far more than that. So when we see them abused, our natural response is the rise of vomit in the throat.

It may be useful to list some of the elements of religions, to see how they are imitated in the world of sports.

If our anthropologists discovered in some other culture the elements they can plainly see in our own world of sports, they would be obliged to write monographs on the religions of the tribes they were studying. Two experiments in thought may make this plain.

Imagine that you are walking near your home and come upon a colony of ants. They move in extraordinary busy lines, a trail of brown bodies across the whitish soil like a highway underneath the blades of grass. The lanes of ants abut on a constructed mudbank oval; there the ants gather, 100,000 strong, sitting in a circle. Down below, in a small open place, eleven ants on one side and eleven on the other contest bitterly between two lines. From time to time a buzz arises from the 100,000 ants gathered in their sacred oval. When the game is over, the long lines of ants begin their traffic-dense return to their colonies. In one observation, you didn't have time to discover the rules of their ritual. Or who made them up, or when. Or what they mean to the ants. Is the gathering mere "escape"? Does it mirror other facets in the life of ants? Do all ants everywhere take part? Do the ants "understand" what they are doing, or do they only do it by rote, one of the things that ants do on a lovely afternoon? Do ants practice, and stay in shape, and perfect their arts?

Or suppose you are an anthropologist from Mars. You come suddenly upon some wild, adolescent tribes living in territories called the "United States of

America." You try to understand their way of life, but their society does not make sense to you. Flying over the land in a rocket, you notice great ovals near every city. You descend and observe. You learn that an oval is called a "stadium." It is used, roughly, once a week in certain seasons. Weekly, regularly, millions of citizens stream into these concrete doughnuts, pay handsomely, are alternately hushed and awed and outraged and screaming mad. (They demand from time to time that certain sacrificial personages be "killed.") You see that the figures in the rituals have trained themselves superbly for their performances. The combatants are dedicated. So are the dancers and musicians in tribal dress who occupy the arena before, during, and after the combat. You note that, in millions of homes, at corner shrines in every household's sacred room, other citizens are bound by invisible attraction to the same events. At critical moments, the most intense worshipers demand of the less attentive silence. Virtually an entire nation is united in a central public rite. Afterward, you note exultation or depression among hundreds of thousands, and animation almost everywhere.

Some of the elements of a religion may be enumerated. A religion, first of all, is organized and structured. Culture is built on cult. Accordingly, a religion begins with ceremonies. At these ceremonies, a few surrogates perform for all. They need not even believe what they are doing. As professionals, they may perform so often that they have lost all religious instinct; they may have less faith than any of the participants. In the official ceremonies, sacred vestments are employed and rituals are prescribed. Customs develop. Actions are highly formalized. Right ways and wrong ways are plainly marked out; illicit behaviors are distinguished from licit ones. Professional watchdogs supervise formal correctness. Moments of silence are observed. Concentration and intensity are indispensable. To attain them, drugs or special disciplines of spirit might be employed; ordinary humans, in the ordinary ups and downs of daily experience, cannot be expected to perform routinely at the highest levels of awareness.

Religions are built upon *ascesis*, a word that derives from the disciplines Greek athletes imposed upon themselves to give their wills and instincts command of their bodies; the word was borrowed by Christian monks and hermits. It signifies the development of character, through patterns of self-denial, repetition, and experiment. The type of character celebrated in the central rituals, more likely than not, reveals the unconscious needs of the civilization—extols the very qualities that more highly conscious formulations are likely to deny. Thus, the cults have a revelatory quality; they dramatize what otherwise goes unspoken.

Religions also channel the feeling most humans have of danger, contingency, and chance—in a word, Fate. Human plans involve ironies. Our choices are made with so little insight into their eventual effects that what we desire is often not the path to what we want. The decisions we make with little attention turn out to be major turning points. What we prepare for with exquisite detail never happens. Religions place us in the presence of powers greater than ourselves, and seek to reconcile us to them. The rituals of religion give these powers almost human shape, forms that give these powers visibility and tangible effect. Sports events in baseball, basketball, and football are structured so that "the breaks" may intervene and become central components in the action.

Religions make explicit the almost nameless dreads of daily human life: aging, dying, failure under pressure, cowardice, betrayal, guilt. Competitive sports embody these in every combat.

Religions, howsoever universal in imperative, do not treat rootedness, particularity, and local belonging as unworthy. On the contrary, they normally begin by blessing the local turf, the local tribe, and the local instinct of belonging—and use these as paradigms for the development of larger loyalties. "Charity begins at home." "Whoever says that he loves God, whom he does not see, but hates his neighbor, whom he does see, is a liar and the truth is not in him."

Religions consecrate certain days and hours. Sacred time is a block of time lifted out of everyday normal routines, a time that is different, in which different laws apply, a time within which one forgets ordinary time. Sacred time is intended to suggest an "eternal return," a fundamental repetition like the circulation of the human blood, or the eternal turning of the seasons, or the wheeling of the stars and planets in their cycles: the sense that things repeat themselves, over and over, and yet are always a little different. Sacred time is more like eternity than like history, more like cycles of recurrence than like progress, more like a celebration of repetition than like a celebration of novelty. Yet sacred time is full of exhilaration, excitement, and peace, as though it were more real and more joyous than the activities of everyday life—as though it were *really living* to be in sacred time (wrapped up in a close game during the last two minutes), and comparatively boring to suffer the daily jading of work, progress, history.

To have a religion, you need to have heroic forms to try to live up to: patterns of excellence so high that human beings live up to them only rarely, even when they strive to do so; and images of perfection so beautiful that, living up to them or seeing someone else live up to them, produces a kind of "*ah!*"

You need to have a pattern of symbols and myths that a person can grow old with, with a kind of resignation, wisdom, and illumination. Do what we will, the human body ages. Moves we once could make our minds will but our bodies cannot implement; disciplines we once endured with suppressed animal desire are no longer worth the effort; heroes that once seemed to us immortal now age, become enfeebled, die, just as we do. The "boys of summer" become the aging men of winter. A religion celebrates the passing of all things: youth, skill, grace, heroic deeds.

To have a religion, you need to have a way to exhilarate the human body, and desire, and will, and the sense of beauty, and a sense of oneness with the universe and other humans. You need chants and songs, the rhythm of bodies in unison, the indescribable feeling of many who together "will one thing" as if they were each members of a single body.

All these things you have in sports.

Sports are not Christianity, or Judaism, or Islam, or Buddhism, or any other of the world religions. Sports are not the civil religion of the United States of America, or Great Britain, or Germany, or the Union of Soviet Socialist Republics, or Ghana, or any other nation.

But sports are a form of religion. This aspect of sports has seldom been discussed. Consequently, we find it hard to express just what it is that gives sports their spirit and their power.

Athletes are not merely entertainers. Their role is far more powerful than that. People identify with them in a much more priestly way. Athletes exemplify something of deep meaning—frightening meaning, even. Once they become superstars, they do not quite belong to themselves. Great passions are invested in them. They are no longer treated as ordinary humans or even as mere celebrities. Their exploits and their failures have great power to exult— or to depress. When people talk about athletes' performances, it is almost as though they are talking about a secret part of themselves. As if the stars had some secret bonding, some Siamese intertwining with their own psyches.

Thus, George Blanda in his exploits in 1970 was not simply a curiosity, like a carnival figure with two long hands or seven ears. He touched something vulnerable in the breasts of millions. He seemed to acquire some form of magic, some miraculous power, some beautiful achievement like the deeds of dreams. He also exemplified the wish of all who grow old that they might retain their powers down the years, against the harsh weathering of time. Some truth about life, some deep vein of ancient emotion and human imagination—this is the chord George Blanda's performances happened to strike. His own body and ordinary self became, as it were, inwardly suffused with a power not his own. Naturally, he made little of the sudden attention; he was doing just what he had always done. Part of his glory was simply the result of modern communications, ballyhoo, and publicity. But for those who saw the actual deeds, their beauty spoke for themselves; their excellence pleased; something true shone out. The tales of *Gawain and the Green Knight*, the *Song of Roland*, the exploits of Ivanhoe—these are the ancient games in which human beings have for centuries found refreshment. The crowds who watched the jousts of old are still cheering, still quenching the dust in their throats with cold drinks between the acts, and still seeing enacted before their naked eyes myths of courage, brains, and skill.

We are so close to sports, so enmeshed in them, that we do not truly *see* them, we do not marvel. We overlook the wonder even the existence of sports should cause, let alone their persistence and their power. Long after the Democratic Party has passed into history, long after the United States has disappeared, human beings will still be making play fundamental to their lives.

Play is the most human activity. It is the first act of freedom. It is the first origin of law. (Watch even an infant at play, whose first act is marking out the limits, the rules, the roles: "This is the road. . . ." The first free act of the human is to assign limits within which freedom can be at play.) Play is not tied to necessity, except to the necessity of the human spirit to exercise its freedom, to enjoy something that is not practical, or productive, or required for gaining food or shelter. Play is human intelligence, and intuition, and love of challenge and contest and struggle; it is respect for limits and laws and rules, and high animal spirits, and a lust to develop the art of doing things perfectly. Play is what only humans truly develop. Humans could live as animals (and often we do, governed by instinct), envying what seems to be the freedom of the wild, the soaring aloft of birds, the unfettered wanderings of jungle felines "born free." But animals are not free, not as humans are. Animals do not multiply cultures and languages, and forms of play, and organizational patterns. Animals play as they have for centuries, while humans ceaselessly invent, produce the multiple varieties of religion and play that establish on the soil of nature the realm of culture, the field of liberty. The religions we have, like the games we have, have issued forth from the historical response of humans to their own liberty.

In all these ways, religions and sports have much in common. Sports belong in the category of religion.

One of the most sensitive of the European professors driven to America by Hitler, Eugen Rosenstock-Huessy, observed at Harvard that his references to European stories, historical or legendary, did not illuminate for Americans the points he was making, as they did for his students in Germany. He tried for several years to find a field of examples of which his American students would have vivid personal experience. Later he wrote: "The world in which the American student who comes to me at about twenty years of age really has confidence is the world of sport. This world encompasses all of his virtues and experiences, affection and interests; therefore, I have built my entire so-

ciology around the experiences an American has in athletics and games."
When he wanted to talk about discipline, excellence, failure, contingency,
community, the sacred, dedication, spirit, a recognition of limits, asceticism,
concentration, mysticism, will, insight, the relation between body and emotion and intelligence, and so on, he chose his examples from experiences his
students had already had with sports. Almost always they could get the point
exactly. Since their attention was turned upon their own experiences, sometimes they could notice elements in those experiences which had eluded him.

Sports constitute the primary lived world of the vast majority of Americans. The holy trinity—baseball, basketball, and football—together with
tennis, bowling, skiing, golf, hiking, swimming, climbing (not to mention
gambling, Monopoly, cards, and other forms of play), are not simply interludes but the basic substratum of our intellectual and emotional lives. Play
provides the fundamental metaphors and the paradigmatic experiences for
understanding the other elements of life. "People preserve their thousand-
year-old experiences," Rosenstock-Huessy writes, "in the world of play."

ALAN R. DRENGSON

Wilderness Travel as an Art and as a Paradigm for Outdoor Education

Many years ago it was my good fortune to teach a course in basic mountaineering. At that time I did not see wilderness travel as the complete
Art that it is with its rich cultural connections. I loved the mountains, had
developed certain skills of travel, had gained a deep appreciation for the
many benefits of mountain living, and simply wanted to share these with others who had not had the good fortune to meet someone willing to help them
to learn these things. In my own case, it was through a neighborhood group
and the inspired efforts of one older man (who devoted his spare time to
young people) that I was first introduced to these things. The spirit of our
group was one of sharing. As younger children were always joining the group,

Originally appeared in *Quest* (1980).

it was the role of the more "experienced" hikers to help the inexperienced learn the ropes. This was done with enthusiasm. We were missionaries for the joys of hiking. Whether someone hiked or not was for us a measure of that person's well-being. When I began to teach basic mountaineering it was with a bit of missionary zeal, but this did not involve a full appreciation for what we were doing. In addition, at that time few appreciated the full educational possibilities of wilderness travel and similar outdoor activities. Through the process of teaching these courses in basic climbing, I perceived the role that serious play and the mixture of group activities and outdoor living could have in the maturation of personal competence. Young people would often come into the first class with a great deal of fear, lack of confidence, and almost zero leadership abilities; however, they would often leave with marked improvement in each of these areas.

One of the initial problems in teaching these courses was a lack of sufficient rope-leaders to aid in the teaching process. One has to rely on the more experienced students to help teach those who are less experienced. The more experienced were taught the skills of rope climbing; and they, in turn, after much practice, shared these skills with others. This was a continuous process as new leaders emerged from each class to replace older ones who were leaving. A point to be noted here is that this process generally produced rather pronounced changes in people who stayed with the program for a couple of seasons. They matured rapidly and began to develop more confidence not only in climbing, but in other areas of life as well. Similar observations have been made in such programs as Earthways in Calgary and Outward Bound, and this is part of their rationale.[1]

Whereas various programs such as Earthways and Outward Bound have articulated aims for outdoor living and wilderness travel as educational activities, my aim is to develop a philosophic perspective on wilderness travel (and by implication other outdoor sports) which enables us to see it as a metaphor for life. Further I will inquire how this process can of itself broaden our perspectives to help us to be well-integrated, whole persons. In a sense I will attempt to look at mountain travel as a Zen art, similar in this regard to Aikido, flower arrangement, archery, or creative poetry. The common features of all learning processes are present in wilderness travel. In this context the aims of learning involve a realization of intuitive intelligence, which corresponds to the creative capacity of mastery; the realization or mastery of the way, and its skills; and finally, the realization, through skillful work or practice together, of community or communion together. To achieve these aims in a wholly integral way with full awareness and oneness with our activities *is* mastery in everyday contexts. In the context of *Zen* this mastery would be said to be zen in everyday life.

THE ART

Let me now specify what will be meant by "Wilderness Travel." I capitalize these words to set them off as a title, for they are meant to be both descriptive and metaphoric. "Wilderness Travel" is used metaphorically for daily life and how the whole process of daily living is reflected in Wilderness Travel. Just as in Wilderness Travel we know a mountain by seeing it from many perspectives under a variety of conditions, so in daily life gaining many perspectives on such dynamic social processes as love and hate, work and rest, leads us to understand them. Just as in Wilderness Travel the routes vary, some difficult, some easy, so too with the paths in daily life. Just as in Wilderness Travel we learn the value of pace and of attention to details, so in daily life we learn the value of care and pace in work. In speaking of Wilderness Travel in this context we must keep these metaphoric levels of meaning in mind.

"Wilderness Travel" will be used descriptively to stand for the outdoor activity that involves cross-country travel and trail hiking while living in wilderness, or semiwilderness, mountainous areas. It is a form of mountain touring in which the level of skill reaches into basic mountaineering. This means that Wilderness Travel involves such skills as the use of ice-axe for self-arrest and belaying; the use and selection of proper alpine boots and equipment; the selection and use of climbing equipment, such as crampons, ropes, slings and such hardware as carabiners and assorted anchors. The alpine tourer must learn the general skills of outdoor living and travel. These involve such things as arranging for shelter, clothing, and proper provisions; planning trip itinerary, meals, and transport. It involves skills in first aid, orienteering, wilderness survival, route finding, glacier travel, ridge running, snow travel, basic rock climbing, and steep side hill traversing. It requires knowing how to handle a variety of possible crises involving injuries, personal conflicts within the group, animal attacks, assessment of avalanche hazards, weather conditions, and management of parties caught on the peaks during lightning storms. It might require plant identification, and certainly requires proper disposal of human wastes. It involves a knowledge of the ethics of outdoor living and perhaps even such things as photography, sketching, and describing mountainous terrain. In addition, it requires stellar navigation, recognizing the hazards of hypothermia, and knowing how to prevent frostbite. These are some of the many skills that comprise the Art of Wilderness Travel.

As is evident from the skills listed, the achievement of their mastery with appropriate attitudes constitutes nothing less than the ability to live outdoors in a self-sufficient way. In a larger sense one must be able to do so safely, with enjoyment and a sense of play, and in such a way that one causes minimal or no damage to the environment or to oneself and companions. Mastery also implies a continuance of development through the Art. Thus, although our development often reaches plateaus, if we continue we eventually go beyond these. All arts are alike in this respect. Learning has no final end—even though we may have mastered the art. Through this learning process we come to understand ourselves and others, and our place in the natural world; but this is a dynamic place—hence learning is continuous. However, Wilderness Travel, as we can see, contains a range of activities, each of which could be pursued on its own. There are people who practice just orienteering and others who are interested primarily or solely in rock climbing. Wilderness Travel involves all of these and more.

Lest we be misled, it is necessary here to note that Wilderness Travel is not simply the mastery of the variety of skills mentioned, for in the actual practice of the Art the level of mastery is a unified practice. Without such unity, mastery of these skills would lack coherence as expressed through the Art. The process of the Art is the travel; the travel that is the Art, is an integrated process. It is not just finding footholds, or only using a compass; these are merely part of the total fluid activity. For the master they form a natural unity within the flow of the journey.

Mastery of Wilderness Travel does not involve planning a strict itinerary to which one then attempts to adhere no matter what the circumstances during the trip. Here flexibility is the key, and the rule is that there are no hard and fast rules. One transcends the book in mastery; the book is no longer needed. All of the specific methods are only attempts to indicate aspects of the Art that are later simply processes within the context of this whole activity as a form of creative improvisations. At the level of mastery one is able to see the significance of each act within the total context. Thus mastery opens unlimited possibilities for creativity; no two trips will ever be exactly the same.

To further explain what Wilderness Travel is, I will describe one of its creations, a trip that would be a clear example of the practice of this Art. This can be done at a superficial level by simply describing the general plan of the trip through a certain area. However, since the trip as a whole involves subjective experiences, feelings, emotions, and thoughts—of individuals and the group—description of rough itinerary is not sufficient as an account. Further, the trip involves the interaction between the group, the travel, and the natural setting itself. This is a very complex process, and it is not my aim to discover all of its elements or describe its phenomenology. Thus, although I describe primarily the physical context as the locus for the illustrative trip, it must be noted that this is shorthand for a more complete description.

Consider, then, the following trip: It will begin in the Hoh Rain Forest and go up the Hoh River to Glacier Meadows on the side of Mt. Olympus. From here the route will go to the summit of the mountain and continue on a southerly and easterly direction over the Blue Glacier, across the Hoh Glacier, and down Hume's Glacier to the head waters of the Queets River. From Queets Basin the route will turn north and head up the backbone of the Bailey Range to Ferry Basin; from there it will cross the steep sideslopes of Mt. Carrie, then the ridge crest known as the Cat Walk. From here it will follow the High Divide Trail and continue to Heart Lake. From Heart Lake it will go along High Divide to Hoh Lake, and from there it will drop back to the Hoh Rain Forest and return to the car via the Hoh River Trail.[2]

This projected trip will take about 10 days. It will involve many miles of heavy backpacking both on trails and off. In addition, it will require roped travel over glaciers, up to Class 3 rock climbing, the negotiation of steep un-trailed side hills and gravel slides; it will require negotiating river canyons and river crossings, mountain passes, steep snow slopes, ridge tops, and the like. A good deal of the trip will be high above the tree line. In clear summer weather this can mean days spent in blistering sun and drying wind. More-over, the days at these elevations are much longer than they are in the valleys below. But time will also be spent in alpine forests and in deep, shady, damp river bottom rain forest. It is not uncommon to encounter at least one storm on this route during a 10-day period, even in summer. These summer storms can be hypothermic killers. In some summers there are very long stretches of clear weather, but experience shows that bad weather on such a trip should be anticipated.

As can be seen from this description, this is a trip demanding a high level of skill in the various facets of outdoor living and mountain travel.[3] It also demands excellent physical conditioning along with a soundly based confidence.

THE LESSONS

Now that we have defined and exemplified the Art of Wilderness Travel, let us consider the lessons which can be learned from it. As we have already seen, Wilderness Travel involves familiarity with a range of practical skills such as compass use, map reading, ice-axe skills, and the like. These are ex-amples of learning which can be described in greater detail. However, the lessons of Wilderness Travel that I want to focus on are not these skills but instead, how this Art contributes to the process of education and personal development as a whole. By "education," then, I do not mean merely train-ing or conditioning. The aim of education in a free society must be the growth and development of well-integrated, confident, whole persons. This definition is somewhat vague and so the following must be added. Education is a process in which the educator is a Socratic midwife whose aim is to aid the development of the capacity to engage in intelligent action and inquiry. The educator leads others to discover their own native intelligence by enabling them to examine their own experiences free of distorting theories, preconceptions, and beliefs. All skills, techniques, and the various methods used are only devices to aid in this process, they are not by themselves education. They all must ultimately be transcended by one who educates and by those who are educated to understand human life as a whole with its interconnected communities, both human and nonhuman. Thus education ultimately turns around the values to be realized in full personhood. This implies such understanding and engenders a commitment to a lifetime of learning.

Outdoor education has a profound contribution to make to this process. Wilderness Travel as a paradigm for outdoor education demands self-knowledge and awareness that brings an understanding of our relationships. The master of Wilderness Travel creates situations in which learners come to know themselves and also the natural world through immediate experience and by means of total immersion in a context that demands action rather than speculation or theorizing.[4] There are elements of risk here, but all development involves risk. Furthermore, the very nature of life is change and demands flexibility, and Wilderness Travel cultivates this understanding. In summary, Wilderness Travel addresses not only the intellect, but makes demands on the resources of the whole person. It requires the capacity to respond intelligently with all of one's emotional, physical, intellectual, and spiritual energies. The last of these is an important dimension of human life often ignored, or even denied, in contemporary secular education. Because this is so, more must be said about it.

The spiritual aspects of such learning come to be appreciated only through one's own experience and not as a result of argument, debate, or theorizing. Without directly conveying these aspects of human growth, Wilderness Travel deepens one's appreciation for other life forms and for the pulse of life that beats within each of us. It helps to balance the forces of modern industrial society that create conditions of doubt, alienation, and nihilism within the person's subjective life and that tend to cut one off from natural community and from one's own larger self. In contemporary society we often know ourselves only as personae, but in a wilderness setting we have an opportunity of grasping our larger personal resources.

As a culture we are often skeptical of traditional approaches to spirituality, but Wilderness Travel can be seen as a form of *Rasa Yoga*, the Yoga which leads to unity of self via an appreciation for the aesthetic qualities of the natural world and of the natural human self. As one travels through the rich silence of the wilderness with its diverse forms of life, one reflects more and more deeply on the source of life and its creative capacities. The deep starry skies overlie the whispered sounds of the night with its timelessness, and the visit of a lone goat to one's darkened camp high on an alpine ridge brings an immediate contact with the mysteries of existence. The sound of falling water and the rush of streams, the cycles of rain and snow, and the high wind in the trees bring us once more into the presence of our own immediate experience with the world. They pull us out of our intellectualizing and our worries about the future and stop our reliving of the past. After several days of arduous mountain journey, one settles into the rhythms of one's own biology and those of the natural world. When hungry, one eats; when sleepy, one sleeps. When under way, one is intensely alive and totally involved in what one is doing. One is not divided in the ways in which we so often are. Eating at home might be accompanied by worry, or by watching TV, or by reading; but in the mountains, one just eats. This totality of involvement makes each experience intensely satisfying. It takes one out of the haste that the tyranny of clock time creates. Time in the latter sense seems suspended; one touches the timeless.

The foregoing comments on the spiritual dimensions of Alpine Travel are meant to convey in only a limited way what some of these features are. In the actual context of travel these are woven into the rich fabric of the total experience. One comes to realize in Wilderness Travel the symmetries between human consciousness and the laws of ecology that pervade the natural world. One can see that each of us is an ecosystem in miniature, and that the lessons to be learned in Wilderness Travel apply to daily life and to life's journey as a whole. We know that just as the rain will cease, the sun will eventually emerge from the clouds once more, so too sadness goes, the clouds of grief dissipate, the sun shines once more. We need some basic orientation in daily life, so too in the mountains; we need meticulous preparation for life's work, so too for extended Wilderness Travel, and so on. Thus, Wilderness Travel is not limited to the mountains; its lessons permeate our whole lives, and we are subtly changed by it. One eventually becomes a Wilderness Traveller in daily life.

One of the most important lessons to be learned from Wilderness Travel is closely connected to the idea of voluntary simplicity.[5] In order to undertake such an adventure as Wilderness Travel one is forced to simplify one's life. This begins with a simplification of one's equipment and gear. One cannot haul vast amounts of equipment to the mountains. The average man or woman can rarely manage more than 25 kg of backpack. Of course, heavier loads are carried, and one can manage twice this weight if one is well-conditioned and strong. But the aim is to reduce weight and gear to a minimum consistent with safety. The elegant traveler is one whose gear has been reduced to include primarily necessities. The practical limit to what one can carry on one's back helps a person to realize how little he or she actually needs in order to survive. In fact, because some of the most rewarding and happy times one will ever experience will be spent in Wilderness Travel under conditions with only bare necessities, one gains perspective on human needs. This has implications for ecologically balanced life styles. Moreover, one realizes well-being and happiness are not dependent on a large number of possessions. On the contrary, possessions can be seen as burdens, as attachments that can prevent one from liberation. It is not so much that one becomes a fanatic about riches and sees poverty as the desirable state for humans. It is rather that one begins to get a perspective on the margins and the range of possibilities for human life in relation to material needs and natural limitations. The limits of our environmental systems are beginning to bring similar lessons home to those who have looked at projections detailing future scenarios under certain assumptions about growth and finite resources.

Simplifying and reducing possessions consistent with comfort, safety, and a manageable load give one perspective on desires in contrast with needs. Simple pleasures come to be so satisfying that one has no desire for the unusual pleasures of the jaded palate. A drink of cold water when one is genuinely thirsty is more satisfying than all of the exotic drinks of civilization. Exotic drinks tend to stimulate further thirst, whereas in an alpine setting a sweat-earned thirst is quenched by fresh cold water. We learn in this context how desire operates and how desires create other desires; how desires of a certain order are self-perpetuating since they are always future oriented. The simplicity of life in Wilderness Travel leads one to appreciate the wisdom in sacred teachings on fewness of desires. It is not that one becomes a rigid ascetic, but rather that one comes to appreciate the wisdom of being liberated from the endless chase of desire.

There are the valuable lessons to be learned from walking itself. In Wilderness Travel one learns the art of pace. Pace refers to the balanced and sustainable forms of rhythmic movements of the legs and upper body, and the beat of the heart, all eventually settling into a state of dynamic harmony. If one learns this art properly, one becomes quite sensitive to the various elements of balance involved in efficient travel achieved by means of adjusting one's pace and posture to conditions. One learns fairly early the importance of a slow steady pace that can be sustained over a long period of time. One learns the folly of haste and frequent stopping. The experience of a "second wind" and seemingly boundless energy become part of one's understanding. In addition, mindful walking is required along with pace, especially in off-trail walking. One cannot walk like a robot; one must be ever mindful of what one is doing. All of one's energies and attentions are focused in walking, and yet one is also able to look at the larger view. One learns to put oneself on "automatic pilot" when the trail is even and well-maintained. One learns that the mind can be free to roam without becoming attached to any one thing. Meditation has been defined as the state of being totally one with what one is doing while remaining fully attentive and aware. Wilderness walking leads one to discover this blissful meditative state.[6] One learns that one does not have to think to be. One can be aware, intelligent, perceptive, without a constant chatter of thought. In our daily lives we tend to lose contact with this state of just being, even though, paradoxically, we are it. Our mental tensions and thoughts tend to obscure this realization. They tend to create an uneasy division within. In the context of Wilderness Travel we empty our minds of these tensions, and the meditative forms of walking with pace, balance, and mindfulness facilitate this process. Not only do sweat and simple diet cleanse our bodies, but reduced sensory input cleans our senses and the whole journey cleanses the mind.

Wilderness Travel increases our understanding in other ways as well. We are put more intimately in contact with one another than we usually are in daily life, where so often we fall into mindless habits and into half-hearted contacts in our interpersonal relationships. We have so many sources of stimulation and so many demands placed on us that the impersonal tends to become a dominant feature of our lives. It is not necessary that this be so, but it is often difficult to appreciate that this *is* so, and furthermore how this tends to interfere with our capacities for sympathy and for acting from the heart. In the context of Wilderness Travel we live together 24 hours a day in situations that are simple, intense, and incredibly beautiful. At the same time one spends several hours a day alone with one's thoughts as the party puffs up along alpine ridges or tramps through the silent woods. This balanced movement between inwardness and intense contact gives rise to possibilities for non-linguistic communion with ourselves, with one another, and with the natural world. This communion occurs unplanned at odd moments. Conflicts are relatively few and simple, experienced authentically without the usual manipulations that so often characterize the games we play. Of course, sometimes these games are carried over to the alpine setting, but there is less and less a tendency to do this as one grows toward mastery of this Art. Of necessity the emphasis in Wilderness Travel is not competition but cooperation.

As we journey on our way the honest physical work enables us to become more and more relaxed. There is a playful attitude toward our minor pains. Insect bites, skinned legs and elbows, sore muscles, and the cold hard ground all become familiar friends.

We also learn the folly of resisting gravity and other natural forces too much. Instead of fighting and resisting hardships so produced, we willingly accept them and enjoy them as the natural contrasts of the whole trip. There are times of intense physical and mental demand, and there are moments of profound relaxation and rest. These are not opposites that are eternally separated but instead are parts of one unified process. They have their sense and significance in their interpenetration, each enhancing the other. We learn both from hardship and from the easy-going parts of the journey. Our mistakes provide some of our deepest learning experiences, just as they do in daily life in the lowlands. The whole experience includes both the heights and valleys.

Finally, but by no means exhaustively, I mention the elements of Wilderness Travel that relate to our current environmental problems. These are elements that have to do with personal responsibility in relation to care for the environment; they include an appreciation for the integrity of the ecosystems that sustain all living things on Earth. Wilderness Travel exposes one in a deep personal way to the natural world, to this biosphere. One comes to know it more intimately. For balance, modern humans who live in isolation from these rhythms need more contact with them to the degree to which they live in contexts more isolated from them. The less we have to do with them directly, the less we appreciate them, and the more we lose contact with our own nature.

The breath-taking beauty of the natural world with all of its unhurried cycles has been a source of inspiration for all great sages and religious figures. When God spoke to Moses it was from a burning bush on a mountain. When Job was confronted by Jehovah it was in the form of a whirlwind. Jesus went into the wilderness for 40 days and 40 nights. Buddha meditated under the Bodhi-tree for several days and nights before attaining illumination under the glow of the morning star. The spirit seekers of many Amerind tribes set off alone to the wilderness. The mountain men of North America and the early climbers in the Alps are also part of the traditions that are blended in this Art. One could go on with this list of reminders, but this is sufficient for our purposes.

Through Wilderness Travel one comes finally to appreciate the other living beings with whom we share this earth. One comes to understand in the silence of the wilderness that we all share in the same creative life force. One begins to understand the cycles of life and energy within the biosphere. One comes to appreciate the interconnectedness of life, how each contributes to the processes, how tensions are resolved. One begins to see that the natural world is neither hostile nor inimical to humankind; each of us is the result of this vast interconnected process that life is. The principles of community, friendship, and human flowering are all "written" in the wind, in the flowers of the field, and in the rivers. Through Wilderness Travel one begins to learn how to read these messages. One returns once more to one's home, to that vital center of one's being that is in harmony with the way of nature and the way of the universe. This is the ultimate lesson to be learned from this Art. It is the same lesson that was learned by Lao Tzu and others in Eastern traditions, as well as by the teachers of our own wisdom and mystical traditions. Its mystical qualities are nothing occult or weird, for they are found in the center of all of our own personal daily experiences once we learn how to be aware and receptive to them. Wilderness Travel is one of many Arts which can lead to this realization. Once we realize this we take joy in whatever life sends to us as the gift that it is, and we are good citizens of the earth.

SUMMARY AND CONCLUSION

Let us now summarize our discussion in order to draw the essential features of Wilderness Travel together in concluson. The elements of Wilderness Travel can be elaborated under the following eight categories:

1. The spiritual elements include the realization of the sacredness of life; a growing sense of wonder and awe; a realization that the biosphere is not hostile but benign; a commitment to a life of increasing awareness and care; a respectful attitude toward life which leads to communion with other persons and even other life forms.

2. The physical elements include the conditioning that results; the skills involving balanced movement and regulation of breath; activities which promote flexibility and confidence.

3. Wilderness Travel as a metaphor for life has elements of integrating power that bring one's understanding of natural processes together with one's daily life whether in human communities, in the complexities of modern technology, or in the natural wilderness.

4. The historical backgrounds of Wilderness Travel point towards its evolution as an Art or (as the Chinese would say) a *Tao* or *Way*. This cultural background is bound together with its contemporary practices, whether navigation in the wilderness, or building a fire in the rain soaked forest. The backgrounds include the practice of the withdrawal from society to the desert— and the return; the Amerind spirit quest; the Hunter's skills; the journeys of the Mountain Men; and more recently the skills of scouting, modern Mountaineering as a sport, Outward Bound, and others. Wilderness Travel against this background can be seen as the Art that connects the values realized in these past things and unifies them in our present lives. (The symbolism inher-

ent in Wilderness Travel has affinities with ancient Alchemical traditions which were about the unification of body and spirit, the transmutation of base elements of the soul to the noble forms.)[7]

5. In the solo wilderness trek one finds a form of self-examination that is intense enough to yield deep self-knowledge; in the group trip one also learns about the nature of the self in its relational interconnections.

6. The elements of environmental awareness associated with wilderness travel are many, including the principles of ecology. The trip can be viewed as a creative expression and celebration of a unified vision of reality as a Cosmos.

7. Wilderness Travel has many elements which become ongoing practices in daily life, such as learning to pace oneself in work, etc.

8. Finally, Wilderness Travel can be viewed as a paradigm for forms of education that involve the aim of developing the whole person, and not just the intellect, or just the body—the whole mind/body, or body-mind, as some would say. In this respect it is a paradigm for outdoor education and embodies elements that outdoor education and all education should have.

NOTES

1. As these have illustrated, the process can be facilitated by such practices as the personal journal and also by solo trips. Compare the case of the latter with the spirit quest practiced by various Amerind tribes.

2. The reader might want to consult a map of the Olympics to aid the imagination. Maps and route descriptions can be found in Robert Wood, *Trail Country* (Seattle: The Mountaineers, 1968).

3. This is not to deny that a beginner could not with luck make this trip on his/her own. Early explorations of the Olympics were carried out by men who often were not masters of Wilderness Travel, although many of them were outdoorsmen. Their trials and mistakes paved the way for the development of this Art, as did the 10th Mountain Division, U.S. Army, the Seattle Mountaineers, The Canadian Alpine Club, The American Alpine Club, the early British climbers, etc.

4. It would be useful to have a specially designed room something like a planetarium, that could be totally darkened and acoustically isolated. If one could then "program" different environments with their visual, auditory, olfactory, and other sensory modes, one would have an experiential model simulator for stimulating perceptual awareness through shifting contrasts. This would be valuable for educational purposes and for purposes of design.

5. "Voluntary Simplicity" was coined in the '30s to describe a life style committed to making less do for more. In its current revived form its advocates are committed to living carefully according to ecological principles. They voluntarily lower their levels of consumption and earning in order to lessen their impacts on the environment.

6. Walking is an art that modern humans often have little occasion to learn. Vehicular travel has made the going more rapid and easy but in itself less valuable.

7. Alchemy was an ancient system whose symbols connected natural process and human spiritual development. For example, the transmutation of baser metals into gold symbolized (among other things) the process of developing the more permanent, higher elements of the soul over its lower natures. In addition, various earth processes were seen as analogues to internal psychic processes. The natural world is an analogue to the self, "as within, so without."

A Guide for Further Study

In Chapter 14 of *Sports: A Reference Guide*, pp. 209–220, Robert J. Higgs evaluates much of the writing on religion and sports and provides an excellent bibliography. In addition, check into Roger Caillois, *Man and the Sacred* and Herbert W. Wind, *The Realm of Sport*. Also, see Higgs's article, "Muscular Christianity, Holy Play, and Spiritual Exercises: Confusion about Christ in Sports and Religion," *Arete: The Journal of Sport Literature* 1 (Fall 1983). To supplement Drengson's little manual on wilderness travel, see George Leonard's autobiographical account of mastering Aikido (a Japanese martial art) entitled *The Ultimate Athlete*. Finally, a recent overview of Christianity and sport is Charles S. Prebisch's "'Heavenly Father, Divine Goalie': Sport and Religion," *The Antioch Review* 42 (1984).

Section II: Sport and the Mythic

BERNARD MALAMUD

Pre-game

R oy Hobbs pawed at the glass before thinking to prick a match with his thumbnail and hold the spurting flame in his cupped palm close to the lower berth window, but by then he had figured it was a tunnel they were passing through and was no longer surprised at the bright sight of himself holding a yellow light over his head, peering back in. As the train yanked its long tail out of the thundering tunnel, the kneeling reflection dissolved and he felt a splurge of freedom at the view of the moon-hazed Western hills bulked against night broken by sprays of summer lightning, although the season was early spring. Lying back, elbowed up on his long side, sleepless still despite the lulling train, he watched the land flowing and waited with suppressed expectancy for a sight of the Mississippi, a thousand miles away.

Having no timepiece he appraised the night and decided it was moving toward dawn. As he was looking, there flowed along this bone-white farmhouse with sagging skeletal porch, alone in untold miles of moonlight, and before it this white-faced, long-boned boy whipped with train-whistle yowl a glowing ball to someone hidden under a dark oak, who shot it back without thought, and the kid once more wound and returned. Roy shut his eyes to the sight because if it wasn't real it was a way he sometimes had of observing himself, just as in this dream he could never shake off—that had hours ago waked him out of sound sleep—of him standing at night in a strange field with a golden baseball in his palm that all the time grew heavier as he sweated to settle whether to hold on or fling it away. But when he had made his decision it was too heavy to lift or let fall (who wanted a hole that deep?) so he changed his mind to keep it and the thing grew fluffy light, a white rose breaking out of its hide, and all but soared off by itself, but he had already sworn to hang on forever.

As dawn tilted the night, a gust of windblown rain blinded him—no, there was a window—but the sliding drops made him thirsty and from thirst sprang hunger. He reached into the hammock for his underwear to be first at break-

From *The Natural* (1952).

fast in the dining car and make his blunders of ordering and eating more or less in private, since it was doubtful Sam would be up to tell him what to do. Roy peeled his gray sweatshirt and bunched down the white ducks he was wearing for pajamas in case there was a wreck and he didn't have time to dress. He acrobated into a shirt, pulled up the pants of his good suit, arching to draw them high, but he had crammed both feet into one leg and was trapped so tight wriggling got him nowhere. He worried because here he was straitjacketed in the berth without much room to twist around in and might bust his pants or have to buzz the porter, which he dreaded. Grunting, he contorted himself this way and that till he was at last able to grab and pull down the cuff and with a gasp loosened his feet and got the caught one where it belonged. Sitting up, he gartered his socks, tied laces, got on a necktie and even squirmed into a suit coat so that when he parted the curtains to step out he was fully dressed.

Dropping to all fours, he peered under the berth for his bassoon case. Though it was there he thought he had better open it and did but quickly snapped it shut as Eddie, the porter, came walking by.

"Morning, maestro, what's the tune today?"

"It ain't a musical instrument." Roy explained it was something he had made himself.

"Animal, vegetable, or mineral?"

"Just a practical thing."

"A pogo stick?"

"No."

"Foolproof lance?"

"No."

"Lemme guess," Eddie said, covering his eyes with his long-fingered hand and pawing the air with the other. "I have it—combination fishing rod, gun, and shovel."

Roy laughed. "How far to Chicago, Eddie?"

"Chi? Oh, a long, long ways. I wouldn't walk."

"I don't intend to."

"Why Chi?" Eddie asked. "Why not New Orleans? That's a lush and Frenchy city."

"Never been there."

"Or that hot and hilly town, San Francisco?"

Roy shook his head.

"Why not New York, colossus of colossuses?"

"Some day I'll visit there."

"Where have you visited?"

Roy was embarrassed. "Boise."

"That dusty sandstone quarry."

"Portland too when I was small."

"In Maine?"

"No, Oregon—where they hold the Festival of Roses."

"Oregon—where the refugees from Minnesota and the Dakotas go?"

"I wouldn't know," Roy said. "I'm going to Chicago, where the Cubs are."

"Lions and tigers in the zoo?"

"No, the ballplayers."

"Oh, the ball—" Eddie clapped a hand to his mouth. "Are you one of them?"

"I hope to be."

The porter bowed low. "My hero. Let me kiss your hand."

Roy couldn't help but smile yet the porter annoyed and worried him a little. He had forgotten to ask Sam when to tip him, morning or night, and how much? Roy had made it a point, since their funds were so low, not to ask for anything at all but last night Eddie had insisted on fixing a pillow behind his back, and once when he was trying to locate the men's room Eddie practically took him by the hand and led him to it. Did you hand him a dime after that or grunt a foolish thanks as he had done? He'd personally be glad when the trip was over, though he certainly hated to be left alone in a place like Chicago. Without Sam he'd feel shaky-kneed and unable to say or do simple things like ask for directions or know where to go once you had dropped a nickel into the subway.

After a troublesome shave in which he twice drew blood he used one thin towel to dry his hands, face, and neck, clean his razor and wipe up the wet of his toothbrush so as not to have to ask for another and this way keep the bill down. From the flaring sky out the window it looked around half-past five, but he couldn't be sure because somewhere near they left Mountain Time and lost—no, picked up—yes, it was lost an hour, what Sam called the twenty-three hour day. He packed his razor, toothbrush, and pocket comb into a chamois drawstring bag, rolled it up small and kept it handy in his coat pocket. Passing through the long sleeper, he entered the diner and would gladly have sat down to breakfast, for his stomach had contracted into a bean at the smell of food, but the shirt-sleeved waiters in stocking caps were joshing around as they gobbled fried kippers and potatoes. Roy hurried through the large-windowed club car, empty for once, through several sleepers, coaches, a lounge and another long line of coaches, till he came to the last one, where amid the gloom of drawn shades and sleeping people tossed every which way, Sam Simpson also slept although Roy had last night begged him to take the berth but the soft-voiced Sam had insisted, "You take the bed, kiddo, you're the one that has to show what you have got on the ball when we pull into the city. It don't matter where I sleep."

Sam lay very still on his back, looking as if the breath of life had departed from him except that it was audible in the ripe snore that could be chased without waking him, Roy had discovered, if you hissed scat. His lean head was held up by a folded pillow and his scrawny legs, shoeless, hung limp over the arm of the double seat he had managed to acquire, for he had started out with a seat partner. He was an expert conniver where his comfort was concerned, and since that revolved mostly around the filled flat bottle his ability to raise them up was this side of amazing. He often said he would not die of thirst though he never failed to add, in Roy's presence, that he wished for nobody the drunkard's death. He seemed now to be dreaming, and his sharp nose was pointed in the direction of a scent that led perhaps to the perfumed presence of Dame Fortune, long past due in his bed. With dry lips puckered, he smiled in expectation of a spectacular kiss though he looked less like a lover than an old scarecrow with his comical, seamed face sprouting prickly stubble in the dark glow of the expiring bulb overhead. A trainman passed who, seeing Sam sniff in his sleep, pretended it was at his own reek and humorously held his nose. Roy frowned, but Sam, who had a moment before been getting in good licks against fate, saw in his sleep, and his expression changed. A tear broke from his eye and slowly slid down his cheek. Roy concluded not to wake Sam and left.

He returned to the vacant club car and sat there with a magazine on his knee, worrying whether the trip wasn't a mistake, when a puzzled Eddie came into the car and handed him a pair of red dice.

"Mate them," he said. "I can't believe my eyes."

Roy paired the dice. "They mate."

"Now roll them."

He rolled past his shoe. "Snake eyes."

"Try again," said Eddie, interested.

Roy rattled the red cubes. "Snake eyes once more."

"Amazing. Again, please."

Again he rolled on the rug. Roy whistled. "Holy cow, three in a row."

"Fantastic."

"Did they do the same for you?"

"No, for me they did sevens."

"Are they loaded?"

"Bewitched," Eddie muttered. "I found them in the washroom and I'm gonna get rid of them pronto."

"Why?—if you could win all the time?"

"I don't crave any outside assistance in games of chance."

The train had begun to slow down.

"Oh oh, duty." Eddie hurried out.

Watching through the double-paned glass, Roy saw the porter swing himself off the train and jog along with it a few paces as it pulled to a stop. The morning was high and bright but the desolate station—wherever they were— gave up a single passenger, a girl in a dressy black dress, who despite the morning chill waited with a coat over her arm, and two suitcases and a zippered golf bag at her feet. Hatless, too, her hair a froth of dark curls, she held by a loose cord a shiny black hat box which she wouldn't let Eddie touch when he gathered up her things. Her face was striking, a little drawn and pale, and when she stepped up into the train her nyloned legs made Roy's pulses dance. When he could no longer see her, he watched Eddie set down her bags, take the red dice out of his pocket, spit on them and fling them over the depot roof. He hurriedly grabbed the bags and hopped on the moving train.

The girl entered the club car and directed Eddie to carry her suitcases to her compartment and she would stay and have a cigarette. He mentioned the hat box again but she giggled nervously and said no.

"Never lost a female hat yet," Eddie muttered.

"Thank you but I'll carry it myself."

He shrugged and left.

She had dropped a flower. Roy thought it was a gardenia but it turned out to be a white rose she had worn pinned to her dress.

When he handed it to her, her eyes widened with fascination, as if she had recognized him from somewhere, but when she found she hadn't, to his horror her expression changed instantly to one of boredom. Sitting across the aisle from him she fished out of her purse a pack of cigarettes and a lighter. She lit up, and crossing her heart-breaking legs, began to flip through a copy of *Life*.

He figured she was his own age, maybe a year or so older. She looked to him like one of those high-class college girls, only with more zip than most of them, and dressed for 6 A.M. as the girls back home never would. He was marvelously interested in her, so much had her first glance into his eyes meant to him, and already felt a great longing in his life. Anxious to get acquainted, he was flabbergasted how to begin. If she hadn't yet eaten breakfast and he could work up the nerve, he could talk to her in the diner—only he didn't dare.

People were sitting around now and the steward came out and said first call for breakfast.

She snubbed out her cigarette with a wriggling motion of the wrist—her bracelets tinkled—picked up the hat box and went into the diner. Her crumpled white rose lay in the ashtray. He took it out and quickly stuck it in his pants pocket. Though his hunger bit sharp he waited till everyone was maybe served, and then he entered.

Although he had tried to avoid it, for fear she would see how unsure he was of these things, he was put at the same table with her and her black hat box, which now occupied a seat of its own. She glanced up furtively when he sat down but went wordlessly back to her coffee. When the waiter handed Roy the pad, he absently printed his name and date of birth but the waiter imperceptibly nudged him (hey, hayseed) and indicated it was for ordering. He pointed on the menu with his yellow pencil (this is the buck breakfast) but the blushing ballplayer, squinting through the blur, could only think he was sitting on the lone four-bit piece he had in his back pocket. He tried to squelch the impulse but something forced him to look up at her as he attempted to pour water into his ice-filled (this'll kill the fever) glass, spilling some on the tablecloth (whose diapers you wetting, boy?), then all thumbs and butter fingers, the pitcher thumped the pitcher down, fished the fifty cents out of his pants, and after scratching out the vital statistics on the pad, plunked the coin down on the table.

"That's for you," he told the (what did I do to deserve this?) waiter, and though the silver-eyed mermaid was about to speak, he did not stay to listen but beat it fast out of the accursed car.

Tramping highways and byways, wandering everywhere bird dogging the sandlots for months without spotting so much as a fifth-rater he could telegraph about to the head scout of the Cubs, and maybe pick up a hundred bucks in the mail as a token of their appreciation, with also a word of thanks for his good bird dogging and maybe they would sometime again employ him as a scout on the regular payroll—well, after a disheartening long time in which he was not able to roust up a single specimen worthy to be called by the name of ballplayer, Sam had one day lost his way along a dusty country road and when he finally found out where he was, too weary to turn back, he crossed over to an old, dry barn and sat against the haypile in front, to drown his sorrows with a swig. On the verge of dozing he heard these shouts and opened his eyes, shielding them from the hot sun, and as he lived, a game of ball was being played in a pasture by twelve blond-bearded players, six on each side, and even from where Sam sat he could tell they were terrific the way they smacked the pill—one blow banging it so far out the fielder had to run a mile before he could jump high and snag it smack in his bare hand.

Sam's mouth popped open, he got up woozy and watched, finding it hard to believe his eyes, as the teams changed sides and the first hitter that batted the ball did so for a far-reaching distance before it was caught, and the same with the second, a wicked clout, but then the third came up, the one who had made the bare-handed catch, and he really laid on and powdered the pellet a thundering crack so that even the one who ran for it, his beard parted in the wind, before long looked like a pygmy chasing it and quit running, seeing the thing was a speck on the horizon.

Sweating and shivering by turns, Sam muttered if I could ketch the whole twelve of them—and staggered out on the field to cry out the good news but when they saw him they gathered bats and balls and ran in a dozen directions, and though Sam was smart enough to hang on to the fellow who had banged the sphere out to the horizon, frantically shouting to him, "Whoa—whoa," his lungs bursting with the effort to call a giant—he wouldn't stop so Sam never caught him.

He woke with a sob in his throat but swallowed before he could sound it, for by then Roy had come to mind and he mumbled, "Got someone just as good," so that for once waking was better than dreaming.

He yawned. His mouth felt unholy dry and his underclothes were crawling. Reaching down his battered valise from the rack, he pulled out a used bath towel and cake of white soap, and to the surprise of those who saw him go out that way, went through the baggage cars to the car between them and the tender. Once inside there, he peeled to the skin and stepped into the shower stall, where he enjoyed himself for ten minutes, soaping and resoaping his bony body under warm water. But then a trainman happened to come through and after sniffing around Sam's clothes yelled in to him, "Hey, bud, come outa there."

Sam stopped off the shower and poked out his head.

"What's that?"

"I said come outa there, that's only for the train crew."

"Excuse me," Sam said, and he began quickly to rub himself dry.

"You don't have to hurry. Just wanted you to know you made a mistake."

"Thought it went with the ticket."

"Not in the coaches it don't."

Sam sat on a metal stool and laced up his high brown shoes. Pointing to the cracked mirror on the wall, he said, "Mind if I use your glass?"

"Go ahead."

He parted his sandy hair, combed behind the ears, and managed to work in a shave and brushing of his yellow teeth before he apologized again to the trainman and left.

Going up a few cars to the lounge, he ordered a cup of hot coffee and a sandwich, ate quickly, and made for the club car. It was semi-officially out of bounds for coach travelers but Sam had told the passenger agent last night that he had a nephew riding on a sleeper, and the passenger agent had mentioned to the conductor not to bother him.

When he entered the club car, after making sure Roy was elsewhere Sam headed for the bar, already in a fluid state for the train was moving through wet territory, but then he changed his mind and sat down to size up the congregation over a newspaper and spot who looked particularly amiable. The headlines caught his eye at the same time as they did this short, somewhat popeyed gent's sitting next to him, who had just been greedily questioning the husky, massive-shouldered man on his right, who was wearing sun glasses. Popeyes nudged the big one and they all three stared at Sam's paper.

WEST COAST OLYMPIC ATHLETE SHOT

FOLLOWS 24 HOURS AFTER SLAYING OF
ALL-AMERICAN FOOTBALL ACE

The article went on to relate that both of these men had been shot under mysterious circumstances with silver bullets from a .22 caliber pistol by an unknown woman that police were on the hunt for.

"That makes the second sucker," the short man said.

"But why with silver bullets, Max?"

"Beats me. Maybe she set out after a ghost but couldn't find him."

The other fingered his tie knot. "Why do you suppose she goes around pickin' on athletes for?"

"Not only athletes but also the cream of the crop. She's knocked off a crack football boy, and now an Olympic runner. Better watch out, Whammer, she may be heading for a baseball player for the third victim." Max chuckled.

Sam looked up and almost hopped out of his seat as he recognized them both.

Hiding his hesitation, he touched the short one on the arm. "Excuse me, mister, but ain't you Max Mercy, the sportswriter? I know your face from your photo in the articles you write."

But the sportswriter, who wore a comical mustache and dressed in stripes that crisscrossed three ways—suit, shirt, and tie—a nervous man with voracious eyes, also had a sharp sense of smell and despite Sam's shower and tooth-brushing nosed out an alcoholic fragrance that slowed his usual speedy response in acknowledging the spread of his fame.

"That's right," he finally said.

"Well, I'm happy to have the chance to say a few words to you. You're maybe a little after my time, but I am Sam Simpson—Bub Simpson, that is—who played for the St. Louis Browns in the seasons of 1919 to 1921."

Sam spoke with a grin though his insides were afry at the mention of his professional baseball career.

"Believe I've heard the name," Mercy said nervously. After a minute he nodded toward the man Sam knew all along as the leading hitter of the American League, three times winner of the Most Valuable Player award, and announced, "This is Walter (the Whammer) Wambold." It had been in the papers that he was a holdout for $75,000 and was coming East to squeeze it out of his boss.

"Howdy," Sam said. "You sure look different in street clothes."

The Whammer, whose yellow hair was slicked flat, with tie and socks to match, grunted.

Sam's ears reddened. He laughed embarrassedly and then remarked sideways to Mercy that he was traveling with a slam-bang young pitcher who'd soon be laying them low in the big leagues. "Spoke to you because I thought you might want to know about him."

"What's his name?"

"Roy Hobbs."

"Where'd he play?"

"Well, he's not exactly been in organized baseball."

"Where'd he learn to pitch?"

"His daddy taught him years ago—he was once a semi-pro—and I have been polishing him up."

"Where's he been pitching?"

"Well, like I said, he's young, but he certainly mowed them down in the Northwest High School League last year. Thought you might of heard of his eight no-hitters."

"Class D is as far down as I go," Mercy laughed. He lit one of the cigars Sam had been looking at in his breast pocket.

"I'm personally taking him to Clarence Mulligan of the Cubs for a tryout. They will probably pay me a few grand for uncovering the coming pitcher of the century but the condition is—and Roy is backing me on this because he is more devoted to me than a son—that I am to go back as a regular scout, like I was in 1925."

Roy popped his head into the car and searched around for the girl with the black hat box (Miss Harriet Bird, Eddie had gratuitously told him, making a black fluttering of wings), and seeing her seated near the card tables restlessly thumbing through a magazine, popped out.

"That's him," said Sam. "Wait'll I bring him back." He got up and chased after Roy.

"Who's the gabber?" said the Whammer.

"Guy named Simpson who once caught for the Brownies. Funny thing, last night I was doing a Sunday piece on drunks in baseball and I had occasion to look up his record. He was in the game three years, batted .340, .260, and .198, but his catching was terrific—not one error listed."

"Get rid of him, he jaws too much."

"Sh, here he comes."

Sam returned with Roy in tow, gazing uncomfortably ahead.

"Max," said Sam, "this is Roy Hobbs that I mentioned to you. Say hello to Max Mercy, the syndicated sportswriter, kiddo."

"Hello," Roy nodded.

"This is the Whammer," Max said.

Roy extended his hand but the Whammer looked through him with no expression whatsoever. Seeing he had his eye hooked on Harriet, Roy conceived a strong dislike for the guy.

The Whammer got up. "Come on, Max, I wanna play cards."

Max rose. "Well, hang onto the water wagon, Bub," he said to Sam.

Sam turned red.

Roy shot the sportswriter a dirty look.

"Keep up with the no-hitters, kid," Max laughed.

Roy didn't answer. He took the Whammer's chair and Sam sat where he was, brooding.

"What'll it be?" they heard Mercy ask as he shuffled the cards. They had joined two men at one of the card tables.

The Whammer, who looked to Sam like an overgrown side of beef wrapped in gabardine, said, "Hearts." He stared at Harriet until she looked up from her magazine, and after a moment of doubt, smiled.

The Whammer fingered his necktie knot. As he scooped up the cards his diamond ring glinted in the sunlight.

"Goddamned millionaire," Sam thought.

"The hell with her," thought Roy.

"I dealt rummy," Max said, and though no one had called him, Sam promptly looked around.

Toward late afternoon the Whammer, droning on about his deeds on the playing field, got very chummy with Harriet Bird and before long had slipped his fat fingers around the back of her chair so Roy left the club car and sat in the sleeper, looking out of the window, across the aisle from where Eddie slept sitting up. Gosh, the size of the forest. He thought they had left it for good yesterday and here it still was. As he watched, the trees flowed together and so did the hills and clouds. He felt a kind of sadness, because he had lost the feeling of a particular place. Yesterday he had come from somewhere, a place he knew was there, but today it had thinned away in space—how vast he could not have guessed—and he felt like he would never see it again.

The forest stayed with them, climbing hills like an army, shooting down like waterfalls. As the train skirted close in, the trees leveled out and he could see within the woodland the only place he had been truly intimate with in his wanderings, a green world shot through with weird light and strange bird cries, muffled in silence that made the privacy so complete his inmost self had no shame of anything he thought there, and it eased the body-shaking beat of his ambitions. Then he thought of here and now and for the thousandth time wondered why they had come so far and for what. Did Sam really know what he was doing? Sometimes Roy had his doubts. Sometimes he wanted to turn around and go back home, where he could at least predict what tomorrow would be like. Remembering the white rose in his pants pocket, he decided to get rid of it. But then the pine trees flowed away from the train and slowly swerved behind blue hills; all at once there was this beaten gold, snow-capped mountain in the distance, and on the plain several miles from its base lay a small city gleaming in the rays of the declining sun. Approaching it, the long train slowly pulled to a stop.

Eddie woke with a jump and stared out the window.

"Oh oh, trouble, we never stop here."

He looked again and called Roy.

"What do you make out of that?"

About a hundred yards ahead, where two dirt roads crossed, a moth-eaten model-T Ford was parked on the farther side of the road from town, and a fat old man wearing a broad-brimmed black hat and cowboy boots, who they could see was carrying a squat doctor's satchel, climbed down from it. To the conductor, who had impatiently swung off the train with a lit red lamp, he flourished a yellow telegram. They argued a minute, then the conductor, snapping open his watch, beckoned him along and they boarded the train. When they passed through Eddie's car the conductor's face was sizzling with irritation but the doctor was unruffled. Before disappearing through the door, the conductor called to Eddie, "Half hour."

"Half hour," Eddie yodeled and he got out the stool and set it outside the car so that anyone who wanted to stretch, could.

Only about a dozen passengers got off the train, including Harriet Bird, still hanging on to her precious hat box, the Whammer, and Max Mercy, all as thick as thieves. Roy hunted up the bassoon case just if the train should decide to take off without him, and when he had located Sam they both got off.

"Well, I'll be jiggered." Sam pointed down about a block beyond where the locomotive had halted. There, sprawled out at the outskirts of the city, a carnival was on. It was made up of try-your-skill booths, kiddie rides, a freak show and a gigantic Ferris wheel that looked like a stopped clock. Though there was still plenty of daylight, the carnival was lit up by twisted ropes of blinking bulbs, and many banners streamed in the breeze as the calliope played.

"Come on," said Roy, and they went along with the people from the train who were going toward the tents.

Once they had got there and fooled around a while, Sam stopped to have a crushed cocoanut drink which he privately spiked with a shot from a new bottle, while Roy wandered over to a place where you could throw three baseballs for a dime at three wooden pins, shaped like pint-size milk bottles and set in pyramids of one on top of two, on small raised platforms about twenty feet back from the counter. He changed the fifty-cent piece Sam had slipped him on leaving the train, and this pretty girl in yellow, a little hefty but with a sweet face and nice ways, who with her peanut of a father was waiting on trade, handed him three balls. Lobbing one of them, Roy easily knocked off the pyramid and won himself a naked kewpie doll. Enjoying the game, he laid down another dime, again clattering the pins to the floor in a single shot and now collecting an alarm clock. With the other three dimes he won a brand-new boxed baseball, a washboard, and baby potty, which he traded in for a six-inch harmonica. A few kids came over to watch and Sam, wandering by, indulgently changed another half into dimes for Roy. And Roy won a fine leather cigar case for Sam, a "God Bless America" banner, a flashlight, can of coffee, and a two-pound box of sweets. To the kids' delight, Sam, after a slight hesitation, flipped Roy another half dollar, but this time the little man behind the counter nudged his daughter and she asked Roy if he would now take a kiss for every three pins he tumbled.

Roy glanced at her breasts and she blushed. He got embarrassed too. "What do you say, Sam, it's your four bits?"

Sam bowed low to the girl. "Ma'am," he said, "now you see how dang foolish it is to be a young feller."

The girl laughed and Roy began to throw for kisses, flushing each pyramid in a shot or two while the girl counted aloud the kisses she owed him.

Some of the people from the train passed by and stayed to watch when they learned from the mocking kids what Roy was throwing for.

The girl, pretending to be unconcerned, tolled off the third and fourth kisses.

As Roy fingered the ball for the last throw the Whammer came by holding over his shoulder a Louisville Slugger that he had won for himself in the batting cage down a way. Harriet, her pretty face flushed, had a kewpie doll, and

Max Mercy carried a box of cigars. The Whammer had discarded his sun glasses and all but strutted over his performance and the prizes he had won.

Roy raised his arm to throw for the fifth kiss and a clean sweep when the Whammer called out to him in a loud voice, "Pitch it here, busher, and I will knock it into the moon."

Roy shot for the last kiss and missed. He missed with the second and third balls. The crowd oohed its disappointment.

"Only four," said the girl in yellow as if she mourned the fifth.

Angered at what had happened, Sam hoarsely piped, "I got ten dollars that says he can strike you out with three pitched balls, Wambold."

The Whammer looked at Sam with contempt.

"What d'ye say, Max?" he said.

Mercy shrugged.

"Oh, I love contests of skill," Harriet said excitedly. Roy's face went pale.

"What's the matter, hayfoot, you scared?" the Whammer taunted.

"Not of you," Roy said.

"Let's go across the tracks where nobody'll get hurt," Mercy suggested.

"Nobody but the busher and his bazooka. What's in it, busher?"

"None of your business." Roy picked up the bassoon case.

The crowd moved in a body across the tracks, the kids circling around to get a good view, and the engineer and fireman watching from their cab window.

Sam cornered one of the kids who lived nearby and sent him home for a fielder's glove and his friend's catcher's mitt. While they were waiting, for protection he buttoned underneath his coat the washboard Roy had won. Max drew a batter's box alongside a piece of slate. He said he would call the throws and they would count as one of the three pitches only if they were over or if the Whammer swung and missed.

When the boy returned with the gloves, the sun was going down, and though the sky was aflame with light all the way to the snowy mountain peak, it was chilly on the ground.

Breaking the seal, Sam squeezed the baseball box and the pill shot up like a greased egg. He tossed it to Mercy, who inspected the hide and stitches, then rubbed the shine off and flipped it to Roy.

"Better throw a couple of warm-ups."

"My arm is loose," said Roy.

"It's your funeral."

Placing his bassoon case out of the way in the grass, Roy shed his coat. One of the boys came forth to hold it.

"Be careful you don't spill the pockets," Roy told him.

Sam came forward with the catcher's glove on. It was too small for his big hand but he said it would do all right.

"Sam, I wish you hadn't bet that money on me," Roy said.

"I won't take it if we win, kiddo, but just let it stand if we lose," Sam said, embarrassed.

"We came by it too hard."

"Just let it stand so."

He cautioned Roy to keep his pitches inside, for the Whammer was known to gobble them on the outside corner.

Sam returned to the plate and crouched behind the batter, his knees spread wide because of the washboard. Roy drew on his glove and palmed the ball behind it. Mercy, rubbing his hands to warm them, edged back about six feet behind Sam.

The onlookers retreated to the other side of the tracks, except Harriet, who stood without fear of fouls up close. Her eyes shone at the sight of the two men facing one another.

Mercy called, "Batter up."

The Whammer crowded the left side of the plate, gripping the heavy bat low on the neck, his hands jammed together and legs plunked evenly apart. He hadn't bothered to take off his coat. His eye on Roy said it spied a left-handed monkey.

"Throw it, Rube, it won't get no lighter."

Though he stood about sixty feet away, he loomed up gigantic to Roy, with the wood held like a caveman's ax on his shoulder. His rocklike frame was motionless, his face impassive, unsmiling, dark.

Roy's heart skipped a beat. He turned to gaze at the mountain.

Sam whacked the leather with his fist. "Come on, kiddo, wham it down his whammy."

The Whammer out of the corner of his mouth told the drunk to keep his mouth shut.

"Burn it across his button."

"Close your trap," Mercy said.

"Cut his throat with it."

"If he tries to dust me, so help me I will smash his skull," the Whammer threatened.

Roy stretched loosely, rocked back on his left leg, twirling the right a little like a dancer, then strode forward and threw with such force his knuckles all but scraped the ground on the follow-through.

At thirty-three the Whammer still enjoyed exceptional eyesight. He saw the ball spin off Roy's fingertips and it reminded him of a white pigeon he had kept as a boy, that he would send into flight by flipping it into the air. The ball flew at him and he was conscious of its bird-form and white flapping wings, until it suddenly disappeared from view. He heard a noise like the bang of a firecracker at his feet and Sam had the ball in his mitt. Unable to believe his ears he heard Mercy intone a reluctant strike.

Sam flung off the glove and was wringing his hand.

"Hurt you, Sam?" Roy called.

"No, it's this dang glove."

Though he did not show it, the pitch had bothered the Whammer no end. Not just the speed of it but the sensation of surprise and strangeness that went with it—him batting here on the railroad tracks, the crazy carnival, the drunk catching and a clown pitching, and that queer dame Harriet, who had five minutes ago been patting him on the back for his skill in the batting cage, now eyeing him coldly for letting one pitch go by.

He noticed Max had moved farther back.

"How the hell you expect to call them out there?"

"He looks wild to me." Max moved in.

"Your knees are knockin'," Sam tittered.

"Mind your business, rednose," Max said.

"You better watch your talk, mister," Roy called to Mercy.

"Pitch it, greenhorn," warned the Whammer.

Sam crouched with his glove on. "Do it again, Roy. Give him something similar."

"Do it again," mimicked the Whammer. To the crowd, maybe to Harriet, he held up a vaunting finger showing there were other pitches to come.

Roy pumped, reared and flung.

The ball appeared to the batter to be a slow spinning planet looming toward the earth. For a long light-year he waited for this globe to whirl into the orbit of his swing so he could bust it to smithereens that would settle with dust and dead leaves into some distant cosmos. At last the unseeing eye, maybe a fortuneteller's lit crystal ball—anyway, a curious combination of circles—drifted within range of his weapon, or so he thought, because he lunged at it ferociously, twisting round like a top. He landed on both knees as the world floated by over his head and hit with a *whup* into the cave of Sam's glove.

"Hey, Max," Sam said, as he chased the ball after it had bounced out of the glove, "how do they pernounce Whammer if you leave out the W?"

"Strike," Mercy called long after a cheer (was it a jeer?) had burst from the crowd.

"What's he throwing," the Whammer howled, "spitters?"

"In the pig's poop." Sam thrust the ball at him. "It's drier than your grand-daddy's scalp."

"I'm warning him not to try any dirty business."

Yet the Whammer felt oddly relieved. He liked to have his back crowding the wall, when there was a single pitch to worry about and a single pitch to hit. Then the sweat began to leak out of his pores as he stared at the hard, lanky figure of the pitiless pitcher, moving, despite his years and a few waste motions, like a veteran undertaker of the diamond, and he experienced a moment of depression.

Sam must have sensed it, because he discovered an unexpected pity in his heart and even for a split second hoped the idol would not be tumbled. But only for a second, for the Whammer had regained confidence in his known talent and experience and was taunting the greenhorn to throw.

Someone in the crowd hooted and the Whammer raised aloft two fat fingers and pointed where he would murder the ball, where the gleaming rails converged on the horizon and beyond was invisible.

Roy raised his leg. He smelled the Whammer's blood and wanted it, and through him the worm's he had with him, for the way he had insulted Sam.

The third ball slithered at the batter like a meteor, the flame swallowing itself. He lifted his club to crush it into a universe of sparks but the heavy wood dragged, and though he willed to destroy the sound he heard a gong bong and realized with sadness that the ball he had expected to hit had long since been part of the past; and though Max could not cough the fatal word out of his throat, the Whammer understood he was, in the truest sense of it, out.

The crowd was silent as the violet evening fell on their shoulders.

For a night game, the Whammer harshly shouted, it was customary to turn on lights. Dropping the bat, he trotted off to the train, an old man.

The ball had caught Sam smack in the washboard and lifted him off his feet. He lay on the ground, extended on his back. Roy pushed everybody aside to get him air. Unbuttoning Sam's coat, he removed the dented washboard.

"Never meant to hurt you, Sam."

"Just knocked the wind outa me," Sam gasped. "Feel better now." He was pulled to his feet and stood steady.

The train whistle wailed, the echo banging far out against the black mountain.

Then the doctor in the broadbrimmed black hat appeared, flustered and morose, the conductor trying to pacify him, and Eddie hopping along behind.

The doctor waved the crumpled yellow paper around. "Got a telegram says somebody on this train took sick. Anybody out here?"

Roy tugged at Sam's sleeve.

"Ixnay."

"What's that?"

"Not me," said Roy.

The doctor stomped off. He climbed into his Ford, whipped it up and drove away.

The conductor popped open his watch. "Be a good hour late into the city."

"All aboard," he called.

"Aboard," Eddie echoed, carrying the bassoon case.

The buxom girl in yellow broke through the crowd and threw her arms around Roy's neck. He ducked but she hit him quick with her pucker four times upon the right eye, yet he could see with the other that Harriet Bird (certainly a snappy goddess) had her gaze fastened on him.

They sat, after dinner, in Eddie's dimmed and empty Pullman, Roy floating through drifts of clouds on his triumph as Harriet went on about the recent tourney, she put it, and the unreal forest outside swung forward like a gate shutting. The odd way she saw things interested him, yet he was aware of the tormented trees fronting the snaky lake they were passing, trees bent and clawing, plucked white by icy blasts from the black water, their bony branches twisting in many a broken direction.

Harriet's face was flushed, her eyes gleaming with new insights. Occasionally she stopped and giggled at herself for the breathless volume of words that flowed forth, to his growing astonishment, but after a pause was on her galloping way again—a girl on horseback—reviewing the inspiring sight (she said it was) of David jawboning the Goliath-Whammer, or was it Sir Percy lancing Sir Maldemer, or the first son (with a rock in his paw) ranged against the primitive papa?

Roy gulped. "My father? Well, maybe I did want to skull him sometimes. After my grandma died, the old man dumped me in one orphan home after the other, wherever he happened to be working—when he did—though he did used to take me out of there summers and teach me how to toss a ball."

No, that wasn't what she meant, Harriet said. Had he ever read Homer?

Try as he would he could only think of four bases and not a book. His head spun at her allusions. He found her lingo strange with all the college stuff and hoped she would stop it because he wanted to talk about baseball.

Then she took a breather. "My friends say I have a fantastic imagination."

He quickly remarked he wouldn't say that. "But the only thing I had on my mind when I was throwing out there was that Sam had bet this ten spot we couldn't afford to lose out on, so I had to make him whiff."

"To whiff—oh, Roy, how droll," and she laughed again.

He grinned, carried away by the memory of how he had done it, the hero, who with three pitched balls had nailed the best the American League had to offer. What didn't that say about the future? He felt himself falling into sentiment in his thoughts and tried to steady himself but couldn't before he had come forth with a pronouncement: "You have to have the right stuff to play good ball and I have it. I bet some day I'll break every record in the book for throwing and hitting."

Harriet appeared startled then gasped, hiding it like a cough behind her tense fist, and vigorously applauded, her bracelets bouncing on her wrists. "Bravo, Roy, how wonderful."

"What I mean," he insisted, "is I feel that I have got it in me—that I am due for something very big. I have to do it. I mean," he said modestly, "that's of course when I get in the game."

Her mouth opened. "You mean you're not—" She seemed, to his surprise, disappointed, almost on the verge of crying.

"No," he said, ashamed. "Sam's taking me for a tryout."

Her eyes grew vacant as she stared out the window. Then she asked, "But Walter—*he* is a successful professional player, isn't he?"

"The Whammer?" Roy nodded.

"And he has won that award three times—what was it?"

"The Most Valuable Player." He had a panicky feeling he was losing her to the Whammer.

She bit her lip. "Yet you defeated him," she murmured.

He admitted it. "He won't last much longer I don't think—the most a year or two. By then he'll be too old for the game. Myself, I've got my whole life ahead of me."

Harriet brightened, saying sympathetically, "What will you hope to accomplish, Roy?"

He had already told her but after a minute remarked, "Sometimes when I walk down the street I bet people will say there goes Roy Hobbs, the best there ever was in the game."

She gazed at him with touched and troubled eyes. "Is that all?"

He tried to penetrate her question. Twice he had answered it and still she was unsatisfied. He couldn't be sure what she expected him to say. "Is that all?" he repeated. "What more is there?"

"Don't you know?" she said kindly.

Then he had an idea. "You mean the bucks? I'll get them too."

She slowly shook her head. "Isn't there something over and above earthly things—some more glorious meaning to one's life and activities?"

"In baseball?"

"Yes."

He racked his brain—

"Maybe I've not made myself clear, but surely you can see (I was saying this to Walter just before the train stopped) that yourself alone—alone in the sense that we are all terribly alone no matter what people say—I mean by that perhaps if you understood that our values must derive from—oh, I really suppose—" She dropped her hand futilely. "Please forgive me. I sometimes confuse myself with the little I know."

Her eyes were sad. He felt a curious tenderness for her, a little as if she might be his mother (That bird.) and tried very hard to come up with the answer she wanted—something you said about LIFE.

"I think I know what you mean," he said. "You mean the fun and satisfaction you get out of playing the best way that you know how?"

She did not respond to that.

Roy worried out some other things he might have said but had no confidence to put them into words. He felt curiously deflated and a little lost, as if he had just flunked a test. The worst of it was he still didn't know what she'd been driving at.

Harriet yawned. Never before had he felt so tongue-tied in front of a girl, a looker too. Now if he had her in bed—

Almost as if she had guessed what he was thinking and her mood had changed to something more practical than asking nutty questions that didn't count, she sighed and edged closer to him, concealing the move behind a query about his bassoon case. "Do you play?"

"Not any music," he answered, glad they were talking about something different. "There's a thing in it that I made for myself."

"What, for instance?"

He hesitated. "A baseball bat."

She was herself again, laughed merrily. "Roy, you are priceless."

"I got the case because I don't want to get the stick all banged up before I got the chance to use it."

"Oh, Roy." Her laughter grew. He smiled broadly.

She was now so close he felt bold. Reaching down he lifted the hat box by the string and lightly hefted it.

"What's in it?"

She seemed breathless. "In it?" Then she mimicked, "—Something I made for myself."

"Feels like a hat."

"Maybe a head?" Harriet shook a finger at him.

"Feels more like a hat." A little embarrassed, he set the box down. "Will you come and see me play sometime?" he asked.

She nodded and then he was aware of her leg against his and that she was all but on his lap. His heart slapped against his ribs and he took it all to mean that she had dropped the last of her interest in the Whammer and was putting it on the guy who had buried him.

As they went through a tunnel, Roy placed his arm around her shoulders, and when the train lurched on a curve, casually let his hand fall upon her full breast. The nipple rose between his fingers and before he could resist the impulse he had tweaked it.

Her high-pitched scream lifted her up and twirling like a dancer down the aisle.

Stricken, he rose—had gone too far.

Crooking her arms like broken branches she whirled back to him, her head turned so far around her face hung between her shoulders.

"Look, I'm a twisted tree."

Sam had sneaked out on the squirming, apologetic Mercy, who, with his back to the Whammer—he with a newspaper raised in front of his sullen eyes—had kept up a leech-like prodding about Roy, asking where he had come from (oh, he's just a home town boy), how it was no major league scout had got at him (they did but he turned them down for me) even with the bonus cash that they are tossing around these days (yep), who's his father (like I said, just an old semipro who wanted awful bad to be in the big leagues) and what, for God's sake, does he carry around in that case (that's his bat, Wonderboy). The sportswriter was greedy to know more, hinting he could do great things for the kid, but Sam, rubbing his side where it pained, at last put him off and escaped into the coach to get some shuteye before they hit Chicago, sometime past 1 A.M.

After a long time trying to settle himself comfortably, he fell snoring asleep flat on his back and was at once sucked into a long dream that he had gone thirsty mad for a drink and was threatening the slickers in the car get him a bottle or else. Then this weasel of a Mercy, pretending he was writing on a pad, pointed him out with his pencil and the conductor snapped him up by the seat of his pants and ran his free-wheeling feet lickity-split through the sawdust, giving him the merry heave-ho off the train through the air on a floating trapeze, ploop into a bog where it rained buckets. He thought he better get across the foaming river before it flooded the bridge away so he set out, all bespattered, to cross it, only this queer duck of a doctor in oilskins, an old man with a washable white mustache and a yellow lamp he thrust straight into your eyeballs, swore to him the bridge was gone. You're plumb tootin' crazy, Sam shouted in the storm, I saw it standin' with me own eyes, and he scuffled to get past the geezer, who dropped the light setting the rails afire. They wrestled in the rain until Sam slyly tripped and threw him, and helter-skeltered for the bridge, to find to his crawling horror it was truly down and here he was scratching space till he landed with a splishity-splash in the whirling waters, sobbing (whoa whoa) and the white watchman on the embankment flung him a flare but it was all too late because he heard the roar of the falls below (and restless shifting of the sea) and felt with his red hand where the knife had stabbed him . . .

Roy was dreaming of an enormous mountain—Christ, the size of it—when he felt himself roughly shaken—Sam, he thought, because they were there—only it was Eddie holding a lit candle.

"The fuse blew and I've had no chance to fix it."

"What's the matter?"

"Trou-ble. Your friend has collapsed."

Roy hopped out of the berth, stepped into moccasins and ran, with Eddie flying after him with the snuffed wax, into a darkened car where a pool of people under a blue light hovered over Sam, unconscious.

"What happened?" Roy cried.

"Sh," said the conductor, "he's got a raging fever."

"What from?"

"Can't say. We're picking up a doctor."

Sam was lying on a bench, wrapped in blankets with a pillow tucked under his head, his gaunt face broken out in sweat. When Roy bent over him, his eyes opened.

"Hello, kiddo," he said in a cracked voice.

"What hurts you, Sam?"

"Where the washboard banged me—but it don't hurt so much now."

"Oh, Jesus."

"Don't take it so, Roy. I'll be better."

"Save his strength, son," the conductor said. "Don't talk now."

Roy got up. Sam shut his eyes.

The train whistled and ran slow at the next town then came to a draggy halt. The trainman brought a half-dressed doctor in. He examined Sam and straightened up. "We got to get him off and to the hospital."

Roy was wild with anxiety but Sam opened his eyes and told him to bend down.

Everyone moved away and Roy bent low.

"Take my wallet outa my rear pocket."

Roy pulled out the stuffed cowhide wallet.

"Now you go to the Stevens Hotel—"

"No, oh no, Sam, not without you."

"Go on, kiddo, you got to. See Clarence Mulligan tomorrow and say I sent you—they are expecting you. Give them everything you have got on the ball—that'll make me happy."

"But, Sam—"

"You got to. Bend lower."

Roy bent lower and Sam stretched his withered neck and kissed him on the chin.

"Do like I say."

"Yes, Sam."

A tear splashed on Sam's nose.

Sam had something more in his eyes to say but though he tried, agitated, couldn't say it. Then the trainmen came in with a stretcher and they lifted the catcher and handed him down the steps, and overhead the stars were bright but he knew he was dead.

Roy trailed the anonymous crowd out of Northwest Station and clung to the shadowy part of the wall till he had the courage to call a cab.

"Do you go to the Stevens Hotel?" he asked, and the driver without a word shot off before he could rightly be seated, passed a red light and scuttled a cripple across the deserted street. They drove for miles in a shadow-infested, street-lamped jungle.

He had once seen some stereopticon pictures of Chicago and it was a boxed-up ant heap of stone and crumbling wood buildings in a many-miled spreading checkerboard of streets without much open space to speak of except the railroads, stockyards, and the shore of a windy lake. In the Loop, the offices went up high and the streets were jampacked with people, and he wondered how so many of them could live together in any one place. Suppose there was a fire or something and they all ran out of their houses to see—how could they help but trample all over themselves? And Sam had warned him against strangers, because there were so many bums, sharpers, and gangsters around, people you were dirt to, who didn't know you and didn't want to, and for a dime they would slit your throat and leave you dying in the streets.

"Why did I come here?" he muttered and felt sick for home.

The cab swung into Michigan Avenue, which gave a view of the lake and a white-lit building spiring into the sky, then before he knew it he was standing flatfooted (Christ, the size of it) in front of the hotel, an enormous four-sectioned fortress. He hadn't the nerve to go through the whirling doors but had to because this bellhop grabbed his things—he wrested the bassoon case loose—and led him across the thick-carpeted lobby to a desk where he signed a card and had to count out five of the wallet's pulpy dollars for a room he would give up as soon as he found a house to board in.

But his cubbyhole on the seventeenth floor was neat and private, so after he had stored everything in the closet he lost his nervousness. Unlatching the window brought in the lake breeze. He stared down at the lit sprawl of Chicago, standing higher than he ever had in his life except for a night or two on a mountain. Gazing down upon the city, he felt as if bolts in his knees, wrists, and neck had loosened and he had spread up in height. Here, so high in the world, with the earth laid out in small squares so far below, he knew he would go in tomorrow and wow them with his fast one, and they would know him for the splendid pitcher he was.

The telephone rang. He was at first scared to answer it. In a strange place, so far from everybody he knew, it couldn't possibly be for him.

It rang again. He picked up the phone and listened.

"Hello, Roy? This is Harriet."

He wasn't sure he had got it right. "Excuse me?"

"Harriet Bird, silly."

"Oh, Harriet." He had completely forgotten her.

"Come down to my room," she giggled, "and let me say welcome to the city."

"You mean now?"

"Right away." She gave him the room number.

"Sure." He meant to ask her how she knew he was here but she had hung up.

Then he was elated. So that's how they did it in the city. He combed his hair and got out his bassoon case. In the elevator a drunk tried to take it away from him but Roy was too strong for him.

He walked—it seemed ages because he was impatient—through a long corridor till he found her number and knocked.

"Come on in."

Opening the door, he was astonished at the enormous room. Through the white-curtained window the sight of the endless dark lake sent a shiver down his spine.

Then he saw her standing shyly in the far corner of the room, naked under the gossamer thing she wore, held up on her risen nipples and the puffed wedge of hair beneath her white belly. A great weight went off his mind.

As he shut the door she reached into the hat box which lay open next to a vase of white roses on the table and fitted the black feathered hat on her head. A thick veil fell to her breasts. In her hand she held a squat, shining pistol.

He was greatly confused and thought she was kidding but a grating lump formed in his throat and his blood shed ice. He cried out in a gruff voice, "What's wrong here?"

She said sweetly, "Roy, will you be the best there ever was in the game?"

"That's right."

She pulled the trigger (thrum of bull fiddle). The bullet cut a silver line across the water. He sought with his bare hands to catch it, but it eluded him and, to his horror, bounced into his gut. A twisted dagger of smoke drifted up from the gun barrel. Fallen on one knee he groped for the bullet, sickened as it moved, and fell over as the forest flew upward, and she, making muted noises of triumph and despair, danced on her toes around the stricken hero.

TOM MESCHERY

To Wilt Chamberlain

He appears from afar
A giant Cimmerian statue
Contested for a goal
He shivers strong ebony beads
Of sweat from his body
Turns suddenly
From inanimate to animal
Coils and springs
Sending men like ripples
Into inevitable nonexistence

Off the court
He is enigma
Tropical and dense
As the jungle
Of his forebears
White men fear
Black men genuflect
And once long ago
We argued
Over a fallen tear.

From *Over the Rim* (1970).

JOHN UPDIKE

Hub Fans Bid Kid Adieu

Fenway Park, in Boston, is a lyric little bandbox of a ballpark. Everything is painted green and seems in curiously sharp focus, like the inside of an old-fashioned peeping-type Easter egg. It was built in 1912 and rebuilt in 1934, and offers, as do most Boston artifacts, a compromise between Man's Euclidean determinations and Nature's beguiling irregularities. Its right field is one of the deepest in the American League, while its left field is the shortest; the high leftfield wall, three hundred and fifteen feet from home plate along the foul line, virtually thrusts its surface at right-handed hitters. On the afternoon of Wednesday, September 28th, 1960, as I took a seat behind third base, a uniformed groundkeeper was treading the top of this wall, picking batting-practice home runs out of the screen, like a mushroom gatherer seen in Wordsworthian perspective on the verge of a cliff. The day was overcast, chill, and uninspirational. The Boston team was the worst in twenty-seven seasons. A jangling medley of incompetent youth and aging competence, the Red Sox were finishing in seventh place only because the Kansas City Athletics had locked them out of the cellar. They were scheduled to play the Baltimore Orioles, a much nimbler blend of May and December, who had been dumped from pennant contention a week before by the insatiable Yankees. I, and 10,453 others, had shown up primarily because this was the Red Sox's last home game of the season, and therefore the last time in all eternity that their regular left fielder, known to the headlines as TED, KID, SPLINTER, THUMPER, TW, and, most cloyingly, misTer WONDERFUL, would play in Boston. "WHAT WILL WE DO WITHOUT TED? HUB FANS ASK" ran the headline on a newspaper being read by a bulb-nosed cigar smoker a few rows away. Williams' retirement had been announced, doubted (he had been threatening retirement for years), confirmed by Tom Yawkey, the Red Sox owner, and at last widely accepted as the sad but probable truth. He was forty-two and had redeemed his abysmal season of 1959 with a—considering his advanced age—fine one. He had been giving away his gloves and bats and had grudgingly consented to a sentimental ceremony today. This was not necessarily his last game; the Red Sox were scheduled to travel to New York and wind up the season with three games there.

I arrived early. The Orioles were hitting fungos on the field. The day be-

---

From *Assorted Prose* (1965). Originally appeared in *The New Yorker* (1960).

fore, they had spitefully smothered the Red Sox, 17–4, and neither their faces nor their drab gray visiting-team uniforms seemed very gracious. I wondered who had invited them to the party. Between our heads and the lowering clouds a frenzied organ was thundering through, with an appositeness perhaps accidental, "You maaaade me love you, I didn't wanna do it, I didn't wanna do it. . . ."

The affair between Boston and Ted Williams was no mere summer romance; it was a marriage composed of spats, mutual disappointments, and, toward the end, a mellowing hoard of shared memories. It fell into three stages, which may be termed Youth, Maturity, and Age; or Thesis, Antithesis, and Synthesis; or Jason, Achilles, and Nestor.

First there was the by now legendary epoch[1] when the young bridegroom came out of the West and announced "All I want out of life is that when I walk down the street folks will say 'There goes the greatest hitter who ever lived.'" The dowagers of local journalism attempted to give elementary deportment lessons to this child who spake as a god, and to their horror were themselves rebuked. Thus began the long exchange of backbiting, bat-flipping, booing, and spitting that has distinguished Williams' public relations.[2] The spitting incidents of 1957 and 1958 and the similar dockside courtesies that Williams has now and then extended to the grandstand should be judged against his background: the left-field stands at Fenway for twenty years have held a large number of customers who have bought their way in primarily for the privilege of showering abuse on Williams. Greatness necessarily attracts debunkers, but in Williams' case the hostility has been systematic and unappeasable. His basic offense against the fans has been to wish that they weren't there. Seeking a perfectionist's vacuum, he has quixotically desired to sever the game from the ground of paid spectatorship and publicity that supports it. Hence his refusal to tip his cap[3] to the crowd or turn the other cheek to newsmen. It has been a costly theory—it has probably cost him, among other evidences of good will, two Most Valuable Player awards, which are voted by reporters[4]—but he has held to it. While his critics, oral and literary, remained beyond the reach of his discipline, the opposing pitchers were accessible, and he spanked them to the tune of .406 in 1941.[5] He slumped to .356 in 1942 and went off to war.

In 1946, Williams returned from three years as a Marine pilot to the second of his baseball avatars, that of Achilles, the hero of incomparable prowess and beauty who nevertheless was to be found sulking in his tent while the Trojans (mostly Yankees) fought through to the ships. Yawkey, a timber and mining maharajah, had surrounded his central jewel with many gems of slightly lesser water, such as Bobby Doerr, Dom DiMaggio, Rudy York, Birdie Tebbetts, and Johnny Pesky. Throughout the late forties, the

Red Sox were the best paper team in baseball, yet they had little three-dimensional to show for it, and if this was a tragedy, Williams was Hamlet. A succinct review of the indictment—and a fair sample of appreciative sports-page prose—appeared the very day of Williams' valedictory, in a column by Huck Finnegan in the Boston *American* (no sentimentalist, Huck):

> Williams' career, in contrast [to Babe Ruth's], has been a series of failures except for his averages. He flopped in the only World Series he every played in (1946) when he batted only .200. He flopped in the playoff game with Cleveland in 1948. He flopped in the final game of the 1949 season with the pennant hinging on the outcome (Yanks 5, Sox 3). He flopped in 1950 when he returned to the lineup after a two-month absence and ruined the morale of a club that seemed pennant-bound under Steve O'Neill. It has always been Williams' records first, the team second, and the Sox non-winning record is proof enough of that.

There are answers to all this, of course. The fatal weakness of the great Sox slugging teams was not-quite-good-enough pitching rather than Williams' failure to hit a home run every time he came to bat. Again, Williams' depressing effect on his teammates has never been proved. Despite ample coaching to the contrary, most insisted that they *liked* him. He has been generous with advice to any player who asked for it. In an increasingly combative baseball atmosphere, he continued to duck beanballs docilely. With umpires he was gracious to a fault. This courtesy itself annoyed his critics, whom there was no pleasing. And against the ten crucial games (the seven World Series games with the St. Louis Cardinals, the 1948 playoff with the Cleveland Indians, and the two-game series with the Yankees at the end of the 1949 season, when one victory would have given the Red Sox the pennant) that make up the Achilles' heel of Williams' record, a mass of statistics can be set showing that day in and day out he was no slouch in the clutch.[6] The correspondence columns of the Boston papers now and then suffer a sharp flurry of arithmetic on this score; indeed, for Williams to have distributed all his hits so they did nobody else any good would constitute a feat of placement unparalleled in the annals of selfishness.

Whatever residue of truth remains of the Finnegan charge those of us who love Williams must transmute as best we can, in our own personal crucibles. My personal memories of Williams began when I was a boy in Pennsylvania, with two last-place teams in Philadelphia to keep me company. For me, "W'ms, lf" was a figment of the box scores who always seemed to be going 3-for-5. He radiated, from afar, the hard blue glow of high purpose. I remember listening over the radio to the All-Star Game of 1946, in which

Williams hit two singles and two home runs, the second one off a Rip Sewell "blooper" pitch; it was like hitting a balloon out of the park. I remember watching one of his home runs from the bleachers of Shibe Park; it went over the first baseman's head and rose methodically along a straight line and was still rising when it cleared the fence. The trajectory seemed qualitatively different from anything anyone else might hit. For me, Williams is the classic ballplayer of the game on a hot August weekday, before a small crowd, when the only thing at stake is the tissue-thin difference between a thing well done and a thing done ill. Baseball is a game of the long season, of relentless and gradual averaging-out. Irrelevance—since the reference point of most individual contests is remote and statistical—always threatens its interest, which can be maintained not by the occasional heroics that sportswriters feed upon but by players who always *care*; who care, that is to say, about themselves and their art. Insofar as the clutch hitter is not a sportswriter's myth, he is a vulgarity, like a writer who writes only for money. It may be that, compared to such managers' dreams as the manifestly classy Joe DiMaggio and the always helpful Stan Musial, Williams was an icy star. But of all team sports, baseball, with its graceful intermittences of action, its immense and tranquil field sparsely settled with poised men in white, its dispassionate mathematics, seems to me best suited to accommodate, and be ornamented by, a loner. It is an essentially lonely game. No other player visible to my generation concentrated within himself so much of the sport's poignance, so assiduously refined his natural skills, so constantly brought to the plate that intensity of competence that crowds the throat with joy.

By the time I went to college, near Boston, the lesser stars Yawkey had assembled around Williams had faded, and his rigorous pride of craftsmanship had become itself a kind of heroism. This brittle and temperamental player developed an unexpected quality of persistence. He was always coming back—back from Korea, back from a broken collarbone, a shattered elbow, a bruised heel, back from drastic bouts of flu and ptomaine poisoning. Hardly a season went by without some enfeebling mishap, yet he always came back, and always looked like himself. The delicate mechanism of timing and power seemed sealed, shockproof, in some case deep within his frame.[7] In addition to injuries, there was a heavily publicized divorce, and the usual storms with the press, and the Williams Shift—the maneuver, custom-built by Lou Boudreau of the Cleveland Indians, whereby three infielders were concentrated on the right side of the infield.[8] Williams could easily have learned to punch singles through the vacancy on his left and fattened his average hugely. This was what Ty Cobb, the Einstein of average, told him to do. But the game had changed since Cobb; Williams believed that his value to the club and to the league was as a slugger, so he went on pulling the ball, trying to blast it through three men, and paid the price of perhaps fifteen points of lifetime average. Like Ruth before him, he bought the occasional home run at the cost of many directed singles—a calculated sacrifice certainly not, in the case of a hitter as average-minded as Williams, entirely selfish.

After a prime so harassed and hobbled, Williams was granted by the relenting fates a golden twilight. He became at the end of his career perhaps the best *old* hitter of the century. The dividing line falls between the 1956 and the 1957 seasons. In September of the first year, he and Mickey Mantle were contending for the batting championship. Both were hitting around .350, and there was no one else near them. The season ended with a three-game series between the Yankees and the Sox, and, living in New York then, I went up to the Stadium. Williams was slightly shy of the four hundred at-bats needed to qualify; the fear was expressed that the Yankee pitchers would walk him to protect Mantle. Instead, they pitched to him. It was wise. He looked terrible at the plate, tired and discouraged and unconvincing. He never looked very good to me in the Stadium.[9] The final outcome in 1956 was Mantle .353, Williams .345.

The next year, I moved from New York to New England, and it made all the difference. For in September of 1957, in the same situation, the story was reversed. Mantle finally hit .365; it was the best season of his career. But Williams, though sick and old, had run away from him. A bout of flu had laid him low in September. He emerged from his cave in the Hotel Somerset haggard but irresistible; he hit four successive pinch-hit home runs. "I feel terrible," he confessed, "but every time I take a swing at the ball it goes out of the park." He ended the season with thirty-eight home runs and an average of .388, the highest in either league since his own .406, and, coming from a decrepit man of thirty-nine, an even more supernal figure. With eight or so of the "leg hits" that a younger man would have beaten out, it would have been .400. And the next year, Williams, who in 1949 and 1953 had lost batting championships by decimal whiskers to George Kell and Mickey Vernon, sneaked in behind his teammate Pete Runnels and filched his sixth title, a bargain at .328.

In 1959, it seemed all over. The dinosaur thrashed around in the .200 swamp for the first half of the season, and was even benched ("rested," Manager Mike Higgins tactfully said). Old foes like the late Bill Cunningham began to offer batting tips. Cunningham thought Williams was jiggling his elbows;[10] in truth, Williams' neck was so stiff he could hardly turn his head to look at the pitcher. When he swung, it looked like a Calder mobile with one thread cut; it reminded you that since 1954 Williams' shoulders had been wired together. A solicitous pall settled over the sports pages. In the two decades since Williams had come to Boston, his status had imperceptibly shifted from that of a naughty prodigy to that of a municipal monument. As his shadow in the record books lengthened, the Red Sox teams around him declined, and the entire American League seemed to be losing life and color to the National. The inconsistency of the new super-stars—Mantle, Colavito, and Kaline—served to make Williams appear all the more singular. And off the field, his private philanthropy—in particular, his zealous chairmanship of the Jimmy Fund, a charity for children with cancer—gave him a civic presence matched only by that of Richard Cardinal Cushing. In religion, Williams appears to be a humanist, and a selective one at that, but he and the abrasive-voiced Cardinal, when their good works intersect and they appear in the public eye together, make a handsome pair of seraphim.

Humiliated by his '59 season, Williams determined, once more, to come back. I, as a specimen Williams partisan, was both glad and fearful. All baseball fans believe in miracles; the question is, how *many* do you believe in? He looked like a ghost in spring training. Manager Jurges warned us ahead of time that if Williams didn't come through he would be benched, just like anybody else. As it turned out, it was Jurges who was benched. Williams entered the 1960 season needing eight home runs to have a lifetime total of 500; after one time at bat in Washington, he needed seven. For a stretch, he was hitting a home run every second game that he played. He passed Lou Gehrig's lifetime total, and finished with 521, thirteen behind Jimmy Foxx, who alone stands between Williams and Babe Ruth's unapproachable 714. The summer was a statistician's picnic. His two-thousandth walk came and went, his eighteen-hundredth run batted in, his sixteenth All-Star Game. At one point, he hit a home run off a pitcher, Don Lee, off whose father, Thornton Lee, he had hit a home run a generation before. The only comparable season for a forty-two-year-old man was Ty Cobb's in 1928. Cobb batted .323 and hit one homer. Williams batted .316 but hit twenty-nine homers.

In sum, though generally conceded to be the greatest hitter of his era, he did not establish himself as "the greatest hitter who ever lived." Cobb, for average, and Ruth, for power, remain supreme. Cobb, Rogers Hornsby, Joe Jackson, and Lefty O'Doul, among players since 1900, have higher lifetime averages than Williams' .344. Unlike Foxx, Gehrig, Hack Wilson, Hank Greenberg, and Ralph Kiner, Williams never came close to matching Babe Ruth's season home-run total of sixty.[11] In the list of major-league batting records, not one is held by Williams. He is second in walks drawn, third in home runs, fifth in lifetime average, sixth in runs batted in, eighth in runs scored and in total bases, fourteenth in doubles, and thirtieth in hits.[12] But if we allow him merely average seasons for the four-plus seasons he lost to two wars, and add another season for the months he lost to injuries, we get a man who in all the power totals would be second, and not a very distant second, to

Ruth. And if we further allow that these years would have been not merely average but prime years, if we allow for all the months when Williams was playing in sub-par condition, if we permit his early and later years in baseball to be some sort of index of what the middle years could have been, if we give him a right-field fence that is not, like Fenway's, one of the most distant in the league, and if—the least excusable "if"—we imagine him condescending to outsmart the Williams Shift, we can defensibly assemble, like a colossus induced from the sizable fragments that do remain, a statistical figure not incommensurate with his grandiose ambition. From the statistics that are on the books, a good case can be made that in the *combination* of power and average Williams is first; nobody else ranks so high in both categories. Finally, there is the witness of the eyes; men whose memories go back to Shoeless Joe Jackson—another unlucky natural—rank him and Williams together as the best-looking hitters they have seen. It was for our last look that ten thousand of us had come.

Two girls, one of them with pert buckteeth and eyes as black as vest buttons, the other with white skin and flesh-colored hair, like an under-developed photograph of a redhead, came and sat on my right. On my other side was one of those frowning chestless young-old men who can frequently be seen, often wearing sailor hats, attending ball games alone. He did not once open his program but instead tapped it, rolled up, on his knee as he gave the game his disconsolate attention. A young lady, with freckles, and a depressed dainty nose that by an optical illusion seemed to thrust her lips forward for a kiss, sauntered down into the box seat right behind the roof of the Oriole dugout. She wore a blue coat with a Northeastern University emblem sewed to it. The girls beside me took it into their heads that this was Williams' daughter. She looked too old to me, and why would she be sitting behind the visitors' dugout? On the other hand, from the way she sat there, staring at the sky and French-inhaling, she clearly was *somebody*. Other fans came and eclipsed her from view. The crowd looked less like a weekday ballpark crowd than like the folks you might find in Yellowstone National Park, or emerging from automobiles at the top of scenic Mount Mansfield. There were a lot of competitively well-dressed couples of tourist age, and not a few babes in arms. A row of five seats in front of me was abruptly filled with a woman and four children, the youngest of them two years old, if that. Someday, presumably, he could tell his grandchildren that he saw Williams play. Along with these tots and second-honeymooners, there were Harvard freshmen, giving off that peculiar nervous glow created when a sufficient quantity of insouciance is saturated with enough insecurity; thick-necked Army officers with brass on their shoulders and steel in their stares; pepperings of priests; perfumed bouquets of Roxbury Fabian fans; shiny salesmen from Albany and Fall River; and those gray, hoarse men—taxi drivers, slaughterers, and bartenders—who will continue to click through the turnstiles long after everyone else has deserted to television and tramporamas. Behind me, two young male voices blossomed, cracking a joke about God's five proofs that Thomas Aquinas exists—typical Boston College levity.

The batting cage was trundled away. The Orioles fluttered to the sidelines. Diagonally across the field, by the Red Sox dugout, a cluster of men in over-coats were festering like maggots. I could see a splinter of white uniform, and Williams' head, held at a self-deprecating and evasive tilt. Williams' conver-sational stance is that of a six-foot-three-inch man under a six-foot ceiling. He moved away to the patter of flash bulbs, and began playing catch with a young Negro outfielder named Willie Tasby. His arm, never very powerful, had grown lax with the years, and his throwing motion was a kind of mus-cular drawl. To catch the ball, he flicked his glove hand onto his left shoulder (he batted left but threw right, as every schoolboy ought to know) and let the ball plop into it comically. The catch session with Tasby was the only time all afternoon I saw him grin.

A tight little flock of human sparrows who, from the lambent and pam-pered pink of their faces, could only have been Boston politicians moved to-ward the plate. The loudspeakers mammothly coughed as someone huffed on the microphone. The ceremonies began. Curt Gowdy, the Red Sox radio and television announcer, who sounds like everybody's brother-in-law, delivered a brief sermon, taking the two words "pride" and "champion" as his text. It began, "Twenty-one years ago, a skinny kid from San Diego, California . . ." and ended, "I don't think we'll ever see another like him." Robert Tibolt, chairman of the board of the Greater Boston Chamber of Commerce, pre-sented Williams with a big Paul Revere silver bowl. Harry Carlson, a member of the sports committee of the Boston Chamber, gave him a plaque, whose inscription he did not read in its entirety, out of deference to Williams' dis-taste for this sort of fuss. Mayor Collins, seated in a wheelchair, presented the Jimmy Fund with a thousand-dollar check.

Then the occasion himself stooped to the microphone, and his voice sounded, after the others, very Californian; it seemed to be coming, excel-lently amplified, from a great distance, adolescently young and as smooth as a butternut. His thanks for the gifts had not died from our ears before he glided, as if helplessly, into "In spite of all the terrible things that have been said about me by the knights of the keyboard up there. . . ." He glanced up at the press rows suspended behind home plate. The crowd tittered, appalled. A frightful vision flashed upon me, of the press gallery pelting Williams with erasers, of Williams clambering up the foul screen to slug journalists, of a riot, of Mayor Collins being crushed. ". . . And they *were* terrible things,"

Williams insisted, with level melancholy, into the mike. "I'd like to forget them, but I can't." He paused, swallowed his memories, and went on, "I want to say that my years in Boston have been the greatest thing in my life." The crowd, like an immense sail going limp in a change of wind, sighed with relief. Taking all the parts himself, Williams then acted out a vivacious little morality drama in which an imaginary tempter came to him at the beginning of his career and said, "Ted, you can play anywhere you like." Leaping nimbly into the role of his younger self (who in biographical actuality had yearned to be a Yankee), Williams gallantly chose Boston over all the other cities, and told us that Tom Yawkey was the greatest owner in baseball and we were the greatest fans. We applauded ourselves lustily. The umpire came out and dusted the plate. The voice of doom announced over the loudspeakers that after Williams' retirement his uniform number, 9, would be permanently retired—the first time the Red Sox had so honored a player. We cheered. The national anthem was played. We cheered. The game began.

Williams was third in the batting order, so he came up in the bottom of the first inning, and Steve Barber, a young pitcher born two months before Williams began playing in the major leagues, offered him four pitches, at all of which he disdained to swing, since none of them were within the strike zone. This demonstrated simultaneously that Williams' eyes were razor-sharp and that Barber's control wasn't. Shortly, the bases were full, with Williams on second. "Oh, I hope he gets held up at third! That would be wonderful," the girl beside me moaned, and, sure enough, the man at bat walked and Williams was delivered into our foreground. He struck the pose of Donatello's David, the third-base bag being Goliath's head. Fiddling with his cap, swapping small talk with the Oriole third baseman (who seemed delighted to have him drop in), swinging his arms with a sort of prancing nervousness, he looked fine—flexible, hard, and not unbecomingly substantial through the middle. The long neck, the small head, the knickers whose cuffs were worn down near his ankles—all these clichés of sports cartoon iconography were rendered in the flesh.

With each pitch, Williams danced down the baseline, waving his arms and stirring dust, ponderous but menacing, like an attacking goose. It occurred to about a dozen humorists at once to shout "Steal home! Go, go!" Williams' speed afoot was never legendary. Lou Clinton, a young Sox outfielder, hit a fairly deep fly to center field. Williams tagged up and ran home. As he slid across the plate, the ball, thrown with unusual heft by Jackie Brandt, the Oriole center fielder, hit him on the back.

"Boy, he was really loafing, wasn't he?" one of the collegiate voices behind me said.

"It's cold," the other voice explained. "He doesn't play well when it's cold. He likes heat. He's a hedonist."

The run that Williams scored was the second and last of the inning. Gus Triandos, of the Orioles, quickly evened the score by plunking a home run over the handy left-field wall. Williams, who had had this wall at his back for twenty years,[13] played the ball flawlessly. He didn't budge. He just stood still, in the center of the little patch of grass that his patient footsteps had worn brown, and, limp with lack of interest, watched the ball pass overhead. It was not a very interesting game. Mike Higgins, the Red Sox manager, with nothing to lose, had restricted his major-league players to the leftfield line— along with Williams, Frank Malzone, a first-rate third baseman, played the game—and had peopled the rest of the terrain with unpredictable youngsters fresh, or not so fresh, off the farms. Other than Williams' recurrent appearances at the plate, the *maladresse* of the Sox infield was the sole focus of suspense; the second baseman turned every grounder into a juggling act, while the shortstop did a breathtaking impersonation of an open window. With this sort of assistance, the Orioles wheedled their way into a 4-2 lead. They had early replaced Barber with another young pitcher, Jack Fisher. Fortunately (as it turned out), Fisher is no cutie; he is willing to burn the ball through the strike zone, and inning after inning this tactic punctured Higgins' string of test balloons.

Whenever Williams appeared at the plate—pounding the dirt from his cleats, gouging a pit in the batter's box with his left foot, wringing resin out of the bat handle with his vehement grip, switching the stick at the pitcher with an electric ferocity—it was like having a familiar Leonardo appear in a shuffle of *Saturday Evening Post* covers. This man, you realized—and here, perhaps, was the difference, greater than any difference in gifts—really desired to hit the ball. In the third inning, he hoisted a high fly ball to deep center. In the fifth, we thought he had it; he smacked the ball hard and high into the heart of his power zone, but the deep right field in Fenway and the heavy air and a casual east wind defeated him. The ball died. Al Pilarcik leaned his back against the big "380" painted on the rightfield wall and caught it. On another day, in another park, it would have been gone. (After the game, Williams said, "I didn't think I could hit any harder than that. The conditions weren't good.")

The afternoon grew so glowering that in the sixth inning the arc lights were turned on—always a wan sight in the day-time, like the burning headlights of a funeral procession. Aided by the gloom, Fisher was slicing through the Sox rookies, and Williams did not come to bat in the seventh. He was second up in the eighth. This was almost certainly his last time to come to the plate in Fenway Park, and instead of merely cheering, as we had at his three previous appearances, we stood, all of us, and applauded. I had never before heard pure applause in a ballpark. No calling, no whistling, just an ocean of handclaps, minute after minute, burst after burst, crowding and running together in continuous succession like the pushes of surf at the edge of the sand. It was a sombre and considered tumult. There was not a boo in it. It seemed to renew itself out of a shifting set of memories as the Kid, the Marine, the veteran of feuds and failures and injuries, the friend of children, and the enduring old pro evolved down the bright tunnel of twenty-two summers toward this moment. At last, the umpire signalled for Fisher to pitch; with the other players, he had been frozen in position. Only Williams had moved during the ovation, switching his bat impatiently, ignoring everything except his cherished task. Fisher wound up, and the applause sank into a hush.

Understand that we were a crowd of rational people. We knew that a home run cannot be produced at will; the right pitch must be perfectly met and luck must ride with the ball. Three innings before, we had seen a brave effort fail. The air was soggy, the season was exhausted. Nevertheless, there will always lurk, around the corner in a pocket of our knowledge of the odds, an indefensible hope, and this was one of the times, which you now and then find in sports, when a density of expectation hangs in the air and plucks an event out of the future.

Fisher, after his unsettling wait, was low with the first pitch. He put the second one over, and Williams swung mightily and missed. The crowd grunted, seeing that classic swing, so long and smooth and quick, exposed. Fisher threw the third time, Williams swung again, and there it was. The ball climbed on a diagonal line into the vast volume of air over center field. From my angle, behind third base, the ball seemed less an object in flight than the tip of a towering, motionless construct, like the Eiffel Tower or the Tappan Zee Bridge. It was in the books while it was still in the sky. Brandt ran back to the deepest corner of the outfield grass, the ball descended beyond his reach and struck in the crotch where the bullpen met the wall, bounced chunkily, and vanished.

Like a feather caught in a vortex, Williams ran around the square of bases at the center of our beseeching screaming. He ran as he always ran out home runs—hurriedly, unsmiling, head down, as if our praise were a storm of rain to get out of. He didn't tip his cap. Though we thumped, wept, and chanted "We want Ted" for minutes after he hid in the dugout, he did not come back. Our noise for some seconds passed beyond excitement into a kind of immense open anguish, a wailing, a cry to be saved. But immortality is nontransferable. The papers said that the other players, and even the umpires on the field, begged him to come out and acknowledge us in some way, but he refused. Gods do not answer letters.

Every true story has an anticlimax. The men on the field refused to disappear, as would have seemed decent, in the smoke of Williams' miracle. Fisher
continued to pitch, and escaped further harm. At the end of the inning,
Higgins sent Williams out to his left-field position, then instantly replaced
him with Carrol Hardy, so we had a long last look at Williams as he ran out
there and then back, his uniform jogging, his eyes steadfast on the ground. It
was nice, and we were grateful, but it left a funny taste.

One of the scholasticists behind me said, "Let's go. We've seen everything.
I don't want to spoil it." This seemed a sound aesthetic decision. Williams'
last word had been so exquisitely chosen, such a perfect fusion of expectation, intention, and execution, that already it felt a little unreal in my head,
and I wanted to get out before the castle collapsed. But the game, though
played by clumsy midgets under the feeble glow of the arc lights, began to tug
at my attention, and I loitered in the runway until it was over. Williams'
homer had, quite incidentally, made the score 4–3. In the bottom of the
ninth inning, with one out, Marlin Coughtry, the secondbase juggler, singled.
Vic Wertz, pinch-hitting, doubled off the left-field wall, Coughtry advancing
to third. Pumpsie Green walked, to load the bases. Willie Tasby hit a double-
play ball to the third baseman, but in making the pivot throw Billy Klaus, an
ex-Red Sox infielder, reverted to form and threw the ball past the first baseman and into the Red Sox dugout. The Sox won, 5–4. On the car radio as I
drove home I heard that Williams, his own man to the end, had decided not
to accompany the team to New York. He had met the little death that awaits
athletes. He had quit.

NOTES

1. This piece was written with no research materials save an outdated record book
and the Boston newspapers of the day; and Williams' early career preceded the dawn-
ing of my *Schlagballewusstsein* (Baseball-consciousness). Also for reasons of perspective
was my account of his beginnings skimped. Williams first attracted the notice of a
major-league scout—Bill Essick of the Yankees—when he was a fifteen-year-old
pitcher with the San Diego American Legion Post team. As a pitcher-outfielder for
San Diego's Herbert Hoover High School, Williams recorded averages of .586 and
.403. Essick balked at signing Williams for the $1,000 his mother asked; he was signed
instead, for $150 a month, by the local Pacific Coast League franchise, the newly cre-
ated San Diego Padres. In his two seasons with this team, Williams hit merely .271
and .291, but his style and slugging (23 home runs the second year) caught the eye of,
among others, Casey Stengel, then with the Boston Braves, and Eddie Collins, the
Red Sox general manager. Collins bought him from the Padres for $25,000 in cash
and $25,000 in players. Williams was then nineteen. Collins' fond confidence in the

boy's potential matched Williams' own. Williams reported to the Red Sox training camp in Sarasota in 1938 and, after showing more volubility than skill, was shipped down to the Minneapolis Millers, the top Sox farm team. It should be said, perhaps, that the parent club was equipped with an excellent, if mature, outfield, mostly purchased from Connie Mack's dismantled A's. Upon leaving Sarasota, Williams is supposed to have told the regular outfield of Joe Vosmik, Doc Cramer, and Ben Chapman that he would be back and would make more money than the three of them put together. At Minneapolis he hit .366, batted in 142 runs, scored 130, and hit 43 home runs. He also loafed in the field, jabbered at the fans, and smashed a water cooler with his fist. In 1939 he came north with the Red Sox. On the way, in Atlanta, he dropped a foul fly, accidentally kicked it away in trying to pick it up, picked it up, and threw it out of the park. It would be nice if, his first time up in Fenway Park, he had hit a home run. Actually, in his first Massachusetts appearance, the first inning of an exhibition game against Holy Cross at Worcester, he *did* hit a home run, a grand slam. The Red Sox season opened in Yankee Stadium. Facing Red Ruffing, Williams struck out and, the next time up, doubled for his first major-league hit. In the Fenway Park opener, against Philadelphia, he had a single in five trips. His first home run came on April 23, in that same series with the A's. Williams was then twenty, and played *right* field. In his rookie season he hit .327; in 1940, .344.

2. See *Ted Williams*, by Ed Linn (Sport Magazine Library), Chapter 6, "Williams vs. the Press." It is Linn's suggestion that Williams walked into a circulation war among the seven Boston newspapers, who in their competitive zeal headlined incidents that the New York papers, say, would have minimized, just as they minimized the less genial side of the moody and aloof DiMaggio and smoothed Babe Ruth into a folk hero. It is also Linn's thought, and an interesting one, that Williams thrived on even adverse publicity, and needed a hostile press to elicit, contrariwise, his defiant best. The statistics (especially of the 1958 season, when he snapped a slump by spitting in all directions, and inadvertently conked an elderly female fan with a tossed bat) seem to corroborate this. Certainly Williams could have had a truce for the asking, and his industrious perpetuation of the war, down to his last day in uniform, implies its usefulness to him. The actual and intimate anatomy of the matter resides in locker rooms and hotel corridors fading from memory. When my admiring account was printed, I received a letter from a sports reporter who hated Williams with a bitter and explicit immediacy. And even Linn's hagiology permits some glimpses of Williams' locker-room manners that are not pleasant.

3. But he did tip his cap, high off his head, in at least his first season, as cartoons from that period verify. He also was extravagantly cordial to taxi-drivers and stray children. See Linn, Chapter 4, "The Kid Comes to Boston": "There has never been a ballplayer—anywhere, anytime—more popular than Ted Williams in his first season in Boston." To this epoch belongs Williams' prankish use of the Fenway scoreboard lights for rifle practice, his celebrated expressed preference for the life of a fireman, and his determined designation of himself as "The Kid."

4. In 1947 Joe DiMaggio and in 1957 Mickey Mantle, with seasons inferior to Williams', won the MVP award because sportswriters, who vote on ballots with ten places, had vengefully placed Williams ninth, tenth, or nowhere at all. The 1941

award to Joe DiMaggio, even though this was Williams' .406 year, is more understandable, since this was also *annus miraculorum* when DiMaggio hit safely in 56 consecutive games.

5. The sweet saga of this beautiful decimal must be sung once more. Williams, after hitting above .400 all season, had cooled to .39955 with one doubleheader left to play, in Philadelphia. Joe Cronin, then managing the Red Sox, offered to bench him to safeguard his average, which was exactly .400 when rounded to the third decimal place. Williams said (I forget where I read this) that he did not want to become a .400 hitter with just his toenails over the line. He played the first game and singled, homered, singled, and singled. With less to gain than to lose, he elected to play the second game and got two more hits, including a double that dented a loudspeaker horn on the top of the right-field wall, giving him six-for-eight on the day and a season's average that, in the forty years between Rogers Hornsby's .403 (1925) and the present, stands as unique.

6. For example: In 1948, the Sox came from behind to tie the Indians by winning three straight; in those games Williams went two for two, two for two, and two for four. In 1949, the Sox overtook the Yankees by winning nine in a row; in that streak, Williams won four games with home runs.

7. Two reasons for his durability may be adduced. A non-smoker, non-drinker, habitual walker, and year-round outdoorsman, Williams spared his body the vicissitudes of the seasonal athlete. And his hitting was in large part a mental process; the amount of cerebration he devoted to such details as pitchers' patterns, prevailing winds, and the muscular mechanics of swinging a bat would seem ridiculous, if it had not paid off. His intellectuality, as it were, perhaps explains the quickness with which he adjusted, after the war, to the changed conditions—the night games, the addition of the slider to the standard pitching repertoire, the new cry for the long ball. His reaction to the Williams Shift, then, cannot be dismissed as unconsidered.

8. Invented, or perpetrated (as a joke?) by Boudreau on July 14, 1946, between games of a doubleheader. In the first game of the doubleheader, Williams had hit three homers and batted in eight runs. The shift was not used when men were on base and, had Williams bunted or hit late against it immediately, it might not have spread, in all its variations, throughout the league. The Cardinals used it in the lamented World Series of that year. Toward the end, in 1959 and 1960, rather sadly, it had faded from use, or degenerated to the mere clockwise twitching of the infield customary against pull hitters.

9. Shortly after his retirement, Williams, in *Life*, wrote gloomily of the Stadium, "There's the bigness of it. There are those high stands and all those people smoking— and, of course, the shadows. . . . It takes at least one series to get accustomed to the Stadium and even then you're not sure." Yet his lifetime batting average there was .340, only four points under his median average.

10. It was Cunningham who, when Williams first appeared in a Red Sox uniform at the 1938 spring training camp, wrote with melodious prescience: "The Sox seem to think Williams is just cocky enough and gabby enough to make a great and colorful outfielder, possibly the Babe Herman type. Me? I don't like the way he stands at the plate. He bends his front knee inward and moves his foot just before he takes a swing.

That's exactly what I do just before I drive a golf ball and knowing what happens to the golf balls I drive, I don't believe this kid will ever hit half a singer midget's weight in a bathing suit."

11. Written before Roger Maris's fluky, phenomenal sixty-one.

12. Again, as of 1960. Since then, Musial may have surpassed him in some statistical areas.

13. In his second season (1940) he was switched to left field, to protect his eyes from the right-field sun.

LYNNE BELAIEF

Meanings of the Body

Fifteen years ago I knew a man who despised his body's existence with a totality that fascinated and terrified me, perhaps in the manner that Devil archetypes fascinate within religious experience. This man, a great poet, wrote of the body as the Heavy Bear Who Goes With Me, of his self which "stretches to embrace the very dear / with whom I would walk without him near" and spoke "of those who are terrified by love, and / those who try— before they / try to die—to disappear / And hide" (16: pp. 74 and 202). A few years later *The New York Times* briefly noted the poet's death at a young age and those who knew, knew why.

There is a thrust in me in recent years to counteract this sad memory by a new knowledge of the body that carries a similar fascination while over-coming the demonic in its negativity although not in its power—an attempt, perhaps, to replace the negative body relation with a narcissism that is not simply positive for the self, but also for others. Western culture provides a spectrum of reinforcements for the odd combination of body interest and body hatred, beginning with the all-time incredible symbol of Original Sin and updated into the modern drama of body odor. This is the body as the Bad Me in the clear-cut term of H. S. Sullivan's school of interpersonal psychol-ogy. The hypochondriac is a possible paradigm here, while racism causes a socially initiated model for those who are despised so deeply and essentially

Originally appeared in *Journal of the Philosophy of Sport* (1977).

that their very bodies are seen as possessing negative powers. At the saddest extreme of human misperception the psychotic is threatened with what is called a Not-Me event concerning his body, and then, of course, his self. In the perfect phrase of another psychiatrist, R. D. Laing, there is an experience of "ontological insecurity," a doubt regarding the very continuity of one's biological existence, as well as its realness and identity for others. The frailty is, incredibly, one that Descartes described as intellectually useful, and for which in recent times LSD has been recommended.

To the degree that this body hatred and alienation is observed by recent social commentators and connected attempts made to re-educate, the direction and stress are typically on sexual beauty and performance, often obsessive, filled with artifice, and, of course, limited recognition of the body's soaring scope of possibilities in meaning and being. In Section One I shall try to show what that scope can be and how it is that through participation in sport we can each experience it and, thereby, encounter the body as the Good Me, in that exquisite and genuine way of knowing that includes perception as well as verbalization. (I delineate sport as that area on the spectrum of games which involves the body directly and competitively in acts which require skills, are bound by rules, and are accompanied by a perspective of playfulness, as discussed further below.)

Further in Section Two I shall attempt to demonstrate that these individual self-encounters in sport would function not only to create personal growth and joy—which, of course, they do—but also as a genuine social event introducing new sets of living symbols and archetypes. These have the universal power capable of building a positive functioning myth for modern man to comprehend his relation to the universe, the purpose of all grand unifying and enlightening myths. Account will be taken of the startling similarity in the intellectual's outrageous disdain for two of the proposed new symbolic identities of the myth—the athlete and the astronaut.

THE BODY AND THE SELF

In every culture the body has been feared as having demonic power to destroy when gripped by primitive nature as its tool, a fear that retains its numenistic intensity even after being long severed from the original mythological sources. Cultures stress different possibilities of the body's feared expressions: in our own it has long resided in the sexualization of the demonic, making the experience of sexual pleasure evil, even when wedded intercourse was endorsed. More importantly, however, is the possibility that behind the varied local representations of evil is always the universal archetypal fear of the body as inhabited by a demonic rage that desires destruction without pause. Functioning cultures introduce counter-active symbols and impressing rituals able to heal the terrified. Today, due to lack of living, compelling ways of healing, it becomes safer to be alienated and apathetic concerning all emotional reality—a self-imposed distancing since the risk of caring is too great. Fearing that power may go berserk, as indeed it may, and knowing there are no convincing modes of help, except institutionalization in mental hospitals or prisons, which, in truth, teach nothing humanly useful, we play dead. In the name of virtue we attempt to decry the emotions in favor of reason and to despise personal power while developing ulcers and the rationalizing skill which keeps modern man relatively sane.

Reflection reveals that the opposite of the hated universal of power is "impotence." Much is said about impotence lately; some is foolish, such as confusions with the otherwise sensible interests in pacifism or in equality. As usual, Rollo May provides wisdom and warnings: knowing, as did Nietzsche, that all life *needs* power, if only for survival, he sees that impotence has the impossible characteristic of being self-destructive. Thus, and this is ultimately fortunate, professing that one does not desire power does not destroy that desire, for it is in truth an ontological function of man to will his own power's development. Repression of this desire, in the misunderstanding that power is inevitably destructive, thus fostering helplessness and impotence in our conscious emotional lives, leads to the eruption of rage when the facade of rational calm breaks down. And it will. Violence is the characteristic result of this breakdown where one's repressed power, reaching its limit of tolerance, strikes out in true blind rage, often in order to feel alive at all. It is here that the impotent can become the truly dangerous, since they often seek a risk-free expression for rage by identifying with a group and by putting that rage in the service of the authoritarian leader of that needy, long impotent, self-hating group. The most demonically skillful manipulator of this balloon was of course Hitler. Jung understood this with horrified clarity as he watched World War II being formed in the unconscious minds of Germans years before the irruption into bodies.

The vicious, terrifying circle spinning here is made clear in May's analysis. Explaining that the demonic does have the potential for violence, but not exclusively, and that it, therefore, needs to be feared as well as respected, directed, and lived, May says that:

The daimonic is any natural function which has the power to take over the whole person. . . . The daimonic can be either creative or destructive and is normally both. When this power goes astray and one element usurps control over the total personality, we have "daimon possession"

[or] psychosis. . . . [It is] a fundamental archetypal function of human experience. (9: p. 123)

The self-alienated individual's terror of his possible demonic has been used by rulers of every society to force men into submission and then gratitude for that gutless opportunity. This is always the purpose of an ethics of fear—cowardice becomes a primary virtue and opportunities for hope and self-trust are, with incredible perversity, secretly perceived as dangerous for society, even when that society is a democracy. More of this is in the second section of the paper.

The demonic creates fascination in relationship. Without it there is no pull toward growth, whether at love or at work. There is only the thin connectedness of mind and consciousness. With it, however, there is always the risk of overwhelming the other's precious individuality by an enthusiasm that is a form of being possessed, of being now no longer able to stop the self-assertion that is devouring and overwhelming, rather than creating encounter. Certainly the risk of all this happening is very great in the isolation and strong intensity of sexual intimacy, presenting a puzzle so difficult that most make a complete split, linking intensity with illegitimacy or pornography (the negative demonic), and emotional carefulness with blandness and marriage. A few, more directly, become physiologically impotent in precise reflection of the conflict.

Is there not a way to become acquainted early with the power of ourselves as embodied which would create joyful and relatively tensionless experiences, a narcissism which is creative and ethically positive, for self and other selves? I would like to suggest that sport is the true situation in which humans can learn all this. Some, I discover, have long done so even within the counter-useful conditions and stresses that often prevail in the sport arenas of today. But, it would also be useful and sensible to discuss the fact that the negative demonic does indeed appear in those arenas, and in discussing learn how to recognize and avoid it. Bill Russell tells about its appearance in one game and its devastation within him. Describing a 1965 N.B.A. final game with L.A., in which the Celtics were vastly outplaying the visiting team, Russell says:

Then it became frightening. More than a mere sports event. We were not just beating this team. We were destroying it. The people were screaming. They were yelling for blood. . . . They were egging us on to destroy, to kill, to reduce an opponent to nothing.

And we were responding. We were, in a basketball sense, killing them, leaving them shattered among the ashes of their pride.

It was my worst moment in sports. There was the horror of destruc-

tion, not the joy of winning. The horror of knowing you are the instrument of the voices of man calling out: Destroy . . . kill . . . ruin.

We ruined them. . . . We knew—and did not know—we sensed, and
did not completely comprehend, that we had taken sports out of the
realm of a game. (15: pp. 118–119)

This is emotionally and intellectually powerful stuff indeed. Having experienced the negative demonic, Russell has had the courage and skill, in that
order, to want to see it and to understand it clearly. Perhaps, although he does
not say, he tells it to us as a warning: that it is sickening and yet fascinating.
It contains the horrified pull one always feels as a response to becoming possessed by the forbidden. If the sexualization of the demonic is expressed by
pornography, in sport it is done by the overwhelming devotion to winning so
that violence, psychological or physical, is allowed. Such situations involve
dehumanization in the form of de-individualization.

Although I do not agree with the notion of Santayana and others, that the
forms of sports need to be changed for finer meaning and pleasure, it is certainly clear that our mode of doing, viewing and talking about sport does
need vast development. For example, we hear much criticism of the excessive
nationalisms within the Olympic Games, the global scale analogues of rooting for the home team, and yet it is sadly clear that much of that conversation
occurs because neither spectator nor journalist knows what else to look for or
to say about the sport itself. Our manner of relating to the realm of sports is so
thin it reminds me of the diner who, in Alan Watts's clever scenario, devours
the menu instead of the dinner. Similarly, there is nothing wrong with a modulated desire to win, unless one misses so much else that is going on because
winning becomes the major or exclusive concern.

This series of thoughts is an attempt to suggest changes that would inevitably occur in the perception and place of sport in experience should we begin
to recognize its central ontological and ethical meaning. The most fundamental, and therefore philosophical, reason why one *can* so regard it, and
why I do, is that man is an ontological unity of mind-body-emotions, in
short, embodied subjectivity, and sport is a most full expression of that totality, as will be evidenced shortly. The perspective is that of Merleau-Ponty
whose phenomenology rejects any ontological models which are dualistic,
whether derived from Descartes or Christianity. It also rejects any attempt to
assign ontological superiority to any of the self's dimensions of expression.
The importance of this position will be discussed later when we try to understand why sport has often been denied serious attention because of its alleged
ontological inferiority—a thoroughly meaningless philosophical claim. It

fails to understand that the body is what relates us to our world and through it meaning arises. Merleau-Ponty states that:

> My body is the seat or rather the very actuality of the phenomenon of expression, . . . [It] is the fabric into which all objects are woven, and it is, at least in relation to the perceived world, the general instrument of my "comprehension." (10: p. 235)

Thus, as suggested earlier, how I perceive my body will fundamentally affect all other perceptions of the world in which I make manifest this embodied subjectivity. Nietzsche was among the first to grasp the importance of this for his total philosophy, and the psychotic, because he does it all so differently, is the most observable victim of what happens when the whole thing goes wrong. When Descartes lost the body he also lost the world, as every psychotic illustrates in painful shock. That the philosopher wished to make the ontology of madness his paradigm has already been noted as inexplicable; we here intend to rid ourselves of this double-entry bookkeeping on the self and embrace the precise alternative of ontological unity. This position may be concisely illustrated with brilliance in the perspective of the painter Cezanne who, because of his intense experience of the visual world, says, "Color is the place where our brain and the universe meet." For others, different paradigms exist, and sport is one. The body, however, is always found to be central. Erich Neumann, the great mythologist, explains how the meaning of the body is the meaning of the world:

> The body scheme, as the archetype of the original man in whose image the world was created, is the basic symbol in all systems where parts of the world are co-ordinated with regions of the body. This co-ordination is to be found everywhere, in Egypt, as in Mexico, etc. . . . Not God alone, but the whole world is created in man's image . . . his body scheme. (12:p. 25)

Let us then see what the body in sport particularly experiences and teaches and what can alone or best be accomplished there; what meanings appear, what results for ethics? First we might elaborate what is meant by stating that sport invites the demonic and teaches its overcoming. As suggested earlier, sport, in its undistorted essence, is a profoundly useful route to the human work of directing power creatively, not, I feel, because it sublimates rage, as is so often glibly stated, but because it avoids the need for the experience of rage which arises as the consequence of impotence. Roger Bannister demonstrates knowledge of this complex event:

> After three months in England I felt the frustration of severe training without a race to release all my pent up energy. This feeling of aggression came as a surprise to me. (2: p. 135)

And it is precisely sport that would have annihilated the feeling of aggression rather than produce it, as is often falsely stated. In parallel meaning, Sheehan insightfully points out that long distance runners, contrary to romanticized belief, are lonely only when they aren't running.

To return to the overcoming of the destructive demonic, we can note that sport's unique essence is to be a challenge to the possibility of the body—the testing of limits of "faster, higher, stronger." Assertiveness, alone or with a team, is requisite to develop the very content of a game within its given form. One cannot remain powerless, passive, and non-creative and also *be* participating in the sport. This is the demand that freedom be expressed (freedom perceived as self-determination within a set of rules we agree to obey). Moreover, freedom exists in the more fundamental sense that we made it all up, we can change the form if desired, and we can void any results that betray the rules, call it a foul and do it again. Sport provides an extraordinary model in depth of levels of human freedom not likely elsewhere in social life and impossible in nature. With this exhilarating freedom comes, as noted, the risk of the negative demonic, the distortion of power into destruction.

Phenomenological analysis may well reveal that different sports have different relations to the destructive demonic and, perhaps, different intensities of relation. These may differ between individual and team types, instrument aided, sports of strength, speed, and so on. In some sports the demonic may be more of a risk toward others, in some toward oneself; the sport itself may be designed such that simply completing its structure is a lofty achievement. Here the paradigm is, of course, the marathon. Although Kokichi Tsuburaya ultimately killed himself over his failure to win the Gold before his countrymen at the Tokyo Olympics, even though he had finished grandly, most seem to truly experience great joy through the successful self-testing, contesting with the self as literally the stretching of the self.

Phenomenological analysis could also reveal which sport types most usefully initiate and change various individual types of pre-existing relations with the demonic. But let the limits be drawn very clearly to show that risk and self-testing in the extreme of severe danger is not the meaning of courage, as Aristotle long ago taught. The exquisite in nature is man in sport, directed, and under fine control. Rashness is slaughter, not sport.

When the destructive demonic does not enter, protected by the structure of the sport and the nobility of the performers, we have the ecstasy, the bordering-on-hysterical joy of triumph over temptation. True winning happens here not in the scoring. What matters to the athlete is the conquest of the personal demonic while testing the self in something of significance, but not yielding to the possibilities of cheating or violence. This is, I believe, the locus of trust in others as well as in oneself, both born in the instant silent recognition of their respect for you in this potentially brutal struggle. A Humanism based in this trust can be begun here should the base broaden. So may the possibility for democracy that is more than legal formalism, that has spirit and embodiment, literally, in each of us. It is not a mere coincidence, I think, that the Greek civilization which gave us the beginning of Humanism and the flash of political democracy revered and understood the human body, in art and sport.

In psychological terms, the self-trust born from successful encounters with risk that need to be personally overcome through one's own freedom, and require courage and self-courage in the temptation of winning, can indeed produce enough stable self-identity that one can now risk trusting others, not irrationally, but hopefully. As the psychologist Erikson disclosed no one can hope if there is no basis of trust and that basis is first in oneself. The experienced self is inevitably the self as embodied, therefore one's sense of identity and the valuation of that identity arises from the self experienced as Merleau-Ponty's "body-subject." We start and end here; that's it. In saying that self trust must be brought out from the experience of the reliable body, I am simply concluding what is obvious; in suggesting that this event can best happen in sport, I add the claim that sport, undefiled by its various degenerated forms through poor management or commercialization, aids the learning more than any other widely available opportunity.

Others have argued that sport and the movement arts, as expressed paradigmatically in dance, accomplish similar values for self-growth through heightened embodiment sense: fewer others further argue that dance is superior in that accomplishment, advising Physical Educators to teach dance exclusively (e.g. 6: pp. 165–174). I do not agree with even the weaker position for three reasons. The first, already discussed in other perspectives, is that sport uniquely addresses the agonistic dimension within life and shows us that we can indeed control and direct it into creative power which can then provide the ground of self-trust and the beginnings of the socialization of trust. In sum, we can learn through achievement that the possession of competitive skill need not lead to its demonic expression, so brutally learned by Bill Russell. Without this element of risk one has lost a dimension of the full human struggle. In an impressionistic comparison I suggest that dance is more like a baseball game being staged for a film than like a baseball game. In Francis Keenan's clarifying phrase, sport has the essence of "competitive co-operation," and also provides a fine model for democratic society (more of which in Section Two). Its failure indicates the failure of democracy and, equivalently, that of the spirit of sport.

A second reason for claiming the superiority of sport to dance for self-growth relates to its possession of intrinsically greater clarity due to the peculiar element, variously expressed, of counting. Taking the form of a score, or a record, or even perhaps betting, the objective fact of measurement is not an accident, but inherent in the structure and meaning of sport. It is the external model of the challenge aspect which, unlike art and like science, has a clarity which makes participation and comprehension potentially universal. For example, journalists around the globe were able to record people gleefully counting Henry Aaron's home run total while in N.Y.C. dance critics continued arguing the merits of a performance without reaching compelling clarity . . . nor should they because they can't.

There are various levels of closure in sport, each functioning as a sort of ritual model of excellence, such as a hole in one, a knock-out punch, a four minute mile, and so on, and, although these can concretely alter as the third example shows, the clarity and meaning of a goal's existence remains as an intrinsic part of the sport's (slowly changing) model. Of course, the athlete himself often inwardly experiences a sense of clarity concerning the excellence of his action, felt with joy. He knows that he knows it, with the certainty and immediacy of all right-sided brain activity. But the score, the record, the model of the goal's clarity persists as part of his direction to himself and exhibits this to the spectator, giving a closure and reward to struggle that compels understanding and assent. This syndrome provides an achievement of justice not elsewhere often found. And because this clarity is a promise of sport in its essence, cheating is not only immoral—as it usually is elsewhere as well—but is more strongly, unintelligible.

If the score does not show the situation accurately, how can one keep score? If at the 1972 Olympics the U.S.S.R.'s three-time loss in the basketball finals nonetheless got them the Gold medal, then it did indeed make great epistemological sense for the U.S. to reject the Silver. The tender of truth, in this case medals, was meaningless because no basketball game was accurately completed. We are here outside the realm of sport in a more fundamental philosophical way than the politicization of the event that occurred in Montreal by the withdrawal of various African countries. In the cheating instance the *essence* of sport is boycotted. And this is certainly frightening because, to paraphrase the philosopher's favorite classroom remark that if someone sincerely asks "why should I be moral?" he simply doesn't comprehend the realm of ethics, I would say additionally that the Soviets didn't even care about at least one pragmatic deterrent to overt injustice, and that is that someone might notice.

It is precisely the competitive structure of sport, including its public retelling in the score and record, that accomplishes the shared sense of fairness that is the result of the genuine game. How odd and sentimental it really is, then, to persist in saying that the competitive element in sport is what makes it less ethically desirable for, say, educating youth. I suggest that one reason it is said is that many of the detractors fail to distinguish competing from winning. Indeed, winning isn't all but completion is, and this requires the structure and coherence of competition. The ending provides an explosive experience of awe, gratitude and joy, knowing that the enactment of that performance has shared and clear meaning for player and audience alike. Additionally valuable in a society increasingly losing coherence, we are definitely communicating, and know this. The performer gains inner self-knowledge and self-trust from the contest, again literally, the stretching and straining of the self by the self. Often the ending will produce the overwhelming need for physical touching and hugging of teammates, neighbors, even members of the opposing team. Anyone serious about understanding the intensity of the body experience in sport has an obligation to attend to this common and fascinating thing: to say, "Why are grown men acting this way?" A center of that answer is that the joyful explosion is not about winning alone but about caring and knowing and communicating, directly in the athlete, by empathy in the spectator. It is as if player and spectator alike inwardly knew that the root meaning of the term game is "to leap joyously"; the body knows it.

I suggest, additionally, that many have had these wonderful experiences in youth but fewer recall the joy and those who do are almost always bewildered or embarrassed about the unique happiness and pride the memory still provides. Drew Hyland has employed Heidegger's fascinating concept, with amendments, of being truly "at home" in the world through his encounter with others in sport. What we need to discuss is why sport can be the place where such clarity is *uniquely* achieved and why this is not trivial. Or, to reverse the question: What is the rest of living like such that this remarkable certitude and its resulting joy are not correctly available? The rest of living occurs in a social world which is ambiguous and chaotic at its core of becoming and change, requiring a continual habit of doubt rather than the comfortable expectation of certainty and closure. That is, the moral perspective within a world that both changes and needs changing by us is precisely the suspension of certitude. This however produces existential (as contrasted to private, neurotic) anxiety which is enormously painful and invites flight. Truly, I suspect that the self-certitude which arises from successful body-based experience in sport—or something like this—is necessary to provide the personal stability from which one can dare to experience the chaos of value and meaning and try to change it. The stunning incoherence and injustice of the social world can otherwise lead to madness or, more typically, to regression back to the false certitudes of dogmatic religion, philosophy or political ideologies. And all of history seems to tell that we will so regress if the universal, passionate and honorable request for self-identity and sanity can find no earned source of certitude. If we cannot stand on our own two feet we will have to be held up. We will later connect these problems with the even more challenging obligation to accept tragedy as inherent in finite human reality: it is in this sense alone that the glib remark that sport has become a substitute for religion can be understood. It provides the courage and the grounding to get on with it, to continue.

Bannister's self-observation reflects this point:

> Only in something like running can finality be achieved, the sort of finality that is almost perfection. But it is not the kind of perfection that leaves you with nothing to live for. You are not your own executioner because sport is not the main aim in life. Yet to achieve perfection in one thing . . . makes it possible to face uncertainty in the more difficult problems of life. (2: p. 183)

None of the false heroics of "conquer all other realms" etc.; just "face the uncertainty."

Third and finally, there is the important quality of avoiding artifice that is the essence of sport in process. Inherent is a directness in the primary goal of doing the job as effectively as possible even though many players fail because they seek extraneous rewards that conflict with effectiveness. A perceptive super-fan named Joseph Epstein made this public confession:

> I have recently begun to play a game called racquet ball, and I find that I would still rather look good than win . . . Men who beat me admire the whip of my strokes, my wrist action . . . When this occurs I feel like a woman who is complimented for the shape of her bottom when it is her mind she craves admiration for. (5: p. 72)

Certainly, form, style, and class are significant esthetic elements sport can exhibit, but they are not its unique essence which is the dynamic, self-directed risk of competing without demonic destruction of self or others regarding esteem and trust, and doing so within a structure of clarity that rewards publicly and truly. One competes, he doesn't pose. How easily young-sters understand this skilled spontaneity, this honesty, and how they love the players for it, for in truth, not many adults provoke or deserve this trust, in-cluding the teachers in the official classrooms. The player is without ar-tificiality or guile while playing, and his effort is so appreciated that we need to believe we are communicating this gratitude through our attention border-ing on devotion. Among other results, we cannot turn the TV off: we are loyal to the end because the end is the essence of the effort. It is the closure of the unknown on the dual level of not knowing what will occur or how effec-tively it will occur—within the limits we do know and admire. We cannot betray a proud promise to help this ritual unfold in its ordered but unknown progression to completeness. No excuses from them and no excuses for us dur-ing this concrete particular enactment of that universal model of the game which men determined from its very initiation. Again, the model can be freely changed but it will not change while one is playing it tonight. The clarity, the demonic risk, the effort, the possibility of failure are visible and compelling and we are grateful to be invited. We are also happy.

Speaking about Joe DiMaggio as an outfielder, Red Smith recounts a voice at a crowded bar saying:

> "I've been watching the guy for 10 years . . . and I've never seen him have a hard chance." Is it possible to pay a greater compliment to an outfielder? "I saw it all the way" Joe used to say when asked about one of his implausible catches. He didn't say "I had it all the way." In his phi-losophy, if you saw it, you had it. (17: p. 3)

Smith is correct; it is a philosophy in the sense of providing a unique perspec-tive for interpreting experience, one that is saying that what we can see is what we can do, and that seeing in its ontological foundation begins with the body. Rollo May's idea of perceptual courage is akin to this. I think sport aids the courage because in its directness it rejects artifice and teaches, literally and then philosophically, how to see well.

This exceptionally responsible way of being in the world is an expression of what I would call, reversing Laing, ontological security, which includes not only a firm sense of one's own existence but of the *rightness* of that existence. And this is the source of the happiness that resides in the wonderful sense of being and rightness which has at its center the full-blown achievement of primary narcissism, some minimal intensity of which is indispensible for sanity and even survival. Its growth occurs when the infant receives the un-conditional love and delighted affirmation of whoever is the mothering figure. Primary narcissism is always rooted in the body's existence for this is the infant's sole reality experience. History records the same series of events in earliest societies, which infancy recapitulates. According to Neumann:

> The body stands for wholeness and unity in general and its total reaction represents a genuine and creative totality. A sense of the body as a whole is the natural basis of the sense of personality. . . . Centroversion [self-identity] manifests itself as narcissism, a generalized body feeling. (12: pp. 288 and 307)

The connection needs to be reinforced throughout adult life to root and expand our sense of identity and its value in response to the truly incredible buffeting we receive from changes of fortune and affection. Our society, with unique thoroughness, fails to do this, believing that the dogma of individualism requires that all happiness be earned, and if you don't have it you don't deserve it. Religious and ethical errors also contribute through augmenting our confusion of centeredness needs with self-centeredness in the negative sense of egotism. Often this confusion is skillfully encouraged by those who know that your loss of self-esteem will lead to your greater dependency on their authority. Incidentally, the two above errors are seriously contradictory and yet often mutually held, however unconsciously.

These are severe charges against society because failure here induces an entire spectrum of psychoanalytical ills of the sort which result from the lack or loss of primary narcissism, originating in relation to one's body. At the extreme, the failure leads to the schizoid condition wherein the person exercises relentless self-scrutiny which is totally negative in valuation. In this preoccupation—which we are insisting is the very opposite of positive narcissism—the person feels as if his very being is about to be robbed. In milder versions, this fear can take the shape of obsessional jealousy where one truly feels deprived of identity to the degree that one's value is negatively estimated. A different sort of psychic failure can be expressed as negative narcissism, an unhappy relation to the body wherein the body is a central but painful preoccupation. Expressions of this would be the hypochondriac and any individual engaged in a psychosomatic illness. A final example of failed relation to the body may be expressed in Sartre's metaphor of Nausea: the body as meaninglessness, a surd, in sum, negativity. Because our society's unconscious still fears and forbids pleasure in the body, willfully misperceiving positive narcissism as self-indulgence and selfishness, many people can get some kind of relation going with their body only through these negative attentions—the body as Bad Me. At least no one can label me self-indulgent if

I can manage to cause enough physical or psychic trouble in my body that it really does need care. It is my claim and my conclusion that sport can present a new relation to the body that undercuts these sad behaviors, allowing true care, self-love and virtue to develop. It provides for all who seek a uniquely intense enjoyment and trust of the self.

THE BODY AND SOCIETY

If this spectrum of the meanings of the body for the self is valid, we need now to inquire whether its positive identification of achievement provides valuable results for social ethics as well. That is, does the achievement of a trusting sense of self through the body's intimate and valued experience of the self in sport, portrayed in Section I, have results in social life that are culturally valuable? And, lastly, what is the character of change that could result should the self-victories become common?

We have already suggested one consequence for ethical life arising from the athlete's confidence in his own power to be and to act, namely, his capacity to responsibly doubt and question his life situation, since he can trust his creative ability and courage to design new meanings when needed. I have, of course, just described Nietzsche's Higher Man, his truly ethical one, and the life-long activity of critical creativity, at its heart the activity of *self*-overcoming. It is based in that firm warm sense of self-hood, being, as it were, at home in one's body and, therefore, capable of temporary alienation from society when necessary. And as noted earlier, anyone not a dogmatist knows that in a chaotic, imperfect, growing world, such courage for separation *will* be necessary.

Now what is the inner message here? It is that no one not possessed of this self-trust *can* have the courage to risk distance from a group identity because his lack of primary narcissism has been long replaced, as compensation, by the shared narcissism of a group, such as family, race or nation. They are all neurotic and productive of evil if growing up ethically includes the ability to risk isolation from authority. Those without firm self-trust cannot succeed, as Dr. Milgrim's grotesque test results showed (11: pp. 76–77). For the self-doubting, the impotent self-hating individual, the anxiety of aloneness can at the extreme be experienced as death. This is quite seriously felt. It seems then that if the freedom to risk questioning is part of virtue one must first be healthy to begin to be virtuous.

Contrary to much of Western ethics, we are today, with the help of psychologists, beginning to comprehend what children always know: when anyone has self-love that person is loving and giving of care to others. When mother, or anyone, feels guilty self-hatred this does not increase virtue, despite the historical concentration on guilt-producing forms of self-relation with the pretense to do exactly so. The experience of one's power and the giving of it through caring produces feelings of well-being that I shall here call happiness. And so I state that the happy one is also the virtuous one. He explodes in creativity in action *because* of the abundance of power and the self-trust that it will be creatively, rather than demonically directed. He has the courage to risk creativity and in causal terms one can say that the cause of this virtue is precisely his happiness, not vice versa. Nietzsche's fullest insights come together here:

> The most general formula on which every [codified] religion and morality is founded is: "Do this, and refrain from this and that—then you will be happy! Otherwise . . ." . . . In my mouth, this formula is changed into its opposite: a well-turned-out-human, a "happy one," *must* perform certain actions and shrinks instinctively from other actions. . . . In a formula, his virtue is the *effect* of his happiness. (13: p. 493)

In hating the self and fearing power and action, one cannot love or give; one is ethically constipated. Guilt decreases virtue, increases the turning from life and the productivity that the world always needs. It produces jealousy for any who are noticeably alive and happy, ontologically expressed in the incredible doctrine and hope of Hell. In stunning contrasts, those in the fullness of their body-trust and joy are among the least envious people one can encounter: they admire effort, theirs or others; they have no false humility depriving them of acknowledged self-love; have no need for revenge on one who is happy (i.e. sinful) when he is not, for indeed he is; and they can contemplate equality or even superiority without pain. They also know that power increases with its expression and stretching and do not hoard creative energy as if afraid that it comes in a finite amount and will be depleted permanently (the well-known scarcity mentality). The athlete hates sitting on the bench and prefers to risk and give, unusual indeed in our typical behavior of minimal effort at work or even in friendship.

When they are very young, those in love with sport often have fantasies of their worth which are truly glowing and lovely to behold and which carry on the work of the original mother initiating this primary narcissism. They feel strong and safe with themselves and it has little to do with being the best or actually always winning. It is about being fuller than before. Challenge replaces guilt as the motivating push; growth as against vengeance. And so I do not agree with the following statement of one athlete:

"For starters," writes the Canadian distance runner, Bruce Kidd, "we should stop preaching about sport's moral values. Sport, after all, isn't Lent. It's a pleasure of the flesh." (8: p. 2)

It is, however, precisely the power and the pleasure of the flesh, when experienced in a non-demonic form, that is far more effective than Lent in creating the opportunity for virtue. In Nietzsche's formula, virtue is the effect of happiness, not of guilt.

Now we need to analyze that other element of sport which is also part of its essence and is often misunderstood: I speak, of course, of playfulness. Play, like virtue, is never a means to an end but arises simply from spontaneous feelings of abundance. In this particularity, playfulness can be seen as a unique way of perceiving or interpreting one's experience and it is clear enough that in this sense it comprises a very serious element of a life. Roochnick has usefully discussed playfulness as a "stance," "a mode of being-toward-the-world" (14: p. 39), which I am grateful for and have adopted. Playfulness expresses our self-esteem and power in a manner that makes it clear we are not following external orders, but our own freedom. No one can command the stance of playfulness any more successfully than that of devotion or love, although, surely, the rituals of pretence can go on—in the former often miserably occurring in coercive sport situations with great pressure on winning, and in the latter, all too often, in family relations.

It may be important to point out that the freedom within playfulness attached to sport is not freedom misunderstood as license, that is, the ability to do whatever one wants to do. This is formless and proves nothing and surely *improves* nothing—all of the greatest significance when freedom in sport is understood, I think correctly, as self-determination overcoming limits which include the risk of the destructive demonic. So it would seem that although playfulness certainly requires spontaneity—it is part of its essence—there is also structure and form to sport which should retain some continuity, for generations to measure each overcoming against the past and towards the future. One freely accepts the wonderful limits, called rules, in order to enter *significant* playfulness.

Playfulness in sport, or sex, or wherever it gracefully appears, is principally the message of non-exploitation. One takes risks because one *can* take risks, not because the situation isn't serious in the sense of "it doesn't matter," but because our courage and energy are leading us on.

The intellectualization of experience and the indirectness and artifice of most modern communication heighten the import of expanding the perspective of playfulness in order to grasp the possibility of self-trust and direct knowledge that sport can provide. With its "hands on" directness and wild variety of types, some convincing individual experience is available to any aiming to escape the vaporization threat posed by our meta-society. The "thereness" is all, and must be provided in non-threatening but supremely serious, exact, and individuated ways. In Nietzsche's perfect phrase: "In my language, light feet are the first attribute of divinity."

As previously explained, we play, as we love, from fullness, not out of duty or external obligation, and this is most fortunate because the causality of duty doesn't work and never has worked, existentially, to move to action. We do what we have to do out of the inner necessity of who we already are. The question for ethics is how to improve this inner state through genuine change because, all our thin conscious effort and so-called "will-power" notwithstanding, it is the total self, including the emotional and bodily unconscious, which will prevail. We can be trusted to be consistent only when we are doing what we thoroughly want to do, for otherwise we will be releasing our unfilled unconscious needs indirectly, but truly, in ways we hope are not provable in court. And although acts of playfulness are not done because we need to prove ourself better, or the need to prove *anything*, they do often have these life-affirming results beyond the realm of sport. This is possible, of course, because the body is the self in one mode of experiencing and, thus, can express its learning in other realms. We do not need two educational tracks, one to treat the mind and one the body, as the philosophical and psychological mind-body dualists suggest and educators innocently accept. It is as if we still do not understand Whitehead's spoof on Descartes: Whitehead imagines a person entering a room and announcing "Here I am and I brought my body with me."

The power of playfulness as a stance in the world does not release man from the tragic dilemma of our finitude since the dilemma is ontological, thus not escapable. We have here gained, however, the subjective guts to accept the tragic without lying, without the pleading for the illusions of salvation, whether of a transcendental sort or Descartes' rationalism and his false *cogito*. Indeed, far from representing the world of illusion, as it is often charged, the realms in which men learn playfulness produce the power to *discard* the urge to illusion; they create, in sum, the power and courage for truth. Sport also provides a model for clarity should one have the courage to seek it, see it, and name it. For example, when someone is "out," he is "out," but when someone is killed, stolen from, or fired we prefer to say, wasting, trashing, or retrenching, respectively. The classical term for how this is prevented is "conscience."

Further, because athletes know that happiness includes pain, suffering and loss, the dignity and drama of sport is quite akin to tragic drama as Keenan has skillfully elaborated. Both are great arenas in which to learn how to bear the actual tragedy of existence in a world we neither created nor control, but suffer within. "The beauty of the 'tragic' athlete is found in his ability to seize a 'spiritual' victory from a natural defeat" (7: p. 325). In sport, competing and striving are part of the essence but winning on the "natural" level is rare and not essential to establish meaning. Sport is indeed a preparation for the most calamitous aspects of being in our world where failure is certain. The habit of calling it "merely a game" is a distraction.

Moreover, that habit has deepened to the point where certain highly dubious philosophical implications arise which involve setting up the classical dualism of reality vs. illusion, an ontological error as distortive as the mind-body dualism dismissed earlier. This position assigns, in Buchler's precise terminology, ontological priorities to types of beings or activities by establishing a hierarchy and attributing degrees of being to entities therein (3: pp. 30–51). The labeling is actually a reflection of preferences, for example, ethical or esthetic—a value judgment reified into the unintelligible notion of degrees of reality. In the case we are discussing, the realm of play is seen as so deficient in value that it lacks full reality (although the official explanation reverses the causality). What is peculiarly disappointing about this error of intelligence is its practical result of degrading sport's significance, namely, that it is precisely when sport *ceases* to be playful that trouble, and perhaps evil, enter human relations. More ironically, although this sort of ontological priority-setting begins in passion, it may persist merely by laziness. I suspect we are in the latter situation now in regard to the original religious condemnation of play, similarly as to sex, except for their alleged results of increasing work and birth rates, respectively.

Now, by severe contrast, the East has long considered playfulness in sport as spiritually significant in itself. Although this sense of importance is indeed laudable, it is not what I mean to conclude here; rather, it is precisely the *human* meaning of the self in sport that is of value.

As we all know, because we painfully experience the loss, modern western society fails to provide symbols and rituals that connect, enhance, and clarify man's place in the universe. Psychologically successful societies do this through symbols and rituals which contain life-affirming archetypes with compelling meaning. One fruit is that life feels important. Failure to receive this basis for meaning often results in apathy bordering on insanity. More dangerously, as noted earlier, the personal vacuum will eventually be filled by a skilled demagogue able to manipulate the deep unconscious needs for meaning and hope, filling them with archetypes of destruction. The repressed needs of the raging and impotent followers will honor the bearer because there was nothing else to honor that had power. Hitler remains the paradigm of the demonic here. We deeply require a new positive, life-loving mythos to counteract the fall-out from this god-forsaken exhibit of necrophilia.

When the new myth arrives it will not be by conscious efforts since, as with all dealings with the universal archetypes, the unconscious gets the message first, traditionally through the poets of the tribe. However, that noble mythologist Joseph Campbell has some clues for us in his marvelously titled book, *Hero with a Thousand Faces*:

> Today all of [the earlier] mysteries have lost their force; their symbols no longer interest our psyche . . . Not the animal world, not the plant world, not the miracle of the spheres, but man himself is now the crucial mystery . . . in whose image society is to be reformed. . . . It is not society that is to guide and save the creative hero, but precisely the reverse. The modern hero-deed must be that of questing to bring to light . . . the lost Atlantis of the co-ordinated soul. (4: pp. 390–391, 388)

For the first time in history the individual must begin the quest by himself for it to *be* authentic, for the quest is for the self. This is modern man's archetypal battle—the search for centering of a coordinated, unique selfhood. And we must do it without false faith in our primary rationality. Even if it were not an illusion, it would not help us here, since the knowledge needed must arise from the body's perceptions, where our being and our individuality begin. The body is, incidentally, no longer the generalized mystical body, but the body as science and sport together can know man—the concrete, individuated, responsible and healthy body.

While the astronaut Aldrin was on the Moon the family's minister included these ideas in that Sunday's sermon:

> Since World War II we are in the advent of the modern worldwide civilization that is based upon science—for the language and technology of science is the same in every country . . . the first symbolic event of that civilization is "the bomb." The second . . . is Apollo 11, the first and most imaginative nondestructive event of a new civilization. (1: pp. 272–273)

We are perhaps also in the presence of a new archetype of global community. It is one that, in this modern era, must be translated into individual expressions so that its enactment is created by each of us, as a new myth of individualism plus world responsibility would require. To Nietzsche, who would believe only in a God archetype who could laugh, I add a God who laughed watching a friend of his named Alan Shepard hit a golf ball off the Moon.

Unlike most myths, but like science, this originating event could be exactly dated. But the language and technology of science in a non-demonic form is applicable to each of us as individual bodies learning about self-overcoming and achievement in the athlete's Olympic model of "faster, higher, stronger." It is genuinely a concrete universal, available and comprehensible and, as discussed, replete with playfulness, assuring its attractiveness. In fact, the act of Captain Shepard on the moon is one of the funniest events to occur in this or any other world.

In conclusion, it is possible to state that sport clearly expresses a new living myth for a new society, namely, that individual human power can be positive rather than destructive. Thus, it need not be feared, renamed or repressed only to leap up in demonic madness years later. Power can be positively actualized as power over oneself and for one's creativity and that is the same thing as saying that the age-long Humanistic faith in the supreme value of individual freedom has true flesh. It is the sensation of power first learned through sport, a learning about the body-self's reliability and responsibility. No ill will or negative demonic from the past can rob from you the fact that you now run faster and stronger than yesterday. The achievement is too clear even for the machinations of the destroyers of self-esteem, indeed clear enough to communicate within a mental hospital.

Now, what will the symbol come to do to society as it continues to be lived concretely in the happily embodied selves of modern men? Among the many strange lacks in our culture two stem from the two important aspects previously noted which achieve almost universal scorn among intellectuals, namely, space and sport, the astronaut and the athlete. I suspect jealousy at the spectacular achievements each makes in the concrete world of space and time to be behind the glib readiness to confuse each with their idolatrous, commercialized forms. More deeply, I suspect terror because each involves a soaring that a society based on repression must deny or distort. Well, then, what did the astronaut and what does the athlete teach? Recalling the mind-bending picture of earth from space, two aspects are relevant here: that there is no giant benevolent hand cradling our lonely, fragile globe; and that, therefore, we, the people, are all in this together. Unlike the intellectual, we are stunned by the picture and must look, but unlike the minister, we cannot expect God, only gods who are ourselves. As we focus beyond the body of the globe to the bodies of people on it, for the first time we may see with the urging empathy of the athletic body that the majority of the other bodies are sick and starving. If we at last comprehend this with the intelligence of the body, and do it with a group force, we may have the new courage to comprehend that this incredible injustice is the demonic in bodily form. We can know this today without becoming mad from the tragedy because today our scientists can change this. When we allow ourselves to see it, then we have become Humanists in the flesh, not merely in the mind.

If it is true that sport tempts and overcomes the individual demonic in our own self, and if it is true that we wish such results to pervade all social reality globally, as our ritualistic speeches say we do, then those who know, because they know the body both as athlete and scientist, have teaching to do. The archetypal model for our world as it is *lived* today is far closer to games of chance than it is like sport. The two could not be more opposed in moral essence and results for personal life regarding, among other variables, justice and joy.

BIBLIOGRAPHY

1. Armstrong, Collins, and Aldrin. *First on the Moon.* Boston: Little, Brown & Co., 1970.

2. Bannister, Roger. *The Four Minute Mile.* New York: Dodd, Mead & Co., 1955.

3. Buchler, Justus. *Metaphysics of Natural Complexes.* New York: Columbia University Press, 1966.

4. Campbell, Joseph. *Hero with a Thousand Faces.* Cleveland: World Publishing Co., 1964.

5. Epstein, Joseph. "Obsessed with Sport." *Harper's,* July 1976. Reprinted in this anthology, pp. 109–118.

6. Kaelin, Eugene F. "Being in the Body." *Sport and the Body: A Philosophical Symposium.* Edited by Ellen Gerber. Philadelphia: Lea and Febiger, 1972.

7. Keenan, Francis. "The Athletic Contest as a 'Tragic' Form of Art." *The Philosophy of Sport.* Edited by Robert G. Osterhoudt. Springfield, Illinois: Charles C. Thomas, 1973.

8. Lipsyte, Robert. "The Joys of Sport and the Drawbacks." *The New York Times,* December 14, 1975, section five, p. 2.

9. May, Rollo. *Love and Will.* New York: W. W. Norton, 1969.

10. Merleau-Ponty, Maurice. *The Phenomenology of Perception.* Translated by Colin Smith. London: Routledge and Kegan Paul, 1962.

11. Milgrim, Stanley. "Obedience to Authority." *Psychology Today* 8 (June, 1974).

12. Neumann, Erich. *The Origins and History of Consciousness.* Part One. New York: The Bolligen Library, 1954.

13. Nietzsche, Friedrich. *Twilight of the Idols.* In *The Portable Nietzsche.* Edited by Walter Kaufmann. New York: The Viking Press, 1968.

14. Roochnick, David. "Play and Sport." *Journal of the Philosophy of Sport* 2 (September, 1975), 36–44.

15. Russell, Bill. *Go Up For Glory.* New York: Berkeley Medallion Books, 1972.

16. Schwartz, Delmore. *Summer Knowledge.* Garden City, N.Y.: Doubleday & Co., 1959.

17. Smith, Red. "Can Joe DiMaggio Be 61?" *The New York Times,* December 14, 1975, section five, p. 3.

HANS LENK

Herculean "Myth" Aspects of Athletics

A "MYTHOLOGICAL" INTERPRETATION OF THE FASCINATION WITH TOP LEVEL SPORT

An aesthetic interpretation of athletics was outlined by Barthes (1). From the spectator's viewpoint, sports contests would represent a modern variant of dramatic struggles between the heroic roles of an almost archetypical symbolic force. This reception by the public of sport encounters encompasses a kind of epic, replete and emotionally laden with interconnections of social unification, partisanship, and personal identification. The spectator experiences the sport contest as a vicarious participant similar to the way he views a drama on the stage.

Barthes referred to the Tour de France and its reception by the public as a dramatic epic. The heroes of the epic are the cyclists. But they are reduced to their "characteristic essences," the "uncertain conflict" of which is the subject of the epic—staged in a Homeric landscape, fought by stylized "supermen" escorted and supported by their vassals. In their roles, the men are matched against each other and against nature. Elements, roles, landscapes are personified, the contestants are somehow "naturalized," styled as quasi-natural forces or elements succumbing to natural forces in a world where only four movements are allowed: "To lead, to pursue, to forge ahead, to fall back" (1: pp. 118, 115).

Barthes and Magnane(8) stressed the "mythical" significance of sport contests for the spectators. Both of them combined this interpretation with a compensatory thesis arguing that the vicarious experience of sports contests somehow compensates for everyday frustration and monotony. According to Barthes, the "myths of sport" express a reconciliation and liberation of man in precise and perfect distinctiveness (1: pp. 118f). Furthermore, Magnane interprets the "modern myths of sports" as a "complete projection system" to explain the world and vicariously to identify oneself with the values of an "unofficial" culture. This projection system not only mobilizes "the psychic forces" which the vocational and family life of common man do not take into consideration, but it also provides a basis for the "explanation of the world" to the sports fan. Estranged from the elusive "official culture," the average

Originally appeared in *Journal of the Philosophy of Sport* (1976).

man tentatively searches for elements of another culture which are based on values he is certain he will be able to grasp. Indeed, he discovers a culture of his own in sports and in the realms of the mass media supporting it. Significant sporting movements in less specific connotations become a special "set of signs." It is this "other culture," this "sporting mythology" by which the relatively uneducated subject "takes revenge" and finds a kind of indemnity for the real disadvantages of fate. Within this reversed image of reality, he finds gross compensation and a source of confidence. Magnane even emphasizes that the "sporting mythology" would fulfill the function of offering frustrated people "in a precultural state" an "access to ontology" (8: pp. 109f).

These metaphoric episodes, conveying a relatively rough compensation thesis about the indemnity function of vicarious sports experiences, are in need of further elaboration and more detailed analysis. The efficacy of myths cannot be reduced to only one unique compensation function. Magnane's own statement, which he did not analyze in any detail, states that sporting myths are "a set of signs" by which the sportive man explains how the world operates (8: p. 97). His single reference to the cathartic function in the sense of theory of ancient theatre could have figured as the point of departure for a more differentiated analysis.[1] The drama of modern day athletic sport displays effects analogous to the theatre of antiquity, although starting from a clearly different, non-religious, basic situation. Being "carried away" relieves the compassionate and enthusiastic adherent of other social and personal problems by vicariously involving him in archetypical struggles between opposing roles within restricted frames of reference. The sport roles symbolically reflect his own problem situation or, at least, some of his problems of tension, stress, anxiety, the dynamics of winning and losing, etc.

The achievement principle in sport is an ideal *abstraction*, a "pure" utopian construction of achievement behavior norms that are scarcely to be found in pure form in the world of labor. This sporting achievement principle may be viewed as representing, relatively speaking, the "pure essence" of achievement behavior, and its standardization and valuation occur through symbolic incarnation, within a realm of exemplification which renders a possibility of strict measurement, visibility, and thus of simple understanding. On the other hand, this abstraction is not carried to an extreme whereby we would lose sight of the correlations, similarities, or analogies of this stylized behavior model to corresponding ones in everyday life. Similarities are present, visibly presented, and maintained to such a degree that the identification of the spectator with his own aims and patterns of behavior is assured, especially since he identifies with the sporting representatives of the group. Therefore, in addition to the "character essences" (Barthes), that is, the "mythical" stylizing of roles, there are similarly stylized, abstract "purified" patterns of *behav-*

ior to be found in sport which might be called "interactional essences" or pure ideal norms of role interaction in the fighting confrontation model. They find their archetypical-"mythical" expressions in the sports contests of top level athletics. If sport is interpreted as a model of an "achieving society" and in this "mythical" and ideal-typical (i.e. pointed, selectively restricted, and yet visible, dynamic incarnation) this might be correctly understood as an interpretation of a "myth," and the analysis as a "mythological" interpretation.

The term 'myth' is most ambiguous. Magnane does not care about defining the term 'myth' or 'mythology' at all. He implicitly refers to the characteristic features of "myths," that is, culturally-historically developed fictional models constituting and conveying sense and meaning by staying with typical examples and incarnation within visible models and images as well as by rendering projections and the explanatory power of this semiological system. In this analysis, 'myth' is understood to mean neither a comprehensive *Weltanschauung* (world view) in images nor an ideological system of belief statements which serve cognitively to justify empirical results or normative convictions. Instead, 'myth' here designates a model symbolizing normative designs, projections, and valuations and how they have developed historically in the cultural tradition. The symbolization is incarnated or represented in typically exemplifying patterned situations and evidenced by dramatic staging in these familiar structures. Myths disclose and constitute sense and significance of the less familiar phenomena. While ideologies serve cognitively to interpret self and the world, myths, by the way of example or exemplification, must provide a *normative* constitution of meaning and ideal images in, typically, perceptible shapes. Myths in this sense, and in contrast to Barthes' (1: pp. 88ff) conception, figure less in closed and hierarchical systems of statements than they do in their stylizing, selective and sense-constituting functions. These might be called the *"mythical functions"* of exemplified action patterns. However, we might follow Barthes in that the consumer of a myth interprets sense composition in a causal-naturalistic way and understands 'meaning' "as a system of facts": "Myth is understood as a system of facts, although it represents only a semiological system," that is, a system which constitutes and mediates significance, sense, and meaning (1: p. 115).

All that has been said about the symbolic-mythical function should not be misinterpreted to mean that sport truly and isomorphically mirrors the principles according to which an industrial society and an "achieving society" is structured. The stating of empirical results about social behavior in any case has little to do with this "mythological" interpretation.

"Sport is a microcosm" and "mirror of social processes," stated Vander-Zwaag recently (9, 10). His thesis that the significance of sport for the individual is derived from interpretations and projections of social processes is clearly relevant for the sport consumer. More specifically, sport as a symbolic microcosmic representation of archetypical role dynamics functions as a modern "myth"; only this additional aspect, refining the microcosm thesis on a semantic level, seems able to explain the fascination of competitive athletics. It is easily compatible with the fact that roles are reduced to the simplest confrontations. Opposition, struggle, in-group, out-group, victory or defeat, representing all-or-nothing or yes-no outcomes—the human tendency to establish and rely on dichotomies and building in-groups against outsiders, clearly denotes an articulation field which renders a dramatic "mythical" incarnation in visible forms.

The thesis about sport as a microcosm of social processes, if understood literally, seems to place too much emphasis on representation while it concentrates on a mapping function. It also neglects the normative character of the model, the "mythical," the archetypical, and the abstractive element. The microcosm hypothesis is descriptive, empirical, and social scientific—and as such, is too general and vague. A philosophical interpretation cannot be totally resolved in an empirical, scientific description or explanation. Sporting life is not only normal life in a nutshell; it does not represent the focus of everyday existence. Sporting life represents a model, but the model is in part an ideal model of a pointed and contrasting life featuring some essential traits and dreams in "mythical" symbolization and exaltation. Sport as a "mythical" model of symbolized, competitive role behavior is governed by archetypical norms. From the spectators' point of view, this "mythological" interpretation may provide a valuable partial explanation, or at least a plausible illustration of the fascination of top level athletics. Projections, worlds of symbols, relative detachment from daily life, microcosm, identification, and dramatic staging all concur in the above "mythological" interpretation and may serve to explain the peculiar position of athletics between usual behavior and abstract ideal patterns. Thus, the "mythological" encompasses the somewhat modified microcosm thesis in a meaningful manner.

A "MYTHOLOGICAL" INTERPRETATION OF THE ATHLETE'S ROLE

The "mythical function" and interpretation of this sport phenomenon developed thus far refer only to the reception of sport contests by the spectators. The athlete as the agent has been neglected in this interpretation. Both Barthes and Magnane deal only with the sports consumer and his tendency to "mythify" the champion as a kind of demigod. A "mythological" interpretation of sport actions *from an actor's perspective* was not designed nor performed by either Barthes or by Magnane. Nonetheless, such an interpretation can be developed in connection with the previously outlined "mythical function" for the sports consumer.

Behavior, motivations, needs, and valuations by the spectator and sport consumer, as significant as they may be for any understanding of top level athletics from a quantitative and theoretical point of view, cannot provide the only basis for a philosophical interpretation of the social realm of sport. Although the top athlete tends to orient his actions toward some aspects of the public response, his action cannot be explained simply by taking into consideration his orientation towards an audience. His behavior cannot be completely resolved in such social categories as an adaptation to social expectations of achievement, the producer on the "achievement market," or the internalization of the collective achievement principle, as some social critics of sport have tried to do. Furthermore, man, as a cultural and symbolic being trying to achieve an active constitution of self, is dependent not only on the satisfaction of biological needs. Even biological needs are overridden by cultural rituals and habits which cultivate a *way* of satisfaction. Man strives to materialize abstract cultural goals, lives up to fictitious values, and abides by normative conventional rules in order to accomplish self-determination and realization, self-differentiation, and self-confirmation. This self-affirmation need not be a conscious, manifest goal at all. Sport achievements which are institutionalized and valued within their proper cultural framework present a particularly attractive medium of demonstrative individualization, self-development, and self-confirmation for younger men with reference to goals and value patterns which are emotionally approved in the culture. Athletics proffer an opportunity for distinction in an otherwise predominantly conforming society—an opportunity which may emphasize individualistic values.[2] Weiss's interpretation of top level athletics as the "concern for excellence" and the desire to excel through bodily action or through the body, gains its relevance and actuality in this connection (11: p. 3 et passim). This ideal-typical interpretation of the athlete as an incarnation of the man who strives for personal distinction is based on the values of Western civilization. There is no evidence that these motivations and values are universals. Cultural historical roots, e.g., the Greek orientation to ideals of agon, or the Christian high valuation of the individual, of individual life and fate including the Protestant ethic of self-confirmation, asceticism, inner-world orientation, and activism as Max Weber had so cogently stressed, are alternate motivations.

Insofar as the athlete strives for ever-improving traits and achievements in athletic performances, he certainly is impregnated by *cultural* factors. The individual, nevertheless, can and may use this cultural challenge in order to constitute and document his uniqueness or peculiarity by personal feats and accomplishments, e.g., by sporting achievements. This is true regarding his self-assessment as well as his regard for his social status. The aspect of self-judgment can be separated only analytically from social assessment. In order to gain self-realization and self-assessment, *social* comparing in the sense of self-classification and social competition seems to be indispensable within the framework of the Western cultural tradition. The guiding norms and principles of athletic behavior and the establishment of goals can be interpreted as being reduced to "essential," "pure" idealized patterns, or quasi-abstract contents—the achievement principle, the competition principle, and the equality principle (3, 4). The latter simply means equality of opportunity. These guiding norms are represented and incarnated in sports contests in an almost ideal-typical, pure, and relatively independent model of realization which certainly has social significance in affecting attitudinal and social orientations.

Although seemingly totally individualistic, even Weiss's interpretation leaves some space for supplementary *social*-philosophical analysis—not only in selecting and institutionalizing criteria and action patterns or in orienting achievement comparisons to competition, but also in the thesis that the athlete must be an ideal incarnation of what man is or man can be through his body. What can be achieved, represents a fascinating plea and request for almost everyone. This normative ideal image of excellence can be seen as constituting a kind of plea which is designed for *social* influence and interaction. In reference to Weiss's interpretation, man as a stance-taking, acting, and valuing being cannot fully ignore the artistic, perfect sport movements in their successions of dynamic tension and release. Sporting action provides a normative image which includes a motor and visual appeal.

Weiss's final metaphysical excursus has to be recalled. Using his freedom with maximum effect, the athlete faces total "actuality." In unification and identification with his body, he is the incarnation of those laws which govern the operation of the perfect, although mortal, body. Therefore, the ideal athlete—"one with those laws"—embodies and displays, in a time-bound limited instantiation, a super-individual and super-temporal "eternal reality" in "co-presence" of "matter" and its "meaning." The ideal athlete represents mankind in the endeavor to achieve maximal results. We would become a part of "eternal reality," somehow symbolically escaping the "remorseless flux of time." The athlete is "sport incarnated, sport instantiated, sport located for the moment" and thus a prominent incarnation of man and his uniqueness in his striving for eternity (11: pp. 243 ff).

If one does not pay too much attention to the Platonistic essentialism in this philosophy of eternity, it might be useful to state that the reference to actuality may present the link necessary to integrate Weiss's views with an existential-philosophical interpretation. More importantly for our argument, the above mentioned eternal reality can only be a *symbolic* one. No eternal laws of nature render the athlete himself "eternal." His example instantiates a symbolic fiction which can be meaningful only as a part of an immaterial cultural system. As a *cultural* idea, it is an incarnation of a norm, which obtains a super-individual significance. It is only in this manner that Weiss is able legitimately to argue that the athlete represents mankind in its maximum endeavor to achieve. The athlete incorporates "*a mythical ideal.*" Is he, then, a Hercules or a Prometheus, or sometimes even a Narcissus? The ideal of cultural achievement beyond the requirements of survival and everyday affairs somehow makes man the culturally creative, spiritual, intellectual, and symbolic being he is. By extending the lines of Weiss's interpretation, the athlete can be interpreted as representing the "myth," instantiating a sort of "mythical" figure of a Herculean-Promethean kind; he is a *cultural god*, capable of extraordinary feats which can only be accomplished by complete devotion.

By implication, Weiss's metaphysics of top level athletics and achievements also leads to the interpretation that sport is a pointed representation of a "mythical" model of symbolized, archetypical competition in which achieving behavior is governed by ideal-typical norms, staged and instantiated in visible dynamic forms. Although Weiss, in his analysis of the athlete, refers only to the achievement capacity of the individual without extending his interpretation to the mentioned "mythological" one, this variation could be easily and harmoniously attached to his analysis. Weiss reduces too individualistically and abstractly what one might perhaps, albeit misleadingly, call the "pure mythical essence." He refers exclusively to the pure personal striving for achievement and excellence in itself. He abstracts from the social modelling situation only in the structure of which, and by the impregnation of which, achievements can be accomplished and compared with each other. The integration of the phenomena of sporting achievement with the ideal-typical social constellation of sport contests, and the culturally developed interpretations, might diminish some of the abstractness, individualistic restriction, and isolation of this interpretation.

The "mythological" interpretation was originally developed as an aspect of the spectator's fascination. It can also be based on an interpretation of the role and function of the athlete himself. Throughout, both interpretations make sense solely and in combination, both of them being partial aspects within the philosophical approach. The social as well as the individual lead to the same model, a model which renders a necessary connection between *social* philosophical and *individualistic* philosophical analyses.[3] From the perspective of an ideal-typical understanding of the athlete's role, different traditional one-factor analyses in the philosophy of sport are also easily arranged around certain core interpretations without a single one of them explaining all phenomena of sport from an actor's point of view. This multifactorial and multifunctional interpretation of sport unites the social philosophical perspectives and the individualistic ones. Partial interpretations are relativized, united, and interlaced. Most differences are reduced to differences of aspect and emphasis. Furthermore, the pluralistic and multifactorial approach allows for a relatively bold and new "*metaphysical*" thesis, namely a cultural-philosophical interpretation of sport as a modern staging of a kind of "myth," a dramatic, visibly instantiated interplay of competitive and archetypical roles, behavior patterns and normative principles.

The "mythological" interpretation presented has yet to be applied to specific sport disciplines in detail. Further differentiations and modifications of a pluralistic interpretation of sport in general have to be elaborated. A single interpretation will always be a selective and ideal-typical one. To be sure, there are characteristic differences between sport disciplines corresponding to different types of basic sport situations, probably implying modifications within the "mythological" interpretation itself. Such typical and essential structural differences are to be found between team sports and individual disciplines; between sports requiring and displaying speed and those kinds which rely purely on bodily strength; between endurance contests and rhythmic-aesthetical performances; between disciplines cultivating skill and control of the body as well as accuracy of movement and those consisting of bodily contact and encounter of man against man; between sports movements coordinating exactness and finely structured phases in detail and those consisting of mastering a strange medium such as water or air and their respective resistances; between sports that upgrade equipment to a degree much closer to perfection and those dispensing with equipment and also with the standardization of the environment which we have in a sporting facility as e.g., in cross-country and orientation running. Between sports where the athlete sits in or on a vehicle like a boat or bicycle and those relying on well-exercised cooperation with an animal, for instance a horse; between sports of conquest of nature, such as mountaineering, which are devoted to the confrontation with and mastering of challenges of nature, and those requiring the mastering of highly artificial equipment, such as shooting; between team sports where the overall score is gained by an addition of points referring to single achievements or those where only a specific transmission event is conducted by the coordination of team members, as in relay running, and those genuine team sports where the overall performance is established by an immediate addition or coordination of forces of the respective members, such as rowing, or where an overall structure of the game is conducted by interaction of special role-holders who make a social network as, for instance, in ball games.

The multiplicity of situations, action patterns, goals and tasks, value aspects, and standardizations is remarkable and far from being exhausted by the previously mentioned list. The attractiveness and fascination of each unique sport depends also on its specific characteristics as perceived by both the athletes and the spectators. Even the symbolic "mythological" interpretation is narrowly connected with such specifics. One might recall the opposition of nature when the mountaineers are challenged by a storm—a symbolic drama against ruthless nature, combined with some attraction of impending existential "boundary situations" of utmost exposure and impending danger. By contradistinction, in what time might a man run a certain distance under standardized conditions of a carefully prepared artificial track? Not even this fascination of speed can be fully explained in a rational way without reference to some symbolic "mythical" basic situation of autonomic and mobile man.

Weiss and others maintain that some laws of nature are revealed in athletic records indicating "what man really is." According to their view, top level athletics and records render some tentative answers to this Kantian question. While this may be true, it probably has less to do with natural laws than with symbolically modelled, "mythical" situations and challenges of man which are, although based on natural conditions, culturally impregnated and do not refer only to his endangered situation within nature, but also to the basic patterns of intra-specific group confrontations—that is, socially structured situations. Although a compulsion to confront nature remains, it is then over-laid by a symbolically interpreted *cultural* model. Toynbee's idea of challenging the "cultural being" by natural conditions has some partial relevance here, even in artificially established and culturally modified "resistances." Top level athletics and sporting achievement in general reflect those basic situations; the active, competitive, or struggling mastery of these situations by goal-oriented, Herculean and Promethean Western man staging the symbolic, dramatic archetype in the form of visible dynamic role interplay.

SOME SIMILARITIES TO "MYTHS" OF TECHNOLOGY

Who is the athlete between Hercules and Prometheus? Prometheus allegedly brought fire and culture to man. Sometimes Prometheus is interpreted as a mythical figure of technology and man's reigning over nature. The link which bridges the gap between a philosophy of technology and philosophy of athletics is still missing. Connecting these subject matters of philosophical interpretation by such a link, or at least by an analogy, is expected to provide fruitful stimulations for both realms. The desire and motivation to extend the frontiers, to cope with challenging risks and adventure in a rationalized and standardized form is deeply characteristic for both phenomena, technology as well as sport.

It is not surprising that the "sporting myth" with its specific tradition and development has progressed along with Western civilization. The dream of reigning over nature by sheer will power and rationality, controlling and increasing vitality, represents a certain power motive which is then transferred to role interactions between men. There is also a rationally controlled comparison of strength, or other sporting capacities, in confrontation with an opponent who is to be overwhelmed, without a serious dependence on power domination and submission existing between two partners or teams. In sport, this actuality and this rational control engender a decrease in seriousness and power dependence. This points to a primary characteristic difference with technology; all the more reason why analogies and similarities as well as characteristic differences and interconnections between technology and sports should be analyzed in the future. Such characteristic differences do exist and should not be minimized by looking for analogies and interconnections. A differentiated analysis has to reveal both commonalities and differences.

Philosophical interpretations of sport as well as of technology along these lines may indicate that "mythological" interpretation and "mythical" functions are not outdated models of a romantic past. In secular form, although mostly hidden, they continue to be effective. The "myth" of technological power over nature and of permanent technological progress certainly represents an essential motivation pattern of Western culture without which, for example, the expenditure for space programs would hardly be understood. The "peaceful" competition of the super-powers in space can also be understood as motivated by a common "myth." It is illusionary and utopian to try to abolish or to suppress this Western ideology. For the analogous "myth" of sport, then, intriguing similarities to some specific variants of the technological "myth" can be stated, although fortunately without the immediate urgency and pressure encountered in technological innovation. Sporting achievements might be compared to space adventures, particularly since the existence of mankind is not dependent on either one. (To travel to another star is another cultural "mythical" dream of mankind.) The analogies referring to top level athletics, which fortunately are not as expensive as spacecraft launching and space expeditions, seem to be found near at hand. The "technological age" is far from being as rational as it pretends to be. Apparently, it needs its own secular "myths." Top level athletics undoubtedly have to be mentioned along with these.

Regarding these parallels and analogies, it is not surprising that the new social criticism of technology and technocracy and the new cultural criticism of sport converge in the criticism of achievement motivation, achievement principle, and achievement behavior. Technocracy may be understood as total dominance of technological processes or mechanization and as a trend, by technical and organizational means and by ruling experts, to subdue human factors (5, 7). Are athletes "technocratic beings" or technocratically manipulated? There is no space to discuss these intriguing problems here. However, with respect to the fashionable social criticism it can be stated that although sports are predominately conservative and technocratically organized and administered today, the actions and the intentions of top athletes are not necessarily so conservative nor technocratic in themselves. Does not the athlete take risks to blaze new frontiers of human achievement behavior? This can never be done by exclusively emphasizing methods, techniques, and procedural requirements; it is achieved by deep personal commitment and devotion. The achieving athlete necessarily displays extraordinary human endeavor and total involvement which cannot be technocratically induced. Herculean-Promethean "myths" as ideal patterns pertaining to human performance exclude conservatism. While it is true that the system of official power elites in sport definitely is in need of a reform, the athlete himself is, at least ideally, though not necessarily individually, beyond the scope of this social criticism.

CONCLUDING REMARKS

Somehow, risk-taking in design and in philosophy is comparable to venturing in sport. This interpretation reveals how far the seemingly everyday phenomenon of sporting achievement is embedded in cultural fiction and argues that sporting contests do symbolize some culturally significant and "mythical" functions which provide reasons for the attraction and fascination of sport from the viewpoint of the athlete as well as the spectator. Despite its tentativeness and simplicity, the "mythological" interpretation may turn out to be very realistic. Stating a "mythological" interpretation does not in itself mean that one subscribes to the "myth." Modern "myths" are real—socially real—in some sense, although secular in make-up. Philosophy, among its other tasks, has to analyze the content, scope, prerequisites and implications of such "myths." Since "myths" and "mythical" functions do impinge on attitudes and social as well as individual basic orientations, it is important for the philosophy of sport to develop further the "mythological" interpretation of athletics especially since the social significance of top level sport in mass media societies is growing even larger.

NOTES

1. However, Aristotle's theory about the cathartic effect of tragedy does not deal with the compensation of everyday frustration. According to Aristotle, the drama reconstructs the impersonal myths of gods. It displays religious significance and provides catharsis as a purification of the spectator from an excessive amount of fear and compassion. The catharsis theory, however, can be analogously exemplified with respect to sport by interpreting sport as a locus for symbolic, "mythological" role confrontation and dramatic staging.

2. One might object that a cult of the individual is superfluous and useless and does not justify the remarkable social expenditures devoted to such institutions as sports. This objection, however, is short-sighted. At first, the concern throughout is with a *social* institution meeting social demands and social requirements of integration, symbolization and "mythical" functions. Furthermore, cultural and social interconnections always materialize via individual actions within institutionalized social frameworks.

3. For a general argument pertaining to the necessity of combining both approaches in a pluralistic philosophy of sport see (6).

BIBLIOGRAPHY

1. Barthes, R. *Mythen des Alltags*. Frankfurt, 1964.
2. Keenan, F. W. "The Athletic Contest as a 'Tragic' Form of Art." *The Philosophy of Sport*. Edited by R. G. Osterhoudt. Springfield, Illinois: Charles C. Thomas, 1973.
3. Krockow, Chr. v. *Sport und Industriegesellschaft*. Munich: Piper, 1972.
4. Krockow, Chr. v. *Sport*. Hamburg: Hoffmann und Campe, 1974.
5. Lenk, H. *Philosophie im Technischen Zeitalter*. 2d ed. Stuttgart: Kohlhammer, 1972.
6. Lenk, H. *Leistungssport: Ideologie oder Mythos?* 2d. ed. Stuttgart: Kohlhammer, 1972.
7. Lenk, H., ed. *Technokratie als Ideologie*. Stuttgart: Kohlhammer, 1973.
8. Magnane, G. *Sociologie du Sport*. Paris, 1964.
9. VanderZwaag, H. J. "Sport as a Microcosm from the Perspective of Social Processes which Lead to Conflict." Paper presented at the Scientific Congress of the Games of the XX Olympiad, Munich, Germany, 1972.
10. VanderZwaag, H. J. *Toward a Philosophy of Sport*. Reading, Mass.: Addison and Wesley, 1972.
11. Weiss, P. *Sport: A Philosophic Inquiry*. Carbondale, Illinois: Southern Illinois University Press, 1969.

A Guide for Further Study

An article packed with illuminating information on the mythical levels in Malamud's novel is Earl Wassermann, "The Natural: Malamud's World Ceres," *Centennial Review* 9 (1965). An interesting piece on contemporary ritual is William Arens, "The Great Football Ritual," *Natural History* (October 1975). Also, see Heinegg's essay in the next section of this anthology, on the philosopher in the playground who contemplates the meaning of sport.

Section III: Sport and the Philosophic

JOHN UPDIKE

Tao in the Yankee Stadium Bleachers

Distance brings proportion. From here
the populated tiers
as much as players seem part of the show:
a constructed stage beast, three folds of Dante's rose,
or a Chinese military hat
cunningly chased with bodies.
"Falling from his chariot, a drunk man is unhurt
because his soul is intact. Not knowing his fall,
he is unastonished, he is invulnerable."
So, too, the "pure man"—"pure"
in the sense of undisturbed water.

"It is not necessary to seek out
a wasteland, swamp, or thicket."
The old men who saw Hans Wagner
scoop them up in lobster-hands,
the opposing pitcher's pertinent hesitations,
the sky, this meadow, Mantle's thick baked neck,
the old men who in the changing rosters see
a personal mutability,
green slats, wet stone are all to me
as when an emperor commands
a performance with a gesture of his eyes.

"No king on his throne has the joy of the dead,"
the skull told Chuang-tzu.
The thought of death is peppermint to you

From *The Carpentered Hen and Other Tame Creatures* (1958). Originally appeared in *The New Yorker* (1956).

when games begin with patriotic song
and a democratic sun beats broadly down.
The Inner Journey seems unjudgeably long
when small boys purchase cups of ice
and, distant as a paradise,
experts, passionate and deft,
wait while Berra flies to left.

WILLIAM HARPER

The Philosopher in Us

What is philosophy? The question spurs an interesting variety of responses. Some would simply say, "That's nice!" and shuffle off to the tennis courts. Others hearing the question might honestly say, "Who cares?" A few sturdy souls might actually try to answer the question, perhaps suggesting that the answer has something to do with wisdom—although exactly what it has to do with wisdom is not certain. Fewer still might approvingly say, "Ah! Philosophy . . . ," but find themselves unable to further respond, paralyzed by the knowledge that the philosophic tradition is old, mostly academic, and seemingly quite beyond their reach. And so the answers might go on.

Common to these (and most) answers about the nature of philosophy are two assumptions. First, it is assumed that philosophy is mostly a subject one can elect to study in a college or university; and second, it is assumed that even when philosophy is studied, what is learned is relatively useless.

But let's think about these assumptions for a few moments. If we pick them over a bit, we will discover that more often philosophy is something one does, not merely studies in school, and that in the deepest sense such philosophizing is useful indeed.

Let's take our beginning from what we know best: our day to day experiences. In fact, let's get specific about a single experience. Not long ago, I received a letter from a young friend. Wedged into the normal chatter was the following paragraph.

Originally appeared in *Journal of Physical Education, Recreation and Dance* (1982).

. . . I must be going crazy! Today I was sitting in one of those semi-fast food places—MacAces? Wendy King? Burger Queen? Dairy Jack?—eating a hamburger. Suddenly, as I gazed straight into the face of this miserable excuse for a hamburger I saw my own life! No, it didn't pass in front of me—the hamburger wasn't that bad. But I looked into this hamburger and thought to myself, "My life is just like this hamburger!" Now think about it for a minute. The hamburger wasn't too hot, kind of cold, actually. Everything in it and on it was off-center: the squirt of mustard in one corner, ketchup in another, the meat-like substance sliding out of the bun, the lettucey stuff dangling from the bun (and my lips). It was layered, stuff separated from stuff, bread between meat, a little of this, then some of that. It was overstuffed, and served in this plastic, flip-top carton which actually crackles at you as you open its mouth. Wouldn't you say that this experience was kind of unsettling? Here I thought I was taking a break from things, deserving a change today, and I find my life staring at me in the form of a $1.25 hamburger: cool, off-center, fragmented, layered, overstuffed, and plastic! On top of that, I didn't even win a prize in their "everybody wins!" contest. What do you make of that?

Well, what should we make of it? Actually we shouldn't make *too* much of it. After all the statement was only a side comment in the letter, probably tongue in cheek as well, and we really can't learn too much from the less than canny observation that "my life is like a hamburger."

Yet we are to make *something* of this paragraph. In it we find an announcement. In this rather ordinary experience we find announced the existence of a rather extraordinary capacity or urge: *the philosopher in us.*

Rising up from we know not where and seizing us in moments not often planned is the philosopher in us. Our hamburger-eating friend was minding his own business when quite suddenly, even rudely, he found his thoughts making connections between the features of the inanimate world (the hamburger—assuming everything in it was dead!) and the animated world of his life. The philosopher in him was at play.

Instead of philosophy being remote and out of reach, we actually find that the basic philosophic activity of *wondering*, of *making connections*, of *asking questions*, is quite close to us—so close, in fact, it almost defines us. As children, we wonder about the names of things; we ask those simple questions, which we know as adults aren't simply answered—sometimes simply avoided—about time and space, about the universe, about where we came from and where we are going, about fear, about death, about why people get angry, about love, about hurting others and being hurt, and in time about all of the most elemental aspects of what it means to be a human being in the world. In later years these questions remain with us (or ought to) and are still put forward, although in sometimes subtle, or sometimes sophisticated ways.

The philosopher in us shows up throughout our lives. In raw form, the basic urge to think about elemental relations among aspects of our world can appear not only while staring at a "miserable excuse for a hamburger," but in many of our daily encounters and situations where we confront ourselves in our world. The urge arises sometimes in our boredom, at other times in our moments of happiness and joy. It pushes through in our loves and our hates, our duties and our careers, our successes and our failures, our courageous acts and our fears. So rather than being a stranger to us, in truth, the philosopher in us is nearby. It is as much in our lives as our lives are to be found in cultivating it.

What if we wanted to cultivate the philosophic impulse? What if we wanted to put this resource to good or better use? By now it should be clear that the meaning of philosophy is not to be found in thinking of it merely as a subject for college or university study. Philosophy, or better, philosophizing, is to be found in the peculiar form of activity which a person somehow does in solitude. At the risk of oversimplifying the distinction, we might say that there are two general, related kinds of philosophic activity: the *contemplative* and the *discursive*.

The attitude of mind holding sway in the contemplative act is an embracing of the individual, concrete things and persons in the world. We take them in. We relax our analytical and reasoning powers. We let things be what they are. We make contact directly with them. Our thoughts come to focus on an object or experience just in the way that the object or experience presents itself. Some have said it is merely letting the soul be still. It is then much more a listening than it is a looking. It is a Socrates standing alone for days in "speechless wonder," knowing that truth is revealed in complete human stillness.

In describing "intuitive knowledge" Henri Bergson (1859–1941) threw light on the contemplative. He spoke of a direct vision without interference or detours—simply a succession, a conscious flow. The act, for Bergson, was "the direct vision of the mind by the mind . . . immediate consciousness, a vision which is scarcely distinguishable from the object seen, a knowledge which is contact and even coincidence." [1] The contemplative act, seen in this way, becomes a continuous creation by the individual thinker. It is a way of doing philosophic activity which brings something new into the world. Bergson even called it a *sympathy*, "by which one is transported into the interior of an object in order to coincide with what there is unique and consequently inexpressible in it." [2] In the end, the act is simple, direct contact with this face, that person, this cloud, that tree—maybe even that hamburger! We aim to *contact*.

If contemplation is embrace, discursive thinking is stiff-arming. We retain the idea of sympathetic disinterestedness, yet in discursive thought we keep our distance from the individual object sought. Instead of suspending our reasoning powers, we gather them. We turn the object of our thinking over and over. We poke at it. We probe. We see how it is or is not like other objects, looking at it from all perspectives. We see what is general within the particular rather than letting the particular speak for itself. It is a wandering about, a wary watching. It yields knowledge no less truthful than the contemplative. And, in fact, the process of such searching makes use of symbols and language, thus is regularly shared with others presumably in pursuit of truth also.

Jose Ortega y Gasset (1883–1955), the Spanish contemporary of the French Bergson, characterized the philosophic act as a tactical act not unlike the discursiveness of the hunt. Of his own study into the question, What is Philosophy? he noted that his work moved in "concentric circles, their radius growing shorter and developing a greater degree of tension each time we swing around . . . making no direct attack, circling slowly around them (philosophic problems)."[3] In another work, Ortega went so far as to say that by definition the hunter is the alert man, and that "like the hunter in the absolute *outside* of the countryside, the philosopher is the alert man in the absolute inside of ideas."[4]

We therefore find that the discursive philosophical act is an effort to capture, not contact. We hunt down our prey, keep a respectful distance, watch for signs of movement and presence, track our critter, all the while keeping our peripheral vision on the nuances of the surrounding landscape. We might be hunting down first order questions about the meaning of life, of justice, the good, or freedom; or we might be looking for the presuppositions of various models, systems, theories, or hypotheses. In any case, we remain alert to the movement of our prey. We aim to *capture*.

Cultivating the philosopher in us asks that we sharpen these capacities. With practice, perhaps with some training, we can take up the contemplative or the discursive on a regular basis. Rather than being victimized by these impulses (as our hamburger-eating friend might have been), we can learn to be the active agents of them. By contacting and by capturing ideas, to the extent that any human being can be, we are in a position to understand and know what can be understood and known.

USEFULNESS

The usefulness of the philosophic way of living—for philosophy is a way of living—lies in the subtle but powerful and important reversal of one's own thought patterns. Contrary to our more routine way of living which finds the philosopher in us more handicap than gift in that what is outside us usually determines what is inside us, cultivating the philosopher in us moves us from the inside out.

Many have said that a major part of living is the need to learn to be socialized. Education, for example, is taken to be an institution whereby human beings are taught the most essential social skills for getting on in society. Yet such thinking may lead to giving persons what they least need, for we are already quite thoroughly socialized well before the school age. It is far more customary that we take our views from others than that we create or discover them for ourselves. Over the years we are subject to others who influence us: parents parenting, ministers ministering, television reporters reporting, teachers teaching, book reviewers reviewing, politicians politicizing, friends befriending, and so on. Being socialized appears to be the least of our problems. We are thoroughly social. Perhaps coming to our own thoughts (by contact and capture) is more of a problem than we care to admit.

In cultivating the philosopher in us, it may be that we may not actually end up thinking all that differently from the parent, minister, teacher, or friend. But what is clearly necessary is that all of us learn to think for ourselves. And herein lies the reversal of our normal way of thinking. It is here that we run smack into the old Socratic "law" that the unexamined life—that is, a life without thinking from the inside out—is not worth living.

But the paradox of living the examined life is that the usefulness of it resides in its being instrumentally useless. In other words, we must not look in the usually "useful" (meaning instrumental) places for philosophy's usefulness. Doing philosophy will not necessarily make one richer in possessions or money. (Witness the income of the teachers who teach it!) Doing philosophy will not necessarily make one a better or more likable person. (Mussolini was a serious student of philosophy.) Doing philosophy will not necessarily give one a trouble-free life. (A number of professional philosophers have had absolutely frightful lives.)

In the end, doing philosophy (or living the circumspect, examined life) is its own reward. Philosophizing is the life source of all that is "useful," and hence cannot itself be "useful." The instrumental uselessness of living in the philosophical way is uniquely valuable and of transcendent usefulness.

This is not to deny the possibility that cultivating the philosopher in us may lead to riches, a well-developed personality, or a trouble-free life. For that matter, neither do we deny that hard and straight thinking on social problems, political theories, or ethical dilemmas ultimately can in fact be "useful" to the world at large. But the good which may come from doing philosophy does not account for our doing it.

We do philosophy because in some sense we have to. Developing the philosopher in us is more a matter of survival than of "usefulness." "If we cannot think," wrote the Trappist monk Thomas Merton, "we cannot act freely. If we do not act freely, we are at the mercy of forces which we never understand, forces which are arbitrary, destructive, blind, fatal to us and our world."[5]

So, what is philosophy? More than a school subject, learning to philosophize is learning a way of living. Useful? Yes, of course it is. But of intrinsic, not instrumental value. To philosophize is to accept that we do not know in advance where our thinking may lead us; we rarely even know what we seek in such thought. We trust that *our* "listening" and *our* "seeing" will guide our pleasures and our progress. The philosopher in us will speak the truth, if cultivated.

NOTES

1. Henri Bergson, *The Creative Mind* (New York: Citadel Press, 1946), p. 32.

2. Ibid., p. 161.

3. Jose Ortega y Gasset, *What Is Philosophy?* (New York: W. W. Norton, 1960), pp. 17–18.

4. Jose Ortega y Gasset, *Meditations on Hunting* (New York: Charles Scribner's Sons, 1972), p. 152.

5. Thomas Merton, *Conjectures of a Guilty Bystander* (New York: Doubleday, 1966).

PETER HEINEGG

Philosopher in the Playground: Notes on the Meaning of Sport

Down through the ages the athlete and the philosopher have never had much to say to each other. In 1970 half a billion people watched the final match of the World Cup soccer championship, but the intelligentsia must have missed the show. Nobody noticed that history's biggest experiment in simultaneous mass consciousness had just taken place—during a *game*. A casual glance at pro sports[1] might lead anyone not hopelessly naive to write the whole thing off as simply organized childishness or another phase of the quest for the almighty dollar. But there's more to it than this.

Of course, sports in this country *are* big business, a highly popular, handsomely packaged, and increasingly expensive consumer item. Players, as their annual wage disputes and occasional strikes remind us, are only members of a glamorous labor union, their inflated wages compensated by bruises, exhaustion, and merciless competition. Professional teams come equipped with a bristling array of bureaucrats, PR men, and capitalist owners, who sell stock in their enterprise, trade players, etc.

But if the people who make their living through sports are trapped in the gears of economic determinism, there is no reason why this should bother the spectator, least of all the living-room contemplative watching the game for free. Insulated from the struggle for survival and success that racks the participants, he can give himself up to purer pleasures. And yet, why does he, why do they, sit there by the tens—or hundreds—of millions staring at the tube? It is time for philosophy to break her silence and say something about this puzzling phenomenon.

Called upon to justify the hours spent indulging his vice, the literate fan might take an aesthetic tack: professional athletes perform with fabulous strength, speed, grace, and coordination. A well-executed power play, fast break, or kick-off return can be awesome.

Even the anti-fan will sometimes stop in his tracks in front of the TV set and admire despite himself. Talented players, clearly, go about their work with as much precision and brio as ballet dancers or violinists.

Originally appeared in *Southern Humanities Review* (1976).

Actually, athletes have an evolutionary superiority over artists. Poetry and French horn playing do not necessarily improve with time, but thanks to better nutrition, coaching, and equipment, players continually surpass their predecessors. The record-book, out of date as soon as published, shelters in its banal pages the myth of infinite perfectibility. Any middle-aged fan can testify that linemen and linebackers are not only bigger and stronger than their counterparts of a generation ago, they are even faster off the mark.

There are a handful of activities, such as dance and gymnastics, where art and sport seem to converge, but such analogies deceive as much as they enlighten. Art is a heightened form of life. Although it ushers us into a realm of fantasy, it always brings us back to earth, to the "real world." Sport, for all its simple-minded concreteness, is essentially a mode of escape from life. Great art inevitably turns to tragedy. Sport is utopian and comic.

One reliable touchstone to test the unreality of sport is sex. We may muse over the phallic quality of billiard cues or the symbolism of "stuffing" in basketball, but sport remains basically sexless. Relationships between men and women create tension and conflict (the very stuff of art), which is too serious for sport to cope with. Institutions that exclude or ignore sex, such as prisons, reform schools, army bases, or seminaries, encourage sports to distract their horny inhabitants. The locker room survives as one of the last unprofaned sanctuaries of maledom, i.e., where grown men can in good conscience behave like boys.

If art reveals the serious, sexually charged world to us by transforming it, sport sets out to build another world altogether. Observe the structure of most games. There is first of all an ideal space, the playing field or court. Here we have a tidy microcosm, carefully lined and ordered, set off from its workaday environment: nature humanized. While real life muddles along in opaque confusion, the ongoing action of sport is luminous, especially for the TV viewer with the advantage of instant replay. The home audience can analyze key plays at its leisure, in slow motion, and from more than one angle. The feeble human eye is suddenly divinized. Video tape fixes what might have flashed by in a peripheral blur, so that the Olympian spectator can pass judgment on it. The beauty and elegance of the fleeting moment are recalled, enjoyed, and then gratefully dismissed.

The soothing clarity of sport comes from its strict adherence to the rulebook. An elaborate system of regulations attends to every imaginable contingency and produces a state of utopian justice. For example, it was recently estimated, on the basis of game films, that calls made by N.F.L. officials were correct 98% of the time. Could any civil judiciary dare to claim such accuracy? And if, *per impossibile*, it did, how could it prove its case? Where else can one find such a flawlessly clear legal code, such quick and disinterested decisions? Where is there less bias, secrecy, or wire-pulling? Sport eliminates the suffering caused by the randomness of existence—the loose ends and ragged edges, the imbalances and anticlimaxes of everyday life. All men are aesthetes to some extent: they fly from the messiness of sick room, bedroom, factory, and market place to the artificial neatness of the playground.

Because of all the improvisation in sport there is enough room for novelty, upsets, flukes, and long shots—and without novelty deadly boredom would ensue. But sport restrains within reasonable bounds the chances that tyrannize human life. Real life may move the bases farther apart while you run them, or let your opponent field twice as many as your side, but sport does not. All in all, the playing field is probably the best place in the world to look for fair play.

Sport, then, is a flight from the pain of existence. As life is perpetual motion—change, growth, and decay—under the rule of time, sport is an attempt to fashion a world of stasis, or ecstasy, a standing apart from the river of time. Sport is a separate universe with a fully articulated structure which is a comic imitation of the real one; an ersatz Creation with both design and purpose (wholly arbitrary, yet consistent). Once you accept a few absurd axioms, everything else follows. Sport of necessity works with the raw materials of everyday life, its desires, energies, and obstacles, but it detoxifies them and renders them pleasurable. Take aggression, for instance. Sport is, among other things, a form of war. In games players can unleash and satisfy the lust for violence that the human race is so far from outgrowing. The spectators share vicariously in this instinctual release. Sport fulfills a perpetual masculine wish: a state of total war without death or serious injury. There are, to be sure, many degrees in the spectrum, from boxing to ping-pong, but violent conflict is always there, expressed or implied.

Sport is a pointless partisan struggle. (What does Green Bay have against Detroit?) It involves a sympathetic identification by the crowd or solitary viewer that can reach the point of frenzy, the end, as Nietzsche might put it, of the principle of individuation. Once again the flight from stern reality, from the shackles of the self to union with the corporate ego of the Home Team. Even when watching a game between unknown teams, the fan willy-nilly takes sides.

The fan roots out of anxiety over the outcome. The equivalent in "reality" to rooting is our concern with the endless cycle of worldly cares and crises. In the outside world we may win or lose any given contest, but new ones supervene to keep us agitated. A similar syndrome occurs in sport, inning after inning, game after game, but most fans feel no real pain, since the outcome makes no difference beyond the stadium walls. Once the score is final, the game has no more interest than an old newspaper. One may wish to review a few highlights, but no more.

The game exhausts itself in the playing. It is, like music, pure act, and produces no artefact. It is, and then is not. But in most concerts the player merely interprets the music of another man, the composer, whereas in sport he is a true innovator, responding to each situation as it comes along. Since this prevents any completely prepared patterns from arising, as in a rehearsed performance, the absorbing question is always "What next?" and the best game is the one which piles up the most brilliant, exciting *coups de théâtre*. But both the joys and the agonies of sport are shortlived (except for the players), which is as it should be. Sport generates a welter of vehement emotions, easily purged (a much better catharsis than tragedy) because they are so insubstantial.

The hero of Sartre's *Nausea* is oppressed and at times sickened by the maddening givenness of reality, its total factitiousness. Reality is *de trop*, a pointless, hypertrophied, overwhelming viscous chaos. To escape this meaningless monster, Roquentin has the habit of playing jazz records, but he might just as well have gone to a soccer match. The cheering throngs there undoubtedly contained many inarticulate sufferers from the same malaise. They (and the radio audience, if any) instinctively sought liberation in sport, and who can say who, the intellectual or the mob, made the better choice?

NOTE

1. And these days high quality in sports and professionalism are all but synonymous: you cannot field a first-rate team without paying it, one way or another. Consider the farce of the "amateur" Soviet national hockey team or the recruiting tactics of American college coaches.

KATHLEEN M. PEARSON

Deception, Sportsmanship, and Ethics

Physical educators, if they are to go beyond the lay person's grasp of their profession, must be willing to undertake the task of dissecting and analyzing the many concepts they employ. Some of the most common concepts with which we deal are only dimly understood. Worse yet, we seem content to live in this twilight world. Status as a profession demands that we make every effort to shine the light of analysis on the many fuzzy concepts with which we constantly must deal.

One of the more troublesome areas with which we struggle is the domain of ethics, and this seems particularly acute for those who work in athletics. I believe that some of the confusion surrounding the nature of ethical conduct in sport can be cleared up through an analysis of the concept of deception in athletics.

At the heart of every athletic activity is the attempt to successfully deceive one's opponent. The thesis presented here is that deception in athletics is not a simple, unitary event. Deception can be analyzed into at least two types: (a) Strategic Deception and (b) Definitional Deception. Finally, a rule of thumb can be established for deciding on the ethics of acts of deception which fall into those two categories.

STRATEGIC DECEPTION

Strategic deception occurs when an athlete deceives his opponent into thinking he will move to the right when he actually intends to move left— that he will bunt the baseball when he intends to hit a line drive—that he will drive the tennis ball when he actually intends to lob it. Examples of this sort of deception are replete in athletic events and need not be elaborated here. The important question is whether these acts of strategic deception are ethical or unethical.

In order to deal with this question, we need a rule of thumb for deciding on the ethics of an act. A standard for deciding if an act of deception is unethical is as follows: If an act is designed by a willing participant in an activity to deliberately interfere with the purpose of that activity, then that act can properly be labeled unethical.

Originally appeared in *Quest* (1973).

What is the purpose of athletic activities? Why even have such things as basketball games, football games, tennis games? I suggest that the purpose of these games, in an athletic setting, is to test the skill of one individual, or group of individuals, against the skill of another individual, or group of individuals, in order to determine who is more skillful in a particular, well defined activity.

How is any particular game defined? A particular game is no more (in terms of its careful definition) than its rules. The rules of one game distinguish it as being different from all other games. Some games may have quite similar rules; however, there must be at least one difference between the rules of one game and those of all other games in order for that game to be distinguished from all other games. If we were to find another game with exactly the same rules between the covers of its rulebook, we would naturally conclude that it was the same game. Thus, problems of identity and diversity of games are decided by the rules for each game. Identical games have identical rules and diverse games have differing rules. A game is identified, or defined, as being just that game by the rules which govern it.

If the purpose of athletics is to determine who is more skillful in a particular game, and if an unethical act is one which is designed to deliberately interfere with that purpose, it is difficult to see how acts of strategic deception could be called unethical. In fact, this sort of deception is at the heart of the skill factor in athletic events. It is the sort of activity which separates the highly skilled athlete from the less skilled athlete, and therefore, is the sort of activity that makes a significant contribution to the purpose of the athletic event. Strategic deception is in no way designed to deliberately interfere with the purpose of athletics.

DEFINITIONAL DECEPTION

Definitional deception occurs when one has contracted to participate in one sort of activity, and then deliberately engages in another sort of activity. An example of this sort of deception might occur if one were to sign a contract to teach political science, be assigned to a political science class, and then proceed to campaign for a particular political candidate.

How does this parallel an act which might be committed in an athletic setting? The paradigm used here suggests that: (a) Under certain circumstances, the commission of a foul in a game falls into the category of definitional deception; (b) Under certain circumstances, the act of fouling can be labeled as unsportsmanlike; and, (c) Certain kinds of fouls can be linked to acts which can be properly labeled as unethical.

It was established earlier that a game is identified, or defined, as being just that game by the rules which govern it. Furthermore, we are all familiar with the fact that it is in compliance with the rules of a particular game that we commit certain acts, while it is against the rules to commit other acts. When one commits an act that is not in compliance with the rules he is said to have committed a foul, and a prescribed penalty is meted out in punishment for that act. The ways in which fouls are committed in athletic contests can be separated into two categories. The first category consists of those fouls which are committed accidentally, and the second is composed of those fouls which are committed deliberately.

Let us first consider the case of accidental fouls. According to our rule of thumb, an act must be designed to deliberately interfere with the purpose of the activity in order for that act to be labeled unethical. Since the criterion of intentionality is missing from the accidental foul, that act has no ethical significance. We would ordinarily expect a person to accept the penalty for that foul, but we would not place moral blame on him.

Next, let us turn to the person who deliberately commits a foul while participating in an athletic contest. If the purpose of the contest is to determine who is more skillful in that game we can say that a player has entered into a contract with his opponent for the mutual purpose of making that determination. In other words, he has contracted with his opponent and the audience (if there is one) to play football, for instance, in order to determine who is more skillful in a game of football.

I have argued earlier that a particular game is defined by its rules—that the rules of a game are the definition of that game. If this is the case, a player who deliberately breaks the rules of that game is deliberately no longer playing that game. He may be playing "smutball," for instance, but he is not playing football. This is a case of deliberate definitional deception. These kinds of acts are designed to interfere with the purpose of the game in which they occur. How can it be determined which of two players (or teams) is more skillful in a game if one of the players (or teams) is not even playing that particular game? If the arguments presented here are correct thus far, we can conclude that the intentional commission of a foul in athletics is an unethical act. Ordinarily, when we refer to unethical acts on the part of athletes, we call these acts unsportsmanlike.

Someone might argue, at this point, that the penalties for fouling also are contained within the rulebook for a particular game, and therefore, fouls are not outside the rules for the game. The obvious rebuttal to this position is that penalties for breaking the law are contained within the law books, but no sensible person concludes, therefore, that all acts are within the law. If this were the case, there would be no sense in having laws at all. Similarly, if this were the case with games, there would be no sense in having rules for games. However, since the definition of a game is its rules, if there were no rules for that game there would be no game. Therefore, even though the penalties for fouling are contained within the rulebook for a game, the act of deliberate fouling is, indeed, outside the rules for that game.

When a teacher or coach has contracted with an institution and with individual students to teach those students how to play a particular game, he is violating that contract when he encourages deliberate definitional deception. The purpose of teaching or coaching a game is to help persons learn to play that game. An act which is deliberately designed to interfere with that purpose is an unethical act. It has already been argued that when a player commits an intentional foul in a game, he is no longer playing that game. Similarly, when a teacher or coach instructs players to commit an intentional foul, he is no longer teaching that game. He is committing an act which is deliberately designed to interfere with the purpose of the contract into which he has entered, i.e., to help students to learn to play that game. Thus, according to our rule of thumb, his conduct is properly labeled as unethical.

A variety of elegant arguments can be produced to indict the deliberate foul. It violates the ludic spirit, it treats the process of playing as mere instrument in the pursuit of the win, and it reflects a view of one's competitor as both enemy and object rather than colleague in noble contest. All of these pleas, however, fall short of the ultimate and most damaging testimony; deliberate betrayal of the rules destroys the vital frame of agreement which makes sport possible. The activity even may go on in the face of such fatal deception, but neither the logic of analysis nor the intuition of experience permit us to call whatever is left a game—for that is shattered.

WARREN FRALEIGH

Why the Good Foul Is Not Good

Understanding how rules function helps sports participants act appropriately and assists rulesmakers state and revise rules. Rules function in relation to a sports contest—an agreed-upon event in which two or more hu-

Originally appeared in *Journal of Physical Education, Recreation and Dance* (1982).

mans oppose one another in attempting to better the other's performance on the same test of moving mass in space and time by means of bodily moves which exhibit developed motor skills, physiological endurance, and socially approved tactics and strategy.[1,2]

How do rules operate to guarantee not only that the contest *exists* but that it may be the *good* contest? In general, rules function in three ways. First, rules contain positive prescriptions for what participants *must do* and what they are *allowed to do*. In basketball, for example, all participants *must* perform actions such as throwing, dribbling and batting the ball and *are allowed to* screen and to choose when they will dribble, pass, or shoot. These prescriptions describe what all other participants must do or can do; thus they define the agreed-upon test which all participants face. Such prescriptive rules may be labeled the *positively prescribed skills and tactics of the contest*.

Second, rules function to identify the within-the-contest goal toward which the performance of the positively prescribed skills and tactics is aimed. The within-the-contest goal in basketball is to throw the ball through your opponent's basket and to prevent the opponent from throwing it through yours. This is what Suits calls the pre-lusory goal of the game; that is, it is a goal which ". . . can be described before, or independently of, any game of which it may be, or come to be, a part."[3] When such a goal can be described and pursued independently from basketball, and is stated in the rules of basketball, *pre-lusory* takes on another meaning. Specifically, the goal of throwing the ball through your opponent's basket and preventing the opponent from doing it to you means that all participants *know* that all opposing participants will be trying to throw the ball through their basket and prevent them from doing the same *before* the contest begins. Thus rules prescribe both a pre-lusory goal and the lusory means by which that goal may be pursued.[4] These lusory means are described earlier in this article as the positively prescribed skills and tactics of the contest. Together, the pre-lusory goal of basketball and the positively prescribed skills and tactics, as stated in the rules, are agreed upon by all participants when they agree to "play basketball." Further, when people agree to play basketball they *know* that everyone else entering the agreement *knows* what the pre-lusory goal is and what the positively prescribed skills and tactics are. That is why basketball players do not ask "Shall we try to throw the ball through the basket?" or "Shall we dribble, pass, and screen?"

Third, rules function to proscribe certain illegal actions. This function is performed by rules statements which identify prohibited actions. Basketball rules, for example, prohibit double dribbles, holding, pushing, tripping, blocking, running with and kicking the ball. Negative proscriptions help to define sport. The inventor of the sport may eliminate certain skills and tactics from the sport, or rulesmakers may add new proscriptions based on the judgment that new skills are inconsistent with the nature of the sport. Basketball rules against goaltending and violations of the free throw lane by an offensive player are proscriptions added by rulesmakers after such actions occurred.

With respect to the contest, rules specify the goal-within-the-contest which all participants must necessarily pursue, the means all participants must use and are allowed to use in pursuing that goal, and the means all participants may not legally use to pursue the goal. These three kinds of rules function together, specifying what all participants in principle agree to when they enter a sport contest and what all participants know all other participants in principle agree to. The three functions of rules operate together to ensure that all participants face the same test mutually—that is, that they are *contesting*. Conversely, if *one* opponent fails to pursue the pre-lusory goal of the sport by not performing the required and permitted skills and tactics and/ or does perform the prohibited skills and tactics then all participants cannot be facing the same test and, thus, the participants cannot be contesting. Obviously participants who cannot be contesting cannot have a good contest.

If we understand that the sport rules function in three ways to ensure the basis for the good sports contest, then we can comprehend why it is crucial that all participants adhere to the *letter* and the *spirit* of the rules. Because the rules of sport are violated, however, it is necessary to analyze the effects of rules violations on the good sports contest. Essentially three types of rules violations affect the good sports contest. Most commonly, rules may be violated inadvertently and unintentionally. A basketball defensive player, attempting to attain or maintain a good defensive position against an opponent who feints and then dribbles toward the basket to score, trips the offensive player unintentionally. Inadvertent rules violation temporarily disrupts the good sports contest and does not destroy the agreed-upon mutual test of entering participants. Diligent practice of the positively prescribed skills and tactics of the sport can reduce the incidence of such inadvertent rules violation and enable sports contests to become good or better.

In the second type of rules violation, a participant knowingly and intentionally violates a rule to gain an advantage, but skillfully attempts to do so while avoiding a penalty. For example, a defensive basketball player can skillfully hold without detection an offensive pivot man so that he is unable to move to receive passes thrown to him. Or a golfer can improve his lie secretly, so that his next shot becomes easier to execute well. Such intentional rules violations constitute cheating and result in deliberate disruption of the agreed-upon mutual test. Cheating destroys the good sports contest because competing, winning and losing in athletics are intelligible only within the framework of rules which define a specific competitive sport; a person may cheat at a game or compete at it, but it is logically impossible for him to do both. To cheat is to cease to compete.[5]

A person who wins a contest as a consequence of cheating may *say* that he has won but, because cheating is not competing, he speaks incorrectly. In short, one may *correctly* say that a person wins only when he/she has been competing in the contest. The one who has been cheating may not claim victory.

The third type of rules violation occurs when a participant knowingly violates a rule to achieve what would otherwise be difficult to achieve, but violates the rules so as to expect and willingly accept the penalty. A "good" foul in basketball occurs where a defensive player, moving behind an offensive player with the ball who is dribbling for an easy lay up shot, intentionally holds the player, forcing him to shoot two free throws to make the same number of points. Such acts are called *good* because it is in the prudent self-interest of the fouling player to force the opponent to shoot twice from a greater distance to make the same number of points as would have been made by shooting once for a lay up. Violating the rules intelligently occurs if we consider *only* the self-interest of the offending player and team.

How does the "good foul" relate to the rules functions described earlier? The "good" foul is intentionally performing skills proscribed by the rules. Holding is proscribed in basketball rules; also among the proscriptions in basketball rules are intentional fouls which carry a penalty of two shots rather than one shot or one-and-one. But, it is argued, the appearance in the rules of statements about special penalties for intentional fouls makes such acts "part of the game" or "within the rules." It should be clear that the *spirit* of such rules as they were codified by rulesmakers was to eliminate or diminish such actions so that they would *not* be part of the positively prescribed skills and tactics of the game. In short, intentional holding, tripping, and so on is not part of the game or within the rules of basketball although, as stated above, it is at times rational and prudent to do such things when one's own self-interest is all that is considered.

How does the "good" foul relate, then, to the good sports contest? The good foul necessarily detracts from the good sports contest precisely because it changes the nature of the test being faced by all participants without clear agreement, in principle, that the test change is being agreed upon. For it cannot be established unequivocally that agreeing to play basketball means for *all* basketball participants that *everyone* will be performing the "good" foul. The "good" foul is a violation of the agreement which *all* participants know that *all* participants make when they agree to play basketball, namely, that all will pursue the pre-lusory goal of basketball by the necessary and allowable skills and tactics and will avoid use of proscribed skills and tactics.

Even the dominant pattern of socialization of basketball participants cannot avoid the detraction of the "good" foul from the good sports contest. Until such acts are established as agreement in principle by the positively prescribed rules and tactics, it cannot be stated unequivocally that all participants agree to performing the "good" foul by agreeing to play basketball. Agreeing to play basketball does not necessarily mean also agreeing to perform the "good" foul, but it necessarily entails the meaning of performing acts of dribbling, shooting, passing, and so on. In summary, then, intentional violation of the rules done for the purpose of achieving an end otherwise difficult to achieve, but performed in such a way that the violator expects to receive and willingly accepts the penalty, detracts from the good sports contest. Although such intentional violations, of which the "good" foul in basketball is used as *one* illustration, are "good" in terms of the rational self-interest of the violator, they are not good in terms of the good sports contest.

NOTES

1. This is a revised definition from Warren P. Fraleigh, "Sport-Purpose," *Journal of the Philosophy of Sport* 2 (1975), p. 78.
2. For a clear exposition on the nature of the sports contest see R. Scott Kretchmar, "From Test to Contest: An Analysis of Two Kinds of Counterpoint in Sport," *Journal of the Philosophy of Sport* 2 (1975), pp. 23–30.
3. Bernard Suits, "The Elements of Sport," in *The Philosophy of Sport*, ed. Robert G. Osterhoudt (Springfield, Ill.: Charles C. Thomas Publisher, 1973), p. 50.
4. Ibid., p. 51.
5. Edwin J. Delattre, "Some Reflections on Success and Failure in Competitive Athletics," *Journal of the Philosophy of Sport* 2 (1975), p. 136.

For a treatment of intentional rules violations see, also, Kathleen M. Pearson, "Deception, Sportsmanship, and Ethics," *Quest* 19 (January 1973), pp. 115–118; reprinted in this anthology, pp. 459–462.

Major concepts in this paper have been abstracted from Warren P. Fraleigh's book *Right Actions in Sport* (Champaign, Ill.: Human Kinetics Publishers, 1984).

CRAIG K. LEHMAN

Can Cheaters Play the Game?

A number of recent philosophers of sport have endorsed the thesis that it is logically impossible to win, or even compete, in a game while at the same time breaking one of its rules (intentionally, at least). For instance, Suits argues:

> The end in poker is not to gain money, nor in golf simply to get a ball into a hole, but to do these things in prescribed (or, perhaps more accurately, not to do them in proscribed) ways: that is, to do them only in accordance with rules. Rules in games thus seem to be in some sense inseparable from ends. . . . If the rules are broken, the original end becomes impossible of attainment, since one cannot (really) win the game unless he plays it, and one cannot (really) play the game unless he obeys the rules of the game. (5: pp. 149–150)

The thesis that cheating in a game is logically incompatible with winning that game may sound initially plausible. I imagine everyone has a vague feeling of having heard it somewhere before—perhaps in high school physical education—but I am going to argue that it is false. Undoubtedly, following some "framework" rules is essential to playing any particular game as we know it, and even violation of rules covering "finer points" may in some cases lead us to say that no game worthy of the name has taken place, no real winner been determined. But counterexamples to the unqualified incompatibility thesis advocated by Suits and others (1, 4) are not hard to come by.

I

Consider, first, what people ordinarily say about certain sporting events in which deliberate violations of the rules are known (or at least thought) to take place. (I take it for granted that the issue here is the conventional meaning of such phrases as "compete in a game," "win a game," "deliberately violate the rules of a game," etc. Of course someone can stipulate a sense in which it is impossible for cheaters to "really" win, but the nontrivial question is whether this conclusion is implicit in the ordinary meanings of the words.)

Originally appeared in *Journal of the Philosophy of Sport* (1981).

For instance, many baseball fans believe that Atlanta Braves' pitcher Gaylord Perry throws a spitball. Throwing a spitball is a violation of the rules of baseball. Suppose these fans are right about Perry. Does anyone seriously want to say that no baseball game is ever played when Perry pitches? Should Perry be ineligible for the Hall of Fame on the grounds that he has never won a game, let alone competed, in baseball? Yet this seems to follow if we accept the unqualified thesis that cheating and competing are incompatible. And, of course, cases like Perry's—many of them more elaborate, some of them legendary—can be multiplied indefinitely.

A second point is as follows: Why, if Suits's argument is sound, should only *intentional* violation of rules be relevant to the question of whether genuine participation in a certain game (and hence victory) has taken place? (In the first sentence of this essay, I tried to be charitable by adding intention as a parenthetical condition of the logical-incompatibility thesis, but it will be noted that Suits himself does not say this.) The major premise of Suits's argument, after all, is just that one cannot play a game without following the rules of that game; or in the words of another proponent (4: p. 117) of the incompatibility thesis, "the rules of a game are the definition of that game." But the failure of something to conform to an established definition or set of rules is not abolished by the absence of an intention to nonconformity on the part of its creator. If I draw a four-sided figure with sides of unequal lengths, then I have failed to draw a square, even if I intended to make the sides equal. Thus, it seems that even unintentional violations of the rules of a game should lead us to say that no game (and hence no victory) has occurred, if the usual argument for the logical-incompatibility thesis is correct.

This points the way to more counterexamples. Amateurs almost certainly commit unwitting violations of some rule or other in any game they play, especially while learning. Even in major professional sports, sharp-eyed commentators (and instant replays) often expose accidental violations of the rules, but no one is tempted to say that no game has therefore occurred. Indeed, in team sports, the presence of just one secret cheater on a squad whose members otherwise intend to follow the rules religiously would render the whole team logically incapable of winning.

Let me approach the matter from a different direction. In "Some Reflections on Success and Failure in Competitive Athletics," Delattre, another defender of the logical-incompatibility thesis, remarks:

Both morally and logically, then, there is only one way to play a game. [That is, by the rules.] Grantland Rice makes clear his appreciation of this point in his autobiography, *The Tumult and the Shouting*. For emphasis, he employs the example of a rookie professional lineman. The athlete responds to Rice's praise for his play during his rookie year by observing that he will be better when he becomes more adept at holding illegally without being caught. Of course, to Rice this confused vision of successful competition is heartbreaking. (1: p. 137)

Now, admittedly, I cannot quite work up a broken heart over this incident, but that is not the main point. My question is rather, what kind of confusion did Rice think his lineman had falley prey to—conceptual confusion, of the sort which fails to notice the impossibility of round squares and married bachelors, or (alleged) moral confusion of the sort which places winning (or, more precisely, "winning") ahead of playing strictly by the rules? The thesis that cheating and competing are logically incompatible would require the former interpretation (and then, perhaps, we should think of the lineman as heartbreakingly stupid), but I strongly suspect that Rice was disappointed in his lineman's alleged moral confusion. I also suspect that the logical-incompatibility thesis draws part of its appeal from being conflated with the moral thesis; Delattre, for instance, speaks of Rice as appreciating "this point," when there are really two points involved.

II

When one cannot see a pattern to them, counterexamples often seem like trivial nit-picking. In this case, however, I think there is a clear pattern, though perhaps not a particularly profound one. The counterexamples all seem to stem from social custom or convenience (i.e., utility). Games are played within a framework of social practices and priorities, and violations of rules must be assessed within this framework to determine whether competition and victory, in the normal sense of the words, have occurred.

Hence, the spitball and offensive holding are a part of the game of baseball and football, respectively, and are techniques sometimes practiced by winners in those sports. Custom seems the primary reason why a game in which the spitball rule is violated is still baseball: The folklore of the game abounds with gleefully told stories of doctored pitches, bats, playing fields, etc., and booing the umpire (i.e., the embodiment of the rules) is a hallowed tradition. On the other hand, the fact that offensive holding can occur in a game of football seems to be mainly a concession to utility: There is simply no practical way for the officials to see everything that occurs in the interior of the line, and the game would probably be much less enjoyable to watch if all the infractions were punished (i.e., the offense would be continually frustrated by penalties, if not by the defensive line).

Of course, as I conceded at the outset, a game cannot be played if too many of its rules are violated. There would be no point in calling an activity a game of baseball if none of the rules of baseball were followed, and it is certainly hard to imagine the point when only a few of the rules are followed. Admittedly, too, one can imagine a society of sanctimonious sports purists who allow that a certain game is played only if every rule of that game is strictly followed. But perfect adherence to every rule is not usually essential to the occurrence of a given game, with a genuine winner.

Between the two extremes of angelic obedience to rules and destruction of a game by wholesale violation of its rules is an interesting set of borderline cases, as in professional wrestling: Here, rules against punching, kicking, strangling, etc., are routinely violated, so that even if the outcome were not fixed, there would be considerable question about whether the resulting show was wrestling. In the social context of certain ultra-violent science-fiction movies, the objective of sport usually seems to be the provision of spectacles of mayhem; perhaps in those societies, "illegal" biting and choking would seem as innocuous as the spitball does in American baseball. But in the actual context of our society, I am not sure what to say about professional wrestling.

So, although I concede that at some (probably hard-to-define) point, excessive rule violations become incompatible with playing a given game, and that there also may be certain ideal cases in which exacting conformity to rules is essential, I maintain that (due to social custom and convenience) it is not in general necessary to the playing or winning of games that every rule of those games be obeyed. Pearson(4: p. 116), however, yet another defender of the logical-incompatibility thesis, remarks that "a particular game is no more (in terms of its careful definition) than its rules." She then goes on, in best Lockean fashion,[1] to state the corollary that "problems of identity and diversity of games are decided by the rules for each game. Identical games have identical rules and diverse games have differing rules." But if I am correct, it should be possible to imagine different games with identical rules (because they are played in the context of different social customs and utilities), and identical games with differing rules (because social customs and utilities negate the difference of rules "in practice"). For example, it seems conceivable (although I do not know this to be the case) that Japanese baseball players are much more earnest about following the rules of the game than American players are. If the spitball were more widely used than it is in American baseball, and if its effect were greater than I think it is, I can easily imagine a Japanese player saying that, because of the spitball, Americans play a different game. In my view, this would be the literal truth rather than just a manner of speech. Also, of course, it is simple to imagine the cases of differential enforcement of rules canceling out differences in rules.

III

So far I have been concentrating on the thesis that cheating and competing are logically incompatible. But the logical-incompatibility thesis often serves as a premise (or at least a background assumption) in moral arguments designed to show that cheating is, without qualification, unethical and/or unsportsmanlike. I therefore want to conclude this essay with a brief examination of one such argument.

The most explicitly worked-out version of this argument that I know of is advanced by Pearson:[2]

> I have argued earlier that a particular game is defined by its rules—that the rules of a game are the definition of that game. If this is the case, a player who deliberately breaks the rules of that game is deliberately no longer playing that game. . . . These acts [i.e., deliberate violations of rules] are designed to interfere with the purpose of the game. If the arguments presented here are correct thus far [and it has been asserted earlier that (1) "the purpose of these games is to test the skill of one individual, or group of individuals, against another . . ." and (2) "If an act is designed by a willing participant in an activity to interfere with the purpose of that activity, then that act can properly be labeled unethical"] we can conclude that the intentional commission of a foul ["an act that is not in compliance with the rules"] in athletics is an unethical act. Ordinarily, when we refer to unethical acts on the part of athletes, we call these acts unsportsmanlike. (4: pp. 116–117)

The major premise of this argument [i.e., item (2) in the brackets] is reminiscent of Kant's second illustration of the first form of the categorical imperative; Pearson also speaks elsewhere of players entering into a contract with their opposition. Obviously, however, discussion of such fundamental principles is beyond the scope of this essay. I grant them for the sake of argument. But consider the other premises.

Understood narrowly enough, I would have no quibble with the assertion that the rules of a game "define" that game; my point has only been that in certain contexts, breaking the rules that "define" a game will not entail that one is not playing that game. Suppose, however, that I am wrong, and the logical-incompatibility thesis is correct. It will still not follow that a player who deliberately breaks the rules of a game is deliberately no longer playing that game. For "deliberately" introduces an intentional context, and validity is not preserved in intentional contexts. (The man behind the arras was Polonius, but it does not follow that in deliberately killing the man behind the arras, Hamlet was deliberately killing Polonius.) Similarly, if someone is too "confused" to appreciate the logical-incompatibility thesis, he or she may deliberately violate a rule without deliberately opting out of the game.

Still, someone might reply, this is irrelevant to Pearson's main point. If her ethical major premise is correct, and if the purpose of games is to test the skill of the participants, then if we just add the premise that someone who deliberately violates the rules of a game is deliberately interfering with a test of the skill of the participants, without trying to deduce it from the logical-incompatibility thesis, the conclusion can still be secured. To be sure, some qualifications might be needed to take care of cases in which rules are deliberately broken for some unusual reason, but the idea would be that in deliberately throwing a spitball (or so we suppose), Perry is deliberately interfering with a test of the batter's skill at hitting a (legal) pitch. In general, cheaters know very well that they are trying to minimize an opponent's chances in a test of skill.

Nevertheless, even if these emendations are allowed, I think the argument is still infected with the same disease I was trying to cure in the last section. For how does one establish that *the* purpose of a game is a test of its participants' skill? So far as I can see, only by supposing a certain romanticized social context in which custom and convenience dictate that games are played solely to test the players' skill within a certain framework of rules. But that, I would argue, is not the social context of most sports as *we* know them. Indeed, to the extent that it is intelligible to talk of sports having purposes at all (an assumption which apparently goes undefended), sports seem to be multipurpose. Baseball, for example, serves the purposes of providing an income for owners and players, an afternoon's diversion for the casual fan, another installment in a unique kind of larger-than-life drama for a passionate devotee of "the national pastime." Of course, competing in or observing an event in which there are tests of skill basically within the framework of a set of (very complicated) rules is a main purpose of almost everyone concerned with baseball, but a pure test of skill featuring saintly observance of every rule is *the* purpose of baseball only to a few purists.

Thus, I think that Pearson's attempt to derive unsportsmanlike conduct from some kind of frustration of the purpose or goal of a game implicitly falls victim to the same oversight as the thesis that cheating and competing are logically incompatible: It assumes that one can read off what a game (or the purpose of a game) is just by examining the rule book. Admittedly, rule books for games do not contain statements of purposes for those games. But they do set down conditions for winning, and they do proceed on the assumption that the rules are rigorously followed; this makes the hypothesis that the purpose of a game is to determine a winner according to its rules by far the most obvious hypothesis.

I suspect, then, that no argument that makes deliberate violation of rules a sufficient condition for unsportsmanlike conduct is likely to apply to many of the sports we know. And this seems to me as it should be: I have no reason to believe that Perry, if he throws a spitball, or offensive linemen, if they hold, are generally regarded as poor sports by their peers or the fans. On the contrary, it seems likely that many of them are regarded as displaying all the essentials of good sportsmanship. Sportsmanship seems to transcend the rulebook, not only in the sense of sometimes requiring more than adherence to the rules, but also in the sense of sometimes permitting less.

NOTES

1. See (3), esp. Bk. II, Ch. 27, sec. 8, "Idea of Identity suited to the Idea it is applied to."
2. For similar views, see (1, 2). Keating does not defend the logical-incompatibility thesis, but he does tie unsportsmanlike conduct to frustration of the goal of sport.

BIBLIOGRAPHY

1. Delattre, Edwin J. "Some Reflections on Success and Failure in Competitive Athletics." *Journal of the Philosophy of Sport* 2 (1975), 133–139.
2. Keating, James W. "Sportsmanship as a Moral Category." *Ethics* 75 (October 1964), pp. 25–35.
3. Locke, John. *Essay Concerning Human Understanding.* Many editions.
4. Pearson, Kathleen. "Deception, Sportsmanship, and Ethics." *Quest* 19 (January 1973), 115–118. Reprinted in this anthology, pp. 459–462.
5. Suits, Bernard. "What is a Game?" *Philosophy of Science* 34 (June 1967), 148–156.

HANS LENK

Prolegomena Toward an Analytic Philosophy of Sport

The analytic philosophy of sport is still in its infancy, but it turns out to have a growing significance. In this short contribution of a rather tentative and limited purpose I shall deal critically with some earlier papers regarding definitional problems and questions of theory construction in the analytic philosophy of sport. I maintain that the general perspective of analytic philosophy has to be broadened beyond the restrictive "ordinary language" brand to guarantee fruitful results. After the looming pragmatic turn, analytic philosophy has to take into account not only scientific results but also practical problems of everyday life in their situational, cultural and social context. This is also true for the analytic philosophy of sport, which should not restrict itself to merely definitional problems without considering their contexts, should not confound definitions and explications, and should also not put aside the construction of theory.

I shall mainly discuss the papers "Sport: The Diversity of the Concept," by Fogelin (1968), "Toward a Non-Definition of Sport," by McBride (1975), and "Toward a Non-Theory of Sport," by Kleinman (1968), and later shall give an example of a helpful application of analytic models for the evaluation of sporting achievements, as outlined by Schubert in his dissertation "Evaluation Problems in Sport Competition" (1980).

Starting from the definition "Sports is the sort of thing written about on sports pages," Fogelin criticizes essentialistic interpretations of sport and sports definitions: traditional philosophy of sport would confound sport language and the philosophical analysis of sport language, thereby falsely hypothesizing a substantial philosophy of sport. Instead, philosophical analysis of sport, according to Fogelin, can only be a Wittgensteinian descriptive analysis of the language of sport.

However, Wittgenstein's *practise* of the philosophy of language games was more creative than his conservative, purely descriptive program of philosophy, which is in fact oriented toward abolishing philosophy. Analytic philosophy has already followed, and will (and should) increasingly follow

Appeared in earlier form in *International Journal of Physical Education* (1981).

Wittgenstein's *practise* in developing substantial approaches, in considering historical and cultural traditions, in contriving language reform proposals and in critically reflecting scientific results. Fogelin, e.g., sticks to a very narrow understanding of analytic philosophy, too strict for an Oxfordianism. He does not get in touch with pragmatic problems of sport practise. Moreover an analysis isolated from theoretical concepts will also turn out to be too abstract to be really meaningful. Since definitional problems only make sense if pertaining to a theoretic framework, not just to problems of language, Fogelin suffers from a negative definitional fallacy and from a too simple theoretic isolationism. Concepts of a family resemblance character like "sport" only function if they are integrated into a seemly theoretic or pragmatic framework. Then, actually, one will find out that sport is indeed *not* "the sort of thing written about on sport pages." He who only knows the sport pages does not know very much about sport. He certainly gets a distorted definition and interpretation.

In a certain sense McBride's critical remarks about a nondefinition of sport also commit the fallacy of theoretic isolationism insofar as he dwells on definitional problems regarding the one expression "sport" without considering the context of problems and theory. This isolationism seems to treat concepts as fetishes, so to speak, rather than as practical problems. He stresses that a precise lexical definition of "sport" will either be too narrow and at the same time too broad in different perspectives, or will end up as a purely stipulative definition. McBride argues by examples like the following one: a definition of sport as "voluntary, having rules, and involving a test of how physically excellent a person can be" will be too narrow (for certain forms of fishing don't test physical excellence) and too broad at the same time (army volunteering meets these features, too). But the concept "sport" is not only vague but also ambiguous (there are for example 127 different usages of "sport" and 176 of "game" listed in the *Oxford English Dictionary*). Therefore, McBride concludes, philosophers should not waste their time attempting a logically impossible task—searching for a precise definition comprising all relevant ordinary language usages of "sport."

However, it can be shown that McBride himself looks for the impossible while confounding explications and definitions and overlooking the general aporia of explication. Any precise explication of a species concept (of a complex social phenomenon at least) is a selective reconstruction and therefore does not encompass *all* the nuances of the vague and ambiguous ordinary language usage. This does not imply that explications and definitions are not possible at all or useless. Indeed, explicative analyses of imprecise concepts are especially important—in order, e.g., to be able to find out the vagueness, ambiguities, incompatibilities, ideological prejudices, etc., and to compare the adequacy of different explications of the same concept. These problems of explicating species concepts are fairly general in all social sciences and humanities; they do not pose any special problem of knowledge for the concept of sport. One should not require the impossible (to convey an explication which is precise and all-comprehensive, covering all established nuances of usage at the same time) and then imply that it is logically impossible to give an explication (or "definition" in that wider sense). This would certainly amount to rendering senseless analytic philosophy in general and an analytic philosophy of sport in particular. On the contrary, we urgently need conceptual analyses and explications (as well as more precise theoretical "stipulative" definitions) in this realm of sport analysis. It is neither logically impossible to (stipulatively) define and to explicate the concepts of "sport," nor to judge the comparative adequacy of the explication or expediency of the definition.

Kleinman in his article "Toward a Non-Theory of Sport" (1968) even extends his criticism regarding the non-definability of "sport" to the thesis that even a theory about sport would be impossible, since sport does not possess a set of necessary and sufficient properties. A theory, however, he thinks would have to provide a "complete explanation" of all characteristic features of sport—which would not be possible if there is no clear-cut set of these essential features.

Kleinman not only exaggerates McBride's concept fetishism but also misunderstands, misinterprets and really overcharges the tasks and functions of a theory. A theory is not a panacea to solve all problems whatsoever by combining complete precision with total comprehensiveness. No theory is all-comprehensive. Any theory has its limits, leaves out some aspects, is to a certain degree a tentative construction. Philosophical theories in particular cannot offer total, complete, and exact explanations; but they should describe important structural and functional features of their subjects by providing an ideal model of conceptualizations and symbolizations in a contextual framework.

Instead of banning theories and theoretical descriptions *per se* one should favor theoretical approaches with a pluralistic and multifunctional perspective which is adequate for dealing with a complex phenomenon. One need not overstress exactness and overcharge theories. Even theories with "blurred edges" may sufficiently work in that regard.

Kleinman favors phenomenological description instead. However, he does not take into account that non-comprehensive description using classifications and symbolic or even abstract concepts still can not dispense with theory and theoretical foundations. If this theoretical impregnation is not stated or seen, it will remain implicit. That means that philosophers merely rely on hidden theoretical concepts of a "naive theory" (in the terminology of the new cognitive psychology). Phenomenological description is certainly a necessary step and a starting point for working out a philosophical interpretation, but is not the last and only word. To take it as such would mean not only an unjustified monopolistic claim but an unintentional undercutting of traditional totally essentialistic conceptions. Theory-free essence, however, being both utopian and useless, remains a mystical or even mythical hypothesized fiction.

To give an example indicating how helpful methods and models of analytic philosophy, including the logic of relations and preference, could be if applied to philosophic interpretations of sport, I chose the problem of judging, grading and ranking sporting achievements. Schubert in his Ph.D. dissertation (1980) succinctly scrutinizes and analyzes several models underlying different models of judgment on sports.

The model of "classical competition" only allows for one and, wherever possible, only one singular victor or winner: "Surpass all competitors!" is accordingly the norm. This model even introduces artificial and fictional differentiation if the achievements of two athletes are equal (e.g. in high jump or weightlifting). By contrast, the so-called "dimensional competition" always ranks equal all the athletes with equal achievements in an event, under the slogan "Reach for the maximum dimension (maximized possible achievement)!" There are no vacant ranks here. Also the modified model of "mitigated competition," following the slogan "Try not to be surpassed by others," basically allows for more than one, even many winners—and there need not be an out-classed loser as in classical competition. Schubert also discusses so-called "exam-like events," contending that records somehow show the characteristic structure of this model. In addition, basis-competition and meta-competition (consisting of a ranking according to the grading and number of wins in several respective basic competitive events) are discussed. He pleads for a meta-competition model for the all-round competitions in track and field, gymnastics, etc.

According to the different analytic models there are different possible ways of filling the ranks in judging a competition, some even allowing for interspersed vacant ranks (e.g. in the classical or mitigated competition models). As to the structure of maximum rank coverage, the classical model is similar to a pyramid (with the winner or victor on top) whereas the models of mitigated and dimensional competitions are similar to an inverted pyramid. By contrast, the exam-like type of events shows a maximum structure of rank-coverage in the form of a square. There might be no single winner (since it is so to speak no competition at all) but one or even many "masters."

Turning to all-round competitions, it is interesting that one and the same running of a set of events can lead to a different winner depending on which model is selected for evaluation. Schubert constructed an informative example for speed skating in which a different athlete is pronounced victor, if you interpret the compound event as a basis-competition, than if you understand it as a meta-competition. Schubert pleads for the meta-competition model: the decision, despite an equal overall result in terms of points, to give the Olympic gold medal in the women's track and field pentathlon in Montreal to one competitor because she was better than her rival in three of the five events would have been right therefore. On the other hand, it would not be possible any longer to compensate weakness in one by strong achievements in other sub-events—which somehow seems to belong to the idea of an all-round competition. The question is how to interpret all-round competition: as a model only of a balanced manysidedness and positive versatility *without* compensation or as an all-round competition *with* the possibility of compensating unbalanced ability or weakness in any event. In addition, world records would logically no longer be possible in all-round competitions if these were taken as meta-competitions. The rules of the pentathlon in athletics (or decathlon, likewise) seem to show a funny mixture of dimension competition with a secondary meta-competition character in case of equal outcomes— apparently motivated by the imperative norm of classical competition, i.e. the "Achilles complex" (Segal): "Always to be the very best, distinguished from every one else"* (Homer, *Iliad* VI, 208; XI, 794).

Indeed, for a simple judgment of sporting adequacy or "justice" of evaluation, it seems to be unfair, unseemly, or even illogical to assign different ranks when competitors earn equal points in an additive event (i.e. an event which sums up points earned).

Obviously, then, different social *philosophical* attitudes or norms underlie the rules of sports and games. A classically harsh orientation toward distinguishing a singular victor—as in the K.O. system—displays quite another basic philosophical tendency than, say, the exam-like type which may produce many "masters" as, e.g., in the German Gymnastics Festival or the pupils' Federal Youth Games. There, the harshness of singular-victor-orientation is mitigated to allow many to be winners (i.e. "masters"). This seems to be very appropriate, social-philosophically speaking.

The exam-like type is much better compatible with sporting partnership, instead of exacerbated sporting opposition which sometimes today seems almost to lead to real *enmity*. In view of the ever-growing exacerbation of top-

---

*"Αἰὲν ἀριστεύειν καὶ ὑπείροχον ἔμμεναι ἄλλων."

level sports competitions it may turn out to be wise to recommend such a moderating model as the mitigated or the dimensional competition.

In summary one may get the insight that approaches and models of analytic philosophy could be fruitfully applied to sport—even such simple models of preference logic as those mentioned. Definitions and discussions of bare concepts, however, do not suffice; one must utilize hypotheses, theoretical models, theoretical concepts if not theories—maybe theories in the "embryonic state" (Feyerabend once wrote that metaphysical theories are scientific theories in their embryonic state)—to lend the capacity of useful differentiation and practical relevance to the necessary development of an analytic philosophy of sport.

BIBLIOGRAPHY

Best, D. *Philosophy and Human Movement*. London, 1975.

Fogelin, R. J. "Sport: The Diversity of the Concept." In *Sport and the Body*. Edited by E. W. Gerber. Philadelphia, 1972. 58–61.

Kleinman, S. "Toward a Non-Theory of Sport." *Quest* (1968), No. 10, 29–34.

Lenk, H. *Leistungssport: Ideologie oder Mythos?* Stuttgart u.a., 1972. (2d ed. 1974.)

Lenk, H. "Bemerkungen zur Notwendigkeit einer philosophischen Analyse des Sports und der Leistungsmotivation." In *Philosophie des Sports*. Edited by H. Lenk, S. Moser, and E. Beyer. Schorndorf, 1973. 9–21.

Lenk, H. *Sozialphilosophie des Leistungshandelns*. Stuttgart u.a., 1976.

Lenk, H. "Zu Coubertins olympischen Elitismus." *Sportwissenschaft* 6 (1976), 404–424.

Lenk, H. *Metalogik und Sprachanalyse*. Freiburg, 1973.

Lenk, H. *Pragmatische Philosophie*. Hamburg, 1975.

Lenk, H. *Team Dynamics*. Champaign, Ill.: Stipes, 1977.

Lenk, H. *Pragmatische Vernunft*. Stuttgart, 1979.

Lenk, H. *Social Philosophy and Athletics*. Champaign, Ill.: Stipes, 1979.

McBride, I. "Toward a Non-Definition of Sport." *Journal of the Philosophy of Sport* 2 (1975), 4–11.

Moser, S. "Analyse des Sports (1945–46)." In *Philosophie des Sports*. Edited by H. Lenk, S. Moser, and E. Beyer. Schorndorf, 1973. 138–162.

Ortega y Gasset, J. "Der Sportliche Ursprung des Staates." In his *Gesammelte Werke*. Stuttgart, 1954. Vol. 1, 428–449.

Ortega y Gasset, J. "Über des Lebens sportlichfestlichen Sinn." In *Jahrbuch des Sports* 1955–56. Frankfurt, 1956. 9–20.

Osterhoudt, R. G. (ed.). *The Philosophy of Sport*. Springfield, Ill., 1973.

van Peursen, C. A. *Phänomenologie und analytische Philosophie*. Stuttgart u.a., 1969.

Rescher, N. *Methodological Pragmatism*. New York, 1977.

Schubert, E. *Wertungsprobleme im Sportwettbewerb*. Vienna, 1980.

Suits, B. *The Grasshopper: Games, Life and Utopia*. Toronto, 1978.

VanderZwaag, H. J. *Toward a Philosophy of Sport*. Reading, Mass., 1972.

Weiss, P. *Sport: A Philosophic Inquiry*. Carbondale, Ill.: 1969.

Weiss, P. "Records and the Man." In *The Philosophy of Sport*. Edited by R. G. Osterhoudt. Springfield, Ill., 1973. 11–23.

Wittgenstein, L. *Philosophische Untersuchungen*. In his *Schriften*, Vol. 1. Frankfurt, 1960.

Zeigler, E. F. "Eine Analyse der These, dass 'Physical Education' zu einem Begriff der 'Familienähnlichkeit' geworden ist." In *Wissenschaftstheoretische Beiträge zur Sportwissenschaft*. Edited by K. Willimczik. Schorndorf, 1979. 158–173.

HANS LENK

Action Theory and the Social Scientific Analysis of Sport Actions

In this paper I intend to show, by epistemological argument and by providing a few examples, how the extensive discussion of the analytical philosophy of action can illuminate social scientific approaches to the analysis of sport.

Let me begin by sketching some of the main dividing lines between the different positions in the analytic philosophy of action, and then describing a new interpretive model of an action theory approach. This new approach seems capable of overcoming most of the difficulties, anomalies, and even contradictions of the traditional action theoretic models underlying social scientific analyses of action. In particular, my analysis suggests that purely behavioristic approaches do not suffice for a full-fledged social scientific analysis of meaningful actions guided by social norms, values, conventions, symbols, etc.

In the analytic philosophy of action three main controversies mark the state of the discussions to date. These are the controversies between:

1) Causalists and logical intentionalists;

Appeared in earlier form in *International Journal of Physical Education* (1979).

2) Particularists and generalists (or repetitionists);

3) Pluralists and reductionists.

Let me give a brief summary of these three controversies.

1) Whereas the logical intentionalists (e.g. A. I. Melden, C. Taylor, R. Taylor, G. H. von Wright) think that there is a logical connection between the concept of an action and the concept of its motivating intention, inasmuch as the intention and the action itself cannot be described independently of one another from a logical point of view, causalists (such as R. M. Chisholm, A. Danto, D. Davidson) think that there are logically independent internal causes contingently causing the action.

The new interpretational and component theoretic approach to be outlined shortly will lead to the result that both these views, if taken strictly, are wrong, but that both are right to a certain degree. Logical intentionalists are right in claiming that there is a conceptual bond between the description of an action and the description of its "grounds," "reason," "motivation," or its mental components in general, inasfar as the set of these components cannot be conceived of as a logically independent cause of the action. As components they are part and parcel of the action description. However, single components can and will depend on independently describable (for example, other physiological) events, which may be construed as causally though not logically necessary conditions of a movement corresponding to an action.

2) Whereas particularists, such as M. Brand, Danto, and Davidson, conceive actions as single and singular, unrepeatable concrete events which can be uniquely identified in space and time, generalists like Chisholm and particularly A. Goldman think that single action events merely exemplify general actions as abstracts, i.e. as repeatable, instantiable entities, which cannot be uniquely characterized in time, but are dependent on findings and statements, i.e. descriptions. (This also holds true, by the way, for events and facts.)

If you choose a descriptive constituent or component approach, this controversy turns out to be a bit terminological in character. The events related by an action description, and their components, may be assigned to a single event-point in time and space, though their description has to take into account general expressions of action properties and action types, without which characterization of the action will be impossible.

3) Whereas reductionists (as again among others Chisholm, Danto, Davidson) claim that there is only a unique sort of entities (namely "bodily movements") characterizing an action and that each statement about actions can be reduced to statements about such primitive movements, pluralists (primarily Goldman) would necessarily assign different actions to different action

descriptions, even if there is only one and the same movement to which both descriptions refer.

One can easily understand that both positions, if taken strictly, are led into grave difficulties. Neither the one-sided reductionist position dealing only with physical movements nor the proliferating world of abundant ontological types of actions (violating Occam's razor principle) can cope with the ramifying variations of real actions and their connection with conceptualizations and descriptions.

A descriptive or interpretational approach, however, can cope with these difficulties without resorting to either too simple or too abundant an ontology of action entities.

Now what are the main suggestions of such a descriptive or interpretational approach combined with a component model like the one recently (1977) developed by I. Thalberg? In his book *Perception, Emotion, and Action* Thalberg suggests not conceiving actions as the sum of movements and additional mental acts (e.g. acts of willing) but understanding the mental phenomena intertwined with the action and its characterization as necessary ingredients, as components or constituent parts, of the action. (Constituent parts cannot be causes but can be correlates of, say, physiological causes.) The set of components, so to speak, defines and identifies the action as such.

Yet Thalberg never distinguishes between sorts of components of an action: the physical or physiological components are treated on a par with psychic or psychological or even social elements. And what is their ontological status, which they must surely have if understood in such a naive and direct way? Undoubtedly one has to add a semantic dimension to avoid these ontological difficulties and moreover to really cope with the details of the social sciences.

Actions are not simply physical movements. This has long been known except by hard-core reductionists and materialists. But what would remain if you subtract the physical movement from an action, what has to be added to a physical movement to make an action? This was a famous question of the later L. Wittgenstein's *Philosophical Investigations* (1960, §621). Wittgenstein answered: "nothing"—i.e. nothing which is existent in an ontological sense, no extra psychic act like a special act of will (H. R. Prichard). But certainly a plain physical movement (e.g. a reflex) *per se* is not an action. Therefore something has to be added. But not necessarily something physical or ontologically mental, no additional act which would really reopen the question of the nature of the action. (To be sure, there may be—and usually are—special nerve impulses, etc., material and physiological components, which distinguish reflexes for example from intentional action; but firstly these added factors are not themselves internal acts, and secondly they are dependent on a chosen interpretation or even consist of a description.)

In short: *An action is not an ontological entity but an interpretational construct, a semantically interpreted entity: Actions are semantics-impregnated.* They can be conceptually analyzed only on a semantic level, they are not concepts of the object language but theoretical concepts referring to interpretations, perspectives, conceptualizations—they are interpretational constructs of observable movements (and the movements are all one can observe). It is the interpretation or description which has to be added to make an action out of a plain physical movement and to make it identifiable as such. Thalberg's components therefore are of different sorts; some of them are based on a semantic dimension and are interpretational.

Now, to take an example from the realm of sport or sport-like behavior: Whether an agent performs a javelin throw as an action of spear hunting, warfare, sport, or other conventional social or political action certainly depends on the social setting and frame of reference as much as on the interpretation and description which the agent himself or participating or nonparticipating observers apply to it. In medieval times, even a vassal's claim to land tenure was sometimes measured by the applicant's ability to throw a stone or spear to the borders of his future acquisition. In early Roman antiquity the priest's throw of a spear at a special place outside the city wall was a decisive symbol of a declaration of war. In each of these cases the agent's physical movement may have taken the same external form; at least let us assume this for the sake of argument. The differences between these actions, and the possibility of assigning them to particular realms of action, clearly depend on the socially impregnated definition of the situation, on the social context with all its norms, rules, traditions, values, frames of reference, and reference groups. All these certainly play a decisive role in perceiving, and all the more so in actively orienting oneself, reacting, and acting.

For the agent as well as for the observing partner and also for the observing, analyzing scientist, actions are therefore interpretive constructs, whose constituents partly belong to the object language proper but also partly (and not least) depend on theoretical perspectives or even on metalanguage concepts. *Action concepts are theoretical concepts of an interpretational character.*

The component theory developed by Thalberg has to be modified in order to take this theoretical-interpretational character of action into account. The component theory therefore has to be enlarged toward *a descriptive-interpretational constituent theory of action.* It is only in this way that the modified component approach can cope with the methodological difficulties and anomalies mentioned above.

Even each possible characterization and classification of actions, prior to each explanatory analysis, depends on a descriptive framework outlined by constitutive rules among other things.

Let us take up again our example from sport—throwing the javelin. Even in looking at this seemingly simple and unproblematic action, which is very closely tied to the agent's physical movement, social criteria for defining an action necessarily play a part. For example, there are conventional social rules of equivalence, substitutivity, equality, etc., which decide whether or not a movement is admissible as a javelin throw: to throw the javelin with the left instead of the right arm is certainly admissible. This would stay within the admissible range of the sport action, conventionally defined by the rules of the International Amateur Athletic Federation.

Yet no movement of throwing the javelin with, say, one's leg, if possible at all, would count as such an admissible action. The thrower would be disqualified at once. Some years ago there was the interesting example of a discovery that did not become an accepted innovation, though it could have done so: a Basque javelin thrower threw the javelin after turning around like a discus thrower, shattering the world record by far. After considerable discussion, but nevertheless quickly, the IAAF banned the then admissible form of movement by *ex post facto* changing the rules. The Basque style was banned. It was not considered an admissible action of sport—of throwing the javelin—any longer. The admissibility class of javelin throwing was restricted by deliberate convention. By contrast, an intelligent innovation in the high jump, the new style of the Fosbury flop, was not hindered by such restrictions. (Maybe this was due to the fact that there was not such a shattering supremacy of the new style as in the case of the Basque javelin thrower.) Certainly the influence of conventional rules defining admissible actions is still far more obvious in team games than in the relatively elementary, quasi-"natural" track and field events. The conventional character of the offside rule in soccer need not be stressed at all.

The upshot of all my theoretical and methodological remarks and of the simple examples so far is that all actions are interpretational constructs, perspectival, contextual and conceptual, even and all the more if we take one of the most distinctive approaches in the philosophy of action, namely a component approach (such as Thalberg's), avoiding the traditional dichotomies of causalists vs. intentionalists and pluralists vs. reductionists. All that has been said is clearly relevant for any social scientific analysis of action whatsoever, in particular for the sociological, social psychological (e.g. research on motivation), and especially social philosophical analysis of sport actions and their methodological problems.

One may easily derive some well-known corollaries like the following:

Kinesiology and biomechanics are certainly very valuable and indispensable scientific disciplines for the analysis of sporting actions, but they certainly cannot cover the whole range of possible important questions connected to this phenomenon, which exhibits ineradicable social roots. Comprehensive studies of sport action have to go beyond the realms of biomechanics and behaviorist approaches in general. Indeed, not even the objects of such a discipline can be identified in a purely behaviorist manner, but only with the help of ultimately social scientific and social philosophical concepts.

A purely behaviorist approach will *a fortiori* not do in a social scientific analysis of sport, although the augmenting of precision and the manipulability of variables makes behavioral and even behaviorist analysis a heuristically fruitful tool to begin with. However, the long-range productiveness of such a methodologically restricted model should not be exaggerated. This judgment rests directly on a thoroughly detailed methodological investigation, and indeed is unavoidable when one considers the philosophical foundation, constitution and analysis of the seemingly hard-core behaviorist or positivist concepts themselves.

These methodological considerations seem to point, indeed, to a necessary integration of the different branches of sport sciences, including philosophical disciplines. The provinces or prospecting grounds of the interscientific frontier are for the most part neatly separated, and we have unfortunately not gone very far in breaking through or even just bridging the disciplinary boundaries—at least not yet. With respect to sport analyses, for instance, the hints of Lüschen and the present author (1975) toward the explicit use of cross-level laws or quasi-laws, which would use both behaviorist and action terms in the social psychology of sport, have not been taken up widely or even been elaborated to a considerable degree. Yet the most interesting problems—at least from a social philosophical and methodological point of view—seem to loom in this interdisciplinary, intertheoretical and intermethodical realm.

BIBLIOGRAPHY

Beckerman, A. and G. Meggle (eds.). *Analytische Handlungstheorie*. Frankfurt: Suhrkamp, 1977.

Brand, M. and D. Walton (eds.). *Action Theory*. Dordrecht: Reidel, 1976.

Brand, M. "Particulars, Events, and Actions." In *Action Theory*. Edited by M. Brand and D. Walton. Dordrecht: Reidel, 1976. 133–175.

Brand, M. (ed.). *The Nature of Human Action*. Glenview, Ill.: Scott Foresman & Co., 1970.

Chisholm, R. M. "Events and Propositions." Nous 4 (1970), 15–24.

Chisholm, R. M. "On the Logic of Intentional Action." In Agent, Action and Reason. Edited by R. Binkley, R. Bronaugh, and A. Marres. Oxford: Blackwell, 1971. 38–80.

Chisholm, R. M. "Problems of Identity." In Identity and Individuation. Edited by M. Munitz. New York, 1972. 3–80.

Chisholm, R. M. "Some Puzzles about Agency." In The Logical Way of Doing Things. Edited by K. Lambert. New Haven: Yale, 1969. 199–217.

Chisholm, R. M. "The Structure of Intention." The Journal of Philosophy 67 (1970), 633–647.

Danto, A. C. Analytical Philosophy of Action. Cambridge: Cambridge U.P., 1973.

Danto, A. C. "Basic Actions." American Philosophical Quarterly 2 (1965), 141–148. Rpt. in Readings in the Theory of Action. Edited by N. S. Care and C. Landesman. Bloomington: Indiana U.P., 1968. 93–112.

Danto, A. C. "What We Can Do." The Journal of Philosophy 60 (1963), 435–445.

Davidson, D. "Agency." In Agent, Action and Reason. Edited by R. Binkley, R. Bronaugh, and A. Marres. Oxford: Blackwell, 1971. 3–25.

Davidson, D. "Events as Particulars." Nous 4 (1970), 25–32.

Davidson, D. "Actions, Reasons, and Causes." The Journal of Philosophy 60 (1963), 685–700.

Davidson, D. "On Events and Event Descriptions." In Fact and Existence. Edited by J. Margolis. Oxford: Blackwell, 1969. 74–84.

Davidson, D. "The Individuation of Events." In Essays in Honor of Carl G. Hempel. Edited by N. Rescher, et. al. Dordrecht: Reidel, 1969. 216–234.

Goldman, A. I. A Theory of Human Action. Englewood Cliffs, NJ: Prentice-Hall, 1970.

Goldman, A. I. "The Individuation of Action." The Journal of Philosophy 68 (1971), 761–774.

Lenk, H. and G. Lüschen. "Epistemological Problems and the Personality and Social Systems." Theory and Decision 6 (1975), 333–335.

Thalberg, I. Enigmas of Agency. London: Allen & Unwin, 1972.

Thalberg, I. Perception, Emotion and Action: A Component Approach. Oxford: Blackwell, 1977.

Thalberg, I. "Singling out Actions, Their Properties and Components." The Journal of Philosophy 68 (1971), 781–787.

Wittgenstein, L. Philosophische Untersuchungen. In his Schriften, Vol. 1. Frankfurt: Suhrkamp, 1960. 279ff.

von Wright, G. H. Erklären und Verstehen. Frankfurt: Athenaum, 1974.

For an extensive elaboration of the interpretation approach see:

Gebauer, G. "Überlegungen zu einer perspektivischen Handlungstheorie." In Handlungstheorie. Edited by H. Lenk. Munich: Fink, 1978. Vol. 2, 351–371.

Lenk, H. "Handlung als Interpretationskonstrukt." In Handlungstheorie. Edited by H. Lenk. Munich: Fink, 1978. Vol. 2, 279–350.

A Guide for Further Study

Higgs's bibliography in *Sports: A Reference Guide*, pp. 222–225 is the starting point for clarifying a diverse volume of available material. A ten year index to the *Journal of the Philosophy of Sport* (volume 10 (1983), pp. 119–125, compiled by Klaus V. Meier) is helpful, along with the bibliographies in *Sport and the Body: A Philosophical Symposium* (2d. ed.; Philadelphia, 1979). *The Philosopher's Index* is also a good place to begin—looking under entries like "sport," "play," and "games." For some books in this area, see Hans Lenk, *Social Philosophy of Athletics*; David Best, *Philosophy and Human Movement*; Bernard Suits, *The Grasshopper: Games, Life and Utopia*; and Peter Arnold, *Meaning in Movement, Sport, and Physical Education*.

Section IV: Sport and the Aesthetic

MARIANNE MOORE

Baseball and Writing

Fanaticism? No. Writing is exciting
and baseball is like writing.
  You can never tell with either
   how it will go
   or what you will do;
  generating excitement—
  a fever in the victim—
  pitcher, catcher, fielder, batter.
    Victim in what category?
Owlman watching from the press box?
    to whom does it apply?
    Who is excited? Might it be I?

It's a pitcher's battle all the way—a duel—
a catcher's, as, with cruel
  puma paw, Elston Howard lumbers lightly
   back to plate. (His spring
   de-winged a bat swing.)
  They have that killer instinct;
  yet Elston—whose catching
  arm has hurt them all with the bat—
    when questioned, says, unenviously,
  "I'm very satisfied. We won."
    Shorn of the batting crown, says, "We";
   robbed by a technicality.

From *The Complete Poems of Marianne Moore* (1967).

When three players on a side play three positions
and modify conditions,
      the massive run need not be everything.
         "Going, going . . ." Is
         it? Roger Maris
    has it, running fast. You will
    never see a finer catch. Well . . .
    "Mickey, leaping like the devil"—why
         gild it, although deer sounds better—
snares what was speeding towards its treetop nest,
         one-handing the souvenir-to-be
         meant to be caught by you or me.

Assign Yogi Berra to Cape Canaveral;
he could handle any missile.
      He is no feather. "Strike! . . . Strike *two!*"
         Fouled back. A blur.
         It's gone. You would infer
    that the bat had eyes.
    He put the wood to that one.
Praised, Skowron says, "Thanks, Mel.
    I think I helped a *little* bit."
         All business, each, and modesty.
         Blanchard, Richardson, Kubek, Boyer.
         In that galaxy of nine, say which
         won the pennant? *Each.* It was he.

Those two magnificent saves from the knee—throws
by Boyer, finesses in twos—
      like Whitey's three kinds of pitch and pre-
         diagnosis
         with pick-off psychosis.
    Pitching is a large subject.
    Your arm, too true at first, can learn to
    catch the corners—even trouble
         Mickey Mantle. ("Grazed a Yankee!
My baby pitcher, Montejo!"
         With some pedagogy,
         you'll be tough, premature prodigy.)

They crowd him and curve him and aim for the knees. Trying
indeed! The secret implying:
    "I can stand here, bat held steady."
        One may suit him;
        none has hit him.
    Imponderables smite him.
    Muscle kinks, infections, spike wounds
    require food, rest, respite from ruffians. (Drat it!
        Celebrity costs privacy!)
Cow's milk, "tiger's milk," soy milk, carrot juice,
        brewer's yeast (high-potency)—
        concentrates presage victory

sped by Luis Arroyo, Hector Lopez—
deadly in a pinch. And "Yes,
    it's work; I want you to bear down,
        but enjoy it
        while you're doing it."
    Mr. Houk and Mr. Sain,
    if you have a rummage sale,
    don't sell Roland Sheldon or Tom Tresh.
        Studded with stars in belt and crown,
the Stadium is an adastrium.
        O flashing Orion,
        your stars are muscled like the lion.

PETER MEINKE

To an Athlete Turned Poet

(for James Dickey)

Fifteen years ago   and twenty
he'd crouch   line-backer   gang-tackler
steel stomach flexing for
contact   contact   cracking
through man after man   weekend hero

From *Trying to Surprise God* (1981).

washing the cheers down
with unbought beer

and now his stomach's soft   his books
press out his veins as he walks
and no one looks

but deep in his bone stadium
the roar of the crowd wells
as he shows them again
crossing line after line
on cracking fingers   heart red-
dogging with rage and joy over the broken backs
of words   words   words

ROBERT WALLACE

The Double Play

In his sea lit
distance, the pitcher winding
like a clock about to chime comes down with

the ball, hit
sharply, under the artificial
banks of arc-lights, bounds like a vanishing string

over the green
to the shortstop magically
scoops to his right whirling above his invisible

shadows
in the dust redirects
its flight to the running poised second baseman

Collected in A Literature of Sports, ed. Tom Dodge (1980). Originally published 1960.

pirouettes
leaping, above the slide, to throw
from mid-air, across the colored tightened interval,

to the leaning-
out first baseman ends the dance
drawing it disappearing into his long brown glove

stretches. What
is too swift for deception
is final, lost among the loosened figures

jogging off the field
(the pitcher walks), casual
in the space where the poem has happened.

PAUL G. KUNTZ

Aesthetics Applies to Sports as Well as to the Arts

If I were to write an essay "Ethics Applies to Sport" there would be little doubt about what there is to discuss: the standards of fairness between contestants, the need of umpires to prevent cheating and foul play. Yet the title "Aesthetics Applies to Sport" produces shock. Since Aesthetics is generally conceived as applying to the arts, the title suggests that athletes are some new kind of artists, that there are performances in the arts and the sports that are comparable and even identical, that sporting events or athletic contests may be viewed as theater or dance and should be judged according to aesthetic standards. All these claims are indeed made in the literature of sport and it is a challenge to assess them fairly.[1]

These difficult conceptual problems arise not because philosophers seek to

Originally appeared in *Journal of the Philosophy of Sport* (1974).

confuse categories but because there is a movement called "art in sport." In this essay I shall limit myself exclusively to what athletes say of themselves, to what persons in physical education and recreation write of their aims and to what critics of sports claim about the values of sporting activities. Because I am fascinated by this body of thought, to which I am so new, I shall spend much time quoting.

I shall not spend time defining "aesthetics" or defining "sports." There are philosophic essays that show that this can be done in such ways that it follows deductively that there is little to talk about except the confusion of categories or that there is an identity between sport and art.[2]

The area called generally "philosophy of sport" is so new an area that we need to examine the questions in the contexts in which they arise. This means much empirical study on the part of philosophers with the dangers of missing the specific meanings developed in the sports, and trenching upon psychology, sociology, history, education. The results of an early survey of a field are indeed likely to be in the stage of inquiry Whitehead called "assemblage." This cannot be helped if one is to avoid premature systematization.[3] I think it sufficient to consider proposed answers to the set of questions that seem to fall under "aesthetics of sport," however we find the categories of aesthetics and of sports used. Is it possible at this stage to know whether we should begin with the athlete who thinks he performs as an artist? We may anticipate difficulties with the intentions and attitudes said to characterize each, and then we have a compounded intentional fallacy. If we begin with the performance, say "the well played game," to ask about it in contrast to an artistic performance, how do we decide which game and which concert or drama or dance performance?[4] We have all seen fallacious generalizations produced not merely by selecting instances of maximum or minimum divergence in the spectrum of performances, but the descriptions of both events are never innocent of theory. If a soccer game is described by a sports critic in dramatic terms, does this then become an artistic event? Politics can be described in the language of games without making politics sport. If we do not take the perspective of the performer or of the spectator, what of the coach or director who is an educator of the performer and the producer of the spectacle? He is deeply committed to the importance of his work and may well characterize it in whatever laudatory language the audience accepts. We all know that sports in a Victorian age were recommended to reduce, like cold showers, sexual desire. In a competitive age coaches stress roughness as preparation for dog eat dog business; in a more cooperative age roughness is a safety valve protecting gentle folks from attack. Are there any values in the activities or only in the attitudes of people towards them? My trust in the description of sporting events is subject to the caveat that the describer may merely project his attitudes and then pretend to have found these values there as though they were facts for every observer. Should we then finally consider how the performance in sport is to be judged? If "the beautiful" is the standard of sports as well as of arts, should we then give the aesthetic theory within which the norm acquires precision, so that we know the modes from "pretty" to "sublime" and their opposites? So great is the ambiguity of aesthetic norms that it is rash to begin without a prolegomenon of massive proportion.[5]

All these problems are involved in a concrete instance. An athlete answered them dogmatically in one way and his coaches were equally dogmatic on the other side. Because the consequences are grave, the case makes us consider our answer as more than a parlor game. Neal Shartar was one of the best Georgia athletes of recent years, who won the state high school championship in 1970. He won a scholarship on the University of Georgia's gymnastic team. The advocacy of the aesthetic value of sport led to difficulty. His coaches laid down the rule that sideburns should not be below the bottom of the ear, the hair shouldn't cover any part of the ear, and shouldn't touch the collar in the back. Two hundred and forty other athletes on scholarships followed the rules. Neal Shartar was out of step with them. His position was that performance is important and the length of hair, when it doesn't interfere with performance, is insignificant. Neal Shartar had become less an athlete obedient to the coaches and more an artist acting from his own conception of himself.

Although he performed beautifully, his old high school coach refused him use of the rings of the gymnasium. "Not in my gym. I'm not part of your protest because I don't agree with you." "Art in sports" cost Neal Shartar his scholarship and he withdrew from the University. There is the consequent cost of a philosophy of sport.

"Other things are more important than being an athlete," he said. "Or winning." "And what is that?" he was asked. "The beauty of it," he said. "Gymnastics is very beautiful. People don't see much of it and so they don't know how beautiful it is, but when they do see it they like it. One should do gymnastics for the beauty of it, not for winning."[6]

The case is regrettable intellectually as well as morally. Does the conception of "artist" require non-conformity and specifically is short hair necessarily the mark of the athlete and long hair of the artist?[7] The general issue of authority in a peculiar application gets confused with the relevant issue of whether a gymnastic performance is to be judged by aesthetic standards and is therefore like an artistic performance. And if it is an artistic performance is it sufficient that it be enjoyed? In conversation some teachers of music, dance and drama have insisted that Shartar is right. Games are played to win. Athletes compete and it is scoring points for victory that is essential to the game.[8] But art events aim to satisfy standards of beauty, and cannot be judged in the competitive situation. If poets and musicians competed at Olympia, the ancient Greeks gave us an example of forcing the wrong categories upon the arts.

Maybe we could resolve the problem by saying that gymnastics conceived as an art belongs more to music, dance and drama and that games, specifically contact sports, are altogether different kinds of bodily activities, even though some analysts bring them all under the one umbrella term "movement."

But this athlete has a much stronger theoretical case that unfortunately the journalist's story could not examine. The journalist reported his aesthetic experience.

> Neal C. Shartar whirls around beautifully on the rings. . . . He can do breathtaking things with such little apparent effort that he seems to have conquered gravity itself. . . . Like ballet, for instance, the gymnast . . . seems to do the impossible. He does in thin air what most of us can't even do on the ground. . . . He might be kin to the angels. . . . And if the gymnast can maintain the illusion, the crowd falls under a certain spell. . . .[9]

The gymnast's aims are defined socially and the judge's standards are fixed institutionally. The "beauty" reported is made rather precise; one may hope, precise enough to be applied in a competitive situation where every decision must be as defensible as a judge's in court of law, subject to some kind of review.

> Movements combining the elements of *balance, agility, strength, elasticity*, jumps and leaps (tumbling) presented in *rhythm* and *harmony*. The gymnast is required to move in different directions, *not using too many* running steps. (The run must be taken in the *right proportion* to the difficulty of the jump or tumbling routine that follows.)
>
> A perfect exercise with a maximum rating is one that is presented with *elegance, ease, precision* and in a *style* and *rhythm* well adapted to the nature of the *aesthetic* performance with no faults in execution. The faults in execution or style are penalized by a deduction in points or fraction of points according to the following directions:
>
> Defects in elegance in general. An exercise, although executed with-

out fault, but presented in a rhythm *too quick* or *too slow*, or with an *ill-proportioned* display of force, counts less than a perfect exercise as described. . . .[10]

Is winning a gymnastic contest an intrusion upon the artistry of the gymnast if the standards are appropriately aesthetic? I have often heard tennis players allowing that one player did indeed win the points that added to victory, and that although within the rules, he played without grace and ease. It is then conceptually possible that the non-aesthetic, even antiaesthetic, element in games is not playing for victory, but failure to award the victory according to appropriate aesthetic standards.

To establish that there are sufficient common characteristics shared by arts and sports, or some arts with some sports, is difficult. Some thinkers have been deeply impressed by the common feature of spontaneity. From the perspective of utility and work, performances in both families of activities belong to "leisure" and are often put to use as "recreation."[11] But the theory of play is itself a difficult concept and produces many paradoxes when artists practice seriously and when athletes train to the point of exhaustion and expose themselves to great pain. I would not wish the argument to rest on a merely verbal similarity that there are "players" in both drama and games, for to "play" in the theater and to "play" on the tennis court may be as accidental as the common word "dog" applied to a hound and a star.

The surest beginning of a positive answer to the problem of exactly how aesthetics applies to sport is to conceive of the performances, some of which are called "arts," such as dance, and others called "sports," such as figure skating. Now the accidental and superficial aspect is that one takes place in a concert hall, a shrine of the muses, and the other in the arena of a palace of sport. The fundamental positive likenesses have been made forcefully and in great enough detail that they cannot be brushed aside.[12] Apart from the "special buildings" in which there are created "special worlds," there are the rules to which both kinds of performers must conform, along with the unities of time and space and special ways of using time and space. Does this analysis maintain a difference? Yes, there is no score or choreography or text in the sports as in music, dance and drama, but only game plans that might be thought approximations. But we will consider the point of whether sports can symbolize reality later.

On the level of physical action there is a kind of aesthetic analysis that applies. This is kinesthesis and empathy (*Einfuhlung*). Something happens physiologically and psychologically between performer and spectator.[13]

When it is said that physical education is being reconceived aesthetically, now we can see precisely what is meant. As far as it goes I find Maureen

Kovich's "Sport as an Art Form" convincing. She is a teacher of physical education in Regina High School, Cincinnati. A merely scientific analysis of movement does not get to the "artistic qualities." These we must state because many people get their art outside of theaters and galleries.

"Art is also being performed in our natatoriums, gymnasiums, and playing fields through the medium of sport. The definition of art needs to be expanded to include the skilled athletic performance." Miss Kovich could footnote her claim with some of the most sophisticated aesthetic analyses: "art" is an open not a closed concept. There is, accordingly, no way to establish that the concept cannot meaningfully be expanded beyond any static definition.[14]

It is not only sports such as figure skating and synchronized swimming that are comparable to dance, but pole vaulting, tennis, gymnastics, and not only stellar performances, but "any skill in movement expressing beauty."

Is there aesthetic value for both the performer and the spectator? The experience of joy, excitement, satisfaction in performing and witnessing can be analyzed and it is instructive to follow her analysis closely.

From the perspective of the performer, any given performance can have qualities of the aesthetic—something of excellence that goes beyond the theoretical perfect. Rebound tumbling, for example, becomes more than mere novelty. The tumbler senses something of brief snatches of freedom, something of precarious balance in unsupported space, of underlying rhythm, and of forces initiated by himself acting upon himself. He becomes sensitive to the elements of space, force, and time in his world of movement. From this viewpoint, we see that it is not just the man's body performing; it is the whole man. The total performer then becomes both artist and material. Man and his movements become the art.

The beauty of any movement depends upon the aesthetic response of the performer or spectator. The performer perceives his movements as art through the working of his kinesthetic perception, his own sense of personal feel. He cannot go outside himself and see his movements simultaneously with their execution, but he does "know" in an intuitive way when the movement "feels right." The evaluation of the performance by a spectator or judge serves only as additional testimony to the trueness of the movement for the performer himself.

The spectator cannot divorce man from his movements. Sport is a truly human form of art, for it is not just the product of man's abilities which is on display; it is man. Research in electromyography has shown that observers mimic in a minute way the movement patterns of the performer, thus inducing a form of restrained participation. As the performer feels the art he is creating, so can a perceptive spectator feel this same quality, although not to the same extent. Whether intended or not, there is silent communication between the performer and the spectator. Empathy with the elements of force, space, and time in the world of the performer and his movements can account, in part at least, for the spectator interpreting the movement as meaningful and beautiful. [15]

An opponent of my thesis that aesthetics applies to sport might at this point grant all that I have argued for: that there are some activities called "sport" that are judged by standards of grace, etc., which we shall call "formal aesthetic norms," that there are indeed many aspects, possibly nearly all, of performance shared in common, and that there is a psychology of aesthetics, the kinesthetic-empathetic, that explains the delight provided by athletic performances. Yet this opponent might say that sports are physical activities with relatively crude animal passions, but arts are refined with subtle emotions and intellectual content.

This is most difficult because we must recognize psychological differences from some who claim to speak for the arts, fine arts and liberal arts, or "culture"; and when these spokesmen call sports "mechanical," "crude," even "brutal," or at best "pop arts," the defender of sport realizes that he may sound like a "prole," or plebian who strayed into the sacred grove of the cultural aristocracy.

Aren't artists and athletes very different sorts? Isn't it painfully obvious that there are artistic boys whose reluctance to fight subjects them to bullying? A contemporary author writes of being forced to play on a team and to ride a horse. He feels a gap between himself and the hearty games-loving boys. "Moreover, when I observed their boisterous play I could not help but feel that I was missing something. Though part of me now rejoiced in music and literature, there was another part of me which longed to be tough and callous." [16] It would seem altogether axiomatic to such a person, become an intellectual, to place the arts at the pinnacle of culture and to regard sports as mere amusement of relatively crude people. He would incline to nod approval when he reads Matthew Arnold, son of Dr. Thomas Arnold of Rugby School: ". . . Bodily health and vigour are things which are nowhere treated in such an unintelligent, misleading, exaggerated way as in England. *Both are really machinery.*" He meant clearly that "games and sports" are *physical activities* only, to which boys and young men are, in his term "sacrificed." [17] This lowly estimate of sport may be based not merely upon dualism of body and mind, now grown increasingly outmoded, but the view of the body as low and the mind exalted in dignity. [18]

Another writer on culture, T. S. Eliot, seems to grant that sporting activities have aesthetic character. But notice his judgment: "Culture includes all the characteristic activities and interests of a people: Derby Day, Henley Regatta, Cowes, the twelfth of August, a cup final, the dog races, the pin table, the dartboard, Wenleydale cheeses, boiled cabbage cut into sections, beetroot in vinegar, nineteenth century gothic churches and the music of Elgar." The first items are sporting events and are aesthetically trivial or aesthetically bad. [19]

Is a sport such as yachting in a class with cheese, boiled cabbage and beetroot? I should rather say that yachting is in the aesthetic category of caviar and champagne. T. S. Eliot mentioned Cowes, didn't he? Had he been to Cowes as a spectator or participant? Had he merely passed over the yachting news in the *Times* as the amusement of empty headed monarchs and millionaires? We should not allow this judgment to pass without confronting the author or reader with the presentation of yachts in the pages of Frank and Keith Beken, *The Beauty of Sail*, or Beken of Cowes, *The Glory of Sail*. [20]

If one turns to the arts for the rich life of emotion, he can be satisfied also in the world of sport. This is the satisfaction particularly in our Olympic games:

> The history of the Olympic games is rich . . . with drama and pageantry, goodwill and controversy, humor and pathos. The Olympics are sports at the summit, and because the stakes are so high and the tension so great, the games seem to bring out and intensify the most basic emotions. Men cry in defeat and sing in victory. Spectators cry too. For the observers and the observed, the Olympic games are the most compelling spectacle in sports.
>
> Yet the Olympics *go beyond sports. They approach art.* They offer ritual in the symbolic freeing of pigeons, the solemn lighting of the Olympic flame, the quiet dignity of the Olympic oath. They offer competition, with the animal excitement of physical combat, strength matched against strength, style against style, stamina against stamina, courage against courage. And, above all, they offer a singular spirit of camaraderie born of shared victories, and an understanding born of shared defeats. [21]

One of the most enlightening sporting autobiographies is Roger Bannister's *The Four Minute Mile*. It was not with him first discipline, then skill, then beauty as a by-product of efficient motor behavior. That is the implicit mechanism of much analysis rejecting an aesthetic of sport. Bannister is in the Platonic not the Democritean tradition. He writes in tones reminiscent of Wordsworth's nature mysticism. The athletic eros is a response to beauty. He stood, as a child,

> barefoot on firm dry sand by the sea. The air had a special quality as if it had a life of its own. The sound of breakers on the shore shut out all others. I looked up at the clouds, like great white-sailed galleons, chasing proudly inland. I looked down at the regular ripples on the sand, and *could not absorb so much beauty*. I was taken aback—each of the myriad particles of sand was perfect in its way. . . .
>
> In this supreme moment I leapt in sheer joy . . . A few more steps. . . . The earth seemed almost to move with me. I was running now, and a fresh rhythm entered my body. No longer conscious of my movement I discovered a new unity with nature. I had found a new source of power and beauty, a source I never dreamed existed.
>
> From intense moments like this, love of running can grow.[22]

Bannister then rejects a scientific "objective" explanation in terms of electrical impulse.

> The electric rhythm produced there is a source of pleasure. Like that caused by music, it has some interplay with rhythms inherent in our nervous systems. But no explanation is satisfying that does not take account of feelings of beauty or power.

Is there an essential will-to-win that differentiates sport from art? Bannister denies it. There is an agonistic element.

> We enjoy struggling to get the best out of ourselves, whether we play games of skill requiring quickness of eye and deftness of touch, or games of effort and endurance like athletics. There is the need to feel that our bodies have a skill and energy of their own, apart from the man-made machines they may drive. . . . The sportsman enjoys his sport even if he has absolutely no prospect of becoming a champion.

Of "running—win or lose" Bannister writes as a source of deep satisfaction. Even running in the mud adds variety and negates boredom. "However strenuous our work, sport brings more pleasure than some easier relaxation. It brings joy, freedom and challenge which cannot be found elsewhere" (p. 13).

I wonder if Bannister's response to beauty could not have led him to become a great ballet artist. He writes that he feels his story applies not only to sports but "beyond" (p. 14). I feel he is a great mystical poetic philosopher of sport.

Of what importance for sports is Bannister's aesthetic analysis? It gives him a reasoned basis of criticism of recent tendencies in athletics. The development of professional skills to break records for national prestige may be the mainspring of Olympic activity, but by Bannister's conception of sport, this athleticism is degenerate sport.

Much as the Greek philosophers who rebuked professionalism and striving for victory, Bannister deplores the present situation. What is wrong with professionalism is

> not . . . unlimited financial reward, but . . . devoting unlimited time and energy to sport. Every country is seeking to enhance national prestige through physical achievements. It may be in establishing new jet-plane speed or altitude records, penetrating the depths of the sea, or scaling the world's highest mountain. Too few questions are asked about the means, provided the end of national glory is achieved. I have tried to show that running refuses to fit into a pattern of this kind.

In this aesthetic view of sport, running is a satisfying expression of human intimacy with nature, and a way to realize the best within us. To break a record is accidental, for mere training to perform more successfully has no intrinsic satisfaction. "Where would it all end? Running would have lost its purpose" (p. 247). "We run, not because we think it is doing us good, but because we enjoy it and cannot help ourselves. It also does us good because it helps us to do other things better" (pp. 248–9).

From this perspective, it is the high emotional quality, like that of music, that makes sports worthwhile. When one applies aesthetics in this sense one must condemn much of what goes under the name of sport as quite poor. Should we reject Bannister's evaluation as merely the characteristic quaint protests of a university bred Englishman? Is this not more of the same old outmoded protest of the amateur against the professional? An American sports writer shifted his justification from moral to aesthetic grounds. John R. Tunis once stressed sport as educationally valuable: sport inculcates "democratic ethics."[23] In the next decade Tunis saw precious little high morality in sport because of American zeal to compete and be successful, to win and break records. Professionalism breeds sport that is "a first-class training ground for a jungle society."[24] Genuine sport, by contrast, is what is taught by a multitude of nameless, faceless coaches and recreation directors: "*poise, coordination, a sense of beauty, and a feeling for their bodies as well as skills beyond measure.*"[25]

In what sense of "aesthetic" other than good form and psychological empathy, can aesthetics be said to apply to sport? There can be great emotional value in the sporting events, such satisfactions as the high points of the Olympic games, and the intense moments of emotional climax and unification described by Roger Bannister. It is valuable to notice that those who defend sports as ends-in-themselves, not appealing to any usefulness, usually talk of the "joy" in the "enjoyment" of participator and spectator.

Whereas all sporting activities may be equally described as kinaesthesis and empathy, only some events have this great consummatory joy. Hence some sporting activities are of lower value than others. The theory must be normative. By employing this standard Bannister condemns professional specialization and making the competitive zeal supreme, and judging achievement solely by quantitative standards.

Beyond the aspects of aesthetic value we have already recognized, is there any further claim? What is beyond form and beyond feeling, is there "significance" or "meaning" or "revelation" or "symbolic import"? This is the most difficult question (or questions) to put precisely, but it is frequently the issue on which some critics of sporting spectacles claim the decisive difference from the arts, and on this issue others affirm that some sporting events are comparable to some artistic.

Put the question another way: if we have recognized the kinesthetic-empathetic response between spectator and performer and given an account of the emotions that are sometimes rich and intense, what other kind of aesthetic value is there in sport? It is sometimes said that the drama of theater has something that the drama of sport lacks. This is perhaps the best way to handle the question of the difference between sporting and artistic performances. Earlier it was pointed out that a stage play has a text and the players are assigned roles to represent the characters and to perform actions. But the players in a game play the places of the team and, governed by the rules, strive to win. The game may have a structure of beginning, middle and end, it may have turning points and a climax, but the structure is not symbolic. What is the game about? Schechner can write that Chekhov's *Three Sisters* is about "going to Moscow (or, having a meaningful love relationship) and 'lives wasted by time.'" But games have no script and do not represent reality. There is indeed, he argues, a continuity of the modes of performance, but there are differences of degree that amount to differences of kind.[26]

If I understand the recent position of Paul Weiss it is that the purpose of a contest is the striving to win, as victory is recorded in points. If there is an element of "style," it is reduced to numbers to be added to the score. He does not question the "accepted way of quantifying style." The position developed here is that the custom is mistaken, that the aesthetic elements of form and feeling are irreducible and that, according to Bannister's *The Four Minute Mile*, the agonistic success of breaking a hitherto unbroken barrier does not exhaust the meaning of his running. Now the issue is whether there is some dramatic excellence other than striving for success in the contest and winning.[27]

There are dramatic aspects of a game, Weiss admits, but a game is only "episodically" dramatic: "the highs occur unexpectedly in the midst of a multitude of flat moments."[28] There are opportunities and there are obstacles but "they are usually not noted in the records, despite the great role they sometimes play in the determination of an important result" (p. 94). Weiss then belittles all but winning. "He who does not try to make maximal use of his body is playing at, not in a sport" (p. 94). To "perform at his best" an athlete must strive to maximize his score. But what follows? "The end to which an athlete is dedicated is narrower than that appropriate to man at his best." The "dedicated" athlete becomes a fanatic, a man of misplaced zeal. So this policy produces a Mark Spitz, with all his excellence in record but lacking the wholeness of a Bannister. For the latter, not for the former, there are also scientific, artistic, religious and ethical goals not alien to the life of sport. One would think that Weiss's whole philosophy would lead him to side with Bannister against fanaticism.

"How do we know what best performance is?" asks Dean Fraleigh.[29] If there are many dimensions of sport, and there is "mimesis" or representation as well as "agon" or contest, then an emphasis on sport as drama is one way to preserve a richer significance.[30] The striving for excellence is not exhausted by the dimensions of *citius, altius, fortius*, stated as goals of the modern Olympics. Even if we do not picture the perfected athlete as a god of Olympus, or even sing his praise as a hero, as did Pindar, we still recognize excellence other than the record. Says Erich Segal of Bannister: "the most eloquent poetry ever composed to praise or describe the spirit of sport."[31] Dean Fraleigh sees "higher" as a symbol of transcendence. "In dance, humans move their bodies to use space, time, and force to produce images of infinity, eternity and omnipotence as the symbolic means of overcoming their 'earthiness.'"[32] Is the meaning then of sport that man strives for and attains divinity?

It is easier to grasp exactly how sporting events are significant in the social context as "a celebration," also in religious terminology. Sporting events surely as ritual festivals strengthen the traditions of a society. "Like the drama . . . sport instructs people by commemorating the glories of the past and by strengthening communal pride."[33]

The view of the sporting contest as a tragic drama has much attraction.[34] It locates the significance not in the product, the score, but in the performance. "The stress on the numerical result, especially a solitary, fixed final structure like winning" obscures "the aesthetic qualities," the "artistry of another's performance." The spectator transcends the narrow partisanship of we-they antagonism in that he views the struggle with "physical distance."[35]

Hence the most explicit criticism of the exclusively agonistic theory of sport.

> Unfortunately, at least from an aesthetic appreciation posture, excellence in athletics has been equated with quantitative measures. Winning has become the necessary condition for achieving excellence. The fetish for the scoreboard does not accurately define the conditions of the contest, or man as athlete engaged in athletic phenomena. This constraint to victory would be a restriction on the freedom of the aesthetician to perceive other forms of beauty and excellence in athletics. (p. 125)

The tragic view of sport is protected from the charge against a simple hedonistic view that sport then becomes mere recreation. The aesthetic value of tragedy requires pain, which can be subsumed into this concept of a bipolar beauty. "When the distasteful can be perceived as a means for further developing and cultivating an experience, it may be viewed as aesthetic and enjoyable" (p. 125).

A game may not have the specific meaning of Chekhov's *Three Sisters*, so that we can say what it is about. Even if there is no text and characters acting out a plot, still there is an answer to the question of what is sport's "significance" or "meaning" or "revelation" or "symbolic import." "The tragedy symbolizes man's struggle with the inequities and paradoxes of life. In tragedy, man is featured in an attempt to overcome hostile forces to which he inevitably must succumb. The display of courage in the face of adversity is prized because it reflects something beautiful about man—the spirit with which he enters marvelous combat with an overwhelming and unpredictable world" (p. 127).

This analysis transmutes the *agon* into *mimicry*, that is the struggle to win is made into a necessary aspect of the imaginary world presented to us. It is a larger perspective that does not glorify winning at any cost, and therefore would tend to reduce the trickery and violence that have become the marks of bad sportsmanship. Hence, although introduced as an "aesthetic" philosophy, it is also a moral philosophy of sport.

Yet even if the athlete plays in a game viewed as a tragic drama, he is not an actor in a tragedy. We must guard ourselves against forgetting we are applying aesthetics to sport, seeing likenesses and making analogies, but not trying to identify sport and art.

Much has been written about sport as tragedy but nothing about sport as comedy.[36] The summer of 1973 will not be forgotten as the time of the battle of the sexes, Bobby Riggs the hustler challenging Billie Jean King. The American public needed relief. Farce is sometimes needed because of the high tension of contest in sports and politics. The great authority on Greek athletics reconstructed the five days of Olympic games. The programme closed with the race in armor. It was popular, picturesque and "afforded a welcome relief" as an obstacle race: runners in helmets and greaves and carrying shields must have been amusing. It returned to the connection of sport with real life.[37]

Paul Weiss makes the thesis of "sport as a form of art" turn on revealing "something of the nature of man." In contrast to art, the "athlete . . . does not seek to convey anything." If it is art to be "removed to a second degree," for the athlete as the artist to grasp the meaning of the sport as a drama, then it seems to me that the philosophy of sport is a move towards making sport more meaningful.[38]

Forms of sport develop and change, and who is to say what these forms will not become? The activity is complex and history shows much mutability. "The preference for agon, alea [favor of destiny], mimicry, or ilinx [pursuit of vertigo, spasm, seizure, shock] helps decide the future of a civilisation."[39]

Once centuries ago the Venetians raced in boats to the Lido for sling practice. From this simple challenge to triumph has come the magnificent Regatta. The first Regatta is recorded in 1315 and the Regatta of 1973 is claimed to be the 670th. It is not nearly as old as the Olympic games (776 B.C. – 393 A.D.), 1,168 years,[40] yet our modern Olympic games, by comparison, are merely 77 years old.

The historic Regatta of Venice is now a combination of gondola races between pairs of gondoliers and crews of a dozen oarsmen in larger boats. There is music and dancing and acrobats building pyramids. All is infused with a great sense of the tradition of the Venetian Republic and its role in history as the trading center connecting East and West. The Grand Canal is alive with tapestries and flags and the event expresses the pride of the people.

As I witnessed this great pageant of the city on Sept. 2, I felt confirmed in my belief that there can be great art in sport, and the Regatta of Venice satisfies all sorts because it is so rich and varied.[41]

NOTES

1. The article "Sports" in *The New Catholic Encyclopedia* (New York: McGraw-Hill, 1967), Vol. XIII, pp. 617ff. is followed by "Sports, Moral Aspect of," p. 620. See also Louis Arnaud Reid, "Sport, the Aesthetic and Art," *British Journal of Educational Studies* 18 (Oct. 1970), pp. 245–258.

2. L. A. Reid, *op. cit.*, does the former. Bernard Jeu, "What is Sport?" *Diogenes* 80, pp. 150–163, does the latter.

3. A. N. Whitehead, *Modes of Thought* (New York: Macmillan, 1938), p. 2.

4. See E. F. Kaelin, "The Well-Played Game: Notes Towards an Aesthetics of Sport," *Quest*, Monograph X, *Towards A Theory of Sport*, May, 1968, pp. 16–28.

5. Dean Warren Fraleigh suggested the questions for my paper. I am not sure, in the light of his "Theory and Design of Philosophic Research in Physical Education" (unpublished mimeographed essay, 48 pp.), that I have been sufficiently careful in formulating the issues.

6. Keith Coulbourn, "Why Neal Shartar Won't Get a Haircut," *The Atlanta Journal and Constitution Magazine*, 23 Jan. 1972, pp. 28–30, 32.

7. One knows coaches who say yes to this and spring to the defense of the University of Georgia's Athletic Department. See Tony Simpson, "Real Men, Short Hair," reprinted from *Texas Coach*, May 1973, in *Intellectual Digest* 4, No. 3 (Nov. 1973), pp. 76, 78.

8. Students of Greek point out that "the single aim in all Greek athletes was—as the etymology (from *athlon*, 'prize') suggests—to win. There were no awards for second place; in fact, losing was considered a disgrace." Erich Segal, "It Is Not Strength, but Art, Obtains the Prize," *Yale Review* 56, No. 4 (Summer 1967), p. 606.

9. Keith Coulbourn, *op. cit.*, p. 28.

10. Article "Gymnastics" in *Sports Rules Encyclopedia*, comp. and ed. by Jess R. White (Palo Alto: National Press, 1966), pp. 293–4 (underscored by present author). Compare the statement on style in diving: "The run shall be smooth, straight and forceful. . . . The take off shall be bold, reasonably high and confident." Ibid., p. 480.

I have searched for essays interpreting the judges' use of these rules and the conceptual problems, but I have failed to find any such. It would also be worth knowing how many "sports" are officially so judged, how many might be so judged, and to what degree.

11. Foster Rhea Dulles, *A History of Recreation: America Learns to Play*, 2d. ed. (New York: Appleton-Century-Crofts, 1965). Paul Weiss, "A Philosophical Definition of Leisure," in *Leisure in America: Blessing or Curse?* ed. by James C. Charlesworth (Philadelphia: American Academy of Political and Social Science, 1964), pp. 21–29.

12. Richard Schechner, "Approaches to Theory/Criticism," *Tulane Drama Review* 10, No. 4 (Summer 1966), pp. 20–53.

13. Vernon Lee, "Empathy," does not seem to apply the theory to sports performances; see Melvin Rader, *A Modern Book of Esthetics: An Anthology*, 4th ed. (New York: Holt, Rinehart and Winston, 1973), pp. 357ff. Herbert Sidney Langfeld, *The Aesthetic Attitude* (New York: Harcourt, Brace & Co., 1920) drew examples from figure skating, swimmers and acrobats, pp. 138–42.

14. Maureen Kovich, "Sport as an Art Form," *JOHPER* 42, No. 8 (October 1971), p. 42.

15. *Ibid.* A less analytic but more curricular recent paper is Linda Kay Moore, "Music, Art, Theater, and Physical Education," *JOHPER* 43, No. 8 (October 1972), p. 21.

16. Robin Maugham, *Escape from the Shadows: An Autobiography* (New York: McGraw-Hill, 1973).

17. Quoted from *Culture and Anarchy* (1869) by Peter C. McIntosh, "Twentieth Century Attitudes to Sport in Britain," *International Review of Sport Sociology: A Yearbook*, edited by the Committee of Sport Sociology of the International Council of Sport and Physical Education (UNESCO), Warsaw, 1966, p. 21. Underscoring mine.

The mechanical view is still with us: "It is not helpful to lump American football, Real Madrid and international athletics with Gordonstoun, fishing or diving off a pier, boating or camping. The only thing they have in common is that some males and fewer females of varying ages are *using their muscles*." M. I. Finley, review of P. C. McIntosh, *Sport in Society*. *New Statesman*, May 22, 1964, underscoring mine.

18. Helen M. Simpson, "Physical Education and the Arts," *Physical Education* 59 (July 1967), pp. 54–60. "Herein lies, at its deepest level, the intimate relationship between physical education and the arts, for trust in the senses and the response to sensuous experience are all-important in the arts of painting, music and sculpture, concerned as they are with colour, sound and shape in significant relationship" (p. 55).

19. Quoted in Peter C. McIntosh, *op. cit.*

20. Frank and Keith Beken, *The Beauty of Sail*, commentary by John Scott Hughes (London: Robert Ross Ltd., 1952). Here E. V. Lucas is quoted about yachts: "Never shall I forget their majestic urgency."

Beken of Cowes, *The Glory of Sail, 1897–1914* (New York: Dodd, Mead and Co., 1966).

21. Richard Schaap, *An Illustrated History of the Olympics*, 2nd ed. (New York: A. A. Knopf, 1967), p. ix, underscoring mine.

It might well be objected that the sports enthusiast is claiming a more worthy cultural degree than is warranted. For are not the emotions those of nationalism and striving for victory among competitors who represent nations, and we are too well aware of hatred and violence. Are not the emotions developed in artistic expression far more subtle and various? The rituals of modern Olympics are not genuine solemn religious festivals of ancient Olympia. There are many protests that the oath is a farce.

> Generally it was a very bad year for American athletic ideals. Our losers, who were numerous, rather than taking defeat gracefully, bellyached piteously. Our winners, who were much rarer, tended to be of the [chess champion Bobby] Fischer type. The most important one after Fischer was Mark Spitz, who already had the reputation of being the spoiled brat of swimming. At the Olympics he quarreled with his teammates, who said they would rather have beaten him than any foreigner, hot-dogged in victory and then went home, not to talk to boys clubs about what he owed to swimming, but to talk to business agents about converting his seven gold medals into half a million dollars worth of endorsements. (Bil Gilbert, "Gleanings from a Troubled Time," *Sports Illustrated* 37, No. 26, December 25, 1972, p. 43.)

We need to stop here to remark that "American athletic ideals" may represent something even more prudish than Frank Merriwell. Is only being a good loser, even if one is never a winner, to be praised? If the art of a sport is truly perfected, does not winning naturally follow?

That the Olympic victor Mark Spitz turned to commercialism is quite irrelevant to his prowess as a swimmer. His critics have neglected aspects of his achievement. In the art of swimming he proved superb in spite of his arrogance. The personality of a brat is unimportant compared with the willingness, from the age of six, to train. He perfected the art of swimming and this resulted in victory. Should we not also say that the commercial use of this achievement, regrettable if we expect an amateur to be always an amateur, is irrelevant to his status artistically? Regardless of how many en-dorsements he gave, or even how many pin-ups posed, his swimming was justly ap-praised as superb.

There is no overwhelming difficulty with the thesis that aesthetics applies to sports as well as to arts. Artists strive with each other and are often spiteful and vindictive. It is very difficult to get support for activities that are set apart from the normal eco-nomic life. Just as philosophy bakes no bread, artists bake no bread, athletes bake no bread. There are prizes for the stars who occupy the status of heroes, and grave temp-tations to use either an art or a sport as a means to fame and wealth.

22. Roger Bannister, *The Four Minute Mile* (New York: Dodd, Mead & Co., 1956), pp. 11–12, underscoring mine. References in following paragraphs are to this edition.

23. *Democracy and Sport* (New York: A. S. Barnes, 1941).

24. John R. Tunis, *The American Way in Sport* (New York: Duell, Sloan & Pearce, 1958), p. 98.

25. *Ibid.*, p. xii, underscoring mine.

26. Richard Schechner, *Public Domain: Essays On the Theatre* (N.Y.: Discus Books, 1969), pp. 86, 102–105.

27. Paul Weiss, "Records and the Man," *Philosophic Exchange* 1, No. 3 (Summer 1972), pp. 89–99. "Strategems and Competition," *Sportwissenschaft* 3, No. 1 (1973), pp. 47–54 continues the same emphasis.

28. "Records and the Man," p. 92. References in following paragraphs are to this article.

29. Warren Fraleigh, "On Weiss on Records and the Significance of Athletic Rec-ords," *Philosophic Exchange* 1, No. 3 (Summer 1972), p. 106.

30. Roger Caillois identifies not only *agon*, competition between adversaries, and *mimicry*, the enjoyment of an imaginary world, but *alea*, favor of destiny or chance, and *ilinx*, pursuit of vertigo, spasm, seizure, shock. See *Man, Play and Games*, tr. Meyer Barash (London, 1962), ch. 3, "The Classification of Games." Reprinted in Eric Dunning, *The Sociology of Sport* (London: Frank Cass & Co., 1971), pp. 26–29.

31. Erich Segal, "It Is Not Strength, but Art, Obtains the Prize," *Yale Review* 56, No. 4 (Summer 1967), p. 609.

32. Warren Fraleigh, *op. cit.*, p. 107.

33. Francis Keenan, "The Athletic Contest as a 'Tragic' Form of Art," *Philosophic Ex-change* 1, No. 3 (Summer 1972), p. 126. Scott Kretchmar introduced the term "cele-bration" from Robert E. Neale's *In Praise of Play* (New York: Harper & Row, 1969) in

"Ontological Possibilities: Sport as Play," *Philosophical Exchange* 1, No. 3 (Summer 1972), p. 117.

34. Morris R. Cohen, "Baseball as a National Religion," *The Faith of a Liberal: Selected Essays* (New York: Henry Holt, 1946), stresses "catharsis." Laurence Kitchin, "The Contenders," *The Listener* 76, No. 1961 (Oct. 27, 1966), pp. 607–09, employs *hamartia*, turning point, climax, as well as modern aesthetic terms such as distance and empathy. Professor Keenan's essay is a far more detailed specification of the Aristotelian categories for sport.

35. Francis Keenan, *op. cit.* The quotations in the following three paragraphs are from this article.

36. Ernest Hemingway characterizes the bullfight as a tragedy in three acts. *Death in the Afternoon* (N.Y.: Scribner's, 1932), Ch. X. The literature of bullfighting is singularly rich. If it has a content that can be discovered by depth psychology perhaps we can go further than to say it is about man's courageous fight with the power of nature. Louis A. Zurcher and Arnold Meadow, "On Bullfights and Baseball, An Example of Interaction of Social Institutions," *The International Journal of Comparative Sociology* 8, No. 1 (March 1967) claim it is about the son (the matador) facing the father (the bull) and conquering. A depth approach presumes any sport to be "revelatory."

On comedy, see "How Bobby Runs and Talks, Talks, Talks," *Time*, Sept. 10, 1973, pp. 50–54.

37. E. Norman Gardiner, *Olympia: Its History and Remains* (Oxford: Clarendon Press, 1925), pp. 310–311.

38. Paul Weiss, *Philosophy in Process*, Vol. V (Carbondale and Edwardsville, Illinois: Southern Illinois University Press, 1971), pp. 706–707.

39. Roger Caillois, *Man, Play and Games*, tr. Meyer Barash (London, 1962), Ch. 3, "The Classification of Games."

40. Hermann Bengtson, *Die Olympischen Spiele in der Antike*, 2. Auflage, Lebendiche Antike, Artemis, Zurich & Stuttgart, 1972, p. 20.

41. See Giulio Lorenzetti, *Venice and Its Lagoons* (Roma: Libraria dello Stato, 1961), pp. 20–21. "Regata Storica in Canal Grando, Venezia," 2. Settembre 1973, 4 pp.

SPENCER K. WERTZ

Artistic Creativity in Sport

I

A rtistic creativity in sport is usually established and discussed by critics
and performers who are appealing to the latter's intentions. These intentions may be more latent than deliberately conscious. The kind of intentions
that they are will vary from case to case. The appeal to intentions in any
context can lead to an unjustified assertion that some x is a member of a set S.
This is especially true when S is "art." In other words, the ascription of intentionality to some event does not suffice to say that it is art. All of this becomes even more problematic when some x is an athletic performance. Our
initial question of inquiry is, then, in what circumstances, if any, do we feel
justified to accept an appeal to an agent's intentions? Such appeals are to assist us argumentatively to establish whether or not an athletic performance is
an artistic one. If we are trying to decide whether something is art or not by
appealing to the agent's intentions, there are difficulties with permitting
blanket appeals. One cannot say that one intends j by his or her actions and
that this alone makes them an S,[1] because there are other relevant considerations involved; if these considerations are ignored, one can draw false statements from true premises. Arguments employing such inferences are not
sound. They must be carefully scrutinized, even though they sound convincing at first. Let me briefly list some of the more fallacious moves. For instance,
there can be "mistaken" intentions: a child may tell you that he has drawn a
horse when in fact the figure is a lion. The same should hold true of an artist
who tells us such things about his or her work. Also, unfulfilled or irrelevant
intentions may be another way an appeal to intention can go wrong. An
agent may intend that some x be art, but that doesn't make it so, either in a
descriptive (classificatory) or evaluative sense, but especially in the latter.[2]

Further, such cases as these are interesting, because they show also that
". . . some specification of the artist's intentions in virtue of which his activity is 'artistic' is also required."[3] What is required, as Phillip Montague sees
it, is that although there need be no particular overriding intention (such as
that of producing or performing art), "the entire process of creating" or per-

Published for the first time in this anthology.

forming "manifests the artist's intentional manipulation of his medium in accord with aesthetic concepts" (p. 185). This latter requirement must obviously be present because something in addition to intention is needed to identify a given activity as "artistic." I cannot produce or perform some work which I could label as "artistic," only by intending to do some *x*, like emptying the garbage or opening the closet door. Something more is needed, which is an aesthetic control over a medium.[4] The manipulation of the agent's or performer's *medium* is an important requirement in order to avoid the logical blunders of the so-called "intentional fallacy."[5] An examination of the medium tells us whether or not those intentions were fulfilled, and whether or not a particular meaning is to be ascribed to some token or a specific utterance of some word or clause. Let us try to explore further what is meant by "an aesthetic control over a medium."

"Aesthetic or critical control" is not easily specified or defined, because this is not a rigid concept which consists of a set of necessary conditions. It is much easier to specify the *lack* of aesthetic control than to specify its presence. Basically, aesthetic control is the sort of activity which artists engage in when they are attempting to solve or resolve problems. They attempt to make assessments (conscious or otherwise) in conformity with their concept of what is aesthetically worthwhile. An artist's product or performance, then, is measured not only by how well he or she succeeds or fails in carrying out those assessments in terms of the medium he or she employs, but also in terms of the goal which is specified by the practice or activity undertaken.

In addition to the notion of success and failure included in the artist's enterprise, the concept of "aesthetic control" implies that his products or performances cannot be *accidentally* made or performed, in the crude sense of the term. In the case where the artist permits such things as mistakes or accidents, he has intentionally left the result unfinished or unrevised.[6] Intentionality as a criterion for "the artistic" rules out actions which would be described as full-fledged mistakes or accidents devoid of any conscious direction or manipulation whatsoever. My point is that there is a middle ground between conscious and unconscious actions, and a discussion of a performer's intentions may best be suited here. In other words, we have some sort of rule-governed behavior occurring here even though the notion of a rule is to be broadly construed.

Another reason why "intention" needs to be understood along the above lines is to permit *experiments*—actions undertaken to explore possibilities as yet undetermined. Experimentation among athletes and performers is an important, but little discussed phase in sport and art. Its importance is further appreciated in that it permits one to distinguish between "practice sessions" during which "aesthetic" actions can be created or revealed, and the later performance situations in which such actions are used. This distinction is present in most, if not all, sports.

If biographical information, like intention, contributes to an observer's direct appreciation and experience of a performance, then intentionalist criticism provides a valuable role in guiding aesthetic appreciation. However, "intention" here is no longer construed as a private, subjective affair which is separate from the performance. As Gene Blocker puts it: "Once the artist [or performer] has embodied his intentions in a publicly communicable form of expression, the intention becomes a part of an art object which is now part of the public domain."[7] So the proper, logical ways for intentionalist criticism to be practiced is captured by the following conditional:

(C) If a performer tells us what his or her performance means and it is possible to discover that meaning in the performance independently of the performer's statement, then it can be claimed that the performance means what its performer claims it means.[8]

We can call this "the criterion of independence" for intentional appeals. The fact that a performer had certain intentions in mind when he performed his maneuver does not guarantee that those intentions are embodied in that maneuver. An appeal to intentions can help clear up what was meant by the maneuver. Such an appeal cannot *change* the meaning of the maneuver, if such a meaning has been established by its performance and acknowledged by others. (This is the point of the above conditional, C.) No claim of intimate knowledge of the agent's intention is implied by the fact that the performer is the author of the maneuver. Whatever meaning claims are made are verified or corroborated by an observer or audience, or could potentially be verified. And in ice-skating, the meanings of maneuvers are usually first recognized and steered by the coach-trainer. It is not claimed here that the intentions of performers have a privileged role to play in the carrying out of understanding an x to be art or in distinguishing whether it is a good or bad (artistic) performance. In other words, a performer's role is not privileged in assessing the meaning of his or her performance. It is measured in the same way critics' comments are; that is, by appealing to observable features of those movements performed or their setting.

II

Now, let us see how this applies to the sportsperson or athlete. As a case study, I shall look at figure-skating. Before Toller Cranston (the Canadian world-class skater) and David Curry (the English skater who developed "Ice Dancing" in the late seventies) came Peggy Fleming. In the 1968 Grenoble Olympics, she initiated the aesthetic movement in figure-skating. Her fellow skaters at the Olympics thought she didn't stand a chance of winning because she was deliberately aesthetic in her approach to ice-skating. Her routines and numbers were guided by a set of aesthetic notions. It was thought that such an addition to a skater's performance would mar the routines and that the skater would be marked down by the judges. Fleming challenged the athleticism of that time, an attitude which was firmly entrenched in the skaters, coaches and judges. (Athleticism conceived of performance purely in terms of the skill and technique of execution of a string of otherwise unrelated jumps, spins, and other actions.) There was much resistance to what she did, not because it broke the rules, but because it changed them, demanding a new and more complex (higher) level of skating.

Let us take a closer look at how "biographical information," especially Fleming's, played a role in these dramatic changes in the sport. Interestingly, for sport performers (like ballet dancers) the biographical information also includes the *physical* characteristics (shape of body, feet, turnout, torso length, musculature and skeletal features) of the person and the history of how those characteristics were trained, what possibilities they offered for individual "creativity" within the "rules." Peggy Fleming's body, for example, with its ballet dancer's turnout (feet can be placed on a straight line, heels touching) and hip flexibility, is different from the sturdier, thicker, more muscular body typical of many of her competitors. This is important in analyzing the notion of aesthetic creativity or control, because it introduces a component of individualism absolutely connected to the qualities of the medium (the athlete's body).

In addition to the trained physical characteristics of the athlete's body being significant in understanding the notion of aesthetic control and creativity, we know several important and novel components of the "set" of aesthetic notions which guided Fleming's routines and numbers: fluid transitions between one action and the next, and the selection of the sequence of moves in order to achieve this fluidity; a deft, tidy execution; arm and torso positions reflective of those of the classical ballet; and a responsiveness to the mood and phrasing of the music. These elements which make up "aesthetic control" in figure-skating yield a distinctive personal style of exceptional grace and precision.

Despite the stimulus of Fleming's performance to a few athletes (including gymnasts, for sure), sport today has typically remained "anti-creative."[9] Cranston still sees the dominance of athleticism in the sports most readily capable of an aesthetic (or artistic) dimension (those being figure-skating, diving and gymnastics). In any event, a tension exists between aestheticism and athleticism today in figure-skating. The conflicting schools of thought are evident in the language of figure-skaters. However, in the remaining space I want to examine the school of thought which harbors aestheticism and artistic creativity in sport.

Fleming's figure-skating consists of two basic components; the rink which is her "stage" and the medium which is the "body-on-ice." The routines which she performed were controlled by aesthetic assessments. In observing these routines, one could see that they were more than just physical or athletic; they had an extra "something" added to them, which we would usually speak of as supplying a coherence and a fluency to her moves. The individual moves were performed and coordinated by a gracefulness consciously imparted by the performer. In discussing these "moves," it is important to view these as more than just physical movements. There is a distinction to be drawn here: 1) in the pre-Fleming and "athletic" skating, all "moves" (a sitzspin, for instance) are single, athletic "events," unconnected to the one before or after except for those preliminary moves (like skating fast) necessary to make them; and 2) aesthetic skating from Fleming on requires the individual moves to be linked—part of a continuum or unbroken unity of the entire routine. In light of this, Fleming's performances were rightfully described as "artistic."

Fleming or other skaters may not have had a particular intention to create art (although she did make such claims later, after Grenoble), but the resulting performance can be classified as such because of the aesthetic control exercised over the medium in question. Imagine a conversation between Fleming and her coach at a rehearsal where she says, "Don't you think holding my leg up here longer would look better?" Of course the aesthetic intention and result only come, historically and biographically, after consummate technical ability—a sort of "what do I do next, since I can already execute these single moves superbly?" But at this point we move beyond discussions of technique and skill, and enter into the realm of aesthetic intent and artistic considerations. An artistic medium can be sport just as easily as it can be clay, paint, notes or words. What Fleming did in figure-skating may be done by other realms of sport, for example gymnastics.[10]

So, one way in which the issue of whether or not sport is art can be settled is by appealing to intentions. But blanket appeals are out of the question. Each case must be looked at individually to see if the concept of aesthetic control is satisfied. As I have sketched above, there are certain activities which must reflect or reveal those intentions, and if they are present, then we can talk legitimately about the artistic in sport or sport as art.

III

In pursuit of this goal, let us now briefly examine some recent criticism released from UPI (United Press International). Critic Fred Ferguson talks about an ice show in New York City, entitled *Ice*, which, he argues, has elevated skating to the level of art.[11] His reasons for making this statement are these. First, "*Ice* is a spectacle designed to show off the artistry of truly fine skating." Second, among the cast of thirty-five stars are three world-class skaters—Fleming, Cranston, and Robin Cousins. Third, a top-notch symphony orchestra accompanies the ensemble, and the skating and music are synchronized—not only in tempo and rhythm (usually even "athletic" skaters synchronize with tempo and often with rhythm) but with mood, richness or spareness of orchestration, and thematic invention. Thus, "the excitement is created less by gimmicks than by artistry." Fourth, the choreography (by ice show veteran Sarah Kawahara) brings the production numbers to the level of artistry. Fifth, the costumes designed by Jef Billings for skating provide "a brilliant array of color." And sixth, *Ice* was staged in New York for a New York audience. Ferguson ends his criticism with this observation:

> Cranston, who has been said to have brought ice skating artistry to the level of ballet, proves it in a series of numbers titled "The Thief." A little tragedy is told. It comes as close to ballet on ice as we have seen.

The reasons, then, for skating to be considered as art were embodied in this particular time or moment. (Nelson Goodman's temporal theory of art is particularly useful here.)[12] Skating becomes a work of art at that moment when we have truly outstanding skaters who can perform the total complex unity. "The excitement" or the awareness of the numbers as artistic was created by the conscious manipulation of the medium by the skaters, as in, for example, Cranston's number "The Thief." So the Tomas-Montague requirement of art—critical or aesthetic control—is clearly exemplified by *Ice*. One way that Ferguson establishes his assessment is by pointing out several times that the skating in *Ice* is not arena skating, as it is in the Ice Follies or the Ice Capades. (Ice Follies is only "tempo" skating.) There are no clown acts, no "canned" music (meaning no combo or taped music), no skating behind the music or gliding over it, and no gimmicks of the sort which are commonly found in the Ice Follies. Since *Ice* could easily be mistaken by novice viewers for one of the performances of the Ice Follies, Ferguson is deliberate in making negative comparisons. These "gimmicks" conceal the skating, whereas the features our critic cites leave the audience's attention on nothing but bodily movement on ice and the performance experience which the skaters' movements compose. The entertainment gimmicks are missing. The music is and was for *Ice* supportive of the skating, not its master. What the Ice Follies has done is to say the medium is body on ice with music. The show is no longer skating but art; or to phrase it better, arena skating has become artistic skating.

An appeal to intentions is needed here—to those of Kawahara, Fleming and Cranston—because the context, the arena, has remained essentially the same. Music is also present in both cases. It is how those actions or movements are performed which gives us a clue as to whether skating is an art or not; it is the whole—a unity of music, movements, and the space of the arena. Moreover, it is the *ice*—a unique surface—that provides the athletic challenge and also the artistic setting for the body's motion. Thus our critic Ferguson's final comment is a bit misleading; it isn't fair to say "ballet on ice." Ice-skating is close to ballet in rigor and grace, but not in its particular medium. Ballet happens on a springy wood floor. Its essentials (the five positions) are predicated by its surface just as skating's (steps, glides, plus leg and foot positions) are by its. The unbroken "glide" of skating is fundamentally different from the "illusion" of gliding a dancer must create with individual steps. But surely it is this "gliding" that is fundamental to skating, providing as it does the momentum for the leaps and spins and surely suggesting an "aestheticism" based on fluidity and unity. In other words, skating tries to be aesthetic with its own medium's givens (both limits and freedoms), not ballet's.

The intentions which reflect a conscious manipulation of the medium by aesthetic concepts are seen in Ferguson's mention of Kawahara's choreography, Billings' costumes, Paul Walberg conducting an orchestra, and the skaters themselves. They all form a "complex" of interrelated intentions which satisfy our notions of creative activity and art. There are designated (and coordinated) sets of intentions which make up such actions as orchestrating, choreographing, skating, and so on. (This case—the show *Ice*— is an extension of my original criterion and case which initially involved only individuals—like Peggy Fleming and her coach—creating or performing art works.)

The coherence of *Ice* derives from an aesthetic necessity, but that "necessity" is more like that found in criticism than in logic. In other words, the sort of "necessity" or coherence is like that found in practical reasoning rather than mathematical deduction. An immediate consequence of this alignment of aesthetic necessity or control to criticism is that there is a link between audience and artist. (Goodman presumes this too; see Note 12.) Hence, there is a unity which underlies a particular art work, and its existence or presence can be taken as support for aesthetic monism.[13]

The point of my extended case here is that much of the formal structure embedded in this little piece of criticism can be used as a "guide" to setting up arguments for other activities falling within the domain of sport. If one traces the Wimbledon stories early each summer, one can find a similar informal logic used by critics who discover artistry in the matches. There is no music, but the other elements are present. It takes just a little imagination to fill in the details. In fact, the sportswriters do it every season when Wimbledon is staged. The same conditions of aesthetic control are expected to be fulfilled at The Lawn Tennis Championships. In tennis, it is the body on grass which is the medium to be negotiated by each player. Each sport has its own occasion when its activities can be deemed "artistic."[14]

NOTES

1. This is where *j* denotes "what one intends to think," and *S* denotes "the set of one's intentions."

2. I do not accept the position of some descriptive theorists of art who hold that merely having "artistic intentions" (with the emphasis on *intentions*) suffices for some *x* to be a work of art. The adjective, artistic, needs to contribute something to the meaning of the phrase, artistic intentions.

3. Phillip Montague, "Art and Creative Activity," *Philosophia* 1, nos. 3–4 (July 1971), pp. 179–189, esp. 182. I am heavily indebted to Montague for his argument on these matters.

4. See Montague again, p. 184; and Vincent Tomas, "Creativity in Art," in *Creativity in the Arts*, Vincent Tomas, ed. (Englewood Cliffs, New Jersey: Prentice-Hall, Inc., 1964), pp. 97–109. Reprinted later in *Art and Philosophy: Readings in Aesthetics*, W. E. Kennick, ed. (2d. ed.; New York: St. Martin's Press, 1979), pp. 131–142. Tomas speaks of "critical control" whereas Montague speaks of "aesthetic control."

5. For the discussion of intention in criticism, see W. K. Wimsatt and Monroe Beardsley, "The Intentional Fallacy," *Sewanee Review* (1946), pp. 468–488; and more recently, George Dickie, *Aesthetics: An Introduction* (Indianapolis: Bobbs-Merrill Co., 1971), ch. 12. For a defense of appeals to intention, see E. D. Hirsch, Jr., *Validity in Interpretation* (New Haven: Yale University Press, 1967); and Frank Cioffi, "Some Problems in Modern Aesthetics," in *British Philosophy in Mid-Century*, C. A. Mace, ed. (London: George Allen and Unwin Ltd., 1957), pp. 359–390; and later Cioffi wrote "Intention and Interpretation in Criticism," *Proceedings of the Aristotelian Society* 64 (1963), pp. 85–106. Following Cioffi's lead, if we adopt Wittgenstein's characterization of philosophy: "putting into order our notions as to what can be said about the world," we have a program for the philosophy of sport: "putting into order our notions as to what can be said about the sports world." In this essay I have tried to put our notion of *aesthetic control* into order within the context of sport.

For more on intentions and for an extension of Cioffi's argument, see Anthony Savile, "The Place of Intention in the Concept of Art," *Proc. Arist. Soc.* 69 (1969), pp. 101–124.

6. See Dickie, p. 110. The locutionary background of "intention" I have in mind comes from J. L. Austin's informal account; see his "A Plea for Excuses" and "Three Ways of Spilling Ink," in *Philosophical Papers* (2d. ed.; London: Oxford University Press, 1970), pp. 175–204 and 272–287.

7. H. Gene Blocker, *Philosophy of Art* (New York: Charles Scribner's Sons, 1979), p. 248.

8. This conditional is a generalization of those features of intentionalist criticism which seem to be valid. See Blocker, p. 249; Dickie, p. 119; and Warren E. Steinkraus, *Philosophy of Art* (new ed.; Washington, D.C.: University Press of America, 1984), ch. II, sec. E.

9. Toller Cranston, "Goals before Golds," in *Sport in Perspective*, John T. Partington, et al, eds. (Ottawa, Ontario, Canada: ISSP 5th World Sport Psychology Congress, 1982), p. 19: "Sport today is anti-creativity. In fact, it is kind of silly for me, it's redundant to talk about it. In fact for me, sport today is old fashioned. I think that I was in the era in figure skating when it was at its height, not because of me but because of all the other people who were exploring, who were interested in creating new and different routines, who were interested in music, who were interested in style and the choreography—well all of that has fallen by the wayside. Because the athletes who are winning today, who are on the top—are the ones, who have a triple jump—it has nothing to do with creativity. I suppose the Turisheva, that kind of athlete, if she is going to compete against somebody who does a double back flip on the mat, how do you compete against that? You can't, because people, spectators, judges, coaches, etc., are so programmed to those technical achievements that they are not able to discern how valuable the fully rounded athlete really is. I don't know in particular why the male skaters use music. I think they should set an obstacle course, and see who can do the most triple jumps, and declare them the winner. Because that's really where it's at today." Cranston sees decline in what Fleming briefly established as a movement in figure-skating.

10. See Paul G. Kuntz's discussion of the gymnast from Georgia, Neal Shartar, who encountered resistance from the sport establishment concerning his aesthetic interests; in "Aesthetics Applies to Sports as well as to the Arts," *Journal of the Philosophy of Sport* 1 (September 1974), pp. 6–35, esp. 9ff., and reprinted in this anthology, pp. 492–509.

11. Fred Ferguson (UPI), "Ice Show Elevates Skating to Art," *The Dallas Morning News* (Tuesday, February 22, 1983), p. 2A. I shall use this little piece as a paradigm case for intentionalist criticism.

12. Nelson Goodman, "When Is Art?" in his *Ways of Worldmaking* (Indianapolis: Hackett Publishing Co., 1978), ch. IV. Goodman's answer to the question, "When is an object a work of art?" is as follows:

> My answer is that just as an object may be a symbol—for instance, a sample—at certain times and under circumstances and not at others, so an object may be a work of art at some times and not at others. Indeed, just by virtue of functioning as a symbol in a certain way does an object become, while so functioning, a work of art. The stone is normally no work of art while in the driveway, but may be so when

on display in an art museum. In the driveway, it usually performs no symbolic function. In the art museum, it exemplifies certain of its properties—e.g., properties of shape, color, texture. The hole-digging and filling [in Central Park (N.Y.) by Oldenburg] functions as a work *insofar as our attention is directed to it as an exemplifying symbol.* (p. 67; my italics)

The word *object* is construed broadly enough to include performances. The activity of skating functions as art in the Ferguson case. The performance of *Ice* directs our attention towards artistic considerations, so the "directing" is the result of successful manipulation of the medium (skating) by aesthetic concepts. The above conditional, C, has been satisfied. Whenever this situation arises in sport, we have that given performance aligned as art or a work of art.

13. See Montague's "In Defense of Aesthetic Monism," *Journal of Value Inquiry* 3, no. 2 (Summer 1969), pp. 126–135; and Blocker, pp. 99–100ff., 141n. Aesthetic monism is the view that there is only one object of aesthetic concern which is the work of art itself. Dual object theorists, like George Santayana (see Blocker), are challenged by aesthetic monists. The debate continues between monists and dual object theorists; see, for example, John W. Hanke, "Can Representational Works of Art Be Physical Objects?" *Journal of Value Inquiry* 10, no. 3 (Fall 1976), pp. 209–219.

14. I wish to thank Frances Osborn Robb (Instructor of Art History at North Texas State University in Denton) for her help with my discussion of figure-skating. And I wish to thank those present at the spring meeting of the North Texas Philosophical Association, Saturday, April 23, 1983, at Texas Christian University, Fort Worth, in particular, Richard F. Galvin, who served as commentator and whose essay follows in this anthology, for their comments and criticisms. They have helped me become clearer on the issues involved in this paper. Also, I am grateful to the Office of Sponsored Projects and Research at Texas Christian University for financial assistance in the development of this essay.

RICHARD F. GALVIN

Aesthetic Incontinence in Sport

In order to have an adequate appreciation for the force of Professor Wertz's argument, it is necessary to focus on the original foe, i.e. David Best and those who would have it that context excludes sport from art, since context

---

Published for the first time in this anthology.

alone determines whether or not x is a work of art.[1] The argument made by Wertz that contextualists such as Best cannot account for conceptual change is persuasive, and this point casts serious doubt on the plausibility of contextualist accounts of art.

However, before turning to the details of Wertz's position, I would like to pause to consider the following issue. It puzzles me that in both Philosophy of Sport and Aesthetics, the examples which are typically produced in the debate surrounding these issues consist of putative instances of what is aesthetically pleasing, or of what is beautiful in sport, music or whatever. Yet even in the time of Plato at least the conceptual dependence between the beautiful and the ugly was identified. Hence, at least prima facie, if sport is art, we should have at least the concept of what would be ugly in sport. It is also arguable that such cases are more interesting; for example, what makes a performance by an athlete aesthetically unpleasant? It is certainly arguable that these cases are more entertaining, if not more conceptually interesting, than those of the aesthetically pleasant. Thus I shall argue that we do have instances of the ugly in sport. If this is true, we would have additional confirmation of the thesis that art does not exclude sport. I shall now proceed to outline a few of my favorite instances of ugly performances in sport.

Where else to start but with Marv Throneberry? I was at the Polo Grounds in 1962, watching the worst team in major league baseball history, viz. the New York Mets of the aforementioned vintage. Marv was a vital cog in this machine. On the day in question he hit a line drive off the right field wall, and was heading for second base with an apparent double. However, midway between first and second base he tripped over his own feet and fell flat on his face. He was tagged out, while lying flat on his back like a beached whale, by a surprised and no doubt amused second baseman. Another similar incident involved Steve Hamilton, a lanky relief pitcher for the Yankees, who was a devout tobacco-chewer. One day, with full chaw, he delivered a pitch which resulted in a fierce line drive which hit him in the midsection. Appropriately startled, he swallowed the tobacco and proceeded to redeposit his lunch on the pitcher's mound. The batter was awarded a base hit.

However, not all examples of the aesthetically unpleasant in sport involve pathos and failure as the above might suggest. Dick Hall was a very effective relief pitcher for the Kansas City Athletics and Baltimore Orioles in the mid '60s. His mode of delivery was the subject of controversy. Unlike the fluid, beautiful pitching form of a Sandy Koufax or Tom Seaver, Hall's motion was likened to that of a "drunken giraffe on roller skates." But he was a very good pitcher.

More examples of this abound. In football we have Joe Kapp, most noted as a Viking quarterback, who was very successful, but whose performances were often criticized as lacking aesthetic beauty. He did not move gracefully, and probably never threw a spiral pass in his life. In the same vein we had the overweight Sonny Jurgenson, who was immobile, ungraceful, and violated most of the rules on how to throw a football. Also in football we have Tom Matte, a halfback whose style rather than productivity earned him the nickname "garbage back."

One example from basketball deserves mention. Mel Counts was an extremely awkward seven-footer who played for Boston and Phoenix in the NBA. It was contended by many that his manner of release in shooting a jump shot was incompatible with its winding up anywhere in the vicinity of the basket. His dribbling, passing and defensive performances were the epitome of lack of grace on the court. But again, he was a very effective player.

Perhaps I am sensitive to this issue because once while pitching in a Little League playoff game, I attempted to make a pickoff throw to first base, caught a spike on the pitching rubber, and fell on my face, watching helplessly as the ball dribbled in the general direction of first base. But I was not called for a balk, and the runner did not advance to second, probably because he was laughing too hard.

There is a moral to these stories, and it is a moral which appears to support Wertz's thesis. The notion of aesthetic control, which plays a central role in Wertz's analysis, appears to be precisely what enables us to identify those performances in sport which are aesthetically pleasing as well as those which are aesthetically unpleasant. Something about how the athletes in these stories manipulated the medium—how they performed in their respective sports— enables us to identify their activities as ugly performances, and it is crucial to note that failure to accomplish the objective of the particular sport is neither a necessary nor a sufficient condition for this assessment. This will ward off the obvious objection that the putatively aesthetic notions applied to performances in sport are merely elliptical references to success or failure at the sport in question.

Having argued that we find instances of both the beautiful and the ugly in sport performances, we should now take a close look at Wertz's argument. Appeals to intentionality are notoriously problematic, and such an appeal plays a crucial role in Wertz's account. The sport-art issue is particularly complex, since there seem to be two sets of intentions relevant here—the intentions of the performer, and the intentions of observers, perhaps especially critics. Each set of intentions deserves close analysis.

One might attempt to produce an argument against Wertz by arguing that the appeal to the intention of the performer to create something artistic, as in the case of Peggy Fleming, is clearly not a *necessary* condition for our identifying a sport performance as a work of art. For example, many have argued that the performances of Joe Namath and Ken Stabler are works of art, in that their play selection, anticipation of defensive strategy, manipulation of the time clock and passing were artistic. Likewise, it is plausible that when quizzed about their intentions, Namath and Stabler would deny intending to produce a work of art, perhaps claiming that they were interested only in winning the game, and disavowing any manipulation of the medium in accordance with any aesthetic concepts whatsoever. Although such testimony is no incontrovertible evidence of one's intentions, it would appear to provide strong evidence which would appear to cut against Montague's position, and might eventually cause problems for Wertz's thesis, which relies upon, e.g., Peggy Fleming's express intention to create an artistic performance on ice.

This problem concerning intentionality is not limited to sport aesthetics alone, but rather applies to aesthetics in general. For example, it is plausible that Michelangelo might deny that his painting of the Sistine Chapel involved an intentional manipulation of the medium in accordance with aesthetic concepts. Perhaps he would claim only to have intended to create an atmosphere which would be conducive to praying, or perhaps to have attempted to produce an accurate pictorial representation of Genesis, with no consideration of the aesthetics of the matter. Likewise, a carpenter might be attempting to solve an engineering problem of sorts, such as constructing a staircase which connects point A and point B. His concerns could be entirely pragmatic—durability, functional efficacy, economy, etc. This appears to have been the case in the construction of a spiral staircase in the Loretto Chapel in Santa Fe, New Mexico. Yet critics have observed that the staircase is a work of art, and have attributed an array of aesthetic properties to it. Still further, archaeologists have discovered numerous objects which are agreed to be beautiful, yet in many cases the intentions of their creators are completely unknown or obviously devoid of any intention to produce a work of art. It is clear that the intention of the performer or artist to accord with aesthetic concepts is not a necessary condition for something's being a work of art, whether in the context of sport or elsewhere. This is troublesome for any account of art which relies on the artist's forming or acting upon such intentions. Since arguments invoking this type of appeal to intentionality will apply to all intentional accounts of art regardless of any inclusion or exclusion relationship claimed between sport and art, these arguments will not establish that art excludes performances in sport.

It might also be objected that an appeal to the intentions of the audience, whether critics or more casual observers, is peculiar. How could it be that the intentions of third parties determine whether or not something is a work of art, when the crucial relationship appears to lie between the creator and the object? At least preanalytically, one wants to say that once the creator completes his task, the object has been created, and it is what it is. It appears strange to maintain that the intentions of third parties can transform an object which is not otherwise a work of art into one which is. An object's taking on such new properties is not at all like Cambridge Dependence, in which, e.g., a woman can acquire the property of "being a widow" by the death of her husband, even though there is no change in the woman herself. Aesthetic properties appear not to fit such a paradigm. The intuition is that the object itself must bear this burden—after all, *it* is the work of art.

This difficulty arises in the appeal to the intentions of third parties in the attempt to explain how sport can be art. For example, it is perplexing at least to hold that what makes a diving stab by a shortstop, who has no intention to create a work of art, take on aesthetic properties is that Howard Cosell feels compelled to heap lavish praise upon the performance, attributing aesthetic properties to it.

But once again, the same objection applies *mutatis mutandis* to *all* other art forms. The composer of a spectacular gospel tune might be intending only to put worshipers in a mental state conducive to enthusiastic praying, which need not have any reference to aesthetics, perhaps only to psychology, and does not intend to manipulate the medium in accordance with any aesthetic concepts. He might know only that certain sequences of sounds are likely to put people in the appropriate mood. The immediate audience might be unaware of any of this, be it intentions to create art or to make people feel like praying. But suppose that this tune is discovered by musicians or critics and praised for its aesthetic properties. This result is just as counterintuitive, as far as the role of third-party intentions is concerned, as the case of the shortstop whose fielding play "becomes" a work of art thanks to the comments of Joe Garagiola. If these really are works of art, they should be so both before and independently of the formation of the "relevant intentions" on the part of third parties. The problem lies not in the "sport as art" thesis, but rather in the intentionality thesis.

My suggestion is as follows. What needs to be explicated is the crucial notion of aesthetic control. This is troublesome not specifically for the sport as art thesis, but rather for aesthetic accounts which rely on the species of appeal to intentions. One could then begin to construct an account of art according to which something is a work of art if (and perhaps only if) it satisfies the notion of aesthetic control. In this way the essential features of Wertz's account would be vindicated. We must, however, be able to produce an account of aesthetic control which does not require the attribution of intentions which involve aesthetic concepts, whether as a necessary or sufficient condition, or make a covert reference to what is to count as an aesthetic medium. Clearly one worry here is fatal overinclusiveness; the other is vicious circularity. We need a principle of aesthetic control which will claim the carpenter's construction of the staircase, the composing of a musical piece, and the performance of Peggy Fleming among its instances, but will exclude things like taking out the garbage, changing a flat tire, and the like. But circularity is the Scylla to this Charybdis—the principle of aesthetic control cannot contain the notion of an aesthetic medium as a crucial term in the analysis. Producing such an account is a major project for the view which Wertz proposes.

Moreover, if what I suggested at the beginning of this paper about the aesthetically unpleasant performance in sport is correct, a further project would appear to be necessary. If we require a principle of aesthetic control in order to account for aesthetically pleasant creations, we would appear to require a similar principle in order to account for aesthetically unpleasant creations. I suggest that we call this "The Principle of Aesthetic Incontinence," whose task it will be to identify and explain instances in which something fails to measure up to the appropriate criteria for the medium in question. And this type of failure is not simply that of "failing to create something aesthetically pleasant," which would appear to include aesthetically neutral products and performances, but rather should account for those products and performances which are ugly. I should also add that performances of both a research and critical nature by academicians, perhaps especially philosophers, should not be excluded from the domain of this principle. Surely the spirit of Marv Throneberry lives on in the classroom, at conferences and in scholarly journals as well as in what once was the area between first and second base at the Polo Grounds.

NOTE

1. David Best, *Philosophy and Human Movement* (London: George Allen & Unwin, 1978), Ch. 5, esp. p. 121; and "Art and Sport," *Journal of Aesthetic Education* 14, no. 2 (April 1980), pp. 69–80.

SPENCER K. WERTZ

Comments on Galvin

When is a comedian a comedian? It's when he or she has the right set of intentions. You can place an individual in the proper setting or context, but that individual may not be a comedian or make people laugh. If we replace Johnny Carson with Wertz on *The Tonight Show*, we would seal its fate. If, however, that individual possesses the relevant, rightful intentions, then we have a comic situation and all of us share in the laughter.

This happens in tracing the aesthetically unpleasant or the ugly in sport with Professor Galvin. Throneberry, Hall and Galvin surely throw into question all those things Roger Angell wrote about baseball and the legendary interior stadium. All that symmetry, balance, grace, and rhythm have been comically displaced by their opposites. Either situation is recognizable by us for what it is—be it the product of aesthetic control or incontinence. This recognition (or potential recognition) of something being one thing rather than another or in addition to another helps us appreciate how we human beings create our social world (*die Umwelt*).

Sport like art is one of the regions of that social world, and the structure of that world is identifiable by those who occupy it or appreciate it for what it is. This is where "third party" intentions come into play, for they assist us in weeding out the more troublesome borderline cases. The conditional I formulated on page 512 is an attempt to summarize the procedure or routine for legitimatizing appeals to intentions when those sorts of appeals seem necessary.

By "intentions" I don't mean psychological inner states which an agent is overtly aware of, but rather I mean to designate a more basic phenomenological feature of human consciousness. Intentional states, in this fundamental sense, are actions directed towards "objects." States of consciousness are always *about* something or directed toward something. If the states are "correlated" with the appropriate objects, then we have the proper genre or class assignment; e.g., where something in "sport" becomes something "artistic." That transformation amounts to a set of correlations being made. (Here again see the conditional and my use of it in the above analysis.) I have tried to provide a logical account of our ability to identify some human movements as certain actions of a type. "Sport as art" is one such process of identification. "Third party" intentions function like auxiliary hypotheses in the logic of

---

Published for the first time in this anthology.

confirmation. They provide for some sort of validation or verification step in the process of reasoning. In other words, they give us *reasons* why we can call something *x* rather than *y*. Hence, some critical or aesthetic control is made by the performers in or on their medium, and it is *that* which is identified.

Galvin is right in suggesting that an account of aesthetic control shouldn't make a covert reference to what is to count as an aesthetic medium. Such a move clearly begs the question and is therefore fallacious: aesthetic is an aesthetic! That doesn't get us anywhere. It is also a reason why I think you can't rule "sport" out of "art." There is something suspicious about ruling a priori or logically that something is not or cannot be something else when we are talking about human institutions, conventions, and practices which all change as we change. In this respect, "sport" and "art" are no different from the other practices which make up our social world.

A Guide for Further Study

Chapter 3, "Sports and Traditional Arts: Sculpture, Painting, Literature," of Higgs's *Sports: A Reference Guide*, pp. 50–68, provides ample reading on the relationship between sport and aesthetics. The only book on the topic which is definitely worth studying is Benjamin Lowe's *The Beauty of Sport: A Cross-Disciplinary Inquiry*, especially chapters 1–5. Moreover, the first three articles in *Philosophy in Context* 9 (1979) are devoted to sport aesthetics. The best recent work is by C. D. Cordner in "Grace and Functionality," *British Journal of Aesthetics* 24 (Autumn 1984), and essays by Boxill, Kupfer, and Bostow in *Journal of the Philosophy of Sport* 11 (1984).

Part IV:

The Dimensions of Sport

Introduction

That sport touches the full range of our experiencing as human beings is the assumption underlying Part IV: The Dimensions of Sport. The five sections on Language, Fantasy, Humor, Time and Space, and Death are only five arbitrary selections out of the multiple possibilities that might be covered. Perhaps you can think of at least ten off hand.

We have all heard sporting language in unlikely contexts and from peculiar sources. Politicians and book reviewers have been known to play "hardball," and academic committees sometimes try an "end run," then decide to "punt." The section on language looks at sportalk in its several forms. Randall Poe's "The Writing of Sports" provides a history of American sportswriting and an evaluative survey of the best contemporary artisans. Michael Novak continues this scrutiny of sportswriters, dividing them into interesting categories: "Jocks, Hacks, Flacks, and Pricks." And he speculates on television's damaging effect on the quality and profundity—even the accuracy—of sportswriting. Novak's critique of Howard Cosell, easily the most famous, or infamous, figure in modern sports journalism, is a thoughtful evenhanded assessment of both Cosell's contributions and his limitations. The phenomenon of sports language pervading politics is the subject of Francine Hardaway's "Foul Play: Sports Metaphors as Public Doublespeak." In this piece, Hardaway concludes that political jock talk is ultimately pernicious in that it deflects the public from thinking about public issues in clear, precise language. Richard Lipsky also ponders the problem in his chapter "Of Team Players and Sky Hooks: The Infiltration of Sports Language in Politics." For Lipsky, the appeal of sports-language usage by politicians is its ability to create linguistic community by drawing upon a common store of symbolic imagery. To see South Vietnam, for example, as one of America's "expansion teams" is a concept graspable by all, yet, at the same time, a bit misleading in its oversimplifying complex issues.

Ordinary language philosophy is a recent movement imported from the

British Isles in the Fifties and Sixties. Michael Martin and Warren Fraleigh attempt to analyze the phrase "a good clutch hitter" and demonstrate that there is no satisfactory quantitative definition. (No one should be surprised by their result.) Baseball's lore is full of acronyms like RBIs—runs batted in. Continuing the convention, Martin and Fraleigh stage a Super Bowl of acronyms for us to feast on.

The crucial question is how "go ahead conditions" (GAC) and "crucial and important games" (CG) are to be clarified in the proposed definitions. Martin attempts to do this in his first essay, giving us "batting average under go ahead conditions in the late innings" (BAGACLI, pronounced "ba-gack-lee"). BAGACLI doesn't escape the vagueness rule for definitions because it leaves out CG. So the idea suggests itself of defining "clutch hitter" as someone who has a high BAGACLI with CG, or for short BAGACLICG. Well, this refinement proves to be vague, too, and Martin concludes that maybe for some purposes this vagueness of ordinary baseball language is desirable. GAC and CG must be "open" textured concepts in order to handle the variety and diversity of the game and its players. To illustrate this situation, we follow the philosophers' debate with a "Stats" piece by Henry Hecht from *Sports Illustrated*, entitled, "Here's the Info on Hitters Who Get Tough When the Going Gets Tough." Does Hecht fall victim to some of Martin's ill-fated formulae or does he illustrate the desirable vagueness or open-texturedness of ordinary baseball language?

Sport is the very stuff of daydream. The name Walter Mitty, Thurber's memorable daydreamer, is synonymous with fantasy, specifically glorious imaginings of sporting triumphs. As well, sport has lent itself to imaginings of the fantastic, the bizarre, a twilight zone where the strange and the improbable are neighbors. The second section, Sport and Fantasy, presents several versions of the imagination at play.

In *The Universal Baseball Association* Robert Coover's nondescript bachelor CPA, age 56, has invented an entire baseball league, a board game, that provides him with a glamorous fictional world in contrast to the boring routine of his accounting career. Yet Henry Waugh's creation ends up dominating his actual world and undermining Henry's sanity. In the opening chapter reprinted here, the reader finds Henry in the seventh inning of a perfect game, the implications of which reveal that more is going on than a lonely man's harmless pastime. That one can lose oneself in fantasy is also a concern of Sam Koperwas's short, surreal story, "Ball." In the driest terms, the story is about the conflict of a Jewish father's pushing his tall son to play basketball while the son has other desires. Yet the story is narrated via a delightfully absurdist technique climaxed by the father's fantasy that his son has grown to cosmic proportions and the father's realization that he has created a monster. Laurence Lieberman's father dreams too, as he tells us in his poem, "My Father Dreams of Baseball." It seems that his father is a betting man, to his family's detriment, who redeems his losses through fantasy. This notion of redeeming life failures through sporting fantasies is the subject of Jim Brosnan's insightful essay, "The Fantasy World of Baseball." An ex-pitcher for Cincinnati, Brosnan anticipated Coover's J. Henry Waugh: "The Inner Fan wants the game played as he thinks it *should* be played. He will create players in his own image—a man making gods—to assure a good sport." In short, sport offers a fantasy of perfection in an imperfect world. That fantasy of perfection is analyzed by Roland Garrett in the closing piece titled "The Metaphysics of Baseball." Garrett illustrates various ways in which baseball shares the concern of metaphysics by showing that baseball, along with other sports, has a contemplative and abstract orientation which demands clarity and intelligibility. Because of this carefully articulated structure, "the game makes reality accessible." Garrett's conclusion is in line with what the other writers in the section think of sport: "The unique perspective of the game makes reality uniquely known and meaningful. The action of rounding the bases, in which the whole person takes part and by which he succeeds, transforms this limited perspective on reality into a timeless, complete, encircling encounter."

While sport is a serious subject, it is also subject to the comic squint. The readings in Section III prove that the arena is a rich source of burlesque, farce, exaggeration, parody, whimsy, and satire. The leaven of laughter relieves and raises the spirits of all.

Baseball with its inherent zaniness, as one might expect, has offered writers the most comic possibilities. The selection from Philip Roth's *The Great American Novel* describes a bizarre contest between the Ruppert Mundys and the inmates of an Ohio insane asylum, an away game that is way, way out, featuring a kleptomaniac shortstop who hides every grounder hit his way in his shirt. The other baseball piece is a chapter from Ring Lardner's classic, *You Know Me Al.* In this chapter, rookie busher Jack Keefe, southpaw hurler and master of the alibi, has made the White Sox roster. The contrast between what he thinks of himself and his performance is Lardner's comic strategy. And it is hilariously effective.

In more recent years, writers have begun to exploit the gridiron for humorous fiction. Ernest W. Speed, Jr., the author of "The Coach Who Didn't Teach Civics," describes a small Texas town's hiring of a new high school football coach whose degree is not in secondary education. Coach Rhodes carries on a side business the nature of which is shrouded in mystery. The players themselves make the discovery much to their delight and to the town's embarrassment. Texans and football are an unbeatable comic team in Dan Jenkins' *Semi-Tough* as well. In this excerpt, Fort Worth oilman Big Ed Bookman regales us with his philosophy of life and his interpretation of God's will on Thursday evening before the all-New York Super Bowl. Jenkins lampoons a mind set that, unfortunately, is not that much of an exaggeration of the way some folks perceive reality, those that see Archie Bunker as a straight shooting speaker of truth.

Sport offers pause for cosmic reflection, compelling us to consider time and space. The four selections in Section IV cause us to contemplate the special time and space of the field as opposed to our experience of time and space in our everyday pursuits.

The illusion of timelessness that baseball creates for the fan is the theme of Rolfe Humphries' poem "Polo Grounds." Yet the individual fan becomes conscious that he grows older every season while the players appear to remain the same age. The poem is a compressed version of the baseball essays by Angell, Grella, and Garrett. The spatial organization of sport, especially baseball and football, intrigues Murray Ross in "Football Red and Baseball Green." His most interesting ideas emerge from his discussion of football, in particular the notion that football converts space into time. Michael Novak, always stimulating, raises the problem of time and space to the metaphysical level in "Sacred Space, Sacred Time." Stadia are "our cathedrals," Novak maintains, places of tales, traditions, and extraordinary acts. Likewise, time in sport is sacred, intensified, in contrast to alarm clocks and calendars. Sport time emphasizes possibilities. So long as outs remain or seconds are left, something improbable can happen. Thus Yogi Berra's famous dictum, "It ain't over till it's over," has echoes of eternal life in it for Novak.

What seems more remote and unthinkable in sport than human mortality? When death casts its shadow on the field, we recoil in shock. Thurman Munson's empty locker gapes like an open grave. Death lacks manners, a sense of tact. In the fifth section, four writers gaze the Reaper in the face. We offer this final section as a kind of memento mori, the skull on the fifty-yard line and in the batter's box.

The chapter reprinted from Mark Harris's novel about a dying catcher, *Bang the Drum Slowly*, concerns Bruce Pearson's first attack and its effect on the team, but it proves to be a false alarm unrelated to his terminal Hodgkin's disease. Pearson, a marginal player of modest skill, is the butt of everyone's jokes until the truth of his condition leaks out to the team. For the narrator, Henry Wiggen, the impact of his roomie's dying is to make Wiggen reappraise his own living, to focus on "what you say *now*." Moving from fiction to fact,

Barnard Collier's piece tells the story of Detroit Lion Chuck Hughes, who died of a heart attack in the fourth quarter of a game with the Chicago Bears in 1971 at age 28. Collier captures the unseemliness, the sheer inappropriateness, of this athlete dying young right in our living rooms on national TV amidst the beer and the popcorn. Mass death is simply benumbing as Robert W. Hamblin's moving elegy to the Evansville University basketball team so eloquently expresses. Perhaps, Hamblin argues, "all opponents are Death/masquerading in school colors."

Hamblin's suggestion becomes a theme for Slusher and Ermler. Failure in sport becomes a metaphor for death. However, there are sports (ones Slusher calls death-centered sports) where failure *does* mean death: "In such sports as boxing, auto racing, bobsledding, and speed-boating, man is constantly performing in the shadow of death." And "facing death makes the man of sport available to an awareness of authentic existence." There is no faking it when the hunter awaits the charge of a wild boar. The recognition of death itself provides the sportsperson with life. How? "As he embraces defeat, as he must death, he learns, indeed, the structure (meaning) of life." Kathy Ermler brightens our outlook by suggesting the responses to defeat or failure need not be tragic. They can be comic or hopeful: "The comic athlete looks forward to a time when there will be another attempt to prove personal worth." And perhaps the greatest insight of all into the playing of a sport she sums up with these words: "Failure, no less than success, may be a means through which to achieve authentic self-understanding." Sport affords us with the opportunity to learn to deal with failure. It is something all of us must learn to cope with.

Ernest Hemingway once remarked that all true stories end in death. This anthology has had a true story to tell, the story of sport.

Section I: Language

RANDALL POE

The Writing of Sports

Well-meaning people often ask sportswriters, even middle-aged sportswriters, what they are going to do when they grow up.

—Robert Lipsyte, author and former
sports columnist for The New York *Times*

Ten-fourteen p.m. in Madison Square Garden. The New York Knicks have just defeated the Boston Celtics and sit in front of their locker stalls like pickups in a singles bar. Swiftly, the sportswriters move in.

"What happened out there?" ask several of them at once.

Earl Monroe, pulling on his red bikini underpants, says it was a case of good team defense. Then, a babble of other questions: Did you lose your temper? (*Newsday*), Why didn't you shoot more? (New York *Post*), Does your foot hurt? (*Boston Globe*).

Bored with Monroe's yes-no replies, the sportswriters head for Dave De-Busschere in the corner. He gives them his Standard Unrevised Victory Analysis: "When you make your shots you can't lose, because the other team has to keep taking the ball out of the hoop and then out-of-bounds, which means they've got to start all over again."

Monroe, a black Bugs Bunny who prefers *Billboard* to the sports pages, listens and grins. He's heard DeBusschere's critique before. A new group of sportswriters closes in.

Monroe grimaces and puts on his matching red socks and a serious face.

"Say, Earl, what the hell happened out there?"

He repeats his message about team defense. When they leave he stands up and says: "Where do all these *questions* come from? They have better seats than I do. You'd think they could see for themselves what happened out there."

The locker rooms of America are full of runty men from the *PosTimes-*

Originally appeared in *Esquire* (1974).

RegisteRecord asking impertinent questions. But this sweaty social intercourse between reporters and athletes has evolved only during the past decade. Before the 1960s, only a few sportswriters—mostly from magazines and afternoon newspapers—hounded jocks to find out *why* things happened. The New York *Times*, whose fifty-six-member sports staff is the largest in the country, has been showing up regularly in dressing rooms for only five or six years.

Traditionally, American sports pages have been scoreboards. Most sportswriters have specialized in game watching. When television proved it could watch the games even better, many editors chased their sportswriters out of the press box in search of things cameras can't show.

Television, however, is only one factor in the shift. The history of sports writing has been a long, wobbly crawl from innocence to skepticism.

The first American sports pages appeared in the 1880s and 1890s. Their ultimate objective was to tell who won and who lost. But the scores often got in the way of rococo description and were overlooked. Gradually, and tentatively at first, a style emerged which I call the Hero Sandwich. It first showed up in 1889 when Joe Villa, sports editor of *The New York Sun*, ran along the sidelines writing the first play-by-play story of a football game. At the turn of the century, the Hero was refined and stylized by Charlie Dryden, the widely imitated Philadelphia sportswriter. He created a glossary of baseball clichés and that you-gotta-believe parochialism which still afflicts sports pages. From then on, the Hero was made from equal parts jock worship, press-agentry and awe.

Sample Dryden: "All the fret and worry have been wiped from the schedule, and the fanatics may seek some needed repose. The Pennant is ours.

"Mr. Mack's tired toilers lost today, 10 to 4, but they can do the shouting, since St. Louis cleaned up Chicago. The doubleheader here tomorrow carries no terrors. If necessary, we can drop both games while the White Sox pound away at the Browns until they are blue in the face. Nothing more doing until the postmortem series to decide which is the dead one—Giants or Athletics. Let us all emit three cheers, anyhow, for luck.

"The Rube broke into the busy whirl today, but he was too rusty to rescue like he once did. Coakley needed help, and Rusty Rube gave the best he had, and which gives promise of the best there is later on."

Between 1914 and 1930, a period known appropriately as "The Golden Age of Sports," the Hero was spiced and fattened. Babe Ruth, Rogers Hornsby, Jack Dempsey, Bobby Jones, Red Grange, Knute Rockne, and Bill Tilden had their whopper byliners in Damon Runyon, Paul Gallico, Bill Corum, Westbrook Pegler, John Kieran, Ring Lardner, Heywood Broun, Grantland Rice, and W. O. McGeehan (who refused to serve the Hero. In fact, throughout this period and later, McGeehan, John Lardner and Red Smith, perhaps the best three sportswriters of this century, always went for critical revelation, presaging the sports writing to come).

More than anybody, Grantland Rice certified and sold the Hero Sandwich. His account of the Notre Dame-Army game in 1924 is probably the most influential sports story ever written. It has caused decades of vocational damage:

"Outlined against a blue-grey October sky, the Four Horsemen rode again. In dramatic lore they are known as Famine, Pestilence, Destruction, and Death. These are only aliases. Their real names are Stuhldreher, Miller, Crowley and Layden. They formed the crest of the South Bend cyclone before which another fighting Army football team was swept over the precipice of the Polo Grounds yesterday afternoon as 55,000 spectators peered down on the bewildering panorama spread on the green plain below.

"A cyclone can't be snared. It may be surrounded but somewhere it breaks through to keep on going. When the cyclone starts from South Bend, where the candlelights still gleam through the Indiana sycamores, those in the way must take to storm cellars at top speed. Yesterday the cyclone struck again, as Notre Dame beat Army 13–7 with a set of backfield stars that ripped and crashed through a strong Army defense with more speed and power than the warring Cadets could meet. . . ."

The famous passage goes on at length, but this lead prompted Red Smith to say, "I wonder what angle Granny watched the game from if he could see them outlined against the blue-grey October sky."

Forgetting the brawling metaphors and foaming hype, Rice hides the score and tells us nothing about the real players on the field. Rice suffered from Oscar Wilde's dictum: that to be natural is to be obvious and to be obvious is to be inartistic.

But Rice released the sportswriter's imagination. He convinced generations of sportswriters to give up their dull habits of accuracy and let fly. He legitimatized the use of those colorful code words—*smash* for hit, *turf* for field, *ripped* for ran—which endure to this day. Rice's influence was the result not only of his technicolor style but of his sunshine philosophy. "In a two-nothing game," he said, "I tend to give the pitcher credit for pitching a good game—instead of belaboring the other team for poor hitting. You might say I go along year to year with this same philosophy."

Fred Russell, a Rice disciple from the *Nashville Banner*, made the point for sportswriters who may have missed it: "Sportswriters are all enthusiasts," he said. "The few who try to be cynical soon get converted or quit."

In *Bury Me in an Old Press Box*, Russell laid out a road map for sportswriters. Rule number one: "Tie goes to the runner. Favor the positive over the negative."

The collapse of the economy and the demise of several major sportswriters moderated the Hero in the 1930s. Many papers pruned their sports sections. Ring Lardner, McGeehan and Heywood Broun died. Westbrook Pegler defected to write a political column.

But more and more sportswriters were now high-school graduates. And some had been to college. Executive sports editors were hired for the first time, such as Arch Ward (*Chicago Tribune*) and Stanley Woodward (*New York Herald Tribune*). In the 1940s, the Hero was challenged by a small group of sportswriters, including Jimmy ("Nobody Asked Me But . . .") Cannon, Stanley Frank, Oscar Fraley, and Red Smith. They held that athletes were not sun gods but people doing interesting things for money. Sometimes, but not often, they even wrote the way they felt (Smith being a conspicuous exception).

The Associated Press sports wire was initiated in 1945. It nationalized and formularized sports coverage. Sports cartoons began showing up regularly on sports pages for the first time.

Still, the Hero prevailed, largely because of gentle Arthur Daley, who inherited John Kieran's New York *Times* column. Daley, the only sportswriter to win a Pulitzer Prize, wrote more than ten thousand columns in his thirty-one years as the *Times* columnist (he died last January). He was not so much a columnist as a sports master of ceremonies, introducing and promoting sports figures he liked and ignoring those he didn't. "I write about good people," he said. Every other day, he seemed to compose hymns to Joe DiMaggio, Joe Louis, Casey Stengel and Vince Lombardi. When a Hero got in trouble, Daley attacked like a member of the family. After the Yankees fired Stengel, Daley wrote: "It's a shabby way to treat the man who has not only brought them glory but also has given their dynasty firmer footing than it had ever had. So long, Case. You gave us twelve unforgettable years."

Says Ed Linn, the perceptive former sportswriter who now writes non-sports books: "Daley was not a good writer and he wasn't a good craftsman. Actually, he wasn't a good anything. But when you read him you could see those pennants flying."

In the late 1940s and 1950s, sports writing turned mawkishly personal, although the Hero still held. Daley was echoed by a passionate school of pundit columnists, including Vincent X. Flaherty (*Los Angeles Examiner*), Bob Considine (Hearst), Joe Williams (Scripps-Howard), Milton Gross (New York *Post*), and Jimmy Burns (*Miami Herald*).

But Smith, John Lardner and Cannon were at the top of their game, steadily subverting the Hero. And an unawed group of magazine writers—Linn, W. C. Heinz, Frank, and Jimmy Breslin—were beginning to deal with the underbelly and psychological impact of sports.

Lardner's 1953 piece on spring training was a signal of what I've named the Sourdough school: "To be fair, spring training is fun for a lot of people. It is fun for sportswriters like myself, who travel the sunshine trails, working lightly and relaxing strongly. Obviously the readers of sports pages, who are hungry for baseball news after three of four months of winter blight, get a certain amount of nourishment, and even pleasure, out of it. But the truth is that baseball has wandered into an odd predicament. In this matter of spring training, modern baseball clubs are in the position of a fellow who, getting up earlier and earlier every morning to keep ahead of his neighbor, finally meets himself coming home to bed."

Then, in the 1960s, a more insolent group of sportswriters appeared. Loaded with unbelief, they wrote about sports as raunchy big business rather than as exalted rite. They described games as charades, as cartoons even. They focused more on feeling than on events.

These pioneers included Larry Merchant (New York Post), Wells Twombly (now of the San Francisco Examiner), Stan Isaacs (Newsday), Robert Lipsyte (New York Times), Phil Pepe (New York Daily News), the late Leonard Shecter (New York Post and magazines), and Stan Fischler (magazines and books). They began hanging around athletes and assaulting them with personal questions. Soon, they were writing more about the players than about plays. They looked at sports from new angles (Isaacs got bored with a baseball game in Kansas City and joined a flock of sheep on a hill overlooking the stadium. He described the game from the sheep's vantage point).

In the beginning, these new Sourdough sportswriters were called chipmunks. Says Isaacs: "The New York Yankees probably did more than anybody to foment this movement. They were an arrogant, humorless organization which let reporters know that it was a privilege just to be covering them. Some of us didn't see it that way. We used to stand around talking and laughing with the players. One day Jimmy Cannon saw Pepe, who has a tooth protrusion, laughing with Jim Bouton. Cannon said: 'Look at them, a bunch of chipmunks.' He said it with derision. But some of us adopted it as a badge of honor."

Shecter may have synthesized the chipmunks' credo when he said: "No press, no interest, no baseball, no twenty-two-year-old shit-kicker making thirty-five grand a year at an animal occupation."

Understandably, most athletes do not endorse the Sourdough school. Conflict, after all, is built into the basic ingredients of the new sports writing. It is semi-intellectual man versus semi-savage. Watching Willie Mays read a newspaper is like watching an archaeologist puzzle over the map of a lost civilization. As sportswriter Roger Kahn observes, the reading experience of most athletes is limited to running their fingers over the pages of *Playboy*. Athletes, who have been trained to view sportswriters as a low form of press agent, are confused by the new enmity. Tommy Nobis, Atlanta's large, child-faced linebacker, stopped talking with sportswriters last season. "They just pulled too many crappy things," he says. "They only want to write personal and negative things, like how bad my legs are and how I walk funny. I've been walking funny since I was a little kid." St. Louis Cardinal pitcher Bob Gibson posted a Jock Manifesto on his locker this spring, pre-answering questions about his thirty-eight-year-old body and his new divorce. It said: "In case I'm not here, knee feels bad. Weather doesn't matter. Arm doesn't feel too good yet. None of your damn business."

Says Gibson, who has learned to look through reporters as if they were window glass: "Sportswriters like to think they make athletes. But I've been setting records for years and all they do is record them. Their stories have never helped me a bit at contract time. I don't read papers anyway. I had to do so much reading in school that I promised myself I'd quit when I got out."

The discomfort is also being felt by jock entrepreneurs. Norman Brokaw, agent for Mark Spitz, notes: "For some reason, these smartasses are starting to ask dumb questions. Like asking Mark when he's going to endorse hemor-rhoids. Can you imagine this country's greatest living hero having to put up with that?"

Although many sports pages now push soft-core skepticism, it is debatable how much sports writing has improved. There is still a lot of lyrical gushing. The general level of sports writing is about the same as in *Screen Stars* (O.J. RECALLS THE LEAN YEARS). Sportswriters still have an incorrigible flair for the obvious, are several months behind a trend, and stand slack-jawed before strength and winners.

The Hero Sandwich, while going stale, is still being served. *Sports Illustrated*'s story on the 1974 Super Bowl began: "They came by land and by air, if not by sea, and they didn't squeak by the Vikings but roared over them in an awesome display of offense and defense to win their second straight Super Bowl." The headline writer then slipped the metaphor baton to Tex Maule. But he took off in another direction: "Super Bowl VIII had all the excitement and suspense of a master butcher quartering a steer. The slaughterhouse was Houston's Rice Stadium and the butcher was Miami quarterback Bob Griese. . . ."

And *The Sporting News*, with minor exceptions, also continues to make the Hero. It is a collection of endless novellas which all seem to ask: CAN HAHN FILL YAWNING GAP IN CENTER?

Only grudgingly does Jim Murray, the *Los Angeles Times* sports columnist whose peers this year named him Sportswriter of the Year for the ninth consecutive year, acknowledge some improvement: "The worst sportswriters are a little better than the worst used to be." Red Smith insists that "the number of good and bad sportswriters remains constant."

Not unexpectedly, the younger sportswriters proclaim a sports-writing renaissance. Wells Twombly, the free-form sports columnist for the *San Francisco Examiner*, says: "Athletes don't realize yet what's happened to the old sports page. It has become the most literate part of the newspaper in most big cities. The volume of cogent, sensitive writing goes steadily up."

And Merchant chimes in: "There may not be any Lardners around, but nearly every big city paper has a very good sportswriter today and that wasn't the case twenty or thirty years ago."

He's right. Virtually every major newspaper and magazine now has at least one excellent sportswriter. Most have more than one. An arbitrary list would have to include William Barry Furlong (Washington *Post*), Melvin Durslag (*Los Angeles Herald-Examiner*), Jack Murphy (*San Diego Union*), Vic Ziegel, Joseph Valerio and Leonard Lewin (New York *Post*), Ron Bergman (*Oakland Tribune*), Peter Gammons (*Boston Globe*), Jerry Izenberg (Newhouse papers), Roy Blount, Barry McDermott, Ron Fimrite and Frank Deford (*Sports Illustrated*), Pete Axthelm (*Newsweek*), Roger Angell (*New Yorker*), Joe Flaherty (*Village Voice*), Dave Anderson, Leonard Koppett and Steve Cady (New York *Times*), Pete Alfano, Joe Donnelly and Ed Comerford (*Newsday*), and Rick Talley (*Chicago Today* and *Chicago Tribune*).

But at least six sportswriters stand out from the pack, blending solid reporting skills with uncommon perception. They are Red Smith, Jim Murray, Dick Young, Merchant, Twombly and Kahn.

RED SMITH

When I was in junior high school, I saw a picture of Smith in the *Denver Post*. He wore a checkered sport shirt buttoned at the neck. For several years, I wore my sport shirts ludicrously buttoned at the neck.

Smith, sixty-nine, has been the most influential single force on American sports writing. He has given sports what Monet gave sunrises—a pure and constantly fresh eye. Smith's hands sometimes tremble and his columns in The New York *Times* often turn watery (his boxers may become "limp as overcooked spaghetti"). But his grace, wit and common sense are intact. Listen to some recent Smith:

On sportscasters: "Those people who make a living reading the scores of games on television."

On players' contract disputes: "If Bob Kuechenberg isn't satisfied opening holes for Larry Csonka, let him get a job opening oysters and see how he likes that."

On Joe Cronin as American League president: "In twenty sinless years as a ball-player in the majors, Joe Cronin was a good enough shortstop, but it was his bat that got him into the Hall of Fame, not the way he handled hot grounders by Babe Ruth or Al Simmons. Today he can't handle the shots Charlie Finley hits his way. How much can an infielder slow down without taking root?"

On kite-flying champion Will Yolen: "Not much larger than a growler of beer, he stands tall in international kite-flying society, where he has recognized himself as world champion ever since he tricked the Maharaja of Bharatpur into diving his kite into a rain forest during a fly-off in Central India."

On Baseball Commissioner Bowie Kuhn: "By this time the owners had a fairly clear idea of what they wanted in a commissioner and were dead sure what they didn't want. What they didn't want most was impartiality, so they chose the lawyer who had acted for them in such matters as the sack of Milwaukee.

"They have not been disappointed. There has never been a commissioner who stood more erect, wore better clothes or kept his shoes more meticulously polished than Bowie Kuhn."

Smith's rule for sportswriters: "Use the Mother Tongue with respect and don't gush. The first duty is still to tell who won, concisely and truthfully. If you can manage that gracefully, so much the better. But some of these amateur psychologists on the sports pages bore me. And when I find a poisonous writer, I quickly turn the page."

Smith often looks back on stuff he's written and starts talking to himself. "I usually say, 'Why did you work so hard at being cute.' Of course, when I used to read John Lardner I would sometimes shake my head and say, 'That son of a bitch is so good I should quit.'"

Do people, even fans, really care about good sports writing? Smith: "The public can't tell good writing when they see it and neither can plenty of editors and publishers. Still, the good writers become popular. I guess they succeed for about the same reason the jury system succeeds. Somehow, Eugene O'Neill and Hemingway and W. Shakespeare managed to make it."

And up ahead? "Well, Granny Rice worked it out. He kept talking about retiring. First it was Florida, then it was California, and then it was going to be Arizona. But he finally keeled over at the typewriter. That's kind of nice."

JIM MURRAY

Jim Murray wrote about politics and movies for *Time* until he was in his mid-thirties. In 1953, *Time* shipped him to *Sports Illustrated* for its dry run. He has been a sportswriter ever since.

Murray's style is slick and foxy, reflecting his longtime employment at *Time*. But his etchings about the habits and postures of sports people are tiny, comic masterpieces. When he is right, which is very often, he achieves what Damon Runyon only set out to do.

Murray knows that professional sports wouldn't exist without sports writing. "Sports, of all things, need dramatization," he says. "TV comes in only after the papers build it up. What athletes do is not basically interesting. There is nothing remarkable about catching or throwing or hitting a ball. Jugglers in Yugoslavia do it better."

While Murray works mostly in the shadows of sports rather than on the plains, the shadows have always been a good place to gather evidence:

On sportswriters and managers: "By and large, baseball writers and baseball managers get along like husband and wife. They respect each other, but not much. I bug Walt Alston something terrible, for instance, because he thinks I don't know anything about the game of baseball. Angel manager Bill Rigney, on the other hand, is different. He *knows* I don't know anything about the game of baseball. Where Alston gets mad and stomps out when I try to be helpful, Rig waits for his laugh. He digs his elbow in my ribs and says, 'What do we do now, maestro—punt?'"

On Mickey Walker: "Edward Michael Walker, the fistfighter, will best be remembered as the middleweight who had the best left hook and the biggest thirst in the business. If it hadn't been for the one, the thirst, the other, the hook, might have made him the only hundred-fifty-pound heavyweight champion in modern history."

On going to Spokane for a hockey game: "The only trouble with Spokane, Washington, as a city is that there's nothing to do there after ten o'clock. In the morning. But it's a nice place to go for breakfast."

On race driver Richard Petty: "In a sport populated by guys known as 'Fireball' and 'Wild Bill' and pioneered by guys driving around mountain passes chased by revenoors shooting at them, Richard Petty's cars come back looking as if they had been owned by two little old ladies from Pasadena. You wouldn't even want to kick the tires.

"Richard Petty has never tried to suit up for Indy or Pocono or Ontario or their hell ovals, or tried to crash the monocle-and-champagne circuits of Europe, but he has made more than two million dollars on the 'you-all' and 'down yonder' country. He prefers thirty-eight hundred pounds of steel around him to eleven hundred pounds of plastic. Besides, he gets four more miles to the gallon."

On Frank Howard: "Watching Frank Howard come out of the dugout to start a game is like watching the opening scene of a horror movie. You know the bit, there's an explosion under a polar ice cap someplace, the earth rumbles and opens up, and out of it comes this Thing."

On *players' names*: "When I was a kid back in Connecticut, I used to love U.S.C. backfields. You had to be fascinated. I remember rolling the names off my tongue. Morley Drury. Homer Griffith. Grenville Landsdell. Gaius Shaver. Irvine Warburton. Orville Mohler. You read them and felt like going out and throwing rocks at your mother and father for naming you Jim."

Murray, who likes to sit invisibly in locker rooms and watch, thinks there might be too much Sourdough now: "The sociology trend started when reporters like Shecter and Merchant began asking players how they felt about things other than the infield-fly rule. It's been overdone. To me, sports writing has never been a matter of schools. When a guy is wonderful you can say he's wonderful. When he isn't, just say that he stinks."

Murray is embarrassed by sportswriters who cheer in the press box. "You see hardened reporters standing up and screaming, 'Hold 'em, Rams, hold 'em.' It's deplorable, but it's caused partly by economics. The sportswriter wants his team to succeed because if it doesn't, the sportswriter may lose his beat. So he yells, 'Go, team, go.'"

Murray asks the same dumb questions other sportswriters ask. "I loved to get Roberto Clemente going. He didn't care for most questions but when one interested him, he would go on for hours. I once asked him what it would take these days to be a four-hundred hitter. For several hours he described everything that he wasn't—a young ballplayer, a left-handed hitter, an unmarked man in the lineup and so on. Another time he gave me a one-hour analysis on why Manny Sanguillen isn't as unhappy as his face suggests."

But still, aren't sports the toy department? "Of course. I always wanted to wear a trench coat, carry a Luger, be a foreign correspondent in Vienna and write plays. When I was with *Time*, I would get mad when they wouldn't carry something I wrote and would take a train up to Hartford. I would sit watching people come out of the factories, shutting down the drill presses and turning off fluorescent lights. After a while I would stop feeling sorry for myself and come back to New York. I guess I'll finish out my days discussing why Roman Gabriel passed instead of ran and describing other important matters to our culture."

DICK YOUNG

Young, who has been writing sports for the New York *Daily News* for thirty-two years, may be the most prolific sportswriter in the country. He writes five columns a week, sometimes seven. He recently delivered thirty columns in thirty-one days.

Young's work is coarse and simpleminded, like cave painting. But it is superbly crafted. When you write on stone, there is no room for large words. Since Young writes the way fans talk, he is able to define basic sports issues more clearly than just about anybody.

He is contemptuous of litterateurs on the sports page. "Young sportswriters think they're writing literature," he says. "They emphasize fluff to camouflage their lack of knowledge about sports. But you can't fool the sports fan. He demands more expertise than any other newspaper reader."

Young has developed running feuds with modern-day sports royalty, such as Howard Cosell, Namath, and Muhammad Ali. His columns are flaming sermonettes on the decline of sports morality.

Listen to Young: "Baseball has gone crooked. There is no delicate way of putting it. There is no other interpretation to be placed on the Braves' announced intention of playing its first three games without Henry Aaron in the lineup, so that he may assault Babe Ruth's ghost on home ground, several days later, in Atlanta, and of course on national television. . . . Thus, once more, even deeper, does television corrupt the sports scene. Thus does baseball grow richer, and poorer."

On the public image of athletes: "Whether we like it or not, it is a fact of life that kids idolize and emulate star athletes. There is a very memorized line of argument among the swinging athletes of today that goes something like this: 'I don't want to be an example for kids. Let them idolize their father.' This, for two reasons, is an unrealistic approach. Few kids idolize their old man. In their very early years, they want to be firemen, or cops, or John Wayne. In their adolescence, they want to be Larry Brown, or Mickey Mantle, or Joe Namath, or Johnny Rodgers. That is part of the obligation, the image, whether athletes want to shoulder it or not. To say, as some do, let the little punks idolize their father, is a cop-out, and unreal, even cruel."

On Namath retiring: "He'll go right on playing football as long as he is physically able, and as long as somebody is willing to pay him for what little he plays these days. He is sure of that two hundred fifty thousand dollars, and perhaps as much again for selling shaving cream and popcorn and stuff. When he is done with football, there will be plenty of time for Joey Baby to get a nose job and make movies. With a new nose, he wouldn't be bad looking."

On players' greed: "Coach Shula, leaping from Baltimore to Miami, is the same thing as Larry Csonka leaping from Miami to Toronto. Man goes where the money is. It was ever thus. It simply seems to be a little more so now because there is more money now.

"Another of the funny things said is, 'There comes a time when a man has to think of the security of his family.' Larry Csonka said that. Don Shula said that when he entered the contractual pole-vaulting event. I'm sure Willie Sutton said that just before ripping off the First Federal.

". . . You amaze me. The resiliency of you, the fan, amazes me. The owner drops you, moving what you thought was your team, and you bounce back. The players drop you, jumping sometimes in the middle of a cheer, but you always bounce back. Silly, innocent, gullible you. The owners don't give a damn. The players don't give a damn. Only you give a damn. You continue to root for a city's name on a shirt. Did you ever stop to wonder why?"

Young doesn't understand why columnists don't have pungent opinions like he does. "I always wondered why more writers don't have opinions. God, don't they react to things going on? I get as mad at William Simon as I do Namath. The other day I read that Simon says we should buy gas only when we need it. It made me want to vomit."

He doubts that sports writing is improving. And its socioeconomic directions disturb him. "Every young sportswriter starts out writing about black athletes in the ghetto. They come back saying how articulate the black athlete is. What does that mean? That he can speak words."

Jackie Robinson called Young a "racist." "Sure, Jackie thought I was a bigot and he told me about it over and over. I reminded him that I had ghosted an article for him for *Jet* magazine. All he said was, 'Yeah, Dick, but you've changed.'"

Namath refuses to talk with Young. "I say hello and he won't answer. He's spoiled. You've got to please him to talk with him. He thinks he's punishing me. Namath has the funny idea that if he doesn't talk to me I won't write about him."

As for Cosell, Young says: "He appears on things like *Nanny and the Professor* and then goes around saying sports are insignificant. Poor Howard."

Young admits to some jock hero worship. "I can't help it, I find myself rooting for nice guys, like Stan Musial and Pee Wee Reese and Bud Harrelson."

He has turned down an offer to write a general column, because he thinks the biggest journalistic challenge is "writing sports well and doing it every day. Other reporters sit around for days doing nothing. But the good sportswriter produces every day. And he doesn't have rewrite men, the headpiece scene, to help him. The sportswriter has to tell people they're full of shit and then go out and face them the next day. Other reporters ask tough questions of grieving widows and then never see them again."

LARRY MERCHANT

Merchant of the New York *Post* is the best of the "non-sports" sports-writers, working in a style which might be called Controlled Blasphemy.

He is brazenly political ("liberal chic," says Young). In Merchant's world, most athletes are running-and-jumping derelicts, and owners are crazed money fiends. Despite his cynicism, his work exudes an adolescent's wonder at the ways sports work. Given the ground he covers, Merchant works at a high level of consistency and originality. He has erased the old-line boundaries of the sports page, writing about such things as the World Monopoly Championship, the importance of the Frisbee, the Boston Marathon as nature study, kite flying in Central Park, and the ruptured Achilles tendon as status symbol.

Two years ago, when the major-league baseball season failed to open because the players went on strike, Merchant cruised the playgrounds of New York. "The crowds were small," he wrote, "but the baseball season opened yesterday, on schedule, in all the important places. . . . It's pointless to get dyspepsia over the baseball strike. Just look around. The season has opened."

When Dick Cavett invited him to be a guest on his show with Ali and Joe Frazier—and then failed to bring him on—Merchant wrote: "I want to show the kind of guy I am by having Dick Cavett as a guest in my column." Then, he began writing about Denny McLain, Alex Karras and Monty Stickles. Finally, in the last paragraph, Merchant sighed: "Gee, this is really embarrassing. Here I am down to my last inch and I haven't gotten around to Dick Cavett."

On the Hank Aaron home-run controversy: "In the spring, a young man's fancy turns lightly toward thoughts of love and streaking, while his elders debate the great issues of the day, like Hank Aaron and home runs. Youth may not be wasted on the young after all."

On George Allen: "He is like a guy without a wristwatch who walks into a room with twenty-five guys who have wristwatches. It's easy for him to get the time, by asking. He takes advantage of everyone else's hang-up about wearing a wristwatch. One of these days, they hope, nobody will give him the right time."

On the Munich Olympics: "A dirge played by the Munich Symphony Orchestra touched a crowd of eighty thousand mourners, but the politicians and jocks had something else in mind: to save their hides. Speech after speech drew applause with appeals to keep those gold medals coming.

"Avery Brundage out-Brundaged himself. With the remaining Israelis sitting in attitudes of bereavement, some of them weeping, Brundage's croaking Olympian tone suggested that the players really had tried to ruin his life's

work, as though someone had urinated in one of his priceless Ming vases."
On the importance of names to sports success: "America knew it instantly. Vida
Blue! Vida Blue tripped off the tongue like Babe Ruth and Ty Cobb and Lefty
Grove. No way that a pitcher named, say, Sonny Siebert could get on the
covers of *Time* and *Newsweek* and draw crowds like the pope. Sonny Siebert
would have to win forty, strike out four hundred and whistle *The Flight of the
Bumble Bee* to do that."

Merchant, who was sports editor of the *Philadelphia Daily News* when he
was twenty-six, is convinced the sports pages are moving in the right direction.

"Sports used to be a sanctuary from the rest of life," he says. "The sportswriter used to be a fan. There are still fans writing sports, but they are becoming the exception. Some sportswriters twenty and thirty years ago just didn't
do their jobs. I was doing a story on Vida Blue's holdout and checked back to
see what was written about Joe DiMaggio's long holdout in the 1930s. There
wasn't a single interview with DiMaggio in any of the New York papers."

He credits Muhammad Ali and the New York Mets with revolutionizing
sports writing. "Ali and the Mets were important litmus tests for the new
breed of sportswriter. Ali was something totally different, a crazy kid who
went around desecrating the sports temple. Most sportswriters began covering him this way. When the chipmunks looked at the early Mets they decided
it was fun and games, not life and death. They emphasized the inadequacies
of the Mets, laughing sympathetically with them. These sportswriters caused
a new celebration between players and fans. People began bringing banners
out to the ball park."

Merchant has no illusions about sports writing being cosmic. "Sportswriters may not be dealing in *War and Peace*," he says, "but their contribution
can be something more than 'Bud Harrelson pilfered the sack.'"

WELLS TWOMBLY

While his daughter was being held for ransom, Randolph Hearst sent a
message to Twombly, an employee, telling him that his columns had given
him his only laughs during the ordeal.

Few athletes find Twombly funny. Some, such as pitcher Sam McDowell,
have tried to eliminate Twombly's smile with their fists. Old-style fans find
him difficult reading. Readers of *The Sporting News* complain they don't understand what he is trying to say.

A chipmunk gone literary, Twombly's work is ornamental and theatrical.
He often uses adjectives the way older women apply rouge. But he is a tough,
diagnostic reporter, getting behind the masks sports people wear. While Murray's work shouts, "No harm meant," Twombly means a lot of harm.

On bullfighting in the U.S.: "This was an important press conference. An announcement of staggering importance was about to be made. Bloodless bullfighting, the greatest athletic spectacle since shadowboxing fell into decline, was returning to Houston, the city of its birth. (Someday the hall of fame may be erected here.) The public demand for its resurrection, said impresario Enrique Abascal, had been so intense that it was now almost nonexistent. In a week or two, it might soar even higher."

On Bobby Riggs defeating Margaret Court: "The two of them met on Mother's Day, with Riggs bowing graciously and presenting his opponent with a huge bunch of red roses, she being a mother and all that. No greater act of gamesmanship has been committed in recent memory. Properly softened, Margaret Court discovered that Riggs's amazing collection of garbage shots totally disrupted her strong, smooth-flowing game.

"She crumpled easily. And when it was over, she seemed—may Germaine Greer forgive her—on the verge of tears. Her head was buried in her lap and she seemed to need the aid and comfort of a husband. Somewhere in the vicinity, Barry Court was carrying the baby. He always carries the baby, a point that ought to make Norman Mailer sick to his tum-tum."

On sportswriters: "The players have a distinct notion that the press constitutes the enemy. Why not? They see the club's policy being repeated word for word, without question, in the daily sports pages. They see reporters in the company of general managers and publicity men on the road. What else are they to think? After all, isn't it the practice for a sportswriter to confuse his pronouns? It takes no more than a few weeks on the baseball beat to start referring to the newspaper that pays your salary as 'them' and the club that provides your free booze as 'us.' The players are also aware that 'us' means management, not labor."

On baseball in San Francisco: "Stiff winds flap across that most beautiful of bays, making baseball a cheerful impossibility on most days when sensible people want to witness the game. Cold weather stalks the shoreline regardless of the time of day. A pitcher must have an arm made out of lead in order to survive. Fog and evil humors are a constant threat, as if somebody up there is making a strong comment about the advisability of playing games in places originally meant as roosting places for gulls and sea lions.

"These are perilous days on the shores of Candlestick Point, where the quaint city of San Francisco built the nation's only brand-new old baseball stadium. The owner of the Giants feels the horrid pinch of Charlie Finley's presence only eight miles across the water."

On the Harlem Globetrotters: "They come prancing out onto the basketball floor to the tune of an extraordinary racist piece of music, their eyeballs rolling, their legs strutting, their bodies moving to the rhythm. They jabber like plantation slaves who have gathered on the front lawn of Old Miasma, the Doric-columned Mississippi estate, to entertain the white folks sipping bourbon up there on the antebellum veranda.

"They are alleged to be comic, but they end up looking grotesque. Their time is long past. They are as contemporary as a minstrel show, with Rastus telling stories about his adventures with Mandy in the kitchen. They belong to an era when blacks had no sense of purpose, when they forgot their pride and buried their dignity."

Twombly joined the *San Francisco Examiner* after a term at *The Houston Chronicle*. He has always viewed sports writing as a valid form of literature.

"I try to write in a literary style and make each column a small magazine piece. I stay away from sizing up the old ball club and making predictions nobody cares about. There's been too much influence by journalism professors, who teach method rather than style. I once took a journalism course. They told me if I put everything in a certain order I would be a journalist."

For Twombly, there was no Golden Age of Sports Writing. "Most of the sports writing in the Twenties and Thirties was written for dolts. Grantland Rice mixes metaphors about twenty-four times in his 'Outlined against a blue-grey October sky.' Today's sports pages have more style and more art than any other part of the paper. Look at Dutton's anthology of sports writing each year and you'll see the steady improvement."

Twombly takes his work, if not himself, seriously. When Reggie Jackson gave him a string of non-answers in an interview, Twombly told him: "I'm as good a writer as you are a home-run hitter. If you want me to write about you, you'll have to call me." Jackson called him back as he walked away.

But Twombly's sports-writing days may be numbered. "The other day I was interviewing a player and found myself framing his answers before I asked my questions. I was about seventy-five percent accurate. A friend of mine says you've heard it all in sports when you reach thirty-five. I'm three years over the limit. Eventually, I'm going to have to get out."

In a way, Twombly "gets out" even on the sports page. After the shootings at Kent State, he concluded that "there are days when you don't feel like writing about children's games, especially when children are lying on the street."

The *Examiner* surprised him. It ran the column.

ROGER KAHN

Kahn's style is soft and straightforward. It is also sentimental.

Since he is the sports columnist for this magazine, his inclusion here may seem to be incestuous, but I couldn't resist because Kahn's influence on sports

writing is clear. (The editor said okay provided Kahn didn't see this until publication day.) He has no peers in conveying the strains—physical and mental—of sports. "This dull pain," Coleridge called it.

With *The Boys of Summer*, Kahn carried sports writing to places it may not
belong, infusing it with a higher sensibility. Bad copies are already on the
field. I'm waiting for a *Girls of Autumn* about women's football.

Kahn's concern is not with the raw results of competition but with the personal effects. He extracts the mysteries of sports by detailing their basic con-
figurations: "Lined up against the four are six offensive players, the center,
two guards, two tackles, the tight end. So, from Lilly's crouch, each play begins six to four against him. A big back lingers near the quarterback as palace
guard. Four against seven. Sometimes two men are assigned to block Bob
Lilly. And sometimes three."

And: "A major leaguer ordinarily has mastered four pitches. The sixty feet,
six inches that lie between the mound and home plate create one element in
a balanced equation between pitcher and batter. No one can throw a baseball
past good hitters game after game."

Kahn is a romantic grown-up who still finds sports slightly incredible.
On Jackie Robinson: "It is now almost a year since Jackie Robinson broke a
dinner date for the most pardonable and least acceptable of reasons. He fell
dead. . . . I loved Jackie Robinson well enough not to have to deify him.
Politically, he was an infant. Successively, Richard Nixon conned him and
Nelson Rockefeller bent him to the expediences of his will. A tough busi-
nessman hired Robinson as a company union man. A talented, sometimes
petty newspaperman reduced him to the sewers of his own pettiness by baiting him with wisecracks. Jack was no philosopher, no reader, and if he knew
that a man named Franz Schubert ever lived, he kept it a secret, at least
from me."
On the emergence of pro football: "The intervening salesmanship has been remarkable. First football offered us a special vocabulary which, as Orwell observed in another context, is essential to a developing ideology. In the old
huddles we said, 'You go out three steps and cut like hell to the right.' This
became a 'square out.' Or, 'Both you guys go long and when you get to the
manhole cover, crisscross, and I'll throw it way up.' The crossing pattern.
Add such jargon as red dog, blitz, stunt, overshift, and it is possible to speak
entire sentences in profootballese without bisecting English.

"The new language also masks unpleasantness. To jab a forearm into someone's throat is a poor show. To *clothesline* a man; well, quel sportiva. We do
violence and we detest admitting that we know we do. Clothesline for assault; incursion for the invasion of Cambodia."
On hockey goalie Glenn Hall: "'The truth is I don't like to play hockey any-

more. Aiyee,' he says, making the pronoun a sound of pain, 'don't like it, but it is a marvelous sport. I like the people, the talk, even the dinners. I love everything about hockey except the games.' His distaste for play is overwhelming. Invariably, as Hall is about to leave the clubhouse to guard the six-by-four-foot entrance to the goal, nausea seizes him. Often he loses the lunch he unhappily devoured six hours earlier."

On Billy Cox, today: "Someone else prattled about niggers. 'You was lucky, Cox. It wasn't like today. You didn't play with no niggers. Campanella was a gentleman. Robinson had been to college. You didn't play with no niggers.' A film fell over the eyes of Billy Cox. He walked to the pool table and began practicing shots.

". . . No one present, I thought, except myself, witnessing this two-a.m. talk of niggers, the ugly woman clouting the sodden man, could have realized that this broad-shouldered, horse-faced fellow tapping billiard balls, missing half a finger on one hand, sad-eyed, among people who would never be more than strangers, was the most glorious glove on the most glorious team that ever played baseball in the sunlight of Brooklyn."

Kahn began writing sports at the *New York Herald Tribune* in the early 1950s. Later, he wrote sports for *Newsweek* and *The Saturday Evening Post.* Now, he writes books and the sports column here.

While Kahn has glided in and out of sports, he still finds sports a perfect match for a writer's calling: "Sports tell anyone who watches intelligently about the times in which we live: about managed news and corporate politics, about race and terror and what the process of aging does to strong men. If that sounds grim, there is courge and high humor, too."

As for his own sports-writing preferences, Kahn says: "I find myself partial to the less urbanely smooth, to the professionals who make a living by writing sports day after day. Man for man they write better than newspapermen did twenty years ago and they would write better yet were it not for the catastrophic collapse of competitive journalism."

Still, he misses the older school and especially Lardner, W. C. Heinz and Linn, all magazine writers. "They were giants in their prime, each with a great sense of the English language."

Kahn has found athletes as difficult to deal with as anybody else. When he asked Henry Aaron if Sal Maglie was throwing at him, Aaron spun on him and shouted: "Don't ever ask a man that kind of question." Then Aaron stalked across the street. When Kahn asked Carl Furillo how he learned to play the right-field wall at Ebbets Field, he got: "I worked, that's fucking how."

Says Kahn, wearing his official Pittsburgh Pirate hat: "You take your journalism lessons where you find them."

The problem is not, of course, getting it all down into the notebook or listening for what Kahn calls "the defiant cadence of truth." The problem is rendering the whole thing pure.

Kahn describes the feeling this way: "Whenever I strike the right story subject, my response is intuitive and overwhelming. I feel a tightening of the solar plexus. My heartbeat quickens. Then the slow unraveling begins."

Almost a boxer's pre-fight emotions, that.

Sadly, there are no real histories of reporting, and of course none of sports journalism. Said Tom Wolfe: "I doubt that it ever occurred to anyone, even in the journalism schools, that the subject might have historical phases."

Even if sports writing is not qualitatively better, but only different, it is entering its most expansive stage. More and more sportswriters are writing books, some of them literate. A few people are putting them on shelves next to Sartre and Nabokov.

And the sports metaphor keeps seeping into more serious sections of the newspaper. Consider Joseph Kraft, reported successor to Walter Lippmann, writing recently about Aleksandr Solzhenitsyn: "A full-court press, largely by the United States, is required. By the willful provocation which led to his expulsion, Solzhenitsyn has asked whether we in the West care enough about peace and freedom to go the distance—to keep the pressure on the Soviet regime."

It's close, but I have always enjoyed good sports writing more even than sports. As Murray says, contests are merely contests without dramatization. It is sports writing which defines the quest, spins the myth, and makes us care.

"It's a tragedy," says Linn, "but sports are covered better than anything else. What is covered as well as the World Series, the Super Bowl, or a heavyweight championship? Not the White House. Not the Pentagon. Not city hall."

The wire-service machines carried roughly 1,160,000 words on the 1974 Super Bowl. Most of this was graceless blather (CSONKA CAME TO PLAY), but it's hard to imagine an aspect of this event that was not critically and comprehensively covered.

If today's sportswriters sniff for life pulses in jockstraps, why not? Kahn: "I find sports a better area than most to look for truth." Merchant: "The way people play gives you some very important clues about a society." Smith: "The oldest standing building in Rome is the Colosseum."

Imagine if political journalists could borrow the sportswriter's schtick—to sit with the President in his underpants six minutes after a State of the Union address and ask him: "What the hell happened out there?"

MICHAEL NOVAK

Jocks, Hacks, Flacks, and Pricks

Years ago, the sports pages were the best-written, most lively, and most informative about the many cultures of this nation than any other pages in the paper. The writers, or at least a good share of them, were poets, lyricists, modest craftsmen. They delighted in the nation and its variety; they loved their beat. Such love is at the heart of any form of art. It forms a secret bond between the artist and his audience. Behind the words in newsprint on the page lay a secret bond of understanding. Readers met the writers in their hearts. *Cor ad cor*, went Cardinal Newman's motto, *loquitur*: Heart says to heart what words do not.

Long ago, one waited for terse accounts of great games or great fights by teletype. Line by line they came, bare, stark, to the point. In imagination, knowing the games and the images of the players, the men gathered round, animation rising and falling, as in their heads they recreated every action, every deed.

On the radio in the past, as one drove a truck or in some other circumstance (painting a bedroom) heard the play-by-play, one learned to love the basic accuracy and the single bare detail that lifted the imagination. For the Ali-Frazier fight of October 1, 1975, those who could not get to the theaters for closed-circuit TV listened for radio summaries, round by round. Not only who hit whom, but with what force and what effect, was suggested in stark and cryptic messages. The mind flew. The inner eye recreated each detail. The stomach churned.

Late for a football game at Notre Dame, I once heard the first half on the car radio. The terse verbal images, the cadences of mounting excitement, the use of the half minute between plays to feed details to the imagination about the substitutions, tempo, and mood reminded me of how objective and to the point sports broadcasting used to be—still is, where television is not watched. There was no pretense that sports is entertainment. One got the basic liturgy, the essential drama.

That one received it through an eyewitness, whose skills and perception one had some reason to doubt (no two witnesses being the same), did not detract from the essential focus of the experience: the game itself. Perhaps things never happened on the field exactly as Bill Stern or Rosie Rosewell

From *The Joy of Sports* (1976).

used to call them. Listening to a portable radio at the game, one could see with one's own eyes whether "racing back on the warning track" really threatened the outfielder with the crash into the wall that the broadcaster seemed to suggest. But excitement in the voice of the broadcaster also helped one to *see* even what in the park one's own eyes "saw"—added form, added consistency, supplied a context for comparison. All the more so when one wasn't present. Not for nothing have millions of men had fantasies of broadcasters' voices in their ears as they practiced shooting baskets, or even weaving through traffic: ". . . *three seconds left to play, 1 point behind, Bradley shoots, it's up, it's good! . . . he's to the 30, gets one block, sidesteps the safety man, he's to the 20, only one man has a shot at him now, the 10, the 5, he's over! Touchdown, Olivieri! . . .*" Even the great Bill Bradley, practicing his shots "around the horn," hour by hour, disciplining himself to make 10 out of 13 from every spot before he moved to another, broadcast his own game with his own lips, cheering himself on, in isolation in Crystal River, Missouri.

The advent of television has made cowards out of many sportswriters, mere chatty, fatuous, and complacent entertainers out of many broadcasters, and shambles out of the religions of sports. It is true that television has given us enormous pleasures, and taught us to watch the games with new eyes. The "instant replay" has helped us to freeze the instantaneous ballet of a runner's moves; but it has rendered the unaided eye weak and undisciplined at a real game. It is harder to concentrate in the stadium; one has to remind oneself that there will only be one chance to see. The game looks totally different in the flesh. One regains there one's peripheral vision. One doesn't have to peer through the limits of the television box, subject to the judgments of a producer about which camera angle shows which portion of the play. One sees the whole. How large it is!

In a stadium, one feels present at a liturgy, at a kind of worship service where delight and fun are proper decorum. There is a sense of presence. Smells, touches, discomforts, the sweat and heaving of one's fellow spectators give one the sense of flesh, humanity, actuality. At home, pleased as one is to settle back and watch the vivid color in contemplative enjoyment, there is, rather, the feeling of being a voyeur; one feels a kind of distance and detachment. To be sure, the power of the drama itself is often so intense that one is drawn "into" the game. One's living-room, hotel room, or bar becomes an arena of its own. One cheers, yells, groans, gets up and walks around, whoops, hollers. It is not as though one were a million miles away. One is *there*, after a fashion.

In between times, however, the broadcasters go back to being entertainers. The game is not allowed to speak for itself. Instead of the steady beat of the radio voice, there is the mindless chatter of a late-night talk show, a Johnny

Carson in a jock. Everything one loathes about the entertainment ethic now obtrudes itself in places where respect is called for. Blessed are they who can listen to the radio while watching the plays on silent television. I find no television broadcaster suited to the demands of sport. The tolerable voices among them would be Frank Gifford, who understands and has accurate sympathies for the ritual he is faithful to; Vince Scully when he is covering the Dodgers (but not at other times); and Curt Gowdy, who is endurable when he does not overpraise or gild or give us pieties. What I admire is a workmanlike performance that allows the game to come to me undiluted. The television voices are far too conscious of themselves, watching Liz Taylor and Doris Day gaining on them over their shoulders, thinking they have to please us with their (God forbid) personalities. *I do not want to be entertained.* I want to experience the event.

Because they establish a level of patter—and what Howard Cosell calls the "chemistry" of interaction—the sportscasters trap themselves in banality; they cannot rise to the level of the high drama right before their eyes. When nothing is happening, they chatter on. When something happens, they can't escape their chatter. Their voices may get louder. Their exclamations are not different from our own. Where the radio broadcaster must describe what happened, carrying its inherent dramatic power, the television broadcaster says: "Did you see that! Did you see that!" They have a naïve faith in the human eye. In all the millions of bombardments the eye receives each second, it needs to know *which* to fasten on. The function of a broadcaster is to give us *form.* The television people have forgotten form. They do not trust the power of the word. They do not remember that Word, not vision, was the name God gave himself. In Hebrew as in Christian thought: God speaks, but is not seen.

The ear, not the eye, is the organ of human fact. And also of thought. The ear is personal (it carries tone and "voice"), holistic, stimulative. The eye distances, makes flat, kills, tames. To hear a great mind lecture is to have access to his thought—and to his heart and seat of judgment—that reading his books does not supply. The liturgy of the churches, is, wisely, centered on the spoken Word. So ought the liturgies of sport to be. Television, in trusting to the eye and renouncing the function of words except as filler, makes sports trivial. The eye is the most superficial sense. Television, the medium of the eye, cheapens us.

Still, sports triumph over television, and are enhanced by it. The use of several different cameras teaches millions about the relativity of standpoints. Was Pete Rose, awarded first base by the umpire, actually hit by the pitch? Three different camera angles show he wasn't. Was Charley Taylor out-of-bounds? Three cameras and a stop-action show he was. Multiple cameras do what the single eye cannot. Instant retrieval helps the eye to see again (but weakens concentration and memory). For those who do not know the game through long exposure, the isolation of a single player or a special match-up illustrates the atomic pieces that compose the whole. In taking one's eye away from the whole, however, these atomic pictures frequently recreate a totally different game.

Football, in particular, is a game of eleven men moving as a unit. While it is useful to understand the small dramas of which each play is the sum, to comprehend the true rhythm and the flow of play one has to grasp the whole. I, for one, would love to see television cameras snap pictures from above, and dramatize the lines of an actual play just as X's and O's diagram it on the coach's blackboard. Newspaper photos sometimes capture at least one instant of a whole play. I remember once a Notre Dame game with North Carolina in which, on a touchdown run to open up the second half, the Irish blockers left not a single opponent standing; it was the vision of the whole field that gave one pleasure. One photo caught it all, I seem to remember.

Basketball, for this reason, is exceedingly difficult for television to cover; the quality of team play and the sense of patterns on the floor are almost excised by television. For baseball, television is almost perfectly suited, in its ability to focus on solitary artistry. The problem baseball poses for television is not due to baseball but to television. Television is a nervous medium, hating "dead" space, irresistibly urged to fill silent moments with something, *anything*. The leisureliness of baseball is one of its deepest pleasures. Television has to jazz it up. It is out of "sync" with baseball.

Television has distorted what we share. The fault is not that of the technology involved. The fault lies in the conception of the sports directors, producers, and sportscasters. They boast endlessly about their skills. The self-hawking of television is revolting, endlessly telling us, as if we did not have schedules every day, what they will do next. A particularly disgusting point was reached in 1975 when ABC used sports shows to shill for Howard Cosell's short-lived extracurricular career as emcee of a variety show. Nothing showed better the corruption of sports by entertainment than this fancy of Cosell's; having turned football into television entertainment, he moved by inexorable logic to what he may have really wanted all along. To argue, as Cosell does, that network shilling is made necessary by money already invested, as well as by the pressures of competition, is the oldest excuse for corruption known to history.

Were television to govern its approach to sports by the nature of sports, rather than by the canons of entertainment, the technology available could do the job. For dozens of years, sports did not bore Americans. Television sports have begun to bore. Iron laws of entertainment so decree. Revulsion gathers.

The most damaging effect of television, however, has been its enervation of sportswriters and their editors. Often it happens that one cannot see the televised game. Then it is almost impossible to find out in the papers the drama of the game itself. The writers take for granted that their readers have seen the game; they write about everything else. They have lost their faith in the power of the written word. For even when one *has* seen a game, either in the flesh or on the tube, the pleasure of reading about it the next day is unabated. One tests one's own perceptions against the reporter's. One rejoices in (or deplores) his way with words. One delights in the poetry of recollecting experience in tranquillity. Words direct the eye and heart. Words sort out diffuse impressions. Words contrive a permanent form for life. The power of words is far vaster than the power of television. Why have newspapers had a failure of nerve? Perhaps the sports pages can usher print media back to the center of our culture, now that the novelty of the cathode ray is wearing off.

For we have seen dozens of politicians on television now. One charismatic leader begins to look like all the others. One wearies of the pretty faces of the anchormen, experts, and politicians. One hungers for words to sink one's imagination into. So also with the parade of athletes, celebrities, and multiple sportscasters on the tube. The game's the thing. One craves words about it.

No pages in the paper used to be, and occasionally still are, such a vivid stimulus to the imagination. No pages give a writer equal scope. Weather, place, local culture, history, strategy, judgments, decisions, moods—all these are part of the reality of every contest, are focused by the contest, make up the drama of the contest. In almost every game, changes of strategy or tactics subtly influence the outcome; even if a team decides simply to "play its game," that phrase begs for analysis into its components. Television, of necessity, almost always fails us here. For two reasons.

A contest is a drama whose meaning is not clear until beginning, middle, and end are seen as one. A television sportscast is too close to the event to render an account of it as a single form. Here is where the writer has a function television does not even attempt. The writer can bring back a portrait, complete, whole, whose end is included in its beginning, whose unfolding he can clearly see. The reporter of an athletic event is rendering a drama as vividly and clearly as he can. The talent required is a craftsman's talent, an artist's talent. Collections of the great sportswriting of the past abound in craftsmanlike examples. One seldom sees them in the papers today.

Second, television sportscasters are merely guessing in advance, or from the press box, precisely what will work or is working on the field. But the writer has an opportunity to find out, and to make it part of his story. For example, a sportscaster can say from the booth, "If the Giants want to win today, they have to pass short." Then, indeed, the Giants may pass short. So said Howard Cosell on October 20, 1975, when the Giants startled everyone, including Cosell and Alex Karras, but not Frank Gifford, who predicted it, by beating the Buffalo Bills 17–14 in the last six seconds. But how many short pass plays do the Giants have? And what, precisely, is the weak spot in the Buffalo defense that will make the short pass work—and where? Which blocking patterns are emerging that allow the Giants to run around end successfully, as they had not been doing for weeks? On a football field, things don't just happen. Someone is thinking about them, probing, trying to make them happen. The writer, after the game, can formulate the critical questions and get the solid answers—if not necessarily from the principals, then perhaps from a scout observing such matters for next week's opponent.

On September 8, 1975, for example, Alabama met Missouri in a televised game. I was reading a biography of Bear Bryant that weekend, and for the first time gained a grasp of what Bear had been trying to do at Alabama and what his traditions at the school meant. The spring before, I had visited Missouri and had sharp images in my mind both of the campus on the plains, the relatively humble stadium there, and the faces of Missouri students. I knew a little of the function of the Missouri team in the state, and a little of its struggles toward greatness. For the first time in my life, my sympathies were very strongly with Alabama, which Bear seemed to hope might become his best team ever. One former Alabama player, now a coach in another league, said before the game that the Alabama squad included the greatest talent ever assembled on one team in the South. Yet Missouri totally mastered Alabama. The frustrations of obviously excellent players were tangible; one wanted, almost, to reach out and help. I couldn't figure out exactly how Missouri was doing it. Two or three offensive plays they used seemed extraordinarily interesting; they worked with such brilliance that I wanted to know the secret.

The next day, I looked in vain in the relatively long accounts of the game in the New York Times and Newsday for an account of those plays, and of the defensive formations that kept Alabama contained as they had seldom been in five years. Gladly would I have exchanged a dozen articles on trades, analyses of financial conflicts, and organizational chitchat about players' unions and corporate bosses for intelligence about the strategic insights that dominated the actual play. A friend of mine in Alabama, blessedly, mailed me the sports page of the Anniston Star. There, precisely diagrammed, were the plays I wanted to know about. That is the sort of intelligent reporting one longs for in the press. Football is delightful because it bears such study. More is always happening than meets the eye. The players and the coaches, appearing for television interviews, have been intimidated by the entertainment format; they seldom get a chance to say abstractly and technically what we need to know—what they would tell their own observers in the booths above. Television, in its hunger to personalize the game, seldom deals with its abstract strategy, its formal design, its team execution. It gossips.

Yet not all the failings of sportswriters today—contrary to self-serving myth, we are unlucky in our generation—are due to cowardice in the face of television. In at least two ways the writers, some of them at least, undercut themselves. Some of them believe that they are superior to those they cover; they believe it is their function to prick the bubble of illusion surrounding sports. For convenience, we may call them pricks. They would prefer, second, to be working on some other section of the paper, covering financial or business news, or investigating city hall. There is some plausibility to their new conception of sports reporting, for it is not often that athletes or coaches in the sports world speak the idiom of our new journalists; and the growth of sports as a plaything of millionaires badly needs to be investigated. Still, it seems astonishing to read writers who do not love their subject.

In early 1975, David Shaw of the Los Angeles *Times* wrote a page-one article of 129 column inches on the new sportswriting, praising his own paper as the best in the country, and lavishly commending its publisher and editors. He had warm enthusiasm for the new breed of sportswriters, the "team" *he* plays for, so to speak. He praised the "quality of their writing," their "questioning minds" and "master's degrees." According to the new breed, to write in this way about a local football team would be to be a rooter. That is wrong. But choosing up sides among writers, and cheering for one's own, is right. Shaw names his own team, and their degree of loyalty, with serenity. The movement started with Larry Merchant, Joe McGinniss, Jack McKinney, and George Kiseda at the Philadelphia *Daily News* in 1957. It has spread to the Los Angeles *Times*, but not to its opposition (Shaw emphasizes) the *Herald-Examiner*; to *Newsday*, the Boston *Globe*, the Philadelphia *Inquirer*. "Only a few other sports sections in the United States [are] now actively moving toward the level of those already mentioned": the Washington *Post*, New York *Post*, Chicago *Tribune*, Chicago *Sun-Times*, Miami *Herald*, and New York *Times* (which has "special problems"). The new sportswriters have a "litmus test" for their side: how a writer covered Muhammad Ali, Joe Namath, and the early New York Mets. The good writers dealt with such symbols "on their own terms, as representatives of a new independence and self-awareness." The good guys saw that the early Mets weren't serious but a diversion, and the good guys "laughed sympathetically" with them. The way you laugh is important nowadays, even in sports.

It is astonishing to read Shaw's description of earlier sportswriting, however: "'Meat and potatoes' sportswriting, it was called, and it consisted almost solely of scores and statistics—batting averages, shooting percentages, earned-run averages, running yardage, passing percentages. . . ." Shaw must not have gained his master's degrees in sportswriting history, nor dipped into anthologies; for the older sportswriting was some of the most sociologically acute, colorful, lyrical, and biting in the history of journalism. What pleasure it affords, nowadays, to read collections of old clippings.

Shaw, however, was deeply moved by "the socio-political upheavals of the 1960s." His interest is ideological, not historical. He writes a trifle ecstatically:

> The times—and the nation's sports pages—they are a changin', and it is now no longer sufficient to write sports stories by the numbers . . . or by the clichés. The more sophisticated and literate reader of today's sports page wants to know more than what happened on the field. He also wants to know how it happened and why (or why not), as well as what may have happened before (or after) the event, in the locker room, the courtroom, the boardroom and the bedroom.
>
> Racism, drugs, sex, religion, gambling, exploitation, psychology, cheating, feminism, dress styles, violence, antitrust legislation—all these subjects, and many more, have been explored in detail on the sports pages in recent months.

Shaw lists several ways in which the new sportswriters are better than the old; his claims sound either untrue or disheartening. The athlete is not romanticized, but "analyzed, criticized, and even condemned." The sporting event is not "treated as seriously as a holy crusade" but dealt with "lightly, humorously, sarcastically or scornfully." We now probe "the athlete's development as an individual, his relations with others (on and off the field) and his attitude toward a whole range of personal, political, and psycho-social issues." This is supposed to be important for grasping what happens on the field (and also for one's daily dose of political education?). In addition, "Where once the sports pages contained some of the worst writing in the newspaper, now—on any given day—the best piece of pure writing in some very good newspapers might well be found on the sports page." Also, "the rooter as writer is a vanishing breed." Finally, "the biggest single change in sportswriting has been the coming of sociology to the sports page."

Shaw, above all, exalts his own new intellectual status. The sports department is no longer "the toy department . . . a sandbox peopled by the idiot children of journalism." The "new-breed sportswriter" is "socially and politically aware, motivated more by his own curiosity and need to write than by a love of sports for sports's sake." The greatest impetus to the new sportswriting, Shaw admits, however, is television. The "good" papers no longer recreate or analyze games; they look for "soft angles" not covered by television.

The new sportswriters do not actually write very well; only Roger Kahn—and he is not really one of them—writes with distinction. The late Leonard Shecter wrote with bite and wit, however, and his book is the fullest statement of the pricks to date. The title of this delightful, wry, and astringent book is itself an insult: *The Jocks*. He describes it as "a sports book by a man who hates sports." Hate, of course, is next to love, and infinitely to be preferred to indifference. Many a good book has had its origin in hate. Passionate attack is as important in writing as in football. What Shecter adds to hate, however, are arrogance and contempt. His own words convey his point: "There are two kinds of sportswriters—those with the good sense and ability to go on to other things and those with neither." He calls his classic chapter on the subject: "To Hell with Newspapermen, You Can Buy Them with a Steak." His own style around the clubhouse when he covered the Yankees may be inferred from comments like these: "The last thing a ball player cares about are the precepts by which a newspaperman is supposed to live. . . . The only thing a ball player wants to know is what you have done for him lately. . . . Why should a ball player have the right to decide when he will talk to a newspaperman? . . . I leaned over backwards to be nice to ball players and was rewarded by arrogance. I accepted the arrogance and even began to feel it was my due. I never get angry. . . . I suppose my major problem, when I first began to cover a baseball team, was that I was more interested in being a newspaperman than a sportswriter."

There is a virulent passion for debunking in the land, one of the consequences, it is said, of the horrors of Vietnam, the sudden visibility of the depth of racism, and Watergate. Perhaps the roots of this passion lie deeper still, however, and the evils mentioned may be merely its occasion. A new class is struggling for power, in the world of sports reporting as in government; its method is contempt for all that has gone before. Its source is not our present theme, but its effects plainly are. In Shecter, as in others, the rage against sports seems overwrought, disproportionate, and off the mark. Sports are symbolic realities, but somehow in these writers sports begin to symbolize *political* evils. It is as though their rage against the nation, and perhaps against themselves, had been misdirected into sports. They do not, by and large, distinguish clearly enough between the realm of the spirit acted out in sports and the impact of mass communications and commercial interests. Rifle shots might hit their targets; they use napalm from a height.

"Nowhere else in the world," Shecter writes, "is such a large portion of the population so consistently engaged in sports and games." One wonders. It is estimated that 2 billion persons saw the World Cup championships in soccer in 1974, outside the United States. It offends him that 228 million Americans paid to attend major sports events in 1967. The figure sounds impressive until we average it out for a population of 200 million: paid attendance is approximately one per person every year. In 1973, by comparison, 112 million Americans visited a zoo. Only 35.9 million attended football games in 1967, according to Shecter; baseball games, 34.7 million; basketball games, 22 million. (These figures are for professional or college games.) Another 67.8 million went to the races. It dismays Shecter that sports have become "a monster, a sprawling five-billion-dollar-a-year industry." This is a large sum. Yet many industries are larger, including the print and broadcast media, the pet industry, and cosmetics. Out of a gross national product of almost $1.4 trillion, $5 billion does not seem disproportionate.

Shecter devotes most of his energy in *The Jocks* to every example of "the dump, the fix, the thrown game, the shaved points" he can find in the history of American sports. He adds little new evidence to familiar allegations, and lists few episodes that are not well known. His point is a good one. Wherever money is involved, it is wise to be cynical, best to be on guard. From his point of view, however, the public gets pitifully little from the hoopla. Sports yield, in his judgment, "a marvelous sense of the importance of the unimportant." His prose is passionate:

> Around the simplicity which most of us want out of sports has grown a monster . . . which pretends to cater to our love for games but instead has evolved into that one great American institute: big business. Winning, losing, playing the game, all count far less than counting the money. The result is cynicism of the highest order. There is no business in the country which operates so cynically to make enormous profits on the one hand, while demanding to be treated as a public service on the other. . . . What we get, as opposed to what we think we get, is what this book is about. . . . It's about the cynicism of American sports. . . . It's about the newspapers and the newspapermen who shill for sports. It's about television, the conscienceless and ruthless partner of sports. It's about the spoiled heroes of sports, shiny on the outside, decaying with meanness underneath. It's about the greedy professionals and posturing amateurs, the crooks, the thieves, the knaves and the fools. These are not trivial things. Sports have a great and continuous impact on American life. . . .

Shecter's passion for purity is a useful contribution. But how will it be executed? If it means that sportswriters will now become investigative reporters whose mission is to prove that men in sports are as venal as men outside of sports, we shall not learn much we don't already know. The more they write about the sports *industry*, the more the new sportswriters involve us in money, contracts, deals, swindles, and a vicious cynicism of our own. With the moral passion of the "chipmunks" (to use Jimmy Cannon's term) we can perhaps agree; everything depends on how they execute. Here is where they contribute to the distortion they deplore.

The main business of a sportswriter is to describe what happened in athletic events. The contests themselves are the forms of his craft. Everything else is secondary, instrumental, and to be judged in that light. The business side of sports smells of rot; but the business side of sports should be reported on the business pages. The politics of sports are rotting, too; but the politics of sports belongs on the national or the city desk. Many of the stories about big money in sports—money made by teams or paid to individual players—are not true; they are exaggerated as part of the hype to attract attention. Nothing should be hidden; everything should be reported. *But not in the sports pages.*

When I read the sports page, I'm not interested in big business, wheeling and dealing, money; all that is part of the mundane world of everyday and belongs on the other, boring pages of the paper, to be read from a sense of duty. On the sports page, I seek clear images of *what happened*; or, in advance, *what is likely to happen* in athletic contests. I expect guidance in learning afterward exactly *how it happened*. I would like sports reporters to be, in this sense, better newsmen. I would like them to give probing, intelligent, and artistic accounts of the one world that here interests me: the events on the field. Let them be reporters. But about the contests on the field, not about the industry. If they want to work for the financial pages, let them; but not at the expense of the events without which sports do not exist. The essential craft of the sportswriter is mimetic: to recreate events, to imitate and to reveal their form, to catch new sides to their significance. The craft is more like that of the novelist or dramatist than like that of the investigative reporter. The craft of the sports columnist, and of those writers not assigned to specific events, too, take their meaning from athletic contests. Without the contests, there would be no sports. No matter what is said, or done, or thought elsewhere, the essential subject is what happens on the field in games.

It is important to our kind of civilization to keep sports as insulated as we can from business, entertainment, politics, and even gossip. Naturally, sports involve all these elements. But none of them must be permitted to obscure the struggle of body and spirit that is their center. The athletic contest has too much meaning for the human spirit to be treated with contempt. Our civilization needs sports, and it needs as well the skillful exercise of the sportswriter's craft. The narrative forms that recount athletic struggles supply millions with a sense of form. These forms express implicitly realities of law, fairness, effort, and spirit.

Who, watching the sixth game of the 1975 World Series in Boston's ancient and angular Fenway Park, as first the Cincinnati Reds and then the Boston Red Sox fought their way back from 3-run deficits and battled for four hours with brilliant play after brilliant play—Lynn of Boston lying immobile after crashing his spine into the centerfield wall; Foster of Cincinnati throwing sharply from left field to make a bases-loaded double play at the plate; Evans of Boston racing back to the seats in right in the eleventh to take away a certain home run; Fisk fighting the night breeze with his hands to pull his twelfth-inning homer far enough inbounds to hit the foul pole and give Boston a 7–6 victory—who, watching this game, could not detect some of the main sources of our civilization's strength, acted out in ritual form? It is ponderous to put it this way; best if one drinks in the pleasure, imitates the attitudes, without too many words. But it is precisely in tacit and unspoken ritual forms that all religions have most effectively taught their hidden mysteries. The account of these rituals, in narrative form, is the main business of the sports page. It is being seriously neglected.

Without narrative forms, a culture flies apart; sorting out the relevant from the irrelevant becomes impossible; living loses zest. Life in its multiplicity overwhelms the brain, blows it out. The opera, the play, the cinema, the short story, the ballet, the modern dance—all these wrest form from chaos. The forms of play, including the narrative forms crafted by sportswriters, are absorbed into the psyche, become the forms through which other forms may be perceived. For this reason, above all, it is important to be vigilant over the corruptions and the range of sports.

Standards of fair play, honesty, courage, scrappiness, law-abidingness, excellence, perfect execution, etc., are all dramatized in a baseball game, in football, and in basketball. These are standards difficult to meet in the contests themselves, in the industry that makes them possible, and in the rest of life. As we have seen, these standards belong not to the players, who may not embody them, but to the inherent structure of the game. Without such standards in its ritual structure, a game could not be played; it would be meaningless. Without such standards in a culture, human beings could not complain of vice, corruption, or incompetence.

Sports are not a sufficient vocabulary of forms for a whole human life; but they are a fundament, a basic vocabulary, around which it is possible to build an ampler human structure. Many athletes and coaches find their work of absorbing interest. For others, athletics are just a job for a certain time in their lives. For most of us, they are part of our mythic world—nourishment for body, soul, and imagination.

It is not uncommon for writers in a given field, even a generation of writers, to lose sight of their essential function. Ever since Theodore H. White's *The Making of the President, 1960,* a generation of political writers has developed a mania for looking under, behind, and around the central actions of politics. There is passionate concern for "inside" stories, but far less concern for grasping clearly the economic consequences of political ideas. So, also, among sportswriters there appears to be at present a damaging and costly failure of nerve. Intellectually, sports have been treated with disdain; commercially, television has intimidated writers and editors, and led them to neglect what they do best and, indeed, what only they can do: clarify the dramatic form of each sports event. Just because people have "seen it on the tube," one ought not to cease describing the event as it occurred outside the limits of the camera lens. Repetition is no enemy of sports; nor of religion; nor of art.

In addition, there are characteristics of sports that differentiate sportswriters from any other writers on the paper. There are two pleasures in sports: first, a perception of the sheer excellence of play; second, the identification of self with the struggle and the outcome. Nourished by the latter, one can with pleasure enjoy from time to time a contest between teams one hardly knows. But true enjoyment does not begin until the self is risked, until there is a part of the self to lose. It is not absolutely essential that one become completely partisan in order to feel this risk. As a Dodger fan, I felt a relative neutrality between Boston and Cincinnati in the World Series of 1975. Or, to put it more exactly, I rooted for Boston in every game until the last. They deserved not to be humiliated, and their spirit was infectious; but after six years of steady excellence, Cincinnati deserved a championship. I wanted Middle America to win one. I would have been pleased, but a little less so, if Boston had won. Such response is more than aesthetic; I find myself identifying, acquiring loyalties, choosing sides, accepting risks, even when the grounds of choice are neither deep nor unchangeable.

One's appreciation for a game, moreover, increases with detailed familiarity with various factors that affect it. Bookmakers take even minor factors into account: the weather, injuries, morale, the place of a game in the schedule, and so forth. Athletic deeds gain part of their significance from the history in which they occur. A home run at the end of a slump, at a critical point, brings a special pleasure. If one knows that a player is hurt, and if one also knows his characteristic moves, one can watch an entire game anticipating, and then enjoying the specific pleasure of a drama adequately "true to form." One recognizes, for example, Joe Namath's relative immobility because of his bad knees, but one also knows that at any moment he can fire an electrifying pass. The long waits between his four or five moments of brilliance may be justified (but were not, really, in 1975) through the pattern they fulfill, linked to a history of previous deeds. One measures an athlete against his remembered form, his best; and one's standards for him grow as he grows. Appreciation in sports requires a grasp of local history.

History, then, is at the heart of sports. Each contest is part of a chain of others. Each is partly self-contained, but each is also linked to others. The excitement of many contests depends on rivalries from the distant past. In part, these are collective rivalries between organizations; in part, personal rivalries between coaches or players. "Last year, they murdered us." "The last three weeks we played badly; tomorrow we have to establish our rhythm, our kind of game." Each game has its stakes; no two raise the same expectations.

But we are not infinite. We cannot appreciate the full traditions of the top twenty college football teams, or of twenty-six professional football teams with one thousand one hundred and eighteen players. The human imagination, heart, memory, and intelligence are finite. The nature of the human psyche is to proceed from what is close to us outward; we cannot without self-deception begin by embracing everything. To claim to love humanity is to carry a very large and thin pane of glass toward a collision with someone you can't abide.

Thus, a sportswriter becomes a folklorist of sorts, steeped in detail and anecdote, practicing a form of intellect from which all others spring, the lore of the wise man of the tribe. Like Arthur Daley and Red Smith, Dick Young and Jim Murray, virtually every veteran writer learns this craft. Knowledge in sports is exceedingly concrete. Great theories and general rules don't carry athletes too far. Each must tailor principles to his own individual circumstance. Particularities, quirks, eccentricities, peculiar preferences, habits, and customs loom large in sports—as everywhere in life except where the rationality of bureaucracy extends, its rules snarling and tangling one another up. The most highly prized form of intellect is concrete.

All these characteristics of the sports world draw the sportswriter into an unusually close relationship with the subjects of his work. Even independently of his need to keep on good terms with his sources, or to avoid friction between his paper and the teams he covers, the attitude of a writer to his subject normally involves ties of long standing, profound loyalties, and deep personal identification. Some critics deplore such developments and speak with contempt of "shills" or "house flacks." Such contempt seems, most of the time, misplaced. For an attitude of love for the subjects of one's writing and even a deep loyalty and rootedness in a particular team are uniquely appropriate in sports reporting. The readers of sports stories in the local paper read from a point of view, with a sense of identification, and also with a passion for perfect play on the part of their team. As they are critical, so the writer may be. Scrappy, independent loyalty is best. I do not find it shocking to imagine sportswriters in the press box shouting hoarsely for the home team and pounding their desks in excitement. The cool modern types may do it differently; in the world of sports, there are many styles. The essential point is to get the drama right for one's readers.

Many readers are intelligent. They are inured to the stupidities of journalism. They delight in craftsmanship lovingly performed. They like to read a writer who challenges and defies them. They want him often, in their stead, to sock it to errant players, management, owners, television, industry, the world. They recognize the difference between loyalty based on love for excellence and sycophancy. They are tolerant, endure a great deal of mediocrity. But work of quality has a way of winning recognition, being cited in conversation, reread, and given thanks at first in private, later perhaps more publicly. Bill Veeck, flamboyant owner of several teams, says he prefers the sharp, pesky, argumentative writer who takes a poke at management. He's interesting. He's reacted to. He does in his craft what the players do in theirs. And he helps both his paper and the team, much as the biggies may dislike the names he calls them.

The writers of the new breed—Shecter, Larry Merchant, Wells Twombly, Robert Lipsyte, as well as the ex-athletes Jack Scott, Dave Meggysey, Chip Oliver, Jim Bouton, and others—often picture themselves as the first frank, critical, and abrasive sportswriters in the nation's history. Yet lovers of the game have always known how to barb, skewer, and roast a charlatan, a fake, a quitter, a tenderskin. Boston writers rode Ted Williams hard; he kicked back. Writers in Atlanta tried to drive Bear Bryant out of football. Years ago, Frank Leahy was the target of vicious criticism, some of which helped force his resignation. Rosie Rosewell used to want the Pittsburgh Pirates to win so bad it hurt to hear him when they made mistakes. (The broadcasters, of course, are hired by the team; they are not exactly "press.")

Since at least the age of nine, I've received one clear message from the papers: that sportswriters would make better managers, and maybe better players, than the fellows on the field. Half the pleasure of the connoisseur is trying to outguess events. His imagination swiftly runs ahead, with keen expectations, and the poor fellows who have to play the ball seldom attain the perfect form anticipation craves. So it is not new for sportswriters to be critical.

What is new is the relatively recent surge of hostility so total it is puzzling, a kind of global disappointment and resentment, as if America and life and sports had let some writers down. It is as though one had a right to expect a nation to be just, true, good, compassionate; as though liberty and justice were easy to attain, and failures to attain them due solely to slack will; as though an intense will for goodness were sufficient. Yet I am not sure the hostility of which I write springs from innocence. It may be futile to try to guess its motives. It has given prominence and power to the pricks, with mixed results.

A prick is a writer who is out of place in sports. He really wants to deal with a world of Serious Subjects. Enlightened, bright, able, interested in facts (without necessarily uncovering many), the prick thinks himself incorruptible. He also writes well, or tries to. The flack, by contrast, is a company man, not in the sense that he is, say, an announcer paid by a ball club, but in the sense that he is sycophantic.

A flack has no independence of mind. A "house announcer" or "house writer" is different from the flack in this respect. His loyalties are plain. Yet he is faithful, as well, to standards that transcend both him and his employer. He does not bite the hand that feeds him; he has room for self-respect; he does not wear a leash. He does not expect sports organizations to operate by a higher morality than newspapers, universities, or other human organisms. He has learned a certain tolerance for human frailty. He often calls himself, self-deprecatingly, a "hack": seldom setting the world on fire; doing a decent job; establishing a solid, if modest, reputation; workmanlike; like most players on most ball clubs or, for that matter, like most human beings. The type, as Lincoln put it, that God loved to duplicate. The sports department of the New York *Times* numbers 53. They can't all be rising stars.

"A baseball club, the public has been brainwashed into thinking, is like a city's army going out to do battle with the mercenaries of another city," writes one prick. Another writes: "Sports act as an important socializing agent for misdirected elitism, nationalism, racism, and sexism, thus tending to turn jocks into proto-fascists." A third writes that he applauds the breakdown of local loyalties by television, as on the *Game of the Week* and *Monday Night Football*. He praises the universalization of sports, although he finds himself less interested than formerly. Even though he is a New Yorker, he writes, he would believe Joe Namath great even if he were playing for the Los Angeles Rams.

These attitudes seem noble and large-spirited. Yet they run counter to the human heart. Intense group loyalties are part of being human. They are important to the survival of the race. They teach forms of fairness, justice, and fellow feeling on which other moral forms are based. In every sport, these local loyalties are transcended by the rules of play. The game is larger than the local passion. Sports help to show how one can be particular and universal at the same time; partisan, yet not self-enclosed; loyal, yet rule-abiding;

attached to one's own, yet capable of recognizing worth in others. Babe Ruth was an idol for millions who weren't Yankee fans. "All-America" teams command respect from all sections and factions. Even those who despise Alabama, or Notre Dame, or Ohio State can—and do—recognize their frequent greatness. To love the Dodgers is not inconsistent with recognizing that the 1975 Cincinnati Reds were a better team, that Oakland and Boston played more exciting baseball, and that the Pittsburgh Pirates were explosive and underrated. Sports fans are often quite objective about the strengths and weaknesses of various teams and players, despite their loyalties. Their judgments are, or can be, settled on the field. I would much rather argue the merits of Notre Dame with an ardent Alabama fan than argue politics with extremists of the right or of the left. Any day.

The pricks, in sum, tend to have large, even global souls. The hacks have humble loyalties. The pricks are strong on principle. For the hacks, morality is rather more familial; their deepest moral bond is likely to be a loyalty between persons, as in the family, rather than a morality of principle, or duty, or universalizable rule, or moral imperative. The prick doesn't trust the easy tolerance of the hack. The hack believes that pricks, like other men of principle, will in the name of moral principles betray their friends every time. The war between pricks and hacks is an ancient war. Often, each has something good to say. It would be silly to be a flack for either one of them.

For all who report sports, however, at least this much can be demanded: a passion for excellence in covering the heart of the matter, the actual contests on the field. Today not many have it. Lacking that, the rest is beside the point.

MICHAEL NOVAK

Humble Howard

Look, there is no damn way you can go up against Liz Taylor and Doris Day in prime-time TV and present sports as just sports or as religion. Sports aren't life and death. They're entertainment.

—Humble Howard

No sports commentator in recent years has stirred the juices as much as Howard Cosell. Why? Commentators are to sports what prophets and theologians are to religion. Howard is the nation's first major non-Christian sports prophet. He never had to learn all those inhibitions that young Christians, particularly those in the heartland of sports, the Bible Belts of the land, drink in with their mother's milk and relearn from their pappy's strap. Every culture carries with it distinctive ideals, and in the case of the Christian athlete, these usually involve a ritual form of modesty, self-effacement, team-consciousness, and oft repeated loyalty. In America, individualism reigns and associations are fluid; hence, assurances of loyalty and conformity are precious. In public, at least, the pieties fall as thick as snowflakes.

Cosell describes himself as a "needler," and he admits frankly to a certain abrasiveness. That he is no great practitioner of self-effacement is obvious, and that modesty is not a virtue he carries to extremes may be glimpsed even in the titles of his books: *Cosell* and *Like It Is*. Cosell gives good reasons for every boast he makes. The usual Christian fashion, not least in the world of sports, is not to boast in public, with or without good reason. Cosell is under no obligation to bow to pieties that inhibit others. He has helped to raise the degree of abrasive frankness in our national discourse. He has added to the repertoire of future sports commentators one more style, one more approach to the subject. For his exaggerations, self-promotions, and violations of cultural taboos, he has paid a certain price—not unlike that paid by other ethnic types in sports (like Namath, Billy Martin, and Muhammad Ali) who do not share the classic pieties.

One recalls Cosell, on his very first regular Monday night broadcast, saying in his own inimitable tone of voice: "Leroy Kelly has not been a *compelling* factor in this game." Cleveland won 31–21. Howard thought the first night a great success. Then the flood of letters and editorial protest startled him.

From *The Joy of Sports* (1976).

"You see," he explains in *Cosell*, "in the spoon-fed Alice in Wonderland world of sports broadcasting, the public was not accustomed to hearing its heroes questioned." But this is nonsense. The Boston sportswriters used to tear Ted Williams apart. Nothing is a more common experience of athletes and coaches than criticism in the press—considerably more accurate and ferocious than Cosell's. Yet thousands of letters came. More than half the mail was about Howard and Muhammad Ali. "I knew instinctively what [it] meant. It was a pattern with which I was painfully familiar: 'Get that nigger-loving Jew bastard off the air. Football is an *American* game.'" Cosell doesn't stop to recognize that half the mail was in defense of Leroy Kelly, a black man. He does not see that his tone says far more than his words, projects his sense of his own superiority. Some of the mail, he is told, "says you can't criticize the players, you never played the game." It is a question of tone. His tone belittles others. No one doubts he can *talk* better than most ex-athletes; has, in his own words, "great verbal dexterity." His tone needn't indicate that he is also better in every other way. Humble Howard!

The second reason for Cosell's capacity to enrage is not so much a question of style as a question of substance. Granted that he is so damn sure of himself, that he pronounces his judgments in a tone of voice that makes him seem almost papal in complacence ("papal bull," one almost wants to say), Cosell also diagnosed the existence of a new constituency for sports. Studies have shown that high numbers of professional people—from managers and executives to lawyers and intellectuals—follow sports with passion. Some 89 percent of managers regularly attend football games or watch on television. The "average sports fan" includes not only drivers of beer trucks or construction workers, but a large majority of the new and swelling professional class. Cosell decided to give them sociology as well as sports. He broke with conventional ideas.

Cosell describes sportscasters tearing copy off the wire machine and reading the results verbatim:

> That was their idea of a sportscast. Not mine. I had my own notion about the business. I felt that the field was wide open for anyone willing to develop the sources and get to the scene. . . . I wanted to explore the issues. The world of sports was about to explode in America. Great changes in technology were coming; an increase of leisure time; the exodus to the suburbs to escape from the great cities. The whole pattern of society was changing, and sports would become ever more important. The influx of black athletes had begun. A whole new set of smoldering problems would emerge. Could we keep giving the country line scores as news?

Cosell tended to side with "change," with the new professional classes, with the advance, so to speak, of New York liberalism across the countryside. In this way, Cosell won the reputation—a valuable one as time went on—of being antiestablishment. The transformation of Cassius Clay into Muhammad Ali was almost perfectly suited to dramatizing Cosell's career. A black man, a dissenter, a colorful and lippy violator of the same pieties of modesty and self-effacement Cosell himself was violating, Ali was also a brave and bold champion. Call him a fraud, if you wished. Call him a coward. Call him all sorts of names—the more you became preoccupied with him, the more valuable he became as a draw. Then in his fights he took the assaults of his enemies' best blows and, while absorbing some defeats, most of the time came back to win. His bouts with Joe Frazier and George Foreman were classics. Ali talked big. But he delivered big, too. His style gave credibility to Cosell's. Their careers benefited each other. At critical stages, each helped the other.

Yet Cosell, as an immigrant outsider, was always deeply involved in his own family; his wife Emmy figures often in his writings, and he remembers that his father was disappointed every day until his death in 1957 that Howard didn't continue as a lawyer. Thus, Cosell had complex sympathies. His essay on Vince Lombardi is a poignant answer to Leonard Shecter's vicious assault on Lombardi in *Esquire*. Cosell understood the intensity of Lombardi's attachment to family values and to the old immigrant ways of excellence. It was as if Cohen (Cosell's original name) well understood Lombardi, rising as they did off the same streets of New York, with a passion for excellence fed by resentment of false pieties. Both of them endured no little abuse from those whose preferred style was different.

On the plus side, then, are Cosell's attack on less than truthful pieties and his insistence on being himself—"integrity" is one of his favorite words, a word one imagines him sticking out his chin to say, his eyes flashing a certain defensive arrogance, his lips already set for counterattack to any challenge. Nevertheless, I hold his influence on the nation's conception of sport to be negative. Cosell grants that sports are not *merely* entertainment, but entertainment and something more. He has wanted to bring "honesty" to sports, he says:

> It must be realized, once and for all, that sports are not separate and apart from life, a special "wonderland" where everything is pure and sacred and above criticism. A football game is not a holy sacrament, and baseball does not truly equate with apple pie and motherhood and the American flag. I suggest that in American society today, it is time to tell it like it is—and that includes sports.

Cosell's critics said he and Don Meredith were making *Monday Night Football*, which changed the social habits of millions of Americans, "entertainment, not football." But Cosell had clearly recognized that sports is *both* news and entertainment. He explains that ABC had to attract 30 million viewers, and each paragraph he wrote needed to earn back "$100,000 a minute." It was big business, a risk; it had to compete, and it had to succeed. The other networks predicted failure, having failed themselves. Against his critics he would reply: "ABC will not be like the others. We'll be number one because we make football entertaining."

For Cosell, the debate is between news and entertainment. He confuses the false pieties of the Anglo-American style with religion. In rejecting sports as something like a sacrament, sacred, profoundly rooted in the human spirit and in a particular people, he thinks he is rejecting a "wonderland" where everything is "pure and sacred and above criticism." Religions aren't like that. Everything in a religion is subject to criticism; people have gone to war over such criticisms. And in treating sports as though they were part news, part entertainment, he misses half the true passion, excitement, and "hot sporting blood" in sports. Cosell's memory about individual players, teams, and even particular plays is truly remarkable, and his ability to draw upon the past often adds enjoyment to a particular deed upon the field. Yet often his comments seem to be either occasions for him to show off or beside the point. He usually doesn't add much to our comprehension of which plays, formations, and strategies are working or not working. He seems to miss the dimensions in which football is like chess. One misses in him the pleasures of connoisseurship. Above all, one finds in his commentary too much flair for the personal grudges, anxieties, career turning points, etc., of the individual players and coaches. He runs the commentary along the lines of gossip, as do journals like *Sport* and the *Sporting News*. Such comments make the game personal. No doubt, they are successful for some, and he knows they will be. But they do change the experience of watching the game, for the worse.

I like to know the specific drama of each contest, for each is different, and on this point Cosell is helpful. His excitement about excellence is contagious, particularly when he supplies the narrative at halftime for the swift review of the previous day's games. His respect for the athletes' endurance, effort, and zest for perfection is also winning. Yet, still, he somehow leaves us with a certain emptiness about the games, an emptiness he himself seems to feel. Often in *Cosell*, he complains about "the disproportionate emphasis placed upon sports in America in which people get so bound up with an event, with winning or losing, that their whole sense of values is discarded in the transitory escape from real life that the event provides." He has a certain contempt for the fan, for middle America, and it often shows. The day after Robert Kennedy was shot, Cosell said in his morning broadcast that he could not speak of sports, and talked instead about "the three assassinations in a decade and why I had to think about what I do and why I do it, and I suggested that it might be the time for everyone to do just that because there was a terrible sickness in the society." He was surprised by the volume and bitterness of the resultant mail, telling him, in effect: "Don't tell me how to live, just give us the scores." Cosell was stunned. "My instant reaction: What hope is there for the country if this is the thinking?"

A great deal of hope. The politicalization of almost everything is a form of totalitarianism. The preservation of parts of life not drawn up into politics and work is essential for the human spirit. In the well-ordered world of baseball, an assassination is a grievous, savage, and blasphemous intrusion. By recounting the meaning of conflict and competition, as these are acted out in sports, Cosell might have made an overpowering point about the murder of Robert Kennedy—the equal of the point Kennedy himself had made, citing a Greek dramatist, when Martin Luther King was brutally gunned down. Kennedy loved sports. Cosell need not have preached, but only used the resources of his métier to make his point. Instead, his political and moral lecture—on the "sickness" he imputes to "our society"—was out-of-bounds, a violation. Under the emotion of the moment, he might be forgiven. But those who reacted with outrage at his words were moved, perhaps, by a good, deep, sound, and true instinct. To politicize sports is to contribute to the politicalization of everything, the blaming of everything on politics, and the despair of many naïve persons with the human condition—which they falsely seem to believe politicians can wave away. I myself was sick at heart that day, devastated, and did not want to hear the scores; but I was glad the world was still going on, the scores were still coming in. My essential faith is not in politics, which is a brutal, ugly business.

Cosell was not alone in departures of this sort. Later, Wells Twombly did the same thing in the San Francisco Examiner, and so did the young editor of the Daily Cal at Berkeley: "It has been a custom for sports columnists and editors to be to the right of Genghis Khan politically, and to be behind Spiro Agnew in insight. The sports world must not sit back and watch everything go to pot all around it. It cannot, as some of its backers would prefer, exist in a vacuum unrelated to the world."

At all times and in all places, sports do have a relation to politics and culture; it would be foolish to believe that sports are apolitical. But the relationship of sports to politics is not simple, nor is it direct. Sports provide elementary metaphors for certain conceptions of fair play and justice, for a sense of constitutionality and due process. These things, too, are rituals and have a

sacred quality. Even during and after an assassination—which violates them—
they retain their force. They go on. Life goes on. To turn to sports, as some
did on those days, is not necessarily an escape. The pretense that life will *not*
go on, the attribution of the foul deed to a curable "sickness"—*that* may be
the escape. The glimpse into the abyss of brutality is an insight into everyday
reality.

That there is evil in the world to be fought; that injustice is relentless; that
death unfairly defeats us all and with special cruelty takes the young—all
these are deeply written into the laws of sport themselves. The metaphors of
sport would be cheapening on such occasions, for actual death exceeds symbolic death, and actual injustice symbolic injustice. But the essential points
are no different. Young athletes have died in their prime; great stallions have
come up lame at the threshold of victory and had to be "put away" before
their promise was fulfilled. Handsome bullfighters have, grotesquely, accidentally, felt their stomachs torn apart by the unpredicted twist of a maddened
animal. Outrageously unfair mistakes of judgment have cost teams World Series games. Cheats, frauds, and unfair tactics have brought about defeat for
the worthy. If sports do not permeate the sports commentator's mind with
images like these, he has not seen beneath the surface entertainment. And
that is sad.

At the heart of sports there is a deep aloneness, a silence, in which one
faces extremities. The cold tearing of the tissues of one's lungs, the strains
upon the fibers of one's heart, the blackness threatening one's brain, are so
intense that it sometimes seems impossible to will another step. One's whole
self groans against defeat. Against death. Yet death comes.

For revolutionaries as well as for those who defend the liberties they have
won, sports are not a poor preparation of the spirit. Jack Scott offers a key to
the real emotion behind the sermons of the new commentators: "The new
breed of college sports writer is also attempting to dispel the stereotype image
of all athletes as being crew-cutted, dumb jocks." One does not dispel this
image by pulling cheap politics over one's superficial metaphysics. Cosell, in
particular, is better than that.

Yet it comes as no surprise when at the end of *Cosell*, Cosell confesses slyly:
"The one thing that would take me out of broadcasting would be the opportunity to serve in the Senate of the United States"; and, later, when Cosell
replies "jocularly" to a questioner about his ambitions for the Senate, "I
doubt that there are ten better qualified persons in the United States." (The
precedents he cites are Ronald Reagan and George Murphy.) Cosell too much
believes that politics is the real world, and sports an escape, to be a reliable
theologian of sports. He treats them as escape. I think I am not alone among
lovers of sports in turning to them for something far more substantial, some-

thing much more basic to my life than that. Just as clergymen sometimes suffer from being too close to holy things, from handling them in their daily work and as a matter of routine, thereby losing their touch for transcendence, so also many athletes, coaches, and commentators have too much of a good thing and lose their touch for its mysteries.

Having done so well in cracking the crust of unreflective pieties, Cosell fails at the most radical level to "tell it like it is." He leaves out the inner power of sports, the power of the human spirit, without which crowds could not be attracted and so much love and energy could not be inspired. In trying to be secular, dry, abrasive; above all, in trying to entertain, he neglects the living roots. Left to his care alone, therefore, one would expect sports to wither on the vine, to begin to bore him, and many others with him.

FRANCINE HARDAWAY

Foul Play: Sports Metaphors as Public Doublespeak

Nobody would argue the place of sports in American life; they are big business. And they are big business because they fit philosophically with the widely accepted American dream of open competition in a free market economy. Americans believe in competition, foster it, and encourage it. They live by its rules. No wonder the language of athletic competition has found its way as metaphor into every aspect of American life. If we are at a disadvantage, we say we've "got two strikes against us," things have "taken a bad bounce," or we're "on the ropes." If we are being aggressive, we "take the ball and run with it," "take the bull by the horns," "come out swinging," or "make a sweep." If the fates still conspire against us, we "take it on the chin," "throw in the towel," or "roll with the punches" until we're "saved by the bell."

It's worth taking some time to think about how these sports metaphors, so ubiquitous and so ignored until Watergate brought them to our attention, describe the quality of life in America.

The purpose of such metaphors is to explain unfamiliar or difficult concepts

---

Originally appeared in *College English* (1976).

in terms of familiar images. But recently there have been some changes in our national self-concept and these changes are duly reflected in sports metaphors. We seem to have changed drastically from a society in which "it isn't whether you win or lose, but how you play the game," to one in which, to use Vince Lombardi's words, "winning isn't everything, it's the only thing." And our sports metaphors have changed with us. "The good fight" and "the old college try" have given way to the more sophisticated "game plans," "play-calling," and quarterbacking rhetoric of Vietnam and Watergate. Sports metaphors now often function as public doublespeak: language meant to manipulate its audience unconsciously. Analyzing sports doublespeak reveals some scary truths about how we Americans look at life. In John Mitchell's words, "when the going gets tough, the tough get going," and we turn out to be a society in which "nice guys finish last," and everybody wants to "be on the winning side."

The rhetoric of the playing field appears in advertising, business, and government. Let's take an obvious example first. President Ford, in publicizing his economic strategies when he first took office, devised the W.I.N. button. An offshoot of Ford's other unfortunate sports metaphor, the promise to "hold the line" on inflation, the W.I.N. button was meant to appeal by familiarity to the sports-minded American who will "get up for the game," and "tackle the job" if the coach just tells him what to do. Ford hoped that the "win" mentality was so strongly ingrained in America that the very word would alter attitudes and behavior.

With the W.I.N. button, Ford hoped to make use of a sports metaphor the way advertising does. He wanted to make the analogy from athletic success to success in other fields. We all expect to be manipulated by advertising, so it is no surprise to see professional athletes advertising hair tonic, shaving cream, even frozen pizza or panty hose. The doublespeak is implicit: use this product, and you will enjoy the same success as Frank Gifford, Arthur Ashe, Joe Namath. Associating the athlete with the product, however, makes another claim for the athlete: it extends his expertise beyond the playing field. Ad agencies hope we will take the advice of these "pros" about shaving cream, hair tonic, frozen pizza, or panty hose; after all, the pro wouldn't make a wrong choice about these products any more than he would throw the ball away at a crucial moment of the game. So the athlete is an expert, as well as a hero. His ability to "score" carries over into financial and sexual arenas as well; there is even a product named "Score."

Since it has been established by advertising that the athlete is both hero and expert, sports metaphors are used more subtly to sell products. In the MGB ad that reads "MGB. Think of it as a well-coordinated athlete," we can see how much athletic ability is admired. No longer do we compare the good athlete or the good team to a well-oiled machine: now we're comparing the machine to the good athlete. Like a well-coordinated athlete, you'll "score" in your MGB.

But advertising is an easy target for doublespeak analysis. More complex by far is the way sports metaphors function in business, where their analysis leads to crucial revelations about American ethics. Business has always been fond of the football analogy, as William H. Whyte, Jr. points out:

> No figure of speech is a tenth as seductive to the businessman. Just why this should be—baseball curiously is much less used—is generally explained by its adaptability to all sorts of situations. Furthermore, the football analogy is *satisfying*. It is bounded by two goal lines and is thus finite. There is always a solution. And that is what makes it so often treacherous.[1]

Business uses the team philosophy, says Whyte, to hedge on moral issues. By making analogies to sports, business convinces the outside world that its decisions aren't truly consequential: they are "games" executed by good "team players." The fact that dollars and human lives may also be involved is not included when the sports metaphor is used, for the sports metaphor imposes automatic limits on the way business activity is seen.

> The goal of sports activity is always unambiguous and non-controversial; participants do not come together to discuss or debate the ends for which the activity has been established, but rather take this end for granted and apply themselves in a single-minded fashion to the task of developing the most efficient means to achieve the predetermined unchanging and non-controversial end: winning.[2]

So the sports metaphor precludes thought; it operates on unconscious and irrational levels, manipulating its users as well as its audiences. Perhaps its use in business, where the idea of competition in the free marketplace still carries moral force, has something to do with man's aggressive nature; what sports and business have in common that allows the sports metaphor to be drawn so often and so successfully by American businessmen is aggressiveness. Sports are an acceptable form of releasing aggressive impulses; if business uses the sports metaphor, isn't the aggressiveness of business automatically acceptable?

> . . . [the] same aggressive impulse which can lead to strife and violence also underlies man's urge to independence and achievement. Just as a child could not possibly grow up into an independent adult if it were not

aggressive, so an adult must needs continue to express at least part of his aggressive potential if he is to maintain his own autonomy.[3]

No wonder the Duke of Wellington was able to observe that "the battle of Waterloo was won on the playing fields of Eton." The skills learned on the playing field by the child are translated into the battles of the adult.

But there is also a certain cynicism associated with the use of the sports metaphor by business.

> What happens to some guys is—well, I'll draw the analogy to sports again. Baseball has its hot players and the next year the hot players cool off, and what happens is that their salaries drop and they get optioned out to Toledo.[4]

In Jerry Della Femina's description of what happens to advertising men who don't produce, the sports metaphor obscures the human position of the advertising executive, the man who has a good year followed by a bad year and suddenly finds himself nursing an ulcer and out of a job. Like most sports metaphors, this one permits the reader to ignore the ethical implications of cut-throat competition among advertising agencies for top talent.

But business still isn't the "Big Game"—that's government. And, as we might now expect, the bigger the game, the more prevalent the sports metaphor as doublespeak. Watergate revealed the wholesale use of the sports lexicon by politicians, but Watergate was neither the beginning nor the end of the sports metaphor. As William Safire points out in his excellent book *The New Language of Politics*,[5] Shakespeare may have been the first to use these comparisons. King Henry V told his troops before Harfleur "I see you stand like greyhounds in the slips, straining upon the start. The game's afoot . . ." But Safire also notes that Shakespeare wasn't the last; the section on "Sports Metaphors" in *The New Language of Politics* is a wonderful compendium of quotations from past political greats beginning with Woodrow Wilson's "I have always in my own thought summed up individual liberty, and business liberty, and every other kind of liberty, in the phrase that is common in the sporting world, 'A free field and no favor,'" and stopping at JFK's "Politics is like football. If you see daylight, go through the hole."

Amusingly enough, politics doesn't content itself with the football metaphor so favored by business. Instead, it inadvertently reveals its seamier side by the frequent use of the horse race analogy. There are front-runners and dark horses, long shots and shoo-ins. The winner takes the reins of government, while the loser is an also-ran who was "nosed out." Harry Truman said, "I am trying to do in politics what Citation has done in the horse races. I

propose at the finish line on November 2 to come out ahead. . . ." It seems
that in politics, more than in advertising or in business, the use of the sports
metaphor reveals more than gamesmanship, competition, or vicarious aggression; it also reveals an affinity with gambling.

But Safire's compendium, while amusing and instructive, is pre-Watergate
and he therefore views the sports metaphor as innocuous. He says,

> Sports metaphors relate closely to many people, which is why politicians
> spend the time to create them; at other times they are tossed off without
> thinking because they are already a part of the language. After a Ken-
> nedy aide appeared on Lawrence Spivak's television panel show *Meet the
> Press*, the President called to say "They never laid a glove on you." It is
> the classic remark of a trainer to a prizefighter who has been belted all
> over the ring. (pp. 421–22)

Since Watergate, we have become more attuned to the way sports metaphors
are often used to make big decisions involving all our lives seem trivial and
inconsequential.

> Nixon's "jocko-macho" talk (as Nicholas von Hoffman called it) was
> amply demonstrated; the limited supply of tough-guy metaphors, akin to
> verbal locker room swaggering of muscle-flexing *machismo* at the beach:
> . . . Years earlier, some critics had felt that Nixon's overt enthusiasm for
> spectator sports (shaking hands with athletes, telegrams and phone calls
> to coaches) was simply a calculated ploy ("a grandstand play") to win
> the favor of certain voters, to create the illusion that he was "just one of
> the guys." It was no illusion. Nixon was not the first politician to use the
> imagery of athletics . . . but the transcripts reveal that the traditional
> emphasis on "fair play," "following the rules," and "good sportsmanship"
> had been replaced by a "win at all costs" mentality.[6]

One need hardly comment further on what Watergate did to the language; its
only good effect was to alert many Americans to the way language does both
form and corrupt thinking. For that, we should probably be grateful.

Unfortunately, the effects of Watergate aren't longlasting. In the midst of
the recent New York City financial crisis, the *Wall Street Journal* carried the
following story:

> After a seven-month game of political brinkmanship, the Ford admin-
> istration has browbeaten New York City into "fiscal responsibility" and
> the city has pressured Washington into limited federal help.

But the path to that outcome proved to be far different than either side had expected, and the ultimate results happier than either would have predicted just a short time ago. There seems to be no clear winner in the long struggle—just losers of varying degrees. . . .

The reconstruction of these events leading up to the Wednesday statement discloses basic miscalculations by every player in the game. . . .

The city's fiscal crisis, surfacing last May, rapidly developed into a high-level game of political chess—played out in Washington and New York and Albany, full of bluff and bombast, maneuver and surprise.[7]

Only the name of the game has changed; the article goes on to discuss how New York's crisis developed into a standoff between Ford and the city, in which participants in the negotiations between New York and Washington felt that "it was hardball both ways, and nothing was spared." The "hardball season" of negotiations ran from September through November, when Ford and New York City finally reached a compromise.

The story illustrates very well the dangers of relying too heavily on sports metaphors. Here a genuine crisis has been reduced for readers to a game in which participants are trying to out-bluff and out-maneuver each other while New York and perhaps the rest of the nation await the consequences. And the crisis is portrayed as a strategy problem, rather than a human problem or a problem in responsible government.

What is the lesson to be learned from looking at our culture's continuing use of sports metaphors to render important situations innocuous in advertising, in business, and in government? If it is true, as Walker Gibson said to the NCTE Convention in 1973, that "learning to read is learning to infer dramatic character from linguistic evidence," then examining the metaphors used in popular culture provides good insight into our character as a nation. And if it is also true, as Orwell remarked in *Politics and the English Language*, that "language can corrupt thought," then sports metaphors become not merely ways of revealing our adolescent preoccupation with aggressiveness, with winning, with games, but also ways of perpetuating those concerns, of glorifying them, of passing them on unexamined to our children through our national culture. It is at least worth a few minutes of our time to wrestle (there it is again) with the decision of whether we really want to see ourselves forever as a nation of teamplayers and sports fans.

NOTES

1. William H. Whyte, Jr., "The Language of Business," in *Technological and Professional Writing*, ed. Herman A. Estrin (New York: Harcourt, Brace & World, 1963),

p. 83. In this part of the paper, I am indebted to an unpublished paper on "Sports Metaphors in Business" by John Driscoll.

2. Ike Balbus, "Politics as Sports: The Political Ascendancy of the Sports Metaphor in America," *Monthly Review*, March 1975, p. 30.

3. Anthony Storr, *Human Aggression* (New York: Atheneum, 1970), p. 59.

4. Jerry Della Femina, *From Those Wonderful Folks Who Brought You Pearl Harbor* (New York: Simon & Schuster, 1971), p. 124.

5. New York: Random House, 1968, p. 421.

6. Hugh Rank, "Watergate and the Language," in *Language and Public Policy*, ed. Hugh Rank (Urbana, Ill.: NCTE, 1974), pp. 7–8.

7. November 28, 1975.

RICHARD LIPSKY

Of Team Players and Sky Hooks: The Infiltration of Sports Language in Politics

We have sort of an expansion ball club that's fighting in Vietnam at the present time. The South Vietnamese will not win every battle or encounter but they will do a very credible job.

—Melvin Laird, former Secretary of Defense

Enter a Pittsburgh bar and listen. "Oh, man! Terry was cool! Three large studs ready to stomp his behind, and he just danced, spotted Lynn, and hit him right on the money! That's my man!" Walk past the playgrounds of New York City. "Oh, sweat! The Doc copped that pill in one hand, skied o'r top three dudes and threw that sucker down!"

Wherever there are sports fans, you will find the talk, the warm, lively retelling of yesterday's game, the playfully serious arguments over players' talents and umpires' calls. The boastful partisan predicting, "No *way* are those turkeys gonna beat us tomorrow." Games and players long since forgotten come back to life with astonishing vividness. Individual exploits take on the cosmic significance of a confrontation between gods.

The talk is not conversation in the usual sense. It is reenactment. Watch

---

From *How We Play the Game: Why Sports Dominate American Life* (1981).

the wildly gesturing arms, the expert imitation of obscure movement, and the festive slapping of palms. In the same way that going to the game lifts us out of mundane reality, talking about the game and the players is itself a form of escape from nagging frustrations and dull routines. The Sportsworld comes to life in talk, and the talk brings life to everyday surroundings.

A few years ago, I went to dinner with a group of lawyers. A young Chicana lawyer was part of our party. All efforts at drawing her out into conversation failed; her replies were short and without emotion. The conversation shifted naturally to sports, and, without warning, the woman enthusiastically jumped in, explaining in animated tones her love for the DePaul University basketball team. She went on about Dave Corzine's moves, Gary Garland's shooting and the muscle work of Joe Ponsetto. Every detail was lovingly described. Just as suddenly, her mother lode obviously tapped out, she withdrew back under her cloak of timidity.

A recent *Sports Illustrated* survey found that 72 percent of all Americans saw themselves to some degree as sports fans. In sharp contrast, those who are knowledgeable and avidly follow the events of the political arena are part of a shrinking population. Because of this widening gulf between sports interest and political apathy, politicians and those who analyze politics increasingly have turned to sports language and sports metaphors in order to generate interest and communicate information about politics.

The rise of sports language and its subsequent use in political discussion says a great deal about the relationship between sports and politics in this country. An understanding of language helps to explain how the Sportsworld is able to create a dramatic power that performs important political and personal functions.

The political turmoil of the 1960s led to the growing politicization of athletics. At the same time, politics itself was being athleticized.

President Nixon frequently was photographed in some scene of sports significance. If he wasn't at the ball park or in the locker room, he was phoning the winning team and its coach to congratulate them. When political demonstrations against the Vietnam war engulfed the capital, the President pointedly watched a football game. Even more significantly, on the morning of the invasion of Cambodia, the President met with a group of protesters at the Lincoln Memorial. After asking them what colleges they attended, he immediately began discussing their football teams.

This breeding of sports and politics is perhaps best exemplified by the increased use of sports language in political communication. Cabinet members are referred to as "team players." The invasion of a country is described as "Operation Linebacker," and the military commander is called the "head coach." Making a job easier for a colleague is referred to as "doing downfield blocking," and an ally that needs a great deal of political and military bolstering is referred to as "an expansion team." Politicians aren't the only people using these sports metaphors. Political commentators have borrowed this "sportugese" and by extension see politics in athletic images.

The proliferation of sporting usage to describe political actions and events indicates a significant relationship between the two worlds. In the first place, the use of sports analogies and the borrowing of actual sports settings point to the pervasive influence of athletics in American life. Red Smith grasps this when he indicates that "one measure of the stature of sports in the American scheme is the extent to which sporting terms are employed away from the playing fields." [1]

It is through language and settings (or "scenes," in a dramatic sense) that we communicate common symbols. A distinct sports language indicates that the Sportsworld is a separate province of meaning. Language, communication, symbolism, and group life are inseparable pieces of a common plot.

The existence of a sports jargon demonstrates that sports fans are linked to a common perspective. The "world view" of sports is embodied in its scenes, slogans, and jargon. If this is true, then the use of "sportspeak" by political leaders and political commentators, as well as the posturing of politicians in front of sports backdrops such as ball fields and locker rooms, means the values and motives of sports have seeped into the conceptualization and carrying out of political action. How this happens and the political consequences of its happening need to be explained.

The appeal of sports language cannot be grasped without first understanding the social context in which its appeal flourishes. We live in an increasingly rational and bureaucratic time that tends to create obstacles to effective communication. Unfulfilled needs for contact and communication rise accordingly.

The increased complexity of industrial society introduces the problem of creating and maintaining a comprehensive set of symbols for the entire society. Older, stable value systems become fragmented or completely erode in the face of industrialization. The problem isn't merely "getting an idea across" but effectively dramatizing a common purpose as well.

Language rests on an emotional and communal basis. It transfers basic emotions into symbolic imagery. As society becomes more complex, though, so does language. Yet as language becomes more scientific and abstract, it becomes less rich and no longer links people together. Style, beauty, and form become downgraded in the face of the "objective uses" of language.

With increased division of labor, each bureaucracy or social subarea develops its own specialized jargon. These scientific and technical vocabularies contain a very low emotional content. Ideally, they are suited for signaling bureaucratic movements, but they lack dramatic power.

The increased use of technical explanations and statistically laden speech deadens human interest. People lose interest in and attachment to the political and social orders once these orders lose the ability to persuade, to entice, and to dramatize a sense of allegiance for their mass audience. The political speech or the public service message is an inconvenient interruption from the more colorful appeals of sports, popular culture, or Dear Abby, for that matter.

The traditional political system and its language cannot convey a sense of human meaning. When there are no answers to the questions of why we are here and where we are going, the path has been cleared for the aggressive return of the mythical. An impersonal and abstract social and political system fails to provide the emotional feedback that human beings seem to thrive on.

Because the political world is bewildering, politics becomes the creature of the language used to describe it. Metaphors and myths are used to simplify the complex events that cause anxiety in people. In turn, the kinds of metaphors or vocabularies we use will inevitably structure the kind of reality we perceive and act on.

In order to make the political world closer, warmer, and more comprehensible, it is necessary to employ metaphors that will convey a warm sense of the familiar. Given a complex and impersonal environment, it is essential for political speech to tap areas where audiences do experience warmth, clarity, and personal satisfaction. Political metaphors can dramatically call forth new worlds in which remedies for personal distress are clearly perceived. This is best accomplished through an accepted vocabulary both speaker and audience understand.

Because politics is threatening, much political communication is repetitious, using a small number of classic themes that continually serve as explanations of political reality. Such repetition cues the listener that the world is moving along familiar routes. These classic expressions have the ability to keep conflict within comfortably circumscribed areas while at the same time closing off fresh insights.

The use of worn-out metaphors can just as easily reduce interest as reduce threat. In a political system with little conflict over basic values, dramatic appeals tend to become stale. Since our candidates tend to be relatively indistinguishable around key issues, alternative ways of generating political interest must be found. The remoteness and threatening impersonality of political action is overcome through the symbolism of entertainment and the arena. As one perceptive observer has noted:

> Failing to organize our politics around politics, we organize it as entertainment; sometimes it is a horse race, sometimes an interminable TV sitcom. Hey—Jimmy Carter just picked up six delegates in Kansas . . . how about that, sports fans? Even our political literature is getting less political these days, tending ever more to dramatic, novelistic forms.[2]

Glamour, personality, and the pure enthusiasm of the political contest turn politics into the consumption of dramatic images generally devoid of ideological content. Politics, no longer an arena for moral indignation, becomes part of popular culture: "Politics is to be appraised in terms of consumer preferences. Politicians are people—and the more glamorous the better. The manner and mood of doing things is quite as important as what is done."[3]

Style and the aesthetic sensibilities of the discriminating shopper become the key ingredients of political success. With the mass media becoming the barker for a political carnival, glamour and gossip are used to combat indifference. Glamour is retailed; our political personalities take their places in the pantheon of *Us* and *People* magazines. Yet something is missing. Because the politics of entertainment or the entertainment of politics is inevitably a weak imitation of those areas where drama, conflict, and heroism exist in pure form, the values and appealing ways of more dramatic arenas begin to strut their stuff on the political stage.

Spectator politics must compete for the entertainment dollar and overcome its poor reputation among the voters. The appeals of the Sportsworld, on the contrary, are already known and loved. As James Reston points out, "The world of sports has everything the world of politics lacks and longs for . . . They have more pageantry and even dignity than most mass occasions in American life; more teamwork, more unity, and more certainty at the end than most things . . ."[4]

The Sportsworld has become the arena where grace, form, and ethical content still survive. It not only creates a seemingly autonomous world with its own ethical imperatives (slogans, morals, legal proscriptions), it also creates a powerful communal bond. The Sportsworld, with its ritual celebrations, its magical performers, and intense audiences, effectively counteracts the decline of emotional connections in the larger society. Arnold Beisser gives us a good illustration:

Everyone needs to feel he has ties with others. With the dispersal of the traditional extended family, the clan and the tribe, this need to be identified with a group of some kind has become more intense. The sports fan has a readily available group to satisfy this need, at least in part. He has a meeting place where he is needed to support the team. He can gather with others, don his Dodger cap or some other identification badge, and yell at the top of his lungs for his teams . . . In effect, by doing all this, he becomes a member of a larger, stronger family group, or collective entity comparable in some sense to the tribe or clan.[5]

The communal bonds that are created in the festivity of the sports drama are sustained in language. "Sportspeak" is the glue that cements the activities of sports into a common emotional package. The rise of sports to its present level of mass involvement cannot be understood without an understanding of the historical evolution of sports language.

The rise of sports language can be traced to the development of the sports page around the turn of the century. The struggle of tabloids for a mass audience saw the development of yellow journalism, comics, and a separate section in the newspaper devoted solely to sports. The newspaper sought to widen—to democratize—its appeal and sports was a vehicle for such an appeal. This is still evident today. A great number of New York "sophisticates" (myself included) read the *Post* and the *Daily News* precisely because of their elaborate, colorful sports coverage.

Democratization slowly gave rise to a "national sports-consciousness" that was inevitably linked to a distinct dialect. As the sports historian John Betts has written:

With the rise of a national press and the popularization of sporting journalism, with millions playing organized games on the playground or the athletic field, with the development of a national sports-consciousness, enrichment of the American language is inevitable.[6]

The sports dialect's democratic appeal was linked to its ability to reach people in a concrete, tangible, and emotional way. As sportswriter Marshall Hunt points out about Captain Patterson and the New York *Daily News*: "It was Patterson from the beginning who saw we would increase circulation by developing a strong sports department. He always wanted us to write in a bouncy way. Very biff, bang, boom stuff."[7]

Style was extremely important in the appeal of the sports page. The 1920s, the "Golden Age of Sports," saw this style become distinct jargon. "Informality of style, originality of composition and a new jargon blossomed onto the sports page—but accompanied by a tendency toward verbosity, triteness and shopworn cliches, synonyms and analogies."[8] It is precisely this use of jargon (overlaid with a stylistic originality) that makes sports language so appealing. Ritualistic language creates a predictable and understandable world of meaning, while at the same time condensing emotional reponses. Sportswriting strives primarily to simplify and vivify. "It is clear that the selection of sports verbs and adjectives is not based solely on the objective content of the events . . . but also to convey part of the color and emotion of the contest . . ."[9]

The effect of dramatic simplification is bolstered by the involved attitude of the reporters themselves. Unlike the political or economic reporters who are supposed to remain neutral, the sportswriter more often than not is an unabashed partisan. In Gallico's words: "I believed in it and was impressed by athletes and what I was seeing. And while the title of your book is No Cheering in the Press Box, I've seen and heard plenty of cheering in press boxes when we sports writers got excited about something."[10]

The sports fan is not only emotionally involved but knowledgeable: "Spectatorship involves more than merely watching. It involves a great deal of cognitive ability on the part of spectators. It involves knowledge, an increasing knowledge. It involves expertise."[11] The fans demand accurate information:

> According to newspapermen . . . no class of readers is more responsive and none demands a higher degree of accuracy than the sports fan. The baseball writer especially is writing for an informed readership, and, if he makes a mistake, both he and his paper will get a dozen letters in the next morning's mail calling attention to that fact.[12]

The development of a "national sports-consciousness" and a distinct medium for its communication paved the way for extending sports symbolism into the political realm. So far, former President Nixon has been the most sophisticated in seeing the possibilities inherent in this extension. Nixon's use of the sports metaphor derived from his complete self-identification with the world of sports. His relatively non-Machiavellian preoccupation with sports has been observed by almost all those who have commented on the former President's sports involvement. After all, only a true fan would have gone—privately—to a Washington Senators' double-header in the 1950s.

As the focal point of the American political system, the President becomes the receptacle for much public expectation and fear. An effective device for identification in American politics has always been the image of "one of the boys." For Richard Nixon, as Gary Wills has underscored, the impression of being an average guy has always been important. Wills reports that Nixon had a genuine dislike of snobbery: "Football was always his way to remain 'common' during his triumphs on the long debating tours of his time." [13] This desire explains the numerous (and politically effective) visits to locker rooms, phone calls to coaches, and receptions for sports figures. The use of sports terms and the "team" metaphor, as William Safire has observed, are useful because "they relate so closely to people." [14] This fits in with the previously reported relationships between democratization and the rise of sports language. If the sports reporter is able to become part of the action he is conveying, and is able to develop a sense of empathy with his audience, it is not hard to envision a similar process between a political leader and a mass public. As a "symbolic leader," the President is for many people the personal link to the political system. Since sports does appear to many as a personal and concrete universe, the identification with its language and scenes is a way to develop a sense of the personal. The vicariousness of this relationship is part of the consumption pattern. It also encourages a sense of "false concreteness" about a complex and abstract political process.

Nixon's self-identification with the world of sports went beyond involvement with its ceremonies. He also seemed to believe that the values of the Sportsworld were those needed to "succeed" in real life. James David Barber and Gary Wills both indicate how Nixon's description of his "six crises" reflects the competitive "never-say-die" ethos of the athlete competitor. It is the ethic of Frank Merriwell and Horatio Alger:

> It became fashionable in the years after Nixon's crushing defeat in 1962 to ask him what kept him running. It was the same thing that kept him on the football field where he did not belong—the sacredness of running, the need to deserve luck eventually by showing the pluck that starts at the bottom and never quits. [15]

That simpler world of competitive "character" and success is anachronistic in the light of the past century's development. Yet it is a world that is preserved in all its symbolic clarity in the realm of sports. The transposition of that value system into a technocratic political system falsely clarifies the new complexity with the images of old simplicity. This is especially true since many of these values still continue to be accepted by many people.

The nature of sports language, warm and vital, emphasizing the concrete and personal at the expense of the abstract and logical, may prevent its users from being able to theorize and universalize. The use of sports language encourages sending complex messages through an oversimplified conceptual and syntactical framework. This inevitably leads to "noise"—but, significantly, "melodious noise."

Sports is a universe of controlled conflict. By using sports symbolism in political discourse the politician or commentator tends to transpose sports' ideologically unproblematic nature onto politics. This has the effect of underscoring the organizational (instrumental) imperatives at the expense of articulating substantive goals. It promotes an interest in who is "winning" or "losing" without looking at the reasons why one *should* win and the other *should* lose.

This tendency is evident in the use of such terms as "team player," "quarterback" (for leader), and "expansion team": The use of the team concept is an attempt to instill an "usness" where victory (which is morally unambiguous) is essential. If the South Vietnamese are an expansion team, for instance, they are first of all typically *American*. Second, what do you have to do with an expansion team? Everybody knows that such a squad must inevitably go through the "building" process of "stockpiling" talent. With the help of the "expansion draft" we eagerly anticipate the rise of the South Vietnamese Rangers into a first division team.

Interest may be piqued and loyalty instilled but not without paying a heavy price. Domestically, a similar process occurs. If a political commentator tells us that "Senator Muskie has been placed in the line-up as a possible Democratic running mate," our attention is focused on whether "Ol' Ed" gets his licks rather than what's in "Ol' Ed's" head. (This, of course, overlooks the atrocious misapplication of this baseball term. If someone is "placed in the line-up," then, barring unforeseen circumstances, he should get his at-bats. Ironically, and almost certainly unintentionally, this "line-up" applies more to the process of picking out a criminal suspect for identification.)

The use of sports symbolism in political discourse is essentially a conservative device that prevents thinking about new policies and directions. Perhaps in order to move forward we must in some ways overcome *and* recover the past, but the Sportsworld is too often a place of refuge from the present. The attempt to transport its genuine apolitical and ahistorical appeals to our political and historical world will, further, make the political present more difficult to comprehend.

The rise of sports language and its subtle transposition to less dramatic arenas underscore the symbolic strength of the Sportsworld itself. Its use as a prop for a disinterested electorate offers neat insight into the evolving relationship between sports and politics. The strength of sports language and drama demonstrates how the symbolic world of sports provides for an emotional network in American society that forms an important foundation for political stability. The power of sports language, as an agent of sports symbolism, forms a network of national and social communication that provides large masses of Americans with communal warmth and personal identity. In such a role, sports language is the glue for a diffuse "rain or shine" attachment to the American system.

NOTES

1. Red Smith, "Spoken Like a True Son of Old Whittier," *The New York Times* (April 30, 1973). See also James Reston, "Sports and Politics in America," *The New York Times* (September 12, 1969). The emphasis on language here is designed to show how symbolism is transmitted or conveyed through language.

2. Meg Greenfield, "Get on the Raft with Taft, Boys," *Newsweek* (June 7, 1976).

3. David Reisman, with Nathan Glazer and Reuel Denney, *The Lonely Crowd: A Study of the Changing American Character* (New Haven: Yale University Press, 1953), p. 189.

4. Reston, "Sports and Politics in America."

5. Arnold Beisser, *Madness in Sports: Psychosocial Observations on Sports* (New York: Appleton-Century-Crofts, 1967), p. 129.

6. John Betts, *America's Sporting Heritage* (Reading, Mass.: Addison-Wesley, 1974).

7. Jerome Holtzman, *No Cheering in the Press Box* (New York: Holt, Rinehart & Winston, 1973), p. 23.

8. Perry Tannenbaum and James Noah, "Sportugese: A Study in Sports Page Communication," in John Loy and Gerald Kenyon, *Sport, Culture, and Society* (New York: Macmillan, 1969).

9. Tannenbaum and Noah, p. 336. See also Robert Lipsyte, *Sportsworld* (New York: Quadrangle, 1976), p. 122. As Erwin Canham of *The Christian Science Monitor* once said, "News must be made more interesting and compelling which means *simplification* and *dramatization* are imperative. The result is that the news is sometimes 'souped-up' to the language of the sports page which finds its way into events that are too grave to be considered in such terms" (Stanley Woodward, *The Sports Page*, New York: Greenwood Press, 1968, p. 420).

10. Jerome Holtzman, p. 72. The preponderance of writers interviewed by Holtzman expressed a similar view. Stanley Woodward in *The Sports Page* feels that sportswriting more and more resembles the rest of the paper. My observation is that this is not necessarily true unless we take the incongruous position that the rise of sports language in the rest of the paper is bringing *it* closer to the sports page rather than the other way around. See Tannenbaum and Noah, "Sportugese," p. 327, for a similar view.

11. C. H. Page, "Reaction to Stone Preservation," in *Aspects of Contemporary Sports Sociology*, G. S. Kenyon, ed. (Chicago: The Athletic Institute, 1969), quoted by Barry McPherson, "Sports Consumption and the Economics of Consumerism," in D. Ball and John Loy, eds., *Sport and the Social Order* (Reading, Mass.: Addison-Wesley, 1975).

12. This is illustrated as well in "Sportugese," where Tannenbaum and Noah note a high communication coefficiency between sportswriters and sports fans. The kinds of verbs that the writer uses indicate to the fan the nature of the final point spread be-

tween teams. "However, for the person who does not read or follow sports, these verbs fail in communicating their message" (Woodward, p. 424).

13. Gary Wills, *Nixon Agonistes: The Crisis of the Self-Made Man* (Boston: Houghton Mifflin, 1970), p. 161.

14. William Safire, *Safire's Political Dictionary: The New Language of Politics* (New York: Random House, 1978), page 633. Mr. Safire was extremely helpful in the preparation of this chapter.

15. Wills, p. 162. See also James David Barber, *Presidential Character* (Englewood Cliffs, N.J.: Prentice-Hall, 1972), pp. 388–393.

MICHAEL MARTIN

Philosophical Analysis at Work: In Search of the Elusive Clutch Hitter

The great Brooks Robinson in his prime was known as a good clutch hitter despite the fact that his batting average was mediocre. The philosopher in every baseball fan might well ask "What is a good clutch hitter?" The answer to the question, I will show, is not easy to give and a precise quantitative definition of a good clutch hitter is hard to come by. Although I suggest some definitions of a clutch hitter in this paper, I am not completely satisfied with any of them. So, if the paper causes other philosophical analysts of sport to improve upon my definition, my efforts will be worthwhile.

I

Before I attempt to construct some definitions of a clutch hitter, the philosophical relevance of such an attempt should be made plain.

Philosophers ever since Socrates have attempted to analyze certain key concepts that we use in ordinary life. Although philosophical analysis may not be the whole of philosophy, it has been and continues to be an important part. Philosophical analysis is made possible by a remarkable linguistic phenomenon. People are able to use a term correctly, that is to apply it to concrete cases, yet not know what the term means in the sense that they are

Published for the first time in this anthology.

unable to give necessary and sufficient conditions for its correct use. For example people might know when to use the word "know," but be unable to specify what it means to say "s knows that p," that is to specify general conditions for knowledge.

Philosophical analysts suggest analyses of knowledge. These analyses are tested by appeal to people's ability to use the word "know" correctly. An analysis is rejected if it conflicts with standard usage, that is if counter examples can be found, examples which conflict with the proffered analysis. If a counter example is found, a new analysis is suggested and the quest for counter examples goes on. The hope is that in the long run an analysis will be constructed to which no counter examples can be found.

Sometimes, of course, the philosophical analyst does not attempt to reflect completely standard usage, but tries to improve upon it. Where ordinary usage is vague, ambiguous or in need of improvement for special purposes, the philosophical analyst may attempt to reflect ordinary usage only partially, perhaps where it is clear or unambiguous. The analyst may also attempt to clarify or improve on ordinary usage by explicating or rationally reconstructing standard usage. In such cases, a philosophical analysis is not just tested by its ability to withstand the search for counter examples, but by its ability to improve upon ordinary usage relative to certain purposes.

It should not be thought that philosophical analysis has been performed just on terms found in standard common everyday language. Philosophers have analyzed technical terms in mathematics, science and the law. Thus philosophers of science have analyzed terms like "functional system" and "operational definition." Here too philosophical analysts may attempt to reflect technical usage up to a point, but also to improve upon it, by clarifying it and showing ambiguities implicit in such usage.

It seems to me that the philosophical analyst of sport is in this long and great tradition of philosophical analysis that reaches back to Socrates. There are many terms used in sport that are in need of philosophical analysis. For example, the term "sport," "clutch hitter," "tough competition," "team player," and "game." People may know how to use these terms in concrete situations and yet have difficulty in saying exactly what they mean. The philosophical analysis of sport depends on this remarkable ability. The analyst suggests analyses and tests them by appeal to ordinary sport usage, eliminating those for which counter examples can be found. The philosophical analyst of sport may also improve on ordinary sport language where usage is ambiguous, making distinctions that ordinary usage does not make explicit.

In what follows many of these general points will be illustrated.

II

On one level the answer to what is a good clutch hitter seems easy. A good clutch hitter is obviously one who hits well in the clutch. But this answer, although quite correct, is completely unhelpful. The question remains: What is hitting well in the clutch?

One thing is clear. The standard baseball statistics are completely inadequate to defining a clutch hitter. Consider RBI's. A batter may lead his league in RBI's and still not hit well in the clutch, for example, if most of the RBI's have come when the team is far out in front.

More promising is someone's batting average with men on base (henceforth referred to as BAMOB). But again, one could have a high BAMOB and still not be a good clutch hitter, for a high BAMOB is compatible with batting well only when one's team is ahead.

A similar point can be made about other standard statistical measures of batting prowess. Clutch batting average is not captured by them.

III

The problem with RBI and BAMOB suggests another definition. Why not say that a good hitter is a hitter who hits well with runners on base when his team is behind? This account certainly seems to be an improvement over the usual RBI and BAMOB measures, but it does not seem to capture completely the meaning of clutch hitter for two reasons.

First, suppose a person hits well with runners on base, but only when his team is down by 12 runs or more; he does not hit well when his team is down by less than 12 runs. Suppose further that since his team usually loses by a very large margin (12 runs or more), his BAMOB is very high. I submit that we would not be willing to call this person a clutch hitter.

Second, a clutch hitter is not someone who *just* hits well with runners on base under certain as yet unstated conditions. A hitter who got leadoff hits in certain situations could be known as a clutch hitter.

The above considerations may suggest that a clutch hitter is someone who hits well when his team is behind when the score is fairly close or when the score is tied. In other words, the hitter's batting average is high under what might be called go ahead conditions (GAC). Let's call this batting average BAGAC. Is the good clutch hitter, then, someone with a high BAGAC? Not quite. One can imagine a person who has a high BAGAC who is not a clutch hitter. Suppose the person hits well under GAC only in the early innings.

Given this problem the idea suggests itself that a clutch hitter is someone who has a high BAGAC in the late innings (LI). Let's call this BAGACLI.

This idea may in fact capture what some people mean by a clutch hitter. But I am not completely satisfied with BAGACLI as a final definition of clutch hitting ability. Before I specify my reservations some unclarities in BAGACLI need to be noted.

First, according to the above account a clutch hitter is a hitter with a high BAGACLI. But how high is high? A hitter with a .380 BA is thought to have a high BA. But what about a person with a .380 BAGACLI? Is this high or not? Well, this depends on the league BAGACLI. If everyone in the league has this high a BAGACLI, then a .380 BAGACLI becomes common and .380 will not be considered high in the league. So what is a high BAGACLI is a function of the league average.

Second, it is not clear what a GAC is. Of course, one has no problem in judging the extremes. If the score is tied or the other team has a one run lead, it is clear that one has GAC. On the opposite extreme is a game in which an opposing team has a 15 run lead. Clearly this is not a GAC. This does not mean, of course, that a 15 run lead can not be erased even in the late innings, but this is highly unusual.

However, these extremes leave lots of room for doubt. Suppose the home team is 3 runs down in the 9th inning and the opposing pitcher is overpowering. Do we have a GAC? (Contrast this with a 6 run lead in the 9th inning when the opposing pitcher has given up lots of hits and runs.) Suppose further (to complicate the situation even more) that the home team has a reputation for coming from behind in the late innings. Do we now have a GAC? All of these considerations suggest that GAC is vague. Consequently BAGACLI has a range of vagueness.

Now it might be suggested in the light of this vagueness that there is a use of GAC, standard in baseball thinking, that would precisely define a GAC and consequently would eliminate any range of vagueness from BAGAC. Let us call this idea of GAC the sportscasters' GAC, or GAC_1 for short. According to this idea, there is a GAC_1 if, should the batter (plus any players who are on base) score, the team at bat would go ahead. Thus, if the opposing team is three runs ahead and the home team loads the bases, the home team would be in a GAC_1. A good clutch hitter then is someone who hits above the league average in GAC_1 in the later innings.

To be sure, with this idea, one would be able to define precisely a clutch hitter. Unfortunately, it does not seem to capture completely what is meant. As I mentioned before, a batter who consistently gets leadoff hits when his team is a couple of runs behind might well be considered a good clutch hitter under certain circumstances. Yet, a GAC_1 would not be present.

The philosophical analyst of sport here has several choices. One may simply note the vagueness of our ordinary notion of a clutch hitter because of the vagueness of GAC, or attempt some improvement in the clarity of GAC. GAC_1 would, of course, clarify GAC at a price; it would not cover all cases where the phrase "clutch hitter" is actually used in baseball discourse. Whether such an improvement is worth the price I will not attempt to answer here. Nor will I attempt to answer whether other ways of clarifying GAC would be better for certain purposes.

IV

Unclarities aside, the GACLI definition of clutch hitting does not seem to me to capture completely what is *sometimes* meant by a clutch hitter, for it leaves out an important dimension of clutch hitting. A good clutch hitter in one sense is not just someone who has a high BAGACLI, whatever the residual vagueness in such a definition, but is someone who has a high BAGACLI in *important games*. One can imagine a ball player who has a very high BAGACLI yet who strikes out consistently in GACLI in crucial games— World Series, playoffs, and other important games during the regular season. In one important sense this player would not be a clutch hitter.

The idea therefore suggests itself of defining clutch hitter as someone who has a high BAGACLI in crucial and important games (CG). Let us call this average BAGACLICG. But what is crucial and important? This may be a matter of some controversy. Certainly there are uncontroversial cases: World Series and playoff games are crucial. But one does not want to define a clutch hitter in such a way that only members of the best teams can be clutch hitters, members of teams that make it to championship games. It is conceivable that the best clutch hitter could be on the worst team. The notion of important game brings to the idea of clutch hitter what seems like an irreducible qualitative dimension and suggests that no precise quantitative definition would be adequate.

After all, how is one to identify what is an important game independent of playoff and championship games? One way would be for the players, coaches and managers of a baseball team to judge which of their games during the year were the most important ones. It is doubtful whether there would be complete agreement on this, but no doubt there would be wide agreement. One could then proceed on the following rule: Eliminate the controversial cases and base a player's BAGACLICG on the uncontroversial cases of CG as judged by members of his own team.

There are two problems with this suggestion. What is an important game for one team may not be an important game for another team despite the fact that both teams played in the game. For one team a certain game was the beginning of a long winning streak that took them into first place; for the other team it had no particular significance. Consequently, the definition of a clutch hitter would be a relative one. Smith may be a good clutch hitter relative to the Red Sox and not to the Yankees. Furthermore, what is an important game to one team may not appear important at the time; it will appear crucial only in retrospect, sometimes not till the end of the season. If this is so, a player's BAGACLICG could not be computed until the season is over; one could not have a BAGACLICG on a day to day basis as one has a BA or even BAGACLI. This idea is reinforced when one recalls that many crucial games come at the end of the year. A clutch hitting average may not be able to be computed until the end of the season even if crucial games could be recognized as they occurred.

However, this suggests that there is something wrong with the idea considered above, that a definition of clutch hitter must take into account performance in crucial and important games, for it does seem possible to have some intuitive sense of who is a good clutch hitter during the season. Yet the BAGACLICG definition seems to make that impossible. On the other hand, hitting well in crucial games does seem essential for being a clutch hitter. There seems to be a paradox here. How can this paradox be reconciled?

V

Perhaps there are two notions of a clutch hitter that need to be distinguished. One notion of a good clutch hitter is defined in terms of BAGACLI: crucial games would be irrelevant. Let us call this idea the standard clutch hitting average. In the other notion, clutch hitting ability is defined in terms of clutch hitting average in important games, that is BAGACLICG. Let us call this crucial game clutch hitting average, or clutch hitting$_1$ average for short. The paradox, I suggest, is generated by confusing these two notions of clutch hitter.

What is a good clutch hitter then? A good standard clutch hitter is a batter with a high standard clutch hitting average relative to the rest of his league (or other appropriate reference group) where standard clutch hitting average is defined as BAGACLI. A good clutch hitter$_1$ has a high clutch hitting$_1$ average relative to his league or other appropriate reference group where this is defined as BAGACLICG. An ideal clutch hitter is both a good standard clutch hitter and a good clutch hitter$_1$.

A good standard clutch hitter may be a good clutch hitter$_1$ but he also may not be. There is no a priori way of telling, short of comparing his standard clutch hitting average and his clutch hitting$_1$ average. The latter average may only be computed at the end of the season and has no clear day to day meaning, as does the standard clutch hitting average. Still, looking at a ball player's record over the year we may be able to make some reliable inductive inferences. Since John Smith's standard clutch hitting average was close to his clutch hitting $_1$ average over the past seven years, one might argue that it is likely that the two will be close this year as well. However, if the above argument is correct, one would not be able to verify conclusively the inductive conclusion until the end of the season.

The two definitions of clutch hitter given above leave open the way in which crucial terms in these definitions are to be clarified. In particular, the question of whether GAC and CG should be clarified and how remains open. Different clarifications may be useful for different purposes and for some purposes the vagueness of ordinary baseball language may be desirable.

NOTE

The idea for this paper was suggested to me by Judson Webb. He is not responsible, of course, for any errors the paper may contain.

WARREN FRALEIGH

Philosophical Analysis and Normative Judgments on Clutch Hitters: A Reaction to Michael Martin

Professor Martin's paper provides many handles to grasp in a reaction. My reactions here will be restricted by (1) the time available here, (2) the time available to prepare this reaction, and (3) the limitations of my knowledge of the technicalities of philosophical analysis. My reaction will be informed by three considerations: (1) my understanding of some portions of Paul Taylor's classic work on *Normative Discourse*, (2) my knowledge of baseball, and (3) my sense of priorities in the philosophy of sport and the relationship of philosophical analysis to such priorities.

Published for the first time in this anthology.

Let me begin by focusing on those delightful linguistic devices called acronyms. Michael Martin has enriched us with some new ones including BAGACLI and BAGACLICG. I would like to offer HHRNP. What does HHRNP mean? A story will illustrate:

When I was the freshman baseball coach at San Jose State College, I had an elaborate system of signs, like most coaches, to communicate tactical advice to players. Now, in about three or four games a season a situation would arise in which my team was a run or two behind in the late innings, and we would have a runner on first base with one or two outs and a power hitter at bat with a count of two balls and no strikes or two balls and one strike. I would save a signal for just such occasions reasoning that regular use of that signal would risk detection of a pattern by the opposing team resulting in a change from normal pitching tactics on the next pitch. The sign used in this unique circumstance meant HHRNP, otherwise called hernip. And, in case you have not already guessed, HHRNP, or hernip, meant *hit home run, next pitch*.

Now, I do not relate this story for idle reasons. For not one of my batters, in approximately fifteen repetitions of the hernip sign over several years, ever responded by hitting a home run. I know that each batter had received the sign on each such occasion. Accordingly, in reading Martin's analysis I was led to wonder what would be necessary for me, or anyone else, to say correctly that player A was a good hernipper or that player B was a poor hernipper or that player C was your average hernipper. Martin's paper encouraged me to explore the logic of *validating standards*, in my case the standards for good hernipping and in Martin's case the standards for good clutch hitting. Would my experience of no successful hernips in fifteen trials indicate that *one* successful hernip be a validated standard for good hernipping? So my reaction to this paper will be informed, partially, by the logic of *validating standards* for making value judgments, whether on clutch hitting or hernipping or automobiles or whatever, as developed by Paul Taylor.[1]

With that introduction I will set out to do two and, time permitting, three things.

First, I would like to evaluate Martin's paper in terms of what characteristics he correctly associates with the concept "good clutch hitter." Also, I would like to suggest that there are some important characteristics which either he does not mention or, if mentioned, he rejects too quickly. Then I will propose a way in which all, or at least most of the included characteristics of good clutch hitting are recognized appropriately. In this last I will be responding to Martin's ". . . if the paper causes other philosophical analysts of sport to improve my definition, my efforts will be worthwhile."[2]

Second, I would like to ascertain whether the standards he proposes for good clutch hitting may be considered to have been validated as the best of those which are possible.

Third, time permitting, I would like to comment briefly upon the kind of potential philosophical relevance Martin's work has for philosophy of sport and the kind of relevance it has for other endeavors which are, essentially, nonphilosophical.

I

What are the good-making characteristics which Martin correctly identifies as being relevant for normative judgments on good clutch hitters? Obviously, batting average of some sort is necessary to such a judgment. Martin rejects, I think correctly, batting average men-on-base or BAMOB. I find his reasons for rejecting BAMOB satisfactory. What he does, correct insofar as it goes, is specify batting average under certain specified conditions such as go-ahead-condition (GAC) and go-ahead-condition-late-innings (GACLI). He includes, also, batting average go-ahead-conditions-late-innings-crucial-games or BAGACLICG. I think this is not correct and will refer to it later.

What are some characteristics which he considers and then rejects? He rejects RBI correctly as the total measure of good clutch hitting but further consideration will show that, under given circumstances, RBI is relevant.

Imagine a go-ahead condition, GAC, with a batter's team tied or one run down with runners on second and third or bases loaded with less than two outs. Suppose that the batter responds by driving in a run with a sacrifice fly and moves the runner on second to third. Or suppose that the batter delivers either a run scoring suicide or safety squeeze bunt in that situation. It would be difficult to account adequately for such performance solely by batting average figures. I suggest we need to add RBIGACSH, run-batted-in-go-ahead-condition-sacrifice-hit, as a good-making characteristic of clutch hitting.

Although entertaining batting average go-ahead-condition, Martin finally rejects this characteristic because of its possibility in early innings. However, it is quite possible on some occasions that delivering a hit under go ahead conditions in early innings may be the deciding event if few or no additional runs are scored. Thus, an early inning BAGAC becomes the functional equivalent of a BAGACLI in a given game. Perhaps there is a different way of including BAGAC.

What are some other good-making characteristics which Martin does not mention which, at the least, deserve consideration and, at most, might be included as good-making characteristics of clutch hitting? Let me suggest three possibilities without arriving at conclusions on their necessity.

How about slugging average under go ahead conditions or go ahead conditions late innings? Is there a better demonstration of clutch hitting than, say, hitting a home run in go ahead conditions late innings, as Ted Williams did in the ninth inning of the 1941 All-Star Game in Detroit? Should extra base hits in such conditions count more in good clutch hitting than singles? A yes answer to that question allows me to get hernipping back into the picture here. Just think of the additional record book entries such as batting average-hit home run next pitch or BAHHRNP, batting average-hit three bagger next pitch or BAHTBNP (pronounced bah-teb-nip) and batting average-hit two bagger next pitch or BAHTBNP$_2$ (pronounced bah-teb-nip$_2$).

How about bases on balls under go ahead conditions late innings or BBGACLI (pronounced bee-bee-gack-lee)? If a batter is facing, say, a Goose Gossage and works him for a walk which moves a baserunner from first to second he deserves some credit for clutch work if not a medal for bravery for staying in the batter's box.

How about sacrifice bunts which move two runners to second and third under go ahead conditions late innings? It is no small feat of clutch performance to bunt successfully when the pitcher is throwing nothing but letter-high pitches and the first and third basemen are charging toward home on the pitch.

There is still another consideration which, I must say, is absolutely essential to an understanding of good clutch hitting. This consideration may be one of the things Martin had in mind when he says the answer to the question, "What is a good clutch hitter?" ". . . is not easy to give and a precise quantitative definition . . . is hard to come by. Although I suggest some definitions . . . I am not completely satisfied with any of them" (p. 592). This unmentioned consideration also makes me reject the crucial game characteristic, at least the way it has been designated by Martin, as a post hoc consideration in clutch hitting which is not relevant, in principle, because it is post hoc.

Simply stated, I reject post hoc characterizations of clutch hitting because what the "clutch" in clutch hitting is must include the individual perception and conception of the batter in a specific situation that the situation does place some unusual psychological stress and demand upon him *then*. For, if the batter does *not* have the personal consciousness of clutch, that is, a crucial situation in his own mind, then all the objective characteristics do not make the situation a real clutch. This characteristic, which must be present for any situation to be a clutch, may be called psychological stress or PS. Its presence or absence is certainly one of the uncertainties to which Martin alludes in characterizing the good clutch hitter.

Now, what can be done to improve upon the fine start which Martin has given us? Simply, I propose developing a kind of formula which will include as many of the objective good-making characteristics of clutch hitting as possible and will give us information on the quality of any one player's performance "on-the-whole." The formula would be such that parts of it could be analytically separate for their practical uses by baseball personnel. (Some managers would, no doubt, want to play the percentages on hernipping.) At the same time, we would need to recognize that no strictly quantitative formula will give us a total assessment of good clutch hitting because it could not include PS.

In addition to building in so many characteristics what else must be in the formula? There must be a weighting of each characteristic so that judgments of good clutch performance "on-the-whole" are impacted upon more heavily by some characteristics than others. From my earlier statements in this reaction, we find that the formula must build in ways of crediting performances which are not, strictly, batting averages. For instance, RBIGACSH, Slugging averages GAC and GACLI, BBGACLI and SHGACLI.

Finally, there must be a *validated* final standard for performance in clutch hitting situations which allows comparisons of the performances of individual players with a relevant class of comparison. Martin suggests all other players in the league as a relevant class of comparison. It is, and there are many other possible relevant classes depending on our purposes including such classes as all-time hernippers. The class of comparison along with the validated standard then allows us to make such normative judgments correctly as Player A performs well in clutch hitting situations, Player B performs poorly in the same and Player C is an average performer.

I would like to illustrate one idea of such a formula. I will specify what the different good-making characteristics are, what their weightings might be and in what measure of "on-the-whole" performance in clutch hitting situations they would result. It must be understood that I am *not* suggesting that this is the best formula possible. I offer it solely to illustrate the *kind* of formula which I am recommending. Please note that the formula includes only objective factors in clutch hitting situations and, by so doing, implicitly recognizes that the condition PS is not being included. Such recognition has significance for validation.

Batting Average Characteristics (BAGAC + 2BAGACLI) + Slugging Average Characteristics (SAGAC + 2SAGACLI) + fixed percent bonuses of (.002 per RBISHGAC + .001 BBGACLI + .001 SHGACLI) ÷ 4 = Performance Effectiveness Average, Objective Clutch Hitting Situations or PEAOCHS.

II

It is now appropriate to turn to the problem of whether or not Martin's standards for good clutch hitting are validated as the best of those possible. First, let me repeat the standards with which Martin concludes his paper.

1. A good standard clutch hitter means a high standard clutch hitting average relative to the rest of the players in the league where standard clutch hitting average is defined as BAGACLI.

2. A good clutch hitter₁ means a high clutch hitting average relative to the rest of the players in the league where high clutch hitting is defined as BAGACLICG.

Both of these standards tell us that "good" means "above the average of all players in the league."

Are these standards validated? In Martin's analysis of the meanings of "good clutch hitter" in common usage he has attempted, also, to arrive at standards by which value judgments on clutch hitting may be made correctly. To *validate* such standards means to justify the act of adopting them (Taylor, p. 77). And how is adopting a standard by which value judgments are to be made justified? Taylor identifies three logical steps. First, the standard must be shown to be relevant (p. 84). Second, it must be shown that neither the situation in which the clutch hitter becomes the clutch hitter nor something out of the ordinary about the clutch hitter allows us to make an exception to the general standard determined in step one (p. 85). Third, it must be shown ". . . either (a) that no other valid standard or rule conflicts with the one being applied, or (b) that, if there is a conflict, the one being applied takes precedence over all those in conflict with it" (p. 85).

I will now relate Martin's two standards to these three steps in validation. This analysis is, clearly, limited.

Step One—Are the standards of above average BAGACLI and BAGAC-LICG relevant? It appears that our prior analysis shows that BAGACLI has *some* relevance. However, BAGACLICG is very doubtful in that it includes, in its description, a necessary post hoc determination which presupposes the presence of PS in all GACLICG situations. There is no way of correctly supposing PS in all CG situations because CG is determined on a post hoc basis.

Step Two—The two standards above average BAGACLI and BAGACLICG assume that a clutch hitter becomes a clutch hitter in a situation constituted by objective factors alone. Unless the necessary qualitative characteristic of the clutch hitting situation is recognized as such then these two standards, because PS is not identified, falsely constitute what the clutch hitting situation is. Because the situation is constituted falsely exceptions to these standards may be identified because PS is a necessary element of clutch. Therefore, unless sorted out, a situation for clutch hitting which does not include PS cannot be properly identified as the situation within which the standards apply.

Step Three—I have attempted to show in my earlier reactions that there are other and, it seems, better standards which, if not in conflict with above average BAGACLI and BAGACLICG, recognize other and more characteristics of good clutch hitting in addition to BAGACLI and BAGACLICG. In this way we can see that the PEAOCHS (performance effectiveness average, objective clutch hitting situation) admits other important characteristics into the standard for judgment and, at the same time, because it directly states that it includes *only objective clutch hitting situations*, avoids the problem which Martin's standards have because they do not explicitly recognize the PS characteristic. By identifying PEAOCHS we have found another standard over which Martin's standards have not been shown to take precedence. The other standards which Martin recognizes and then rejects are BAMOB, RBI and BAGAC. But his rejection of these standards is not that they are valid, albeit less worthy of precedence than BAGACLI and BAGACLICG, but that they are *not* relevant standards for good clutch hitting.

I would like to finish by stating a few more things about various possible and, I believe, more definitive meanings of "good" in good clutch hitting or in good performance effectiveness average in objective clutch hitting situations. If we use the word good as meaning above average batting average or above average performance effectiveness average we get only a very rough evaluation, namely, one group of above average players and another group of below average players. If we use other treatments we can derive much more definitive results. We could, for instance, compute all of the players' averages and then rank all players from highest to lowest average. We would then know who was the very best performer in clutch situations, the second best and so on down to the poorest performer. As still another instance, we could compute the averages of all players and then divide those who are above average into three classes called the best performers, the better performers and the good performers while dividing those below average into classes of poor, poorer and poorest performers.

III

The philosophic analysis of crucial concepts can be very useful in the better philosophic understanding of sport. Many sport-relevant concepts are badly in need of clarity. For the sake of philosophic comprehension of sport, I suggest that the concept of the good clutch hitter is one facet, among many, of a broader concept which if clearly understood would enhance our understanding of all sport, including baseball. I refer to a concept which has to do with player ability to perform well under pressure in perceived crucial situations. All sports exhibit such occasions whether in the ability to hold off an opponent at triple match point in tennis, to complete the fifty yard bomb in the last seconds of a football game or to sink the birdie putt on the eighteen hole of a tight golf match. Analysis of the *generic* competencies and their standards which characterize this ability correctly in all sport would help us to unravel one more mystery in the maddening power of sport.

NOTES

1. Paul W. Taylor, *Normative Discourse* (Englewood Cliffs, New Jersey: Prentice-Hall, Inc., 1961), chapter 4. Subsequent references to this work will be noted in the text.
2. Michael Martin, "Philosophical Analysis at Work: In Search of the Elusive Clutch Hitter," delivered at the conference of the Philosophic Society for the Study of Sport, Hartford, Connecticut, October 17, 1981; reprinted in this anthology, pp. 592–598. Subsequent references to this essay will be noted in the text.

MICHAEL MARTIN

Comments on Fraleigh

I would like to respond to some of Warren Fraleigh's most serious criticisms. (1) Fraleigh argues that my fifth definition—the batting average under go ahead conditions in the late inning definition—is too limited; it does not take into account enough of the characteristics that make up a good clutch hitter. Although he admits that someone's batting average in go ahead conditions in the late innings is relevant to evaluating whether someone is a good clutch hitter, he says that other things are as well. According to Fraleigh, one must take into account a batter's ability to make sacrifice bunts, hit sacrifice

---

Published for the first time in this anthology.

flies and even get walks in clutch situations in any completely adequate definition of a clutch hitter. But this I do not do in any of my definitions.

How can I respond to this serious charge? In this way, I think Fraleigh and
I are talking about clutch hitters in two different senses. (One value of his
comments is that the ambiguity became clear to me after reading them.)

In a broad sense a hitter in baseball is a batter, i.e. the person at the plate.
People at the plate do various things to help their team: they get hits, sacrifice
flies, sacrifice bunts and walks. But in a narrow sense, the sense I had in
mind, a hitter is simply a person who gets hits. In my paper I was trying to
capture the narrow sense of hitter in the expression "clutch hitter."

To put my point in a different way. There are clutch hits, clutch sacrifice
flies, clutch sacrifice bunts and clutch walks. I was interested in giving an
account of what it means to say that someone is good at getting clutch hits.
This is what I mean by a good clutch hitter. I was not interested in what it
means to say that someone is good at getting either clutch hits or clutch sacrifice flies or clutch sacrifice bunts or clutch walks.

The difference between Fraleigh and me on this point, I suggest, is based
on attempts to analyse different concepts, concepts that are ambiguously referred to by the same term "clutch hitter." Fraleigh is attempting to analyse
the concept of a clutch hitter in a broad sense—a person who does various
things beside get hits in the clutch. In order to avoid ambiguity I suggest that
such a person be called a clutch *batter*, not a clutch hitter.

I think both notions—a clutch batter and a clutch hitter—are important
in baseball and Fraleigh has made an important contribution in outlining
some of the characteristics of good clutch batters (in contrast to good clutch
hitters).

So, correctly understood there is no disagreement between Fraleigh and me
on this point at least.

(2) However, Fraleigh says some things that this distinction cannot handle.
He argues at one point that my Definition 5 is inadequate in another way. For
he maintains that someone's hit in go ahead conditions in the early innings
may be decisive if few or no runs are scored in later innings. This, he seems to
think, shows that the fifth definition requiring a higher batting average in
GAC in late innings is inadequate as an account of a clutch hitter.

However, I have trouble with this suggestion. First of all, this idea seems
to conflict with his emphasis on psychological stress as being essential to
the concept of a clutch hitter. For unless a player has precognition he or she
would not ordinarily feel the psychological stress of a clutch situation in the
early innings. How can the player know in the early innings that what he or
she does will be decisive? Second, I wonder if Fraleigh is not really talking

about something other than clutch hitting here. A player who gets decisive hits in early innings in GAC, hits that ultimately decide the game, would not, I believe, be called a clutch hitter. I am not sure baseball has an appropriate term for such a player, but let us introduce one. Let us call such a player a "decisive hitter" and define a decisive hitter in this way:

> A person P is a decisive hitter IFF P has a high batting average in go ahead conditions and but for P's hits in go ahead conditions P's team would often lose games.

So although I think that Fraleigh is getting at an important aspect of baseball hitting here, I question whether what he is talking about is clutch hitting.

(3) Fraleigh also brings up some considerations that he believes show that my sixth definition is inadequate, that of clutch hitter in terms of BAGAC-LICG. I take it that his argument is that it is essential to the concept of a clutch that a clutch hitter must be under psychological stress (PS). He assumes that this definition does not provide for this because, as I argue, what is a crucial game can sometimes not be known except in retrospect. Consequently the player at the time he or she is hitting in a crucial game cannot know he or she is in a crucial game and will not feel any psychological stress. Now, I do not believe that Fraleigh's idea that psychological stress is an essential part of a clutch hitter is correct, but even if it is, my definition in a way takes this into account.

Does a clutch hitter have to experience PS while hitting? Surely not. There may be some batters—the Bjorn Borgs of baseball—with ice water running through their veins who feel no stress in the clutch; indeed they may even be calmer and steadier in the clutch than ordinarily. Are we really going to say that because of their remarkable psychological endowment they cannot be clutch hitters? I think not. I think Fraleigh would be on much safer ground if instead of emphasizing PS he emphasized knowledge. He perhaps should argue that a clutch hitter must know he or she is hitting in a clutch but that whether the hitter feels stress or not is irrelevant.

Now my sixth definition allows for a clutch hitter to know he or she is hitting in a clutch and even to feel psychological stress because of this. It even allows that the hitter *sometimes* knows he or she is hitting in a crucial game and feels stress because of this knowledge. After all, it is very often the case that players know they are in crucial games since often crucial games are playoffs, World Series and the like. What my definition does provide for is that *on occasion* a hitter may not know he or she is hitting in a clutch *in a crucial game* since the crucial quality of this game is clear only in retrospect.

But this is quite compatible with the player knowing he or she is hitting in a clutch and feeling PS because of this. What the hitter may lack is knowledge of the crucial nature of the game, not the clutch situation of the game.

But my definition does have a peculiar implication and this is perhaps what Fraleigh was really responding to. Since sometimes what is a crucial game can only be known in retrospect a player might be a good clutch hitter, but only in crucial games that are not known to be crucial at the time he or she hits in the clutch. (I hasten to point out that this is a purely hypothetical example and I seriously doubt whether there are any such players.) How might we explain the behavior of such a player?

One idea would be that the player's behavior is a coincidence. It just happens by chance that he or she gets clutch hits in such games. But suppose (to make the case even more hypothetical) this player continues to be a clutch hitter over many baseball seasons only in crucial games whose crucial quality could be known only in retrospect. The idea that this can be explained by coincidence now seems implausible.

Parapsychologists might suggest that the player has some remarkable ESP ability, in particular that the player has precognition: that he or she can unconsciously see into the future and unconsciously rise to the occasion, that the significance of the present can be known only by ESP. But we need not carry these speculations further, since however such remarkable ability is explained, it is allowed for by my sixth definition of a clutch hitter. I am inclined to suppose that this is an advantage rather than a defect in my definition. I, for one, would not want to exclude from the definition of a clutch hitter behavior that in the light of our present knowledge is mysterious. To do so would be to restrict the definition too much to what is explainable by present knowledge.

HENRY HECHT

Here's the Info on Hitters Who Get Tough When the Going Gets Tough

B y now, just about every baseball fan is aware of the game's newest official stat—it's only three years old—the game-winning RBI, the ribbie that puts a team ahead to stay. It means that if you lead off a game with a home run and your team goes on to win 11−10 without surrendering the lead, your first-inning homer is the GW-RBI. Don Baylor, who signed a $3.675 million contract with the Yankees in December, was the best clutch hitter in baseball last season as a California Angel, with 93 RBIs, of which 21 were "gamers." He led the American League and tied the Giants' Jack Clark and the Cardinals' Keith Hernandez for the major league lead in GW-RBIs.

But that's only part of the story. Baylor was the top clutch hitter because of the way those gamers were distributed: 10 of them came after the sixth inning, when throats get dry, Adam's apples start bobbing and batting averages often plummet. No one else hit double figures for the late innings, though the Royals' Amos Otis, who tied for second with the Orioles' Eddie Murray in the American League with 20 gamers, had nine of them after the sixth. A second-year player for the Red Sox, Reid Nichols, was the percentage leader—all six of his GW-RBIs came late in games. Nichols was at once pleased and mildly chagrined when told how heroic he'd been. It seems he'd just signed his 1983 contract and wished he had known that stat beforehand.

Reggie Jackson, stat freak and pressure hitter, has some strong opinions about what makes a man perform in the clutch. "It's an ability to concentrate, and it entails a certain strength of character," says Jackson, a teammate of Baylor's last season. "I really think that strength of character is the most important aspect, and it's something you've got to *have*, something you can't make or fabricate."

Hernandez certainly proved his character in the last three games of the 1982 World Series, in which he went 7 for 12 and drove in eight runs after going 0 for 15 in the first four, but only three of his 21 gamers in the regular season came after the sixth inning. Clark did better, with eight. All told, 665 of the 1,968 major league gamers, or 33.8%, came in the final third of the game.

Originally appeared in *Sports Illustrated* (1983).

Says Jim Palmer, pitcher, pitchman and philosopher, "Mature, confident hitters don't expand their strike zones in late-inning clutch situations. They don't swing at the pitcher's pitch. I think the hitter has the advantage, but I'm not so sure most of the hitters realize that."

But Baylor does. As Palmer says, "He's the last guy you want coming up."

"Sometimes you try so hard you get too tight," says Baylor himself. "If you're not relaxed, you'll hit at a pitcher's pitch and make a foolish out. And there are still times for me when I have to step out of the batter's box and rewind myself."

But when he is rewound and relaxed, this is what happens: "When I'm totally tuned in," Baylor says "it's like I'm looking down a tunnel where there's nothing else but the pitcher. I'm aware of the fans, I can hear the noise, but it doesn't bother me."

Clutch hitting can have a powerful impact on a team's overall performance. The Angels, with Baylor, made it to the American League playoffs. The surprising '82 Giants, who were in the pennant race through Game 161, got a lift not only from Clark, but also from Joe Morgan; five of his 10 gamers came after the sixth. The Giants had the highest percentage of late-inning game-winning RBIs (45.1) in the major leagues.

But sometimes a team doesn't need that kind of heroics. The Brewers made it into the Series and led the majors in home runs and runs scored, but they had the lowest percentage (23.0) of late-inning gamers. This was for the best of reasons—seems like they usually led 8–0 after two innings.

And even though a three-run homer in the first inning may sometimes be as important to the outcome of the game as an eighth-inning single, it's those late-game hits with the winning run on second that people remember.

"Some people rise to the situation and some people don't," says San Francisco Manager Frank Robinson, whose own hitting under pressure helped him win MVP awards in both leagues. "Me? I didn't get uptight or panic. There was the challenge."

Last year no one met that challenge better than Baylor.

A Guide for Further Study

Believe it or not, Howard Cosell has a few choice words about sport language in his *Cosell*. Higgs has a comprehensive section on language in his *Sports: A Reference Guide*, pp. 69–73. An entertaining and informative analysis of sport verbiage is Percy N. Tannenbaum and James E. Noah, "Sportugese: A Study of Sports Page Communication," collected in Loy and Kenyon, *Sport, Culture, and Society: A Reader on the Sociology of Sport*.

Philosophical analyses can be found in the *Journal of the Philosophy of Sport*: "Toward a Non-definition of Sport" by Frank McBride, in volume 2 (1975); "What Makes Physical Activity Physical?" by Robert Paddick, volume 2, (1975); "A Critique of Mr. Suits' Definition of Game Playing" by Frank McBride, volume 6 (1979); "McBride and Paddick on *The Grasshopper*" by Bernard Suits, volume 8 (1981). See also Hans Lenk's "Prolegomena Toward an Analytic Philosophy of Sport" (reprinted in this anthology, pp. 474–480).

Section II: Fantasy

ROBERT COOVER

The Perfect Game

Bottom half of the seventh, Brock's boy had made it through another inning unscratched, one! two! three! Twenty-one down and just six outs to go! and Henry's heart was racing, he was sweating with relief and tension all at once, unable to sit, unable to think, *in* there, *with* them! Oh yes, boys, it was on! He was sure of it! More than just another ball game now: *history!* And Damon Rutherford was making it. Ho ho! too good to be true! And yes, the stands were charged with it, turned on, it was the old days all over again, and with one voice they rent the air as the Haymaker Star Hamilton Craft spun himself right off his feet in a futile cut at Damon's third strike—zing! whoosh! *zap! OUT!* Henry laughed, watched the hometown Pioneer fans cheer the boy, cry out his name, then stretch—not just stretch—*leap up* for luck. He saw beers bought and drunk, hot dogs eaten, timeless gestures passed. Yes, yes, they nodded, and crossed their fingers and knocked on wood and rubbed their palms and kissed their fingertips and clapped their hands, and laughed how they were all caught up in it, witnessing it, how he was all caught up in it, this great ball game, event of the first order, tremendous moment: *Rookie pitcher Damon Rutherford, son of the incomparable Brock Rutherford, was two innings—six outs—from a perfect game!* Henry, licking his lips, dry from excitement, squinted at the sun high over the Pioneer Park, then at his watch: nearly eleven, Diskin's closing hours. So he took the occasion of this seventh-inning hometown stretch to hurry downstairs to the delicatessen to get a couple sandwiches. Might be a long night: the Pioneers hadn't scored off old Swanee Law yet either.

A small warm bulb, unfrosted, its little sallow arc so remote from its fathering force as to seem more akin to the glowworm than lightning, gleamed outside his door and showed where the landing ended; the steps themselves were

From *The Universal Baseball Association, Inc., J. Henry Waugh, Prop.* (1968). Title supplied by the editors.

dark, but Henry, through long usage, knew them all by heart. Cold bluish streetlight lit the bottom, intruding damply, seeming to hover unrelated to the floor, but Henry hardly noticed: his eye was on the game, on the great new Rookie pitcher Damon Rutherford, seeking this afternoon his sixth straight win . . . and maybe more. Maybe: immortality. And now, as Henry skipped out onto the sidewalk, then turned into the front door of Diskin's Delicatessen, he saw the opposing pitcher, Ace Swanee Law of the hard-bitten Haymakers, taking the mound, tossing warm-up pitches, and he knew he had to hurry.

"Two pastrami, Benny," he said to the boy sweeping up, Mr. Diskin's son—third or fourth, though, not the second. "And a cold six-pack."

"Aw, I just put everything away, Mr. Waugh," the boy whined, but he went to get the pastrami anyway.

Now Swanee Law was tough, an ace, seven-year veteran, top rookie himself in his own day, one of the main reasons Rag Rooney's rubes had finished no worse than third from Year L through Year LIV. Ninety-nine wins, sixty-one losses, fast ball that got faster every year, most consistent, most imperturbable, and most vociferous of the Haymaker moundsmen. Big man who just reared back and hummed her in. Phenomenal staying power, the kind old Brock used to have. But he didn't have Brock Rutherford's class, that sweet smooth delivery, that virile calm. Mean man to beat, just the same, and to be sure he still had a shutout going for him this afternoon, and after all, it was a big day for him, too, going for that milestone hundredth win. Of course, he had a Rookie catcher in there to throw to, young Bingham Hill, and who knows? maybe they weren't getting along too well; could be. Law was never an easy man to get along with, too pushy, too much steam, and Hill was said to be excitable. Maybe Rooney had better send in reliable old Maggie Everts, Law's favorite battery mate. What about it? Haymaker manager Rag (Pappy) Rooney stroked his lean grizzly jaw, gave the nod to Everts.

"How's that, Mr. Waugh?"

"Did you put the pickle?"

"We're all out, sold the last one thirty minutes ago."

A lie. Henry sighed. He'd considered using the name Ben Diskin, solid name for an outfielder, there was a certain power in it, but Benny spoiled it. A good boy, but nothing there. "That's okay, Benny. I'll take two next time."

"Working hard tonight, Mr. Waugh?" Benny rang up the sale, gave change.

"As always."

"Better take it easy. You been looking a little run-down lately."

Henry winced impatiently, forced a smile. "Never felt better," he said, and exited.

It was true: the work, or what he called his work, though it was more than that, much more, was good for him. Thing was, nobody realized he was just four years shy of sixty. They were always shocked when he told them. It was his Association that kept him young.

Mounting the stairs, Henry heard the roar of the crowd, saw them take their seats. Bowlegged old Maggie Everts trundled out of the Haymaker dugout to replace Hill. That gave cause for a few more warm-up pitches, so Henry slowed, took the top steps one at a time. Law grinned, nodded at old Maggie, stuffed a chaw of gum into his cheek. In the kitchen, he tore open the six-pack of beer, punched a can, slid the others into the refrigerator, took a long greedy drink of what the boys used to call German tea. Then, while Law tossed to Everts, Henry chewed his pastrami and studied the line-ups. Grammercy Locke up for the Pioneers, followed by three Star batters. Locke had been rapping the ball well lately, but Pioneer manager Barney Bancroft pulled him out, playing percentages, called in pinch-hitter Tuck Wilson, a great Star in his prime, now nearing the end of his career. Wilson selected a couple bats, exercised them, chose one, tugged his hat, and stepped in.

Henry sat down, picked up the dice, approved Everts' signal. "Wilson batting for Locke!" he announced over the loud-speaker, and they gave the old hero a big hometown hand. Henry rolled, bit into pastrami. Wilson swung at the first pitch, in across the knuckles, pulling it down the line. Haymaker third-sacker Hamilton Craft hopped to his right, fielded the ball, spun, threw to first—*wide!* Wilson: safe on first! Henry marked the error, flashed it on the scoreboard. Craft, one of the best, kicked the bag at third sullenly, scrubbed his nose, stared hard at Hatrack Hines, stepping now into the box. Bancroft sent speedster Hillyer Bryan in to run for Wilson.

"Awright! now come on, you guys! a little action!" Henry shouted, Bancroft shouted, clapping his hands, and the Pioneers kept the pepper up, they hollered in the stands.

"Got them Rubes rattled, boys! Let's bat around!"

"Lean into it, Hatrack, baby! Swanee's done for the day!"

"Send him down the river!"

"Dee-ee-eep water, Swanee boy!"

"Hey, Hatrack! Just slap it down to Craft there, he's all butter!"

The dice rattled in Henry's fist, tumbled out on the kitchen table: *crack!* hard grounder. Craft jumped on it this time, whipped the ball to second, one out—but young Bryan broke up the double play by flying in heels high! Still in there! Bancroft took a calculated risk: sent Hatrack scampering for second on Law's second pitch to Witness York—*safe!* Finishing his sandwich, Henry wondered: Would the Rookie Bingham Hill, pulled for inexperience, have nailed Hines at second? Maybe he would have. Pappy Rooney, the graybeard

Haymaker boss, spat disdainfully. He knew what he was doing. Who knows? Hill might have thrown wild.

Anyway, it didn't matter. Pioneer Star center fielder Witness York stepped back in, squeezed his bat for luck, swung, and whaled out his eleventh home run of the season, scoring Hines in front of him, and before Law had got his wind back, big Stan Patterson, Star right fielder, had followed with his ninth. Wham! bam! thank you, ma'am! And finally that was how the seventh inning ended: Pioneers 3, Haymakers 0. And now it was up to Damon Rutherford.

Henry stood, drank beer, joined in spirit with the Pioneer fans in their heated cries. Could the boy do it? All knew what, but none named it. The bullish roar of the crowd sounded like a single hoarse monosyllable, yet within it, Henry could pick out the ripple of Damon's famous surname, not so glorified in this stadium in over twenty years. Then it was for the boy's father, the all-time great Brock Rutherford, one of the game's most illustrious Aces back in what seemed now like the foundling days of the Universal Baseball Association, even-tempered fireballing no-pitches-wasted right-handed bell-wether of the Pioneers who led them to nine pennants in a span of fourteen years. The Glorious XX's! Celebrated Era of the Pioneers! Barney Bancroft himself was there; he knew, he remembered! One of the fastest men the UBA had ever seen, out there guarding center. Barney the Old Philosopher, flanked by Willie O'Leary and Surrey Moss, and around the infield: Mose Stanford, Frosty Young, Jonathan Noon, and Gabe Burdette, timid Holly Tibbett behind the plate. Toothbrush Terrigan pitched, and Birdie Deaton and Chadbourne Collins . . . and Brock. Brock had come up as a Rookie in Year XX— no, XIX, that's right, it would have to be (Henry paused to look it up; yes, correct: XIX), just a kid off the farm, seemed happy-go-lucky and even lackadaisical, but he had powered his way to an Ace position that first year, winning six straight ball games at the end of the season, three of them shutouts, lifting the long-suffering Pioneers out of second division into second place. A great year! great teams! and next year the pennant! Brock the Great! maybe the greatest of them all! He had stayed up in the Association for seventeen years before giving way to age and a troublesome shoulder. Still held the record to this day for total lifetime wins: 311. 311! Brock Rutherford . . . well, well, time gets on. Henry felt a tightness in his chest, shook it off. Foolish. He sighed, picked up the dice. Brock the Great. Hall of Fame, of course.

And now: now it was his boy who stood there on the mound. Tall, lithe, wirier build than his dad's, but just as fast, just as smooth. Smoother. More serious somehow. Yes, there was something more pensive about Damon, a meditative calm, a gentle brooding concern. The calm they shared, Rutherford gene, but where in Brock it had taken on the color of a kind of cocky,

almost rustic power, in Damon it was self-assurance ennobled with a sense of
. . . what? Responsibility maybe. Accountability. Brock was a public phenomenon, Damon a self-enclosed yet participating mystery. His own man,
yet at home in the world, part of it, involved, every inch of him a participant, maybe that was all it was: his total involvement, his oneness with the
UBA. Henry mused, fingering the dice. The Pioneer infielders tossed the ball
around. Catcher Royce Ingram talked quietly with Damon out on the mound.

Of course, Pappy Rooney cared little for the peculiar aesthetics of the moment. It was his job not only to break up the no-hitter, but to beat the kid.
Anyway, old Pappy had no love for the Rutherfords. Already a Haymaker
Star and veteran of two world championships, four times the all-star first
baseman of the Association, when Dad Rutherford first laced on a pair of
cleats for the Pioneers, Rag Rooney had suffered through season after season
of Haymaker failure to break the Pioneer grip on the UBA leadership, had
gone down swinging futilely at Brock's fireball as often as the next man. So
maybe that was why it was that, when the Haymaker right fielder, due to lead
off in the top of the eighth, remarked that the Rutherford kid sure was tough
today, Rooney snapped back: "Ya don't say. Well, mister, take your goddamn
seat." And called in a pinch hitter.

Not that it did any good. Henry was convinced it was Damon's day, and
nothing the uncanny Rooney came up with today could break the young Pioneer's spell. He laughed, and almost carelessly, with that easy abandon of old
man Brock, pitched the dice, watched Damon Rutherford mow them down.
One! Two! Three! And then nonchalantly, but not arrogantly, just casually,
part of any working day, walk to the dugout. As though nothing were happening. *Nothing!* Henry found himself hopping up and down. One more inning! He drank beer, reared back, fired the empty can at the plastic garbage
bucket near the sink. In there! *Zap!* "Go get 'em!" he cried.

First, of course, the Pioneers had their own eighth round at the plate, and
there was no reason not to use it to stretch their lead, fatten averages a little,
rub old Swanee's nose in it. Even if the Haymakers got lucky in the ninth and
spoiled Damon's no-hitter, there was no reason to lose the ball game. After all,
Damon was short some 300-and-some wins if he wanted to top his old man,
which meant he needed every one he could get. Henry laughed irreverently.

Goodman James, young Pioneer first baseman making his second try for a
permanent place in the line-up after a couple years back in the minors,
picked out a hat, stepped lean-legged into the batter's box. Swanee fed him
the old Law Special, a sizzling sinker in at the knees, and James bounced it
down the line to first base: easy out. Damon Rutherford received a tremendous ovation when he came out—his dad would have acknowledged it with
an open grin up at the stands; Damon knocked dirt from his cleats, seemed

not to hear it. Wasn't pride. It was just that he understood it, accepted it, but was too modest, too *knowing*, to insist on any uniqueness of his own apart from it. He took a couple casual swings with his bat, moved up to the plate, waited Law out, but finally popped up: not much of a hitter. But to hear the crowd cheer as he trotted back to the dugout (one of the coaches met him halfway with a jacket), one would have thought he'd at least homered. Henry smiled. Lead-off man Toby Ramsey grounded out, short to first. Three up, three down. Those back-to-back homers had only made Law tougher than ever. "It's when Ah got baseballs flyin' round mah ears, that's when Ah'm really at mah meanest!"

Top of the ninth.

This was it.

Odds against him, of course. Had to remember that; be prepared for the lucky hit that really wouldn't be lucky at all, but merely in the course of things. Exceedingly rare, no-hitters; much more so, perfect games. How many in history? two, three. And a Rookie: no, it had never been done. In seventeen matchless years, his dad had pitched only two no-hitters, never had a perfect game. Henry paced the kitchen, drinking beer, trying to calm himself, to prepare himself, but he couldn't get it out of his head: *it was on!*

The afternoon sun waned, cast a golden glint off the mowed grass that haloed the infield. No sound in the stands now: breathless. Of course, no matter what happened, even if he lost the game, they'd cheer him, fabulous game regardless; yes, they'd love him, they'd let him know it . . . but still they wanted it. Oh yes, how they wanted it! Damon warmed up, throwing loosely to catcher Ingram. Henry watched him, felt the boy's inner excitement, shook his head in amazement at his outer serenity. "Nothing like this before." Yes, there was a soft murmur pulsing through the stands: nothing like it, electrifying, new, a new thing, happening here and now! Henry paused to urinate.

Manager Barney Bancroft watched from the Pioneer dugout, leaning on a pillar, thinking about Damon's father, about the years they played together, the games fought, the races won, the celebrations and the sufferings, roommates when on the road several of those years. Brock was great and this kid was great, but he was no carbon copy. Brock had raised his two sons to be more than ballplayers, or maybe it wasn't Brock's work, maybe it was just the name that had ennobled them, for in a way, they were—Bancroft smiled at the idea, but it was largely true—they were, in a way, the Association's first real aristocrats. There were already some fourth-generation boys playing ball in the league—the Keystones' Kester Flint, for example, and Jock Casey and Paddy Sullivan—but there'd been none before like the Rutherford boys. Even Brock Jr., though failing as a ballplayer, had had this quality, this poise, a gently ironic grace on him that his dad had never had, for all his raw jubilant power. Ingram threw the ball to second-baseman Ramsey, who flipped it to shortstop Wilder, who underhanded it to third-baseman Hines, now halfway to the mound, who in turn tossed it to Damon. Here we go.

Bancroft watched Haymaker backstop Maggie Everts move toward the plate, wielding a thick stubby bat. Rookie Rodney Holt crouched in the on-deck circle, working a pair of bats menacingly between his legs. Everts tipped his hat out toward the mound, then stepped into the box: dangerous. Yes, he was. The old man could bring the kid down. Still able to come through with the clutch hit. Lovable guy, old Maggie, great heart, Bancroft was fond of him, but that counted for nothing in the ninth inning of a history-making ball game. Rooney, of course, would send a pinch hitter in for Law. Bancroft knew he should order a couple relief pitchers to the bull pen just in case, but something held him back. Bancroft thought it was on, too.

Rooney noticed the empty bull pen. Bancroft was overconfident, was ripe for a surprise, but what could he do about it? He had no goddamn hitters. Even Ham Craft was in a bad slump. Should pull him out, cool his ass on the bench awhile, but, hell, he had nobody else. Pappy was in his fifteenth year as Haymaker manager, the old man of the Association's coaching staffs, and he just wasn't too sure, way things were going, that he and his ulcer were going to see a sixteenth. Two pennants, six times the league runner-up, never out of first division until last year when they dropped to fifth . . . and that was where his Rubes were now, with things looking like they were apt to get worse before they got better. He watched Everts, with a count of two and two on him, stand flatfooted as a third strike shot by so fast he hardly even saw it. That young bastard out there on the rubber was good, all right, fast as lightning—but what was it? Rooney couldn't quite put his finger on it . . . a little too narrow in the shoulders maybe, slight in the chest, too much a thoroughbred, not enough of the old man's big-boned stamina. And then he thought: shit, I can still beat this kid! And turning his scowl on the Haymaker bench, he hollered at Abernathy to pinch-hit for Holt.

Henry realized he had another beer in his hand and didn't remember having opened it. Now he was saying it out loud: "It's on! Come on, boy!" For the first time in this long game, the odds were with Damon: roughly 4-to-3 that he'd get both Abernathy and—who? Horvath, Rooney was sending in Hard John Horvath to bat for Law. Get them both and rack it up: the perfect game!

Henry hadn't been so excited in weeks. Months. That was the way it was, some days seemed to pass almost without being seen, games lived through, decisions made, averages rising or dipping, and all of it happening in a kind of fog, until one day that astonishing event would occur that brought sudden

life and immediacy to the Association, and everybody would suddenly wake
up and wonder at the time that had got by them, go back to the box scores,
try to find out what had happened. During those dull-minded stretches, even
a home run was nothing more than an HR penned into the box score; sure,
there was a fence and a ball sailing over it, but Henry didn't see them—oh,
he heard the shouting of the faithful, yes, they stayed with it, they had to,
but to him it was just a distant echo, static that let you know it was still going
on. But then, contrarily, when someone like Damon Rutherford came along
to flip the switch, turn things on, why, even a pop-up to the pitcher took on
excitement, a certain dimension, color. *The magic of excellence.* Under its
charm, he threw the dice: Abernathy struck out. Two down, *one to go!* It
could happen, *it could happen!* Henry reeled around his chair a couple times,
laughing out loud, went to urinate again.

Royce Ingram walked out to the mound. Ten-year veteran, generally acknowledged the best catcher in the UBA. He didn't go out to calm the kid
down, but just because it was what everybody expected him to do at such a
moment. Besides, Damon was the only sonuvabitch on the whole field not
about to crap his pants from excitement. Even the Haymakers, screaming for
the spoiler, were out of their seats, and to the man, hanging on his every
pitch. The kid really had it, okay. Not just control either, but stuff, too. Ingram had never caught anybody so good, and he'd caught some pretty good
ones. Just twenty years old, what's more: plenty of time to get even better. If
it's possible. Royce tipped up his mask, grinned. "Ever hear the one about the
farmer who stuck corks in his pigs' assholes to make them grow?" he asked.

"Yes, I heard that one, Royce," Damon said and grinned back. "What
made you think of that one—you having cramps?"

Ingram laughed. "How'd you guess?"

"Me too," the kid confessed, and toed a pebble off the rubber. Ingram felt
an inexplicable relief flood through him, and he took a deep breath. We're
gonna make it, he thought. They listened to the loudspeaker announcing
Horvath batting for Law. "Where does he like it?"

"Keep it in tight and tit-high, and the old man won't even see it," Ingram
said. He found he couldn't even grin, so he pulled his mask down. "Plenty of
stuff," he added meaninglessly. Damon nodded. Ingram expected him to
reach for the rosin bag or wipe his hands on his shirt or tug at his cap or
something, but he didn't: he just stood there waiting. Ingram wheeled around,
hustled back behind the plate, asked Horvath what he was sweating about,
underwear too tight on him or something? which made Hard John give an
uneasy tug at his balls, and when, in his squat behind the plate, he looked
back out at Rutherford, he saw that the kid still hadn't moved, still poised
there on the rise, coolly waiting, ball resting solidly in one hand, both hands

at his sides, head tilted slightly to the right, face expressionless but eyes alert. Ingram laughed. "You're dead, man," he told Horvath. Henry zipped up.

Of course, it was just the occasion for the storybook spoiler. Yes, too obvious. Perfect game, two down in the ninth, and a pinch hitter scratches out a history-shriveling single. How many times it had already happened! The epochal event reduced to a commonplace by something or someone even less than commonplace, a mediocrity, a blooper worth forgetting, a utility ball-player never worth much and out of the league a year later. All the No-Hit Nealys that Sandy sang about . . .

N-o-O-O-o Hit Nealy!
Won his fame
Spoilin' Birdie Deaton's
Per-her-fect game!

Henry turned water on to wash, then hesitated. Not that he felt superstitious about it exactly, but he saw Damon Rutherford standing there on the mound, hands not on the rosin bag, not in the armpits, not squeezing the ball, just at his side—dry, strong, patient—and he felt as though washing his hands might somehow spoil Damon's pitch. From the bathroom door, he could see the kitchen table. His Association lay there in ordered stacks of paper. The dice sat there, three ivory cubes, heedless of history yet makers of it, still proclaiming Abernathy's strike-out. Damon Rutherford waited there. Henry held his breath, walked straight to the table, picked up the dice, and tossed them down.

Hard John Horvath took a cut at Rutherford's second pitch, a letter-high inside curve, pulled it down the third-base line: Hatrack Hines took it backhanded, paused one mighty spellbinding moment—then fired across the diamond to Goodman James, and Horvath was out.

The game was over.

Giddily, Henry returned to the bathroom and washed his hands. He stared down at his wet hands, thinking: he did it! And then, at the top of his voice, "WA-HOO!" he bellowed, and went leaping back into the kitchen, feeling like he could damn well take off and soar if he had anyplace to go. "HOO-HAH!"

And the fans blew the roof off. They leaped the wall, slid down the dugout roofs, overran the cops, flooded in from the outfield bleachers, threw hats and scorecards into the air. Rooney hustled his Haymakers to the showers, but couldn't stop the Pioneer fans from lifting poor Horvath to their shoulders.

There was a fight and Hard John bloodied a couple noses, but nobody even bothered to swing back at him. An old lady blew him kisses. Partly to keep Rutherford from getting mobbed and partly just because they couldn't stop themselves, his Pioneer teammates got to him first, had him on their own shoulders before the frenzied hometown rooters could close in and tear him apart out of sheer love. From above, it looked like a great roiling whirlpool with Damon afloat in the vortex—but then York popped up like a cork, and then Patterson and Hines, and finally the manager Barney Bancroft, lifted up by fans too delirious even to know for sure anymore what it was they were celebrating, and the whirlpool uncoiled and surged toward the Pioneer locker rooms.

"Ah!" said Henry, and: "Ah!"

And even bobbingly afloat there on those rocky shoulders, there in that knock-and-tumble flood of fans, in a wild world that had literally, for the moment, blown its top, Damon Rutherford preserved his incredible equanimity, hands at his knees except for an occasional wave, face lit with pleasure at what he'd done, but in no way distorted with the excitement of it all: tall, right, and true. People screamed for the ball. Royce Ingram, whose shoulder was one of those he rode on, handed it up to him. Women shrieked, arms supplicating. He smiled at them, but tossed the ball out to a small boy standing at the crowd's edge.

Henry opened the refrigerator, reached for the last can of beer, then glanced at his watch: almost midnight—changed his mind. He peered out at the space between his kitchen window and the street lamp: lot of moisture in the air still, but hard to tell if it was falling or rising. He'd brooded over it, coming home from work: that piled-up mid-autumn feeling, pregnant with the vague threat of confusion and emptiness—but this boy had cut clean through it, let light and health in, and you don't go to bed on an event like this! Henry reknotted his tie, put on hat and raincoat, hooked his umbrella over one arm, and went out to get a drink. He glanced back at the kitchen table once more before pulling the door to, saw the dice there, grinned at them, for once adjuncts to grandeur, then hustled down the stairs like a happy Pioneer headed for the showers. He stepped quickly through the disembodied street lamp glow at the bottom, and whirling his umbrella like a drum major's baton, marched springily up the street to Pete's, the neighborhood bar.

N-o-O-O-o Hit Nealy!
Won his fame
Spoilin' Birdie Deaton's
Per-her-fect game!

The night above was dark yet the streets were luminous: wet, they shimmered with what occasional light there was from street lamps, passing cars, phone booths, all-night neon signs. There was fog and his own breath was visible, yet nearby objects glittered with a heightened clarity. He smiled at the shiny newness of things springing up beside him on his night walk. At a distance, car head lamps were haloed and taillights burned fuzzily, yet the lit sign in the darkened window he was passing, "DIVINEFORM FOUNDATIONS: TWO-WAY STRETCH," shone fiercely, hard-edged and vivid as a vision.

The corner drugstore was still open. A scrawny curlyheaded kid, cigarette butt dangling under his fuzzy upper lip, played the pinball machine that stood by the window. Henry paused to watch. The machine was rigged like a baseball game, though the scores were unrealistic. Henry had played the machine himself often and once, during a blue season, had even played off an entire all-UBA pinball tourney on it. Ballplayers, lit from inside, scampered around the basepaths, as the kid put english on the balls with his hips and elbows. A painted pitcher, in eternal windup, kicked high, while below, a painted batter in a half-crouch moved motionlessly toward the plate. Two girls in the upper corners, legs apart and skirts hiked up their thighs, cheered the runners on with silent wide-open mouths. The kid was really racking them up: seven free games showing already. Lights flashed, runners ran. Eight. Nine. "THE GREAT AMERICAN GAME," it said across the top, between the gleaming girls. Well, it was. American baseball, by luck, trial, and error, and since the famous playing rules council of 1889, had struck on an almost perfect balance between offense and defense, and it was that balance, in fact, that and the accountability—the beauty of the records system which found a place to keep forever each least action—that had led Henry to baseball as his final great project.

The kid twisted, tensed, relaxed, hunched over, reared, slapped the machine with a pelvic thrust; up to seventeen free games and the score on the lighted panel looked more like that of a cricket match than a baseball game. Henry moved on. To be sure, he'd only got through one UBA pinball tourney and had never been tempted to set up another. Simple-minded, finally, and not surprisingly a simple-minded ballplayer, Jaybird Wall, had won it. In spite of all the flashing lights, it was—like those two frozen open-mouthed girls and the batter forever approaching the plate, the imperturbable pitcher forever reared back—a static game, utterly lacking the movement, grace, and complexity of real baseball. When he'd finally decided to settle on his own baseball game, Henry had spent the better part of two months just working with the problem of odds and equilibrium points in an effort to approximate that complexity. Two dice had not done it. He'd tried three, each a different color, and the 216 different combinations had provided the complexity, all right, but he'd nearly gone blind trying to sort the colors on each throw. Finally, he'd compromised, keeping the three dice, but all white, reducing the total number of combinations to 56, though of course the odds were still based on 216. To restore—and, in fact, to intensify—the complexity of the multicolored method, he'd allowed triple ones and sixes—1–1–1 and 6–6–6—to trigger the more spectacular events, by referring the following dice throw to what he called his Stress Chart, also a three-dice chart, but far more dramatic in nature than the basic ones. Two successive throws of triple ones and sixes were exceedingly rare—only about three times in every two entire seasons of play on the average—but when it happened, the next throw was referred, finally, to the Chart of Extraordinary Occurrences, where just about anything from fistfights to fixed ball games could happen. These two charts were what gave the game its special quality, making it much more than just a series of hits and walks and outs. Besides these, he also had special sacrifice bunts, and squeeze plays, still others for deciding the ages of rookies when they came up, for providing details of injuries and errors, and for determining who, each year, must die.

A neon beer advertisement and windows lit dimly through red curtains were all that marked Pete's place. Steady clientele, no doubt profitable in a small way, generally quiet, mostly country-and-western or else old hit-parade tunes on the jukebox, a girl or two drifting by from time to time, fair prices. Henry brought his gyrating umbrella under control, left the wet world behind, and pushed in.

"Evening, Mr. Waugh," said the bartender.

"Evening, Jake."

Not Jake, of course, it was Pete himself, but it was a longstanding gag, born of a slip of the tongue. Pete was medium-sized, slope-shouldered, had bartenders' bags beneath his eyes and a splendid bald dome, spoke with a kind of hushed irony that seemed to give a dry double meaning to everything he said—in short, was the spitting image of Jake Bradley, one of Henry's ballplayers, a Pastimer second baseman whom Henry always supposed now to be running a bar somewhere near the Pastime Club's ball park, and one night, years ago, in the middle of a free-swinging pennant scramble, Henry had called Pete "Jake" by mistake. He'd kept it up ever since; it was a kind of signal to Pete that he was in a good mood and wanted something better than beer or bar whiskey. He sometimes wondered if anybody ever walked into Jake's bar and called him Pete by mistake. Henry took the middle one of three empty barstools. Jake—Pete—lifted a bottle of VSOP, raised his eyebrows, and Henry nodded. Right on the button.

The bar was nearly empty, not surprising; Tuesday, a working night, only six or seven customers, faces all familiar, mostly old-timers on relief. Pete's cats scrubbed and stalked, sulked and slept. A neighborhood B-girl named Hettie, old friend of Henry's, put money in the jukebox—old-time country love songs. Nostalgia was the main vice here. Pete toweled dust from a snifter, poured a finger of cognac into it. "How's the work going, Mr. Waugh?" he asked.

"Couldn't go better," Henry said and smiled. Jake always asked the right questions.

Jake smiled broadly, creasing his full cheeks, nodded as though to say he understood, pate flashing in the amber light. And it was the right night to call him Jake, after all: Jake Bradley was also from the Brock Rutherford era, must have come up about the same time. Was he calling it that now? The Brock Rutherford Era? He never had before. Funny. Damon was not only creating the future, he was doing something to the past, too. Jake dusted the shelf before putting the cognac bottle back. He was once the middle man in five double plays executed in one game, still the Association record.

Hettie, catching Henry's mood apparently, came over to kid with him and he bought her a drink. A couple molars missing and flesh folds ruining the once-fine shape of her jaw, but there was still something compelling about that electronic bleat her stockings emitted when she hopped up on a barstool and crossed her legs, and that punctuation-wink she used to let a man know he was in with her, getting the true and untarnished word. Henry hadn't gone with her in years, not since before he set up his Association, but she often figured obliquely in the Book and conversations with her often got reproduced there under one guise or another. "Been gettin' any hits lately?" she asked, and winked over her tumbler of whiskey. They often used baseball idiom, she no doubt supposing he was one of those ball-park zealots who went crazy every season during the World Series and got written up as a character—the perennial crank—in the newspapers, and Henry never told her otherwise. Since she herself knew nothing at all about the sport, though, he often talked about his Association as though it were the major leagues. It gave him a kind of pleasure to talk about it with someone, even if she did think he was talking about something else.

"Been getting a lot," he said, "but probably not enough." She laughed loudly, exhibiting the gaps in her teeth. "And how about you, Hettie, been scoring a lot of runs?"

"I been scorin', boy, but I ain't got the runs!" she said, and whooped again. Old gag. The other customers turned their way and smiled.

Henry waited for her to settle down, commune with her drink once more, then he said, "Listen, Hettie, think what a wonderful rare thing it is to do something, no matter how small a thing, with absolute unqualified utterly unsurpassable *perfection!*"

"What makes you think it's so rare?" she asked with a wink, and switching top knee, issued the old signal. "You ain't pitched to me in a long time, you know."

He grinned. "No, but think of it, Hettie, to do a thing so perfectly that, even if the damn world lasted forever, nobody could ever do it better, because you had done it as well as it could possibly be done." He paused, let the cognac fumes bite his nostrils to excuse the foolish tears threatening to film his eyes over. "In a way, you know, it's even sad somehow, because, well, it's done, and all you can hope for after is to do it a second time." Of course, there were other things to do, the record book was, above all, a catalogue of possibilities . . .

"A second time! Did you say *perfection* or *erection?*" Hettie asked.

Henry laughed. It was no use. And anyway it didn't matter. He felt just stupendous, not so exultant as before, but still full of joy; and now a kind of heady aromatic peace seemed to be sweeping over him: ecstasy—yes, he laughed to himself, that was the only goddamn word for it. It was good. He bought another round, asked Pete: "How is it you stay in such good shape, Jake?"

"I don't know, Mr. Waugh. Must be the good Christian hours I keep."

And then, when the barkeep had left them, it was Hettie who suddenly turned serious. "I don't know what it is about you tonight, Henry," she said, "but you've got me kinda hot." And she switched top knee again: call from the deep.

Henry smiled, slowly whirling the snifter through minute cycles, warming the tawny dram in the palm of his hand. It was a temptation, to be sure, but he was afraid Hettie would spoil it for him, dissipate the joy and dull this glow, take the glory out of it. It was something he could share with no one without losing it altogether. Too bad. "It's just that nobody's bought you two straight drinks in a long time, Hettie," he said.

"Aw," she grumbled and frowned at her glass, hurt by that and so cooled off a little. To make up for it, he ordered her a third drink. He'd had enough, time to get back, had to make it to work in the morning, old Zifferblatt had been giving him a hard time for weeks now and was just looking for a chance to raise hell about something, but Pete poured him one on the house. Not every day you pitched perfect games and got VSOP on the house. "Thanks, Jake," he said.

"Henry, hon', gimme some money to put in the jukebox."

Coins on the bar: he slid them her way. Stared into his snifter, saw himself there in the brown puddle, or anyway his eye.

> It was down in Jake's old barroom
> Behind the Patsies' park;
> Jake was settin' 'em up as usual
> And the night was agittin' dark.
> At the bar stood ole Verne Mackenzie,
> And his eyes was bloodshot red . . .

"The Day They Fired Verne Mackenzie": Sandy Shaw's great ballad. Dead now, Verne. First of the game's superstars, starting shortstop on Abe Flint's Excelsiors back in Year I, first of the Hall of Famers. But he got older and stopped hitting, and Flint, nice a guy as he was, had to let him go. And they all knew how Verne felt, even the young guys playing now who never knew him, because sooner or later it would be the same for them. Hettie leaned against him, head on his shoulder, humming the jukebox melodies to herself. He felt good, having her there like that. He sipped his brandy and grew slowly melancholy, *pleasantly* melancholy. He saw Brock the Great reeling boisterously down the street, arm in arm with Willie O'Leary and Frosty Young, those wonderful guys—and who should they meet up with but sleepy-eyed Mose Stanford and Gabe Burdette and crazy rubber-legged Jaybird Wall. Yes, and they were singing, singing the *old* songs, "Pitchin', Catchin', Swingin'" and "The Happy Days of Youth," and oh! it was happiness! and goddamn it! it was fellowship! and boys oh boys! it was significance! "Let's go to Jake's!" they cried, they laughed, and off they went!

"Where?" Hettie mumbled. She was pretty far along. So was he. Didn't realize he had been talking out loud. Glanced self-consciously at Pete, but Pete hadn't moved: he was a patient pillar in the middle of the bar, ankles and arms crossed, face in shadows, only the dome lit up. Maybe he was asleep. There was only one other customer, an old-timer, still in the bar. The neon light outside was probably off.

"To my place," he said, not sure it was himself talking. Could he take her up there? She leaned away from his shoulder, tried to wink, couldn't quite pull it off, instead studied him quizzically as though wondering if he really meant it. "Hettie," he whispered, staring hard at her, so she'd know he wasn't kidding and that she'd better not spoil it, "how would you like to sleep with . . . Damon Rutherford?"

She blinked, squinted skeptically, but he could see she was still pretty excited and she'd moved her hand up his pantleg to the seam. "Who's he?"

"Me." He didn't smile, just looked straight at her, and he saw her eyes widen, maybe even a little fear came into them, but certainly awe was there, and fascination, and hope, and her hand, discovering he could do it, yes, he could do it, gave a squeeze like Witness York always gave his bat for luck before he swung, and she switched knees: *wheep!* So he paid Jake, and to-gether—he standing tall and self-assured, Hettie shiveringly clasped in his embrace—they walked out. As he'd foreseen, the neon light was out; it was dark. He felt exceedingly wise.

"What are you, Henry?" Hettie asked softly as they walked under the glow-ing nimbus of a mist-wrapped street lamp. His raincoat had a slit in the lining behind the pocket, and this she reached through to slip her hand into his coin pocket.

"Now, or when we get to my place?"

"Now."

"An accountant."

"But the baseball . . . ?" And again she took hold and squeezed like Wit-ness York, but now her hand was full of coins as well, and they wrapped the bat like a suit of mail.

"I'm an auditor for a baseball association."

"I didn't know they had auditors, too," she said. Was she really listening for once? They were in the dark now, next street lamp was nearly a block away, in front of Diskin's. She was trying to get her other hand on the bat, gal can't take a healthy swing without a decent grip, after all, but she couldn't get both hands through the slit.

"Oh, yes. I keep financial ledgers for each club, showing cash receipts and disbursements, which depend mainly on such things as team success, the buy-ing and selling of ballplayers, improvement of the stadiums, player contracts, things like that." Hettie Irden stood at the plate, first woman ballplayer in league history, tightening and relaxing her grip on the bat, smiling around the spaces of her missing molars in that unforgettable way of hers, kidding with the catcher, laughing that gay timeless laugh that sounded like the clash of small coins, tugging maybe at her crotch in a parody of all male ballplayers the world over, and maybe she wasn't the best hitter in the Association, but the Association was glad to have her. She made them all laugh and forget for a moment that they were dying men. "And a running journalization of the activity, posting of it all into permanent record books, and I help them with basic problems of burden distribution, remarshaling of assets, graphing fluc-tuations. Politics, too. Elections. Team captains. Club presidents. And every four years, the Association elects a Chancellor, and I have to keep an eye on that."

"Gee, Henry, I didn't realize . . . !" She was looking up at him, and as they approached the street lamp, he could see something in her eyes he hadn't

seen there before. He was glad to see it had come to pass, that she recognized—
but it wouldn't do when they got to bed, she'd have to forget then.

"There are box scores to be audited, trial balances of averages along the
way, seasonal inventories, rewards and punishments to be meted out, life histories to be overseen." He took a grip on her behind. "People die, you know."

"Yes," she said, and that seemed to excite her, for she squeezed a little
harder.

"Usually, they die old, already long since retired, but they can die young,
even as ballplayers. Or in accidents during the winter season. Last year a
young fellow, just thirty, had a bad season and got sent back to the minors.
They say his manager rode him too hard." Pappy Rooney. Wouldn't let go of
the kid. "Sensitive boy who took it too much to heart. On the way, he drove
his car off a cliff."

"Oh!" she gasped and squeezed. As though afraid now to let go. "On
purpose?"

"I don't know. I think so. And if a pitcher throws two straight triple ones
or sixes and brings on an Extraordinary Occurrence, a third set of ones is a
bean ball that kills the batter, while triple sixes again is a line drive that kills
the pitcher."

"Oh, how awful!" He didn't tell her neither had ever happened. "But what
are triple sixes, Henry?"

"A kind of pitch. Here we are."

Even climbing the stairs to his place, she didn't want to release her grip,
but the stairway was too narrow and they kept jamming up. So she took her
hand out and went first. From his squat behind the box, the catcher watched
her loosening up, kidded her that she'd never get a walk because they could
never get two balls on her. Over her shoulder, she grinned down upon him, a
gap-tooth grin that was still somehow beautiful. Anyhow, she said, I *am* an
Extraordinary Occurrence, and on that chart there's no place for mere passes!
The catcher laughed, reached up and patted her rear. "You said it!" he admitted, letting his hand glide down her thigh, then whistle up her stocking underneath the skirt. "An Extraordinary Occurrence!"

She hopped two steps giddily, thighs slapping together. "Henry! I'm
ticklish!"

He unlocked the door to his apartment, switched on a night light in the
hall, leaving the kitchen and Association in protective darkness, and led her
toward the bedroom.

"We're at your place," she said huskily when they'd got in there, and
squeezed up against him. "Who are you now?" That she remembered! She
was wonderful!

"The greatest pitcher in the history of baseball," he whispered. "Call me . . . Damon."

"Damon," she whispered, unbuckling his pants, pulling his shirt out. And "Damon," she sighed, stroking his back, unzipping his fly, sending his pants earthward with a rattle of buckles and coins. And "Damon!" she greeted, grabbing—and that girl, with one swing, he knew then, could bang a pitch clean out of the park. "*Play ball!*" cried the umpire. And the catcher, stripped of mask and guard, revealed as the pitcher Damon Rutherford, whipped the uniform off the first lady ballplayer in Association history, and then, helping and hindering all at once, pushing and pulling, they ran the bases, pounded into first, slid into second heels high, somersaulted over third, shot home standing up, then into the box once more, swing away, and run them all again, and "Damon!" she cried, and "Damon!"

SAM KOPERWAS

Ball

A flower grows for every drop of rain that falls. Don't tell me no. In the middle of the darkest night, there is still a candle that is glowing. This I believe. *Glowing.* If a lost person wanders in the street, somebody will come along to find the way for him. I would swear it on bibles. I *believe.*

It is my son who does not believe.

He stands in front of me, six-five. His arms hang down to his knees, to his ankles. You don't know how much I love him, my boy. I jump up to hug him. I press my face into his chest.

"You're a basketball player," I yell up to him. "Become a Knickerbocker, son. Listen to your father. Be a Piston, a Pacer."

I stuff vitamins into all his openings. In the house he has to wear lead weights under his socks if he wants to eat.

My son hates a basketball.

He reads books about blood circulation and heart conditions. Set shots he doesn't want to know from. I have to twist the boy's arm before he'll stand up straight.

Originally appeared in *Esquire* (1975).

"Floods wiped out a village in Pakistan," he cries to me. His shoulders slump like rooftops caving in. "Puerto Ricans push carts in the gutter. Beaches are polluted. Where has the buffalo gone?"

"Grow up!" I shout. "What kind of talk is this from a boy? Play basketball and make money. Practice sky hooks. Forget floods, forget buffalo—you're not even a teen-ager yet. What I want from you are slam dunks. God made you tall. Run! Dribble!"

"Pop," he sobs to me.

"My boy," I say.

The kitchen tells the story. A history book of inches and feet is here. Growth is here, all the measurements right from the start.

"This is you," I holler. I point to pencil scratches on a leg of the kitchen table. "Right from the hospital I stood you up on those fabulous legs of yours."

I touch one mark after another. Tallness, like a beautiful beanstalk, climbs up the broom closet, up the refrigerator, a ladder of height. The inches add up, interest in the bank.

The boy stoops over. These measurements are making him sick. He takes his size like you take a ticket for speeding.

"I can't, Dad. Rapists and inflation and tumors are everywhere."

I grab the boy by the arm. I pull him to the refrigerator, push him against the door, stand him up tall. I point with a father's finger to faint key scratches on the door.

"Nursery school!" I scream. "Right here, son. What a smoothy you were, what a natural. Slop from the table you palmed with either hand. This is your father talking to you. When I cut your bites too big to finish, swish in the garbage bag you dunked them. I saw an athlete, son. I saw a millionaire."

My boy shuts his eyes. He sees stethoscopes behind them. I see basketballs.

The do-gooder, he refuses to shoot basketballs. Instead, he reaches for the encyclopedia. My son curls up to read.

Six-six, and growing every day like good stocks. This is an athlete. This is handsome, long and tall, and getting big and getting bigger.

I give him rabbit punches in the kidneys.

"Son," I explain to him.

"Dad," he mumbles.

I take my boy to the school yard. Above us is a basket. I point.

"Here is a ball. Shoot it!" I shout.

My son looks at the ball in his hands. Then he looks down at me.

"I can't, Pop."

Tears plip on his huge sneakers.

"I don't see little rubber bumps, Dad. I see faces of tiny orphans all over the world. Instead of black lines I see segregation and the bald eagle that's becoming extinct. I see unhappiness and things that have to be stitched back together."

He drops the ball, klunk.

I chase after the ball. My boy runs next to me. Frazier does not run smoother, believe me. It breaks my heart.

I bounce the ball to my son and it hits his stomach. He doesn't move the hands that could squash watermelons.

"Wilt Chamberlain has a swimming pool in his house!" I scream up to the boy. "Your father is talking to you. In the *house!*"

Closer to six-eight than to six-seven and larger every day, every day shooting up like the price of gold. I need a chair to measure him.

"I won't play basketball," he cries to me. "I want to be something. A heart surgeon. I have to help people. How can I play basketball after what we've done to the Navaho and the Cherokee?"

I reach up and grab the boy's ear. I drag him to the basket. I shove the ball into his hands.

"Shoot!" I yell. "Stuff it in! Dribble like Maravich. This is your father speaking to you. Spin the ball on a finger. Make it roll down your arms and behind your neck. Score baskets, son! Make money. Bring scouts. Bring Red Holzman. I want contracts on the doorstep, I want promises."

I stand toe to toe with the boy, nose to stomach.

I slam the ball into his belly.

"Son," I whisper.

"Pop," he moans.

You should eat an apple every day. This is a proven fact. Every prayer that comes out of your mouth gets listened to. This also is proven. Nobody can tell me different. Somebody up there hears every single word. Argue and I'll slap your eyes out. We live in the land of opportunity.

My boy will be a basketball player.

I slip the ball into his bed at night. I put it on the pillow next to his big sad face.

The boy opens his eyes. They are round, like hoops.

"Dad."

"Son."

Under his bed there are electric basketball games covered with dust. Coloring books of basketball players turn yellow in his closet. Basketball pajamas the boy has outgrown I will never throw away.

"Dad."

"Son."

I am with him at the table when he eats. I love the boy. I marvel at his appetite, whole shipments he packs away. My son can shovel it in. Lamb chops I set before him with gladness. My eyes are tears when he clears the table, the hamburgers and the shakes and the fries. I make him drink milk. Inside, he is oceans of milk.

"Eat!" I scream. "Get tall and taller. Grow to the skies."

My son rips through new sneakers every two weeks. Owners, managers, franchisers would kill for him right now.

"People starve," the boy says. "There are earthquakes in Peru that don't let me sleep nights. Squirrels are catching cold in the park. Drug addicts and retarded children walk the streets."

My flesh and blood weeps before me, my oil well. Cuffs never make it past the boy's ankles. In less than a week any sleeve retreats from his wrists.

"I'm not even thirteen," he sobs. "There's so much to do. Workers without unions get laid off. Every day the earth falls a little closer into the sun. Kidneys fail. I don't know what to do, Pop. Mexicans get gassed. Puppies have to pick grapes."

I run over to the boy. He stoops to hug me.

"You're hot property," I shriek up to him. "Listen to your father. You're land in Florida, son. Scoop shots and pivots. I'm your father. Bounce passes and free throws. Listen to me."

I run to the bedroom. I drop the ball at his feet.

"Look, son. Red, white, and blue. What more could a boy ask for?"

He doesn't pick it up. I have to put the ball in his arms. He cries. He lets the ball drop to the floor. Tears pour down on me from above.

"Son," I say.

"Pop," he says.

I lead my boy to a gymnasium. I push him under a basket.

"Turn-around jumpers and tip-ins," I shout up. "That's what I want from you. I want rebounds."

"Please, Pop."

"You're just a boy," I beg. "Listen to your father."

I hold the ball out for him to take.

"Pop," he says.

"Son," I say.

He takes the ball.

A baby cries and I am moved. A leaf gets touched and I melt. A son bends to take a ball from his father's hands, and . . . I . . . know . . . why . . . I . . . believe.

My son *spins* the ball. My son *eyes* the seams. My son *pats* the ball. My son *tests* the weight.

"I don't know, Pop."

I reach up a fatherly hand. I tap my boy on the chest.

"Factories murder the air. Russians steal fish."

"It was meant for you, son. Try it."

My son drops the ball with just a hint of English and it comes right back to him. He spins the ball again. It bounces back.

My son smiles.

He performs, he does tricks, he experiments. The kid is Benjamin Franklin with a kite, Columbus with a boat. Tears run from our eyes. This is an athlete in front of me. He is happy and tall.

My son is bouncing the ball.

I point to the net. He squeezes the ball. He shakes it. He shoots.

Swish.

My son makes baskets. Shot after shot, swish.

I love him. He sinks hook shots, jumpers from half court.

"Dad," he shouts.

"My boy," I scream.

He stands up tall. He tosses in baskets from everywhere. He reaches up and drops it through. He holds it with the fingertips of one hand. My six-tenner, he dunks it backward.

He runs, he jumps. He grows. His shoulders straighten, knees straighten. My son is a tree.

He zooms up taller, my seven-footer. I love him. He is enormous.

Buttons pop. The boy tears through his clothing. He grows taller. He throws it in with his eyes closed. His head grows over the rim, over the backboard. His fingers reach from one end of the court to the other.

"Son," I call up to him.

"Pop, Pop, Pop."

He grows taller still. He blasts through the ceiling. My son stands tall and naked. His head is in the sky. I love him, my monster.

He pushes himself up higher. He skyrockets above us. The boy is taller than buildings, bigger than mountains.

"Son," I call.

"Pop, Pop, Pop," he bellows from afar.

The boy is gigantic.

He pushes aside skyscrapers. He swallows clouds. He grows. He swats airplanes from the sky with either hand, crushes them between his fingers. He blots out the light.

My son keeps growing. There is thunder when he speaks, an earthquake when he moves. People die.

The boy grows and grows.

"Son," I sob.

"Pop, Pop, Pop!"

He grows in the sky. He stretches to the sun. My boy leaps past stars.

"Pop, Pop, Pop!"

But it is no longer a human voice I hear from the heavens. When my son speaks, it is the crashing of meteors, the four corners of the galaxy wheeling, wheeling, wheeling toward that outer horizon where the Titans themselves lob a furious ball in lethal play, and the score is always climbing. It is the playground where suns and moons careen in hopeless patterns. It is a void where victors hold frivolous service and cause thunder with tenpins, where old men shower the rain with unholy weeping, where solar systems are deployed in the secondary and every atom is a knuckle ball.

In this I sadly believe.

"Son," I say.

"Pop."

The boy is beside me. He is a good boy, a boy who wants to help people: he is young. This boy knows compassion, tenderness, genetics. His head is not in the clouds.

I buy microscope sets for him, medical journals. I bring home tongue depressors for the boy. We dissect frogs together. We cure diseases.

"I've seen things, Dad," he tells me. "My eyes have been opened."

"We'll make remedies, son. You'll heal the sick, comfort the needy."

"I can't explain it, Dad. It's all more than a basketball."

"You'll patch holes in the earth, son. You'll feed Biafrans, help birds fly south in winter. You'll bring peace to the Mideast, equal rights to women."

My son spins the ball in front of him. My son eyes the seams. My son pats the ball. My son tests the weight.

"You'll plug up radium leaks, son, solve busing problems. You'll put the business to venereal disease. You'll grow bananas that don't spoil. Listen to me. You'll invent cars that don't shrink, cotton goods that run on water. I am your father."

The boy does not hear. Nobody does. Babies are born every second and every one of them cries. Leaves by the millions turn brown in the street. The sky is all poisonous particles.

"Son."

"Dad?"

He shoots the ball at a basket. *Swish.* He spins them in off the backboard. *Swish.* Flips from corners. *Swish.*

I clutch at my chest.

"Here comes a lefty hook, Pop."

Swish.

I collapse at his feet. The boy looms over me. Cancers strike at my vitals.

Seizures grip me. Plagues and pestilence and uncertainty flood my veins. Pandora's box breaks open in my heart.

My son looks down at me. He twirls the ball on a terrible finger. I look up at a son whose hands could cradle nations.

"Son," I beg.

"Not now, Pop."

He bounces the ball on my stomach. Once, twice, three times for luck. He dribbles between his legs, behind his back. My son flies to the basket. My son soars to his laurels over my dead body.

LAURENCE LIEBERMAN

My Father Dreams of Baseball

On hot September nights, when sleep is scarce,
in place of sheep Dad counts home runs that carry
the left-field fence and fly clean out of the ball park.

    Father snaps off the twi-night doubleheader.
    Behind his back, the screen door loosens a hinge.
    He escapes to the backyard retreat to rant at the ump.
    Hopped-up in the Porsche, he's off for an all-night binge.
    By morning, Mother's throat has a telltale lump.
    He takes his losses hard, a heavy bettor.

In his dreams, white dashing figures circle the bases.
Their caps dazzle in the sun like lights on a scoreboard.
The diamond is worn a foot deep under hammering cleats.

    He attends home games. Through Dad's binoculars
    the power hitters charge home plate like bulls,
    and make the picador pitcher's heart stand still.
    (A curve ball is a lance that bull's-eyes skulls.)

From *The Unblinding* (1968). Originally appeared in *The Atlantic Monthly* (1963).

My father in the stands directs the kill
like a black matador in Madrid spectaculars.

Just inches inside the foul line, a figure is poised
three feet in the air, his arm outstretched for the catch.
His mouth is pinched with the pain of a near-miss.
The features are fixed with the dull metallic glow
of an ancient face, cast in bronze or brass.

JIM BROSNAN

The Fantasy World of Baseball

The public, even the private, lives of major league ball players are an open book. Writers dissect the players, biographers idolatrize them, psychologists study them. They are cheered for winning, booed for losing; they are loved or hated in equal, and equally irrational, measure; they are objects of devotion, amusement, pity, scorn.

What, on the other hand, is a fan? Which one of them in his seat in the stands cheers, and why? Who boos? What, after all, is he doing up there, playing *his* game?

Charles Comiskey, a legendary baseball figure, first called clubhouse visitors "fanatics," and Ty Cobb called fans "bugs," a scurrilous slang synonym for "zealot" or "enthusiast." Cobb occasionally rushed into the grandstands to stamp his opinion on the face of the customer who criticized his play. Fans, thus subdued, lose some of their original character.

In the word world "extravagant fancy" pinch-hits for "fantastic." A fantastic mental image is a substitute fantasy. Those persons who derive pleasure and pain, frustration and gratification, from vicarious participation in professional sports live, for such moments, in a world of their own. In pursuit of an unattainable happiness they create a fantasy world.

The professional baseball fan is an American cultural phenomenon. His fund of quotable statistics, his trove of memorable traditions, his collections

---

Originally appeared in *The Atlantic Monthly* (1964).

of valueless mementos comprise a mine of guilt-edged insecurity. Although he can neither do nor teach, he regards himself as a player-coach.

The average baseball fan, according to surveys of one professional club, attends two or three games per season. His infrequent actual attendance does not preclude a wholehearted daily interest. Fostered by the promotional genius of Organized Baseball, interest in the game between May and October each year becomes a preoccupation with most Americans. Radio, television, newspapers and magazines, barroom and living room conversations feed the fan's obsession with the intimate experiences of five hundred major league athletes. No other sport exerts so much influence with so much trivia on persons who have so little personal involvement in the whole affair.

To the fierce, ardent, leather-lunged professional fan, baseball is life itself, a motive for breathing, the yeast that helps his spirit, as well as his gorge, rise.

Fans are made, not born. Interest in baseball starts in childhood and reaches its peak in puberty. Acquaintance with rules of play is a definite perquisite but not a prerequisite for being a fan. Everyone can talk about baseball, the fan assumes, because he *ought to know* something about the game.

The fan, whether or not he identifies with the players and thus vicariously participates in the game, is free to take pleasure in losing most of his inhibitions—to shout, wave his arms, jump up and down. He may criticize umpires, players, and even the hot dog vendors without incurring responsibility for his emotional outburst. "Much of the discharge of energy and the sense of participation in baseball," says Social Research, which has made a psychological study of the game, "is gained vocally."

Baseball as a ritual has no deep and mystical meaning. It depends upon personalities to maintain the fanatic fervor of the fancy. Fans want the player to be not what he inherently is but what they think he ought to be. Even the moderately indifferent fan, according to Social Research, thinks that "the players owe it to their public to set good examples." Ball players, as representatives of all baseball virtues, are considered to be healthy and vigorous humans, virile and skillful men, friendly and approachable fellows. They deserve idolatrization, and whether they like it or not, they sometimes get it.

Ardent baseball fans come in two emotional sizes. The preternaturally optimistic fan assumes that any big league ball player is a good, true, clean-living, home-loving American boy. The negative fan, subconsciously concerned that baseball is just a game, feels that major leaguers must be essentially immature adolescents, juvenile delinquents in social responsibility, and therefore proper objects of scornful criticism.

The fan club, a half-noteworthy institution, attests to the idealization practiced by active, positive fans. A major league fan club is frequently formulated in the passionate thoughts of pre-teen-age girls. Any ball player who has had two headline notices in a metropolitan newspaper can expect one request from a chubby-cheeked girl to start a fan club in his name. The zealous enthusiasm with which this jean-clad vestal virgin pursues her personal idolatrization depends upon the player's reaction, which may run the gamut from indifference to embarrassment. It is a rare young athlete who sits comfortably on a pedestal.

In Wichita, Kansas, an organization calling itself the National Baseball Fan's Club suggests that the "distinguished individuals" who are members of the NBFC "play a conspicuous and active part in baseball." Activity apparently includes the wearing of emblems, the reading of rules and statistics, and the paying of five dollars for the privilege. The NBFC is two years old, and its commercial success would seem to be limited. The abstract "baseball" would not appear to have the appeal of the flesh-and-bone baseball player.

The most unusual, and without a doubt the jolliest, fan club of baseball history is devoted to an extinct organization, a team with no live ball players. The St. Louis Browns' Fan Club was created on the day the team disbanded.

Bill Veeck, the man who put the team out of business, once said: "I found out the Brown fans were a myth. You heard about 'em, but you never saw 'em." As owner of the Browns, Veeck had searched river bottom and wheatland in and around St. Louis for customer-fans. Unfortunately for him they were in Chicago, where they paid the White Sox a nominal fee for bleacher tickets. There they cheered for the Browns, who epitomized the All-American underdog.

"They needed us," says Bill Leonard, a charter member of the SLBFC and a columnist for the Chicago *Tribune*. "They didn't have anything else."

On the last weekend of the 1953 baseball season the SLBFC traveled to St. Louis to see the final games played by the Browns.

"They lost," wrote Leonard. "We were unsurprised and undaunted."

Today the SLBFC carries on its motto: "To perpetuate the proud name of the St. Louis Browns, file progress reports on the reincarnation of the Browns, drink toasts in nut-brown ale, and maintain jolly times."

As fans, they're out of this world.

The simplicity of motivation in the Inner Fan distinguishes him from the millions. His single-minded desire to seek absolute identification with the player demonstrates high purpose if not poverty of imagination. His inability to establish communication with the player causes elemental frustration. He quickly, naturally, assumes grandstand leadership of the jowly, unathletic loudmouths who cluster in bunches—sour gripes, yelling and cursing at men working.

Consider Off-side Smitty.

To the National League ball players who work in the northeast corner of Connie Mack Stadium in Philadelphia, the voice of the average fan belongs to a man named Smith. Philadelphia bleacherites are a raucous breed, sensitive to player performances, their critical appreciation sounded from the bottom of their hearts.

The bass bawl of Off-side Smitty is particularly penetrating. An ex-soccer player who apparently could not control his enthusiasm in that sport either, Off-side Smitty has the face of a losing pugilist, an encyclopedic memory for player names and performances, and an attendance record of awesome breadth. Off-side never misses a game.

Smitty's persistence has the quality of desperate affability. His nagging, sometimes profane, judgments beg for an explanation, consideration, understanding.

"How can you be such a bum, you bum!" he yells, saying to himself simultaneously, "How can you disappoint me who loves you and wants you to be good!"

Smitty occasionally gets a response from the player, a malicious rebound from a pride-thick hide that reacts only to Smitty's needle. Gracelessly, Smitty smarts under player-voiced needling. A tormentor tormented, he wilts in a cross fire of personal insults.

"Meet me outside after the game, you—!" he eventually yells. Then he exits during the seventh inning, unwilling or too old to stretch his acquaintanceship. Back he comes the next day, evincing his Fan's True Love. The harder he's hit, the harder he falls.

The Inner Fan projects the Ideal Ball Player and begs every fumbling, fallible major leaguer to emulate that image.

Consider Dirty Louie.

The knowledgeable New York City baseball fan is the wisest of them all. He watches, he studies, he pursues the game like a philosopher seeking the truth. Disenchantment with any play or player can turn him into a crank. (Primitive baseball fans were called "cranks," whether they got wound up by baseball or not.)

Dirty Louie is a massive man, three hundred pounds of wisecracking fan. He would rather watch baseball than bathe. His creative and often funny critical comments would please his chosen audience—ball players who work at either New York stadium—if he had a cleaner delivery. (In the old Polo Grounds, Louie was once showered with packaged soap bars by a bullpen crew whose names were mud from then on, the way Louie told it.)

Rumor has it that Louie carries a large salami in one pocket of his dirty gray overcoat, the better to spice his vitriol. In a grandiloquent voice he spews kosher comment on fumbles, foul balls, and other futile efforts of what he calls bush leaguers. Any major leaguer who is not dead or in baseball's Hall of Fame is a busher to Louie.

Dirty Louie has no close followers among other fans. He is a lonesome prophet, hailing a redeemer who will swing like Babe Ruth, throw like Christy Mathewson, and run like Ty Cobb.

The Inner Fan wants the game played as he thinks it *should* be played. He will create players in his own image—a man making gods—to assure a good sport.

Consider Jack Barron.

In southern California the sun is hot and refreshments are often stimulants because water is scarce. On the dusty playground of his own imagination Jack Barron is revolutionizing baseball techniques. He has invented, so far, the Cosmic Swing and the Astro-Naut Pitch, two developments which will do for baseball what the White Queen did for logic. Barron has for years conducted a campaign for scientific progress, for an investigation of corporate ownership and slave labor in baseball, and for a place in the game for his son who, dutiful boy, believes in Daddy.

Many fans, experts with free advice, write to ball players during the season. They counsel pitchers, correct batting stances, offer tips on proper training and sermons on moral living. Jack Barron mimeographs pages of wisdom, reams of good counsel, and he has even published books to improve the game.

Barron would like to reorganize Organized Baseball, with the help of God, the Internal Revenue Service, and J. Edgar Hoover (who claims he's not interested). The moguls of O. B. tend to disregard True Fan Barron, who professes progress and illustrates his theme by teaching pros how to throw a ball and swing a bat.

"The Astro-Naut Pitch," says Coach Barron, "starts in the head. The pitcher thinks through his spinal cord down to his feet and up through his back. The spine is his axis and the back muscles have got to flip off the hip action. His gut is tight to his belt and flexed for ballast and free intake and deflation of air. When he makes a decision to unload, his back will flip out of the coil—like a pair of wrists off the hip action."

Most professionals can't see this pitch, though it literally seems fantastic.

The Cosmic Swing depends on a batter's ability to coil and uncoil gyroscopically into the back swing and out.

"Adjust your thinking so that the legs accept tension and rebound through the back. Pinch your buttocks and brace your hip off the back swing and allow your topside to idle circlewise for a good look. Your front foot will trigger a rising thrust from shoulder and back muscles and the shoulder blades. Your arms will rise and orbit the ball like a cat's paw."

Duke Snider, a clean-living, home-loving, all too approachable big league star, agreed publicly to try Barron's swinging theories. The Los Angeles Dodgers, unamused, sold Snider to the Mets, a unique baseball club that has many far-out fans of its own in faraway New York.

The Inner Fan spurns fealty to one team. He grudgingly responds to the plea: "Support your home town Tigers!"

Loyalty to the Team is more directly applicable to undergraduate and alumni audiences. Organized Baseball businessmen do better when they sell Baseball as an institution and Baseball Players as personalities.

One Houston business executive was delighted when the Texas metropolis first obtained a big league franchise. He bought a box seat ticket, "because I'm a baseball fan and I wanted to prove that Houston could support the Colts." He attended most of the home games in more or less silent approval of an unexciting, losing team. During the second season his fancy turned to more basic fulfillment.

"I kept my mouth shut for one whole year. But now I've got to let myself go. If I didn't have the Colts' third baseman to yell at I don't know what I'd do." He seldom missed a game that season either.

Pen-in-hand baseball fans frequently express their personal regard for the professionals who give them pleasure. Along with thousands of letters from adolescents who wish to exchange flattery for autographed mementos come such sympathetic analyses of fan-observing fans:

> Only maladjusted people yell and holler at the ball players on the field. Usually they are insolent persons anyway, or intoxicated, drunk, stoned, or cracked. Personally I never plan to boo or yell at ball players. That is *extremely rude!*

Or the quizzical note:

> Maybe ball players don't expect respect from fans. That couldn't be possible! (Could it?)

Most fan mail is favorable and not always favor-requesting. Occasionally a male fan offers to help the struggling young athlete and promises at the same time to attend future efforts of the player if he will just pay attention:

I was thinking for a long time if I should do this then I thought no harm can come. What I was trying to tell is by bending the first finger at the knuckle and holding the ball throwing it as a fast ball you will get a good sinker and the *slower* you throw it the *bigger* the sinker. Tell everybody to do this and the next time you are pitching I will be there to see that you are using this pitch.

The out-and-out negative correspondents reveal by their handwriting evidence of disturbed minds. Big letters, rambling script, disconnected sentences full of nonsense. My own favorite closing paragraphs from a decade of fan mail collecting are these:

You were my favorite player last season. What's wrong with you this year. YOUR A BUM TIL YOU START WINNING!
(Signed) Your fan

And:

What's more you don't even know how to spell your own name!
(Signed) W. J. Bresnahan

It was inevitable, I suppose, that the fan's wish to be a ball player should find, as a correlation, an equal duty for the player to be the fan.

Times have changed, and the factors which created the world of the baseball fan may be losing significance. Self-reliance, the leit-motiv of the late nineteenth-, early twentieth-century American, is no longer the prime ethic of American culture. Now the emphasis is on standardization—of personal ambition, performance, and morality.

Baseball is unique among team sports in its glorification of the individual, his opportunity to excel being limited only by his willingness to cooperate in a lawfully delineated competition. As a spectacle, baseball owes its popularity in great measure to the way it satisfies psychic needs. The spectator receives his wish fulfillment through identification with the player in action rather than through the action itself.

But the major league ball player himself sometimes contributes to the desecration of his image as a special sort of folk hero. His public preoccupation with future security in the form of a valuable early retirement pension makes him a mere transient idol. He prefers business contacts to the camaraderie of fans. Instead of endorsing Mother, the Flag, and Little Leaguers, he promotes merchandise on national television that makes him no more than equal to the average shaver, BO sufferer, or fungus-footed shoe clerk.

The world of baseball is fan-made. The fan's interest is sentimental in the sense that sentimentality is an emotion in excess of its cause. His interest is also coincidental, for baseball just happens to offer the best means to obtain a wishful end. The tensions of a changing world may reproduce new symptom formations. The neurotic compromise that the fan makes between his interest in baseball and his inability to attain absolute pleasure from it could produce a regressive turn to other sports. Like football, that bloody game.

ROLAND GARRETT

The Metaphysics of Baseball

It may appear strange to find the two words "baseball" and "metaphysics" joined in the title of a single essay. Baseball is ordinarily an affair of the schoolyard, stadium, or television set. It seems to be a matter of physical exercise or leisure, at most a local event of history and culture. Metaphysics, on the other hand, is viewed as a complex of ideas, books, and rugged formal education, always searching for greater levels of abstraction and generality. To join the two topics may seem like mixing oil with water, or the department of physical education with the department of philosophy. Even oil and water can be mixed, however—with soap. If we clarify and, as it were, cleanse our thinking, then we will see that the knowledge of metaphysics and the knowledge of baseball can contribute to one another.

The point I will try to establish is quite simple. But perhaps the issues will be clearer if we follow philosophical tradition and begin with a commentary on the meanings of words. We do not need precise definitions of either the word "baseball" or the word "metaphysics." But a brief discussion of their meanings will illuminate our inquiry.

Metaphysics has, as its subject-matter, reality in general. It asks questions about the nature of reality, the fundamental types of real things, and the general traits which distinguish the basic types or are shared by all. In the development of metaphysics, many familiar concepts and distinctions have become important, including those of unity and plurality; appearance; form and matter; possibility and actuality; space and time; relation, order, change, and

Originally appeared in *Philosophy Today* (1976).

causation. As these concepts are used and developed to describe more specialized subjects, we often find a sort of applied metaphysics. Thus we have the metaphysics of experience, the metaphysics of literature, or the metaphysics of abstract painting. In each of these areas some of the fundamental problems or categories of metaphysics are used to illuminate the distinctive nature of the more limited sphere, to show how and with what significance it expresses the broader reality denoted by the categories in their more common usage. From another point of view, such studies involve an analysis of the fundamental principles of a narrower field in their, and its, broader import. So also for the present study of baseball.

Setting aside the problem of giving a formal definition of metaphysics, we can roughly suggest what is included by contrasting what we are here calling metaphysics with other approaches to baseball.

Baseball, as a human institution, has a history. Consequently there are written histories of the sport, which describe its emergence from earlier ball games, its formalization a century and a quarter ago, the development of its rules, the growth of the leagues, the great figures of the game, and so forth. But knowledge of this kind, useful as it is, does not provide a metaphysics of the game. Likewise if we were to focus on the economics of baseball, its technology, its unique physiological or medical demands on participants, its involvement in American social customs, the aesthetics of bodily movements typical of the game, the psychology of players or fans, or parallels that anthropologists and archeologists might discover in other cultures. None of this is metaphysics.

There are some studies in what may be called the mathematics and physics of baseball, including an entire, and quite technical, book on baseball devoted to probabilities. In the *American Journal of Physics* a few years ago there was an article offering a physicist's answer to the question: How does a fielder judge a fly ball? An outfielder normally will not run at top speed to the point where he expects the ball to drop and then stop and wait for the ball. What does he do? In the answer given, the fielder "will arrive at the right place at the right time to catch a fly ball if he runs at the only constant velocity for which the rate of change of [the] tangent of the elevation angle of the ball and the bearing angle of the ball both remain constant." *Scientific American* expressed this conclusion nicely by saying that a fielder unwittingly solves a problem in trigonometry.[1] This is fascinating, and it has implications for the theme of our discussion. But, in itself, lacking the requisite generality and focus, it is not a contribution to the metaphysics of the game.

I do not think psychoanalysis is more intelligible than physics, but perhaps it can provide an illuminating additional contrast. I am not talking now about the psychoanalysis of participants or spectators but the psychoanalytic significance of the game itself. In baseball, it might be said, the competition of pitcher and batter represents the age-old conflict between father and son. The pitcher-father attempts to reach home with a thrown ball, representing semen, while the batter-son uses his bat, a phallus, to deflect and scatter the semen-ball. The pitcher-father gains success when a pitched ball either enters the strike zone or (after being hit) enters a glove of his teammates. The batter may be put out either way. But if, by getting a hit, the batter-son can prevent the pitcher-father from attaining sexual union at home, he can himself attain it by rounding the bases and reaching home again.

There are flaws in this psychoanalytic interpretation of baseball. But before it is rejected out of hand, let us remind ourselves of some pertinent facts. Among the Berbers in Libya, there has been a game, similar to baseball in some respects, called *Om el mahag*. Translated, this means the "pilgrim's mother," and the one base to which the batter runs on hitting the ball, before he runs home again, is called "the mother." Among the Slavs the leader of the catching party in another similar game is called "mother" even when all players are male. In one version of a ball game from which baseball grew, a runner was put out by dropping the ball in a hole, as in golf, before the runner could insert his bat. Finally, baseball, like many other ball games, grew out of ball play in ancient fertility rites. One might still laugh and say: "But contemporary American baseball has nothing to do with sex!" However, baseball is now one of the prime devices by which social leaders in this country, through the agency of "physical education," attempt to divert the sexual interests and energies of the young. And how else than through psychoanalysis are we to explain baseball's fascination with the number three, the magic number of psychoanalysis?

Nevertheless, even if the psychoanalytic interpretation of baseball were valid, which I do not believe, it would not be metaphysics. I formulate the theory here in order to give a concrete example of what the metaphysics of baseball is not. A valid psychoanalysis of baseball could perhaps form part of a comprehensive metaphysics of the game, but only if it were grounded in an analysis of other features of it. Baseball is a complex of activities and aims within a certain limited structure of space and time. We need not assume that experience is oriented around sexuality in order to study how it is organized in and by this limited context.

A few words now on the meaning of the word "baseball." In the official rules that govern professional baseball and much amateur baseball in America, baseball is defined as "a game between two teams of nine players each, under direction of a manager, played on an enclosed field in accordance with these rules, under jurisdiction of one or more umpires."[2] Obviously this is not a good definition. It exaggerates the formalities of the game—direction by a manager, the enclosed field, the jurisdiction of umpires—but it does not identify or even hint at the uniqueness of the activities of the players. To be sure, the definition incorporates within itself the official rules, which describe these activities. Yet the rules are elaborate and complex, containing much that is not essential to baseball. This makes the official definition of baseball a poor beginning for a metaphysics of the game.

Like any complex form of human activity, baseball is difficult or impossible to define with precision. It undergoes historical changes and it is typically mixed with phenomena that are not necessary to it. But, as a game, it is subject to a special difficulty. Its rules, including those rules that are essential to its identity, are significantly arbitrary. Indeed the aims of the players (outs, hits, and runs) are significantly arbitrary. The rules and aims are not compelled by the nature or circumstances of people or things associated with the game but form a deliberately artificial framework for competition. Consequently, any specific definition of baseball, however based on familiar rules and aims, necessarily incorporates some arbitrariness. Its defense must rest primarily, not on the intrinsic relationship of the forms or activities it describes, but on common linguistic usage and the mere social dominance of one set of rules.

These comments can be made more concrete by reflection on a dictionary definition of baseball. According to Webster's Third, baseball is "a game played with a ball, bat, and gloves between 2 teams of 9 players each on a large field centering upon 4 bases that form the corners of a square 90 feet on each side, each team having a turn at bat and in the field during each of the 9 innings that constitute a normal game, the winner being the team that scores the most runs." This definition fails to mention some essentials of the game that ought to be included. But it is good enough to illustrate the necessary arbitrariness of any definition. Why should a game be called baseball if there are 9 players on each team but not if there are 8 or 10? Why should it be called baseball if there are 4 bases but not if there are 3 or 5? If the base paths form a square but not if they form an elongated rectangle or an unrectangular diamond? And so on. Perhaps it will be agreed that all of these conditions are inessential and that any game would remain a game of baseball despite minor variation in them. Then it appears that Webster's Third, like the definition in the official rule book, has not penetrated to the heart of the game.

There are some qualities that I trust everyone will agree are necessary to baseball. The batter attempts to hit a pitched ball with the bat; he becomes a runner if the ball is struck fair; the fielders attempt to defeat the runner by some form of stopping, catching, or handling the ball; the runner attempts to score by running the bases in order and home again at the risk of being put out while off base; the person or team with the highest score wins. However, these abstract conditions are consistent with many possible types of game that would not normally be called baseball. For the purposes of this essay, therefore, I shall not merely rely on or interpret such abstract conditions. Rather, I shall follow the dictionaries and common usage in attributing to baseball a pie-shaped fair territory with a right angle at the point; a square diamond marked by four bases at the narrow end of the pie; the division of players into two competing teams; competitive pitching as well as competitive batting, fielding, and base-running; and the familiar framework of batting order, base order, strikes, balls, outs, and innings. Indeed I shall use the familiar numerical determinations and take American major league baseball as a paradigm. Assuming that these qualities describe or determine the game of baseball, we may return to our primary questions. One result of our inquiry will be a reduction in the apparent arbitrariness of the rules, many of which will be rationalized and integrated with one another. Moreover, our conclusions may be applicable with minor modifications to modified versions of the game.

A game of baseball is a largely self-contained universe of reference with distinctive activities aiming at success. Now, as a game, it has artificial limits and purposes that make possible a sharp clarity of success. Moreover, like many other games, including some which are sports and some which are not sports, it refines and simplifies the judgment of success by quantifying it. When a group of people race against one another, they will be classified at the finish line as first, second, third, and so on. Likewise in baseball, the competition creates a winner and a loser; and victory is determined by the relative number of runs. Each team strives to increase its number, and the team with the highest number at the conclusion of the game is the winner. Thus when the game is over the competing teams are judged, in numerical comparisons, impersonally, objectively, and with striking clarity.

In the game similar to baseball that was discovered among the Berbers in Libya, we are told, "no account of score is kept. The fun lies in keeping the bat as long as possible."[3] Likewise, children in America will sometimes play baseball without any attention to the counting of runs. But this is rare, I think. And when it does occur, the desire and struggle for victory is merely compressed into each isolated run, which is in itself a mark of some achievement and superiority within the game. If there were no interest in attaining the kind of success represented by runs, there would be no baseball.

It would be possible to establish fixed penalties for losses in a game. I am reminded of the ball game in India in which every person on the losing team must carry an opponent back and forth between two points on the playing field as many times as the difference between the two scores. Again, a similar principle often governs the games of our children. But the rules of baseball, like those of most other sports, purify and intellectualize the achievement of victory within each game not only by rigid quantification but by the utter abstractness of the result. The rules of the game define no reward for success or punishment for failure.

There are several additional ways in which baseball shares with other sports a contemplative and abstract orientation. For example, the rules are elaborate and strict, they apply equally to all players, and during play they are unchallengeably interpreted by the umpires or referees. Players in organized baseball cannot mingle with or incite spectators and spectators do not have a defined role in directing the course of the game, which is strictly a contest, not between individuals or crowds, but between two formal organizations or teams. Players wear numbers on their backs, are carefully attended for their medical needs, and typically participate in an impersonal, indeed humble manner. Contrast these traits, as some sociologists have done,[4] with a sport such as bullfighting, with a proud and colorfully dressed matador, the expressive individuality of the fight, the matador's unwillingness to let serious injury keep him from fighting, the overt responses to the demands of the crowd.

However, baseball goes beyond not only bullfighting but many other team sports in its demand for clarity and intelligibility. When Harold Seymour, an historian of baseball, attempted to explain the rapidly expanding interest in baseball in its early years, he suggested, as one of several reasons, that "it was an open game in which every play was apparent to the audience."[5] And Roger Angell, the baseball columnist for the New Yorker, has written that baseball is "perhaps the most visible sport ever devised." "Almost never," Angell claims, "is there a baseball play which cannot be instantly seen and understood by everyone in the park; almost never does the baseball fan have to ask, 'What happened?'"[6] These judgments are overstated. But let us consider what it is about baseball that leads people to make them.

The game is celebrated for its intelligibility primarily because of the way in which it divides and separates action. I shall call this quality of baseball articulation. By turning now to articulation in baseball, we are finally getting down to business with the metaphysics of the game.

We may begin by noting that in the official rules of baseball, unlike those of many other sports such as football and basketball, there is no free substitution of players. When a player leaves a game of baseball, he is permanently out of that game. Thus the small world of the game, which has its own forms of action and success, is more tightly bound to itself and differentiated from ordinary life, to which the departing player returns. Moreover, the roles of the two baseball teams on the playing field are strictly distinct. In football or basketball it is possible to intercept a pass or steal the ball and score, but in baseball there is no way a fielder can score—except by taking his chance at bat when his turn comes, and satisfying the other requirements in order. Thus action that can produce scoring is sharply separated from action that can't.

Baseball is one of the sports where players on a team can have jobs that are clearly quite specialized. All or nearly all must hit, but few can serve as pitcher or catcher, and a shortstop will be required to do things that a first baseman will never have to do. The spatial structure of the game, which creates or influences these specialized roles, is perhaps the most obvious agency of articulation. The fielders are separated from one another in space. They do not hand the ball off to one another, or cross paths in a sudden common offensive, as in football or basketball. Instead their responsibilities are relatively fixed, tied to certain positions or areas; and they more frequently and characteristically transfer the ball to teammates across larger distances. Never does a swarm of players gather around and move collectively with or against the ball as in football. Both fielders and baserunners tend to move, like the ball itself in baseball, either in straight lines or in broad, sweeping curves. There is no such thing in baseball as a wobbly pass, and an occasional bad hop is not like the chaotic bounce of a football. The result is greater intelligibility.

Because of the spatial structure of baseball and the resulting way in which the ball is transferred, there is less opportunity for disguise and faking. The most important faking in baseball, corresponding to the faked passes and faked changes of bodily movement especially found in other sports, lies in the direction of the pitched ball. To an expectant batter, the ball seems to come one way from the pitcher, but then curves, sinks, or appears to rise. However, it is in the nature of baseball's interest in intelligibility that the batter is given a clear opportunity to see and interpret the disguised movement. To demand action from the batter—that is, to be a potential strike—the ball must enter a narrow area, the strike zone, from a fairly definite point a fairly definite distance away. Moreover, a round ball, however it spins, cannot curve very sharply as it travels to the strike zone. Thus the disguise of the ball's movement can only take place within narrow limits that contain the deception. And the batter is warned of it all by a familiar wind-up. Compare this process with the deception involved in a faked hand-off, a couple of faked passes, and the jagged, twisting, rarely or never repeated motions of a halfback in football who finds his way through the opposing team.

Baseball is a relatively slow game. Given the large amount of time taken up with changes in inning, managerial or player conferences, changes in batter, delays between pitches, and so forth, it can be shown that, in a two-and-a-half-hour game, there is on the average only about five or ten minutes of actual play.[7] The relative inactivity of the game is given as one reason for its appeal to intellectuals. It offers enormous scope to the imagination. In basketball there is a continuing, total absorption of players and spectators in what one writer has called "action heaped upon action, climax upon climax."[8] Using the terminology of Nietzsche, we may classify basketball as a Dionysian sport. Baseball, however, with its relative quiet and its characteristic separation of events, is Apollonian.

Baseball is not less exciting than other sports, such as basketball. But its excitement is more carefully modulated. The game is constructed so that alternating roles, repeated circumstances, and sharp punctuations in the temporal order can build tension and suspense without perpetual action. An analogy may help. Instead of, let us say, merely presenting and forming sound, the game gives both silence and sound, making the silence meaningful by its relationship to sound and giving a new dimension to sound by a patterned infusion of still mysterious and internally timeless silence. One strike, out, or inning is just another unit of time; it has the same formal role and limitations as others of its kind; but because of its unique position, it is given special significance by what has already happened and what can happen. Other sports typically lack such a formal similarity of independent self-contained units of temporal measurement. They therefore cannot present the same sort of tension. In basketball, players are always changing their location, direction, and relationship to others, often moving sharply or speeding the length of the court. But there is not more excitement in that than when in baseball a single base-runner stands tensely off base, teasing the pitcher, watched carefully by the pitcher, and testing the pitcher's ability to throw him out. Baseball dramatizes tension and creates psychological pressure in this instance not by complex motions and counter-motions, not by a swarm of conflict around the ball or by speed and agility, but by freezing action, by stopping time, as it were, for the purpose of observation, analysis, and competing predictions. There is something of this in the stance of the first baseman ready to receive the throw, in the slow wind-up of the pitcher, in the stance of the batter, and in the tense readiness of the catcher or any other fielder who threatens but temporarily suspends a throw, at the same time freezing the runner. More generally, in baseball as in chess (as one writer has noted[9]) power radiates from stationary figures. Baseball is unlike chess in that the figures do interact. But it does not merely refine and dramatize action. Rather, it dramatizes the relationship of action to what is not action, of action to stillness, the enigmatic transition from what can be to what is. Relying on the ancient categories of metaphysics, we may say then that baseball dramatizes the relationship of the potential and the actual.

Baseball is carefully articulated in both space and time. In space the action is spread out over distant but definite and easily recognizable positions of significance. The entire field is, in a sense, a simple geometry of lines and points, the clear lines formed by the paths of balls, runners, and fielders, and the fixed points where these paths can be seen or estimated to converge. In time the game is meticulously divided and subdivided, the game into innings, the innings into half-innings, the half-innings into outs, the outs into strikes. Now, just as the fielding team locates itself in and takes shape around a fixed pattern of space, so the batting team orders itself in relation to this fixed pattern of time. It is the institution of the batting order that achieves this. The players on the batting team are arranged in a certain numerical order governing individual appearances at bat. Here the team is broken down into its elements, each unit of the team (that is, each player) corresponding to the possibility of an out. Thus time is articulated not only by formal divisions and subdivisions, but by a distinction between this formal structure and a second time-like structure, the batting order, which overlaps it, connects its elements, and gives it substance and direction.

The articulation of space and time in a single phenomenon in the game is illustrated by the rules that two base-runners cannot find sanctuary at the same base, and that one base-runner cannot pass another. Two runners can be at different bases at the same time, or at the same base at different times, but, in the rules of baseball, they cannot be at the same place at the same time. Significant scoring entities (that is, runners) are kept distinct and their progress kept orderly. Thus does baseball measure and control action, providing an intelligible spectacle. In baseball more profoundly than in other sports, the clarity of the spectacle sharpens the clarity of the result, victory or defeat, success or failure. Appropriately, the rules of organized baseball, unlike those of, say, football, do not permit ties.

Let us consider more carefully the complexity of the contrasts in baseball involving space and time. As umpires know, there is no rule requiring three fielders in the outfield or four near the base paths. "Except the pitcher and the catcher," the rules say, "any fielder may station himself anywhere in fair territory . . ."[10] However, some arrangements of fielders are more effective than others. Thus the fielding team is forced, in view of the nature of the game, to pattern itself after the pattern of the playing field. The batting team, in contrast, must, by the rules, arrange itself in a fixed batting order. The game begins, and its time becomes separated from ordinary time, when the umpire receives the home team's batting order, in effect obtaining jurisdiction over the portion of reality constituting the game. However, the order of time by which the game as a whole proceeds is not that of batting but that of strikes, outs, and innings. We can see from this that the two teams are distinguished by their relative positions in space and time. The fielders exist in a spatial order and attempt to create a temporal order of strikes, outs, and innings.

The batters exist in a temporal order, the order of batting and running, but try to infuse it with a spatial order, the circle of the bases.

Furthermore, the two structures of time, the order of batting and the order of innings, are related in a way that refines even more thoroughly the contrast between space and time. By getting hits, the batting team can continue at bat. The game's order of strikes, outs, and innings will then be suspended and replaced by the batting order of one of the teams. Thus whereas the fielding team, to be successful, must mold itself around the spatial pattern of the game, the batting team, by being successful, can mold the temporal pattern of the game around itself. Sport is a creature of action, and action is ephemeral. But, in a sense, baseball offers action the opportunity of permanence by suspending and restructuring time according to success. Appropriately, the runners in baseball (in contrast to those in the English game rounders, from which it grew) proceed around the bases *counter-clockwise*, and the first baseball team, which formalized this and other new rules, played in a park in Hoboken, New Jersey, called the Elysian Fields.

One further point about space and time. The deliberate contrasts in the game between space and time are subtly reflected in its numerical dimensions. There are four bases and four basepaths, forming a square at one end of the field. At one corner of the square, that is, home plate, there is another square, this one vertical, called the strike zone, which is invisible and different for each batter but nonetheless real in the game. The combination of these two squares defines fair territory, which is thus based on the number four. This is the primary spatial structure of the game, reflected also in the atemporal influence of a walk, four pitched balls outside the strike zone; in the rectangular boxes for batter and catcher; and in the irregular pentagonal shape of homeplate, which is formed by two overlapping squares, one defined by the base lines and one fronting the pitcher. The temporal structure of the game, however, is based on the number three: three strikes to an out, three outs to an inning, at least three appearances at bat for each of the nine players who last a nine-inning game. Accordingly, space and time are contrasted in the game not only by their associations with the competing teams but by their very numerical foundations. The elementary measurement of distance in space or time in ordinary life is based on a confusing array of numbers, multiples of 2, 3, 4, 5, 6, and 7. Thus there are 3 feet to a yard, 4 seasons to a year, 7 days to a week, 12 inches to a foot, 12 months to a year, 24 hours to a day, 60 seconds to a minute, 60 minutes to an hour. There is a dominant pattern here, however, the use of multiples of 3 and 4. What baseball does is break down the complex combinations and separate the numbers. The confusing array of numbers for measuring space and time in ordinary life is replaced in the game with a fairly clear distinction, 4 the number of space and 3 the number of time.

"Therefore is Space, and therefore Time," Emerson said, "that man may know that things are not huddled and lumped, but sundered and individual."[11] As we may put it, space and time are media of articulation. In baseball the distinctiveness of their nature and influence is itself carefully articulated. The result is that in each inning, in order to score, the batting team tries to go faster than time: it has to cover four bases but is given only three outs. At the very least it must suspend time: the batter has to get four balls to get on base with a walk, but he is given only three strikes.

Baseball came into being and grew up in the mid-nineteenth century, a period marked by industrialization. The division of roles, action, time, and space in baseball parallels the division of labor in the factory and in new bureaucracies. The game developed in the cities and represents an application of urban industrializing order to the patches of country, the parks, that could be found in or near cities. It should not be surprising, then, to find a real division of labor, not only implicated in the framework of the game, but apparent in its typical activities. First the pitcher throws the ball, then the batter hits it, then the third baseman fields it, then the first baseman receives the throw from third. As in a factory, the chores are done one by one in quick sequence by different people. To be sure, there is simultaneous action. While the pitcher winds up, the third baseman may be running in for a bunt; while the third baseman throws the ball, the batter darts to first. But the simultaneous activities derive their meaning, as, indeed, in a factory, from the contribution they make to clearly defined linear processes, the movement of the ball from person to person or the course of the runner around the bases. There is a serious imperfection in the industrial analogy, however. For each fielder is not simply like a participant in an assembly line but like a separate artisan. He has a unique position and often distinctive tasks but he may not know when he will be called on to perform distinctively or which of his teammates he will relate to.

From this discussion of the analogy between patterns of individuality in baseball and in industry, we may turn to the general representation of individuality in the game. In the larger spectacle of the game we encounter the individual in a variety of appearances: as an undefined member of a vague group (that is, sitting on the bench waiting to bat); as a batter uniquely located in the batting order, capable of scoring on his own or just helping the team; as a base-runner whose value depends on successes by his teammates or errors by his opponents; and as a fielder, who can perform individually with a grand play or serve as a mere agent in relay of the ball. It is rare for a sport to create such a variety of roles for a single player and then articulate them so carefully. Instead of density, group awareness around the ball, and spontaneous mass movement out of which unique, unpredictable individual directions may break, as in football, there is a studied classification of ways in which the individual achieves by himself, ways in which he relies on others, and ways in which others rely on him. Thus baseball analyzes the relationship of the individual and the group. Again using the ancient categories of metaphysics, we may say that it analyzes the relationship of the one and the many. It shows the patterns of uniqueness, separation, relation, direction, and movement that create the whole. It distinguishes functions which another sport may provide partially and still another may provide primarily in a single, inclusive, corporate display.

Before closing our discussion of clarity and articulation in baseball, we may note another obvious implication. Because of the way in which baseball is articulated, it can be readily translated into numbers and more easily remembered. As Roger Angell has said, the "clean lines [of the game] can be restored in retrospect."[12] Hence the unusual popular interest in the statistics, box scores, great events, and mythic figures of the game. But rather than argue that baseball expresses abstractly the metaphysical foundations of history, I will turn to another dimension of our theme.

In the metaphysics of baseball there are two fundamental categories, articulation and perspective. Let us consider now perspective, which is the more fascinating and profound of the two but which can do with a less elaborate account.

A perspective is like a point-of-view, a view of reality from a single point. It is a complex relationship of things and events as they all are themselves related to a unique position or frame of reference. A painting, for example, can possess perspective. What this normally means is that relationships within the painting are constructed so that they are consistent in size and pattern with the unique viewpoint of the spectator. Trees and mountains understood as farther away from the spectator will cover a shorter length of canvas than a human being up close, because, from the standpoint of the spectator, that is indeed how they will appear. Obviously, any two different positions and directions of sight will provide different visual perspectives on reality. The same is true, although less obviously, for modes of contact with reality other than sight. Thus a symphony will sound slightly different from different parts of the auditorium; and there will be often negligible but nonetheless real differences in the way the body will react to its surroundings if it is located or positioned differently.

Perspective is important in philosophy and in the social sciences because experience is a complex of simultaneous, successive, and overlapping perspectives. The structure of experience is often explored through novel and combined perspectives, as when Picasso, in a single painting, drew both a left and a right profile on the same face, or as when a student of history reads both French and Russian accounts of the Napoleonic invasions. Education, and indeed life itself, is a broadening and supplementation of perspectives, the mere acquisition of information creating new orders of relationship and relative importance. Later we shall see what this has to do with baseball.

The playing field in baseball is divided into fair territory and foul, the inside and outside of two fixed rays extending from home plate. Both fair and foul territory play a role in the game; foul balls have defined functions; but a batter seeks success by hitting the ball fair. Since, however, the fair and foul lines are understood to be extended indefinitely, a batter can hit fairly as far as he can—a home run over the fence or out of the park. Thus the batter, standing in the batter's box and looking toward the pitcher, is given by the geometry of the game a unique visual perspective on reality. Since the angle of the foul lines is 90 degrees, the batter's attention and effort are riveted on what he may do, near or far, in one quarter of reality, roughly what is in, or in line with, his field of vision. Accordingly, the baseball field is, in a sense, a formalization of the batter's perspective. It is the world from *his* point-of-view, or from the standpoint of the strike zone uniquely defined by his batting stance. Reality is classified by its relationship to this perspective as ball or strike; foul ball or fair; infield or outfield. Indeed the baseball field, unlike other sports fields, has the property of handedness. Corresponding to the importance of right-handed and left-handed pitchers and batters, there are two batter's boxes, left and right; hits to the left side and to the right side; a left field, center field, and right field. Just as a mirror image of a left hand has the thumb on the opposite side, so a mirror image of a baseball field has first base on the opposite side. You rarely if ever will find a left-handed third-baseman. Thus perspective is integrated into the spatial medium of the game.

The unique perspective of the playing field is reflected in the directional words that describe relationships on the field, as outlined several years ago in some notes in the linguistic journal, *American Speech*. A pitcher or an infielder may be said, in common baseball language, to throw *over to* a base, and infielders can be said to throw *over to* the pitcher. However, the same phrase, *over to*, is not used to describe throws to or from home plate. Instead such throws are *up to* the plate, *out to* the pitcher, *down to* second, and so forth. Similarly, the catcher is not said to throw *across to* second, whereas from the bases throws are said to be *across* the diamond. "Apparently," a puzzled linguist reasons, "*across* is suitable only for fielders, regardless of the actuality of the throw; for certainly it is as *across* from second to home and from the plate to second as it is from first to third and back again."[13] Actually, however, it is not as *across*. For the perspective of the field gives a unique role to home plate. A ball thrown to or from home would not *cross* the field of vision of someone at home plate, or seem to go *over* from one point to another, although it could appear to go *up*, *down*, *out*, and so on. The adverb *in* illustrates the built-in perspective of the playing field even more clearly. In direction, the linguistic journal reports, the adverb *in* "always refers to the home plate or to somewhere on the home-plate side of the player. 'A run is in'; 'a player throws in from right field'; 'a batter steps in [into the batter's box] for his turn'; 'a runner takes second on the throw-in'; 'a pitcher looks in [to the catcher for his signal] and deals'; 'a fly drops in [short of the outfielders] for a safe hit.'"[14] The place that is most *in* is home plate in that other, distant points are given relevant spatial meaning by their relationship to it. And of course the fielders are all "out."

The perspectival structure of baseball is not exhibited merely in the diagrammatic structure of the playing field or the language commonly used to describe field directions. It is exhibited also in the nature of the fundamental activities of the game. The four bases are positioned symmetrically, as if they were on the circumference of a circle, with all base-paths equal. So much for clarity and articulation. But the bases function differently since they are not equidistant from or equivalent in the game's action. There is a simple, practical expression of this principle in the fact that players will often steal second but rarely even attempt to steal third.

Home plate is the point from which balls are scattered. Just as the spatial order of the field is determined by a single point, so balls in fact emanate unpredictably from that point to distances and heights all over the field. Moreover, home plate is the center of violence and intensity in the action of the game. There the ball, which can reach speeds of around 100 miles an hour from the pitcher's hand, is met with sharp, powerful blows from the bat. Most of the ball-playing interaction among members of the fielding team involves the pitcher and the catcher; next most, the infielders, who guard the bases and relay balls as well as field balls; finally come the outfielders, who merely field balls and have very little fielding interaction among themselves, tending to return the ball in the general direction of home plate.[15]

In a sense there is greater definiteness, as well as more action, near home plate. We have seen that the pitcher and catcher, the two fielders closest to home, are required to occupy the appropriate field positions, while other fielders choose positions on the basis of the need for effective fielding. Infielders naturally group themselves close to marked points, the bases, while outfielders work on an unmarked expanse of grass. Moreover, home plate is the position at which a vaguely pictured team on the bench becomes an actual temporal series of individuals capable of interrupting the normal time of the game through hits. It is thus the position at which the regularized succession of strikes, outs, and innings can be replaced by a unique temporal perspective, the batting order of the batting team as it gets on base. And, most obviously, home plate is the source and culmination of the runner's journey around the bases. It defines success in the journey. In a sense, fielding and guarding bases are a mastery of the unpredictable emanations, the hits and the runners, from home plate.

In all of these ways, the game of baseball establishes a perspective based on a single point. Philip Roth, in his comic baseball novel entitled *The Great American Novel* made baseball pointless and funny in part by a symbolic disregard of this principle: he made his baseball team homeless, with no city from which to leave and to which to return to give meaning to its journeys. Again, in the recent baseball movie, *Bang the Drum Slowly*, the dying man is a catcher, whose view and experience of life is made more poignant by his position outside the primary spatial order of the game and his assumption during play of the batter's visual perspective on its activities.

Other sports in addition to baseball possess articulation and perspective in varying ways. For instance, football is spatially articulated according to elaborate patterns of field and players and temporally articulated into halves, quarters, ball possessions, first downs, and downs. It has a perspective, a left and right, a center of attack, for each team. But it does not have a unique perspective. One team's left is another's right. Thus it does not articulate a single game perspective, a symbolic perspective assumed by each player, except in the sense that the game is itself a focus of everyone's attention. And it does not articulate the relationships of space, time, and action that baseball does, with or without perspective. Cricket is like baseball in that it has a pitcher and batter, bases and base-running, fielders and fielding. But it seems to deliberately avoid uniqueness of perspective. Thus in cricket there is no distinction between fair and foul territory, all deflections of the ball counting truly as hits; there are no fixed dimensions to the outer boundaries of the playing field; there are only two running bases, at home and at the pitcher's area, without a visual perspective spatially defined by field action; and there are frequent changes of position by batter and pitcher, giving each a new viewpoint. Since in cricket every batter bats in every inning, the batting order does not unify the innings or create a distinctive temporal perspective in each, as it does in baseball.

Here, and in this entire discussion, my point is not that baseball is better than other sports, either as sport or as social activity. In these comparisons I argue only that baseball is different in its foundations.

It is well to recognize, of course, that apparent differences among sports can mask genuine similarities. Thus golf, for example, seems to me to share significant traits with baseball. Unlike football and basketball, golf is not pressed by two-minute warnings, thirty-second rules, or three-second rules. It is essentially articulated in both space and time by greens, holes, and strokes; the order of holes in the course provides a unique perspective, shared in its general traits by all competitors; and the golfer, like a runner in baseball, ends up where he started. Informality is introduced through the golfer's walk as it is through the batters' bench. But there are vast differences as well between golf and baseball. Golf is played over a much larger and more complex space, indeed a different space for each course. The greens are positioned to produce an irregular zig-zag journey. Yet golf has a far more elementary temporal structure, simply reflecting space and ability in a distinct linear dimension. And a golfer cannot stop time by succeeding in the game, as players can in baseball or cricket, but can merely compress time by clear limited amounts, approaching the ideal but absolute minimum of eighteen strokes for eighteen holes.

Let us consider generally now the meaning of baseball. As we have seen, the game is organized around the principles of articulation and perspective. We may now ask: What does it do with these traits? Is there a meaning to the attainment of success in this unique structure?

Football seems to be organized after the pattern of the old Roman and British armies, with formal lines of soldiers facing one another. It is a symbolic rendering of territorial conflict in war, each side pressing against the other to move an imaginary dividing line and extend the boundaries of its own land. Basketball is characterized by constant, rapid, relatively chaotic activity; mutual harassment; rapid scoring; quick and frequent reversals in ball possession; and frequent scoring immediately upon gaining possession. Basketball players are often restricted in needless ways by the rules of the game; they are pursued up and down court by officials watching for breaches of the rules; and they are interrupted by the frequent assignment of penalties. They often play by balancing possible penalties against possible strategic advantages which would be gained by a violation of the rules. One sociologist has therefore suggested that the game of basketball, which was devised in America, is a reflection of American middle-class life, with its complex regulations, its strategic attitude toward regulations, and its rapid changes of fortune.[16] This interpretation of basketball can be generalized, as it must since the sport is now played around the world. How should baseball be interpreted?

We have already encountered a couple of positions on the meaning of baseball. For example, I constructed a possible psychoanalytic view, which interpreted the game as a sexual conflict between father and son.[17] However, such an interpretation has many flaws. It is hard to tell whether the pitcher or the batter should be classified as the father. Moreover, psychoanalysis seems unable to interpret important details of the sport, such as the number and order of bases; the pie-shaped fair territory; and the nature of the competition as between, not just pitcher and batter, but elaborately organized teams.

In addition to the psychoanalytic theory, we considered the view of baseball as an expression of the division of labor and the transformation of the country by the city, features of industrialization. But this view similarly can't explain many unique and important features of baseball. There are any number of ways in which a sport might divide and articulate experience.

In 1744 a children's book was published in London entitled *A Little Pretty Pocket-Book*. This book includes a poem that we can use to introduce a third interpretation of the game:

> BASE-BALL
> *The* Ball *once struck off,*
> *Away flies the* Boy
> *To the next destin'd Post,*
> *And then Home with Joy.*
>
> Moral
> *Thus Britons for Lucre*
> *Fly over the Main:*
> *But, with Pleasure transported,*
> *Return back again.* [18]

In this old poem, there is an economic interpretation of the runner's journey in the game. Unfortunately, however, the poem does not really tell us much about the game. Thus it contains no rationale, based on the rules, for the economic interpretation it provides. A bare economic theory like this might be used to explain in part the activities of professional players, managers, and sportswriters. But it does not explain the activities of children and amateurs, who preceded professionals in the formation of the game. Nor does it explain the activities of fans, who now sustain professionals. And it could not explain the unique features of baseball, since there are professionals in most sports.

In a recent essay in *Sports Illustrated* comparing baseball and cricket, there is a more elaborate version. The suggestion is that, in both baseball and cricket, as in football, there is a reflection of economic and military conflict. I quote from this essay:

> In their deepest imagery both sports [baseball and cricket] are about protecting property against attack (in cricket slang the home-plate stumps

are even known as the "castle") and the corollary need to go out and raid to survive. In both games there is a delicious ambivalence of assault and defense, of slipping through siege lines, of setting traps and ambushes, making false sacrifices . . .

Though I like the various forms of football in the world, I don't think they begin to compare with these two great Anglo-Saxon ball games for sophisticated elegance and symbolism. Baseball and cricket are beautiful and highly stylized medieval war substitutes, chess made flesh, a mixture of proud chivalry and base—in both senses—greed. With football we are back to the monotonous clashed armor of the brontosaurs.[19]

This is a powerful interpretation of baseball. It seems to me, however, to misunderstand some details. A batter in baseball does not merely try to deflect a pitch or protect home plate but has a positive interest in getting a hit, giving the ball new impetus. The author, John Fowles, a Briton, has had more experience with cricket, where, as we have seen, merely deflected balls, which would be foul in baseball, can produce baserunners and runs. Moreover, if the runner in rounding the bases is on a symbolic raid, why is there nothing symbolic for him to receive, handle, and try to carry home, as in relay races? The other team does the ball-handling. All the runner gets is occasional sanctuary, the experience of the journey, a new relative status marked by abstract success, and the pleasure referred to in the children's poem. The economic and military analogies are provocative but, I think, in the final analysis, unconvincing. In any event, there is still the more obvious shortcoming in the Fowles theory, since it is an interpretation of both cricket and baseball. Even if it were true, one would still have to consider the meaning of the unique activities of each sport.

In baseball as in chess, one finds safe places in foreign territory, behind enemy lines, as it were. But the objective in baseball, again as in chess, is not the symbolic acquisition of territory. In the early days of the sport, a runner standing off base threatening to run to the next base was said to "take ground." But the phrase was misleading and has come to be replaced by the phrase "lead off," which suggests merely the initiation of movement from some fixed point. To be sure, there is a territorial interest in baseball, and not only in the batter's so-called protection of the plate. The fielders try to catch a fly ball before it hits the ground, in a sense protecting their territory from the batter. They try to keep any hit ball from reaching into their territory enough to permit the batter to become a runner. But the fielding team is protecting territory it already has, not trying to acquire new territory. Indeed it tries to obtain enough outs so that it can leave the field. A team scores, as we have seen, not by possessing space but, as a series of batters, by merely passing through space and possessing time. It must sufficiently acquire and control time in order to make runs.

Now, a run is a particle of action and experience. Again, in the early days of the game, runs were called "aces." This was consistent with the abstraction and articulation of baseball, for an "ace" is etymologically a bare unit. Runs are now called runs, however, because fundamentally they are units of running, the experience of the runner who scores. To the fielding team, the hit ball is poison to the land; hence the interest in catching balls on the fly. To the batting team, however, the ball is poison to the person, who hits it away from himself and who can be tagged out with it while running. Since a runner need not carry a ball around the bases with him to score, since even a home run is not scored until a runner gets to and tags home plate, it is in baseball (more precisely than in other sports, like football) the player or his action that scores. Thus the individual is not celebrated primarily in his effects as in these other sports, nor in his beauty or strength as in still other sports, but in his action.

The centrality of the person and his action in baseball is shown also by the decisive historical change that marked the origin of the game. In rounders, the earlier game, a fielder could put a runner out by throwing the ball at him and hitting him while he was off base. The replacement of this practice by tagging led to the introduction of a harder ball, faster play, and more excitement. But the change had a symbolic significance too. It was itself a transformation of violence into symbol. The power to get outs lay now more strictly in the fielder, not in the ball apart from the fielder. Thus for both fielding and scoring, it is the person or his action that counts. This fact provides a clue to the larger meaning of the game.

Our task now is to explain what baseball signifies about the person, his action, or his experience. In order to do this, let us draw together the various lines of our analysis.

Baseball is an articulated and intellectualized sport, providing fundamentally a realm of intelligibility and clarity. The batter views the field from its central perspective at home plate. The pitcher attempts to deceive and master the batter with his pitches, while the batter attempts to control and project the pitcher's device, the ball. By getting a hit, the batter in a sense assimilates the ball and redirects it according to his own perspective, the perspective he assumes by standing at home plate. A ball hit fair is like a ray proceeding from home plate and staying within the batter's original field of vision. It is a constituent and extension of his own action and experience into territory which he can see but which in fact belongs to and is guarded by others, the fielders. As an extension of the batter into the fielders' own territory, the hit entitles the batter to become a runner, to actually enter and explore what belongs to others. Then, as a runner looking toward home, toward the pitcher, or toward the next base, he sees the small reality of the game in a variety of new perspectives. Thus his experience is enlarged. Nor is this just a matter of seeing. The runner's experience is different on each base due to the different functions of the bases in the action of the game, which is structured by the game's perspective.

Now, if the runner is touched by the ball while off base, he in a sense returns to the limited perspective of his hit from home, and he is out. But by making a complete journey around the bases, the runner expands his experience of the field and its action. At home plate, as a batter looking out into the field, he had a 90 degree vision of reality. But in traversing the base paths, each of which is 90 feet long, the runner goes 360 feet, symbolizing the 360 degrees of a complete circle. Indeed by getting a double or triple or home run, or by traversing at any one time more than one side of the diamond, the runner is able to round the corners of the diamond and create a symbolic circle in his own action. The 360 degrees of the circle extend to completion the original 90 degree perspective.

Thus success in baseball is ultimately a ritual expansion and universalization of the limited and unique perspective of home. The game is an image of growth in knowledge, experience, action, adventure, and life itself. It is an image of growth in the person or group which experiences the running and success. In terms of the traditional categories of metaphysics, perspective is appearance, the appearance of reality from a single point. Baseball is therefore an extension of appearance, the local perspective, to include all of reality. The base-runner tries to break down the very distinction between appearance and reality, which metaphysics teaches. In the stylized contest of the game, fielders as such are compelled to arrange themselves to guard bases and land, restricted to what they already possess. But they try to get outs so they can succeed in the larger adventure.

Jacques Barzun once said: "Whoever wants to know the heart and mind of America had better learn baseball."[20] One conclusion of our inquiry is that baseball has a closer link to American history than any mere reflection of industrialization. It has broader meaning for human experience than is given by mere sexual, economic, or military striving. The carefully articulated structure of the game makes reality accessible. The unique perspective of the game makes reality uniquely known and meaningful. Finally, the action of rounding the bases, in which the whole person takes part and by which he succeeds, transforms this limited perspective on reality into a timeless, complete, encircling encounter.

NOTES

1. Seville Chapman, "Catching a Baseball," *American Journal of Physics* 36 (1968), pp. 868–870; reported in "Trigonometric Outfielding," *Scientific American* 220 (January 1969), pp. 49–50.

2. *1973 Official Baseball Rules*, Section 1.01. Annual editions of the rules are available in many sporting goods stores for about 25¢.

3. Corrado Gini, "Rural Ritual Games in Libya (Berber Baseball and Shinny)," *Rural Sociology* 4 (1939), p. 286.

4. Louis A. Zurcher, Jr. and Arnold Meadow, "On Bullfights and Baseball: An Example of Interaction of Social Institutions," *International Journal of Comparative Sociology* 8 (1967), pp. 99–117.

5. Harold Seymour, *Baseball: The Early Years* (New York: Oxford, 1960), p. 30.

6. Roger Angell, *The Summer Game* (New York: Popular Library, 1973), p. 160; "Baseball—the Perfect Game," *Ten Years of Holiday*, ed. Editors of *Holiday* Magazine (New York: Simon and Schuster, 1956), p. 401.

7. Cf. Mark Harris, "Maybe What Baseball Needs Is a Henry David Thoreau," *New York Times Magazine* (May 4, 1969, Section 6), p. 67.

8. Roger Kahn, "Intellectuals and Ballplayers," *American Scholar* 26 (1957), p. 349.

9. Stefan Kanfer, "The Greatest Game" (Time Essay), *Time* 101 (April 30, 1973), p. 82.

10. *1973 Official Baseball Rules* Section 4.03(c).

11. Ralph Waldo Emerson, "Nature," *Complete Works of Ralph Waldo Emerson*, (Boston and New York: Houghton Mifflin, 1903), Vol. I, p. 38.

12. Angell, *Summer Game*, p. 308.

13. Robert Donald Spector, "Baseball, Inside Out and Upside Down," *American Speech* 31 (1956), pp. 305–306.

14. A. L. H., "Editorial Note," *ibid.*, p. 306.

15. Cf. Oscar Grusky, "The Effects of Formal Structure on Managerial Recruitment: A Study of Baseball Organization," *Sport, Culture, and Society: A Reader on the Sociology of Sport*, ed. John W. Loy, Jr. and Gerald S. Kenyon (London: Macmillan, 1969), pp. 408–415.

16. Edgar Z. Friedenberg, "Foreword," *Man, Sport and Existence: A Critical Analysis*, by Howard S. Slusher (Philadelphia: Lea and Febiger, 1967), pp. ix–x.

17. Cf. Adrian Stokes, "Psycho-analytic Reflections on the Development of Ball Games, Particularly Cricket," *International Journal of Psychoanalysis* 37 (1956), pp. 185–192.

18. Quoted in Robert W. Henderson, *Ball, Bat and Bishop: The Origin of Ball Games* (New York: Rockport Press, 1947), p. 133.

19. John Fowles, "Making a Pitch for Cricket," *Sports Illustrated* 38 (May 21, 1973), p. 108.

20. Quoted in Seymour, *op. cit.*, p. v.

A Guide for Further Study

Fantasy is omnipresent in baseball-centered fiction. *Shoeless Joe* by W. P. Kinsella imagines the resurrection of Shoeless Joe Jackson, one of the Black Sox of 1919 barred from baseball for participating in the World Series fix. Anything by George Plimpton, that latter-day Walter Mitty, describes fantasies become actual. For an account of living counterparts of J. Henry Waugh, see Thomas Boswell, "Of Dice and Men," in his *Why Time Begins on Opening Day.*

Section III: Humor

PHILIP ROTH

The Asylum Keepers

One sunny Saturday morning early in August, the Ruppert Mundys boarded a bus belonging to the mental institution and journeyed from their hotel in downtown Asylum out into the green Ohio countryside to the world-famous hospital for the insane, there to play yet another "away" game—a three-inning exhibition match against a team composed entirely of patients. The August visit to the hospital by a P. League team in town for a series against the Keepers was an annual event of great moment at the institution, and one that was believed to be of considerable therapeutic value to the inmates, particularly the sports-minded among them. Not only was it their chance to make contact, if only for an hour or so, with the real world they had left behind, but it was believed that even so brief a visit by famous big league ballplayers went a long way to assuage the awful sense such people have that they are odious and contemptible to the rest of humankind. Of course the P. League players (who like all ballplayers despised any exhibition games during the course of the regular season) happened to find playing against the Lunatics, as they called them, a most odious business indeed; but as the General simply would not hear of abandoning a practice that brought public attention to the humane and compassionate side of a league that many still associated with violence and scandal, the tradition was maintained year after year, much to the delight of the insane, and the disgust of the ballplayers themselves.

The chief psychiatrist at the hospital was a Dr. Traum, a heavyset gentleman with a dark chin beard, and a pronounced European accent. Until his arrival in America in the thirties, he had never even heard of baseball, but in that Asylum was the site of a major league ball park, as well as a psychiatric hospital, it was not long before the doctor became something of a student of the game. After all, one whose professional life involved ruminating upon the extremes of human behavior, had certainly to sit up and take notice when

From *The Great American Novel* (1973). Title supplied by the editors.

a local fan decided to make his home atop a flagpole until the Keepers snapped a losing streak, or when an Asylum man beat his wife to death with a hammer for calling the Keepers "bums" just like himself. If the doctor did not, strictly speaking, become an ardent Keeper fan, he did make it his business to read thoroughly in the literature of the national pastime, with the result that over the years more than one P. League manager had to compliment the bearded Berliner on his use of the hit-and-run, and the uncanny ability he displayed at stealing signals during their annual exhibition game.

Despite the managerial skill that Dr. Traum had developed over the years through his studies, his team proved no match for the Mundys that morning. By August of 1943, the Mundys weren't about to sit back and take it on the chin from a German-born baseball manager and a team of madmen; they had been defeated and disgraced and disgraced and defeated up and down the league since the season had begun back in April, and it was as though on the morning they got out to the insane asylum grounds, all the wrath that had been seething in them for months now burst forth, and nothing, but nothing, could have prevented them from grinding the Lunatics into dust once the possibility for victory presented itself. Suddenly, those '43 flops started looking and sounding like the scrappy, hustling, undefeatable Ruppert teams of Luke Gofannon's day—and this despite the fact that it took nearly an hour to complete a single inning, what with numerous delays and interruptions caused by the Lunatics' style of play. Hardly a moment passed that something did not occur to offend the professional dignity of a big leaguer, and yet, through it all, the Mundys on both offense and defense managed to seize hold of every Lunatic mistake and convert it to their advantage. Admittedly, the big right-hander who started for the institution team was fast and savvy enough to hold the Mundy power in check, but playing just the sort of heads-up, razzle-dazzle baseball that used to characterize the Mundy teams of yore, they were able in their first at bat to put together a scratch hit by Astarte, a bunt by Nickname, a base on balls to Big John, and two Lunatic errors, to score three runs—their biggest inning of the year, and the first Mundy runs to cross the plate in sixty consecutive innings, which was not a record only because they had gone sixty-seven innings without scoring earlier in the season.

When Roland Agni, of all people, took a called third strike to end their half of the inning, the Mundys rushed off the bench like a team that smelled World Series loot. "We was due!" yelped Nickname, taking the peg from Hothead and sweeping his glove over the bag—"Nobody gonna stop us now, babe! We was due! We was *overdue!*" Then he winged the ball over to where Deacon Demeter stood on the mound, grinning. "Three big ones for you, Deke!" Old Deacon, the fifty-year-old iron-man starter of the Mundy staff, already a twenty-game loser with two months of the season still to go, shot a string of tobacco juice over his left shoulder to ward off evil spirits, stroked the rabbit's foot that hung on a chain around his neck, closed his eyes to mumble something ending with "Amen," and then stepped up on the rubber to face the first patient. Deacon was a preacher back home, as gentle and kindly a man as you would ever want to bring your problems to, but up on the hill he was all competitor, and had been for thirty years now. "When the game begins," he used to say back in his heyday, "charity ends." And so it was that when he saw the first Lunatic batter digging in as though he owned the batter's box, the Deke decided to take Hothead's advice and stick the first pitch in his ear, just to show the little nut who was boss. The Deacon had taken enough insults that year for a fifty-year-old man of the cloth!

Not only did the Deke's pitch cause the batter to go flying back from the plate to save his skin, but next thing everyone knew the lead-off man was running for the big brick building with the iron bars on its windows. Two of his teammates caught him down the right-field line and with the help of the Lunatic bullpen staff managed to drag him back to home plate. But once there they couldn't get him to take hold of the bat; every time they put it into his hands, he let it fall through to the ground. By the time the game was resumed, with a 1 and 0 count on a new lead-off hitter, one not quite so cocky as the fellow who'd stepped up to bat some ten minutes earlier, there was no doubt in anyone's mind that the Deke was in charge. As it turned out, twice in the inning Mike Rama had to go sailing up into the wall to haul in a long line drive, but as the wall was padded, Mike came away unscathed, and the Deacon was back on the bench with his three-run lead intact.

"We're on our way!" cried Nickname. "We are on our God damn way!"

Hothead too was dancing with excitement; cupping his hands to his mouth, he shouted across to the opposition, "Just watch you bastards go to pieces now!"

And so they did. The Deke's pitching and Mike's fielding seemed to have shaken the confidence of the big Lunatic right-hander whose fastball had reined in the Mundys in the first. To the chagrin of his teammates, he simply would not begin to pitch in the second until the umpire stopped staring at him.

"Oh, come on," said the Lunatic catcher, "he's not staring at *you*. Throw the ball."

"I tell you, he's right behind you and he is too staring. Look you, I see you there behind that mask. What is it you want from me? What is it you think you're looking at, anyway?"

The male nurse, in white half-sleeve shirt and white trousers, who was acting as the plate umpire, called out to the mound, "Play ball now. Enough of that."

"Not until you come out from there."

"Oh, pitch, for Christ sake," said the catcher.

"Not until that person stops staring."

Here Dr. Traum came off the Lunatic bench and started for the field, while down in the Lunatic bullpen a left-hander got up and began to throw. Out on the mound, with his hands clasped behind his back and rocking gently to and fro on his spikes, the doctor conferred with the pitcher. Formal European that he was, he wore, along with his regulation baseball shoes, a dark three-piece business suit, a stiff collar, and a tie.

"What do you think the ol' doc's tellin' that boy?" Bud Parusha asked Jolly Cholly.

"Oh, the usual," the old-timer said. "He's just calmin' him down. He's just askin' if he got any good duck shootin' last season."

It was five full minutes before the conference between the doctor and the pitcher came to an end with the doctor asking the pitcher to hand over the ball. When the pitcher vehemently refused, it was necessary for the doctor to snatch the ball out of his hand; but when he motioned down to the bullpen for the left-hander, the pitcher suddenly reached out and snatched the ball back. Here the doctor turned back to the bullpen and this time motioned for the left-hander *and* a right-hander. Out of the bullpen came two men dressed like the plate umpire in white half-sleeve shirts and white trousers. While they took the long walk to the mound, the doctor made several unsuccessful attempts to talk the pitcher into relinquishing the ball. Finally the two men arrived on the mound and before the pitcher knew what had happened, they had unfurled a straitjacket and wrapped it around him.

"Guess he wanted to stay in," said Jolly Cholly, as the pitcher kicked out at the doctor with his feet.

The hundred Lunatic fans who had gathered to watch the game from the benches back of the foul screen behind home plate, and who looked in their street clothes as sane as any baseball crowd, rose to applaud the pitcher as he left the field, but when he opened his mouth to acknowledge the ovation, the two men assisting him in his departure slipped a gag over his mouth.

Next the shortstop began to act up. In the first inning it was he who had gotten the Lunatics out of trouble with a diving stab of a Bud Parusha liner and a quick underhand toss that had doubled Wayne Heket off third. But now in the top of the second, though he continued to gobble up everything hit to the left of the diamond, as soon as he got his hands on the ball he proceeded to stuff it into his back pocket. Then, assuming a posture of utter nonchalance, he would start whistling between his teeth and scratching himself, as though waiting for the action to *begin*. In that it was already very much underway, the rest of the Lunatic infield would begin screaming at him to take the ball out of his pocket and make the throw to first. "What?" he responded, with an innocent smile. "The ball!" they cried. "Yes, what about it?" "Throw it!" "But I don't have it." "You *do*!" they would scream, converging upon him from all points of the infield, "You do too!" "Hey, leave me alone," the short-stop cried, as they grabbed and pulled at his trousers. "Hey, cut that out—get your hands *out* of there!" And when at last the ball was extracted from where he himself had secreted it, no one could have been more surprised. "Hey, the *ball*. Now who put that there? Well, what's everybody looking at *me* for? Look, this must be some guy's idea of a joke. . . . Well, Christ, *I* didn't do it."

Once the Mundys caught on, they were quick to capitalize on this unex-pected weakness in the Lunatic defense, pushing two more runs across in the second on two consecutive ground balls to short—both beaten out for hits while the shortstop grappled with the other infielders—a sacrifice by Mike Rama, and a fly to short center that was caught by the fielder who then just stood there holding it in his glove, while Hothead, who was the runner on second, tagged up and hobbled to third, and then, wooden leg and all, broke for home, where he scored with a head-first slide, the only kind he could ne-gotiate. As it turned out, the slide wasn't even necessary, for the center-fielder was standing in the precise spot where he had made the catch—and the ball was still in his glove.

With the bases cleared, Dr. Traum asked for time and walked out to center. He put a hand on the shoulder of the mute and motionless fielder and talked to him in a quiet voice. He talked to him steadily for fifteen minutes, their faces only inches apart. Then he stepped aside, and the center-fielder took the ball from the pocket of his glove and threw a perfect strike to the catcher, on his knees at the plate some two hundred feet away.

"Wow," said Bud Parusha, with ungrudging admiration, "now, that fella has a arm on him."

"Hothead," said Cholly, mildly chiding the catcher, "he woulda had you by a country mile, you know, if only he'd a throwed it."

But Hot, riding high, hollered out, "Woulda don't count, Charles—it's dudda what counts, and I dud it!"

Meanwhile Kid Heket, who before this morning had not been awake for two consecutive innings in over a month, continued to stand with one foot up on the bench, his elbow on his knee and his chin cupped contemplatively in his palm. He had been studying the opposition like this since the game had gotten underway. "You know somethin'," he said, gesturing toward the field, "those fellas ain't thinkin'. No sir, they just ain't usin' their heads."

"We got 'em on the run, Wayne!" cried Nickname. "They don't know *what* hit 'em! Damn, ain't nobody gonna stop us from here on out!"

Deacon was hit hard in the last of the second, but fortunately for the Mundys, in the first two instances the batsman refused to relinquish the bat and move off home plate, and so each was thrown out on what would have been a base hit, right-fielder Parusha to first-baseman Baal; and the last hitter, who drove a tremendous line drive up the alley in left center, ran directly from home to third and was tagged out sitting on the bag with what he took to be a triple, and what would have been one too, had he only run around the bases and gotten to third in the prescribed way.

The quarrel between the Lunatic catcher and the relief pitcher began over what to throw Big John Baal, the lead-off hitter in the top of the third.

"Uh-uh," said the Lunatic pitcher, shaking off the first signal given by his catcher, while in the box, Big John took special pleasure in swishing the bat around menacingly.

"Nope," said the pitcher to the second signal.

His response to the third was an emphatic, "N-O!"

And to the fourth, he said, stamping one foot, "Definitely *not!*"

When he shook off a fifth signal as well, with a caustic, "Are you kidding? Throw him that and it's bye-bye ballgame," the catcher yanked off his mask and cried:

"And I suppose that's what I want, according to you! To lose! To go down in defeat! Oh, sure," the catcher whined, "what I'm doing, you see, is deliberately telling you to throw him the wrong pitch so I can have the wonderful pleasure of being on the losing team again. Oh brother!" His sarcasm spent, he donned his mask, knelt down behind the plate, and tried yet once more.

This time the pitcher had to cross his arms over his chest and look to the heavens for solace. "God give me strength," he sighed.

"In other words," the catcher screamed, "I'm wrong *again*. But then in your eyes I'm *always* wrong. Well, isn't that true? Admit it! Whatever signal I give is *bound* to be wrong. Why? Because *I'm* giving it! I'm daring to give *you* a signal! I'm daring to tell *you* how to pitch! I could kneel here signaling for the rest of my days, and you'd just stand there shaking them off and asking God to give you strength, *because I'm so wrong and so stupid and so hopeless and would rather lose than win!*"

When the relief pitcher, a rather self-possessed fellow from the look of it, though perhaps a touch perverse in his own way, refused to argue, the Lunatic catcher once again assumed his squat behind the plate, and proceeded to offer a seventh signal, an eighth, a ninth, a tenth, each and every one of which the pitcher rejected with a mild, if unmistakably disdainful, remark.

On the sixteenth signal, the pitcher just had to laugh. "Well, that one really takes the cake, doesn't it? That really took brains. Come over here a minute," he said to his infielders. "All right," he called back down to the catcher, "go ahead, show them your new brainstorm." To the four players up on the mound with him, the pitcher whispered, "Catch this," and pointed to the signal that the catcher, in his mortification, was continuing to flash from between his legs.

"Hey," said the Lunatic third-baseman, "that ain't even a finger, is it?"

"No," said the pitcher, "as a matter of fact, it isn't."

"I mean, it ain't got no nail on it, does it?"

"Indeed it has not."

"Why, I'll be darned," said the shortstop, "it's, it's his thingamajig."

"Precisely," said the pitcher.

"But what the hell is that supposed to mean?" asked the first-baseman.

The pitcher had to smile again. "What do you think? Hey, Doc," he called to the Lunatic bench, "I'm afraid my battery-mate has misunderstood what's meant by an exhibition game. He's flashing me the signal to meet him later in the shower, if you know what I mean."

The catcher was in tears now. "He made me do it," he said, covering himself with his big glove, and in his shame, dropping all the way to his knees, "everything else I showed him wasn't *good* enough for him—no, he teases me, he taunts me—"

By now the two "coaches" (as they were euphemistically called), who had removed the starting pitcher from the game, descended upon the catcher. With the aid of a fielder's glove, one of them gingerly lifted the catcher's member and placed it back inside his uniform before the opposing players could see what the signal had been, while the other relieved him of his catching equipment. "He provoked me," the catcher said, "he always provokes me—"

The Lunatic fans were on their feet again, applauding, when their catcher was led away from the plate and up to the big brick building, along the path taken earlier by the starting pitcher. "—He won't let me alone, ever. I don't want to do it. I never wanted to do it. I *wouldn't* do it. But then he starts up teasing me and taunting me—"

The Mundys were able to come up with a final run in the top of the third, once they discovered that the second-string Lunatic catcher, for all that he sounded like the real thing—"Chuck to me, babe, no hitter in here, babe—" was a little leery of fielding a bunt dropped out in front of home plate, fearful apparently of what he would find beneath the ball upon picking it up.

When Deacon started out to the mound to pitch the last of the three innings, there wasn't a Mundy who took the field with him, sleepy old Kid

Heket included, who didn't realize that the Deke had a shutout working. If he could set the Lunatics down without a run, he could become the first Mundy pitcher to hurl a scoreless game all year, in or out of league competition. Hoping neither to jinx him or unnerve him, the players went through the infield warm-up deliberately keeping the chatter to a minimum, as though in fact it was just another day they were going down to defeat. Nonetheless, the Deke was already streaming perspiration when the first Lunatic stepped into the box. He rubbed the rabbit's foot, said his prayer, took a swallow of air big enough to fill a gallon jug, and on four straight pitches, walked the center-fielder, who earlier in the game hadn't bothered to return the ball to the infield after catching a fly ball, and now, at the plate, hadn't moved the bat off his shoulder. When he was lifted for a pinch-runner (lifted by the "coaches") the appreciative fans gave him a nice round of applause. "That's lookin' 'em over!" they shouted, as he was carried from the field still in the batting posture, "that's waitin' 'em out! Good eye in there, fella!"

As soon as the pinch-runner took over at first, it became apparent that Dr. Traum had decided to do what he could to save face by spoiling the Deacon's shutout. Six runs down in the last inning and still playing to win, you don't start stealing bases—but that was precisely what this pinch-runner had in mind. And with what daring! First, with an astonishing burst of speed he rushed fifteen feet down the basepath—but then, practically on all fours, he was scrambling back. "No! No!" he cried, as he dove for the bag with his outstretched hand, "I won't! Never mind! Forget it!" But no sooner had he gotten back up on his feet and dusted himself off, than he was running again. "Why not!" he cried, "what the hell!" But having broken fifteen, *twenty*, feet down the basepath, he would come to an abrupt stop, smite himself on his forehead, and charge wildly back to first, crying, "Am I crazy? Am I out of my *mind?*"

In this way did he travel back and forth along the basepath some half-dozen times, before Deacon finally threw the first pitch to the plate. Given all there was to distract him, the pitch was of course a ball, low and in the dirt, but Hothead, having a great day, blocked it beautifully with his wooden leg.

Cholly, managing the club that morning while Mister Fairsmith rested back in Asylum—of the aged Mundy manager's spiritual crisis, more anon—Cholly motioned for Chico to get up and throw a warm-up pitch in the bull-pen (one was enough—one was too many, in fact, as far as Chico was concerned) and meanwhile took a stroll out to the hill.

"Startin' to get to you, are they?" asked Cholly.

"It's that goofball on first that's doin' it."

Cholly looked over to where the runner, with time out, was standing up on first engaged in a heated controversy with himself.

"Hell," said Cholly, in his soft and reassuring way, "these boys have been tryin' to rattle us with that there bush league crap all mornin', Deke. I told you fellers comin' out in the bus, you just got to pay no attention to their monkey-shines, because that is their strategy from A to Z. To make you lose your concentration. Otherwise we would be rollin' over them worse than we is. But Deke, you tell me now, if you have had it, if you want for me to bring the Mexican in—"

"With six runs in my hip pocket? And a shutout goin'?"

"Well, I wasn't myself goin' to mention that last that you said."

"Cholly, you and me been in this here game since back in the days they was rubbin' us down with Vaseline and Tabasco sauce. Ain't that right?"

"I know, I know."

"Well," said the Deke, shooting a stream of tobacco juice over his shoulder, "ain't a bunch of screwballs gonna get my goat. Tell Chico to sit down."

Sure enough, the Deacon, old war-horse that he was, got the next two hitters out on long drives to left. "Oh my God!" cried the base runner, each time the Ghost went climbing up the padded wall to snare the ball. "Imagine if I'd broken for second! Imagine what would have happened then! Oh, that'll teach me to take those crazy leads! But then if you don't get a jump on the pitcher, where are you as a pinch-runner? That's the whole idea of a pinch-runner—to break with the pitch, to break *before* the pitch, to score that shutout-breaking run! That's what I'm in here for, that's my entire purpose. The whole thing is on *my* shoulders—so then what am I doing *not* taking a good long lead? But just then, if I'd broken for second, I'd have been doubled off first! For the last out! But then suppose he hadn't made the catch? Suppose he'd dropped it. Then where would I be? Forced out at second! *Out*—and all because I was too cowardly. But then what's the sense of taking an unnecessary risk? What virtue is there in being foolhardy? None! But then what about playing it too safe?"

On the bench, Jolly Cholly winced when he saw that the batter stepping into the box was the opposing team's shortstop. "Uh-oh," he said, "that's the feller what's cost 'em most of the runs to begin with. I'm afraid he is goin' to be lookin' to right his wrongs—and at the expense of Deacon's shutout. Dang!"

From bearing down so hard, the Deacon's uniform showed vast dark continents of perspiration both front and back. There was no doubt that his strength was all but gone, for he was relying now solely on his "junk," that floating stuff that in times gone by used to cause the hitters nearly to break their backs swinging at the air. Twice now those flutter balls of his had damn near been driven out of the institution and Jolly Cholly had all he could do not to cover his eyes with his hand when he saw the Deke release yet another fat pitch in the direction of home plate.

Apparently it was just to the Lunatic shortstop's liking too. He swung from the heels, and with a whoop of joy, was away from the plate and streaking down the basepath. "Run!" he shouted to the fellow on first.

But the pinch-runner was standing up on the bag, scanning the horizon for the ball.

"Two outs!" cried the Lunatic shortstop. "Run, you idiot!"

"But—where is it?" asked the pinch-runner.

The Mundy infielders were looking skywards themselves, wondering where in hell that ball had been hit to.

"Where *is* it!" screamed the pinch-runner, as the shortstop came charging right up to his face. "I'm not running till I know where the *ball* is!"

"I'm coming into first, you," warned the shortstop.

"But you can't overtake another runner! That's against the law! That's *out!*"

"Then *move!*" screamed the shortstop into the fellow's ear.

"Oh, this *is* crazy. This is exactly what I *didn't* want to do!" But what choice did he have? If he stood his ground, and the shortstop kept coming, that would be the ballgame. It would be all over because he who had been put into the game to run, had simply refused to. Oh, what torment that fellow knew as he rounded the bases with the shortstop right on his tail. "I'm running full speed—and I don't even know where the ball is! I'm running like a chicken with his head cut off! I'm running like a madman, which is just what I don't want to do! Or be! I don't know where I'm going, I don't know what I'm doing, I haven't the foggiest idea of what's happening—and I'm running!"

When, finally, he crossed the plate, he was in such a state, that he fell to his hands and knees, and sobbing with relief, began to kiss the ground. "I'm home! Thank God! I'm safe! I made it! I scored! Oh thank God, thank God!"

And now the shortstop was rounding third—he took a quick glance back over his shoulder to see if he could go all the way, and just kept on coming. "Now where's *he* lookin'?" asked Cholly. "What in hell does he see that I can't? Or that Mike don't either?" For out in left, Mike Rama was walking round and round, searching in the grass as though for a dime that might have dropped out of his pocket.

The shortstop was only a few feet from scoring the second run of the inning when Dr. Traum, who all this while had been walking from the Lunatic bench, interposed himself along the foul line between the runner and home plate.

"Doc," screamed the runner, "you're in the way!"

"That's enough now," said Dr. Traum, and he motioned for him to stop in his tracks.

"But I'm only inches from pay dirt! Step aside, Doc—let me score!"

"You just stay vere you are, please."

"*Why?*"

"You know vy. Stay right vere you are now. And giff me the ball."

"What ball?" asked the shortstop.

"You know vat ball."

"Well, I surely don't have any ball. I'm the *hitter*. I'm about *to score*."

"You are not about to score. You are about to giff me the ball. Come now. Enough foolishness. Giff over the ball."

"But, Doc, I haven't got it. I'm on the offense. It's the *defense* that has the ball—that's the whole idea of the game. No criticism intended, but if you weren't a foreigner, you'd probably understand that better."

"Haf it your vay," said Dr. Traum, and he waved to the bullpen for his two coaches.

"But, Doc," said the shortstop, backpedaling now up the third-base line, "*they're* the ones in the field. *They're* the ones with the gloves—why don't you ask them for the ball? Why me? I'm an innocent base runner, who happens to be rounding third on his way home." But here he saw the coaches coming after him and he turned and broke across the diamond for the big brick building on the hill.

It was only a matter of minutes before one of the coaches returned with the ball and carried it out to where the Mundy infield was now gathered on the mound.

The Deacon turned it over in his hand and said, "Yep, that's it, all right. Ain't it, Hot?"

The Mundy catcher nodded. "How in hell did *he* get it?"

"A hopeless kleptomaniac, that's how," answered the coach. "He'd steal the bases if they weren't tied down. Here," he said, handing the Deacon a white hand towel bearing the Mundy laundrymark, and the pencil that Jolly Cholly wore behind his ear when he was acting as their manager. "Found this on him too. Looks like he got it when he stumbled into your bench for that pop-up in the first."

The victory celebration began the moment they boarded the asylum bus and lasted nearly all the way back to the city, with Nickname hollering out his window to every passerby, "We beat 'em! We shut 'em out!" and Big John swigging bourbon from his liniment bottle, and then passing it to his happy teammates.

"I'll tell you what did it," cried Nickname, by far the most exuberant of the victors, "it was Deacon throwin' at that first guy's head! Yessir! Now that's my kind of baseball!" said the fourteen-year-old, smacking his thigh. "First man up, give it to 'em right in the noggin'."

"Right!" said Hothead. "Show 'em you ain't takin' no more of their shit no more! Never again!"

"Well," said Deacon, "that is a matter of psychology, Hot, that was somethin' I had to think over real good beforehand. I mean, you try that on the wrong feller and next thing they is all of them layin' it down and then spikin' the dickens out of you when you cover the bag."

"That's so," said Jolly Cholly. "When me and the Deke come up, that was practically a rule in the rule book—feller throws the beanball, the word goes out, 'Drag the ball and spike the pitcher.' Tell you the truth, I was worried we was goin' to see some of that sort of stuff today. They was a desperate bunch. Could tell that right off by their tactics."

"Well," said the Deke, "that was a chance I had to take. But I'll tell you, I couldn't a done it without you fellers behind me. How about Bud out there, throwin' them two runners out at first base? The right-fielder to the first-baseman, *two times in a row*. Buddy," said the Deacon, "that was an exhibition such as I have not seen in all my years in organized ball."

Big Bud flushed, as was his way, and tried to make it sound easy. "Well, a' course, once I seen those guys wasn't runnin', I figured I didn't have no choice. I *had* to play it to first."

Here Mike Rama said, "Only that wasn't what *they* was figurin', Buddy-boy. You got a one-arm outfielder out there, you figure, what the hell, guess I can get on down the base line any old time I feel like it. Guess I can stop off and get me a beer and a sangwich on the way! But old Bud here, guess he showed 'em!"

"You know," said Cholly, philosophically, "I never seen it to fail, the hitters get cocky like them fellers were, and the next thing you know, they're makin' one dumb mistake after another."

"Yep," said Kid Heket, who was still turning the events of the morning over in his head, "no doubt about it, them fellers just was not usin' their heads."

"Well, maybe they wasn't—but *we* was! What about Hot?" said Nickname. "What about a guy with a wooden leg taggin' up from second and scorin' on a fly to center! How's that for heads-up ball?"

"Well," said Wayne, "I am still puzzlin' that one out myself. What got into that boy in center, that he just sort of stood there after the catch, alookin' the way he did? What in hell did he want to wait fifteen minutes for anyway, before throwin' it? That's a awful long time, don't you think?"

They all looked to Cholly to answer this one. "Well, Wayne," he said, "I believe it is that dang cockiness again. Base runner on second's got a wooden leg, kee-rect? So what does Hot here do—he *goes*. And that swellhead out in center, well, he is so darned stunned by it all, that finally by the time he figures out what hit him, we has got ourselves a gift of a run. Now, if I was managin' that club, I'd bench that there prima donna and slap a fine on him to boot."

"But then how do you figure that shortstop, Cholly?" asked the Kid. "Now if that ain't the strangest ballplayin' you ever seen, what is? Stickin' the ball in his back pocket like that. And then when he is at bat, with a man on and his team down by six, and it is their last licks 'n all, catchin' a junk pitch like that inside his shirt. Now I cannot figure that out nohow."

"Dang cockiness again!" cried Nickname, looking to Cholly. "He figures, hell, it's only them Mundys out there. I can do any dang thing I please— well, I guess we taught him a thing or two! Right, Cholly?"

"Well, nope, I don't think so, Nickname. I think what we have got there in that shortstop is one of the most tragic cases I have seen in my whole life of all-field-no-hit."

"Kleptomaniac's what the coach there called him," said the Deacon.

"Same thing," said Cholly. "Why, we had a fella down in Class D when I was just startin' out, fella name a' Mayet. Nothin' got by that boy. Why, Mayet at short wasn't much different than a big pot of glue out there. Fact that's what they called him for short: Glue. Only trouble is, he threw like a girl, and when it come to hittin', well, my pussycat probably do better, if I had one. Well, the same exact thing here, only worse."

"Okay," said Kid Heket, "I see that, sorta. Only how come he run over to field a pop-up and stoled the pencil right off your ear, Cholly? How come he took our towel away, right in the middle of the gosh darn game?"

"Heck, that ain't so hard to figure out. We been havin' such rotten luck this year, you probably forgot just who we all are, anyway. What boy *wouldn't* want a towel from a big league ball club to hang up and frame on the wall? Why, he wanted that thing so bad that when the game was over, I went up to the doc there and I said, 'Doc, no hard feelin's. You did the best you could and six to zip ain't nothin' to be ashamed of against big leaguers.' And then I *give* him the towel to pass on to that there kleptomaniac boy when he seen him again. So as he didn't feel too bad, bein' the last out. And know what else I told him? I give him some advice. I said, 'Doc, if I had a shortstop like that, I'd bat him ninth and play him at first where he don't *have* to make the throw."

"What'd he say?"

"Oh, he laughed at me. He said, 'Ha ha, Jolly Cholly, you haf a good sense of humor. Who efer heard of a first-baseman batting ninth?' So I said, 'Doc, who ever heard of a fifty-year-old preacher hurlin' a shutout with only three days' rest—but he done it, maybe with the help of interference on the last play, but still he done it.'"

"Them's the breaks of the game anyway!" cried Nickname. "About time the breaks started goin' our way. Did you tell him that, Cholly?"

"I told him that, Nickname. I told him more. I said, 'Doc, there is two kinds of baseball played in this country, and maybe somebody ought to tell you, bein' a foreigner and all—there is by the book, the way you do it, the way the Tycoons do it—and I grant, those fellers win their share of pennants doin' it that way. But then there is by hook and crook, by raw guts and all the heart you got, and that is just the way the Mundys done here today.'"

Here the team began whooping and shouting and singing with joy, though Jolly Cholly had momentarily to turn away, to struggle against the tears that were forming in his eyes. In a husky voice he went on—"And then I told him the name for that. I told him the name for wanderin' your ass off all season long, and takin' all the jokes and all the misery they can heap on your head day after day, and then comin' on out for a exhibition game like this one, where another team would just go through the motions and not give two hoots in hell how they played—and instead, instead givin' it everything you got. I told the doc the name for that, fellers. It's called courage."

Only Roland Agni, who had gone down twice, looking, against Lunatic pitching, appeared to be unmoved by Cholly's tribute to the team. Nickname, in fact, touched Jolly Cholly's arm at the conclusion of his speech, and whispered, "Somebody better say somethin' to Rollie. He ain't takin' strikin' out too good, it don't look."

So Cholly the peacemaker made his way past the boisterous players and down the aisle to where Roland still sat huddled in a rear corner of the bus by himself.

"What's eatin' ya, boy?"

"Nothin'," mumbled Roland.

"Why don'tcha come up front an'—"

"Leave me alone, Tuminikar!"

"Aw, Rollie, come on now," said the sympathetic coach, "even the best of them get caught lookin' once in a while."

"Caught *lookin'*?" cried Agni.

"Hey, Rollie," Hothead shouted, "it's okay, slugger—we won anyway!" And grinning, he waved Big John's liniment bottle in the air to prove it.

"Sure, Rollie," Nickname yelled. "With the Deke on the mound, we didn't need but one run anyway! So what's the difference? Everybody's gotta whiff sometimes! It's the law a' averages!"

But Agni was now standing in the aisle, screaming, "You think I got caught *lookin'*?"

Wayne Heket, whose day had been a puzzle from beginning to end, who just could not really take any more confusion on top of going sleepless all these hours, asked, "Well, wasn't ya?"

"You bunch of morons! You bunch of idiots! Why, you are bigger lunatics even than they are! Those fellers are at least locked up!"

Jolly Cholly, signaling his meaning to the other players with a wink, said, "Seems Roland got somethin' in his eye, boys—seems he couldn't see too good today."

"You're the ones that can't see!" Agni screamed. "*They were madmen! They were low as low can be!*"

"Oh, I don't know, Rollie," said Mike Rama, who'd had his share of scurrying around to do that morning, "they wasn't *that* bad."

"They was *worse!* And you all acted like you was takin' on the Cardinals in the seventh game of the Series!"

"How else you supposed to play, youngster?" asked the Deacon, who was beginning to get a little hot under the collar.

"And you! You're the worst of all! Hangin' in there, like a regular hero! Havin' conferences on the mound about how to pitch to a bunch of hopeless maniacs!"

"Look, son," said Jolly Cholly, "just on account you got caught lookin'—"

"*But who got caught lookin'?* How could you get caught lookin' against pitchers *that had absolutely nothin' on the ball!*"

"You mean," said Jolly Cholly, incredulous, "you took a *dive?* You mean you throwed it, Roland? *Why?*"

"*Why?* Oh, please let me off! Let me off this bus!" he screamed, charging down the aisle toward the door. "I can't take bein' one of you no more!"

As they were all, with the exception of the Deacon, somewhat pie-eyed, it required virtually the entire Mundy team to subdue the boy wonder. Fortunately the driver of the bus, who was an employee of the asylum, carried a straitjacket and a gag under the seat with him at all times, and knew how to use it. "It's from bein' around them nuts all mornin'," he told the Mundys. "Sometimes I ain't always myself either, when I get home at night."

"Oh," said the Mundys, shaking their heads at one another, and though at first it was a relief having a professional explanation for Roland's bizarre behavior, they found that with Roland riding along in the rear seat all bound and gagged, they really could not seem to revive the jubilant mood that had followed upon their first shutout win of the year. In fact, by the time they reached Keeper Park for their regularly scheduled afternoon game, one or two of them were even starting to feel more disheartened about that victory than they had about any of those beatings they had been taking all season long.

ERNEST W. SPEED, JR.

The Coach Who Didn't Teach Civics

It is not hard to discover what motivates the average small town Texan. You can get into a conversation with anybody from a small town on just about any subject but sex, and before you know it, you are listening to the feats accomplished by "their" football team for the last ten years. Anna Rose is like that. When our people go to the Auction Barn in Alice or the County Fair in George West there is more talk about the time Arriba Jones drug three would-be tacklers 27 yards for the tie-breaking touchdown than there is conversation about the price of shoats or the drawbar pull of the latest Farmall tractor. This was the way things went for many years, but after 1956 our folk started talking more about hog prices and tractors than football.

Our old coach passed away that summer and the school board decided to go all out and bring in a real big-name coach. They put ads in all the major papers, and for weeks a string of hopeful young men ate chicken-fried steak and cream gravy and discussed their philosophy of sport with the board members in the Sunshine Cafe banquet room, where the Lions Club met on Tuesdays. My father was on the school board and I heard him talk to my mother about the various applicants for the job. One man was well qualified but had been divorced, so that automatically excluded him. The coach from over at Bluntzer applied, but when they found out he had a tattoo of a naked woman on his chest they burnt his application. It was three weeks before school began when the board announced they had found the man that would establish Anna Rose as a real football power for decades to come. My father told me the new coach was college-educated, had a small business of his own, and had studied under the coach at the University of San Patricio.

Originally appeared in *Quartet* (1975–76).

The town first met Coach Tom Rhodes at a public gathering in the school gym. Our principal, Mr. Parker, explained to the students, the school board, and the assembled parents that our new coach had business interests and would be the first coach the school had ever had who would not teach civics. Mr. Parker had a canned speech he used on all occasions. He told us what a fine school board we had and how these men were recognized for their ability to choose the proper person for every job that affected the well-being of the young people of Anna Rose. When Coach Rhodes finally got to say something, he told us that even though he would not be teaching any classes, he was always available for counseling and students should feel free to see him any time they had a problem. He said he had taken a sociology course in college and was aware of all the problems facing young people. When we drifted out into the hot August night a few minutes later, we all felt like a people on whom God had cast a favorable eye.

We were suited out and standing on the forty-yard line when Coach Rhodes drove up for the first practice. He drove a brand new Ford panel truck that, as we soon learned, was always kept locked. Tom Rhodes looked like a coach was supposed to look. He wore a baseball cap over his flat-top, a whistle around his neck, and he carried a clipboard close to what we called a beer belly. We gathered around him on one knee. This is part of football that most people don't notice. All players gather around their coach on one knee. I think it's some kind of worship—one knee for the coach and two knees for God. It didn't take us long to find out that Coach Rhodes felt we should be on two knees. "Men," he drawled, "there is something ya'll gotta remember if you're gonna play on my team. You better play clean, live clean, and be clean, or you're never gonna see those uniforms except from the stands. Now goddammit, take four laps and let's get it on." We loped around the field four times and then came in and got back down on one knee while the Coach passed out the plays we were going to use in what we called "our years of glory." At the top of the sheet he had written in large, neat letters: PLAY CLEAN—LIVE CLEAN—BE CLEAN. Underneath were the same T-formation plays our former mentor had found in some coaching books back in 1948.

Coach Rhodes was late the next day, so we took the positions we had had the year before and were running plays when he drove up. I can't say he liked that much. The first day of school he had put up a notice on the bulletin board asking everyone interested in trying out for the football team to sign it, but no one had. There was no point in it. Everybody in town knew who was going to play, and what position they were going to play, and had known since the last season. Our backfield was 75 percent Gonzales. Jerry, the youngest of the three Gonzales boys, was our quarterback and could throw a football or a cantaloupe into a basket sixty yards away. He was also good at throwing other things, for he once sailed a dried cow pie through the second story window of the Anna Rose Hotel. He had run the T-formation two years and he knew the plays well enough to run them blindfolded. Jerome, who was surely the oldest and probably the meanest sophomore in the State of Texas, played fullback. He was nineteen, weighed 199 pounds, and spoke only broken English. The middle brother, Jesus, was eighteen and he was our real star. He was affectionately known as "greasy Jesus Gonzales" and was the greatest open-field runner ever seen in Live Oak County.

Coach Rhodes watched us for a minute or two and then blew his whistle. "I don't know who told you these are the positions you're gonna play cause I'm gonna decide that." We all said "Yessir," and then broke to take our four laps. Since my dad was on the school board, Coach thought I should play quarterback, but I knew I was a safety, and after I fouled up about six plays, he agreed and decided to try Jerry Gonzales at the man-under spot, for he had been completing forty-yard passes when Mr. Rhodes had driven up.

Practice soon grew routine and we developed a precision offense. Every afternoon, Coach Rhodes drilled us on clean living and sportsmanship. When we went home, our fathers taught us the finer points of Texas schoolboy football. Joe Youngblood's dad had patented a way to penalize the other team in a key situation and instructed his son, a defensive guard, in its subtleties. Joe told us about it and used it in our first game against the Bishop Bears. They had us third-and-goal on our six-yard line. Their quarterback had just called "Down" when Joe leaned toward the offensive guard and said, "You ignert sonofabitch." When the kid looked up, Joe spit in his eyes. The poor kid rocked back and we charged across the line while the Bears got penalized five yards for illegal motion. We developed other ways of getting illegal motion penalties. On various occasions our linemen would faint, simulate epileptic fits, or when the officials were not looking, bite the other quarterback on the nose, which affected his signal calling somewhat.

But cheating was not our only weapon. Our offense was really good and we averaged over two hundred yards a game. I didn't play a whole lot, but my dad had said, "Marcel, when we have the ball you shouldn't feel bad," and I really didn't. I had very little desire to get smashed by a big running-back, and if it hadn't been for my dad, I probably would have been in what he called "that bunch of fairies out there blowin' horns and beatin' their drums."

We won our first five games and began to get little four-inch write-ups in the Laredo and Kingsville papers. Word even got out that the head coach from The University of Texas was coming down to see that "cantaloupe chunkin' Meskin," but when he found out Jerry was just a junior, he sent word he had changed his plans, but that he would come the first chance he got. He did show up eventually, but it was the third week in June, the thermometer read 102 in the shade, and every Gonzales in Live Oak County was loading watermelons over around Devine, some eighty miles away. Unfortunately, Jerry never did play for *The* University, or any other university.

Our sixth game was a rough one. We were playing Hondo and they had a big, strong team, as a lot of those German towns did. Their star was Albert Bippert, a 255-pound fullback who liked to run straight up the middle and over as many people as possible. The biggest thing we had was Jerome Gonzales, so we put him at middle linebacker. Jerome had been well coached by his boss, the owner of the feed store, and on the first play from scrimmage, when big Al came roaring up the middle, Jerome calmly and quickly kicked him in the balls. Jerome was also the place-kicker for our team and I would not have been surprised to see Albert Bippert's family jewels sail through the uprights. Four men carried the hopes of the Hondo Owls off the field and we were penalized fifteen yards for unnecessary roughness. Though certainly much better than an even trade, that incident almost cost us the game. It fired up the Hondo team and we were lucky to win it, 12 to 7. Besides the two extra points, Jerome also missed three field goal attempts, one from inside the five. Going home on the bus after the game, we discovered he had played all but the first down with two broken toes.

As far as anyone can remember, only one secret was ever kept for more than a week in Anna Rose, and that was the nature of the business Coach Rhodes had as a sideline. He never discussed it and we were all too "sociable" to come right out and ask him just what line of work he was in. All we knew was that he came wheeling up to the football field every day at 3:15 and locked his truck. We tried every excuse in the world to see what was in that damn thing, but we never got so much as a peek for over two months. Finally, in the middle of November, on the night we beat Pearsall to win the Regional Class A championship, the riddle of the green panel truck was solved.

The town had been absolutely wild for three weeks, ever since we had beaten Freer to clinch the district title. When the team drove in from Pearsall, our fathers surrounded the Coach the moment he stepped off the bus and took him down to Chapa's Dance Hall for all the free beer he could drink. As soon as they pulled out of the parking lot, the whole team headed for the truck. We had long been convinced that there must be something in that truck worth stealing or Coach Rhodes wouldn't have kept it locked. We didn't know anybody in the world that locked their house, much less their truck. We finally pried the hinges off the back and pulled the doors off. Mickey Ray Busby and Joe Youngblood had taken flashlights from the schoolbus, and they played them up and down the inside of the truck. We looked, fell silent with mouths agape, then began to murmur in awesome wonder: "Man, oh Man, oh Man! Sheee-it! Will you look at that!" The truck was filled with cardboard cases and about twenty long metal containers that bore the words, "TROJANS—The Perfect Prophylactic." I could not take my eyes off those machines. I read with rapt fascination and mounting excitement— "Two for 25¢. You can be sure," "The Perfect Fit," "The Velvet Touch," "Millions of Satisfied Users," and, of course, "Sold for the Prevention of Disease Only."

There were probably twenty-five cases of rubbers in that truck, but we went on and stole them all. I managed to get a whole case for myself and hid the rubbers in the garage. Each case contained 150 gross of rubbers, and as I went to bed that night it dawned on me I had enough rubbers for at least a quarter century of continual sex. The next week, every member of the team carried at least a dozen rubbers to school every day. We showed them around, discussed our proposed sexual conquests, and passed them out to friends. We felt pretty grown up carrying all those rubbers around and I guess we would still have some of them if we hadn't lost the Quarterfinals game the next week.

Our opponent was to be a Baptist high school from Waco and we were to play an afternoon game at Alamo Stadium in San Antonio, which was a neutral site. As a reward for our "Season of Glory," the Lions Club had raised money to put us up in the Gunter Hotel, and we were going to spend the night after the game in the big city. We all packed pretty much the same things: an extra pair of socks, a change of underwear, a pair of Levis, our best sport shirt, our letter jacket, and of course our rubbers. I had heard there were a lot of women in San Antonio and, in an optimistic moment, I threw in an extra four dozen rubbers.

We got trampled. At the half the Baptists led, 28 to 7, and we were mad as hell. We cheated, played dirty, used every trick we knew, but we could not get moving. They were just too big and too fast. When the final gun went off, the scoreboard said, "Waco Bapt.—56 . . . Anna Rose—14." The Anna Rose Wranglers had never been good losers. In the dressing room after the game, Mickey Ray started it by slamming his shoulder pads against a locker and speculating loudly about the sexual preferences, human and animal, of "those uppity Baptist Bastards." One thing led to another and it wasn't long until we were gleefully blowing up all the rubbers we had packed in our suitcases.

We raced around to the Baptists' parking area and gave each member of their team and several of their rooters a victory balloon, as a sign of our good will and best wishes for their success in the Semifinals. They were mightily impressed. One of their assistant coaches, who was also a part-time preacher, even made a little speech about how well we embodied the ideals of good sportsmanship. We smiled and kicked at the gravel, then waved at our conquerors as they climbed into their cars and buses and headed back to Waco with their collection of rapidly deflating condoms.

It was their coach who got Anna Rose placed on Interscholastic League probation for two years, and almost got us beat to death by our parents in the bargain. The best we were able to piece it together, his six-year-old daughter had got one of our balloons and started chewing on it after most of the air escaped. Somewhere about five miles south of New Braunfels, he turned around and saw his little girl sucking on a spent condom and went into such a state of shock that he ran the car off the road into a field, where he wound up buying two registered Holstein milk cows.

Our yearbook, the Round-Up, omitted pictures of the football team that year, and Coach Tom Rhodes took his whistle and clipboard and green panel truck somewhere else. We never did find out where. Anna Rose didn't give up football. No amount of embarrassment or scandal could have that drastic a result. But some families did de-emphasize the game. My father decided it might not be a bad idea for me to get some musical training, and as our team marched out on the field the following year, I got a little misty-eyed as I puckered up and blew into the big gold tuba.

(For Betty and Rhoda)

RING LARDNER

A New Busher Breaks In

Chicago, Illinois, March 2.

FRIEND AL: Al that peace in the paper was all O.K. and the right dope just like you said. I seen president Johnson the president of the league today and he told me the peace in the papers was the right dope and Comiskey did not have no right to sell me to Milwaukee because the Detroit Club had never gave no wavers on me. He says the Detroit Club was late in fileing their claim and Comiskey must of tooken it for granted that they was going to wave but president Johnson was pretty sore about it at that and says Comiskey did

From *You Know Me Al* (1916).

not have no right to sell me till he was positive that they was not no team that wanted me.

It will probily cost Comiskey some money for acting like he done and not paying no attention to the rules and I would not be supprised if president Johnson had him throwed out of the league.

Well I asked president Johnson should I report at once to the Detroit Club down south and he says No you better wait till you hear from Comiskey and I says What has Comiskey got to do with it now? And he says Comiskey will own you till he sells you to Detroit or somewheres else. So I will have to go out to the ball park to-morrow and see is they any mail for me there because I probily will get a letter from Comiskey telling me I am sold to Detroit.

If I had of thought at the time I would of knew that Detroit never would give no wavers on me after the way I showed Cobb and Crawford up last fall and I might of knew too that Detroit is in the market for good pitchers because they got a rotten pitching staff but they won't have no rotten staff when I get with them.

If necessary I will pitch every other day for Jennings and if I do we will win the pennant sure because Detroit has got a club that can get 2 or 3 runs every day and all as I need to win most of my games is 1 run. I can't hardly wait till Jennings works me against the White Sox and what I will do to them will be a plenty. It don't take no pitching to beat them anyway and when they get up against a pitcher like I they might as well leave their bats in the bag for all the good their bats will do them.

I guess Cobb and Crawford will be glad to have me on the Detroit Club because then they won't never have to hit against me except in practice and I won't pitch my best in practice because they will be teammates of mine and I don't never like to show none of my teammates up. At that though I don't suppose Jennings will let me do much pitching in practice because when he gets a hold of a good pitcher he won't want me to take no chances of throwing my arm away in practice.

Al just think how funny it will be to have me pitching for the Tigers in the same town where Violet lives and pitching on the same club with her husband. It will not be so funny for Violet and her husband though because when she has a chance to see me work regular she will find out what a mistake she made takeing that left-hander instead of a man that has got some future and soon will be makeing 5 or $6000 a year because I won't sign with Detroit for no less than $5000 at most. Of coarse I could of had her if I had of wanted to but still and all it will make her feel pretty sick to see me winning games for Detroit while her husband is batting fungos and getting splinters in his unie from slideing up and down the bench.

As for her husband the first time he opens his clam to me I will haul off and bust him one in the jaw but I guess he will know more than to start trouble with a man of my size and who is going to be one of their stars while he is just holding down a job because they feel sorry for him. I wish he could of got the girl I married instead of the one he got and I bet she would of drove him crazy. But I guess you can't drive a left-hander crazyer than he is to begin with.

I have not heard nothing from Florrie Al and I don't want to hear nothing. I and her is better apart and I wish she would sew me for a bill of divorce so she could not go round claiming she is my wife and disgraceing my name. If she would consent to sew me for a bill of divorce I would gladly pay all the expenses and settle with her for any sum of money she wants say about $75.00 or $100.00 and they is no reason I should give her a nichol after the way her and her sister Marie and her brother-in-law Allen grafted off of me. Probily I could sew her for a bill of divorce but they tell me it costs money to sew and if you just lay low and let the other side do the sewing it don't cost you a nichol.

It is pretty late Al and I have got to get up early tomorrow and go to the ball park and see is they any mail for me. I will let you know what I hear old pal.   Your old pal,   JACK.

Chicago, Illinois, March 4.

AL: I am up against it again. I went out to the ball park office yesterday and they was nobody there except John somebody who is asst secretary and all the rest of them is out on the Coast with the team. Maybe this here John was trying to kid me but this is what he told me. First I says Is they a letter here for me? And he says No. And I says I was expecting word from Comiskey that I should join the Detroit Club and he says What makes you think you are going to Detroit? I says Comiskey asked wavers on me and Detroit did not give no wavers. He says Well that is not no sign that you are going to Detroit. If Comiskey can't get you out of the league he will probily keep you himself and it is a cinch he is not going to give no pitcher to Detroit no matter how rotten he is.

I says What do you mean? And he says You just stick round town till you hear from Comiskey and I guess you will hear pretty soon because he is comeing back from the Coast next Saturday. I says Well the only thing he can tell me is to report to Detroit because I won't never pitch again for the White Sox. Then John gets fresh and says I suppose you will quit the game and live on your saveings and then I blowed out of the office because I was scared I would loose my temper and break something.

So you see Al what I am up against. I won't never pitch for the White Sox again and I want to get with the Detroit Club but how can I if Comiskey won't let me go? All I can do is stick round till next Saturday and then I will see Comiskey and I guess when I tell him what I think of him he will be glad to let me go to Detroit or anywheres else. I will have something on him this time because I know that he did not pay no attention to the rules when he told me I was sold to Milwaukee and if he tries to slip something over on me I will tell president Johnson of the league all about it and then you will see where Comiskey heads in at.

Al old pal that $25.00 you give me at the station the other day is all shot to peaces and I must ask you to let me have $25.00 more which will make $75.00 all together includeing the $25.00 you sent me before I come home. I hate to ask you this favor old pal but I know you have got the money. If I am sold to Detroit I will get some advance money and pay up all my dedts incluseive.

If he don't let me go to Detroit I will make him come across with part of my salery for this year even if I don't pitch for him because I signed a contract and was ready to do my end of it and would of if he had not of been nasty and tried to slip something over on me. If he refuses to come across I will hire a attorney at law and he will get it all. So Al you see you have got a cinch on getting back what you lone me but I guess you know that Al without all this talk because you have been my old pal for a good many years and I have all-ways treated you square and tried to make you feel that I and you was equals and that my success was not going to make me forget my old friends.

Wherever I pitch this year I will insist on a salery of 5 or $6000 a year. So you see on my first pay day I will have enough to pay you up and settle the rest of my dedts but I am not going to pay no more rent for this rotten flat because they tell me if a man don't pay no rent for a while they will put him out. Let them put me out. I should not worry but will go and rent my old room that I had before I met Florrie and got into all this trouble.

The sooner you can send me that $35.00 the better and then I will owe you $85.00 inclusive and I will write and let you know how I come out with Comiskey.   Your pal, JACK.

Chicago, Illinois, March 12.

FRIEND AL: I got another big supprise for you and this is it I am going to pitch for the White Sox after all. If Comiskey was not a old man I guess I would of lost my temper and beat him up but I am glad now that I kept my temper and did not loose it because I forced him to make a lot of consessions and now it looks like as though I would have a big year both pitching and money.

He got back to town yesterday morning and showed up to his office in the afternoon and I was there waiting for him. He would not see me for a while but finally I acted like as though I was getting tired of waiting and I guess the secretary got scared that I would beat it out of the office and leave them all in

the lerch. Anyway he went in and spoke to Comiskey and then come out and
says the boss was ready to see me. When I went into the office where he was
at he says Well young man what can I do for you? And I says I want you to
give me my release so as I can join the Detroit Club down South and get in
shape. Then he says What makes you think you are going to join the Detroit
Club? Because we need you here. I says Then why did you try to sell me to
Milwaukee? But you could not because you could not get no wavers.

Then he says I thought I was doing you a favor by sending you to Milwaukee because they make a lot of beer up there. I says What do you mean?
He says You been keeping in shape all this winter by trying to drink this town
dry and besides that you tried to hold me up for more money when you allready had signed a contract allready and so I was going to send you to Milwaukee and learn you something and besides you tried to go with the Federal
League but they would not take you because they was scared to.

I don't know where he found out all that stuff at Al and besides he was
wrong when he says I was drinking to much because they is not nobody that
can drink more than me and not be effected. But I did not say nothing because I was scared I would forget myself and call him some name and he is a
old man. Yes I did say something. I says Well I guess you found out that you
could not get me out of the league and then he says Don't never think I could
not get you out of the league. If you think I can't send you to Milwaukee I will
prove it to you that I can. I says You can't because Detroit won't give no
wavers on me. He says Detroit will give wavers on you quick enough if I
ask them.

Then he says Now you can take your choice you can stay here and pitch for
me at the salery you signed up for and you can cut out the monkey business
and drink water when you are thirsty or else you can go up to Milwaukee and
drownd yourself in one of them brewrys. Which shall it be? I says How can
you keep me or send me to Milwaukee when Detroit has allready claimed my
services? He says Detroit has claimed a lot of things and they have even
claimed the pennant but that is not no sign they will win it. He says And
besides you would not want to pitch for Detroit because then you would not
never have no chance to pitch against Cobb and show him up.

Well Al when he says that I knowed he appresiated what a pitcher I am
even if he did try to sell me to Milwaukee or he would not of made that remark about the way I can show Cobb and Crawford up. So I says Well if you
need me that bad I will pitch for you but I must have a new contract. He says
Oh I guess we can fix that up O.K. and he steps out in the next room a while
and then he comes back with a new contract. And what do you think it was
Al? It was a contract for 3 years so you see I am sure of my job here for 3 years
and everything is all O.K.

The contract calls for the same salery a year for 3 years that I was going to get before for only 1 year which is $2800.00 a year and then I will get in on the city serious money too and the Detroit Club don't have no city serious and have no chance to get into the World's Serious with the rotten pitching staff they got. So you see Al he fixed me up good and that shows that he must think a hole lot of me or he would of sent me to Detroit or maybe to Milwaukee but I don't see how he could of did that without no wavers.

Well Al I allmost forgot to tell you that he has gave me a ticket to Los Angeles where the 2d team are practicing at now but where the 1st team will be at in about a week. I am leaveing to-night and I guess before I go I will go down to president Johnson and tell him that I am fixed up all O.K. and have not got no kick comeing so that president Johnson will not fine Comiskey for not paying no attention to the rules or get him fired out of the league because I guess Comiskey must be all O.K. and good hearted after all.

I won't pay no attention to what he says about me drinking this town dry because he is all wrong in regards to that. He must of been jokeing I guess because nobody but some boob would think he could drink this town dry but at that I guess I can hold more than anybody and not be effected. But I guess I will cut it out for a while at that because I don't want to get them sore at me after the contract they give me.

I will write to you from Los Angeles Al and let you know what the boys says when they see me and I will bet that they will be tickled to death. The rent man was round to-day but I seen him comeing and he did not find me. I am going to leave the furniture that belongs in the flat in the flat and allso the furniture I bought which don't amount to much because it was not no real Sir Cashion walnut and besides I don't want nothing round me to remind me of Florrie because the sooner her and I forget each other the better.

Tell the boys about my good luck Al but it is not no luck neither because it was comeing to me.   Yours truly,   JACK.

Los Angeles, California, March 16.

AL: Here I am back with the White Sox again and it seems to good to be true because just like I told you they are all tickled to death to see me. Kid Gleason is here in charge of the 2d team and when he seen me come into the hotel he jumped up and hit me in the stumach but he acts like that whenever he feels good so I could not get sore at him though he had no right to hit me in the stumach. If he had of did it in ernest I would of walloped him in the jaw.

He says Well if here ain't the old lady killer. He ment Al that I am strong with the girls but I am all threw with them now but he don't know nothing about the troubles I had. He says Are you in shape? And I told him Yes I am.

He says Yes you look in shape like a barrel. I says They is not no fat on me and if I am a little bit bigger than last year it is because my mussels is bigger. He says yes your stumach mussels is emense and you must of gave them plenty of exercise. Wait till Bodie sees you and he will want to stick round you all the time because you make him look like a broom straw or something. I let him kid me along because what is the use of getting mad at him? And besides he is all O.K. even if he is a little rough.

I says to him A little work will fix me up all O.K. and he says You bet you are going to get some work because I am going to see to it myself. I says You will have to hurry because you will be going up to Frisco in a few days and I am going to stay here and join the 1st club. Then he says You are not going to do no such a thing. You are going right along with me. I knowed he was kidding me then because Callahan would not never leave me with the 2d team no more after what I done for him last year and besides most of the stars generally allways goes with the 1st team on the training trip.

Well I seen all the rest of the boys that is here with the 2d team and they all acted like as if they was glad to see me and why should not they be when they know that me being here with the White Sox and not with Detroit means that Callahan won't have to do no worrying about his pitching staff? But they is four or 5 young recruit pitchers with the team here and I bet they is not so glad to see me because what chance have they got?

If I was Comiskey and Callahan I would not spend no money on new pitchers because with me and 1 or 2 of the other boys we got the best pitching staff in the league. And instead of spending the money for new pitching recruits I would put it all in a lump and buy Ty Cobb or Sam Crawford off of Detroit or somebody else who can hit and Cobb and Crawford is both real hitters Al even if I did make them look like suckers. Who wouldn't?

Well Al to-morrow A.M. I am going out and work a little and in the P.M. I will watch the game between we and the Venice Club but I won't pitch none because Gleason would not dare take no chances of me hurting my arm. I will write to you in a few days from here because no matter what Gleason says I am going to stick here with the 1st team because I know Callahan will want me along with him for a attraction.   Your pal, JACK.

San Francisco, California, March 20.
FRIEND AL: Well Al here I am back in old Frisco with the 2d team but I will tell you how it happened Al. Yesterday Gleason told me to pack up and get ready to leave Los Angeles with him and I says No I am going to stick here and wait for the 1st team and then he says I guess I must of overlooked something in the papers because I did not see nothing about you being appointed manager of the club. I says No I am not manager but Callahan is manager and

he will want to keep me with him. He says I got a wire from Callahan telling me to keep you with my club but of coarse if you know what Callahan wants better than he knows it himself why then go ahead and stay here or go jump in the Pacific Ocean.

Then he says I know why you don't want to go with me and I says Why? And he says Because you know I will make you work and won't let you eat everything on the bill of fair includeing the name of the hotel at which we are stopping at. That made me sore and I was just going to call him when he says Did not you marry Mrs. Allen's sister? And I says Yes but that is not none of your business. Then he says Well I don't want to butt into your business but I heard you and your wife had some kind of a argument and she beat it. I says Yes she give me a rotten deal. He says Well then I don't see where it is going to be very pleasant for you traveling round with the 1st club because Allen and his wife is both with that club and what do you want to be mixed up with them for? I says I am not scared of Allen or his wife, or no other old hen.

So here I am Al with the 2d team but it is only for a while till Callahan gets sick of some of them pitchers he has got and sends for me so as he can see some real pitching. And besides I am glad to be here in Frisco where I made so many friends when I was pitching here for a short time till Callahan heard about my work and called me back to the big show where I belong at and nowheres else.   Yours truly,   JACK.

San Francisco, California, March 25.

OLD PAL: Al I got a surprise for you. Who do you think I seen last night? Nobody but Hazel. Her name now is Hazel Levy because you know Al she married Kid Levy the middleweight and I wish he was champion of the world Al because then it would not take me more than about a minute to be champion of the world myself. I have not got nothing against him though because he married her and if he had not of I probily would of married her myself but at that she could not of treated me no worse than Florrie. Well they was setting at a table in the cafe where her and I use to go pretty near every night. She spotted me when I first come in and sends a waiter over to ask me to come and have a drink with them. I went over because they was no use being nasty and let bygones be bygones.

She interduced me to her husband and he asked me what I was drinking. Then she butts in and says Oh you must let Mr. Keefe buy the drinks because it hurts his feelings to have somebody else buy the drinks. Then Levy says Oh he is one of these here spendrifts is he? and she says Yes he don't care no more about a nichol than his right eye does. I says I guess you have got no hollor comeing on the way I spend my money. I don't steal no money anyway. She says What do you mean? and I says I guess you know what I mean. How about that $30.00 that you borrowed off of me and never give it back, Then her husband cuts in and says You cut that line of talk out or I will bust you. I says Yes you will. And he says Yes I will.

Well Al what was the use of me starting trouble with him when he has got enough trouble right to home and besides as I say I have not got nothing against him. So I got up and blowed away from the table and I bet he was relieved when he seen I was not going to start nothing. I beat it out of there a while afterward because I was not drinking nothing and I don't have no fun setting round a place and lapping up ginger ail or something. And besides the music was rotten.

Al I am certainly glad I threwed Hazel over because she has grew to be as big as a horse and is all painted up. I don't care nothing about them big dolls no more or about no other kind neither. I am off of them all. They can all of them die and I should not worry.

Well Al I done my first pitching of the year this P.M. and I guess I showed them that I was in just as good a shape as some of them birds that has been working a month. I worked 4 innings against my old team the San Francisco Club and I give them nothing but fast ones but they sure was fast ones and you could hear them zip. Charlie O'Leary was trying to get out of the way of one of them and it hit his bat and went over first base for a base hit but at that Fournier would of eat it up if it had of been Chase playing first base instead of Fournier.

That was the only hit they got off of me and they ought to of been ashamed to of tooken that one. But Gleason don't appresiate my work and him and I allmost come to blows at supper. I was pretty hungry and I ordered some stake and some eggs and some pie and some ice cream and some coffee and a glass of milk but Gleason would not let me have the pie or the milk and would not let me eat more than ½ the stake. And it is a wonder I did not bust him and tell him to mind his own business. I says What right have you got to tell me what to eat? And he says You don't need nobody to tell you what to eat you need somebody to keep you from floundering yourself. I says Why can't I eat what I want to when I have worked good?

He says Who told you you worked good and I says I did not need nobody to tell me. I know I worked good because they could not do nothing with me. He says Well it is a good thing for you that they did not start bunting because if you had of went to stoop over and pick up the ball you would of busted wide open. I says Why? and he says because you are hog fat and if you don't let up on the stable and fancy groceries we will have to pay 2 fairs to get you back to Chi. I don't remember now what I says to him but I says something you can bet on that. You know me Al.

I wish Al that Callahan would hurry up and order me to join the 1st team. If he don't Al I believe Gleason will starve me to death. A little slob like him don't realize that a big man like I needs good food and plenty of it.

Your pal.   JACK.

Salt Lake City, Utah, April 1.

AL: Well Al we are on our way East and I am still with the 2d team and I don't understand why Callahan don't order me to join the 1st team but maybe it is because he knows that I am all right and have got the stuff and he wants to keep them other guys round where he can see if they have got anything.

The recrut pitchers that is along with our club have not got nothing and the scout that reckommended them must of been full of hops or something. It is not no common thing for a club to pick up a man that has got the stuff to make him a star up here and the White Sox was pretty lucky to land me but I don't understand why they throw their money away on new pitchers when none of them is no good and besides who would want a better pitching staff than we got right now without no raw recruts and bushers.

I worked in Oakland the day before yesterday but he only let me go the 1st 4 innings. I bet them Oakland birds was glad when he took me out. When I was in that league I use to just throw my glove in the box and them Oakland birds was licked and honest Al some of them turned white when they seen I was going to pitch the other day.

I felt kind of sorry for them and I did not give them all I had so they got 5 or 6 hits and scored a couple of runs. I was not feeling very good at that and besides we got some awful excuses for a ball player on this club and the support they give me was the rottenest I ever seen gave anybody. But some of them won't be in this league more than about 10 minutes more so I should not fret as they say.

We play here this afternoon and I don't believe I will work because the team they got here is not worth wasteing nobody on. They must be a lot of boobs in this town Al because they tell me that some of them has got ½ a dozen wives or so. And what a man wants with 1 wife is a mistery to me let alone a ½ dozen.

I will probily work against Denver because they got a good club and was champions of the Western League last year. I will make them think they are champions of the Epworth League or something.   Yours truly,   JACK.

Des Moines, Iowa, April 10.

FRIEND AL: We got here this A.M. and this is our last stop and we will be in old Chi to-morrow to open the season. The 1st team gets home to-day and I would be there with them if Callahan was a real manager who knowed something about manageing because if I am going to open the season I should ought to have 1 day of rest at home so I would have all my strenth to open the season. The Cleveland Club will be there to open against us and Callahan must know that I have got them licked any time I start against them.

As soon as my name is announced to pitch the Cleveland Club is licked or any other club when I am right and they don't kick the game away behind me.

Gleason told me on the train last night that I was going to pitch here today but I bet by this time he has got orders from Callahan to let me rest and to not give me no more work because suppose even if I did not start the game tomorrow I probily will have to finish it.

Gleason has been sticking round me like as if I had a million bucks or something. I can't even sit down and smoke a cigar but what he is there to knock the ashes off of it. He is O.K. and good-hearted if he is a little rough and keeps hitting me in the stumach but I wish he would leave me alone sometimes espesially at meals. He was in to breakfast with me this A.M. and after I got threw I snuck off down the street and got something to eat. That is not right because it costs me money when I have to go away from the hotel and eat and what right has he got to try and help me order my meals? Because he don't know what I want and what my stumach wants.

My stumach don't want to have him punching it all the time but he keeps on doing it. So that shows he don't know what is good for me. But he is a old man Al otherwise I would not stand for the stuff he pulls. The 1st thing I am going to do when we get to Chi is I am going to a resturunt somewheres and get a good meal where Gleason or no one else can't get at me. I know allready what I am going to eat and that is a big stake and a apple pie and that is not all.

Well Al watch the papers and you will see what I done to that Cleveland Club and I hope Lajoie and Jackson is both in good shape because I don't want to pick on no cripples.   Your pal,   JACK.

Chicago, Illinois, April 16.

OLD PAL: Yesterday was the 1st pay day old pal and I know I promised to pay you what I owe you and it is $75.00 because when I asked you for $35.00 before I went West you only sent me $25.00 which makes the hole sum $75.00. Well Al I can't pay you now because the pay we drawed was only for 4 days and did not amount to nothing and I had to buy a meal ticket and fix up about my room rent.

And then they is another thing Al which I will tell you about. I come into the clubhouse the day the season opened and the 1st guy I seen was Allen. I was going up to bust him but he come up and held his hand out and what was they for me to do but shake hands with him if he is going to be yellow like that? He says Well Jack I am glad they did not send you to Milwaukee and I bet you will have a big year. I says Yes I will have a big year O.K. if you don't sick another 1 of your sister-in-laws on to me. He says Oh don't let they be no hard feelings about that. You know it was not no fault of mine and I bet if you was to write to Florrie everything could be fixed up O.K.

I says I don't want to write to no Florrie but I will get a attorney at law to write to her. He says You don't even know where she is at and I says I don't care where she is at. Where is she? He says She is down to her home in Waco, Texas, and if I was you I would write to her myself and not let no attorney at law write to her because that would get her mad and besides what do you want a attorney at law to write to her about? I says I am going to sew her for a bill of divorce.

Then he says On what grounds? and I says Dessertion. He says You better not do no such thing or she will sew you for a bill of divorce for none support and then you will look like a cheap guy. I says I don't care what I look like. So you see Al I had to send Florrie $10.00 or maybe she would be mean enough to sew me for a bill of divorce on the ground of none support and that would make me look bad.

Well Al, Allen told me his wife wanted to talk to me and try and fix things up between I and Florrie but I give him to understand that I would not stand for no meeting with his wife and he says Well suit yourself about that but they is no reason you and I should quarrel.

You see Al he don't want no mix-up with me because he knows he could not get nothing but the worst of it. I will be friends with him but I won't have nothing to do with Marie because if it had not of been for she and Florrie I would have money in the bank besides not being in no danger of getting sewed for none support.

I guess you must of read about Joe Benz getting married and I guess he must of got a good wife and 1 that don't bother him all the time because he pitched the opening game and shut Cleveland out with 2 hits. He was pretty good Al, better than I ever seen him and they was a couple of times when his fast ball was pretty near as fast as mine.

I have not worked yet Al and I asked Callahan to-day what was the matter and he says I was waiting for you to get in shape. I says I am in shape now and I notice that when I was pitching in practice this A.M. they did not hit nothing out of the infield. He says That was because you are so spread out that they could not get nothing past you. He says The way you are now you cover more ground than the grand stand. I says Is that so? And he walked away.

We go out on a trip to Cleveland and Detroit and St. Louis in a few days and maybe I will take my regular turn then because the other pitchers has been getting away lucky because most of the hitters has not got their batting eye as yet but wait till they begin hitting and then it will take a man like I to stop them.

The 1st of May is our next pay day Al and then I will have enough money so as I can send you the $75.00.   Your pal,   JACK.

Detroit, Michigan, April 28.

FRIEND AL: What do you think of a rotten manager that bawls me out and fines me $50.00 for loosing a 1 to o game in 10 innings when it was my 1st start this season? And no wonder I was a little wild in the 10th when I had not had no chance to work and get control. I got a good notion to quit this rotten club and jump to the Federals where a man gets some kind of treatment. Callahan says I throwed the game away on purpose but I did not do no such a thing Al because when I throwed that ball at Joe Hill's head I forgot that the bases was full and besides if Gleason had not of starved me to death the ball that hit him in the head would of killed him.

And how could a man go to 1st base and the winning run be forced in if he was dead which he should ought to of been the lucky left handed stiff if I had of had my full strenth to put on my fast one instead of being ½ starved to death and weak. But I guess I better tell you how it come off. The papers will get it all wrong like they generally allways does.

Callahan asked me this A.M. if I thought I was hard enough to work and I was tickled to death, because I seen he was going to give me a chance. I told him Sure I was in good shape and if them Tigers scored a run off me he could keep me setting on the bench the rest of the summer. So he says All right I am going to start you and if you go good maybe Gleason will let you eat some supper.

Well Al when I begin warming up I happened to look up in the grand stand and who do you think I seen? Nobody but Violet. She smiled when she seen me but I bet she felt more like crying. Well I smiled back at her because she probily would of broke down and made a seen or something if I had not of. They was not nobody warming up for Detroit when I begin warming up but pretty soon I looked over to their bench and Joe Hill Violet's husband was warming up. I says to myself Well here is where I show that bird up if they got nerve enough to start him against me but probily Jennings don't want to waste no real pitcher on this game which he knows we got cinched and we would of had it cinched Al if they had of got a couple of runs or even 1 run for me.

Well, Jennings come passed our bench just like he allways does and tried to pull some of his funny stuff. He says Hello are you still in the league? I says Yes but I come pretty near not being. I came pretty near being with Detroit. I wish you could of heard Gleason and Callahan laugh when I pulled that one on him. He says something back but it was not no hot comeback like mine.

Well Al if I had of had any work and my regular control I guess I would of pitched a o hit game because the only time they could touch me was when I had to ease up to get them over. Cobb was out of the game and they told me he was sick but I guess the truth is that he knowed I was going to pitch. Crawford got a couple of lucky scratch hits off of me because I got in the hole to him and had to let up. But the way that lucky left handed Hill got by was something awful and if I was as lucky as him I would quit pitching and shoot craps or something.

Our club can't hit nothing anyway. But batting against this bird was just like hitting fungos. His curve ball broke about ½ a inch and you could of wrote your name and address on his fast one while it was comeing up there. He had good control but who would not when they put nothing on the ball?

Well Al we could not get started against the lucky stiff and they could not do nothing with me even if my suport was rotten and I give a couple or 3 or 4 bases on balls but when they was men waiting to score I zipped them threw there so as they could not see them let alone hit them. Every time I come to the bench between innings I looked up to where Violet was setting and give her a smile and she smiled back and once I seen her clapping her hands at me after I had made Moriarty pop up in the pinch.

Well we come along to the 10th inning, o and o, and all of a sudden we got after him. Bodie hits one and Schalk get 2 strikes and 2 balls and then singles. Callahan tells Alcock to bunt and he does it but Hill sprawls all over himself like the big boob he is and the bases is full with nobody down. Well Gleason and Callahan argude about should they send somebody up for me or let me go up there and I says Let me go up there because I can murder this bird and Callahan says Well they is nobody out so go up and take a wallop.

Honest Al if this guy had of had anything at all I would of hit 1 out of the park, but he did not have even a glove. And how can a man hit pitching which is not no pitching at all but just slopping them up? When I went up there I hollered to him and says Stick 1 over here now you yellow stiff. And he says Yes I can stick them over allright and that is where I got something on you.

Well Al I hit a foul off of him that would of been a fare ball and broke up the game if the wind had not of been against it. Then I swung and missed a curve that I don't see how I missed it. The next 1 was a yard outside and this Evans calls it a strike. He has had it in for me ever since last year when he tried to get funny with me and I says something back to him that stung him.

So he calls this 3d strike on me and I felt like murdering him. But what is the use?

I throwed down my bat and come back to the bench and I was glad Callahan and Gleason was out on the coaching line or they probably would of said something to me and I would of cut loose and beat them up. Well Al Weaver and Blackburne looked like a couple of rums up there and we don't score where we ought to of had 3 or 4 runs with any kind of hiting.

I would of been all O.K. in spite of that peace of rotten luck if this Hill had of walked to the bench and not said nothing like a real pitcher. But what does he do but wait out there till I start for the box and I says Get on to the bench you lucky stiff or do you want me to hand you something? He says I don't want nothing more of yourn. I allready got your girl and your goat.

Well Al what do you think of a man that would say a thing like that? And nobody but a left hander could of. If I had of had a gun I would of killed him deader than a doornail or something. He starts for the bench and I hollered at him Wait till you get up to that plate and then I am going to bean you.

Honest Al I was so mad I could not see the plate or nothing. I don't even know who it was come up to bat 1st but whoever it was I hit him in the arm and he walks to first base. The next guy bunts and Chase tries to pull off 1 of them plays of hisn instead of playing safe and he don't get nobody. Well I kept getting madder and madder and I walks Stanage who if I had of been myself would not foul me.

Callahan has Scotty warming up and Gleason runs out from the bench and tells me I am threw but Callahan says Wait a minute he is going to let Hill hit and this big stiff ought to be able to get him out of the way and that will give Scotty a chance to get warm. Gleason says You better not take a chance because the big busher is hogwild, and they kept argueing till I got sick of listening to them and I went back to the box and got ready to pitch. But when I seen this Hill up there I forgot all about the ball game and I cut loose at his bean.

Well Al my control was all O.K. this time and I catched him square on the fourhead and he dropped like as if he had been shot. But pretty soon he gets up and gives me the laugh and runs to first base. I did not know the game was over till Weaver come up and pulled me off the field. But if I had not of been ½ starved to death and weak so as I could not put all my stuff on the ball you can bet that Hill never would of ran to first base and Violet would of been a widow and probily a lot better off than she is now. At that I never should ought to of tried to kill a lefthander by hitting him in the head.

Well Al they jumped all over me in the clubhouse and I had to hold myself back or I would of gave somebody the beating of their life. Callahan tells me I am fined $50.00 and suspended without no pay. I asked him What for and he says They would not be no use in telling you because you have not got no brains. I says Yes I have to got some brains and he says Yes but they is in your stumach. And then he says I wish we had of sent you to Milwaukee and I come back at him. I says I wish you had of.

Well Al I guess they is no chance of getting square treatment on this club and you won't be surprised if you hear of me jumping to the Federals where a man is treated like a man and not like no white slave. Yours truly,   Jack.

Chicago, Illinois, May 2.

Al: I have got to disappoint you again Al. When I got up to get my pay yesterday they held out $150.00 on me. $50.00 of it is what I was fined for loosing a 1 to 0 10-inning game in Detroit when I was so weak that I should ought never to of been sent in there and the $100.00 is the advance money that I drawed last winter and which I had forgot all about and the club would of forgot about it to if they was not so tight fisted.

So you see all I get for 2 weeks' pay is about $80.00 and I sent $25.00 to Florie so she can't come no none support business on me.

I am still suspended Al and not drawing no pay now and I got a notion to hire a attorney at law and force them to pay my salery or else jump to the Federals where a man gets good treatment.

Allen is still after me to come over to his flat some night and see his wife and let her talk to me about Florrie but what do I want to talk about Florrie for or talk about nothing to a nut left hander's wife?

The Detroit Club is here and Cobb is playing because he knows I am suspended but I wish Callahan would call it off and let me work against them and I would certainly love to work against this Joe Hill again and I bet they would be a different story this time because I been getting something to eat since we been home and I got back most of my strength.

Your old pal,   Jack.

Chicago, Illinois, May 5.

Friend Al: Well Al if you been reading the papers you will knew before this letter is received what I done. Before the Detroit Club come here Joe Hill had win 4 strate but he has not win no 5 strate or won't neither Al because I put a crimp in his winning streek just like I knowed I would do if I got a chance when I was feeling good and had all my strenth. Callahan asked me yesterday A.M. if I thought I had enough rest and I says Sure because I did not need no rest in the 1st place. Well, he says, I thought maybe if I layed you off a few days you would do some thinking and if you done some thinking once in a while you would be a better pitcher.

Well anyway I worked and I wish you could of saw them Tigers trying to hit me Cobb and Crawford incluseive. The 1st time Cobb come up Weaver catched a lucky line drive off of him and the next time I eased up a little and Collins run back and took a fly ball off of the fence. But the other times he come up he looked like a sucker except when he come up in the 8th and then he beat out a bunt but allmost anybody is liable to do that once in a while.

Crawford got a scratch hit between Chase and Blackburne in the 2d inning and in the 4th he was gave a three-base hit by this Evans who should ought to be writeing for the papers instead of trying to umpire. The ball was 2 feet foul and I bet Crawford will tell you the same thing if you ask him. But what I done to this Hill was awful. I give him my curve twice when he was up there in the 3d and he missed it a foot. Then I come with my fast ball right past his nose and I bet if he had not of ducked it would of drove that big horn of hisn clear up in the press box where them rotten reporters sits and smokes their hops. Then when he was looking for another fast one I slopped up my slow one and he is still swinging at it yet.

But the best of it was that I practally won my own game. Bodie and Schalk was on when I come up in the 5th and Hill hollers to me and says I guess this is where I shoot one of them bean balls. I says Go ahead and shoot and if you hit me in the head and I ever find it out I will write and tell your wife what happened to you. You see what I was getting at Al. I was insinuateing that if he beaned me with his fast one I would not never know nothing about it if somebody did not tell me because his fast one is not fast enough to hurt nobody even if it should hit them in the head. So I says to him Go ahead and shoot and if you hit me in the head and I ever find it out I will write and tell your wife what happened to you. See, Al?

Of coarse you could not hire me to write to Violet but I did not mean that part of it in ernest. Well sure enough he shot at my bean and I ducked out of the way though if it had of hit me it could not of did no more than tickle. He takes 2 more shots and misses me and then Jennings hollers from the bench What are you doing pitching or trying to win a cigar? So then Hill sees what a monkey he is makeing out of himself and tries to get one over, but I have him 3 balls and nothing and what I done to that groover was a plenty. She went over Bush's head like a bullet and got between Cobb and Veach and goes clear to the fence. Bodie and Schalk scores and I would of scored to if anybody else besides Cobb had of been chaseing the ball. I got 2 bases and Weaver scores me with another wallop.

Say, I wish I could of heard what they said to that baby on the bench. Callahan was tickled to death and he says Maybe I will give you back that $50.00 if you keep that stuff up. I guess I will get that $50.00 back next pay day and if I do Al I will pay you the hole $75.00.

Well Al I beat them 5 to 4 and with good support I would of held them to 1 run but what do I care as long as I beat them? I wish though that Violet could of been there and saw it.   Yours truly,   JACK.

Chicago, Illinois, May 29.

OLD PAL: Well Al I have not wrote to you for a long while but it is not because I have forgot you and to show I have not forgot you I am encloseing the $75.00 which I owe you. It is a money order Al and you can get it cashed by takeing it to Joe Higgins at the P.O.

Since I wrote to you Al I been East with the club and I guess you know what I done in the East. The Athaletics did not have no right to win that 1 game off of me and I will get them when they come here the week after next. I beat Boston and just as good as beat New York twice because I beat them 1 game all alone and then saved the other for Eddie Cicotte in the 9th inning and shut out the Washington Club and would of did the same thing if Johnson had of been working against me instead of this left handed stiff Boehling.

Speaking of left handers Allen has been going rotten and I would not be supprised if they sent him to Milwaukee or Frisco or somewheres.

But I got bigger news than that for you Al. Florrie is back and we are living together in the spair room at Allen's flat so I hope they don't send him to Milwaukee or nowheres else because it is not costing us nothing for room rent and this is no more than right after the way the Allens grafted off of us all last winter.

I bet you will be supprised to know that I and Florrie has made it up and they is a secret about it Al which I can't tell you now but may be next month I will tell you and then you will be more supprised than ever. It is about I and Florrie and somebody else. But that is all I can tell you now.

We got in this A.M. Al and when I got to my room they was a slip of paper there telling me to call up a phone number so I called it up and it was Allen's flat and Marie answered the phone. And when I rekonized her voice I was going to hang up the phone but she says Wait a minute somebody wants to talk with you. And then Florrie come to the phone and I was going to hang up the phone again when she pulled this secret on me that I was telling you about.

So it is all fixed up between us Al and I wish I could tell you the secret but that will come later. I have tooken my baggage over to Allen's and I am there now writeing to you while Florrie is asleep. And after a while I am going out and mail this letter and get a glass of beer because I think I have got 1 comeing now on account of this secret. Florrie says she is sorry for the way she treated me and she cried when she seen me. So what is the use of me being nasty Al? And let bygones be bygones.   Your pal,   JACK.

Chicago, Illinois, June 16.

FRIEND AL: Al I beat the Athaletics 2 to 1 to-day but I am writing to you to give you the supprise of your life. Old pal I got a baby and he is a boy and we are going to name him Allen which Florrie thinks is after his uncle and aunt Allen but which is after you old pal. And she can call him Allen but I will call him Al because I don't never go back on my old pals. The baby was born over to the hospital and it is going to cost me a bunch of money but I should not worry. This is the secret I was going to tell you Al and I am the happyest man in the world and I bet you are most as tickled to death to hear about it as I am.

The baby was born just about the time I was makeing McInnis look like a sucker in the pinch but they did not tell me nothing about it till after the game and then they give me a phone messige in the clubhouse. I went right over there and everything was all O.K. Little Al is a homely little skate but I guess all babys is homely and don't have no looks till they get older and maybe he will look like Florrie or I then I won't have no kick comeing.

Be sure and tell Bertha the good news and tell her everything has came out all right except that the rent man is still after me about that flat I had last winter. And I am still paying the old man $10.00 a month for that house you got for me and which has not never done me no good. But I should not worry about money when I got a real family. Do you get that Al, a real family?

Well Al I am to happy to do no more writeing to-night but I wanted you to be the 1st to get the news and I would of sent you a telegram only I did not want to scare you.   Your pal,   JACK.

Chicago, Illinois, July 2.

OLD PAL: Well old pal I just come back from St. Louis this A.M. and found things in pretty fare shape. Florrie and the baby is out to Allen's and we will stay there till I can find another place. The Dr. was out to look at the baby this A.M. and the baby was waveing his arm round in the air. And Florrie asked was they something the matter with him that he kept waveing his arm. And the Dr. says No he was just getting his exercise.

Well Al I noticed that he never waved his right arm but kept waveing his left arm and I asked the Dr. why was that. Then the Dr. says I guess he must be left handed. That made me sore and I says I guess you doctors don't know it all. And then I turned round and beat it out of the room.

Well Al it would be just my luck to have him left handed and Florrie should ought to of knew better than to name him after Allen. I am going to hire another Dr. and see what he has to say because they must be some way of fixing babys so as they won't be left handed. And if nessary I will cut his left arm off of him. Of course I would not do that Al. But how would I feel if a boy of mine turned out like Allen and Joe Hill and some of them other nuts?

We have a game with St. Louis to-morrow and a double header on the 4th of July. I guess probily Callahan will work me in one of the 4th of July games on account of the holiday crowd.   Your pal,   JACK.

P.S. Maybe I should ought to leave the kid left handed so as he can have some of their luck. The lucky stiffs.

DAN JENKINS

The Wool Market

I don't know how all of the other great book writers do it but I like a little quiet and semi-solitude myself.

It's after one A.M. right now, which means that it has turned Saturday, the day before the game.

I am laying here on the bed where Cissy Walford has gone to sleep in a mound of movie magazines. Everybody left our palatial suite pretty early, about midnight.

That was just what me and Shake wanted to have. An early night.

All we did was sit around, mostly, and talk about how we were going to dough-pop the dog-ass Jets.

Elroy Blunt got out his guitar and sang about seven thousand tunes, which was fun, and relaxing.

Big Ed and Big Barb don't go much for country music and they kept requesting things like "Moon Over Karakaua," and "Palm Frond Mamba," and "You're the Twist in My Cocktail."

Once, Big Ed and Big Barb tried to do their version of the Fort Worth Slide when Elroy sang "You Can't Peel the Bark on a Redwood."

It wasn't so good.

Right in the middle of the evening Shoat Cooper showed up, as he is known to do. He was having his usual case of pregame second thoughts and worry.

He wanted me and Shake to go out in the hall with him and have a "gut check."

From *Semi-Tough* (1972).

Shoat said he had been down in Hose Manning's room chewin' on his cud, as he put it, and there was something troubling him about the game.

"I believe our defense is ready to stick 'em," he said. "I ain't worried about the defense. Their navels is gonna be screwed to the ground and they'll scratch and bite and spit at 'em."

Shoat said he figured our defense could hold the dog-ass Jets to seventeen or maybe twenty-one points. Twenty-four at the most.

"What this means," he said, "is that our offense is gonna have to stay off the toilet seat."

Me and Shake shook our heads in agreement.

"What troubles me," he said, "is that I dreamed the other night that they ain't gonna stay in their tendency defense. I think them sumbitches have so much respect for our runnin' game they're apt to give us a new look."

Shake said, "They can't overload anywhere. We got too many ways to fuck 'em."

Shoat said, "They can do one thing we ain't thought about."

Me and Shake looked at each other, and back at Shoat.

"They can Man you with Dreamer," Shoat said, looking at Shake Tiller. "And send the whole rest of their piss ants after stud hoss here."

"Dreamer can't play Man on Shake," I said. "Shake'll dust his ass off."

Shoat said, "Why's that?"

"He just will," I said. "Nobody's ever been able to play Man on Shake. And the best have tried."

"Dreamer ain't tried," said Shoat.

"So what?" I said.

"It's just something that come to me in my sleep," said Shoat. "It'd be a gamble for 'em. But I think it's what I might try, if I had me a Dreamer Tatum."

We all stood there in the hall and looked down at our feet.

"What else this means," said Shoat, "is that you're gonna take some licks in there, stud hoss. You got to hang onto that football out there Sunday. We can't give them piss ants anything."

I hardly ever fumble, by the way, and I reminded Shoat Cooper of that.

I looked at Shake as if to ask him about all this.

Shake said, "Coach, if I had one wish in life it would be for Dreamer Tatum to cover me Man. The whole fuckin' game."

Shoat Cooper thought about that. Then he said:

"Well, it would be an interestin' thing to look at in the screening room some day, or maybe at a coaching clinic. But I don't know as though it would help us win this football game."

Shake said, "If he tries to cover me Man, he'll get at least three interference calls, and I can beat his black ass all day on deep."

"He cheats," I said to Shoat.

"He wouldn't cheat if his job wasn't to stop no sweeps or pitches," said Shoat. "If his job was only to intimidate old Eighty-eight here and climb inside his shirt, he wouldn't cheat for the run."

We stood there some more, and I made up my mind.

"If they use Dreamer that way they're more dog-ass dumb than I ever thought," I said.

"It's just somethin' that bothered me in my sleep," said Shoat. "I just wanted to know what you studs thought about it."

Shake said, "What'd Hose think?"

Shoat pawed at the hall carpet and said:

"Aw, old Hose, he just smiled. He said he kind of hoped Dreamer would be Man on you because at least if he was, then Hose wouldn't have to worry about gettin' blind-popped from a corner blitz."

We grinned, me and Shake.

"Everything's cool, coach," said Shake. "If they play that way, old Billy C. here might not get his hundred and thirty-five rushing but we'll get everything else."

"You hosses feelin' good?" Shoat asked.

"Ready as we'll ever be," I said.

"Feelin' *fierce*, coach," said Shake, hugging old Shoat on the back. "Ready to rape, ravage and plunder."

Shoat said, "You hosses get a lot of rest in these last few hours. I want them legs to have spring in 'em. It's gonna be nigger on nigger out there Sunday."

"We're ready," I said again.

And we said goodnight to old Shoat, who probably went and drew circles and x's for five or six more hours.

Shake and me stayed in the hall after Shoat walked off.

I said, "Is there any possibility whatsoever that Shoat could be right?"

Shake said, "None."

"No team gives up its basics and takes chances in a big game," I said.

"Right," said Shake.

"It's all down to who executes. And besides that, they're favored," I said. "Or were."

"They think they can play normal and cover us *up* with busy," said Shake.

"And they can," I said.

Shake had started back into our palatial suite, but he stopped and grinned and said:

"Goddamn, Billy C. Nobody ever said it wasn't gonna be semi-tough."

On Thursday night when we had dinner with Big Ed and Big Barb we had a fairly pleasant night, as it turned out. Which was an upset.

You don't just go looking up Big Ed and Big Barb for dinner. Mainly you don't because you know that Big Ed will take you through the whole history of the "oil bidness" again. And he'll go right from that to what's wrong with pro football, specifically the coaching.

Generally, Big Ed will also get mad at one or two waiters or waitresses, so much so that people at other tables will stare at you. And so much so that the food and service will be pretty miserable for everybody.

But, anyhow, it wasn't bad. We went to that steak place on Rodeo where a place called the Daisy used to be. The name of it was Beef Jesus.

Big Ed was on his good behavior, as I say. Except for a few remarks about Hollywood having more Jews than it used to have—in a fairly loud voice.

"Sorry you kids missed Hollywood back in the days when you could tell the women from the men," he said.

Another time, he said, "By god, I loaned some Jews out here some money one time and came out to check up on it and had me a hell of a time. That was before you, Mrs. Bookman."

Big Barb only smiled the whole time and kept glancing around Beef Jesus to see what the other women were wearing.

Big Ed did have a bit of a problem with the menu and the waiter, who looked and was dressed like straight Jesus and carried a big cardboard cross on his back as part of his costume.

"Hi, there," said the waiter. "I'm Jesus Harold. I've *come back* to serve you."

Big Ed spoke half to Jesus Harold and half to his menu.

"I don't know where you came back from, young man, but it looks like you didn't grab anything but your underwear when you left," he said.

And Big Ed looked around the table to see if any of us thought that was funny.

The waiter said, "The menu doesn't actually mean much. The specials, I think, will intrigue you a lot more. The menu is mostly for, well, you know, people from *Iowa*, or somewhere."

Jesus Harold adjusted his cross and stood with one hand on his hip.

Cissy Walford wanted to know what the specials were.

"To start," said Jesus Harold, "I've got avocado and aku, *cold*, of course, with Macadamia nut dressing. Very nice. I've got spinach and mushroom pie. Unbelievable. I've got asparagus soup, *cold*, of course, with some heavenly little chunks of abalone in it. I've got celery spears stuffed with turkey pâté. Incredible. And I've got civiche *without* pitted olives. It's terribly marvelous."

Big Ed looked up at Jesus Harold and said:

"Now tell us what you've got to eat."

I was on Big Ed's side for once.

Jesus Harold said, "On the *menu*, I'm sure the light in here is good enough for you to find a shrimp cocktail, a salad with roquefort, and a New York cut."

Jesus Harold looked away while he was writing on his pad.

"A little dish of vanilla for dessert?" he said. "All around?"

Big Ed said for Jesus Harold to hold on there for a minute. He said he wasn't interested in any of the specials. And he didn't think any of the rest of us were. What we really wanted was some good beef. Nothing to start. Just bring us some more drinks and six good pieces of beef with maybe some asparagus and sliced tomatoes.

"I don't suppose you've got a sixteen-ounce T-bone out there, do you?" said Big Ed.

Jesus Harold said, "If we do, I will *personally* rope it and drag it out here."

We all smiled at Jesus Harold, who wrote down our order. Or Big Ed's.

"Thank you very much," said Jesus Harold. "I'll tell Jesus Barry to bring you another round of drinks."

"Those are all medium rare," said Big Ed.

"Of course they are," said Jesus Harold. "Life *itself* is medium rare."

Our waiter left, straightening the cross on his back and clomping his sandals across the floor.

The steaks weren't bad. Big Ed and Big Barb asked Cissy Walford several questions about her parents. They decided they knew some rich people her parents knew. Big Barb asked Barbara Jane if she had done several things to her apartment since they had last seen it.

Big Ed discussed a number of things that were wrong with the current economy. He reviewed TCU's football season for us. They were three and eight. He also reviewed next season's prospects and said that one of TCU's problems was they had too many niggers on offense and a couple of Jesus Harolds in the secondary.

As Big Ed always does, he proposed a toast when dinner was over and Jesus Harold had sent Jesus Barry around with some stingers. It was the same old toast.

It was the toast where Big Ed says that you come into the world naked and bare, or something, and you go through the world with trouble and care. Then he says you go out of the world you know not where. But if you're a thoroughbred *here*, he says, getting louder, you're a thoroughbred *there*.

Me and Shake and Barb have learned to listen to the toast with blank expressions. We raised our glasses again when Big Ed finished.

And Big Ed said, "Goddamned if I don't love a thoroughbred in life. And we've got a whole table of 'em right here."

Big Ed then spoke for a while on how he had molded most of our lives and helped us become thoroughbreds. Except for Cissy Walford, of course.

He said her daddy, being a wealthy man, had probably done the same thing for her. He said he and her daddy had a lot in common. "Respect for the American dollar," he said. "What's good for America is good for the world," he said. "If the world stops believing that, we may have to kick 'em in their chink asses again," he said.

Big Ed went through some of his fond memories about me and Shake and Barb. Big Barb joined in occasionally. Cissy Walford yawned once or twice.

Big Ed said he couldn't be happier to have turned out such a handsome daughter who seemed to have all of her mother's good taste. He said he didn't understand some of her wit, but, hell, this was another generation.

Only a couple of things had disappointed him, he said.

He said he was sorry a few years ago that Barbara Jane had refused to become a Fort Worth debutante like her mother had planned it. Which would have been the exact same year her mother got herself elected president of the Assembly and the Junior League and the Republican Women for White Freedom—the triple crown, so to speak. The Assembly was a club that picked debutantes.

Big Ed said he would have thrown a hell of a debutante party for Barb. He said he would have brought in Freddy Martin's orchestra and Bert Parks and a lot of other show biz celebrities that he knew.

He said he was sorry, too, that Barbara Jane had gone to TCU instead of a place like Mrs. Bellard-Ronald's in upstate New York. "I'm for TCU as far as our town's concerned," he said. "What the hell we got down there, other than a bomber plant and a bunch of goddamned apartment builders on the city council? But you can go too far with your loyalty. Barbara Jane should have gone off to a lady's school."

"Clarice Stuart in Ironwood, Virginia, would have been *perfect*," Big Barb said.

Barb said, "Terrific."

Big Ed said his other major disappointment was when his very own daughter and some other girls got caught spending the night in the athletic dorm at TCU.

"I never expected such a thing from a Bookman," said Big Ed.

We began laughing.

"I've never *felt* so destroyed," Big Barb said.

Shake said, "It all worked out. It was a joke, anyhow."

And Big Ed said, "You goddamn right it worked out. After I *worked* it out. I thought for a while I'd have to buy the Fort Worth *Light & Shopper*, and I'd just as soon own a dry hole in Egypt."

"Bookman Heiress Shacks Up with Football Studs," said Barb, teasing. "Hell of a story. Aw, come on, Daddy. Jim Tom Pinch wouldn't have ever printed the story. You know that."

"It's funny now, huh?" said Big Ed.

"It's pretty funny, I think," I said. "That was some night. That was the night after the varsity picnic at Lake Worth. The spring before our junior season."

Shake said. "The night we scuttled Bobby Roy Simpson's forty-footer."

Barb said, "You mean the night Bubba Littleton did."

"Well, Bubba did the work but I think it was our idea." Shake grinned.

Big Ed said, "Wait a minute. Somebody sank somebody's boat that night?"

Shake said, "It didn't matter. Bobby Roy Simpson was a rich kid who liked to hang around with the football studs. He had several boats."

Big Ed said, "Well, I've got several boats myself but I'll be goddamned if I want anybody sinkin' 'em."

Barbara Jane laughed and looked at us.

"It didn't matter, Daddy. It really didn't," she said. "If you had known Bobby Roy Simpson, you would have sunk his boat with him *in* it."

Big Ed said it still didn't seem right, somehow. A man's boat and all. A private property deal.

Shake said, "I don't remember why we thought it would be all right to bring the girls back to Tom Brown Hall. It seemed like the thing to do, though."

I said, "Wasn't that the same night that Bubba Littleton tore the pay phone out of the wall?"

"Sure was," said Barbara Jane. "And threw the Coke machine down two flights of stairs. Double-header."

Shake said, "Well, you know why he was so hot?"

Me and Barb broke up. We knew.

Bubba Littleton was hot because Honey Jean Lester had caught him that afternoon flogging it underneath the dock as I have mentioned earlier.

"I don't see how any human being who's white could do things like that," Big Ed said.

"He was just mad at his date about something," I said.

"Well, Bubba Littleton wasn't a good enough football player at TCU to get away with things like that," Big Ed said. "Destroying property is what chinks and Commies want."

"He was a pretty mean tackle," Shake said. "He'd hit somebody."

I said, "He was about half-mean all the way around."

Shake said, "How about those poor Aggies?"

I wished Shake hadn't said that just when I had my young stinger up to my face. I nearly spit in it from laughing.

On a Friday night in Fort Worth one time before a game we had against Texas A&M, Bubba Littleton went downtown to a pep rally the Aggie cadet corps was having because he wanted to get him some Aggies as captives, for a joke.

I never knew any other TCU man who would go around an Aggie rally by himself. But Bubba of course could go anywhere he wanted to. He used to go look up truck drivers and try to get them to fight him to see who bought the beer.

Anyhow, Bubba went downtown and got him four Aggie cadets and brought them back to his dorm room. The first thing he did was shave off all of their hair, what little they had, being Aggie cadets. Then he made them get naked and shave all the hair off of each other's bodies and vital parts.

They were just scrawny little old Aggies whose daddies had made them go there in the first place, to Texas A&M, I mean, which is kind of like going to Sing Sing. So they couldn't do anything except what Bubba Littleton wanted them to do, not unless they wanted to get an arm broke.

The next thing Bubba did was take some purple paint—purple is TCU's color—and make the Aggies stand at attention while he painted something on each one's chest. What he painted so that you could read it when they stood in a certain order was: AGGIES . . . IS . . . SEMI- . . . RURAL.

Bubba finally let the poor souls go after they sang the TCU fight song to his satisfaction, and after they had a beat-off contest.

We carried on a little more with Big Ed and Big Barb about our growing-up days.

Big Ed said that one of the things which pleased him the most is that me and Shake and Barbara Jane had never needed any of his money.

Like all rich guys, Big Ed said he didn't have a whole lot of money but that he had managed to keep *some* from the government. And he said it was always there if any of us ever needed it for something important.

Big Ed said that what he planned to do with what little money he had, when he died, if none of us needed it for something important, was leave it to various things around Fort Worth, in his memory.

He said he hoped TCU would take some of his money and upperdeck the entire stadium and call it Big Ed Bookman Coliseum.

He said the family's first oil pump was still out in Scogie County but that he hoped the city would one day want to bring it to town and put it on the lawn of the Convention Center. He said it would be interesting history.

"Who are you going to leave your heart to?" Barbara Jane asked in a wry way.

Big Ed looked at Barb as if she was a Communist.

"Big Ed's heart goes with Big Ed," he said. "That's just goddamn foolishness, giving up things like that."

Big Ed said, "Wouldn't I be in a fine fix to come back on Earth some day without a goddamn heart?"

Barbara Jane howled.

"I don't want to talk about that kind of thing," said Big Ed. "I know everybody has different ideas these days. I just don't give one goddamn how many transplant cases are walking around healthy. They're supposed to be dead, like God wanted 'em to be."

Shake said, "Damn right. If God wanted a man to have two hearts, he'd have given him two hearts. If God had wanted a man to drink more, he'd have given him two mouths."

Big Ed said, "Go ahead and be funny about it. But I'll tell you this, Eighty-eight. You go out and get yourself a nigger's heart and then we'll see how many footballs you catch on Sunday."

"Can you *believe* it?" said Barbara Jane, looking at us.

Big Ed said we'd do well to listen to him. He said he guessed he would have to educate us, once and for all. Why in the hell did we think Barbara Jane was such a beautiful and great girl? Why was that?

He said, well, he would explain it to us. By God, it was because she was a thoroughbred, he said. She came from good stock. Bookman stock. And don't think that didn't mean plenty, he said.

Big Ed said that God wasn't so dumb that he didn't know there had to be a few people around in history to see that the world ran right.

He said that God tried to turn it all over to mankind once and it just didn't work. A whole goddamn bunch of chinks and niggers got born, along with a whole lot of spicks and Mongol hordes. That pissed God off, he said. So God took over again and God's been trying to straighten it out ever since, without ruining his image.

He said God would sneak a tidal wave in every now and then, or an earthquake, or a volcanic eruption, and then a few wars, to get rid of several million undesirables outside of America.

It's a slow process, Big Ed said, because it got so far out of hand, and God has to be careful and do it slowly, and not make everybody so hot they won't like God any more.

Now then, he said, sipping on his stinger.

While all of this has been going on, God has allowed some carefully selected people he could trust to get born and take rich and be able to run things.

These are people, he said, like all of the great rulers and businessmen of history. Well, he said, they're people like the Murchisons and Hunts were, or like some corporation presidents he had known, and some generals, and himself.

The Bookmans, he said, went back a long way. God sent the first Bookman over on the Mayflower to help get America started off right. The reason, he said, was because God knew that America would be able to get the rest of the world to shape up. Eventually. Like today.

The Bookmans, he said, distinguished themselves in all of the wars, including his own self in World War II, which none of us could much remember, he guessed. The big war, where we kicked the shit out of those that had it coming, and did it right.

He said that God obviously didn't want him to get killed in that war, basically because he had some big money to earn and some jobs to provide later on, and that's why God had given him the intelligence and the aristocracy to go into the army as a colonel at the age of twenty.

He said God knew what he was doing when he worked it out that Big Ed got to stay in Washington, D.C., throughout the big war and help out with many of the important decisions that were made about who to kill next.

Now then, Big Ed said again.

One of the wonderful things that came out of him being preserved and not killed, as God had shown the good sense to do, was that he got to meet Big Barb in college when they were at the University of Texas, after the big war. Big Barb had come from a fine family herself, he said. The Huckabees from Waco, he said.

And out of this union had come Barbara Jane, he said, with her hair of streaked butterscotch, her deep brown eyes, her olive complexion, her splendid cheekbones, her full lips, her perfect teeth, her big bright smile and her keen mind and, according to her mother, her flawless carriage and good taste and her incredible body.

"It took a lot of Bookmans to produce that," said Big Ed in conclusion.

"And one hell of a lot of earthquakes," said Barbara Jane.

A Guide for Further Study

Of the wealth of comic sports-centered novels, we suggest Dan Jenkins' satiric look at golf in *Dead Solid Perfect*. On baseball, Jerome Charyn's *The Seventh Babe* and James F. Donahue's *Spitballs and Holy Water* are great fun. Almost all the fiction mentioned in previous guides contains comic episodes, in particular *The Natural*, *North Dallas Forty*, and *Joiner*.

Section IV: Space and Time

ROLFE HUMPHRIES

Polo Grounds

Time is of the essence. This is a highly skilled
And beautiful mystery. Three or four seconds only
From the time that Riggs connects till he reaches first,
And in those seconds Jurges goes to his right,
Comes up with the ball, tosses to Witek at second
For the force on Reese, Witek to Mize at first,
In time for the out—a double play.

(Red Barber crescendo. Crowd noises, obbligato;
Scattered staccatos from the peanut boys,
Loud in the lull, as the teams are changing sides) . . .

Hubbell takes the sign, nods, pumps, delivers—
A foul into the stands. Dunn takes a new ball out,
Hands it to Danning, who throws it down to Werber;
Werber takes off his glove, rubs the ball briefly,
Tosses it over to Hub, who goes to the rosin bag,
Takes the sign from Danning, pumps, delivers—
Low, outside, ball three. Danning goes to the mound,
Says something to Hub, Dunn brushes off the plate,
Adams starts throwing in the Giant bullpen,
Hub takes the sign from Danning, pumps, delivers,
Camilli gets hold of it, a *long* fly to the outfield,
Ott goes back, back, back, against the wall, gets under it,
Pounds his glove, and takes it for the out.
That's all for the Dodgers. . . .

From *Collected Poems of Rolfe Humphries* (1965).

Time is of the essence. The rhythms break,
More varied and subtle than any kind of dance;
Movement speeds up or lags. The ball goes out
In sharp and angular drives, or long, slow arcs,
Comes in again controlled and under aim;
The players wheel or spurt, race, stoop, slide, halt,
Shift imperceptibly to new positions,
Watching the signs, according to the batter,
The score, the inning. Time is of the essence.

Time is of the essence. Remember Terry?
Remember Stonewall Jackson, Lindstrom, Frisch,
When they were good? Remember Long George Kelly?
Remember John McGraw and Benny Kauff?
Remember Bridwell, Tenney, Merkle, Youngs,
Chief Myers, Big Jeff Tesreau, Shufflin' Phil?
Remember Matthewson, and Ames, and Donlin,
Buck Ewing, Rusie, Smiling Mickey Welch?
Remember a left-handed catcher named Jack Humphries,
Who sometimes played the outfield, in '83?

Time is of the essence. The shadow moves
From the plate to the box, from the box to second base,
From second to the outfield, to the bleachers.

Time is of the essence. The crowd and players
Are the same age always, but the man in the crowd
Is older every season. Come on, play ball!

MURRAY ROSS

Football Red and Baseball Green

Every Superbowl played in the 1970s rates among the top television draws of the decade—pro football's championship game is right up there on the charts with blockbusters like *Rocky*, *Roots*, *Jaws*, and *Gone with the Wind*. This revelation is one way of indicating just how popular spectator sports are in this country. Americans, or American men anyway, seem to care about the games they watch as much as the Elizabethans cared about their plays, and I suspect for some of the same reasons. There is, in sport, some of the rudimentary drama found in popular theater: familiar plots, type characters, heroic and comic action spiced with new and unpredictable variations. And common to watching both activities is the sense of participation in a shared tradition and in shared fantasies. If sport exploits these fantasies without significantly transcending them, it seems no less satisfying for all that.

It is my guess that sport spectating involves something more than the vicarious pleasures of identifying with athletic prowess. I suspect that each sport contains a fundamental myth which it elaborates for its fans, and that our pleasure in watching such games derives in part from belonging briefly to the mythical world which the game and its players bring to life. I am especially interested in baseball and football because they are so popular and so uniquely *American*; they began here and unlike basketball they have not been widely exported. Thus whatever can be said, mythically, about these games would seem to apply to our culture.

Baseball's myth may be the easier to identify since we have a greater historical perspective on the game. It was an instant success during the Industrialization, and most probably it was a reaction to the squalor, the faster pace and the dreariness of the new conditions. Baseball was old-fashioned right from the start; it seems conceived in nostalgia, in the resuscitation of the Jeffersonian dream. It established an artificial rural environment, one removed from the toil of an urban life, which spectators could be admitted to and temporarily breathe in. Baseball is a *pastoral* sport, and I think the game can be best understood as this kind of art. For baseball does what all good pastoral does—it creates an atmosphere in which everything exists in harmony.

Consider, for instance, the spatial organization of the game. A kind of con-

Appeared in earlier form in *Chicago Review* (1971). Revised 1982.

trolled openness is created by having everything fan out from home plate, and the crowd sees the game through an arranged perspective that is rarely violated. Visually this means that the game is always seen as a constant, rather calm whole, and that the players and the playing field are viewed in relationship to each other. Each player has a certain position, a special area to tend, and the game often seems to be as much a dialogue between the fielders and the field as it is a contest between the players themselves: will that ball get through the hole? Can that outfielder run under that fly? As a moral genre, pastoral asserts the virtue of communion with nature. As a competitive game, baseball asserts that the team which best relates to the playing field (by hitting the ball in the right places) will win.

I suspect baseball's space has a subliminal function too, for topographically it is a sentimental mirror of older America. Most of the game is played between the pitcher and the hitter in the extreme corner of the playing area. This is the busiest, most sophisticated part of the ball park, where something is always happening, and from which all subsequent action originates. From this urban corner we move to a supporting infield, active but a little less crowded, and from there we come to the vast stretches of the outfield. As is traditional in American lore, danger increases with distance, and the outfield action is often the most spectacular in the game. The long throw, the double off the wall, the leaping catch—these plays take place in remote territory, and they belong, like most legendary feats, to the frontier.

Having established its landscape, pastoral art operates to eliminate any reference to that bigger, more disturbing, more real world it has left behind. All games are to some extent insulated from the outside by having their own rules, but baseball has a circular structure as well which furthers its comfortable feeling of self-sufficiency. By this I mean that every motion of extension is also one of return—a ball hit outside is a *home* run, a full circle. Home— familiar, peaceful, secure—it is the beginning and end. You must go out but you must come back; only the completed movement is registered.

Time is a serious threat to any form of pastoral. The genre poses a timeless world of perpetual spring, and it does its best to silence the ticking of clocks which remind us that in time the green world fades into winter. One's sense of time is directly related to what happens in it, and baseball is so structured as to stretch out and ritualize whatever action it contains. Dramatic moments are few, and they are almost always isolated by the routine texture of normal play. It is certainly a game of climax and drama, but it is perhaps more a game of repeated and predictable action: the foul balls, the walks, the pitcher fussing around on the mound, the lazy fly ball to center field. This is, I think, as it should be, for baseball exists as an alternative to a world of too much action, struggle and change. It is a merciful release from a more grinding and insistent tempo, and its time, as William Carlos Williams suggests, makes a virtue out of idleness simply by providing it:

The crowd at the ball game
is moved uniformly
by a spirit of uselessness
Which delights them. . . .

Within this expanded and idle time the baseball fan is at liberty to become a ceremonial participant and a lover of style. Because the action is normalized, how something is done becomes as important as the action itself. Thus baseball's most delicate and detailed aspects are often, to the spectator, the most interesting. The pitcher's windup, the anticipatory crouch of the infielders, the quick waggle of the bat as it poises for the pitch—these subtle miniature movements are as meaningful as the home runs and the strikeouts. It somehow matters in baseball that all the tiny rituals are observed: the shortstop must kick the dirt and the umpire must brush the plate with his pocket broom. In a sense baseball is largely a continuous series of small gestures, and I think it characteristic that the game's most treasured moment came when Babe Ruth pointed to where he subsequently hit a home run.

Baseball is a game where the little things mean a lot, and this, together with its clean serenity, its open space, and its ritualized action is enough to place it in a world of yesterday. Baseball evokes for us a past which may never have been ours, but which we believe was, and certainly that is enough. In the Second World War, supposedly, we fought for "Baseball, Mom and Apple Pie," and considering what baseball means, that phrase is a good one. We fought then for the right to believe in a green world of tranquility and uninterrupted contentment, where the little things would count. But now the possibilities of such a world are more remote, and it seems that while the entertainment of such a dream has an enduring appeal, it is no longer sufficient for our fantasies. I think this may be why baseball is no longer our preeminent national pastime, and why its myth is being replaced by another more appropriate to the new realities (and fantasies) of our time.

Football, especially professional football, is the embodiment of a newer myth, one which in many respects is opposed to baseball's. The fundamental difference is that football is not a pastoral game; it is a heroic one. One way of seeing the difference between the two is by the juxtaposition of Babe Ruth and Jim Brown, both legendary players in their separate genres. Ruth, baseball's most powerful hitter, was a hero maternalized (his name), an epic figure destined for a second immortality as a candy bar. His image was impressive but comfortable and altogether human: round, dressed in a baggy uniform, with a schoolboy's cap and a bat which looked tiny next to him. His spindly legs supported a Santa-sized torso, and this comic disproportion would increase when he was in motion. He ran delicately, with quick, very short steps, since he felt that stretching your stride slowed you down. This sort of superstition is typical of baseball players, and typical too is the way in which a personal quirk or mannerism mitigates their awesome skill and makes them poignant and vulnerable.

There was nothing funny about Jim Brown. His muscular and almost perfect physique was emphasized further by the uniform which armored him. Babe Ruth's face was sensual and tough, yet also boyish and innocent; Brown's was an expressionless mask under the helmet. In action he seemed invincible, the embodiment of speed and power in an inflated human shape. One can describe Brown accurately only with superlatives, for as a player he was a kind of Superman, undisguised.

Brown and Ruth are caricatures, yet they represent their games. Baseball is part of a comic tradition which insists that its participants be above all human; while football, in the heroic mode, asks that its players be more than that. Football wants to convert men into gods; it suggests that magnificence and glory are as desirable as happiness. Football is designed, therefore, to impress its audience rather differently than baseball.

As a pastoral game, baseball attempts to close the gap between the players and the crowd. It creates the illusion, for instance, that with a lot of hard work, a little luck, and possibly some extra talent, the average spectator might well be playing, not watching. For most of us can do a few of the things the ball players do: catch a pop-up, field a ground ball, and maybe get a hit once in a while. Chance is allotted a good deal of play in the game. There is no guarantee, for instance, that a good pitch will not be looped over the infield, or that a solidly batted ball will not turn into a double play. In addition to all of this, almost every fan feels he can make the manager's decision for him, and not entirely without reason. Baseball's statistics are easily calculated and rather meaningful; and the game itself, though a subtle one, is relatively lucid and comprehendible.

As a heroic game, football is not concerned with a shared community of near-equals. It seeks almost the opposite relationship between its spectators and players, one which stresses the distance between them. We are not allowed to identify directly with Jim Brown any more than we are with Zeus, because to do so would undercut his stature as something more than human. Pittsburgh's Mean Joe Green, in the now classic commercial, walks off the battlefield like Achilles, clouded by combat. A little boy offers him a Coke, reluctantly accepted but enthusiastically drunk, and Green tosses the boy his jersey afterwards—the token of a generous god. Football encourages us to see its players much as the little boy sees Mean Joe: we look up to them with something approaching awe. For most of us could not begin to imagine ourselves playing their game without risking imminent humiliation. The players are all much bigger and much faster and much stronger than we are, and even as fans we have trouble enough just figuring out what's going on. In baseball what happens is what meets the eye, but in football each play means eleven men acting against eleven other men: it's too much for a single set of eyes to follow. We now are provided with several television commentators to explain the action to us, with the help of the ubiquitous slow-motion instant replay. Even the coaches need their spotters in the stands and their long postgame film analyses to arrive at something like full comprehension of the game they direct and manage.

If football is distanced from its fans by its intricacy and its "superhuman" play, it nonetheless remains an intense spectacle. Baseball, as I have implied, dissolves time and urgency in a green expanse, thereby creating a luxurious and peaceful sense of leisure. As is appropriate to a heroic enterprise, football reverses this procedure and converts space into time. The game is ideally played in an oval stadium, not in a "park," and the difference is the elimination of perspective. This makes football a perfect television game, because even at first hand it offers a flat, perpetually moving foreground (wherever the ball is). The eye in baseball viewing opens up; in football it zeroes in. There is no democratic vista in football, and spectators are not asked to relax, but to concentrate. You are encouraged to watch the drama, not a medley of ubiquitous gestures, and you are constantly reminded that this event is taking place in time. The third element in baseball is the field; in football this element is the clock. Traditionally heroes do reckon with time, and football players are no exceptions. Time in football is wound up inexorably until it reaches the breaking point in the last minutes of a close game. More often than not it is the clock which emerges as the real enemy, and it is the sense of time running out that regularly produces a pitch of tension uncommon in baseball.

A further reason for football's intensity is that the game is played like a war. The idea is to win by going through, around or over the opposing team and the battle lines, quite literally, are drawn on every play. Violence is somewhere at the heart of the game, and the combat quality is reflected in football's army language ("blitz," "trap," "zone," "bomb," "trenches," etc.). Coaches often sound like generals when they discuss their strategy. Woody Hayes of Ohio State, for instance, explained his quarterback option play as if it had been conceived in the Pentagon: "You know," he said, "the most effective kind of warfare is siege. You have to attack on broad fronts. And that's all the option is—attacking on a broad front. You know General Sherman ran an option through the south."

Football like war is an arena for action, and like war football leaves little room for personal style. It seems to be a game which projects "character" more than personality, and for the most part football heroes, publicly, are a rather similar lot. They tend to become personifications rather than individuals, and, with certain exceptions, they are easily read emblematically as embodiments of heroic qualities such as "strength," "confidence," "grace," etc.— clichés really, but forceful enough when represented by the play of a John Riggins, a Joe Theisman, or a Cliff Branch. Perhaps this simplification of personality results in part from the heroes' total identification with their mission, to the extent that they become more characterized by what they do than by what they intrinsically "are." At any rate football does not make as many allowances for the idiosyncrasies that baseball actually seems to encourage, and as a result there have been few football players as uniquely crazy or human as, say, Casey Stengel or Dizzy Dean.

A further reason for the underdeveloped qualities of football personalities, and one which gets us to the heart of the game's modernity, is that football is very much a game of modern technology. Football's action is largely interaction, and the game's complexity requires that its players mold themselves into a perfectly coordinated unit. Jerry Kramer, formerly all-pro guard of the Green Bay Packers, explains how Lombardi would work to develop such integration:

He makes us execute the same plays over and over, a hundred times, two hundred times, until we do every little thing automatically. He works to make the kickoff team perfect, the punt-return team perfect, the field-goal team perfect. He ignores nothing. Technique, technique, technique, over and over and over, until we feel like we're going crazy. But we win.

Mike Garrett, the halfback, gives the player's version:

After a while you train your mind like a computer—put the ideas in, and the body acts accordingly.

As the quotations imply, pro football is insatiably preoccupied with the smoothness and precision of play execution, and most coaches believe that the team which makes the fewest mistakes will be the team that wins. Individual identity thus comes to be associated with the team or unit that one plays for to a much greater extent than in baseball. To use a reductive analogy, it is the difference between *Bonanza* and *Mission Impossible*. Reggie Jackson is mostly Reggie Jackson, but Franco Harris is mostly the Pittsburgh Steelers. The latter metaphor is a precise one, since football heroes stand out not only because of purely individual acts, but also because they epitomize the action and style of the groups they are connected to. Kramer cites the obvious if somewhat self-glorifying historical precedent: "Perhaps," he writes, "we're living in Camelot." Ideally a football team should be what Camelot was supposed to have been, a group of men who function as equal parts of a larger whole, dependent on each other for total meaning.

The humanized machine as hero is something very new in sport, for in baseball anything approaching a machine has always been suspect. The famous Yankee teams of the fifties were almost flawlessly perfect, yet they never were especially popular. Their admirers took pains to romanticize their precision into something more natural than plain mechanics—Joe DiMaggio, for instance, became the "Yankee Clipper." Even so, most people seemed to want the Brooklyn Dodgers (the "bums") to thrash them in the World Series. Perhaps the most memorable triumph in recent years—the victory of the Amazin' Mets in 1969—was memorable precisely because it was the triumph of a random collection of inspired rejects over the superbly skilled, fully integrated and almost homogenized Baltimore Orioles. Similarly, in the seventies, many fans watched with pleasure as the cantankerous Oakland A's went to work dismantling Cincinnati's self-styled "Big Red Machine." In baseball, machinery seems tantamount to villainy, whereas in football this smooth perfection is part of the unexpected integration a championship team must attain.

It is not surprising, really, that we should have a game which asserts the heroic function of a mechanized group, since we have become a country where collective identity is a reality. Football as a game of groups is appealing to us as a people of groups, and for this reason football is very much an "establishment" game—since it is in the corporate business and governmental structures that group America is most developed. The game comments on the culture, and vice versa:

> President Nixon, an ardent football fan, got a football team picture as an inaugural anniversary present from his cabinet. . . .
>   Superimposed on the faces of real gridiron players were the faces of cabinet members. (A.P.)

In one of the Vietnam war demonstrations, I remember seeing a sign that read, "49er fans against War, Poverty, and the Baltimore Colts." The notion of a team identity appeals to us all, whether or not we choose establishment colors.

Football's collective pattern is only one aspect of the way in which it seems to echo our contemporary environment. The game, like our society, can be thought of as a cluster of people living under great tension in a state of perpetual flux. The potential for sudden disaster or triumph is as great in football as it is in our own age, and although there is something ludicrous in equating interceptions with assassinations and long passes with moonshots, there is also something valid and appealing in the analogies. It seems to me that football does successfully reflect those salient and common conditions which affect us all, and it does so with the end of making us feel better about them and our lot. For one thing, it makes us feel that something can be released and connected in all this chaos; out of the accumulated pile of bodies something can emerge—a runner breaks into the clear or a pass finds its way to a receiver. To the spectator, plays such as these are human and dazzling. They suggest to the audience what it has hoped for (and been told) all along, that technology is still a tool and not a master. Fans get living proof of this every time a long pass is completed; they appreciate that it is the result of careful planning, perfect integration and an effective "pattern," but they see too that it is human and that what counts as well is man, his desire, his natural skill and his "grace under pressure." Football metaphysically yokes heroic action and technology by violence to suggest that they are mutually supportive. It's a doubtful proposition, but given how we live, it has its attractions.

Football, like the space program, is a game in the grand manner, and it is relatively sober sport too—at least when set against the comic pastoral vision baseball regularly unfurls. Heroic action is serious business, and in the late fall and winter, when it is getting cold and miserable and brutal outside, football merely becomes more heroic, though sometimes the spectacle seems just absurd. I remember seeing the Detroit Lions and the Minnesota Vikings play one Thanksgiving in a blinding snowstorm, where—except for the small flags in the corners of the end zones—the field was totally obscured. Even with magnified television lenses, you could see only huge shapes come out of the gloom, thump against each other and fall in a heap, while occasionally, in desperation, the camera would switch to show us a cheerleader fluttering her pompoms in the cold and silent stadium. For the most part this game was a kind of theater of oblivion, and it's not hard to understand why some people find football pointless, a gladiatorial activity engaged in by moronic monsters. Yet these bleak conditions are also the stuff of which heroic legends are made. It was appropriate, I think, that what many regard as the greatest game of all time (the 1967 championship between the Packers and the Cowboys, won when the Arthurian Bart Starr plunged over the goal line in the final seconds behind Jerry Kramer's block) happened to be played when the temperature was a cool thirteen degrees below zero, the coldest December day in Green Bay history. These guys from Camelot had to beat the Cowboys, the clock and the weather too, so it's no wonder that Kramer waxed so ecstatic about his team. In the Detroit-Minnesota game I have just described, the pathetic monotony of the action was suddenly relieved when Jim Marshall, a veteran defensive end, intercepted a pass deep in his own territory. Marshall's off-season hobby is bobsledding, and he put his skills to good use here, rumbling upfield with a clumsy but determined authority through the mud, the snow, and the opposing team—then lateraling at the last moment to a teammate who scored the winning touchdown. It was a funny play, but it had something epic about it, and it was doubtless hailed in the bars of Minnesota with the same kind of rowdy applause that a good story once earned in the legendary halls of warrior kings.

Games like these get rarer and rarer, mostly because baseball and football have become so much more businesslike. It doesn't make good business sense to play outside where it might rain and snow and do terrible things; it isn't really prudent to play on a natural field that can be destroyed in a single afternoon; and why build a whole stadium or park that's good for only one game? More and more, both baseball and football are being played indoors on rugs in multipurpose spaces. The fans at these games are constantly diverted by huge whiz-bang scoreboards that dominate and describe the action, while the fans at home are constantly being reminded by at least three lively sportscasters of the other games, the other sports and the other shows that are coming up later on the same stations. Both pro football and pro baseball now play vastly extended seasons, so that the World Series now takes place on chilly October nights and football is well under way before the summer ends. From my point of view all this is regrettable, because these changes tend to remove the games from their intangible but palpable mythic contexts. No longer clearly set in nature, no longer given the chance to breathe and steep in their own special atmospheres, both baseball and football risk becoming demythologized. As fans we seem to participate a little less in mythic ritual these days, while being subjected even more to the statistics, the hype and the salary disputes that proceed from a jazzed-up, inflated, yet somehow flattened sporting world—a world that looks too much like the one we live in all the time.

Still, there is much to be thankful for, and every season seems to bring its own contribution to mythic lore. Some people will think this nonsense, and I must admit there are good reasons for finding both games simply varieties of decadence.

In its preoccupation with mechanization, and in its open display of violence, football is the more obvious target for social moralists, but I wonder if this is finally more "corrupt" than the seductive picture of sanctuary and tranquility that baseball has so artfully drawn for us. Almost all sport is vulnerable to such criticism because it is not strictly ethical in intent, and for this reason there will always be room for puritans like the Elizabethan John Stubbes who howled at the "wanton fruits which these cursed pastimes bring forth." As a long-time dedicated fan of almost anything athletic, I confess myself out of sympathy with most of this; which is to say, I guess, that I am vulnerable to those fantasies which these games support, and that I find happiness in the company of people who feel as I do.

A final note. It is interesting that the heroic and pastoral conventions which underlie our most popular sports are almost classically opposed. The contrasts are familiar: city versus country, aspirations versus contentment, activity versus peace and so on. Judging from the rise of professional football, we seem to be slowly relinquishing that unfettered rural vision of ourselves that baseball so beautifully mirrors, and we have come to cast ourselves in a genre more reflective of a nation confronted by constant and unavoidable challenges. Right now, like the Elizabethans, we seem to share both heroic and pastoral yearnings, and we reach out to both. Perhaps these divided needs account in part for the enormous attention we as a nation now give to spectator sports. For sport provides one place where we can have our football and our baseball too.

MICHAEL NOVAK

Sacred Space, Sacred Time

SACRED SPACE

The feeling athletes have for the arena in which they struggle is a secret feeling not often voiced. If you have ever walked on Paratroopers' Hill in Jerusalem, in the trenches and in the dugouts, recalling the fierce nighttime chaos in the barbed wire where men's bodies were shredded by rockets and automatic weapons, and where the liberation of the city was made possible;

From *The Joy of Sports* (1976).

or if you have walked the fields of Gettysburg, reconstructing in imagination the movements and the courage; perhaps then you understand how certain places are hallowed by deeds.

An athlete trains everywhere he can: boys shoot baskets by the hour in the driveways, in playgrounds, in scores of gyms. Yet there is a special awe that arises when one enters for the first time—or at any time—one's high school gym, or Madison Square Garden, or Pauley Pavilion, or wherever the symbolic center of achievement may be. Each arena is a little different: one concrete place, one patch of earth, one England. The athlete needs to internalize the ambience, to dig his cleats at the turf, to root his senses and instincts there, to bounce the ball experimentally on the floor, to learn by sixth sense the slightest fixtures, signs, and contours of the place. Baseball, basketball, and football do not take place just anywhere. There are consecrated places.

It is a stirring occasion to walk in Notre Dame stadium when no other soul is present. One feels the proximity of every seat. Even when the place is packed, so perfect is the oval that the most distant fan can hear a coach shout from the bench. The drainage slope gives the visitor an upward lift as he walks across the well-kept grass. Images and voices arise from the past. The mind's eye sees Johnny Lujack, Emil Sitko, George Connor, Leon Hart, imagines the Gipper.

Each time I pass the stadium at any of the universities where I sometimes lecture, I feel the presence of such ghosts. I may not know the local traditions, but I know, at Nebraska, at Missouri, at Michigan, at Harvard, at Princeton, that great tales await my learning. Vividness, color, injury, impossible catches, courage, crushing disappointments (Michigan's two devastating ties with Ohio State in 1973 and 1974) await attention.

Sports arenas are storied places. Universes of tales. One sits in them surrounded by ghostly ancestors, as at the Mass one is surrounded by the hosts who have since Abraham celebrated a Eucharist. Even a new stadium, as at Oakland, is a place where tradition instantaneously begins. Impoverished in memory, a new arena is a tabula rasa for new impressions. Records are set. Achievements are fixed in memory.

Three religions in the world, especially, are religions of place; perhaps all religions are, each in its different way. For Judaism, one land is holy. Not a rich land, mainly desert. Not a clearly defined land with sharp natural borders, and not an especially beautiful land—except in its starkness, in the sheer power of hostile nature that one feels in its hills and deserts, and in the extraordinary lucidity of its air and light. Yet all of the longing of the religious tradition focuses upon this land as the symbol of the Divine Presence for the Jewish people and a symbol for the transcendence of God. Judaism is concrete and thisworldly. It is a religion of particularity, of universality *through* particularity. God chose a people, for his own reasons, in his own way. This singular people is a people gathered around a land and a city: Jerusalem. For Catholics, Rome is a special city, but *historically* special, not holy in itself. The Vatican could be located anywhere; only tradition would be violated. But Jerusalem is valued not only for historical reasons, or as a traditional place; it is, as it were, a sacrament of longing and unique graciousness.

Christianity, too, is a religion of particulars, a religion of pilgrimages. God is everywhere, but certain places are especially alive with His presence. From early times, to enter a church was to enter a territory no longer part of the state, a sanctuary which soldiers of the state could not penetrate; the roots of notions of the separation of church and state arose from this sense of sacred space.

In Islam, too, Mecca is a holy city, and toward it all the faithful turn in prayer (just as Christian churches point toward Jerusalem). In a subordinate way, Medina and Jerusalem are also holy places. Because Muhammad is believed to have ascended into heaven from the Tomb of Abraham in Jerusalem, that place is held to be the "center of the world," the "navel of the universe." The place is universal, touching all humans, but locatable, finite, particular—and sacred.

So it is with many national monuments and historical homes, battlegrounds, meetinghouses, and so forth. Where great deeds have been done, places are lifted out of ordinary life and gain a certain aura. It is like that for athletic arenas. Players often feel it. Places where they struggle, where they may suffer injury, where opportunity comes and their careers blossom or, on the other hand, suddenly decline or fail to materialize—places where they meet their trial and testing—have a certain fascination over them. A ball field, a court, a gridiron are, after all, such small and finite spaces, and the thought that within these confined precincts so much that affects their personal destiny will occur presses itself deep in the cells of their flesh and organs. Being traded, going to another place, sometimes tears the unconscious self more than the mind allows; the feeling vibrates in the body more than in the mind. The spirit belongs anywhere, but the body belongs in particular spaces and grows accustomed to them. The body sometimes has an almost physical dread about being transplanted, almost like the dread the body feels in being forced by rational will to enter through an airplane door. The mind says it is as safe as any other kind of travel, no reason to worry, but the body dreads the unnatural environment.

The space in which athletic events occur is not only familiar but also awesome. Not just rookies feel it, in their first entrance onto the playing surface, but even veterans. Deeds done here depend so much on Fate. For one thing, opportunities for the sort of dramatic play that marks greatness come at their own time; the individual cannot control either their advent or their frequency. For another, his response is as much a matter of instinct, chance, timing, and placement as of intention or will. Most great athletic deeds are not thought through or entirely foreseen. One must react to opportunity, however it presents itself, from whatever stance in which one finds oneself. The Fates that govern this one small space have a great deal to do with one's own deeds. There are players who dread, who hate certain arenas in which they must play, because their showing there is consistently unflattering; and others who for some odd reason seem to prosper in certain parks or on certain fields, who play there with a lightness and brilliance they seldom achieve anywhere else. Being unable to control such factors, athletes often harbor feelings about particular arenas which they cannot describe coherently or with secular matter-of-factness.

Sports are carriers of traditions, of rituals. They war against traditionless modernity. They satisfy the most persistent hungers of the human heart—for repetition (how many cocktail parties have you attended? how many dinners?) and for solemn ritual, for pageantry and for uncertain outcomes. For centuries, human beings have gathered so. Sports are our brotherhood with ancient and medieval times. Sports are religions of place, of particulars, of deeds done *here* and at a concrete hour.

When an athlete kicks at the dust of the infield, or digs his cleats into turf or carpet, or squeaks his sneakers on the reflection-yielding floorboards, he gains a sense of concentration: all the hours of practice, all the years of discipline, all the frustrations of getting ready, have their focus here. The arena draws inward the multiplicities of life and weaves them into a tapestry. Once woven, the threads remain entwined forever. Arenas are like monasteries; individual games imprint on memory single images blazing as if from an illuminated text. Awesome places, a familiar, quiet sort of awe. Our cathedrals.

SACRED TIME

Baseball is unlike basketball or football in its relationship to time. Baseball pays no attention to the clock. However long an inning takes, it takes; games may last two hours or five. The game should last 9 innings, but anything over 4½ will count (if the home team is winning), in case of rain; and games as long as 17 or 19 or 24 innings have not infrequently occurred. In baseball, clock time does not exist. Time is measured by outs—three outs for each side per inning. Baseball is more intent on equality and fairness than on the clock. From each according to his abilities; to each according to an equal number of outs and innings. "Well, we had our innings," the combatants can say. As nearly as possible, baseball is free of alibis. The bounces of the ball are part of the game.

Still, the time of a baseball game is a special time, measured in outs rather than in minutes. The clock time required to play a game is always listed in the box score, as though to assist one in translating one time measure into another. Every baseball game has its own distinctive clock time. Each *is* its own distinctive unit of time: "One complete game." One hundred and sixty-two complete games constitute a year (not counting exhibition games or play-offs)—the baseball year.

It is almost like being a Catholic and living according to the calendar of the liturgy, or being Jewish and counting the seasons and years along another axis of memory. For Catholics, the year begins four Sundays preceding Christmas, and then day by day the life of Jesus is relived until Good Friday, Easter, and Ascension. Ten days later comes Pentecost, Sunday of Sundays, and then for twenty-odd Sundays the public preaching of Jesus is recounted, until Advent comes again. The secular calendar, January to December, is an abstract convenience, a tool of measurement; it does not recount the inner life of memory and identification—not for Catholics (or Christians generally), not for Jews, and not for devotees of baseball or the other sports. (I knew an Irish Catholic priest once, a friend of Whitey Ford and chaplain to the football Giants; his friends tease him that *his* liturgy begins with the football season, is moved along by basketball, and hits the high holy days when baseballs begin to fly in Florida.)

In basketball, sacred time is measured parsimoniously by two clocks: the stopwatch ticking off the seconds of the game, halted when whistles blow or the ball goes out of bounds; and the 24-second clock (in professional basketball) ticking off the number of seconds allowed before the offensive team must put the ball up toward the basket. Ordinary, secular time is disregarded. Especially toward the end of the game, when classic strategies have been developed for stopping the clock and setting up the final crucial plays, three minutes of sacred time may last as long as fifteen minutes on the pagan clock. The basketball player must be alert, then, to four separate times: profane time, game time, shooting time, and the end time.

In football, there is as in basketball a special game clock, stopped on canonized occasions: a ball out-of-bounds, a signal from the referee. There is, as well, a timer to speed up the offensive team: twenty-five seconds from the end of one play to the snapping of the ball for another. The sixty minutes of official playing time take more than two hours of pagan time. Since play is not continuous, but requires changes of personnel and special units, huddles and conferences, the actual time of action is very short. The execution of each play from the time the ball is snapped until the ballcarrier is driven out of bounds or tackled may last three to ten seconds, seldom much longer. There may be, perhaps, 120 plays a game. Only ten or twelve minutes out of sixty are spent in actual contact. Yet so furious and intense is the physical exertion in these few minutes that exhaustion, even of the most splendidly conditioned athletes, is apparent. Years of practice and preparation are funneled toward these highly charged and limited moments. However well one has performed in practice, only here in these sacred moments does performance count. A quarterback may complete a given pass play thousands of times in practice, and try it three times in a game and miss each one; the preceding thousand do not matter. The pressures under sacred time invite perfection-on-demand. A tight end may be called upon for only three or four passes; a halfback may carry the ball but six times; a defensive tackle may have a real shot at only five tackles. Years of training focus tightly down to narrow opportunities.

In this sense, football is far more intense than either basketball or baseball. In baseball, each batter gets his turns at bat, usually four or five per game; and a batted ball is handled by each defender singly, or in discrete sequence. In basketball, each of the five players is absorbed with duties every second, whether on offense or on defense. In football, not only are substitutions more frequent, and not only are specialists called upon in continuous rotation, but also the shifting directions and demands of the game allow some players on virtually every play to commit themselves only partially to action: to carry out feints or fakes, to engage in only brush blocks or tentative charges, on the ready, but not necessarily called upon. Only when the action directly engages them are they in a spotlight where their deeds are critical to success or failure. Some players, of course, carry the brunt of duty on almost every play: the quarterback, the offensive front line, the most frequently called upon runners or receivers, the defensive front four, and the linebackers. But football is so corporate an effort that one player's performance alone can be singled out from others' only by abstraction. Most observers of the game cannot keep track of the efforts of all eleven men, or even of more than three or four on any single play. In baseball and basketball, the individual performer is almost constantly in the spotlight of attention. In this sense, they are sports of greater intensity than football.

The final two minutes of a football game are among the most dramatic in any sport. They take a long time—in secular time—to play. Time-outs have commonly been hoarded (each team is allowed three per half). The offensive team, if it is behind, tries to run each play out-of-bounds, to stop the clock, forcing the game clock to record only the three to ten seconds of concentrated action required for each play. Enormous amounts of action can be compressed into two minutes. Harvard, losing 20–3 to Yale in one recent game, scored three times in the last minutes and won.

A feature of sacred time is its emphasis on life and possibility. As long as there are seconds on the clock, anything can happen; maximal efforts may be crowned with success. Athletes probe the forces and the sources of life, press against them, court them to their uttermost. "With a score of 6–0, two outs, two strikes, nobody on, only an average batter at bat, bottom of the ninth," William Saroyan has written of baseball, "it is still possible, and sometimes necessary, to believe that something can still happen—for the simple reason that it *has* happened before, and very probably will again. And when it does, won't that be the day? Isn't that alone almost enough to live for, assuming there might just be little else? To witness so pure a demonstration of the unaccountable way by which the human spirit achieves stunning, unbelievable grandeur?"

Sacred time is sacred because it stores up possibilities of the heroic; so long as sacred time exists, the heroic is in incubation. Sacred time teaches humans never to quit, to count upon and to entrust themselves to the potencies of life, redemption, beauty. One never knows. Deep in the resources of each of us may be ripening at least one supremely lovely act. Attentive, alert, ever pressing, we may allow it, when the circumstances most desperately call upon it, to flower into being, like a night watchman, a judge, a congressman lifted by the Fates to sudden vindication of their long careers.

I recall vividly, when my son was four or five, just old enough to watch football with me, how discouraged he became when Stanford fell far behind Michigan in the Rose Bowl. "I quit," he said. "This is a lousy game. They lost it. They lost." He had been born in Stanford hospital. He was too young to relish identifying himself, risking himself, and losing. I told him, a little angrily, not to quit, to stay and watch: "You never know. There's lots of time. You cannot be a quitter." Randy Vataha and Jim Plunkett of Stanford made at least one father in America feel a little less pompous, for they stormed back in the second half and devastated the bigger, stronger, crisper Big Ten team. Ever since, when I hear my son tell me, or his friends, or himself, "You never know, there's still lots of time," I am grateful to football. (The memory in his mind is vivid; I have heard him cite that game—and he remembers that Plunkett's first name was Jim, and that it was Michigan, not Ohio State, as I had written in my first draft, which he corrected.)

In certain African religions, a distinction is drawn between profane time, real time, and the time of the heroes. These times are not so much spoken of in words as observed in practice. Profane time is practical time, time spent in work and utilitarian necessities. Real time is time aware of the swiftness and uncertainty of life, of the illusoriness of practical time (which, indeed, "kills" real time, allows one to forget). For the time of the heroes, one imagines that in every human life is cocooned an ideal form, the ideal beauty of which the human race is capable. By their deeds, the heroes of the past raised their lives to these high, clear, stirring forms at least momentarily; they broke from the daily mediocrity of human life, beyond the veils. These higher levels always beckon human beings. Imagine that we walk through our days on hidden tracks, in cycles round and round, and at foreordained moments we are lifted out of the ordinary sphere and allowed to live momentarily in the eternal "time of the heroes." The true form of humanity then radiates briefly from our deeds: this is what we are truly like, what our usually unfulfilled possibilities dimly point to.

In the sacred time of sports, the time of the heroes occasionally breaks through. No one dictates the moment. It comes when it comes. But by preparing oneself, by laboring steadily, by forcing one's attention and concentration to the highest pitch possible, one may not lose the opportunities which suddenly and surprisingly appear. Such moments do not come frequently. Unhappy is the one whose mind is drifting when the instant comes—the defensive back who drops an easy interception, the touchdown lost because the mind made it before the hands held the ball. Living in the time of the heroes requires intensity. One must often practice raising the quality of one's attention to every instant as it arises, staccato-like, from the void.

Both the real time and the time of the heroes in sports are tokens of eternal life. At moments of high intensity, there seem to be no past, no future. One experiences a complete immersion in the present, absorption in an instantaneous and abundant now. In what seems like an instant, hours of profane time elapse unnoticed. From this experience, the descent into ordinary time is like exchanging one form of life for another. The most acute and disturbing pointer to the form of life high traditions have spoken of as "eternal life"— life in a different mode from that of the life we normally lead in time—arises for saints in contemplation, for artists in the joy and intensity of creation, and for all of us ordinary sinners in the festivals of sport.

It is from experiences like these that the myth of eternity arises. While some, especially among the educated, are properly skeptical, many human beings trust these intimations in themselves of another form of life: butterfly in a cocoon, longing to break free. To live at such instantaneous intensity forever, all gathered up like the sweetness of a plum at peak of ripeness, would be joy indeed. It would be cowardly of me not to say that such life seems to me the truth of human destiny, more credible than its opposite. Yet if it is not true, then the intensities of sports, and art, and love have been enough. If these fail as signs, in themselves they do not fail.

A Guide for Further Study

In the Fantasy section, Roland Garrett's metaphysics of baseball has a discussion of space and time which is worth thinking about in connection with this section. Two other articles in this area are: William J. Morgan, "A Preliminary Discourse Concerning Sport and Time," *Journal of Sport Behavior* 1 (1978); and Jean-Rene Vermes, "The Element of Time in Competitive Games," *Diogenes* 50 (1965). The section on human time in *The Philosophy of Time: A Collection of Essays*, edited by Richard M. Gale, is a good one to explore in relation to sport; also consult his bibliography on pp. 504–506. *The Discovery of Time* by Stephen Toulmin and June Goodfield discusses the historical development of our ideas of time as they relate to nature, human nature and human society. Also, see the entries "Time" and "Time, Consciousness of" in *The Encyclopedia of Philosophy*, Paul Edwards, ed., vol. 8. Finally, see "The Lived Body as a Phenomenological Datum," by Calvin O. Schrag in *The Modern Schoolman* 39 (1962).

Section V: Death

MARK HARRIS

The False Alarm

The following Thursday night he either had the attack or else only thought he did. I never stopped to worry which it was but flew out of bed and started waking up doctors. "Get back in bed and keep warm," said I, and finally a doctor answered, a fellow name of Charleston P. Chambers, M.D., and I give him our room and told him get over in a hurry.

"Wait now," said he. "Just what is the trouble?" and I told him, and he told me tell him get back in bed and keep warm, which I already knew from the sheet the doctors give me in Minnesota, and the doctor yawned a couple times and said he would be right over as soon as he was shaved and dressed and located his chauffeur, and he begun telling me he had this loony chauffeur that had a wife in 2 different places, one on the east side and one on the west, and he was never sure which wife he might be at.

"Never mind your chauffeur," I said. "I will have a fellow meet you in a cab," and I wrapped a towel around me and flew down the hall and pounded on Goose's door, and Horse opened it and said, "Come on in, Author," and I shoved past him and shook Goose awake and said, "I need help."

"What for?" he said.

"You know," said I.

"Oh," he said, and he was out of bed and in his pants in 15 seconds. "What do I do?" he said. "You can talk. Horse knows, for I told him."

"I thought you promised you would never tell a soul in the world," I said.

"Only my roomie," he said.

I give him the doctor's address and went back to Bruce. He looked OK, only breathing a little hard was all, and cold, and I piled blankets on him and stuck a hot water bottle in bed and sat down beside him. The sky was just beginning to light up a little, the quiet time when all the air is clean and you

---

From *Bang the Drum Slowly* (1956). Title supplied by the editors.

can hear birds, even in the middle of New York City, the time of day you never see except by accident, and you always tell yourself, "I must get up and appreciate this time of day once in awhile," and then you never do. Don't ask me why. "I am sorry to of woke you," he said.

"Make it back to me some other time," I said.

"I do not think there will be another time," he said. "Tomorrow is my birthday. I suppose my mother put a package in the mail. You can keep it when it comes, or cash it in if it is something you do not need. Give Katie a call."

"Lay still and save your energy," I said.

"I wish Katie was here," he said. "Probably Dutch will bring Piney Woods up. He is from Georgia, and that is something, ain't it? You know, I will bet I am the first ballplayer ever died at the top of the Sunday averages." He was 12 for 7, 583. "Tell Sid I hope he beats Babe Ruth."

"All these things you will take care of yourself," said I, "if you will only lay still and save your energy."

"Is the doctor coming?"

"Yes," said I. "Goose went after him."

"Why Goose?" said he.

"Why not?" said I. "He was the first person I thought of. He has a heart of gold underneath."

"It just never really showed before," he said.

"People are pretty damn OK when they feel like it," I said.

"Probably you told him or something," he said.

"I never told a soul," said I.

"Probably everybody be nice to you if they knew you were dying," he said.

"Everybody knows everybody is dying," I said. "That is why people are nice. You all die soon enough, so why not be nice to each other?"

"Hold on to me," he said, and I took his shoulder and held it, and he reached up and took my hand, and I left him have it, though it felt crazy holding another man's hand. Yet after a while it did not feel too crazy any more.

Soon the doctor walked in, all shaved and dressed, which really made me quite annoyed that he took so much time, and Goose and Horse with him. "Who is the sick ballplayer?" he said. "You do not look sick. Open your mouth." He whipped out a thermometer and stuck it in, and he took his pulse, looking up at Horse and saying, "Who are you?"

"Horse Byrd," said Horse.

"How did you ever get such a name?" said the doctor.

"I am a little large," said Horse.

"I would of never noticed," said the doctor, and he read the thermometer and shook it down, and he read the "Instructions for the physician" and went back and examined Bruce some more and asked him questions, and when he was done he sat down on the other bed and thought awhile. "I think it is something else," he said.

"You mean something else besides what they said in Minnesota?" I said. My heart jumped up.

"I could not say about that," he said. "I only mean I can see no danger as of this minute."

"It sure felt like it," said Bruce.

The doctor got up and walked back and forth, now and then stopping and looking at Bruce and asking one more question, then walking again. Finally he begun packing away his gear. "Boys," said he, "pardon me for asking a stupid question. But I actually thought Babe Ruth died some while ago."

"He actually did," I said.

"Yet I keep seeing Babe Ruth down there in the corner of the page every morning, plus this other boy."

"Goldman," I said.

"Which club is Goldman with?"

"Ours," I said.

"Pardon me for asking one more stupid question," he said. "No doubt I am no better than an Australian or somebody for not knowing a thing like this, but what club are *you* with?"

I told him. "Now you can do *me* one favor," I said. "You can send the bill @ me in Perkinsville, New York, and also not leak anything to the paper."

"I am not in the habit of leaking my house calls to the paper," he said. "Tell Goldman I hope he strikes out Babe Ruth."

I lost to Chicago that night, though they are usually the softest touch in the world for me. But I never got back to sleep until noon, and when I did it was one of these hot, sweaty sleeps. Goose was tired, too. He been catching all week, Dutch benching Jonah and hoping Goose would power up the lower end of the order. He done so, too. We won 4 in a row between the game I won Memorial Day and the game I lost Friday night to Chicago which I would of never lost if I had any sleep under my belt. Dutch said he believed he would now rotate me every 5 days instead of every 4, which he done, rotating Van Gundy every 6 instead of 5, starting Lindon Burke and Blondie Biggs fairly regular now, and spot-pitching Piss against right-hand clubs if his hay fever wasn't acting up too bad. Around this time of year you wake up one morning short pitchers. In the beginning you look around you, and you say, "We are certainly loaded with pitching," and then all of a sudden doubleheaders start piling up and people give out or get hurt or just simply don't show quite the stuff they had in May.

We dropped back to the 1½ cushion over Washington, though we picked it up again Saturday, a real slaughter, beating Chicago 13–3, the most runs we scored all year so far. Sid hit 2 and was now 2 up on Babe Ruth, and Pasquale and Vincent and Canada and Goose hit one apiece.

The paper now took some notice of Goose. He wrote an article called "How I Hit the Comeback Trail at 35" which a writer name of Hubert W. Nash wrote and sold and give him $250 for and the magazine said it would print when his birthday rolled around in August, but it never did. I mean the magazine never printed it. I took 200 of the 250 and applied it against premiums and with 40 more he bought his wife a dress, saving out 10 for taxes which I told him to or else have the United States Bureau of Internal Revenue kicking down his door all winter. I did not like him hanging with the writers, for they will pump things out of you. He said he never said a word about it, and never would.

Saturday night after dinner there come a knock on the door, and in walks Goose and Horse with a birthday cake and 4 quarts of ice cream. I said to myself, "Buddy, now you seen everything." "Happy birthday," they said, and they laid the cake on the dresser and tore open the ice cream. There were 2 candles on the cake, one for the years and one to grow on. "Many happy returns of the day to you, Bruce old pal," they said, and we said, "Same to you, boys," and we dug in. They also brung a carton of Days O Work, and Bruce said "Thanks" and picked out a chew and passed the box around, though nobody else took. "There looks like enough there to last you 15 or 20 years," said Goose.

"Do not lay it on too thick, boys," said I to myself, and I am glad to say they did not. They polished off the cake and cream and got up and took off.

Goose busted up both ends of the doubleheader Sunday with 2 doubles in the first game and a single with the bases loaded in the second, pinch-hitting for Jonah, which give us 3 out of 4 over Chicago, 7 wins in the last 8 starts.

Monday morning Bruce said to me, "You forgot to write away to Arcturus," and I snapped my finger and said, "So I did. As soon as I get back from drill I will." It was an open day, but Dutch calls drills on open days if things are going good, believing in keeping in stride. He also calls them when things are going poorly, believing that a drill on an open day will *break* your stride. I guess he knows because it works, or else he just misses being away from the park. Whatever it was we drilled, and all the way up and all the way back and all the while getting dressed Bruce said to me, "Do not forget and write that letter," and I told him I would if he ever stopped asking.

I was standing around shagging flies when Roberto Diego come running out. "Mister," he said, "Dutch is wishing you," and in I went.

"Author," said Dutch, "meet Mr. Rogers. Mr. Rogers, meet Henry Wiggen. Author, Mr. Rogers is a detective. Close the door and sit down. Mr. Rogers been down to Bainbridge and is now on the way up to Rochester, Minnesota, filling in some facts for me. However, you can save him a trip and the club some cash by filling in the rest of the story which Mr. Rogers begun."

"I will certainly try my darnest," I said.

"Tell him what you told me," said Dutch, and Mr. Rogers begun.

"I went and hung in Bainbridge a week," said he, "and I developed the following information." He had it all jotted down on little scraps of paper, and he kept looking at them. "I seen the following people," he said. "On May 19 I seen Mr. Randy Bourne at the crate and box plant, and on May 20 I seen Mr. Dow McAmis at the Country Club, and on May 21 I seen a colored man name of Leandro."

"Never mind the facts," said Dutch. "Get down to the details."

"Well," said Rogers, "I was told that along about the end of October Mr. Pearson told these various people that he was not feeling so good and went to the hospital in Atlanta, and they told him why not try up in Rochester, Minnesota, and see what been ailing you. He drove up to Minnesota and returned in January with Mr. Wiggen, telling everybody he was cured of what he had. Him and Mr. Wiggen hung in Bainbridge a month and then drove off with a girl."

"My wife," I said. "Big exciting mystery."

"I developed the information that nobody knew what was ailing him," said Rogers. He folded his papers and laid them on Dutch's desk.

"Do you get paid for doing this?" I said. "Because you developed absolutely nothing that I could not of told you and saved you a hot trip down there this time of year, plus which you developed actually less than half the truth, which I will personally fill in now for Dutch and wind up the whole matter once and forever and get back out and drill where I ought to be keeping in stride."

"Do not stall," said Dutch.

"I actually developed a lot more than this but am only giving you the bare particulars," said Rogers.

"If you actually spoke to anybody worth the while," said I, "you would of learned that Bruce has this rotten habit of running off to Atlanta maybe once or twice a month. No doubt you developed this much."

"Well, yes, as a matter of fact I did," said Rogers, "but I did not think it worth mentioning."

"Because as a detective you are from hunger," said I. "No need telling you

where he went in Atlanta. Everybody knows. And you know what you sometimes pick up in them places, which he did and which he rather not have
them treat in Atlanta nor anywheres else near home for fear of it getting back
and troubling his mother with her heart trouble. He was ashamed. You no
doubt developed the information that when he went up to Minnesota he
took along his fishing and hunting gear though when he got there found all
the rivers 9 feet deep in ice. He checked in, got himself shot with a few miracle drugs, flirted with the nurses, checked out, met me in Cannon Falls, went
hunting, changed his mind, and back down home again."

"Goddam it," said Dutch, and he flung open his door. "Diego Roberto!
Run out and get Pearson in here." Then he picked up the phone and called
Doc Loftus. "Come up here," he said, and the 2 of them wandered in about
the same time. "Take down your pants," said Dutch. "Are you over the clap
yet?"

"Yes sir," said Bruce. "Long ago."

"Check him over," said Dutch. "All I need is the clap running through my
ball club."

"Do not forget to write that letter," said Bruce to me, standing there while
Doc checked him over.

"What did you do for it?" said Doc.

"Got shot with miracle drugs," said Bruce.

"He looks fine to me," said Doc. He went over and washed his hands.

"Should I head out and develop this information further in Rochester,
Minnesota?" said Rogers.

"Stay with it," said Dutch. "Some things have yet to be explained."

"While I am here I might as well write out a bill," said Rogers.

"If you charge more than $1.50 you are a swindler," I said, and I went out
whistling.

That night I wrote the letter, saying, "Dear Sir, please send me a change of
beneficiary form for my insured, Mr. Bruce William Pearson, Jr.," and his policy number underneath, and I showed it to him and slid it in the envelope
and told him I would mail it this instant before I forgot, and I done so, sending it up to Holly.

Cleveland moved in, and we took 2 out of 3 and they moved out and St.
Louis in, and we split 2 with them, Friday night washed out, and we went
west 3 games to the good.

I pitched the first afternoon in Chicago and was really my top, which was a
good thing, too, because the power was off. It is usually always off in Chicago
because the wind in from right plays hell with Sid and Pasquale and Vincent.

You might as well stay home some days as buck that wind with left-hand hitters. Sid only hit one home run in Chicago all year.

The second day Dutch moved Pasquale back to Number 6, moving Canada up to 3 and Coker to 5 and lifting Vincent altogether and playing Lawyer Longabucco in left, and then finally how we won it Bruce hit a home run in the eighth, batting for F. D. R. who relieved, the first home run Bruce hit since Friday, July 25, 1952, according to the paper, and the first home run he *ever* hit in the pinch, a high and gliding type of a drive that started out too much towards left-center but then got hung in the wind and washed over towards left, and in. Gil Willowbrook mopped up in the ninth.

But Thursday you couldn't of bought a breeze, and we sat around in the clubhouse going through the old routine where the first fellow says, "I wish I was dead," and the second fellow says, "Why do you wish you were dead?" and the first fellow says again, "Because I will go to hell." Somebody is supposed to ask, "But why should you wish to go to hell?" I asked it myself one day in St. Louis my first year up, and I had to buy everybody a coke.

"I wish I was dead," said Gil.

"Why do you wish you were dead?" said Herb.

"Because I will go to hell," said Gil, and everybody waited, and now Wash Washburn said, "But why should you wish to go to hell?"

"Because hell will be cooler than Chicago," said Gil, "and that will be cokes all around," and Wash looked at Perry, and Perry said, "I guess it will, Wash," and it was, and Dutch come out and give the lineup, Goose catching, and Goose said, "Dutch, I am hot and tired." He was breathing, and he looked beat.

"Very well," said Dutch. "Brooks will catch," and he told Doc fork out some heat pills, and Doc brung them out and we passed them around and the boys swallowed them down with their coke, all except me and maybe 3 or 4 others. No doubt they are good pills, green for heat, white for weariness, blue and yellow for pain, depending where the pain is, for many of the boys been taking them for many years, and they sometimes help, and others been taking them rather than hurt Doc's feelings, but I believe they are all the same pill colored different. "Goose," said Dutch, "why not hang in town over the weekend and meet us in Pittsburgh Monday?" and Goose said he would. He took his wife and kids to the beach and was pretty much a new man by Monday.

I believe Dutch might of regretted it, but he never said a word. We lost to Chicago on getaway day, and then we lost 2 straight in Cleveland, the first time all year we lost 3 in a row, our cushion now skinned back to 1½ again, the power sometimes off and sometimes on and many people blaming Jonah, for even if it was on it was never on in the 8 spot, and Dutch benched Jonah and started Bruce, my day to work, warm but not hot, a perfect day for baseball and a great Sunday crowd.

I was hooked up with Rob McKenna, a left-hander. I beat Rob in a 16-inning ball game one night in July of 52, Chapter 28 in "The Southpaw" if you wish to read it again, one of the ball games of my life that I remember best, but he beat me after that more than I ever beat him, or anyhow beat the club, not me. We simply never hit him. He has an overhand fast ball that fogs through with a kind of downspin, almost a sinker, and even if you hit it you hit it in the dirt. He fogged it through that afternoon like always, and we had holes in our bats, and it made me mad because I was working good and hate to see hard work end up in the lost column. Bruce said, "He sure burns them through."

"Damn it," I said. "Do not sit there admiring him. Think how to hit the son of a bitch."

"I am thinking," he said, and I believe he must of been. He had his chew up between his front teeth, where he keeps it when he is thinking, not chewing but only thinking, for he can not do both. "I been thinking I can never hit his fast ball but can whale his curve a mile."

"I rather see you whale it than talk about it," said I.

"I could whale it," said Bruce, "if I knew when it was coming, or else I am meeting it late."

"Then study him," said I, "and figure out when it will be coming."

"I am keeping a book," he said.

"What does it say?" said I.

"It says he will throw me a curve after 2 strikes and try and clip the corner, and if he misses he will throw me still another a little closer in."

But Bruce went on hitting in the dirt all afternoon, and the boys as well, all but Sid. Sid parked Number 20 in the stands in the fourth. He was now 2 behind Babe Ruth, and we went into the eighth trailing 2 – 1, Canada opening it with a single, Vincent Carucci trying to push him along but bunting foul twice and finally fanning, and Coker topping a fast ball and sending a slow roller towards short which if it been any faster would of been 2 for sure, but was slow, Coker beating the relay to first, and Dutch said, "Lawyer, if Pearson gets on you hit for Author." Bruce took the 2 strikes, and he leaned in and waited for the curve, and it come, and it was maybe an inch or 2 out, and Bowron called it a ball, Cleveland beefing hard, and the crowd as well, and I remember Dutch crying above the sound, "Good eye, Pearson," Bruce leaning on his bat and waiting for Cleveland to calm, and then stepping back in, his jaw working and saying, "Rob McKenna is only a country boy like me, or else a country boy from the city," Rob looking down at Coker on first, then looking in, and kicking and pitching, Bruce counting on the curve, set for it, swinging, and when he hit it you knew it was hit and never looked for it, Coker tearing for second full speed and then slowing and jogging on around and waiting at the plate for Bruce, and shaking his hand. Longabucco sat down, and I took my swipes, looking for the 2 strikes first, and then the curve, and swinging on the curve, but fanning. The damn trouble is that knowing what is coming is only half the trick. You have still got to hit it. We took it, 3–2.

Goose caught the rest of the way through the west, and things held up. We played 3 at night in Pittsburgh, and 2 out of 3 at night in St. Louis, and it was cooler. I knew Goose would not last the year, and I am positive Dutch did, too, but Dutch was now past worrying about the year. He was nursing things along day by day, now 2, now 2½, pretty much stuck with what he had. There was no use hoping for miracles. Catchers do not drop out of the sky. You have the people you have, and you know what you are up against, and all you can hope is your people will pull together, and if they do you will also get a little help from wind and weather and Mother Luck and the schedule and the umps and charity bounces.

Goose brung his boy back to Pittsburgh with him, halfway through High School with pimples all over his face name of Andy, the first time in his life he ever been out of Chicago. Doc give him pills for the pimples, and he stood with us until around July 4, a nice kid, but tough, always trying to talk out of the side of his mouth and swearing like 90 when Goose wasn't around. He drilled with us, all style but no results until Jonah told him one day, "Boy, catch the ball first and pose for your photo later." Goose left him strictly alone on the ball field.

St. Louis beat me 3–0. How can you win without runs? I had an 11–5 record when we started home from St. Louis Sunday night, but I actually never give it much of a thought nor stopped to think how close I was to the bonus clause. I know that nobody will ever believe me, so why I even bother to write it down is beyond me, but it is true. When your roomie is libel to die any day on you you do not think about bonus clauses, and that is the truth whether anybody happens to think so or not. Your mind is on *now* if you know what I mean. You might tell yourself 100 times a day, "Everybody dies sooner or later," and that might be true, too, which in fact it is now that I wrote it, but when it is happening sooner instead of later you keep worrying about what you say *now*, and how you act *now*. There is no time to say, "Well, I been a heel all week but I will be better to him beginning Monday" because Monday might never come.

BARNARD LAW COLLIER

On Chuck Hughes, Dying Young

In the fourth quarter of the Sunday-afternoon pro-football game on TV, a twenty-eight-year-old Detroit Lion named Chuck Hughes dropped dead of a heart attack on the fifteen-yard line in front of the gathering of millions of Americans.

You did not know right away he was dead, but you knew something was very wrong. The cameras showed a close-up of Dick Butkus of the Chicago Bears standing over him and waving in a scared and frantic way for the referees and then for the doctors on the Lions bench. A player must wave for the referees before the doctors can come out on the field or it is a violation of the National Football League rules. A player might be lying there faking an injury to stop the clock. The Lions were behind by five points and they needed a touchdown before the clock ran out in order to win. But an incomplete pass had already stopped the clock, so Chuck Hughes had no reason to fake. He must have looked very bad off to Dick Butkus, because you knew that Butkus is mean and ornery when he is out there on the football field and doesn't normally come to the aid of an injured man who is not on his team.

The doctors ran out and started moving around too fast. You knew from looking at it on TV that this wasn't just a man with the wind knocked out of him. He was too still. Nothing of him moved. The doctors were working too hard. Instead of just loosening his pants like they do when a man is down with the wind knocked out, they went for his chest and mouth.

One doctor was pounding on Chuck's chest with his fist, and the other gave mouth-to-mouth breathing. This football player was not going to get bravely to his feet and walk off the field under his own steam, hanging from the shoulders of the trainers and dragging a leg. This man was not just injured. You knew from watching on TV that this man was badly hurt. In fact, you could tell by that funny feeling you get inside when death comes that there was a dead football player on the field. It was like the feeling the Indians must have gotten when they watched the spirits of their dead braves and chiefs rise out of the bodies and float up the chimney to fly away into the other world. Somehow, on TV, you could practically see the spirit leaving the body.

Chuck's wife Sharon was in the stands. She did not know that he was dead.

Originally appeared in *Esquire* (1972).

She thought maybe he had swallowed his mouthpiece, or his tongue, which is something football players sometimes do. When they do, it looks very bad as they gag and choke for air. But if the doctor gets out there in time with the little gadget he carries in his back pocket to pull the tongue back out, there usually is no problem. The man can breathe again and he gets back into the game. But Chuck was so motionless. Then Sharon knew that her husband was very bad off and she started screaming.

It seemed to her like ten minutes before Butkus stopped waving at the referees and the doctors got out there.

The doctors told some newspapermen later that in our society a man is dead only when he is pronounced dead. Chuck was pronounced dead at a hospital forty-five minutes after he fell down. But a doctor said, "In my heart I know he was dead out there on the field about ten seconds after I got to him."

They waved Sharon down from the stands, and she climbed into the ambulance with Chuck. Now she was sure he was dead. But maybe they could revive him. They seemed to be trying so hard. But the ambulance drivers: "Where is the key?" "I don't know. You got the key." "No I don't, you got it." "Maybe it's in the back." "I thought you had it." She wanted to scream, "For God's sake, one of you find the key and let's get going!"

She stared at what the doctors were doing and she watched as Chuck's ear turned slowly black and blue. Now it did not make that much difference to her when the ambulance got to the hospital. Now she knew Chuck was beyond reviving. After that, time slowed down so much that hurrying did not matter.

She kept thinking about their marriage and how much Chuck was in love with football.

When Chuck was a little boy in Breckenridge, Texas, he carried a football around with him nearly all the time. He started playing football with his brother Johnny when they were in the third and fifth grades of the elementary school. Johnny was ahead. They played competitive football very young in Texas: in the grade schools a boy with the talent and the gifts could learn the fundamentals and grow up to make Texas proud of its football crop.

Chuck was a little blond kid. His father was a small, tough Irishman who went off to World War II as one of those flying sergeants in the Air Force. He flew planes over the Hump in Burma and crashed a couple of times but came away okay. Then he cracked one up in Labrador, and it mashed him up so badly inside that the Air Force gave him a one-hundred-percent disability rating and retirement. But Chuck's father said, "If I can't fly a plane, I'll fly a desk." He was never the same though, and his heart gave out one night in his sleep four years later.

Chuck's mother was a sweet, delicate, small lady who bore sixteen children. She loved each one as well as the other. One little girl died when she was only two. The rest were all alive when Mother Hughes died at age fifty-two from what the doctors said was a worn-out heart. Chuck was fifteen years old then, in the Summer of 1958. Johnny and Chuck went to a farm to live with a relative until the end of the school year in Breckenridge before they went to live with Tom, their big brother, and his wife in Abilene.

For brothers, Chuck and Johnny were good buddies. Except that Johnny liked to pick on his little brother. For some reason bees did not sting Johnny. So he used to catch bees and wasps in his hands and slap them on Chuck. The bees would sting Chuck good, and Chuck would get roaring mad and start to cry and to fight wildly. But he never could get a solid lick in on his bigger brother. Perhaps Johnny gave Chuck so many handfuls of bees because he was angry inside that his little brother was better at football. Chuck was a very good athlete.

He had a pair of the quickest hands anyone in that part of Texas had seen in a long time. If you have any sense for it, you can spot quick hands in a boy without looking too long. But in Texas people seem to have some extra sensitivity to it. Maybe it is a little leftover skill from the old days when Texas men wore pistols and had to sense whether a stranger was quicker before seeing him draw.

Chuck also had good moves. He could fake a defender out so badly that the man would stand there looking stupid while Chuck was taking off four or five steps in the clear behind him.

Chuck loved to catch the football. He loved to catch it and feel it in his hands and then run. He was too small and skinny to catch the ball and run over people, so his coaches all told him: "Chuck, you must never, never try to run over people. You get the ball in your good hands and run *away* from them." Chuck would get the ball in his good hands if it was flying by anywhere in his vicinity and run away.

He also had something else. He was never the kind of receiver who would do what they call "listening to the footsteps." That means that when the defense man is running at you from behind like a mad steer, and the ground is thumping, and you know you are going to get creamed as soon as your fingers even brush the football, you don't listen. You don't listen to the footsteps.

Chuck never listened to the footsteps and in college he was a star receiver and a record-maker for Texas Western, where he went on a scholarship. Chuck was chosen to be an All-American.

He was small and he was skinny—at best he was six feet tall and one hundred and seventy pounds when he was a sophomore on the team—but he worked himself harder than anybody to get into shape. He ran pass patterns time and time again. He always made sure he started out on the right foot every time and he got the timing down to the split second in his head.

He had decided he was going to be a pro, and now he carried a football everywhere. Once a coach told him that a great pass receiver has got to know the feel of a football. You've got to know it like you know your own body. You've got to know how it feels when it's right and when it's wrong. The only way to know it is by carrying it, by touching it, feeling it, getting used to it, rubbing it. Chuck's brother Tom, who raised Chuck and six other children after their mother died, says that Chuck could tell exactly where the seams of the football were even if the ball was handed him behind his back. Chuck carried the football to the dinner table with him and put it in his lap; he touched it first thing in the morning when he woke up and last thing before bed at night.

He met Sharon in his sophomore year. She was Homecoming Queen, a short, pretty girl with long hair. Chuck was just the most beautiful man she had seen. He wasn't a big brute like the other football players, and only just a little too sure of himself for her taste. And his muscles were magnificent. She told her girl friends that his muscles were just what the doctor ordered for her. She wanted to get married right away; all the other sophomore girls were getting married.

Chuck said no. He couldn't get married right away if he was going to be a pro. And he was going to be a pro. He would marry her when he signed a pro contract. He carried the football the whole time. When they studied together it was there; it rested between them on the seat of the car at the drive-in movies. When Chuck signed a pro contract with the Philadelphia Eagles in February of his senior year, they got married. Sharon was twenty-one years old.

The rookie year is the toughest year in the pros, especially if you don't have a no-cut contract. Without the no-cut clause they can cut you from the team right up to the last day of training camp with no questions asked. Chuck and Harry Jones were both rookies the same year and they roomed together in the college dormitory the Eagles used to house their players during the eight weeks of camp. Harry had a no-cut contract and he was safe, but Chuck didn't and he went through hell.

All day on the field he tortured his body to make it do just that much more than any of the coaches thought it could. Some days he was spectacular, and all of his extra effort, the straining, the extra wind sprints, the extra concentration paid off with some wonderful catches. But some days he called up everything extra he had and it still was not enough to make him stand out as the best. Both Chuck and the coaches knew it.

Athletes and coaches are extremely critical. In pro football no player gets away with anything for very long. Coaches and players watch the game films and run them back and forth looking for the weaknesses in themselves and their opponents. The opposing side is also looking at the game films and the scouting reports hunting for weaknesses. Now there are computer programs that pick out statistical weaknesses in a team that human minds cannot always spot. A team must take advantage of every knowable percentage to win over the long haul.

The "game" we see every Sunday in the pro-football part of the year is actually an incredibly complicated one of advanced military-style strategy and tactics between two teams who are probably better equipped and informed and sophisticated about the battle they are fighting than any army in the world. When they find a weakness, they are completely ruthless about exploiting it. You don't say in pro football, "Well, let's not take unsportsmanlike advantage of their left defensive tackle because he's pretty banged up and slower than usual." You run right over him. You punish him with contact early. If he shows any signs of weakening you call your plays to his side. In the pros you know the difference between victory and defeat, and if a man is weak in any way, nobody is too polite or too kind or too sorry to let him know it.

Chuck had a weakness. It was a glaring, uncorrectable, inherited weakness for a wide receiver. As they say, "He didn't have 'the great speed.'"

To be a starting wide receiver on a winning team in the pros you must have "the great speed." You must be able to take off away from your defender with the kind of acceleration that leaves him panting just out of reach. That is the kind of runner that gets the breakaway play and makes the catch for the big touchdown when you need it. Coaches look always for "the great speed" and they program it into the team's offensive plays.

Chuck did not have it, or as they said, "Chuck wasn't blessed with 'the great speed.'"

Still, Chuck made the cut for the Eagles on the last day in training camp and the night he found out they made him drink whiskey with beer chasers and he got drunk and sick because he was not accustomed to hard liquor. But he said it was the best sickness of his whole life.

The Eagles kept Chuck because of his good hands and the fakes. They kept him to use in the emergency, when the number-one wide receiver is hurt and you need a man in there with a good chance to hang on to something if he's really hot that day. Of course you can't start him because of the weakness. If you have a man who has good hands and fakes and "great speed" too, you have to play him ahead of a man like Chuck who has only two out of three. Otherwise it would be like playing five-card stud with just four cards.

On the Eagles, Chuck sat on the bench. But, really, Chuck never sat *down* on the bench during a game. He was always standing up as close to the coach as he could get, with his helmet in his hand, yelling for the team, making

funny jokes, ready to run in there whenever the coach needed him. He figured that if he put himself in the coach's line of vision often enough, the
coach would recognize him and send him in. But on the Eagles Chuck was
behind two fast wide receivers. They could run the hundred in nine-four and
nine-six. Maybe, at his best, Chuck could do the hundred in ten flat. Those
tiny parts of a second make and break careers in pro football.

In the summers, Chuck and Harry Jones used to follow each other in different cars from Texas to the Eagles training camp. Chuck would insist that they
stop at a motel at five o'clock so that he could put himself through a hard
workout before the sun went down. He would run wind sprints, and then his
precise pass patterns. He and Harry would play catch. When Chuck got to
training camp he wanted to be in shape. He wanted them to know that he
had the makings of a star wide receiver if they'd only let him start.

A kind of unexplainable thing for non-athletes happens to pro-football
players in training camp. Harry Jones says the closest he can come to describing it is to remember how he and Chuck, who was his roommate, used to lie
in bed so sore they couldn't move and talk about *everything* until they finally
fell asleep at two or three o'clock in the morning. For eight weeks, without
any wives or girl friends, it was kind of like being married to somebody who
could really understand what you went through. Somebody who could say the
things that got your confidence up for the next day.

One night Chuck said he was thinking about how his father and his mother
and his brother Pat, who was just thirty-four, had all died of heart attacks.
Chuck said he sometimes worried about that, and he hoped the same thing
wasn't in store for him.

It was one of those things you put out of your head when a friend confides
in you about it. Harry Jones nearly forgot it. Chuck never bothered to tell
Sharon about it.

Chuck got traded to the Lions after three years and he was happy about it.
He hoped he would get a better chance to play. He liked it in Detroit, and
the Lions and their fans liked old "Coyote," as they called him. It was a nickname he picked up on the Eagles because his nose was long and sharp like the
coyote that chased the roadrunner in the *Roadrunner* cartoons on TV. The
nickname went well with his West Texas drawl and the handmade alligator or
turtle cowboy boots, and his Western suits and his Texas hats.

But it was not much better for him on the Lions. He did get to play more
often than on the Eagles, and the Lions were a winning team with good
spirit. But Chuck had the bad luck to be behind two more wide receivers with
"the great speed," and they had to get hurt before he got in. He could not get
a start no matter how hard he tried. On Thanksgiving Day in 1970, in a play
that his brother Johnny remembers they reran on instant replay six times,

Chuck made a turn-in catch where he threw himself straight out into the air about three feet off the ground and flew like a human arrow for about five feet to snag a football with his fingertips. And he held on to it when he crashed into the cold hard ground. It had to be an extraordinary catch to be rerun six times on instant replay: the film stands as a record of the kind of effort Chuck could make.

Last fall, he'd come home to Sharon and their two-year-old son, Brandon Shane, and Sharon would ask him how practice went. He did not like to talk what he called "business" at home. He would say, "I had a rotten day." Or, "I had a great day. I can't understand why I'm not in the lineup, but I had a great day."

And that's all he would say to Sharon about business. She wanted to massage his sore feet, his sore legs, his aching Achilles tendons, and rub his head. But seldom would he let her. He told her that she couldn't understand how it was with pro-football players.

His favorite record was a country-western song by Tammy Wynette called *Stand By Your Man*. Chuck would play it over and over for Sharon and other Lions wives when the Lions and their wives went to each other's houses. The song said that a woman should stand by her man no matter what, even though she doesn't understand. He would sing it in a twangy, flat voice: "Sometimes it's hard to be a woman . . . giving all your love to just one man. You'll have bad times . . . and he'll have good times . . . Doin' things that you don't understand. Stand by your man . . . And tell the world you love him. . . . Keep giving all the love you can . . . Stand by your man."

Sharon and the other wives hated it. They didn't understand and they were close friends with each other because of their lack of understanding. They would fume and sulk about how the men got off practice at two-thirty and spent the next two hours in a tavern drinking beer together and patting the behinds of their playmates. But Sharon knew Chuck was under tremendous pressure because he wasn't playing. Playing was the only thing he wanted to do—had ever wanted to do. So Sharon made less and less fuss, and they seemed happy.

The only odd thing Sharon noticed that last week before the Bears game was that whenever she came back from the grocery store Chuck would ask her if she had bought Alka-Seltzer. Sharon never remembered his using much Alka-Seltzer before. Other than that he looked very well. He had gotten sandwiched between two tacklers in a pre-season exhibition game with Buffalo and that put him in the hospital twice with terrible pains in his chest. The doctors gave him every test they could think of in case it was a heart condition that caused the pain, but none of the tests showed anything wrong. And the pain eventually went away.

So on the Sunday of the Bears game Chuck was in his usual laughing, happy mood, standing down there near the coach when one of the Lions' wide receivers got hurt. The coach recognized Chuck and sent him into the game. It was the moment he had been waiting for. It was already late in October and it was only the second time they had put him in a game since the official football season opened.

Nobody in the press box knew Chuck had come on the field. Somebody yelled "Who the hell is that?" when Chuck ran a post pattern downfield and made a spectacular leaping, third-down clutch catch of the football for a thirty-two yard gain.

"It's Chuck Hughes," somebody called out after looking up the number.

They ran the great catch back on instant replay.

Then the press and the TV talent knew Hughes was in there and they were going to keep an eye on him when he went deep. They would put an isolated camera on him, too.

The next two plays went deep, but to the other side of the field. Chuck had run perfect patterns and had faked his man out and was open down in the end zone all by himself. But the plays went the other way.

Chuck walked out of the end zone after the second play and trotted slowly back to the huddle down the middle of the gridiron. At the fifteen-yard line he looked as if he had tripped. Then somebody in the press box saw him pile up flat on his face in the grass.

They turned the TV cameras on him for us until the spirit left him, and then they turned away. For millions of Americans to intrude on the unfortunate death of a football player was no longer appropriate.

ROBERT W. HAMBLIN

On the Death of the Evansville University Basketball Team in a Plane Crash, December 13, 1977

And now we know
why coaches rage,

Originally appeared in *The Cape Rock* (1978).

kick benches,
curse rivals and referees.

Here, on this corpse-strewn hill
where grief smothers hope
with an obscene fog,
finality the only prize,
the orphaned heart knows
that every contest is do or die,
that all opponents are Death
masquerading in school colors,
that each previous season
is mere preliminary for encounter
with this last, bitter cup.

Yet we would not have it so,
it must not be so:
man is not made for death.
Cry foul. Shriek protest.
Claim a violation.
Even in losing, dying,
herald the perfect play.

So scream, all-knowing coaches,
admonishing priests, scream.
Swear, chew asses, make us work.
Never quit.
What else sustains
in nights when dreams
plummet downward in darkness
to question the betraying earth?

HOWARD S. SLUSHER

Sport and Death

Typically, man views death as an external phenomenon. He sees it as something away from the self. It is the one thing that man cannot and has not *experienced*. He can experience pain; or he might be near death; and he even knows of some person who has died. But for him, *as a person*, death is one phenomenon he does not experience during his existence. It is not surprising therefore that death is normally viewed as not *immediately* imperative. It is real. We know it is present. But it is removed from man's realm for he only sees it as a spectator.

> When death appears in its true form as the lean and joyless reaper, one does not behold it without terror; but when, to mock men who imagine they can mock it, it comes upon the scene disguised, when only the spectator sees that this is death, this unknown figure which captivates all by his courtesy and causes all to exult in the wild abandonment of pleasure—then a profound horror seizes him. (Kierkegaard, 1944, p. 83)

Indeed, the presence of death keeps most men as viewers of the future. Knowing we will all die, *at some time*, man enters into life almost laughing at death, for it is not to be regarded as *specific*. Yet all his laughter and talk about death, plus his obvious avoidance, implies the importance of death.

In a way, sport flirts with death. We have already seen that sport encourages the *intensification* of actual experience in a real-unreal world. The drama of competition encompasses the extremes of joy and suffering, and rightfully "toys" with death much like a little girl would tease her big brother.

Most often sport provides man the opportunity for false bravado in the name of death. For all the ruggedness and fierceness of football, soccer and rugby, *real* death is much an accident and not really a transformation of the actual probabilities. The athlete may well think he is a noble warrior facing the perils of death, while in reality he is greatly protected from the ultimate. Thus, actual death is indeed accidental to sport. Certainly it is a realistic possibility for the baseball player to be mortally injured when "beaned." The basketball player can take a final vicious fall. And the skier may well meet his

From Man, *Sport and Existence: A Critical Analysis* (1967).

end on the slopes. Yet the thought of death is not a *reality* for most sport participants.

Notice what occurs immediately following a serious injury on the football field. After an initial, almost "I-hope-nobody-sees-me," look at a teammate or opponent the performers will turn away from the injured athlete. Their action almost indicates a kind of refusal to admit the obvious. Namely, that injury and death are *real*. Man faces death almost as a *nonentity*. He tries not to acknowledge the unpleasant, much less death. Man must face death as an individual. There is no one or thing that can share this with him. He is *finally* alone.

In the so-called death-centered sports, performers overtly talk about death only in the rarest of situations. They tend to act as if it does not exist. One should not mistake this for a lack of concern, for they are *all* aware of the *coming*. But death is treated as something that is there but not *recognized* as tangibly affecting their lives (overtly). It simply hounds them. It is in this area that one can see how much man refuses to face the truth of his own existence. Authentically to encompass death is beyond the grasp of personal reality. "Death is the impossibility of possibility" (Heidegger, 1929, p. 19).

Prior to his tragic death, Donald Campbell, England's great speedboat racer, told reporters, "You boys will see me carried away in a box one of these days. That's what you're all really here for" (Scorecard, 1967, p. 7). Perhaps when the sportsman relates daily and directly to death he comes to recognize, with a little greater clarity, the almost inhuman desires of his fellow man. In a way, Campbell seemed aware of the certain desire for man to almost *wish and know* that nature cannot be continually thwarted. But when man is really *compelled* by the spirit of sport, life becomes a risk we all must take, for without the risk there is no *real living*. There is only *mere* existence. "There are things in life you must do . . . It's darned difficult to get inside yourself and find out why. All you know is that there is a fire burning inside" (Scorecard, 1967, p. 7). After reaching speeds of almost 320 mph, *Bluebird*, his boat, started tramping. Suddenly the end was there. Campbell lost to nature.

Indeed, Donald Campbell probably did not know why he remained in this sport. Many of us do not. Perhaps it *is* the uniqueness of the being of each sport. But one must wonder if like life, death brings a meaning to our existence, that is, in part, responsible for this uniqueness. And in so doing, man lives as if he is almost awaiting death. "All life is colored by the expectation of impending death" (Kaufmann, 1956, p. 87). It is really difficult to know. Is it not? Our intense efforts are to ignore this final departure; yet, we can't really escape from its prevailing presence in the world of sport. It becomes an *inclusive* segment of the total experience; and as such must be assimilated within the realm of realistic choices that are to be made. Its presence is both

real and personal. Its significance lies in the "availability" to man, an availability that renders our efforts meaningless (Storer, 1966, p. 2).

Sport is to be lived, by the living and for the living. Death is the end of life
and thus irreconcilable with sport. The athletic is his life; and he becomes
little beyond his performance. In truth, the athlete lives constantly with the
thought of death. However, like most men he knows not the *fact* of death; nor
will he admit the *concept* of awareness. In such sports as boxing, auto racing,
bobsledding, and speed-boating, man is constantly performing in the shadow
of death. Performers in these areas are constantly arranging a rendezvous with
the ultimate. More often than not, the desire to participate in "high-risk"
sports gives man the attitude of "complete" living. The feeling of excitement
is generated by what might be called an attempt to escape *death*, and not life
as is more commonly thought. Man hides his anxiety about death through a
process of actually testing the *object* of death. Death, in this way, is not a
reality; rather, *fear* of death becomes the reality. By facing fear the performer
is more often than not stimulated to new heights. In defeating fear he assumes he has defeated death. In truth, he has done little more than suppress
and conceal the actual. His performance is enhanced and man sees himself as
more than what he is. As Kaufmann indicates, the expectation of impending
death actually does enrich life.

Sport, unlike many other areas of human involvement, provides for increased satisfactions and wonder as the participation is repeated. In too many
of man's habitual day-to-day activities life is little more than a "daily routine." Life almost appears to be commonplace if not a bore. It almost appears
that the more years man lives (is endure a better word?), the closer he comes
to merging the extremes of novelty and repetition.

When man faces death, he really faces life. Sport provides for a voluntary
and regulated expression of this confrontation. Man tends to be most authentic when close to death. At this point there is no need to fake. The hunter
must stop "playing at being a hunter," when he awaits the charge of a wild
boar. Now the superficial and superfluous are not necessary. There is no one
to impress. Now he faces the ultimate reality. Is man capable of passing the
test? It is *real* ability that counts. It is rather paradoxical that man needs to
escape the "real" world (which might not be so *real* after all) and enter into
the artificial realm of sport in order to determine the authentic self. He now
must admit real existence to the self, something he can usually manage to
avoid. To this degree, the man of sport is closer to truth. He learns his potentiality. He realizes what, perhaps, he has already and always known—namely,
who he is. He no longer needs or can fool himself. He faces the finality of life
and in so doing sees the *Gestalt* of his existence. To the degree that he can be

"objective," in what was and presently is a most subjective existence, man is forced to realize his own worth.

The sportsman faces life with one last moment. How does he use his freedom to mediate between the *worthy* life and mere living? Death is not faced as a "just" sentence to the evils of man's ways. Rather it is the result of one of many choices man has made. Apparent finality is little more than one truth in the life of men. Perhaps it is with value that sport presents this opportunity to achieve meaningful inner discussion—a process that might well yield a significant impact to personalized existence.

Facing death makes the man of sport available to an awareness of authentic existence. Performance, faced with such extreme stakes, will tend to represent authentic being. Putting it another way, man is rarely as moral as when he is facing death. Death tells man to "face up" to life. Meaning comes to the performer when he becomes aware of the end. The totality is taken into account.

No one is "short-changed." Sport now becomes real for man. "Authentic action is not a chaos, but an ordered pattern based upon the structure of human nature" (Wild, 1955, p. 240). The man of sport is not as acutely faced with this problem. In fact, he often enters sport to find escape from boredom. Each event, each day, is *new*. Tomorrow *is* another day. The event of today is never quite like the one of yesterday. And tomorrow's encounter will be still different. Each *meeting* on the field reveals the elements of nature and man as an experience that refuses to allow man the opportunity to become blasé. Death therefore is paradoxically present and not present. It *is* there but not of the conscious. In this light sport provides a realm to escape the boredom of years and the necessity of common tasks. Sport acts as a solvent, dissolving the constant experience, which can be truly repetitious and thus lead to boredom, by providing *cycles* of activities (Lamont, 1965, pp. 29–36). These full patterns, such as innings, seasons, rounds and periods provide both completeness and variety. Thus, looking at sport as an exciting venture, man can face each activity with a type of heroic encounter. Lose—well at least I played. Win—and I am the one who did the unexpected. I am the hero! With courage and fortitude man can face battle and still maintain the relative security guaranteed by the "controls" of the situation. If one can be frequently successful, then truth begins to leave the subjective. Man's efforts become regular and thereby expected. If success is extremely constant then, in a sense, man's efforts live on.

THE HERO AND IMMORTALITY

Death is always a reality. But sport provides man with "everlasting" life. It offers the common man *immortality*. The great performance is remembered and man's name becomes a part of all the stages of time. The performance on the high school football team keeps man alive. It places him in *retrospect* to the unfolding history of time. In a sense he attains immortality because of his identification as a "football player." But in another way his *performance* is what lives, not the performer. In some small, but significant way, each participant is related to the unfolding history of sport and life.

For example, in talking of one of golf's greatest upsets, Jack Fleck defeating Ben Hogan in the United States Open Championship of 1955, Jim Murray the perceptive sports columnist of the *Los Angeles Times* more than hinted at the "unforgivables" in life.

> The public doesn't forgive guys who beat Jack Dempsey, break Ruth's record, replace Stan Musial in right field. People who thwart romance, dispel myths, flout legend, get to go stand on a corner the rest of their lives. To paraphrase a British earl, not losing to Ben Hogan is a kind of agnosticism that has no place in a decent society. (Murray, 1966, III, p. 1)

Indeed, man does not enjoy facing death. To maintain immortality in the sporting hero is one way for each of us to keep our association with the far-reaching past. In this way, we each stay alive a little longer and our life is also that much richer.

Perceiving the sport performer in this manner brings to attention the image of the daring and the brave. To this degree all performers possess a quality of heroism. Certainly this is most obvious in sport folklore. Gipp, Grange, Thorpe, DiMaggio, Mikan, Cousy, Richard, Owens, Bannister, Palmer and Dempsey are only a few of the numerous examples of performers personifying heroic stature. The legend of sport is the legend of heroes. But let this not be misleading. That is to say, it is not that sport is founded in the image of the "Saturday Hero," as much as man looks to sport for heroic realization. It is the rare youngster who, in his fantasy, did not hit the 3−2 pitch "out of the park" to win the World Series.

No matter if the hero be romantic or realistic, the performer in sport is forever mindful of the *individual*. Through *one* stroke of the bat, one last-minute shot from half-court, or one desperate lunge for the over-thrown pass, each man *can* be a hero. The fact that this is rarely achieved only increases the perception of glory.

The reader could well be skeptical. Certainly man doesn't really expect to be the "one in a million." Does man play golf on weekends so he can be the hero? Do youngsters play on the sandlots because of heroic desires? The immediate answer must be a resounding no. But I say, yes! I don't pretend to know the motivation of man. But I do *feel* that the chance for the "hole-in-one" keeps many a man returning to the golf course. And it is not the rare youngster who constantly daydreams, while playing the outfield, of his opportunity to make the leaping catch against the outfield wall. *To a degree*, man seeks the spectacular. Sport provides for the rational possibility.

The quality of existence is not foreign to analysis of the sport hero. The performer of heroic magnitude is theoretically self-directed. Yet the obvious paradox is present. Namely, man enters sport via externalized stimuli and proceeds to internally discipline himself toward heroic ends.

Because of the "tomorrow is another game" doctrine, sport gives man an opportunity to be a hero each and every time he participates. It is important to note that this explanation admits no qualities to man. He *is* neither a hero nor a coward. He is what he is. Each and every sporting phenomenon gives him the opportunity *to be* a hero.

> Man is free. This means he cannot be a coward in the same way, for instance, that a table is a table. He may be a coward on some particular occasion, but every new occasion that presents itself offers him a completely clean sheet, to be a coward again, or to be a hero. Observe . . . the phrase "be a coward *again*" rather than "continue to be a coward." He may have acted like a coward on *every* occasion, yet it is still not true to say he *is* a coward. He is free . . . for his essence he has no qualities. . . . he just is. (Wilson, 1959, p. 110)

Thus, man's involvement *characteristic* is a function of choice. Each and every decision points to his existence and not his essence.

The *immortals* in sport are legends known to most men. Joe McCarthy, Amos Stagg, Nat Holman, Dean Cromwell, Knute Rockne, Babe Ruth, Ty Cobb, Lou Gehrig and Florence Chadwick are only a few of the many who will always be linked to the past. In each case they are *symbolic* of a sport feat which in some significant way their performance stretched beyond the bounds of the ego. These are individuals who have actualized, fulfilled, affirmed and lived up to the maximum potential. Their bodies have passed on or will pass on, but their self (*being*) will continue to live. The ego immortalizes the *concept* of man, if not man. The Owens, Cousys, Gibsons, Hudsons and Rudolphs will continue *to be*.

Since man knows of death, it is with great courage that he accomplishes more than mere survival. Not many baseball fans will forget the final speech of Lou Gehrig, a man knowledgeable of his immediately impending end. In his last dark moments he maintained the courage that was indicative of the quality that immortalized all that he represented. The "Iron Man" is gone but his being is ever with us. He affirmed the pinnacle of selfhood, much beyond skill as an athlete. He remains, as he was, a deathless spirit.

Death is non-relative. But its potential, as a reminder of *life*, is all the more significant. To say life can again be duplicated by the same mortal is beyond the scope of this analysis. But to recognize for each of us that there is the *hope*, in sport, no matter how average our ability, that perhaps, just perhaps, someday we might make *that* leaping catch, or bowl that 300 game. In some little way we might have an association with both the past and the future. In a way, this softens our responsibility toward that end which we know will come to us, as it does to all.

Death terminates existence. But somehow it is part of the game. Tragic? Yes. But only for the moment. It is an element of integration. Certainly the tragedy is registered on the individual, close relations and friends. Even those who are not known personally are shocked. The *deaths of immortals* (a rather unusual phrase) such as Thorpe, Gehrig, and Ruth grieve us all. But this is what it means, in part, to attain a meaningful existence. The despair of the actual end for each of these individuals gets transformed into the lives of the living. Even when death is not caused *in* sport, and is a "relief" from painful illness, the *end* is tragic. All that is left is solitude. If it does occur *in* sport the feeling is perhaps even more distasteful. In a sense we ask, "Was it really necessary? Did he really have to take this chance?" Of course this attitude is one that recognizes the "make-believe" quality of sport and the real quality of life, as if man can separate his necessity from his need.

The element of death stands in man's path as a barrier for actualization. Not only is the performer cognizant of advancing age, which in itself is related to the approach of death as a deterrent of his *being*, but he must face the possibility of each performance being his final *appearance*. What sport does for man is bring this awareness closer. The "death sentence" makes man aware of his wholeness in that as long as the awareness of death is present, man is *not* whole. It is a rather unusual turn that projects the performer into his own recognition of what he does not possess. It is only when man takes time, a feature not often afforded to the man of sport, that he can *really* consider his total existence. When man finally encompasses death, he is then said to have *ceased life*. Once man is aware of his death he can understand the self in a way that sport typically does not encourage. It is almost sublime that man thinks of sport participation as the cultural avenue where he faces death and stares it in the face, when in truth it is sport that negates his view of death in any meaningful way. To bring death to an awareness is to pursue the authentic life.

Death is uniquely personal. Perhaps this is another reason why it honestly is not faced in sport. Namely, sport does not lend itself to sensitivity of *the personal*. The emphasis is placed on the impersonal, the collective, and man's ability to demonstrate his skills on and to the mass. Always seeking fulfillment and perfection man realizes that the very concept of death is a direct contradiction to the process man must undergo to really be *of sport*.

The indefiniteness of the *time* of death leads the sportsman into the pain of this inevitable conflict. The dynamics of sport allow man to "lose" himself and to forget his personhood; but at the same time he loses the sensitivity that is essential to the development of the impending crisis—the crisis of non-awareness. In this light, we see that the recognition of death becomes a personal responsibility. Man must appraise his personal world and decide if sport is going to be *used* to hide the inevitable or if it will be a mecca for the attainment of actualization. To run away is not to escape but to delay.

If, therefore, the ordinary man reacts to the thought of death with numbing fright, it is not because the ordinary man resists the consciousness of death, flees from it, in order to protect the mundane values which he has not the courage to abandon even though the consciousness of death has revealed their pettiness to him. The courageous man, on the contrary, will embrace the consciousness of death as an agent of liberation. He will not flee from it nor from the anguish which accompanies it because he knows that it is absurd for a finite being to expect fulfillment and well-being as traditionally conceived and because he is aware of the values which the consciousness of death carries with it. (Olson, 1962, p. 72)

Death is a human experience. To avoid its realization, by participating with vigor in sport, is to avoid the former and misuse the latter.

Death provides man with a viewpoint for sport. It asks man to accept death as a *real happening*, and to develop the necessary abilities to thwart death. But typically this just does not happen. Man naturally wishes to escape death and thereby develops his skills with extreme precision. But in the forestalling of death, through competency, the process of means and ends are reversed. In man's refusal to approach death, and take it into his existence, his high degree of skill reflects not his ability as much as his refusal to encounter the primary concern. Running in a frenzied effort for greater development in sport, he hopes he can shut out the reality of finitude. But he cannot. The anxiety increases and, as with any doubt, leaves little room for authentic living. All the trophies, medals and recognitions provide increased layers of "glare," not allowing man to focus or, for that matter, see the reality of life.

It is easy to see that man usually participates in sport in an unauthentic manner, hiding from his person the thoughts that are most related to him. Therefore, it is not surprising, if man lives and plays unauthentically, that he should die unauthentically. Always running from reality, attempting to avoid the final confrontation, man never allows for affirmation of his own existence. "To die authentically is to live in such a way that death is constantly anticipated in one's projects" (Heidegger, 1949, p. 188). The sport performer must see beyond the immediate. To think the game *is* life speaks most sadly for life. Man will not be afforded the opportunity to have a substitute take his place in the final game. He must be there at the end *himself*.

Then why play each game from the bench? Why, in the avoidance of death, do we allow ourselves to "get" less from sport than we easily could achieve? What is needed is man's honest insistence upon the responsibility for his own life. By becoming aware of death, he unites himself to his parts and to the elements of time (history as well as tempo); he comes closer to making both sport and life personal.

Since we cannot avoid death, it seems reasonable that it be brought into the consciousness. In sport man *can* (it is within his potential of *being*) become aware of the authentic life. I don't think it takes a restructuring of sport as much as it requires a new orientation to conflict. To say it takes concern, courage and awareness is to state the minimal. To speak of its importance in the development of humanity is to state the obvious.

To recognize death as a part of sport is to admit it is part of life. This is hardly enlightening. But what is crucial is man's appreciation of death and his perception of the *awareness* of death as a sign that one is capable of freeing the self for meaningful pursuits. Each defeat that is suffered in sport, and what is more important, the recognition of the potential for defeat, gives man the opportunity to achieve *meaning* for all of life. As he embraces defeat, as he must death, he learns, indeed, the structure of life. It is a shame that many "play" at sport for many a year and never come to this anticipation. But then there are many more that "play" at life and, too, never recognize their own self until the game is all but over. To say that sport is a reflection of life is, perhaps, not admitting the whole story. But then maybe the whole story is not known, that is until man knows the end. It is odd, but maybe not *that* odd, that the *recognition* of death itself provides the man of sport with *life*.

BIBLIOGRAPHY

Heidegger, Martin. *Existence and Being*. Chicago: Regnery Co., 1949.

Heidegger, Martin. *Vom Wesen des Grundes*. Halle: Max Niemeyer, 1929.

Kaufmann, Walter. *Existentialism from Dostoevsky to Sartre*. Cleveland: World Publishing Co., 1956.

Kierkegaard, Soren. *The Concept of Dread*. W. Lowrie, trans. Princeton: Princeton University Press, 1944.

Lamont, C. "Mistaken Attitudes toward Death." *Journal of Philosophy* 52 (1965), 29–36.

Murray, J. "Fleck's Infamy." *Los Angeles Times*, June 17, 1966, Part III, 1.

Olson, R. G. *An Introduction to Existentialism*. New York: Dover Publications, Inc., 1962.

Scorecard. *Sports Illustrated* 26, No. 7 (1967).

Storer, D. "Significance of Death in Sport." Unpublished paper, University of Southern California, 1966.

Wild, J. *The Challenge of Existentialism*. Bloomington: Indiana University Press, 1955.

Wilson, Colin. *The Age of Defeat*. London: Victor Gollancz Ltd., 1959.

KATHY L. ERMLER

Two Expressions of Failure in Sport

Such literary figures as Shakespeare's Hamlet and Miller's Willy Loman exemplify ways the resolution of failure is portrayed in literature. Hamlet responds to his own inability to vindicate the murder of his father by berating himself and his own impassioned inaction. Willy Loman, in *Death of a Salesman*, is a man whose misdirected desire for the wrong things drives him to suicide. He exclaims, "A man can't go out the way he came in . . . a man has got to add up to something . . . Does it take more guts to stand here the rest of my life ringing up to zero?" [1] Each character, in his own way, responds tragically to his personal failure.

Sport philosophers, biographers, and journalists are perhaps the most avid exponents of tragedy and its metaphoric applications to failure. The "tragedy of a missed goal/catch/putt" is the kind of phrase which comes easily to the sportswriter and is accepted even more readily by the reader. Man's emotional response to his failure in sport has been questioned philosophically.

Originally appeared in *Journal of Physical Education, Recreation and Dance* (1982).

What is anger and rage and violence but a goal thwarted by ill-fates, or ill-winds, or poor choices? What is sorrow and despair but loss of something valued because we "blew it," because we misperceived, misunderstood, gave up or just plain were not good enough.[2]

Failure in sport, no less than in life, is perceived all too frequently as having tragic characteristics.

RESPONDING TO FAILURE

However, it is possible that a person's response to failure may assume a different and polar form: a comic expression. Briefly, a comic expression relative to failure in sports refers to an athlete's ability to see past the immediate failure and to establish and seek future goals. Many college football players who do not make the pros exemplify tragic failure. After years of training they assume, having "put all their eggs in one basket," that they cannot do anything else once their football careers are terminated. Other athletes, such as Arnold Palmer or Jack Nicklaus, may be said to represent the comic response to failure. While sport is an important and serious aspect of their lives, they also realize that no failure represents total failure. In essence, a comic response to failure indicates that the athlete is aware that no *single* goal in sport or life can ever define what an individual is and can be.

Implicit in the word *failure* is the idea that an individual is unable to achieve his desired goals. But unlike the tragic athlete, focusing hopelessly on the past, and *overcome* by failure, the comic athlete, focusing hopefully on the future, *overcomes* his failure. Slusher contends, "It is at this point (defeat) that one experiences the relief of carrying the burden of hope."[3] Perhaps it is the comic athlete's ability to "carry this burden of hope" that assists his transition from the past to the future.

THE COMIC OPTION

The following statements illustrate the potentiality of the comic expression of failure in sport.

Quit? . . . Now? After one defeat? . . . Definitely, this is not the time to quit. . . . How could I live with myself?[4]

Sometimes you have to go all the way down to go back up.[5]

I ran and did the best I could, coming in fifth, but I didn't make the

Olympic team. I was a little disappointed, but I know now that if I had qualified for the team then, it might have been the ruination of me.[6]

Adversity has the effect of eliciting talents which under prosperous conditions may have remained dormant.[7]

Hope, the central element in the comic response, is reflected in some ath-letes' descriptions of their failures.

You can't be a better runner unless you are willing to be beaten. That's how I feel. If I am beaten, I say, "O.K., you're better than I am, but next time I'll try to beat you."[8]

Losing can sometimes bolster you. It gives you energy. You say I can do better. You go to work.[9]

There will be a next time for the comic athlete, a next time for which to be better prepared and better skilled. Although the next time will be a new "world," the goals toward which the athlete is working are similar to those of the previous "world"; i.e., failure has the quality of preserving a semblance of the previous situation. Perhaps in defeat, the comic comes to realize, if only subconsciously, that the *striving for* rather than the *achievement of* a goal is the ultimate occupation of man.

And who knows . . . perhaps the only goal on earth to which mankind is striving lies in the incessant process of attaining, in other words, in life itself, not in the thing to be attained . . .[10]

It may be that the comic athlete apprehends personal failure as a momentary reprieve from reaching a destination from which there will be nothing further to seek.

Man . . . feels that when he has found it there will be nothing for him to look for. . . . He loves the process of attaining, but does not quite like to have attained, and that is very absurd. In fact, man is a comical creature.[11]

Having failed in an attempt to achieve a personal goal, the comic athlete looks forward to a time when there will be another attempt to prove personal worth.

CHOOSING HOPE

It is important to emphasize that the ability to perceive failure comically is not inborn; it is not something that some people have and some people don't. Everyone is capable of personally *choosing* either a tragic or a comic response to failure. Few individuals understand that failure need not be experienced as a tragic event. Potentially, failure can expand or contract personal understanding, can strengthen or weaken commitment and desire to achieve a goal, can limit or enlarge potentialities.

An athlete's selection of a tragic or a comic response to failure is often due to the influence of a teacher/coach role model. Physical educators and coaches deal with failure regularly. Yet too often, the teacher or coach leaves the athlete to deal with his failure alone. Rather than leaving a person to wallow in failure, overcoming failure should become a teaching function. Rather than allowing the individual to remain at an easy and unchallenging level, assisting the athlete to re-examine defeat so as to establish new priorities and goals should be an educational objective. While assisting an athlete with failure is not simple, it is integral to the learning process. Teachers and coaches can help athletes cope with failure not only through the attitude they assume toward it, but by creating an environment in which the student feels safe to try and to fail. Only in this situation can the student/athlete come to realize that failure need not be an end but may signify a new beginning—not a place from which travel is no longer possible, but a place from which to depart. Failure, no less than success, may be a means through which to achieve authentic self-understanding.

NOTES

1. Arthur Miller, *Death of a Salesman* (New York: Penguin Books, 1976), pp. 125–126.
2. Carolyn Thomas, "The Sportsman as a Tragic Figure," in *Sport and the Humanities*, ed. William J. Morgan (Knoxville: University of Tennessee Press, 1980), p. 17.
3. Howard Slusher, *Man, Sport and Existence: A Critical Analysis* (Philadelphia: Lea and Febiger, 1967), p. 4.
4. Floyd Patterson, "How I Lost the Title," *Sports Illustrated*, June 4, 1962, p. 40.
5. Jerry Kirshenbaum, "The Golden Moment," *Sports Illustrated*, August 20, 1979, p. 72.
6. Frances Sabin, *Women Who Win* (New York: Random House, 1975), p. 49.
7. Ray Kennedy, "It's :00 Ara, Time to Say Goodbye," *Sports Illustrated*, October 7, 1974, p. 27.
8. S. Pileggi, "Rush Hour in the Big Apple," *Sports Illustrated*, October 29, 1979, p. 25.

9. Patterson, *Op. cit.*, p. 23.
10. Fyodor Dostoevsky, *Notes from Underground*, in Walter Kaufmann's *Existentialism from Dostoevsky to Sartre* (New York: New American Library, 1975), p. 77.
11. *Ibid.*, p. 78.

A Guide for Further Study

In addition to Harris's novel, we recommend the fine film version of *Bang the Drum Slowly*, and the book and film, *Brian's Song*. The classic A. E. Housman poem, "To an Athlete Dying Young," establishes all the issues later writers have elaborated on. Mortality is never far from the foreground in Malamud's *The Natural*. Athletic retirement as social death is explored in studies by Edwin Rosenberg and Stephen Lerch in *Sport and the Sociological Imagination*, edited by Nancy Theberge and Peter Donnelly. These issues also emerge in the stories which open this anthology.

SELECTED BIBLIOGRAPHY

The titles below are intended to supplement those listed in the Guides for Further Study.

LITERARY CRITICISM OF SPORTS-CENTERED WORKS

Books

Berman, Neil D. *Playful Fictions and Fictional Players.*
Coffin, Tristram Potter. *The Old Ball Game: Baseball in Folklore and Fiction.*
Greenberg, Martin H., and Joseph D. Olander, eds. *Run to Starlight: Sports Through Science Fiction.*
Higgs, Robert J. *Laurel and Thorn: The Athlete in American Literature.*
Johnson, William O. *Super Spectator and the Electric Lilliputians.*
Messenger, Christian K. *Sport and the Spirit of Play in American Fiction: Hawthorne to Faulkner.*
Oriard, Michael V. *Dreaming of Heroes: American Sports Fiction 1868–1980.*
Siner, Howard, ed. *Sports Classics: American Writers Choose Their Best.*
Umphlett, Wiley Lee. *American Sport Culture: The Humanistic Dimensions.*
Umphlett, Wiley Lee. *The Sporting Myth and the American Experience: Studies in Contemporary Fiction.*

Journal Articles

Maddocks, Melvin. "Jock Lit 101." *Time* 107 (June 28, 1976).
Smith, Leverett T. "Five Books About Sports in American Fiction." *Journal of the Philosophy of Sport* 10 (1983), 92–106.
Vanderwerken, David L. "Sports Literature Anthologies: A Scorecard." *Journal of the Philosophy of Sport* 6 (1979), 95–100.
Vanderwerken, David L. "The Joy of Sports Books: A Tout Sheet." *The Georgia Review* 33 (1979), 707–712.

PHILOSOPHY

Books

Best, David. *Expression in Movement and the Arts: A Philosophical Enquiry.*
Fraleigh, Warren P. *Right Actions in Sport: Ethics for Contestants.*
Hyland, Drew A. *The Question of Play.*
Keating, James W. *Competition and Playful Activities.*
Kupfer, Joseph H. *Experience as Art: Aesthetics in Everyday Life*, ch. V.
Lenk, Hans, ed. *Topical Problems in Sport Philosophy.*

McIntosh, Peter. *Fair Play: Ethics in Sport and Education.*
Mihalich, Joseph C. *Sports and Athletics: Philosophy in Action.*
Ortega y Gasset, Jose. *Meditations on Hunting.* Translated by Howard B. Wescott.
Simon, Robert L. *Sports and Social Values.*
Sourian, Paul. *The Aesthetics of Movement.* Translated and edited by Manon Sourian.
Steinkraus, Warren E. *Philosophy of Art.* Revised edition. Appendix C.
Thomas, Carolyn E. *Sport in a Philosophic Context.*
VanderZwaag, Harold J. *Toward a Philosophy of Sport.*
Whiting, H. T. A., and D. W. Masterson, eds. *Readings in the Aesthetics of Sport.*

Journal Articles

Arnold, Peter J. "Sport, Moral Education and the Development of Character." *Journal of Philosophy of Education* 18 (1984), 275–281.
Aspin, David. "Ethical Aspects of Sport and Games and Physical Education." *Proceedings of the Philosophy of Education Society of Great Britain* 9 (July 1975), 49–71.
Aspin, David. "Kinds of Knowledge, Physical Education and the Curriculum." *Journal of Human Movement Studies* 3 (1977), 21–37.
Best, David. "Sport Is Not Art." *Journal of the Philosophy of Sport* 12 (1985).
Carr, David. "Practical Reasoning and Knowing How." *Journal of Human Movement Studies* 4 (1978), 3–20.
Carr, David. "The Language of Action." *Journal of Human Movement Studies* 6 (1980), 75–94.
Carr, David. "The Language of Ability and Skill." *Journal of Human Movement Studies* 6 (1980), 111–126.
Lenk, Hans. "Toward a Social Philosophy of Achievement and Athletics." *Man and World* 9 (February 1976), 45–59.
Radford, Colin. "The Umpire's Dilemma." *Analysis* 45 (March 1985), 109–111.
Wertz, S. K. "A Response to Best on Art and Sport." *Journal of Aesthetic Education* 18 (Winter 1984), 105–108.
Wertz, S. K. "Representation and Expression in Sport and Art." *Journal of the Philosophy of Sport* 12 (1985).
Wertz, S. K. "Sport and the Artistic." *Philosophy* 60 (July 1985).

MISCELLANEOUS

Books

Allen, Dorothy J., and Brian W. Fahey, eds. *Being Human in Sport.*
Baker, William J., and John M. Carroll, eds. *Sports in Modern America.*
Bale, John. *Sport and Place: A Geography of Sport in England, Scotland and Wales.*
Bandy, Susan, ed. *Coroebus Triumphs: The Alliance of Sport and Literature.*

Boswell, Thomas. *Why Time Begins on Opening Day.*

Caillois, Roger. *Man, Play, and Games.*

Ehrmann, Jacques, ed. *Game, Play, Literature.*

Lasch, Christopher. *The Culture of Narcissism: American Life in an Age of Diminishing Expectations*, ch. V.

Mihalich, Joseph C., ed. *Sports in the American Mind: Views and Perspectives.*

Murphy, Michael, and Rhea A. White, eds. *The Psychic Side of Sports.*

Okrent, Daniel. *Nine Innings.*

Stone, Gregory P. *Games, Sport and Power.*

VanderZwaag, Harold J., and Thomas J. Shechan. *Introduction to Sport Studies: From the Classroom to the Ball Park.*

Zeigler, Earle F. *Philosophical Foundations for Physical, Health, and Recreation Education.*

Zeigler, Earle F. *Physical Education and Sport Philosophy.*

Journal Articles

Frey, James H., ed. "Contemporary Issues in Sport." *The Annals of the American Academy of Political and Social Science* 445 (September 1979), 1–165.

O'Muircheartaigh, I. G., and J. Sheil. "Fore or Five?—The Indexing of a Golf Course." *Applied Statistics* 32 (1983), 287–292.

Renick, Jobyann. "The Structure of Games." *Journal of Human Movement Studies* 3 (1977), 193–206.

Shotter, John. "Prolegomena to an Understanding of Play." *Journal of the Theory of Social Behaviour* 3 (1973), 47–89.

Zeigler, Earle F. "Philosophy of Sport and Developmental Physical Activity." *The Sport Sciences* 4 (1983).

INDEX OF AUTHORS AND TITLES

ACKNOWLEDGMENTS

SPORT INSIDE OUT: READINGS IN
LITERATURE AND PHILOSOPHY

The selections in this anthology are reprinted by the kind permission of the following authors, publishers, and representatives:

Roger Angell. "The Interior Stadium" reprinted from *The Summer Game* by Roger Angell. Copyright © 1971, 1972 by Roger Angell. Reprinted by permission of the author and Viking Penguin Inc. Originally appeared in *The New Yorker*.

Lynne Belaief. "Meanings of the Body" reprinted from *Journal of the Philosophy of Sport*. Copyright © 1977 by the Philosophic Society for the Study of Sport. Reprinted by permission of the editor.

Jim Brosnan. "The Fantasy World of Baseball" reprinted from *The Atlantic Monthly*. Copyright © 1964 by the Atlantic Monthly Company, Boston, Massachusetts. Reprinted by permission of the publisher.

Edwin H. Cady. "Pop Art and the American Dream" and "The Sort of Sacred, Sometimes Ritual" excerpted from Chapter 4 of *The Big Game: College Sports and American Life* by Edwin H. Cady. Copyright © 1978 by the University of Tennessee Press. Reprinted by permission of the publisher.

Barnard Law Collier. "On Chuck Hughes, Dying Young" reprinted with permission from *Esquire* (February, 1972). Copyright © 1972 by Esquire Associates.

Robert Coover. Chapter 1 reprinted from *The Universal Baseball Association, Inc., J. Henry Waugh, Prop.* Copyright © 1968 by Robert Coover. Reprinted by permission of the author, Random House, Inc., and Georges Borchardt, Inc.

Frank Deford. "Religion in Sport" reprinted from *Sports Illustrated* (19 April 1976, 26 April 1976, 3 May 1976). Copyright © 1976 by Time Inc. Reprinted by permission of *Sports Illustrated*.

Don DeLillo. "The Exemplary Spectator" excerpted from Chapter 19 of *End Zone* by Don DeLillo. Copyright © 1972 by Don DeLillo. Reprinted by permission of Houghton Mifflin Company and Wallace & Sheil Agency, Inc.

James Dickey. "For the Death of Vince Lombardi" reprinted with permission from *Esquire* (September, 1971). Copyright © 1971 by Esquire Associates.

Alan R. Drengson. "Wilderness Travel as an Art and as a Paradigm for Outdoor Education" reprinted from *Quest*. Copyright © 1980 by Human Kinetics Publishers. Reprinted by permission of the author and the Publications Director.

Joseph Epstein. "Obsessed with Sport" reprinted from *Harper's*. Copyright © 1976 by Joseph Epstein. Reprinted by permission of the author and Georges Borchardt, Inc.

Kathy L. Ermler. "Two Expressions of Failure in Sport" reprinted from *Journal of Physical Education, Recreation and Dance*. Copyright © 1982 by the American Alliance for Health, Physical Education, Recreation and Dance. Reprinted by permission of the author and the Director of Publications.

Frederick Exley. "Frank Gifford and Me" excerpted from Chapter 2 of *A Fan's Notes* by Frederick Exley. Copyright © 1968 by Frederick Exley. Reprinted by permission of the author, Random House, Inc., and International Creative Management, Inc.

Gerald R. Ford. "In Defense of the Competitive Urge" reprinted from *Sports Illustrated* (8 July 1974). Copyright © 1974 by Time Inc. Reprinted by permission of *Sports Illustrated*.

Warren Fraleigh. "Philosphical Analysis and Normative Judgments on Clutch Hitters: A Reaction to Michael Martin" is an original essay published by permission of the author.

Warren Fraleigh. "Why the Good Foul Is Not Good" reprinted from *Journal of Physical Education, Recreation and Dance*. Copyright © 1982 by the American Alliance for Health, Physical Education, Recreation and Dance. Reprinted by permission of the author and the Director of Publications.

Richard F. Galvin. "Aesthetic Incontinence in Sport" is an original essay published by permission of the author.

Roland Garrett. "The Metaphysics of Baseball" reprinted from *Philosophy Today* (Fall, 1976), Carthagena Station, Celina, Ohio 45822. Reprinted by permission of the author and editor.

Gary Gay. "Ishmael in Arlis" reprinted from *The Bi-Centennial Collection of Texas Short Stories*. Copyright © 1974 by the Texas Center for Writers Press. Reprinted by permission of the publisher.

Peter Gent. "Monday" reprinted from pages 3–16 of the first chapter of *North Dallas Forty* by Peter Gent. Copyright © 1973 by Peter Gent. Reprinted by permission of William Morrow & Company and the Sterling Lord Agency, Inc.

Bil Gilbert and Lisa Twyman. "Violence: Out of Hand in the Stands" reprinted from *Sports Illustrated* (31 January 1983). Copyright © 1983 by Time Inc. Reprinted by permission of *Sports Illustrated*.

George Grella. "Baseball and the American Dream" reprinted from *The Massachusetts Review*. Copyright © 1975 by *The Massachusetts Review*. Reprinted by permission of the editors and *The Massachusetts Review*, Inc.

Allen Guttmann. "The Sacred and the Secular" excerpted from Chapter 2 of *From Ritual to Record: The Nature of Modern Sports*. Copyright © 1978 by Columbia University Press. Reprinted by permission of the publisher.

Robert W. Hamblin. "On the Death of the Evansville University Basketball Team in a Plane Crash, December 13, 1977" reprinted from *The Cape Rock* (Winter, 1978). Copyright © 1978 by Robert W. Hamblin. Reprinted by permission of the author.

Francine Hardaway. "Foul Play: Sports Metaphors as Public Doublespeak" reprinted from *College English* 38, No. 1 (September, 1976), 78–82. Reprinted by permission of the National Council of Teachers of English.

William Harper. "The Philosopher in Us" reprinted from *Journal of Physical Education, Recreation and Dance*. Copyright © 1982 by the American Alliance for Health, Physical Education, Recreation and Dance. Reprinted by permission of the author and the Director of Publications.

Mark Harris. Chapter 11 reprinted from *Bang the Drum Slowly* by Mark Harris. Copyright © 1956 by Mark Harris. Reprinted by permission of the author and the Fox Chase Agency, Inc.

William Harrison. "Roller Ball Murder" reprinted from *Roller Ball Murder* by William Harrison. Copyright © 1973, 1974 by William Harrison. Reprinted by permission of William Morrow & Company and Robson Books Ltd. Originally appeared in *Esquire* (1973).

Henry Hecht. "Here's the Info on Hitters Who Get Tough When the Going Gets Tough" reprinted from *Sports Illustrated* (21 March 1983). Copyright © 1983 by Time Inc. Reprinted by permission of *Sports Illustrated*.

Peter Heinegg. "Philosopher in the Playground: Notes on the Meaning of Sport" reprinted from *Southern Humanities Review* 10, No. 2 (Spring 1976), 153–156. Copyright © 1976 by Auburn University. Reprinted by permission of the editors.

Ernest Hemingway. "Fifty Grand" reprinted from *The Snows of Kilimanjaro and Other Stories* by Ernest Hemingway. Copyright © 1927 by Charles Scribner's Sons; Copyright © renewed 1955. Reprinted by permission of Charles Scribner's Sons. Reprinted also from *The First Forty-Nine Stories* by Ernest Hemingway; reprinted by permission of Jonathan Cape, Ltd., and the Executors of the Estate of Ernest Hemingway.

David Hilton. "The Poet Tries to Turn in His Jock" reprinted from *Huladance*. Copyright © 1976 by The Crossing Press. Reprinted by permission of the publisher.

Rolfe Humphries. "Night Game" and "Polo Grounds" reprinted from *The Collected Poems of Rolfe Humphries*. Copyright © 1965 by Indiana University Press. Reprinted by permission of the publisher.

Drew A. Hyland. "Playing to Win: How Much Should It Hurt?" reprinted from *The Hastings Center Report* (April, 1979). Copyright © 1979 by the Institute of Society, Ethics and the Life Sciences. Reprinted by permission of the editor.

Dan Jenkins. "The Wool Market" and "Game-Face" excerpted from *Semi-Tough* by Dan Jenkins. Copyright © 1972 by Dan Jenkins. Reprinted by permission of Atheneum Publishers, Inc. and The Sterling Lord Agency, Inc.

Roger Kahn. "Lines on the Transpontine Madness" reprinted from *The Boys of Summer* by Roger Kahn. Copyright © 1971, 1972 by Roger Kahn. Reprinted by permission of the author, Harper & Row, Publishers, Inc., and the William Morris Agency, Inc.

Sam Koperwas. "Ball" reprinted with permission from *Esquire* (February, 1975). Copyright © 1975 by Esquire Associates.

R. Scott Kretchmar. "'Distancing': An Essay on Abstract Thinking in Sport Performances" reprinted from *Journal of the Philosophy of Sport*. Copyright © 1982 by the Philosophic Society for the Study of Sport. Reprinted by permission of the editor.

Paul G. Kuntz. "Aesthetics Applies to Sports as Well as to the Arts" reprinted from *Journal of the Philosophy of Sport*. Copyright © 1974 by the Philosophic Society for the Study of Sport. Reprinted by permission of the editor.

Ring W. Lardner. "A New Busher Breaks In" reprinted from *You Know Me Al* by Ring W.

Lardner. Copyright © 1916 by Charles Scribner's Sons; copyright © renewed 1944 by Ellis A. Lardner. Reprinted by permission of Charles Scribner's Sons.

Craig K. Lehman. "Can Cheaters Play the Game?" reprinted from *Journal of the Philosophy of Sport*. Copyright © 1981 by the Philosophic Society for the Study of Sport. Reprinted by permission of the editor.

Hans Lenk. "Action Theory and the Social Scientific Analysis of Sport Actions" and "Prolegomena Toward an Analytic Philosophy of Sport" reprinted from *International Journal of Physical Education* (1979, 1981). Copyright © 1979, 1981 by Hans Lenk. Reprinted, in revised form, by permission of the author and editor.

Hans Lenk. "Herculean 'Myth' Aspects of Athletics" reprinted from *Journal of the Philosophy of Sport*. Copyright © 1976 by the Philosophic Society for the Study of Sport. Reprinted by permission of the editor.

Laurence Lieberman. "My Father Dreams of Baseball" reprinted from *The Unblinding* by Laurence Lieberman. Copyright © 1963 by Laurence Lieberman. Reprinted by permission of Macmillan Publishing Company. Originally appeared in *The Atlantic Monthly*.

Richard Lipsky. "Of Team Players and Sky Hooks: The Infiltration of Sports Language in Politics" reprinted from *How We Play the Game: Why Sports Dominate American Life*. Copyright © 1981 by Richard Lipsky. Reprinted by permission of Beacon Press.

Bernard Malamud. "Pre-game" reprinted from *The Natural* by Bernard Malamud. Copyright © 1952, renewed © 1980 by Bernard Malamud. Reprinted by permission of Farrar, Straus and Giroux, Inc. and Russel & Volkening, Inc.

Michael Martin. "Philosophical Analysis at Work: In Search of the Elusive Clutch Hitter" and "Comments on Fraleigh" are original essays published by permission of the author.

John McMurtry. "The Illusions of a Football Fan: A Reply to Michalos" reprinted from *Journal of the Philosophy of Sport*. Copyright © 1977 by the Philosophic Society for the Study of Sport. Reprinted by permission of the editor.

Peter Meinke. "To an Athlete Turned Poet" reprinted from *Trying to Surprise God* by Peter Meinke. Copyright © 1981 by Peter Meinke. Reprinted by permission of the University of Pittsburgh Press.

A. James Memmott. "Wordsworth in the Bleachers: The Baseball Essays of Roger Angell" reprinted from *Journal of American Culture*. Copyright © 1982 by *Journal of American Culture*. Reprinted by permission of the author and editor.

Tom Meschery. "To Wilt Chamberlain" reprinted from *Over the Rim* by Tom Meschery. Copyright © 1970 by Tom Meschery. Reprinted by permission of the author. Originally published by McCall Publishing Company.

Alex C. Michalos. "The Unreality and Moral Superiority of Football" reprinted from *Journal of the Philosophy of Sport*. Copyright © 1976 by the Philosophic Society for the Study of Sport. Reprinted by permission of the editor.

Marianne Moore. "Baseball and Writing" reprinted from *The Complete Poems of Marianne Moore*. Copyright © 1961 by Marianne Moore. Reprinted by permission of the Estate of Marianne Moore, Viking Penguin, Inc., and Faber and Faber Ltd.

Michael Novak. "Regional Religions," "The Natural Religion," "Jocks, Hacks, Flacks, and Pricks," "Humble Howard," and "The First Two Seals: Sacred Space, Sacred Time" reprinted from *The Joy of Sports: End Zones, Bases, Baskets, Balls, and the Consecration of the American Spirit* by Michael Novak. Copyright © 1976 by Michael Novak. Reprinted by permission of Basic Books, Inc., Publishers.

Kathleen Pearson. "Deception, Sportsmanship, and Ethics" reprinted from *Quest*. Copyright © 1973 by Human Kinetics Publishers. Reprinted by permission of the author and the Publications Director.

Randall Poe. "The Writing of Sports" reprinted with permission from *Esquire* (October, 1974). Copyright © 1974 by Esquire Associates.

Murray Ross. "Football Red and Baseball Green." Copyright © 1982 by Murray Ross. Reprinted by permission of the author. An earlier version of this article appeared in *Chicago Review*.

Philip Roth. "The Asylum Keepers" excerpted from Chapter 3 of *The Great American Novel* by Philip Roth. Copyright © 1973 by Philip Roth. Reprinted by permission of the author, Holt, Rinehart and Winston, Publishers, and Jonathan Cape Ltd.

Irwin Shaw. "The Eighty-Yard Run" reprinted by permission of the author and the Irving Paul Lazar Agency. Originally appeared in *Esquire* (1941).

Howard S. Slusher. "Sport and Death" excerpted from Chapter 5 of *Man, Sport and Existence: A Critical Analysis* by Howard S. Slusher. Copyright © 1967 by Howard S. Slusher. Reprinted by permission of Lea & Febiger.

Adam Smith. "Sport Is a Western Yoga" reprinted from *Powers of Mind* by Adam Smith. Copyright © 1975 by Adam Smith. Reprinted by permission of the author.

Ernest W. Speed, Jr. "The Coach Who Didn't Teach Civics" reprinted from *Quartet* 7, Nos. 51–53 (1975–76), 32–36. Reprinted by permission of the editor.

Jack Spicer. "God is a big white baseball . . . ," the fourth of "Four Poems for the St. Louis Sporting News" reprinted from *The Collected Books of Jack Spicer*, published by Black Sparrow Press. Copyright © 1975 by the Estate of Jack Spicer. Reprinted by permission of the publisher.

Margaret Steel. "What We Know When We Know a Game" reprinted from *Journal of the Philosophy of Sport*. Copyright © 1977 by the Philosophic Society for the Study of Sport. Reprinted by permission of the editor.

Glendon Swarthout. "The Ball Really Carries in the Cactus League Because the Air Is Dry." Copyright © 1978 by Glendon Swarthout. Reprinted by permission of the author and the William Morris Agency, Inc. Originally appeared in *Esquire* (1 March 1978).

John Updike. "Hub Fans Bid Kid Adieu" reprinted from *Assorted Prose* by John Updike. Copyright © 1960 by John Updike. Reprinted by permission of Alfred A. Knopf, Inc. Originally appeared in *The New Yorker*.

John Updike. "Tao in the Yankee Stadium Bleachers" reprinted from *The Carpentered Hen and Other Tame Creatures* by John Updike. Copyright © 1956 by John Updike. Reprinted by permission of Alfred A. Knopf, Inc.

Harold J. VanderZwaag. "The Interior Stadium: Enhancing the Illusion" is an original essay published by permission of the author.

George Vecsey. "Fans" reprinted with permission from *Esquire* (October, 1974). Copyright © 1974 by Esquire Associates.

Robert Wallace. "The Double Play." Copyright © 1960 by Robert Wallace. Reprinted by permission of the author.

Peter S. Wenz. "Human Equality in Sports" reprinted from *The Philosophical Forum* (Spring, 1981). Copyright © 1981 by *The Philosophical Forum*. Reprinted by permission of the author and editor.

Spencer K. Wertz. "Artistic Creativity in Sport" and "Comments on Galvin" are original essays published by permission of the author.

Typesetting by G & S, Austin
Printing and binding by *Edwards Brothers*, Ann Arbor
Design by *Whitehead & Whitehead*, Austin